SCIENCE
FOR THE MASSES

NUMBER TWENTY-TWO: EASTERN EUROPEAN STUDIES

STJEPAN MEŠTROVIĆ
SERIES EDITOR

SCIENCE
FOR THE MASSES

THE BOLSHEVIK STATE, PUBLIC SCIENCE,
AND THE POPULAR IMAGINATION
IN SOVIET RUSSIA, 1917-1934

JAMES T. ANDREWS

TEXAS A&M UNIVERSITY PRESS
COLLEGE STATION

Copyright © 2003 by James T. Andrews

Manufactured in the United States of America

All rights reserved

First edition

Library of Congress Cataloging-in-Publication Data

Andrews, James T., 1961–

　Science for the masses: the Bolshevik state, public science, and the popular
imagination in Soviet Russia, 1917–1934 / James T. Andrews. — 1st ed.

　　p. cm. — (Number twenty-two ; Eastern European studies)

　ISBN 1-58544-247-X (cloth : alk. paper)

　　1. Science and state—Soviet Union—History—20th century. 2. Science—
Soviet Union—History—20th century. I. Title. II. Series.

　Q127.S696 A737 2003

　509.47—dc21

2002153966

∞ The paper used in this book meets the minimum requirements of the American National
Standard for Permanence of Paper for Printed Library Materials, Z39.48–1984.
Binding materials have been chosen for durability.

To Maggie and our beautiful daughter, Elena Sophie

"In this bright future, you can't forget your past. . . ."
—Robert Nesta Marley

CONTENTS

ILLUSTRATIONS

ACKNOWLEDGMENTS

Many scholars in Russian studies offered their support of this manuscript; however, a few stand out who read all or part of this book prior to its publication. Scott J. Seregny has been friend and colleague since Gorbachev's perestroika days when we met on the stairs outside the Lenin Library in Moscow. He read two drafts of this manuscript offering critical commentary that helped sharpen my arguments. I value his collegiality, admire his unselfish generosity, and cherish his friendship. Larry Holmes read an earlier draft and gave me voluminous comments that helped dramatically streamline the book and focus my analysis. Using his keen eye as a seasoned author, Paul Josephson poured over an earlier draft and also provided key suggestions for revision. Lewis Siegelbaum read the chapter on TekhMass and ZOT, offering detailed suggestions for revision. Donald J. Raleigh's insights forced me to reconsider my contribution to local/provincial history and also my take on the cultural-revolution debates. Finally, Lynne Viola has been a supportive colleague, showing enthusiasm for my forays into the early Stalinist era and graciously chairing panels at conferences that I organized on Stalinist culture and that relate to the end of this book.

Several scholars with expertise in the history of Russian science and technology also provided much support for this project from its outset. Over the years, Loren R. Graham has offered support and guidance for my research on the cultural history of science; I am grateful for his generous help and the effort he has taken to read my work. Susan Gross Solomon invited me, through an SSRC Fellowship, to the University of Toronto in the early 1990s, offering helpful insights at an early stage in the project. Mark B. Adams, in our conversations in St. Petersburg and East Germany, encouraged me to expand on the analysis of prerevolutionary popular science that had fibers of connection with the early Soviet era. Douglas R. Weiner introduced me to a variety of Russian specialists in Moscow at the Academy and shared his valuable insights on my work at an early stage. Three Russian scholars stand out who helped me in so many ways. On a snowy January during the twilight of the former Soviet Union, on the steps outside the Russian Academy of Sciences in Moscow, Danya Alexandrov, Kirill Rossianov, and Irina Sirotkina met me to share their insights on my work and to introduce me to their new cohort of social historians of Russian science. From that day on, they have all been invaluable colleagues, offering insightful suggestions for my archival work and providing illuminating discussion of my papers that I presented in Russian at their wonderful conferences in Moscow and Leningrad/St. Petersburg.

Although this book is dramatically different from its early manuscript, it is fundamentally based on my University of Chicago doctoral dissertation on the topic of science popularization in Revolutionary Russia. I therefore wish to thank my dissertation advisors for their continual help, encouragement, and generous commentary of my work. From the day I entered graduate school, Richard Hellie offered endless support and critical commentary of my research. Jeffrey P. Brooks helped me create a nexus between my past knowledge of the natural sciences and my then-recent interest in Russian popular culture. Robert J. Richards introduced me to the diverse field of the history of modern science and was generous with his time and advice. Finally, Sheila Fitzpatrick, my dissertation supervisor, offered voluminous commentary on my research, as well as incisive advice on Soviet archival research when the archives were first opening en masse in the former Soviet Union. I greatly appreciate Sheila's continued interest in my research on Soviet society and culture, and admire her genuine concern for the long-term professional development of her former students.

A number of colleagues at various universities where I have recently taught offered much support for this book and my work in general. More than anyone else, Andrejs Plakans has been friend, colleague, and faculty mentor in the truest sense of all those words. He brought me to Iowa State several years ago and has followed my work carefully; I am grateful for his generosity and advice, and I admire his scholarship. I wish to thank my past chair at Iowa State University, George McJimsey, for his academic support and collegiality. Several members of Iowa State's Center for the Historical Studies of Technology and Science, where I am an affiliate, have offered much support for my work. I wish to thank the director of the program, Alan Marcus, for his collegiality in integrating me into the program. Hamilton Cravens read the entire manuscript and offered critical remarks and suggestions. David Wilson, former director of Iowa State's STS program, also showed much support for my research, particularly on provincial science and society. At the University of Connecticut at Storrs, my former chair Altina Waller has been a constant advocate of my historical research while generously offering me her advice and collegial respect. At the University of Texas at Austin, Michael Katz, the former director of Russian Studies, followed my work carefully and showed much support and interest for my research on popular culture. Two Germanists at Austin, Peter Jelavich and David Crew, gave me the benefit of their interest in my analysis of the cultural history of the Soviet 1920s.

This book would not have been realized without the aid of specialists in a variety of libraries. A host of archivists and librarians throughout Russia helped enormously by guiding me through their rich collections and by offering their advice on my topic, over chai (tea) in the drafty halls of their institutions in Moscow, St. Petersburg, Iaroslavl', and throughout the Northern Volga Region. In the United States, five libraries and special collections stand out for their importance to this study. I wish to thank Edward Kasinec and the fine staff at the New York Public Library's Slavonic Reading Room; June Farris and the staff at the University of Chicago's Regenstein Library; Harold Leich and the Library of Congress's European Division and Slavic Collection; Joseph Dwyer and the fine collections, catalogued and uncatalogued, at the Hoover Institution's Library at Stanford University; and, finally, the Russian bibliographic staff at the University of Illinois, Urbana-Champaign.

Several grant institutions, university grant funds, and Russian academic institutions helped either to finance research or to offer academic affiliation while I was in Russia over several long-term trips. I would like to thank the Social Science Research Council in New York, the International Research Exchange Board, the American Council of Teachers of Russian (with funds from the U.S. State Department and Fulbright-Hays), the University of Chicago Research Fund, the former Moscow State Historical-Archival Institute, the Russian Academy of Sciences Institute for the History of the Natural Sciences and Technology, and, finally, the Iowa State University Science, Technology, and Society Fund.

I would also like to thank the editorial staff and production team at Texas A&M University Press (TAMU) for their diligent work on my manuscript. Lastly, my freelance editor at RedLine Editorial Services, Bard Young, is among the finest in the business. His proficient copyediting, conceptual recommendations, and overall engagement with the text went beyond the call of duty.

I dedicate this book to my love and intellectual comrade-in-arms, my wife Maggie (Margaret Rose LaWare). More than anyone, she has watched this book go through various permutations, offering her love, support, and critical advice while traveling with me in Russia or back home in Iowa, where we lead our mutual life as professors. I also dedicate the book to my daughter, Elena Sophie Andrews, who reaffirms for me on a daily basis the beauty of the human spirit and how joyous life can be with a young, vivacious toddler. My parents, Thomas James and Helen Raisides Andrews, have been an everlasting fountain of support for the pursuit of my goals; I love them dearly. Finally, my brother, William T. Andrews (Will), and sister-in-law, Ann Andrews, have been consistently supportive throughout my career as an academic. I am tremendously thankful for their warmth, love, and understanding.

Lastly, in the 1970s Mildred K. Lasky of the former Andrew Warde High School in Fairfield, Connecticut, taught a wonderful course on comparative Russian and Japanese world literature that opened the eyes of an impressionable teenager to the complexities of Russian intellectual life. Daniel M. Mulholland's brilliant and witty lectures at Tufts University in the late 1970s and early 1980s, were, to borrow a phrase from Lenin, an intellectual "spark which ignited the flame" that continues within me and powers my study of modern Russian/Soviet history.

SCIENCE
FOR THE MASSES

Introduction

RUSSIAN SCIENCE, PUBLIC CULTURE,

AND THE BOLSHEVIKS

On a July 1933 evening in Moscow, over two hundred workers packed into an auditorium in the city to view an instructional film and to have a discussion with teachers from the voluntary technical educational group Technology for the Masses (TekhMass). After the showing, a fiery debate broke out between Communist technical activists and Soviet workers from various Moscow factories. The workers were interested in the practical, instructional aspects of such films dealing with, for instance, electro-welding. The films, however, much to the dismay of workers, also carried propagandistic messages of the virtues of Soviet technology in comparison to the capitalist West. On this particular night, workers boldly told activists to scrap the propaganda and to get on with the business of giving them needed, basic technical education these newly minted workers had never received from the countryside, or shop floor for that matter. Various TekhMass activists were stunned by the workers' critiques, which were blatantly apolitical; however, they also realized that they had to placate their complaints. Furthermore, the activists realized that, politics aside, their efforts toward scientific popularization depended on a core ethos that saw science as a practical tool with utilitarian goals for the everyday laborer.

The experience of various activists in the early Stalinist era demonstrates how Bolsheviks sought to bring a new science to the masses after 1928. Science during the Stalinist period took on an increasingly narrow meaning in the public realm. The Stalinist temple of science was the factory-shop floor and the machine, and productive capacity became an end in itself as scientific knowledge and epistemological inquiry were relegated to the background. Yet, this was not always the case in the early Soviet era before Stalin's revolution in 1928. There was actually great continuity between the tsarist and Soviet periods with regard to communicating the virtues of science to the undereducated. This was part of a greater European cultural movement stretching back to the roots of the Enlightenment. Furthermore, Russian scientists and educators of science themselves shaped to a large degree their own agenda and in the process contributed to a civic, public sphere before and after 1917.

Scientists and popularizers of science adopted rhetorical strategies to combat and accommodate initiatives by a Bolshevik state seeking to support but also to control and politicize their work. A symbiotic relationship developed between the state and those scientists because the Bolsheviks realized their dependence on such specialists to enlighten the masses. Yet, even before 1928 this relationship was paradoxically marked by great tension as well as cooperation. The science-popularization movement was a microcosm of the Bolsheviks' struggle during the twenties to develop their own cultural programs while they were still highly dependent on the old intellectual elite of Russia. Ironically, they shared many of the same values in the scientific realm, educationally speaking, even if they differed on the politicizing of knowledge.

However, efforts by militant atheists and radical activists hostile to compromise became increasingly successful after 1928 as the Stalinist state underscored the importance of nationalism, class warfare, and a myopic utilitarianism united with the immediate goals of industrialization and collectivization. Nevertheless, the science popularizers and the Stalinist regime still found reasons to cooperate, and the Stalinists recognized that they needed the popularizers to lead workers, many of them recent migrants from the Russian countryside, toward an appreciation of technology and to teach them particular technical skills useful at their job sites. To understand this evolving tension and cooperation between scientists and the Soviet state, one must consider the subtle sociopolitical patterns that arose in early Soviet society: namely, the simultaneous cooperation and struggle between regional and central agencies; considerable infighting among Soviet institutions of government; an encroaching bureaucratization and institutionalization of Soviet life after 1917; and finally, yet critically, the persistence of civil society across the revolutionary divide into the 1920s, and to a limited extent in the early Stalinist era.

The Soviet effort to popularize science in revolutionary Russia therefore provides a base from which to view and understand the expansion of public culture across the revolutionary divide, especially in the early Soviet era. Nevertheless, no major effort has been made in Western literature to analyze popular science in early Soviet (nor late tsarist) Russia. Historians of Russian science have not extensively analyzed the cultural resonance of science in revolutionary Russia,[1] nor have they focused singularly on the civic activity of these scientists.[2] Equally unaddressed, at least in any comprehensive way, are the intricate venues through which science was popularized in revolutionary Russia, the broad textual media involved in popular science, and how science reached beyond the educated elite.[3]

Historians of late Imperial and early Soviet Russian popular culture have also touched on public science, but only in a peripheral sense.[4] Furthermore, those who have looked at futuristic elements of Bolshevik culture mostly focus on the abstract, utopian concerns of Russian intellectuals (and Bolsheviks in particular) and not necessarily on the more public or even utilitarian, technical components of science that struck an imaginative chord with Russians from all walks of life: laborers, lower-middle-class functionaries, professionals, and others.[5] It was in the interest of the state, as well as that of Russian intellectuals of the older generation, to connect with those undereducated Russians and to teach them the practical and visionary aspects of scientific inquiry. Early Bolshevik culture can be reconceptualized though an understanding of these eclectic elements, the practical and utopian. During the 1920s the Soviet state also had to accommodate the interests of both the old and new intellectual elite.

Only recently have historians of Russian science attempted to address the broad issue of scientific "public" discourse. Douglas Weiner, in his newest work on Russian nature protection, has argued that the ecologists in Stalin's Russia maintained a sense of what he calls "scientific public opinion." They formed defense mechanisms, which he describes as "protective coloration," in order to survive and to continue their ecological work even under the repressive Stalinist regime. Yet, Weiner's case study uncovered how ecologists formed a sense of public opinion that was elitist in nature; as they directed their critiques at the boorish regime, they believed that only they were the harbingers of true knowledge. Weiner also contends that his research on Russian ecologists points to their need to maintain preexisting corporate social identities, as well as independent professional positions. They were effectively shutting themselves off from the public's more mundane interest in environmental concerns.[6]

Science popularizers displayed a different kind of public scientific discourse. Popularizers formed "public scientific opinion," like other scientific subgroups, but they also uniquely supported broad, popular civic culture. Their interests both diverged and converged with the mass-enlightenment agenda of the Bolshevik regime. So, instead of looking down on Soviet mass, voluntary activity, popularizers embraced it and by doing so attempted to maintain their independent civic domains. Furthermore, science popularizers, unlike other scientific subgroups, represented radically diverse professional and ideological positions. They were unique, as an amorphous cohort, since they attempted to transgress professional, discursive, social, and class boundaries. These scientists and educators offer a case in point for analysis of how groups coexisted with the Bolsheviks and actively affected the Soviet state's cultural agendas.

Science popularizers, unlike other Russian professional caste-like elites, represented a point at which state, society, and scientists all converged in an expanding and contracting public sphere. As a group of Russian intellectuals, the popularizers were somewhat of an anomaly because they did not represent a singular corporate identity. Lastly, although the popularizers lobbied the new Bolshevik state for patronage, they manipulated their "protective coloration" in a manner that made their relationship with the state different from the relationship that shaped groups such as the Russian ecologists. Science popularizers highlighted their public enlightenment activities to show how their programs could converge with the atheistic state's scientific vision of popularization. They adopted the rhetorical constructs of the Soviet state while accentuating those parts of their agenda that converged with the state's pervasive platform. Since popularizers had supported public educational programs as part of their operations for decades before the revolution of 1917, fulfilling the Soviet state's extra-curricular mission came naturally to them. Their activities represented strong continuities in scientific practice and civic activity across the divide separating tsarist and revolutionary Russia. Furthermore, an appreciation of the role of the popularizers highlights how the Soviet state's enlightenment campaigns in the early period were not necessarily an innovation, or inherently Communist, but connected to prerevolutionary Russian trends.

After the October 1917 Revolution, the Bolshevik state supported the enlightened ideas of prerevolutionary Russian science popularizers, as well as young Communist scientists and activists who were interested in public culture. The goals and cultural vision of the Bolsheviks intersected and converged with those of prerevolutionary Russian intellectuals who also cherished the notion of bringing science out of the walls of academe and into the public realm. Both the Bolsheviks and scientific intellectuals saw science enlightenment as an inherently transformative venue for shaping Russian culture. From the very beginning of the Revolution in late 1917 and early 1918, even under adverse conditions, the Commissariat of Enlightenment's Scientific Department (Glavnauka) donated huge sums of money to societies that had been the central source of science enlightenment in the late tsarist era.

Indeed, early Bolshevik culture can be viewed as having had a public scientific ethos at its core that would change and evolve at different stages, especially throughout the early Stalinist era. Recently, Nikolai Krementsov has emphasized, contrary to conventional wisdom, how Russian scientists fought and manipulated the Soviet system to maintain the purity of their scientific work and the coherence of their insular laboratory research after 1917.[7] This scenario, while true for research biologists, does not properly describe the general rule for all science educators. On the contrary, though perhaps Russian scientists in the post-1917 era "worked" the Soviet state to maintain their independent scientific research domains, they did not turn inward in an insular manner, away from both the state and society. Rather, Russian scientists seemed inherently driven to create a public domain for the discussion of science's role in society, both in the pre- and post-1917 era. Understanding the historical roots of public scientific activity in Russia might even offer a better understanding of the civic movement for public discussion of social issues during the 1970s and beyond that was spearheaded by scientific elites such as Andrei Sakharov and others.

Ultimately, the Soviet state itself fostered and supported the expansion of public science in the early 1920s and 1930s. Viewing and analyzing Bolshevik culture through the medium of science popularization allows us to bring together under one rubric many aspects of the modernization paradigm of that early revolutionary government: industry and the city v. the backward countryside; science v. religious superstition; futuristic and imaginative concepts v. the insular old world.

Chapters 1 and 2 look at the critical prerevolutionary development of the science-popularization movement in publishing and the rise of scientific societies as catalysts for this activity. Russian intellectuals in late Tsarist Russia were missionary in their zeal to popularize the virtues and importance of *nauka,* a term they used not only for science but also for progress and enlightenment. Although the Imperial Russian state under Peter the Great and subsequent tsars was originally interested in the utilitarian applications of scientific and technological developments, the task of spreading science beyond the walls of academe and into the public realm was left primarily to Russian popularizers. This diverse group of intellectuals included scientists, editors, educators, and teachers. They did not represent simply one corporate, professional identity, nor did they all espouse the same ideological perspective.

In the eighteenth century the process was undertaken by important scientific figures like M. Lomonosov and G. F. Muller, who had an institutional base in the Russian Imperial Academy of Sciences. During the early 1700s, state patronage was the driving engine behind the development and popular diffusion of scientific information in Russian society. However, later in the century during the time of Catherine the Great, independent enlightened publishers, like N. Novikov at Moscow University, used their new presses to spread science via popular pamphlets and journals. This development paralleled the similar efforts of French encyclopedists to spread Newtonian mechanics and scientific thought throughout Western Europe. As time progressed, enlightened intellectuals in Russia began to take control of the movement and connect it more to a developing public culture.

Popular geographic works were among the most widely distributed forms of popular-scientific literature up to the late eighteenth century in Russia. A certain patriotic and nationalistic sentiment in these publications surveyed Russia's vast territory and resources as the imperial empire expanded on its periphery. State sponsorship of certain geographical and geological publications emphasized the underlying importance of those works as textual media that spread ideas describing Russia's wealth and power.

Throughout the nineteenth century the movement to popularize scientific information among a broad sector of the populace in Russia became inextricably linked to the development of programs and journals in self-education. The movement caught on as well in America and Europe after the early 1800s, where science popularization was closely allied to adult-education programs. By the mid-nineteenth century, the development of natural-history museums and scientific societies in Russia altered the nature of scientific popularization. From that point onward the transmission of scientific ideas was not strictly limited to printed textual media. Popular-scientific lectures and exhibits in new museums were a potent tool in the spread of scientific ideas to various elements of the public. Russian natural-history museums spread in the capital and provincial cities, and they sometimes emulated, without wholesale copying, their European and American counterparts.

At the turn of the twentieth century in Russia, the production of popular-scientific works became more market driven. Publishing firms in St. Petersburg and Moscow promoted books on popular scientific themes. The popular reader was interested in a variety of themes, including the origin of the Earth, human evolution, and astronomy. The result was an increase in the publication of popular-scientific journals. The journal was a cheap and accessible source of scientific information for the Russian reader. As in the West popular journals contained advertisements to supplement revenue from subscriptions for the publishing houses.

In both Europe and Russia after the era of the French Revolution, science popularizers, voluntary organizations, and educators were thus involved in a much broader social process. Science popularization entailed sponsoring adult education, moving ideas out beyond the walls of academe, and creating public museums for wider social participation. This civic activity was part of a more general process of expanding the dimensions of the public sphere in Russian society.

Science educators and scientific societies continued to foster civic activity as they broadened the public sphere across the 1917 revolutionary divide. Chapter 3 begins the analysis of the post-1917 era by discussing the relationship between the non-Communist (and Communist) scientists in the 1920s and their new Soviet patron—Glavnauka, the Scientific Department of *Nar-*

kompros, the Commissariat of Enlightenment (or Ministry of Education). Pre-revolutionary scientists were as ingenious as young Communists in lobbying the new Soviet state for finances. They were able to use the language and rhetoric constructed by Narkompros to show how they would be an influential part of the Soviet state's cultural and scientific enlightenment campaign. After 1928 their lobbying efforts would become less successful, but they struggled all the same until their organizations in many instances were liquidated in the early 1930s. By adhering to and manipulating elaborate rituals in their dealings with Soviet state institutions, scientific societies were able to maintain their own independent sense of public identity within certain political limits. Science popularizers not only entered into symbiotic relationships with Narkompros, but skillfully kept the state from interfering in the direction of their public educational activities during the twenties.

Chapters 4 and 5 focus on popular culture during the twenties in Soviet Russia and on how the new Bolshevik scientific vision actually converged with the dreams and imagination of many urban Russians. A market for popular science had existed prior to the revolution of 1917, and at least until 1928 the public demand continued and was fulfilled by the explosion of popular-scientific journalistic activity in Soviet Russia. Though less the case for rural inhabitants, urban Russians from a variety of social backgrounds were fascinated with popular scientific material on a range of topics including air flight, new technology, and exploration of Russia and the globe. The Bolsheviks helped foster these publishing ventures that temporarily fulfilled the state's goal of scientizing Russian cultural norms and educational curricula. Furthermore, Russian readers in the 1920s were fascinated with the feats of foreign technology, and the regime did not attack that cosmopolitan perspective until the mid-1930s. The topical interests of the urban public converged with those promoted by the state in this interim period. This convergence is manifest in the comparison of thematic content, covered in chapters 4 and 5, between non-party and Communist Party/Soviet state publications in the 1920s.

Chapter 6 will view the antireligious campaign as an outgrowth of the Bolshevik cultural vision of bringing "science to the people." In this unconventional interpretation, the antireligion campaign can be seen more as a means to achieve a scientized culture—a venue for science popularization—and less as an end in itself. An analysis of the scientific content of antireligious propaganda is critical to a broader understanding of the Bolshevik program of cultural enlightenment in the 1920s. The Communist Party modified its antireligious propaganda due to much resistance in the local and rural areas and settled instead on long-term scientific, educational planning. That long-term strategy involved sponsoring science popularizers' activities in aiding antireligious activists, as well as promoting Darwinism and diverse evolutionary theory in the schools and popular press. The regime became dependent on those non-Communists in the scientific and educational community to spread evolutionary and antireligious doctrine.

The era of the New Economic Policy (NEP, 1921–27) is a complex time for cultural historians to analyze because the NEP was a transitional era wedged between two radical periods of cultural transformation: namely, the Russian Civil War (1918–20) and the Stalinist Great Break (1928–32).[8] During the period of the NEP the Communist Party and Soviet state (specifically Glavnauka) generously sponsored the popular-enlightenment efforts of many scientific societies, institutions, and publishers, while avoiding any severe political interference in their work. This approach accorded with the early Bolshevik concept of cultural revolution, which called for a gradual raising of educational, scientific, and cultural levels. With the end of the NEP in 1928, the Soviet state continued as the prime funding source for these societies and their enlightenment work. However, radical Communist factions and groups of intellectuals now launched an aggressive challenge to the authority of the prerevolutionary scientific intelligentsia. While their initiative might have come from below, these groups lent support to party resolutions and directives from above that demanded that all enlightenment activities buttress the socialist reconstruction of the economy.[9] Chapter 7 offers an analysis of those confrontations within the larger discussion of science popularization in the era of the Stalinist "Great Break." In 1928 the Stalinist state, managing from above, and radicals, fomenting from below, broke away from the mixed economies of the NEP era as well as from tolerance of the old cultural elite, which characterized NEP Russia.

Scholars have debated for some time the extent of "Bolshevization" of scientific and educational institutions in the period before Stalin's revolution from above. Nikolai Krementsov, in his monograph on Stalinist science, has argued that in contrast to the accommodating Bolshevik policy toward existing scientific research institutions in the 1920s, the Bolsheviks supported a more aggressive attitude toward educational institutions in the sciences.[10] Krementsov concurs with Michael David-Fox, who argues that in addition to reforming existing educational structures the Bolsheviks created a number of new "Communist" institutions, like the Communist Academy, in order to form slowly a Communist intelligentsia.[11] Other scholars, like David Joravsky, see the process of "Bolshevization" of scientific institutions as a more gradual development leading up to the late 1920s.[12]

The "Bolshevization" of scientific and educational institutions was less well defined during the period of the NEP than previous analysts are willing to concede. In the 1920s, prerevolutionary scientific societies were able to justify their work and the funding they received from Narkompros by using the rhetoric of the Communist Party itself. They lobbied Narkompros officials to support their activities, arguing that their societies would actively take part in "enlightenment for the masses." Both non-Communist intellectuals and Bolsheviks alike used the rhetoric of "practical enlightenment" to coexist in the period of the NEP. By 1929, however, the Bolsheviks were attempting to reorganize professional societies and organizations dominated by the prerevolutionary scientific and technical intelligentsia. Although radical Marxists had already begun to draw battle lines during the mid-1920s, they had been unable to muster enough support to purge completely the older generation of popularizers of science.

Throughout the course of the Stalinist cultural revolution (1928–31) tensions grew between young militants and the older generation of professors in the sciences. In the scientific realm, specific institutions, like VARNITSO (All Union Society of the Workers of Science and Technology for the Promotion of Socialist Construction), covered in chapter 8, helped to coalesce attacks against prerevolutionary societies and to serve as a spearhead for further criticism. VARNITSO, a powerful central organization, had ties to key Communist Party members, and its attacks against specialists modified the nature and restricted the extent of the public discussion of scientific issues during the 1930s and beyond. VARNITSO dictated to older established institutions the parameters of popular scientific and technical education and defined more clearly the new politicized rhetoric. During the Great Break, radical science pedagogues, grouped in organizations like VARNITSO, criticized those educators who did not link science education to practical economic tasks. Even within Glavnauka, the radicals openly challenged their associates, whom they accused of propagating material and a point of view divorced from immediate economic and industrial needs.

An analysis of rhetorical and survival strategies as a methodological approach can reconceptualize the dynamic process of cultural revolution by highlighting fundamental sociological tensions and patterns. Scientists and educators came up with a variety of survival tactics before and even during the period 1928–32. Prerevolutionary organizations and intellectuals tenaciously shaped their public personas within the changing parameters constructed by the Soviet state. Scientists and educators in the early Stalin era attempted to "work the system" even when many did not support the state politically or ideologically. Unfortunately, by the early to mid-1930s, many of their attempts both to survive and to cultivate public culture became problematic, given the new political and bureaucratic constraints from above.

Scientists and educators continued to use the Communist Party's rhetoric as a means to gain financial support. During the period of the Great Break, however, the new militants were more effective at using the rhetorical phrases of "class war," "utilitarianism," and "Marxist dialectics" that the Party had unleashed. Independent, voluntary Communist organizations fashioned their own public images and lobbied state institutions for patronage support. The young militants isolated their opponents and placed them on the defensive throughout the early 1930s. Science educators from the old and new generation were competitors in an era of limited resources and politicized educational policy.

In the early Stalin era, Soviet state officials believed that the spread of science and technology had to coalesce with the Communist Party's utilitarian needs to revive the industrial sector of the economy.[13] Initially, radical scientists and propagandists attacked older, prerevolutionary voluntary societies for not aiding the socialist reconstruction of the economy. Eventually, these Communists organized their own mass organizations to aid the economy and to fulfill other tasks, like educating workers. TekhMass, discussed in chapter 9, was one of the new voluntary organizations designed to promote the technical education of workers in order to integrate them into the factory environment of the First Five-Year Plan (FFYP). This extensive organization relied on operating cells throughout the former USSR, and its functioning reflected how the nature of science popularization changed during this era. Although they were fostering the Party's mass propagandistic and economic agendas, Communist voluntary societies, like TekhMass, also provided basic needs for those laborers who wanted more guidance in areas where they never received formal educational training. These organizations converged with the needs and demands of the undereducated worker-peasants entering the urban areas who were interested in more utilitarian forms of science and technology. These new workers became fascinated with journal articles that applied to their jobs and life in a practical sense. Workers' criticisms and petitions to technical educators well illustrate the degree to which laborers were emphatic in their demands. These petitions provide further evidence of public criticism in Stalin's Russia, especially in the scientific and educational realms.[14]

This convergence of the demands of the new Stalinist state, the focus of new Communist voluntary societies, and the needs of the changing work force was reflected in both public policy and in the content of the popular scientific media. Chapter 7 analyzes the fundamental changes in the content of popular science in Stalin's Russia during the cultural revolution. Unfortunately, after 1932 even the Communist educators who were militant members of these organizations came under the control of the party. By then the Soviet state prompted the name change of TekhMass to *Za Ovladenie Tekhnikoi* (All-Union Society for the Mastering of Technology—ZOT) in order to harness its resources for use in Stalin's mass propaganda campaign "The Party and Workers Should Master Technology . . . Technology Decides All." Societies like TekhMass were reorganized, given new names, and became conveyor belts for Stalinist cultural campaigns in the mid-1930s. The Stalinist mass technology campaign was a pervasive focus of many editorials in popular science journals and the popular press during the early Stalin era. This new technologically oriented popularization campaign was of primary importance to key Communist Party leaders and reflects the emphasis the Party placed on popular-technological education programs.

Ultimately, a series of new convergences, different from the NEP period, occurred in the arena of mass technical education and Stalinist popular culture. Workers, who did not have any formal training in specific areas, received needed advice and technical courses at night to improve their qualifications during a tumultuous period. The program and vision of various Communists in the new technical organizations were simultaneously supported by their targeted audience below and reinforced by the regime from above. Finally, the Stalinist state harnessed young Communist scientific activists to fulfill its utilitarian goals of practical technical education, while promoting its own cultural vision of the new, modernized, futuristic society. This Stalinist vision emphasized applied science and how the Soviet Union would become a technologically advanced society. Although that vision built on earlier scientific constructs developed during the NEP by the Bolsheviks, it changed those approaches and tied them more directly to industrial development. It was a futuristic cultural vision of technology shaping and supporting mass Soviet society. In essence the enlightened, imaginative vision of public science that crossed the revolutionary divide became transformed after 1928 into applied science and technology for the masses of workers at the job site. What eventually arose from this cultural ferment was a new Stalinist proletarian temple of science.

Part I

ENVISIONING PUBLIC SCIENCE IN THE TSARIST ERA

Chapter 1

THE BIRTH OF POPULAR PUBLISHING
AND PUBLIC SCIENCE IN TSARIST RUSSIA

Popular science publishing in Russia followed relatively the same developmental path it had taken in Europe. Until the first quarter of the nineteenth century, science popularizers in Russia concentrated on spreading information on geography, concrete astronomical conceptions of the universe, and utilitarian scientific inventions. Much of this effort was sponsored institutionally by the Academy of Sciences and subsequently by scientific scholars and private publishers. By the second quarter of the nineteenth century, science popularizers began to publish basic educational material in all areas of the natural sciences. Even more than their European counterparts, Russian intellectuals believed that science had to be spread through popular media to enlighten the broadest segments of the populace concerning new discoveries and to bring them up to the level of European scientific consciousness. Furthermore, Russia had its own unique tradition of public scientific lectures and traveling science exhibits that continued into the twentieth century. This notion of science for the people begun in the tsarist era connected well with the later Bolshevik notion of mass enlightenment in the early Soviet era.

Yet Russia had also borrowed Western European traditions predating its own movement to spread science to the people. Western European science popularization was more prevalent than in Russia as far back as the early 1600s. At that time, much of the science popularization in early modern Europe was conducted by individual scientists or professors. One of the first important science popularizers in Europe was the author of early theories on physics and celestial dynamics, the Italian scientific thinker Galileo Galilei. In the 1620s and 1630s Galileo launched a publishing campaign to introduce other scientists and educated laymen to Nicholas Copernicus's views on the heliocentric design of the universe and to Galileo's own approaches to the study of dynamics.[1] The work of Sir Isaac Newton then built on Galileo's theories to produce a new system of mechanics. In 1687 Newton published his famous *Principia Mathematica Philosophiae Naturalis.*[2] As time progressed, many scientists and scholars had to defend Newton's scientific theories publicly. At the turn of the century Roger Cotes, Cambridge University professor of astronomy and mathematics, was one of the greatest defenders of

Newton's scientific method. Cotes was one of the few scientists at the time who could both understand Newton's mathematical theories and explain them to a wider body of educated laymen.[3]

During the seventeenth and early eighteenth centuries, a movement began that lent an institutional basis to science popularization. In England, as Newton expounded on his theory of gravity, King Charles II gave the title "Royal" to a group of British natural philosophers in London. In 1662 this society took the formal name the Royal Society. Its most important member, Henry Oldenburg, the Society's Secretary, conceived of a journal called *Philosophical Transactions,* which was first published in 1665. Oldenburg translated and published correspondences between great scientific figures for the scientific and educated community at large. This publication had profound ramifications, since it would be a forerunner to the modern scientific journals of later days and a means to spread knowledge among the scientific and educated lay community.[4] England was certainly not the only European country where these societies developed and popularized science through lectures, exhibits, and newly founded journals.[5] Galileo's disciples formed a similar academy in Florence in 1657, the Accademia del Cimento. It publicly promoted the usefulness of the experimental sciences. Its secretary, Lorenzo Magalotti, published the findings of the academy's experimental discoveries, which the educated public read avidly.[6] These early European societies served as passageways for new scientific ideas to leave the walls of academe and enter the public realm, and Russians would learn from and build on these foundations when creating their own scientific societies.

During the middle and later parts of the eighteenth century, enlightened thinkers and publicists stressed the importance of spreading new scientific ideas through popular publications. The French *philosophes* believed one of their most important tasks was to popularize the ideas of Newtonian science on the continent. The chief catalyst for this movement was the French journalist Denis Diderot, and his new medium for change was the *Encyclopedie* he had been editing since 1747. The popularizing writers scorned superstition and most of all proclaimed Newtonian methods and physics. Articles on industry, science, and new devices also filled the pages of the encyclopedia's several volumes.[7] The Russians would have their own enlightened publicists, like Nikolai Novikov, who fashioned themselves after their European counterparts, the encyclopedists. Novikov and other Russians would use their newly minted private presses in the late eighteenth century to popularize scientific concepts throughout the empire.

During the nineteenth century printing technology advanced dramatically, and new facilities encouraged new publishers and scientists to expand publications in the natural sciences for a broader reading public. In Victorian England this technological revolution enhanced attempts to educate the working classes in both theoretical and applied science and technology.[8] As the nineteenth century progressed, educators, publishers, and liberal intellectuals joined scientists to spread new ideas. In Great Britain mechanics' institutes[9] were designed to provide a largely working-class audience with scientific and technical knowledge through lectures and short courses. These institutes were supported by working-class organizations and liberal politicians and educators in Britain. Henry Brougham, the Whig parliamentarian, promoted these institutes and the movement to popularize science in general among the working classes.[10] In Russia as in Europe, specialists in newly founded scientific societies, and liberal educators like Nicholas Rubakin, paid particularly close attention in the late nineteenth and early twentieth centuries to the needs of working-class citizens, determined to expand their knowledge of science.

As an increasing number of educators and publishers became involved in the European science popularization movement, more thought was given to how popular scientific texts and articles were actually created and to the kinds of language and symbols that could appropriately be used.[11] This forced all popularizers, including scientists, to consider how ideas would be received by ordinary readers and how to react to the demands of the market.[12] As the nineteenth century came to a close in Europe, popular-scientific literature became more market generated. Publishers of popular-scientific journals packaged publications with concise and appealing articles and themes. Journals sought out advertisers to supplement revenue from subscriptions and newsstand sales. European editors anticipated not only the most appealing trends but also the competing disciplines in modern science at the dawn of the twentieth century.[13]

In Russia popular literature in the natural sciences first appeared later than it had in Europe; however, it followed relatively the same institutional and editorial trajectory. The first Russian publications, printed in the late seventeenth century, outlined the study of the European parts of the country and also the early expeditions to Siberia. Public information on the Siberian expeditions of I. Rebrov, S. Dezhnev and E. Khabarov were made accessible in works such as *Kratkie sibirskie letopisi* (short Siberian annals) and *Chertezhnaia kniga Sibiri* (book of maps of Siberia). One of the first popular-scientific texts, published in Moscow in 1710, was a collection of materials and essays on world geography. It included basic information on the world's continents, as well as statistical information on thirty-three Russian towns. It was also the first book in Russian to give a popular explanation of the systematic view of the scholar Nicholas Copernicus.[14]

In 1740 the Imperial Academy of Sciences in St. Petersburg published the Russian translation of Bernard Fontenel's *Conversations on the Multitude of Worlds*. Fontenel, secretary of the French Academy of Sciences, said that *Conversations* would, he hoped, spark the curiosity of ordinary people to know how the Earth was formed and whether there were other worlds similar to ours.[15] At this time the Imperial Russian Academy of Sciences had concentrated in its hands all publishing activities in the sciences. The spread of natural-scientific knowledge by the academy was also transmitted through textual means, such as popular calendars having a wider distribution than popular books.[16] Calendars were printed with scientific popular articles containing information on world geography, exploration, and astronomical themes.[17] Demand for these calendars grew in the middle of the century, and by 1750 the Academy of Science's press had printed 10,020 copies of various calendars.[18]

The Imperial Academy of Sciences published a wide range of popular scientific media. In 1726 the journal *Sankt-Peterburgskie vedomosti* (St. Petersburg gazette) was handed over to the Academy. To explain some of the scientific articles more clearly, a supplement was published along with the gazette. By the 1730s, the basic content of the supplement, entitled *Primechanie* (commentary) and edited by G. F. Muller, consisted of popular-scientific articles on astronomy, geology, and other themes. As one of the first popular scientific publications in Russia, this monthly periodical was geared more toward the general public than the Academy's *Sankt-Peterburgskie vedomosti*.

The supplement appeared simultaneously in Russian and German. The journal's editors were careful not to focus on scholastic sciences, focusing more on farming, hygiene, anatomy, geography, and mathematics. It was also one of the first periodicals to spread popular-geographical information on recent expeditions to Siberia and the Far East, and it contained archaeological and anthropological articles on Siberian tribes.[19] The scientific level of the journal, however, was still geared more to the specialist than to the basic reader. Therefore, Muller and M. Lomonosov[20] met with the Academy and came out with another periodical that was set aside for the "less-prepared" reader: *Ezhemesiachnye sochineniia* (monthly works).[21]

During the eighteenth century, much of the history of the popularization of science in Russia was tied to the efforts of the Academy of Sciences to spread scientific views of nature through mass journalistic means.[22] In the first half of the eighteenth century, religious publications were still the dominant category in Russia. Between 1725 and 1755 religious books made up 41 percent of all titles published, while science and technology constituted only 5 percent of all titles.[23] But this does not reflect the enormous scientific publishing effort carried out by the academy nor how prominent a role science and technology played in that campaign.[24] By the middle of the eighteenth century the Academy of Sciences had become the most important secular publishing house in Russia, and it was the only outlet for the publication of tracts not containing religious or official state topics. Between 1727 and 1755 the Academy of Sciences Press printed over 75 percent of all books coming from secular publishing houses.[25]

The Academy's monopoly on science publishing changed with the founding of Moscow University in 1755. Between 1756 and 1800 the publishing house of the university produced twenty-seven hundred books of a scientific character, not only for scholars and students but also for a wider circle of readers. N. I. Novikov promoted science popularization through Moscow University's press, in the 1780s printing close to a thousand books. In 1788 Novikov published the first entry of *Magazin natural'noi istorii, fiziki i khimii* (magazine of natural history, physics, and chemistry). This work was encyclopedic in form and written to serve the interests of many generations seeking to understand contemporary scientific problems like the formation of the universe.[26] Novikov became the first enlightened publisher in Russia to popularize scientific tracts for a broad audience in the tradition of the European editors like Diderot.

Novikov was involved in translating and publishing contemporary European popular-scientific material for the small, yet growing, Russian reading public in the late eighteenth century. He helped translate into Russian the well-known "Natural History" of Georges-Louis, comte de Buffon. Buffon's multivolume "Natural History" outlined new causal theories for the formation of the world. In several volumes he argued that evolution and change of species were produced by factors such as climate and food. Novikov believed that Buffon had a unique gift for making material intelligible for the widest audience without losing the strength of his argument.[27]

In 1783 a state decree on publishing authorized the opening of private publishing houses without the sanction of the Russian Senate. This would temporarily help to continue and foster the growth of popular-scientific material published in Russia. However, the tsarist state revoked this law on private publishing in 1796 in the aftermath of the revolutionary developments in Western Europe. Under Paul I the production of books was sharply curtailed to 120 per year, compared to the average of 350–400 per year during the 1780s. Up until 1801 it was practically impossible to import foreign books, with the exception of sheet music, into Russia.[28]

In the first decades of the nineteenth century, journalistic activity in Russia rose sharply. From 1801 to 1811, eighty-four new periodicals were started in the Russian capital cities—sixty journals, nine newspapers, and fifteen *sborniki* (collections).[29] Probably, the most widely distributed form of popular-science literature during the first quarter of the nineteenth century was the *puteshestvie* (journey). Explorers at this time published travel notes of a sentimental nature and books of adventure tales, going beyond the academic reports of scholarly expeditions. Furthermore, some of these explorers took part in round-the-world expeditions, and their reports were published for popular consumption.[30]

In the second quarter of the nineteenth century, many accessible popular-scientific works, articles, and lectures became more directed toward adult and extra-curricular education. Journals and books were used by readers, from varied social backgrounds, interested in gaining scientific knowledge outside of formal educational establishments. In Europe at this time most learning for underprivileged adults, at least, took place outside of formal educational institutions. Popular science and other forms of nonfiction benefited from the great reading revolution in Europe in the nineteenth century. Alfred Kelley has argued that in Germany, for instance, small home libraries for the middle class were by the late 1800s rarely without a volume or two of popular science, and the workingman was already using popular science as the main tool of his self-education.[31]

This reading revolution developed more gradually in Russia and extended broadly to the middle and lower classes only later in the nineteenth century, in comparison to Western Europe. However, even under the constrained political and educational environment under Nicholas I (1825–55), scientific publications for the popular reader expanded greatly. Nicholas Riasanovsky has revised our notion of this period by contending that this was indeed an era when publishers and journalists expanded reading material for the public and independently developed public opinion on issues outside the state's purview. The periodical press developed in the reign of Nicholas I, reflecting the expansion of the educated public, while a journalistic explosion occurred between 1838 and 1855.[32] Popularizers thus consistently published popular-science tracts through progressive and conservative reigns in the tsarist era.

In Russia, popularizers like N. Pisarevskii wrote works that were of a general character in order to target the demand for scientific self-education books. Pisarevskii's 1852 *Obshcheponiataia fizika* (physics comprehensible to all) was the first popular-scientific work on physics published in Russia. Pisarevskii believed that science could be interesting to all readers from varied social backgrounds, not just academic scientists or professors.[33] In response to the growing demand for popular educational works, publishers beginning in the mid-1840s produced scientific encyclopedias containing basic information on the major natural scientific disciplines. In the late 1840s the first edition of a broad science encyclopedia for the beginning reader was published in Russia—*Priroda s ee tainstvami i bogatstvami* (nature with its secrets and riches). The first entry on astronomy explained the form and development of the Earth and the stars.[34]

During the second quarter of the nineteenth century, one of the more successful publications used for the purposes of self-education was N. Polevoi's *Zhivopisnoe obozrenie* (pictorial survey). The survey was an illustrated journal for self-education with the goal of spreading useful information among readers in central and provincial arenas.[35] The journal had seven departments, including Geography and history, Natural Sciences, and Science, Art, and Knowledge. The publication was one of the early popular-scientific journals with such a broad range of topics covered within its pages. A large majority of the articles and drawings were taken from the British *Penny Magazine* that was published in London—with a circulation of over two hundred thousand copies—by the Society for the Spread of Widely Useful Knowledge. Some of the material for the Russian journal was also taken from the French *Magazine Pittoresque*. However, articles were not simply translated from these foreign magazines, but adjusted for the Russian reader.[36]

As early templates, European self-education journals and programs helped catalyze Russian editors and scientists to publish indigenous works for the Russian market, sparking a trend roughly between 1830 and 1855 to publish popular-science journals with a particular didactic or educational focus. A perfect example of these new publications was *Biblioteka dlia chteniia* (library for reading). This journal was founded in 1834 by O. I. Senkovskii, and its goal was to serve a young, semieducated clientele. The seven-branch program of the journal included sections on science as well as on industry and agriculture. Many of the articles in the natural sciences were written by science professors.[37] Both *Biblioteka dlia chteniia* and *Zhivopisnoe obozrenie* reflected the early connections between the movement to produce self-educational material for the Russian reader, on the one hand, and, on the other, the spread and popularization of the natural sciences and technology in Russia.[38]

Popular-scientific journals were also published by organizations and scientific societies that had recently been formed. One of those early societies was the St. Petersburg–based Vol'noe obshchestvo liubitelei slovesnosti, nauk i khudozhestv (voluntary society of the lovers of philology, the sciences, and arts), which also established chapters in Khar'kov and Vilnius (1804) and in Kazan' (1819). This society was associated with the secret organization of the first Russian revolutionaries (Decembrists), entitled Soiuz blagodenstviia (union of prosperity). The union, reorganized as the *Soiuz spaseniia* (union of salvation) in 1818, was involved in the spreading of knowledge about science and the arts.[39] The Decembrists also published an almanac that propagated scientific and philosophical ideas in Petersburg—*Poliarnaia zvezda* (polar star).[40]

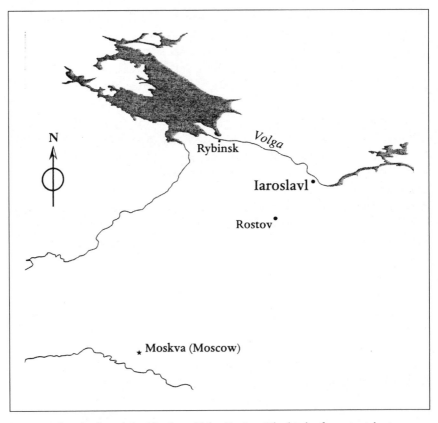

Moscow, Iaroslavl', and the Northern Volga Region. The birth of provincial science societies was spawned in towns in and around Iaroslavl' in the 1860s where a vibrant community of naturalists and field biologists assembled in established organizations up until the 1930s.

Two other science societies, established at this time under the auspices of Moscow University, were the *Obshchestvo ispytatelei prirody* (society of the investigators of nature, in 1804), and the *Obshchestvo meditsinskikh i fizicheskikh nauk* (society of medical and physical sciences, in 1805). Professors of Moscow University who were members of these societies took part in the publication of journals such as the *Zhurnal poleznykh izobretenii v iskusstvakh, khudozhestvakh i remeslakh i noveishikh otkrytii v estestvennykh naukakh* (journal of useful inventions in craftsmanship, the arts, trades, and new discoveries in the natural sciences, 1806–8). The articles in the journal were meant to introduce new inventions to manufacturers and to give the reader a survey of new technological discoveries and trends in the natural sciences.[41]

These Russian journals were very similar to the early eighteenth- and nineteenth-century European popular-science journals that also emphasized the practical application of science and technology for the lay reader. Russian professors used these new popular journals and societies as media to popularize scientific and technical knowledge. At the turn of the twentieth century popular science information would become more oriented toward the consumer market. In the second half of the nineteenth century, however, Russian popularizers still had an enlightened mission, as they had during the earlier periods of the eighteenth century. More than any other organizations, scientific societies utilized popularization to broaden public culture and to urge voluntary association with that effort. In Russia, these societies and their publications had a dual mission: to establish professional associations for scientific scholars and to bring science to the people.

Chapter 2

SCIENTIFIC SOCIETIES AND THE PUBLIC
SPHERE IN LATE IMPERIAL RUSSIA

In tsarist Russia, voluntary societies encouraged citizens from a variety of social backgrounds to participate and become more engaged in civic activity. The scientific society played a significant role in the grand, ambitious movement to popularize scientific ideas. They served as nexus points for various social groups and were loci for tsarist Russia's developing public sphere. Some of the first scientific societies in Russia developed in Moscow in the early nineteenth century. One of the oldest was the Society of the Investigators of Nature (Obshchestvo Ispytatelei Prirody), formed at Moscow University in 1804. Scientific societies began to multiply throughout St. Petersburg and the provinces as the nineteenth century progressed. Besides providing an informal atmosphere for scholars to congregate, they were involved in organizing popular scientific excursions, public lectures, and the establishment of scientific exhibits at museums. These societies served as conduits for the movement of scientific ideas between the intelligentsia and other social groups and were an integral factor in the adult education movement *(vneshkol'noe obrazovanie)*.[1] As voluntary associations scientific societies gave intellectuals, activists, and popularizers an arena in which to sponsor public education. T. I. Vzdorpov suggests that public meetings of various voluntary societies provided a common ground for exchange among members of various prerevolutionary estates *(sosloviia)*. These societies were conveyers of Russian *obshchestvennost'*, a sense of public duty and civic spirit.[2]

Geoffrey Eley and David Blackbourn argue that in nineteenth century Germany an increasingly dense network of voluntary associations provided a conduit for the middle classes to set the tone in the cultural sphere of civil society.[3] Samuel Kassow believes that if we look beyond political development toward more complex social phenomena, we can also see the development of a new public culture in late Imperial Russia. Like Eley and Blackbourn, he lists the rise of voluntary and professional associations as just one of those signs.[4] This recent comparative European historiography points to the development of a public sphere in Russia in the Habermasian, communicative sense. Jürgen Habermas articulates this public sphere as a place mediating between state and society in which European public opinion formed and developed.[5] Scientific societies and science educators helped to develop this space in pre-1917 Russia for an articulation of public discourse.

According to Habermas, as the commercial market expanded so did the rapidly expanding reading public and cultural realm. Periodicals replaced private correspondences as the important medium of discourse, and museums institutionalized public and lay opinions on art and science. In Russia, as in Europe, periodicals, societies, and museums helped expand the distribution of scientific information in the public realm. As the eighteenth century continued and the Enlightenment developed, the public sphere, according to Habermas, became an arena for educational change where one could publicize new ideas in the realms of art and science: "[A] public reflected critically in public on what they had read, thus contributing to the process of enlightenment which they together promoted . . . [T]he first public library was founded; book clubs, reading circles, and subscription libraries shot up."[6]

Habermas's sociohistorical perspective is too limited, however, to describe fully the development of the public sphere in particular geopolitical contexts. He isolates the bourgeoisie as the only class or group with the ability to transform the public sphere. His analysis, therefore, leaves little room for understanding how other classes or social groups came to take part in that public realm.[7] Historians of science in Britain, particularly those who study European popular culture, have attempted to define the public sphere in a broader sense, incorporating the participation of a variety of social groups. Stephen and Eileen Yeo have consistently argued in their work that working-class cultural movements in nineteenth-century England competed with middle-class philanthropic societies for public meeting places. In a study on working-class culture and constraint, Eileen Yeo shows that the halls of science, for instance, competed with the mechanics' institutes. Between 1839 and 1841 socialists built halls of science in towns from Manchester to London and Birmingham. These "halls," much like the Chartist institutes and people's halls, were intended as independent working-class controlled territory. They were places for workers to congregate, listen to lectures, and socialize.[8]

Geoff Eley and Eileen Yeo's analysis seems to encompass a broader definition of the developing public realm as a place where various social groups accommodate one another as citizens. In nineteenth- and early twentieth-century Europe, including Russia, this movement to expand the public sphere was certainly spearheaded, as Habermas points out, by the developing bourgeoisie. Eley and Blackbourn see the development of professional and voluntary organizations as defining elements of the new public culture and the middle class as leading participants in this movement. Yet other social groups, as Vzdorpov reminds us, took an active part in shaping this public sphere within the context of various organizations. In tsarist Russia the scientific societies and their public meetings were arenas where middle-class scientific specialists and educators could interact vibrantly with laymen from a variety of classes above and below them on the social ladder. Furthermore, in Russia, this public arena continued to foster scientific exchange across the 1917 revolutionary divide, mixing scientists, bureaucrats, educated laymen, and commoners alike. We can look to these scientific organizations and their gathering places as potent sites of public, civic activity well into the early Stalinist era, when they were finally extinguished.

The Russian naturalist societies had a particularly public vision, creating an atmosphere in which amateurs could learn more about science and participate in public events, lectures, and excursions. Some, like the St. Petersburg Society of Natural Scientists,[9] even accepted membership from all interested citizens regardless of their academic qualifications.[10] In prerevolutionary Russia the first learned scientific associations were undifferentiated naturalist societies—that is, having no specialist divisions—like the Moscow Society of Naturalists. This scientific club provided a place where scholars could discuss their work in an informal atmosphere. The Moscow society also sponsored advanced scientific work by awarding funds to scientists engaged in research in a number of fields.[11] More differentiated, national learned societies—such as the Russian Geographical, Mineralogical, and Astronomical Societies—began to sponsor scientific research and publication along with popular scientific enlightenment. These groups were interested in the utilitarian application of science to the needs of society.[12]

In the late nineteenth century in Russia, a new type of naturalist society emerged that became the focal point for scientific popularization. These newer naturalist societies sponsored a broad range of scientific work—from observing natural phenomena and collecting museum specimens to modern scientific research. One of the best examples of this type of naturalist society was the St. Petersburg Society of Natural Scientists. The society was an advanced, differentiated learned society divided into specialized departments, each with its own membership and interests. It helped organize natural history excursions led by various experts in geology, physical geography, and botany; and the organization conducted a campaign among zemstvo,[13] or council, authorities to establish science exhibits in local museums. Petersburg naturalists participated in the various national congresses of Russian naturalists and physicians and opened the society's doors to all interested citizens regardless of their scientific or academic qualifications. Furthermore, private citizens interested in science were included on the research committees of the society.[14] According to Alexander Vucinich, the acceptance of nonacademics as members in the naturalist societies helped create an "organic unity of scientific inquiry and civic spirit." Although some learned societies received government assistance, most of them, particularly the naturalist societies, depended on private donations.[15]

By the end of the nineteenth century, nationally recognized naturalist societies combined collective research projects with the popularization of science as a new system of knowledge.[16] The reorganized St. Petersburg Society of Natural Scientists, though founded in the 1860s, was officially sanctioned as a scientific establishment by the tsarist Ministry of Education on May 24, 1901. The new 1901 constitution of the society stated that the organization would participate in the scientific investigation of nature and serve as a gathering place for natural scientists. But the society's new statutes underscored its popularization goals, as indicated in the second paragraph of its constitution, which states a commitment to spread and popularize natural-historical knowledge in Russia.[17] The constitution declared that the organization would promote public lectures and organize excursions for members and the general public to investigate and observe nature.[18]

Naturalists' societies involved in the popularization of science also spread throughout the provincial centers of Russia. Of all provincial naturalist societies, none had as long a tradition of popularizing and spreading natural-scientific ideas in Russia as the Iaroslavl' Natural-History Society. Founded in Iaroslavl' in 1864, with somewhat later branches formed in Rybinsk and Rostov, the Iaroslavl' society's goals were the study of nature in the Iaroslavl' region and also the spread of natural-historical knowledge among the populace. The society was founded on the initiative of A. S. Petrovskii, a botany professor who taught at the Demidovskii Lycee in Iaroslavl'. The 1864 charter statutes urged members to read public lectures, take part in public exhibitions, and popularize agricultural, economic, and biological knowledge by relying on the society's museum.[19] This local society served as a catalyst and example for a small, yet growing, number of provincial societies to open their doors to the public, not just in the Northern Volga region but also in parts of the Urals and southern Russia.

The Iaroslavl' Natural-History Society provides an excellent case study for understanding the rise and fall of scientific societies as public institutions. It had strong links to the local entrepreneurial community, which provided the society with financial support. The board of the society was made up of well-trained chemists and biologists educated at Russia's central universities. It conducted research on the local ecology and on the biology of the Northern Volga area, thus providing its provincial constituency with scientific analysis of the region. Furthermore, it would cultivate its civic, enlightened mission in the 1920s to garner state subsidies before being liquidated during the Stalinist cultural revolution.

As the oldest and most active provincial scientific society in Russia, the Iaroslavl' society provides a rubric for understanding the changes in popular science in the provinces from the era of the Great Reforms through Stalin's cultural revolution. Founded in 1010 A.D., Iaroslavl' was one of the oldest towns of Kievan Rus'. It continued to have a vibrant economy during the imperial period, fostering voluntary civic organizations and the growth of a wealthy merchant class that donated much money to the building of beautiful Orthodox churches. Located along the northern Volga River, the industries and craft houses of Iaroslavl' fostered a developing working class that also showed interest in scientific themes. Furthermore, the diverse river ecology provided an ideal environment in which ecologists and field biologists could study nature.

The Iaroslavl' Natural-History Society was first housed in the local Demidovskii Lycee and received an official approval from the Ministry of Education in late 1864. Unlike the central scientific societies, provincial organizations had to find schools with which to associate themselves where universities had not yet developed.[20] A. Sokolov, director of the Lycee, helped to give the society an institutional home and was quite supportive of the founder of the society, A. S. Petrovskii (a botany professor at the school). Sokolov helped Petrovskii develop the formation of the society's natural-history museum in 1865.[21] Iaroslavl' did not have a university until 1918, and the naturalists therefore turned to the secondary lycee for support.[22]

In the prerevolutionary era, the Iaroslavl' society depended largely on its members' dues, sales of journals, receipts from excursions, and visitors to its museum. Those funds, as well as donations from wealthy merchants and entrepreneurs, made up the bulk of its budget before late 1918. It also sought funding from the Imperial Ministry of Education, provincial and district zemstvos, and the city government (duma).[23] Wealthy merchants and entrepreneurs, especially those from prominent local families, provided links between the zemstvos and the organizational committees of provincial societies like the naturalists in Iaroslavl'. For instance, L. P. Sabaneev (a zoologist) and his brothers, who were from a prominent Iaroslavl' family, were active participants in the Iaroslavl' scientific society and served as important leaders who helped to secure patrons from the local entrepreneurial community.[24]

In the first fifty-three years of its existence, Russia's first provincial naturalist society conducted public scientific lectures and short courses, guided excursions, and professionally guided tours of its museum. Educated, middle-class laymen and students made up the bulk of the society's early participants in courses and excursions. The Iaroslavl' society founded the first natural-history museum in provincial Russia, with smaller satellite museums in towns on the northern Volga, like Kostroma.[25] The museum contained specimens of local flora and fauna collected from Iaroslavl' province, fossils of preexisting animals from the area, and a general scientific collection and public library. It charged ten kopecks per visitor and registered between twelve thousand and sixteen thousand visitors per year.[26]

Throughout prerevolutionary Russia, museums (and itinerant exhibitions) were potent vehicles in the popularization of ideas about science and technological progress. The Museum of Science and Industry in Moscow, organized by various groups including the Moscow Society of Natural Science and Anthropology, began its tours in 1878. The Moscow museum sponsored public lectures and exhibits, as well as courses in the natural sciences and medicine.[27] In the capital cities, as in the provinces, special scientific exhibitions served a function similar to that of the permanent exhibit museum. These exhibitions included the Moscow Exposition of Science and Industry in 1872 and the Moscow Electricity Exhibit in 1892.[28]

However, as the first regional group of its kind, the Iaroslavl' Natural-History Society served as a provincial model for the construction of local museums in other places, like Ekaterinburg. In the view of the members of these provincial scientific societies, their natural-history museums were the ideal educational centers for the spread of new scientific ideas and knowledge, and they also understood that broadly spreading scientific knowledge among laymen in Russia would require a huge effort on the part of regional institutions with close ties to the provincial public outside the more cosmopolitan cities, that is, their societal museums. Local natural history museums in Russia emulated Western European and American models, and their work actually displayed much knowledge of foreign institutions. The ideal of the provincial museum as the engine of lay science education was elaborated by S. G. Lepneva, a member of the Iaroslavl' Natural-History Society, at the outset of her 1914 speech entitled "On the Expansion of the Museum of the Iaroslavl' Natural-History Society with the Goals of the Popularization of Scientific Knowledge," given at the Social-Industrial Congress in Iaroslavl': "It is absolutely essential that all Russians—every person who is involved in our economic-industrial complex—learn about new scientific discoveries. A majority of the Russian people must understand basic scientific concepts. One of the most important goals of the Iaroslavl' Society of Natural History is to popularize natural science in Russia."[29]

In her speech Lepneva stated that the museum needed an overhaul in order to serve as a popular-exhibition site. She argued that in America and Western Europe most natural-history museums were both attractive and instructive. In her view the guiding principle of the National Museum in Washington, D.C., for example, was that "one should not exhibit a single specimen or object that does not represent a special educational goal, does not interest a majority of the public, and does not serve an important general, educational objective." The director of the Iaroslavl' museum agreed that the complex should be a place of cultural enlightenment, accessible and useful to all its visitors. With this goal in mind the director had organized a section of comparative anatomy, which gave visitors to the museum a chance to view skeletons of various local animal species. The director also developed a "living nature" section, which contained an aquarium featuring a variety of fish species and a terrarium including snakes and birds from various parts of Russia.[30]

Lepneva believed that the museum had to create an atmosphere where visitors could both observe the permanent collection and become practically familiar with the achievements of science. She helped create a visitors' laboratory in the museum, where patrons could use simple apparatuses under the guidance of a professional scientist.[31] By the eve of the first World War, and as a result of the efforts of local naturalists, the Iaroslavl' Natural-History Museum had become one of the most important provincial museums of any type in Russia. By 1914 it boasted not only a specific department involved in public education but also sections specializing in comparative anatomy, geology, botany, entomology, and ornithology.[32]

In addition to the work of the naturalists, other amateur scientific societies developed in Russia in the nineteenth century and were also potent forces for the spread of science. S. M. Selivanov, a popularizer working with organizations of amateur scientists, believed that amateur scientific investigation had been one of the essential components of the empirical research process. By the turn of the century, according to Selivanov, the participation of amateurs in Russian science through the formation of voluntary amateur scientific societies had taken on the character of a mass-movement.[33]

One of the most important amateur scientific groups in Moscow involved in science popularization was the Society of the Amateurs of the Natural Sciences, Anthropology, and Ethnography. It was founded in Moscow on October 15, 1863, with the goal of spreading popular enlightenment and criticizing the more scholastic, insular, and dogmatic aspects of scientific development. The society was one of many amateur groups having a thoroughly inclusive orientation and supporting public participation in scientific observation and education. The society helped found the famous Moscow Polytechnic Museum, which lasted well into the late twentieth century. That museum became a central place for large public scientific lectures on a range of topics both before and after the First World War. Some of Russia's most famous scientists, such as K. Timiriazev and V. Vernadskii, gave frequent popular lectures at the Polytechnic to huge audiences. Timiriazev, for instance, popularized Darwinism and evolutionary ideas in several of his public lectures at the Polytechnic Museum at the turn of the century.

The society helped promote the formation of two university museums in Moscow—anthropological and geographical—and helped in procuring exhibition materials for such university museums as the Moscow Zoological Museum.[34] The society organized several important public scientific exhibitions in Moscow in the late nineteenth century. These exhibitions included the Ethnography Exhibition of 1867, the Moscow Polytechnic Exhibition of 1872, the Moscow Anthropological Exhibition of 1879, and the Moscow Geographical Exhibit of 1892. Through its public lectures, the society attempted to bring science closer to the common man. It also helped connect professional organizations with scientific intellectuals to create a symbiotic relationship between science and industry.[35]

Amateur scientific societies throughout the provincial centers of Russia were also involved in popular-scientific education in the late imperial period. The Ural Society of the Amateurs of Natural Science was founded in Ekaterinburg in 1871. This society organized a public natural-history museum with exhibits in archeology, botany, geology, zoology, and fossils of the Urals. It created a meteorological station that helped monitor climatic changes in the Urals and helped organize a number of scholarly expeditions in that region, in addition to expeditions for manufacturers, industrialists, and trappers to understand better the geography and geological conditions of the Urals.[36] The organization united scientists with those people active in the local economy and served as a facilitator between the two groups. The Ural Society became a trendsetter in the eastern provincial areas of Russia, and other amateur groups began to emulate its organizational structure and popularizing methods. In 1887 the Ural Society organized the Urals West-Siberian Scientific-Industrial Exhibit. It conducted public courses, lectures, and conferences on themes such as fishing, forestry, and wildlife of the Urals.[37] In many respects the Ural Society was a perfect example of how scientific societies functioned as an essential component of the *kraevedenie* (regional study of lore, history, and economy) movement.

Amateur scientific societies were involved in a myriad of scientific arenas, and some in the capital cities were particularly involved in popularizing astronomy. Astronomy became very popular in Russia, particularly because amateurs could easily engage in this discipline by spotting shooting stars and identifying planets using telescopes at observatories. The Russian Society of Amateur Investigators of the Natural World was one of the most active in this regard. This Russian amateur astronomy society, founded in St. Petersburg, published a popular journal entitled *Mirovedenie* (study of the natural world), which concentrated on astronomy and physical-mathematical knowledge. Professional scientists also worked for the society and wrote articles for its journal. This enabled amateurs and trained scientists to integrate their work, and laymen could be exposed to more sophisticated methods and theories in astronomy.

Between 1909, the year of its foundation, and 1916 the society financed its activities primarily through membership dues, revenues from the sales of its publication *Mirovedenie,* and other sources. In 1909 the society sponsored several popular-scientific lectures for the public in St. Petersburg, with a special emphasis on popular astronomical themes. The first meetings of the society were conducted on the premises of the St. Petersburg Conservatory. The society formed a public library, which had to be kept in the private apartments of members. In 1909 the director of the Tenishev School in St. Petersburg offered the society the use of its relatively large telescope and other refractory instruments. With the help of members, the society was able to procure a 175-mm refractor, the second largest in St. Petersburg at the time, and some other instruments. The observatory served both the scientific work of the society and the educational needs of the school. Once or twice a week the observatory was open to the public free of charge. Members of the society helped visitors view stars, planets, and other objects, while offering explanations for various stellar configurations. The refractor was transferred to a building in the Petrograd Biological Laboratory after 1914, and the society formed the same symbiotic relationship with the laboratory as it had with the school.[38] As in the case of the Iaroslavl' Natural-History Society, these amateur associations formed symbiotic bonds with local schools and institutions to get off the ground initially. Furthermore, they served as conduits between the scholarly community and the local public.

The Russian Society of Amateur Investigators of the Natural World received public support, and its membership grew at a remarkably fast pace. It sponsored the publication of popular-scientific works for the lay reader. Some of the new publications the society printed included pamphlets for amateur astronomers, such as Professor K. D. Pokrovskii's *Instructions on the Observation of Shooting Stars* (1913) and A. V. Bochek's *Changes on the Lunar Surface* (1915).[39] Pokrovskii's popular work included a guide to the main meteor movements and showers and an explanation of how to follow the path of falling meteors. Astronomy, cosmology, and even the possibilities of spaceflight were among several themes capturing the popular imagination in Russia both before and after the First World War and the Bolshevik Revolution. Readers anticipated the publications of articles, books, and pamphlets written by experts on stellar configurations and on the general analysis of the solar system and its planets.

Whether spreading ideas on flora, fauna, or the universe's expanse, scientific societies substantiated themselves in late Imperial Russia as public institutions, relying heavily on public and private donations. Although registered with the Ministry of Education, they generally received limited funding from the ministry. As in the developing private sector within the economies of the West, these societies in Russia lobbied for their participants' help in keeping their organizations financially afloat and also depended on revenues from journal subscriptions, public events, and membership dues. Their activities helped to expand the Russian public sphere outside the purview of the tsarist state and to create a space for the interaction of varied social groups, laymen and scientific elites alike.

In the aftermath of war, revolution, and the rise of the new Bolshevik bureaucracy, these societies would lobby the new Soviet secular state for funding.[40] In turn the Bolsheviks would use these societies as a means to spread their cultural vision of a rational, irreligious social order. These organizations would struggle to maintain their control, separate identity, and autonomy in this dynamic process in the 1920s. These societies would expand their civic and public educational activities, fostering a continued sense of that Russian ideal of public duty and civic spirit, *obshchestvennost'*, across the revolutionary divide into early Soviet Russia. Along with publishers, scientific societies were crucial components in the spread of science to the Russian public and in the maintenance of a limited, yet viable, "public sphere" in the new Soviet scientific realm.

Part II

THE SOVIET STATE, BOLSHEVIK CULTURE,

AND PUBLIC SCIENCE, 1917–27

Chapter 3

PATRONIZING SCIENCE

Glavnauka and Scientific Societies, 1917–27

The Bolshevik Revolution in 1917 radically transformed the administrative, institutional, and fiscal landscape in which scientific societies had to operate. After the Bolshevik Revolution, all scientific societies in Russia were funded primarily by the Soviet state and made subject to registration and auditing by Glavnauka, the Scientific Department of Narkompros (the Commissariat of Enlightenment) and the People's Commissariat of Internal Affairs (Narkomvnudel or NKVD). The state required that a scientific society send Glavnauka its statutes, a list of its members, and various departments, along with an estimated budget of its yearly expenses. The estimate included what funds it was requesting from Narkompros. Narkompros would then send this material to the NKVD with its registered approval of the association. The NKVD would keep detailed records on which societies were registered by the state and their yearly financial status.[1]

A paradoxical, yet symbiotic, relationship then developed as former independent voluntary societies became housed under Glavnauka, thus receiving their financial sustenance from the Soviet state. The new state funding allowed these societies to continue their scientific and public work, and the leaders of these organizations continued to support independent activities outside the state's purview. Glavnauka, in fact, was a key patron of prerevolutionary scientific groups, helping them to survive the upheaval of the Bolshevik Revolution into the 1920s. On more than one occasion, Glavnauka and its head, F. N. Petrov, directly intervened to help prerevolutionary scientific groups, sometimes in the face of caustic political accusations against the older groups by rival Soviet organizations, like Vesenkha (Supreme Council of the National Economy, or VSNKh). Petrov, an old Bolshevik Party member, strongly believed in supporting public scientific discussion in Soviet Russia. He had joined the Social Democratic Party in 1896, organized alongside Lenin during the revolution, and subsequently became an important member of the Soviet Council of Ministers. He was a key supporter of the role of science in shaping Soviet culture.

STATE PATRONAGE, PUBLIC SCIENCE EDUCATION, AND THE NEW BOLSHEVIK CULTURAL VISION

Narkompros in general, as well as Petrov's Glavnauka, had certain agendas in mind. They were interested in funding and registering societies that especially promoted popular enlightenment programs. Therefore, some societies tried to promote their popularizing activities and mass-enlightenment work in order to gain large monetary subsidies from Narkompros. Many of these societies had been involved in science popularization for some time before the revolution. In the post-October period, some tried to show that the new state needed the work of these organizations in raising the scientific level of the common Soviet citizen.

An example of this interaction is the application to Narkompros from the Moscow based Society of the Amateurs of Natural Sciences, Anthropology, and Ethnography. In a 1918/1919 budget estimate, the society requested 50,000 rubles from Narkompros for its science popularizing activities, which included public courses, lectures, educational excursions, and popular-scientific publications. The rhetoric employed in that budget request shows how these societies cleverly used the catch-phrases that Narkompros officials themselves had coined to promote Soviet cultural enlightenment:

> The popularization of scientific knowledge has been conducted by the society since its foundation. The society, along with the Polytechnic Museum in Moscow, since 1872, has attempted to interest people of all ages in the natural sciences. The society is reworking various projects and programs of popularization in the area of excursions, lectures, and popular-scientific publications. With 50,000 rubles a year, we can organize many useful popularization activities, which today is an important enlightenment task for Soviet power.[2]

The societies rhetorically worked the system of state patronage and succeeded financially at the new game. Their budget requests made prominent use of such phrasings as, "We can accomplish important enlightenment tasks," which echoed the language of Glavnauka's official pronouncements.

Narkompros's Glavnauka department was quite generous in funding these scientific societies, and the sums transferred were remarkable, given the financial and administrative turmoil during the Russian Civil War. The estimated budget of the Petersburg-based Russian Society of Amateur Investigators of the Natural World for 1919 was 115,500 rubles. The society received 58,000 from Narkompros, after the total budget was recalculated by Glavnauka officials at 90,891 rubles.[3] In 1919, therefore, the society received 63.8

percent of its total budget from the Commissariat of Enlightenment's Scientific Department.[4] The rest of the budget was covered by membership dues, journal subscriptions, and charges for public activities.

On occasion societies asked for supplementary funding, outside of the yearly budget, for new projects or specific public lectures and exhibits. Exploiting the popularity of astronomy among the Russian people, the Natural World Society lobbied for funds in 1923 to build an enlarged telescope for an observatory in Odessa. The society requested 3,500 rubles from Narkompros, hoping to conduct public viewings of the astronomical opposition of the planet Mars in August of 1924.[5] Scientific groups like the Natural World Society would add to their budgets and justify their requests by highlighting for Narkompros officials the public-enlightenment value of these supplementary projects.

After the Bolshevik Revolution, other established Petrograd scientific societies continued their work of popularizing science among broad segments of the populace. In May of 1918 the secretary of the Russian Technical Society (RTS) requested government subsidies from Narkompros to keep the society running. He too, realizing the importance of rhetorical strategies, argued that the RTS had been involved in cultural enlightenment for the preceding fifty years and had achieved much success.

Much of the activity of the organization involved disseminating information and organizing informal discussion sessions. Technical education for the public was an important aspect of the society's original agenda. The society fostered a number of schools for workers at various industrial enterprises. Under the leadership of E. Andreev, a number of specialized schools offered the public technical training in a variety of areas. These included courses on printing technology, basic concepts in electricity, and various technical skills.[6] Glavnauka was particularly interested in societies that could offer technical education to workers outside of traditional schools, and the RTS was adept at showing the new state how they could provide those services.

The secretary of the RTS complained that during the war the society was ruined by governmental war taxes and other fees. He further argued that the society needed credit in the amount of approximately 100,000 rubles.[7] In July of 1918, Narkompros responded to this request by ordering its finance commission to send 20,000 rubles to the technical society for the second half of 1918.[8] The presidium of the society contained several key Petrograd scientific figures, including mineralogist and academician A. E. Fersman and chemistry professor M. A. Blokh. In 1919 the society was involved in organizing adult-education courses on technological topics and publishing popular technical works. The RTS was concerned with the application of new technology to agriculture, noting in its 1919 report that it needed to popularize methods of melioration or land improvement (either by drainage or by proper methods of irrigation). Lastly, the society believed it was necessary to spread useful knowledge concerning municipal planning and proper building construction by publishing public norms that were accessible to all.[9] The RTS fulfilled several utilitarian tasks for Glavnauka outside the purview of typical educational institutions and in other ways was a useful organization to Narkompros officials, thus solidifying the society's position with the state's principal agency of support.

With the advent of the New Economic Policy (NEP) in 1921, and the beginning of cost accounting in general, the Bolshevik state introduced across-the-board cutbacks in government spending and subsidies for voluntary organizations. Factories and organizations were instructed to keep close balance-account sheets. A mixed economy was introduced in which the state owned and operated the commanding heights, while significant portions of light industry and retail trade were privatized. Though many scientific societies were affected by the cuts in government subsidies, the state was still the principal financial supporter of those organizations.[10] For example, the Petrograd Society of Natural Scientists continued its work after the Bolshevik Revolution. Its postrevolutionary executive committee was headed by Academician I. P. Borodin.[11] After the transfer to the NEP, the society was deprived of subsidized train transportation for its excursions and printing subsidies, which it had enjoyed during the period of War Communism (1918–20), when most of the centralized economy was state operated. Nevertheless, with other government subsidies and funds from public lectures, excursions, and popular publications, the society was able to survive the difficult change to the NEP.[12]

After the introduction of the NEP, the Russian Society of Amateur Investigators of the Natural World needed increased funding. In a November 1921 memorandum to all members in the society's journal, the director of the society stated that it was necessary to increase the membership fees and asked for donations from individual members. The government subsidy, for the most part, paid for the publication of the journal and support of staff workers. Besides new scientific work, the society had increased its cultural-enlightenment effort and therefore had a larger yearly budget.[13]

However, even under the NEP, government subsidies were responsible for the vast majority of the operating funds of the Russian Society of Amateur Investigators of the Natural World. In 1923 73 percent of the general budget of the organization was provided by Narkompros subsidies; 12 percent came from membership dues, 10 percent from sales of the journal and other popular publications, and 5 percent came from popular lectures. The figure of 73 percent government sponsorship did represent a small drop in state subsidies; and inflationary pressure also played a role in the need for new funds. The society's director therefore argued that the membership fees had to rise for the coming fiscal year.[14] The increase in dues caused a temporary exodus of members during 1924. Over the course of the year, memberships dropped from 849 to 639. Furthermore, the society calculated that approximately 350 members did not pay their dues in full for 1924. The society believed this would not affect the work of the organization. They stressed that only a small number of the more active members would actually leave the society. They were also confident that they would receive a majority of their operating costs from Glavnauka.[15]

The effect of the NEP, therefore, did not necessarily mean that the state would abandon voluntary scientific organizations in Russia. Furthermore, some continuity remained with the earlier period of 1917 to 1920. Conventional descriptions of the NEP era usually paint a picture of the state's abandonment of civic organizations, as it reintroduced a modicum of private economics into Russia. But that picture might not be a good analytical framework for understanding the period, especially since established scientific organizations were able to develop close patronage ties to certain Soviet institutions. Glavnauka was the main funder for the scientific intelligentsia, and the voluntary scientific organizations benefited considerably between 1917 and 1928 because of the close working relationship they actively cultivated.

Along with the positive benefit of Soviet state subsidies came some state interference in the work of the scientific societies. Civic scientific organizations interacted with various Soviet institutions, some of which were sympathetic, some not so sympathetic. From the beginning of 1918, the Russian Society of Amateurs Studying the Natural World insisted on trying to maintain its private status even though it was registered with Glavnauka and received government subsidies. In a 1922 report the society complained to Glavnauka that its broad, science-popularizing activities were being curtailed because the society was required to take part in political-enlightenment work in Petrograd at the request of the Petrograd Gubpolitprosvet (Regional Political Enlightenment Organ).[16] The society demanded that Glavnauka intervene and protect it from the local Gubpolitprosvet.

The Scientific-Technical Department (NTO) of Vesenkha had also been critical of Glavnauka's support of prerevolutionary scientific societies and their popular-enlightenment work. In general this criticism reflected a growing and important power struggle between these two institutions throughout the 1920s that would lead to NTO's displacing Glavnauka by 1928 and taking over the jurisdiction of some of the latter's scientific research institutes.[17] Vesenkha's NTO believed that Glavnauka took an almost "ivory scholarly tower" approach to scientific research and popular enlightenment.

Paul Josephson has noted the growing Soviet distrust of research science during this period, that Vesenkha's officials complained that Glavnauka actually preserved prerevolutionary attitudes about the importance of theoretical science while ignoring more applied science and production.[18] In terms of popularization, Vesenkha was highly critical of Glavnauka's support of the popular cultural activities of scientific societies and educators in the 1920s. Vesenkha was more concerned with popularization that would have some immediate utilitarian gains for the Soviet state, economy, and workers and favored spreading useful technical ideas related to production and industry.

Branches of Vesenkha meddled in the affairs of societies in certain key industrial areas containing valuable natural resources. Some of the scientific societies had been involved in intensively studying the region around a major provincial center. After the October 1917 revolution, Vesenkha realized that such societies could provide much-needed information about the industrial, agricultural, and mineral wealth of these areas. Yet scientific societies complained persistently to Narkompros officials asking for protection.

One case where Narkompros successfully intervened on behalf of a society in the Urals against Vesenkha is instructive. In March of 1920 A. V. Lunacharskii, commissar of Narkompros, received a letter from the president of the Urals Society of the Amateurs of Natural Sciences. This was one of the older, more well-established public scientific societies in eastern European Russia and was based in Ekaterinburg. The president of the society complained directly to Lunacharskii that the Urals Scientific-Technical Branch of Vesenkha had practically decided to nationalize his society and incorporate its various establishments into already existing Soviet organizations. The President stressed the fifty-year commitment his society had made to a wide variety of scientific and public-enlightenment activities.[19] A year later Lunacharskii and Narkompros successfully intervened on behalf of the Urals Society. On July 21, 1921, Narkompros officially certified the Urals Society as a scientific establishment under Glavnauka, the Scientific Department of Narkompros. Narkompros enabled the society to conduct its affairs with relative independence, certainly not under the jurisdiction of Vesenkha. This infuriated Vesenkha officials who believed Glavnauka was shielding bourgeois activists from working for the economic growth of the new Soviet state. This example demonstrates that scientific societies had strong patronage support at the very pinnacle of the Soviet cultural hierarchy. They were able to appeal directly to Lunacharskii, commissar of Narkompros, who became personally involved in specific disputes on a case-by-case basis. Like Petrov, Lunacharskii believed that the old scientific elite in both the capitals and provinces could help raise the cultural and technical level of the Soviet people.

The People's Commissariat of Internal Affairs (NKVD) also persistently monitored the functioning of preexisting science societies and, on occasion, intervened to subsume them under new Soviet institutions. Since the NKVD was responsible for officially registering science societies with the Soviet state, it tried to closely oversee their budgets and affairs. Occasionally, Glavnauka had to come to the societies' defense. For example, in a circular sent to Glavnauka in July of 1923 by the Petrograd Provincial Executive Committee, Narkompros was informed that the NKVD was reviewing the statutes of the Russian Society of the Amateur Investigators of the Natural World. The NKVD claimed that there was no need for such a society in view of the existence of many analogous societies such as the Association of Physicists and the Mathematical Society. Therefore, the NKVD proposed merging this amateur society with one of the other existing societies.[20] Such plans for "reorganization" caused great fear among many societies, whose members worried that they might be engulfed by a new umbrella organization more suitable to Soviet political officials.

In a rebuttal to the NKVD, Petrov, the director of Glavnauka, argued that this Russian amateur naturalist society had existed since 1909, with some eleven-hundred present members and a number of provincial branches. Furthermore, he pointed out, it was subsidized by Glavnauka and performed a number of significant works and activities. According to the director, there were no other existing analogous organizations, contrary to the view expressed by the NKVD in its report.[21] Glavnauka cleverly used the rhetorical constructs of "educational utility to the state" to defend these organizations from outside interference. Here too, Petrov, an old Bolshevik in a powerful position as director of Glavnauka, intervened directly in the affairs of critical scientific societies to save them from the clutches of other Soviet institutions. In this manner both Lunacharskii and Petrov skillfully competed with other Soviet institutions in the bureaucratic turf wars of the 1920s.

Another battle erupted in January 1923 after the NKVD sent a letter to Deputy Commissar of Enlightenment M. N. Pokrovskii[22] requesting a decision regarding whether or not to confirm and reestablish the Society for the Spread of Natural-Historical Education.[23] That natural-history society was founded in St. Petersburg in 1907 and headed by Professor B. E. Raikov, a prominent science pedagogue and member of the Petersburg intelligentsia. Raikov and V. A. Vagner edited the society's journal, *The Natural Sciences in School*. In a September 1923 reply to the NKVD's Administrative Branch, Ivanov (of Narkompros's Branch of Scientific Establishment) successfully argued that the society trained natural science teachers and popularized natural-historical knowledge. He noted that along with its central organization the society had five hundred long-standing members and twenty affiliate members in other cities. He believed that the Society for the Spread of

Natural-Historical Education was unique in the Russian Republic for its ability to unite pedagogues, natural scientists, and teachers in higher institutions.[24] In essence, Ivanov's responses to the NKVD's complaints might make or break the continued existence of many preeminent scientific and educational institutions with a long and distinguished record of public service in Russia which predated the October Revolution of 1917.

Glavnauka received a series of complaints from various scientific societies concerning the NKVD's interference. However, it was the NKVD's responsibility to check on the registration and financial support of various organizations. Given its role as a Soviet institution, the NKVD would understandably want to reject support for certain organizations that seemed redundant or superfluous. However, the NKVD, on the one hand, was also weary of the continued, forthright independent stance of prerevolutionary, voluntary societies. Glavnauka, on the other hand, was a generous patron of scientific societies during the twenties. In many respects, especially regarding national funding, Glavnauka's patronage represented a marked improvement over the prerevolutionary period during which the tsarist Ministry of Education offered little financial support for these societies. These groups not only had a state financial patron in Glavnauka; they also had a protector against Vesenkha's NTO and the NKVD's random checks. During this "golden age" of Soviet science under the NEP, Glavnauka not only protected fundamental scientific research in Soviet Russia from encroachment by government officials, but more importantly was able to protect the broad cultural-enlightenment efforts of scholars, societies, and publishers.

PROVINCIAL SCIENTIFIC SOCIETIES, PUBLIC CULTURE, AND THE BOLSHEVIK STATE

Scientific societies in the provinces were requesting government subsidies from Glavnauka, and they, too, received generous funding because of their ability to lobby Narkompros. Even under the difficult conditions of the early years of Soviet rule, these societies were able to maintain their enlightenment activities. The Bolsheviks saw them as important cultural organizations to support and nurture financially. In turn, the scientific societies in provincial Russia continued to be important purveyors of civic culture in the post-1917 Soviet era. They brought together various social classes that might not have mixed in other arenas. They continued to sponsor a sense of shared community and vision in those regions. These scientific organizations provided Narkompros with a foothold in existing cultural circles that encompassed intellectuals in provincial settings in Russia. The young Soviet state saw the societies as key players to win over and sponsor during a time when the Bolsheviks' political position was tenuous in those areas. The Bolsheviks lacked qualified cadres in provincial settings and relied on the older, scientific intelligentsia and its networks.

By 1918 Glavnauka successfully began registering the provincial societies with Narkompros and winning the favor of Gosbiudzhet (Government Budget Organization) by releasing funds to the societies in business-like fashion on a yearly basis. In the spring of 1918 Glavnauka actively drew more and more provincial organizations into its administrative network. In May of 1918 V. T. Ter-Oganesov—at the time in charge of Glavnauka's financial and accounting department—sent out an important administrative circular affecting regional scientific societies throughout the Russian Republic. The circular stated that Glavnauka requested all regional scientific organizations and societies to send yearly budgetary accounts and organizational records for the period 1915 to mid-1918 to Narkompros officials. The circular added that these societies would then have to be officially registered with the NKVD. Ter-Oganesov mentioned that only then could Glavnauka begin to instruct Gosbiudzhet to transfer government subsidies to provincial societies (usually distributed through the local Gubnarodobraz, or Provincial People's Ministry of Enlightenment Branch).[25]

Even throughout the difficult period of the Russian Civil War, Glavnauka persisted in its efforts to register and patronize local scientific societies. The societies, in turn, lobbied their patron with meticulous budgetary proposals detailing their monthly activities and financial needs. As with societies in Moscow and Petrograd, symbiotic relationships developed through which Glavnauka provided stability, protection, and funding to these organizations and, in return, the societies agreed to report their accounts and activities regularly to these new state institutions. Provincial societies also lobbied the local soviets, which had replaced all municipal dumas. After 1917 local soviets had educational departments that funded scientific societies as long as they claimed to popularize science for workers and other classes beyond the intelligentsia. Given the political turmoil and collapse of prerevolutionary local patrons, older science organizations (such as those in the Northern Volga region) saw this as a chance to gain state subsidies. They quickly registered their societies and requested large government subsidies.

Provincial scientific societies had proliferated in many geographic areas in Russia: for example, in the south (Voronezh), east (Ekaterinburg and other Ural towns), and northeast (especially those on the northern Volga like Iaroslavl', Kostroma, Rybinsk, and Rostov-Velikii). In the south of Russia in 1919, the Society of Natural Scientists at Voronezh State University requested 40,000 rubles from Narkompros for the first half of the fiscal year. The society requested funding for the printing of its protocols, various popular-enlightenment lectures, excursions, and research projects, like the study of malaria in the region.[26] The organization stressed to Narkompros officials the work's practical applications, particularly how the work could be a model for other scientific societies in the area. Other scientific societies in Voronezh also sent budgetary accounts to Glavnauka for funding on a yearly basis, particularly in support of the biological and medical information they could provide to both the local public and the Soviet state.

In eastern Russia, especially in the Urals, various societies served as centers for science popularization. The Urals Society of the Amateurs of Natural Sciences was inextricably involved in building public scientific exhibits and museums. Ekaterinburg was known for its high concentration of scientific societies involved in uniting scientists with professionals to promote understanding of the regional distinctions of the area and its economy. The industrial nature of Ekaterinburg, as well as its network connecting to the surrounding natural wealth of the East, made it an ideal place for scientists to publicize the utilitarian virtues of technology. Although the society had run into trouble with the local branch of Vesenkha before the NEP, by 1922 it was already vigorously at work on extracurricular science-educational tasks. The society was once again busy collecting artifacts and specimens for the archaeological and mineralogical exhibits in its museum. The museum was a provincial center for the study of mineralogical deposits and natural resources. The entomological section of the society conducted a number of research projects in the region and published a number of popular brochures on the struggle with vermin. Lastly, the excursion bureau conducted over thirty excursions for the regional public in 1922 alone.[27] The societies of naturalists in Ekaterinburg were eclectic in their pursuits and scientific interests and, probably more than anywhere else in Russia, focused on the study of regional culture and resource potential. Regional scientific organizations were important both to Vesenkha and to Narkompros officials for the knowledge they commanded on local natural resources and industrial potential. Soviet political agencies naturally saw in the regional scientific societies excellent potential for support of the state's secularizing and modernizing goals.

The most developed and oldest provincial scientific organizational structures were in northeastern Russia, particularly in the area around Iaroslavl' province and other towns in the Northern Volga basin. For this reason I will focus on Iaroslavl' as a case in point to demonstrate how these institutions more specifically related to the developing state. The naturalists in the region had formed the earliest science museums and societies in provincial Russia. They organized branches in many towns including Iaroslavl', Kostroma, Rybinsk, and Rostov-Velikii, and their members traveled to Moscow and St. Petersburg and had numerous foreign connections. After 1917 they vigorously and methodically lobbied Glavnauka for financial and material support. Records show that even during the anarchy of the Civil War, the Iaroslavl' Natural-History Society sent elaborate budget requests to central state agencies. They particularly detailed how this funding would in turn benefit the state's extracurricular scientific-enlightenment campaign. Furthermore, they showed how they could provide the state with a valuable cultural resource in provincial areas where Communist rule was not yet firmly entrenched.

The Iaroslavl' Natural-History Society requested 100,000 rubles from the Glavnauka for the 1918 and 1919 fiscal years. This sum equaled the budgets of some of the large, urban societies. The society skillfully requested funds during the Civil War by arguing that it could provide a social service to the young Bolshevik regime:

> Since 1864, the Iaroslavl' Society had been the first to promote popular-educational lectures in the natural sciences, and sponsored the formation of the first provincial public science museums. However, the society needs to pay for certain expenditures at the present time. The Zoological and Botanical Gardens will not be able to conduct popular-scientific activities without proper funding. Therefore, the society believes that 100,000 rubles should be sufficient for the work of the organization, which would benefit the new Soviet state in its ability to spread science to the masses.[28]

The Soviet state's fulfillment of that budgetary request further validates the importance the Bolsheviks placed on these provincial science organizations.

In January 1917 the Iaroslavl' society, along with the Iaroslavl' Physical-Mathematics Circle, was successful in starting a people's university[29] in Iaroslavl'. The society arranged to have scholars at the natural-history museum give lectures at the people's university. Several members of the society delivered popular-scientific lectures at the newly founded university during the autumn of 1917 and winter of 1918.[30] These activities would place the society in the good graces of Glavnauka officials.

The Iaroslavl' society also lobbied the local soviet for funding. On June 18, 1918, the local soviet in Iaroslavl' sent a representative to observe the proceedings of the Iaroslavl' Natural-History Society to verify the necessity of the 5,000-ruble request for funds.[31] The representative reported back to the soviet by approving the need for those funds. Subsequently, on September 16, 1918, the society sent Glavnauka a lengthy report documenting its history and goals, its former financial budget and donors, as well as its projected needs for the second half of 1918 and first half of the 1919 fiscal year.[32] Two months later on November 13, 1918, Glavnauka responded by saying it had approved 47,390 rubles to be sent to the society for its operating costs until mid-1919, and it officially sent out the funds on December 2, 1918.[33]

In 1918 the society was moving ahead with the reorganization of the Iaroslavl' Natural-History Museum. During that year, the Iaroslavl' provincial executive committee donated another building in town to the museum. The society decided that the museum should be more contemporary and also serve as an educational center for the entire region. A special scientific-popular department was organized within the museum. The society had opened an auditorium for public science lectures in the museum, and its staff conducted four to five guided tours a day for school children from areas throughout the Northern Volga. There was little interference from the local-soviet executive committee, and the society was able to continue its business as it had prior to 1917.

The society believed that the popularization of science and its methods could influence the teaching of the natural sciences in the schools. The society's summer biological station set up a program of visitation for teachers so that they could gather better practical knowledge of the research and investigation of natural processes. The society requested 20,000 rubles in government subsidies in 1918 from Narkompros to strengthen its programs for science teachers. It also requested 25,000 additional rubles for organizing the Iaroslavl' Botanical and Zoological Gardens to enhance their public displays. The gardens featured diverse flora and fauna from the northern Volga River Basin and had an extensive collection of insects and butterflies.[34]

During 1920 and 1921, in order to spread and popularize natural-historical knowledge, the society began short courses for the public. The courses averaged approximately sixty hours in length over a defined period, and each course usually contained sixty adult students. They became even more popular as the 1920s progressed and the political environment in the country became more stable. The activities in the courses included listening to popular-scientific lectures, participating in practical scientific labs, and also going on various nature excursions. The excursions were broken into sections concentrating on various flora and fauna of the forest and other environmental settings surrounding Iaroslavl'. During 1920 over eight thousand people visited the society's natural-history museum, and this number continued to rise after 1921.

After 1921 the Iaroslavl' museum continued to receive government subsidies and was even helped by generous grants from private citizens in the sum of 75,000 rubles.[35] Throughout the NEP the society had to rely on membership dues, some private funding, and funds from lectures and short courses for which it charged the public. However, it was still able to receive large subsidies from Narkompros's Glavnauka, which served as its major patron throughout the 1920s. The NEP did not mean that provincial scientific societies would be left to fend for themselves and rely primarily on private donations. However, as the decade progressed, Narkompros officials became more concerned with intensively documenting all societies' inventories, members' backgrounds, and financial expenditures. During the NEP, a positive, yet strained, relationship developed between the new patron (Glavnauka) and client (provincial science societies). Scientific societies benefited from Glavnauka's subsidies and its protection against the encroachment of other Soviet institutions. These organizations remained independent to continue their scientific research and popular educational activities. Slowly, however, the arm of the ever-encroaching central state began keeping closer and closer tabs on their minute local activities and provincial records. The continued success of established local scientific organizations was paradoxical: their ability to remain independent and garner state subsidies suggests only incremental sovietization of cultural organizations in provincial Russia during the NEP; however, fiscal reliance on the state was simultaneously leading to gradual sovietization by the late 1920s.

Starting in 1922 and 1923 Glavnauka sent out circulars to provincial scientific organizations asking them to have their charters and revised statutes filed with their *gubispolkom* (regional executive committee). Glavnauka requested that an overview of their key tasks and activities, especially public enlightenment work, be sent along to the regional executive committees.[36] By 1924 Glavnauka requested that detailed questionnaires (*ankety*) be filled out by all members of local scientific societies, museums, and libraries. The completed questionnaires documented that very few of these naturalists were actually Communist Party members. Glavnauka sent circulars to local Narkompros branch departments, housed within the local gubispolkom, making sure that local Soviet authorities verified membership, activity, and party affiliation of those in the societies.[37]

Glavnauka made it clear in its circulars to local organizations that no funding or institutional support would be forthcoming in the absence of these completed questionnaires, along with the mandatory budgetary reports. In December of 1924 Glavnauka stepped up its administrative demands by requiring much more detailed documentation from these societies. Petrov, the head of Glavnauka, sent out a circular to all societies in the Russian Republic stating that funding and continued state registration would be dependent on the successful and prompt completion of new yearly reports. Responses to Petrov's circular were remarkable in just how detailed their inventories were, listing practically all possessions and equipment down to office chairs. Furthermore, Petrov's office sent out form templates to guide societies on how to organize these inventories and yearly *otchety* (activity records and accounts). This remarkably incisive attention to detail and inventory control would soon come to characterize the Bolshevik state as its bureaucracy developed more firmly in the locales.[38]

As long as they did not experience enormous interference in their daily activities, provincial scientific societies continued to play the administrative game required by Glavnauka, to assure substantial funding. By the mid-1920s, provincial scientific societies, like the Iaroslavl' naturalists, started sending letters to the local gubispolkomi notifying them of their public-enlightenment activities and how their work was oriented toward popular lectures, courses, and exhibitions. A January 1926 letter to the Iaroslavl' Gubispolkom from the local society sent along a list of public lectures by their members. Some were of general interest, such as overviews of the flora and fauna of the area, while others pertained to more detailed scientific subjects, like plant ecology.[39] The society sent advertisements of public events to local newspapers, offering editors an occasional synopsis of practical public lectures. On June 7, 1926, a letter was sent to A. N. Zeverov, editor of the local newspaper *Severnyi rabochii* (the northern worker), asking him to advertise public lectures and exhibitions of the society and its museum.[40] A list of lectures would then generally appear in the paper, sometimes in the popular section entitled "News of Science and Technology." Such utilitarian public lectures, which certainly had intrinsic scientific value, put the society in the good graces of local Soviet authorities.[41]

Many regional newspapers carried science sections popular with readers. Though they were intrigued by foreign feats of aviation and news on astronomy, readers also focused on scientific issues relevant to the local province. The Iaroslavl' Soviet Executive Committee published its newspaper under the title *Vlast' Truda* (the power of work). This popular and cheap four-page newspaper had a section entitled "Local Life," which featured announcements for local science clubs including amateur astronomers, aviators, and naturalists. The newspaper also carried articles on science and technology and those pertaining to local industries, ecological problems in the area, and the geography of the Iaroslavl' region.[42]

The civic activity of local scientific organizations became transformed for Glavnauka into work that served the new Bolshevik state. A 1926 public lecture on water utilization, by V. Iaroslavksii of the Iaroslavl' Natural-History Society, which had been advertised in the local paper, included a detailed account on how to make sure drinking water was boiled properly. This public lecture had detailed charts and graphs to simplify concepts for the average viewer. At the end of the lecture, other society members in the auditorium, which was filled to capacity, had suggestions for the public on how to carry out what had been learned from the lecture. They passed out captioned notes for local residents, who were evidently obsessed with hygiene and worried about water contamination from local factories. Since paper was expensive, local residents had to share handouts; though specialists complained that residents unfortunately had to fight over copies, the incident reflected the public's interest in the scientific analysis of their daily surroundings.[43]

Lectures that discussed local ecology and biology were particularly popular with residents. On occasion, lecturers complained that there were not enough seats in the small auditorium for eager citizens who were curious about ecological issues. Provincial naturalists also lectured on similar topics, such as air flight and astronomy, which were popular with Russians all across the country. However, naturalists also catered to local laymen's interest in understanding their natural surroundings and thereby helped to foster civic and regional pride. Between August of 1924 and September of 1925, the society's yearly report mentioned an abundance of lectures given by naturalists focusing on scientific topics of local interest. In this way, the society could indeed emulate the large, central societies while specifically defining their own image and scientific mission in the provinces.

In the Iaroslavl' society's auditorium, which seated about one hundred persons, local citizens eagerly listened to lectures with titles such as "History of the Iaroslavl' River Bank," "Study of the Northern Volga's Plant and Animal Life for Amateur Naturalists," and "Local Ecology and Natural Resources of the Volga River Basin." Though seemingly mundane topics, they offered ordinary citizens and nature lovers a scientific understanding of their natural surroundings. B. A. Fedchenko, a biologist who lectured for the society, noted that in 1925 the lectures on local science captivated audiences, who believed they could now understand the technical relevance of those topics when applied to their province's ecology. He linked the lectures to the strong interest in nature excursions run by the society's museum and educational department.[44]

In the Fall of 1925 many excursions planned by the Iaroslavl' society had an educational purpose while also offering local residents an opportunity to see certain plants and animals in their natural settings. Naturalists and field guides in September 1925 took several groups on botanical excursions up and down the Volga River from Iaroslavl' to Kostroma. Participants rode in boats and took nature walks at various points along the river, and they even helped identify and collect plants for the museum in Iaroslavl'. Fedchenko noted that participants mounted horses to take rides further away from the Volga's banks when searching out particular areas naturalists had identified containing rare plant species. Participants expressed enthusiasm for these adventurous and informative trips on which they learned a good deal about the ecology of the area. The Iaroslavl' society also expanded these excursions to target schoolchildren, who were frequent visitors of the museum. However, local schoolteachers and professionals also frequented the excursions to expand their scientific knowledge.[45]

Ultimately, besides catering to local interests, the provincial societies knew that they had to lobby the central Glavnauka officials using evidence of the progress of their popular-enlightenment programs. Beginning in 1925 and 1926, the Iaroslavl' Natural-History Society sent, along with its yearly reports, detailed accounts of its popular-enlightenment efforts in a section entitled "popularization activities." In a February 26, 1926, circular to scientific organizations in the Iaroslavl' area, Glavnauka officials made it clear to these societies that they must discuss at length their "popular-enlightenment work." New questionnaires regarding public activities were sent to local scientific societies with sections asking: (1) what popular publications did you produce this year; (2) for what kind of readers are your publications geared, 'the wide masses?'; (3) which public lectures did you conduct; (4) describe your activities with regard to public exhibitions, short courses, and excursions; (5) analyze the social categories and interests of your listeners, viewers, and readers (do you get enough worker and Red Army personnel?).[46]

Glavnauka officials' attention to "social categories" and "public utility" was both characteristic of the Soviet 1920s and indicative of more stringent times to come under Stalin. Glavnauka's questionnaires were part of a general trend toward sociological analysis for political purposes and organizational control on the part of the regime. This trend was especially evident in provincial areas where Bolshevik control was more precarious after the 1917 Revolution. As controlling as these bureaucratic requests were, provincial societies responded favorably because they wanted to maintain their activities and gain access to state patronage. This was true even though many members were neither affiliated with the Communist Party nor political supporters of the Bolshevik Revolution. The society found funding to be generous during the post-1917 era and, given the general Soviet political constraints, wanted to continue the favorable working relationship with Glavnauka.

The Iaroslavl' Natural-History Society was always prompt in replying and thereby won the good graces of Narkompros officials. Furthermore, Narkompros officials realized it was the oldest provincial science society in Russia, and its actions would be observed by other local science organizations. In March of 1926 the society sent a detailed list of its 1925/26 popularization activities back to Glavnauka. This list included examples of public lectures on popular topics like astronomy, as well as lists of more practical scientific lectures on agronomy and disease control in the area.[47] During the twenties, instead of choosing the road of confrontation, they chose administrative cooperation, while maintaining independent control of their public activities and scientific research.

Glavnauka's Petrov seemed very pleased with the responses he received from local scientific organizations by 1926. In turn, Petrov offered local societies not only funding but even opportunities to engage in dialogue over public science education with Narkompros officials. In a March 1926 circular sent specifically to local scientific societies, Petrov requested feedback as to whether they believed it would be advantageous if foreign scholars were invited to Russia to give public lectures in local areas popularizing new themes in science. Petrov asked officials of local science organizations to send Glavnauka their opinions on the benefits of this proposal and the names of qualified foreign academics.[48] The response from local societies was healthy and quite interactive. The Iaroslavl' society thought this a great idea and offered lists of foreign scholars, like the famous American geneticist Thomas Hunt Morgan, who could come to the USSR to give detailed scientific and broad popular lectures.[49]

During the NEP, scientific societies filled out and sent detailed questionnaires, which included profiles of their members, to central-Narkompros officials. Profiles of major and minor figures in these organizations included their social, educational, and political backgrounds. Since the Bolsheviks were interested in collecting detailed sociological information of members of prerevolutionary organizations, the *ankety* usually included one's name, party affiliation (if any), educational background, job before and after 1917, and present institutional affiliation. Most of those in the Iaroslavl' Natural-History Society, for instance, were not Communist Party members. Yet the society's collegium certainly contained some party members who had regular positions in Soviet organizations such as the *rabfaki* (workers' faculties/ preparatory schools) or various *teknikumy* (technical schools). Many came from middle-class university educated backgrounds, but not all of them. Most of those in the Iaroslavl' society's leadership positions were educated either in Moscow or St. Petersburg (generally before the revolution) before coming back to provincial Iaroslavl'. Some assistants, graduate students, and researchers came from more humble socioeconomic backgrounds.

The backgrounds of a typical segment of the membership indicate a wide variety of interested citizens. Major figures in the Iaroslavl' society who held positions in the collegium were well educated with diverse scientific training. N. I. Shakhanin, a director of the museum, was a biology teacher in secondary school between 1918 and 1920 and then taught at Iaroslavl' University. P. A. Bogdanovich, who volunteered for the museum, taught mathematics at local secondary schools. V. P. Kazanskii, who taught at Iaroslavl' University, was also an agronomy specialist who consulted for the society and helped in creating excursions to rural areas.[50]

Some volunteers to the Iaroslavl' society had more mixed educational and economic backgrounds. In a response to a 1924 anketa, or questionnaire, Elena F. Vichel' (twenty-two years old) indicated she had been volunteering in the society's museum as a curator and was interested in local natural history. Her father (deceased) had been an agronomist, but she listed her mother as uneducated and living in the countryside. Elena had been a student during the early 1920s at Iaroslavl' University before it closed in 1924[51] and indicated she wanted to further her knowledge of natural sciences while working at the museum.[52]

The records document how educated people (such as teachers in the sciences) searched for provincial institutions to carry out their scientific interests after the revolution. V. V. Shestakova, a thirty-two-year-old from a noble family who had been a science teacher in Petersburg before the revolution and Civil War, now sought out work in the Iaroslavl' museum as a science librarian. She indicated on her questionnaire that she had been educated in St. Petersburg and had had trouble finding teaching jobs (maybe because of her class background). She therefore sought out the society in Iaroslavl'.[53] Shestakova's plight is an example of those intellectuals with checkered class backgrounds who sought out provincial organizations to hide or 'mask' their prerevolutionary affiliations. Such individuals were needed in provincial scientific organizations and were made welcome by local communities of intellectuals. This conclusion is supported by the records that show a high percentage of scientists returning to the provinces during the post-1917 era. Kendall Bailes has argued that this out-migration of scientists from the center to the provincial periphery was typical during the Civil War and immediately after. Bailes attributes this to the difficult conditions for scholars in the central cities between 1918 and 1920. This out-migration of highly qualified scholars helped solidify scientific research and organizational foundations in provincial settings.[54]

With the help of a well-educated and qualified staff during the NEP, the scientific society in Iaroslavl' set up a series of popular scientific lectures oriented toward educating the public on basic scientific topics.[55] The lecture series was entitled *Azbuka nauki* (the ABC's of science). They also set up an excursion bureau for various social and institutional groups. Although in the prerevolutionary era these excursions were oriented mainly toward educated middle class intellectuals such as schoolteachers, in the 1920s they were offered to students, schoolchildren, local intellectuals, and workers, as well as to visiting naturalists, teachers, and agronomists. On that level the revolution did have a democratizing effect on the clientele of the society, concentrating its efforts on the popularization of science. Of the 5,560 visitors it registered for the first half of 1922, 4,337 of those were students, including those in specialist schools. In addition the museum had a branch that dealt with extracurricular education in the natural sciences for schoolchildren. The museum received a working budget (mostly from Glavnauka) of 99,000 rubles for 1922 out of the society's total yearly budget of 512,820 rubles (by 1922, inflationary prices had raised budgets dramatically in comparison to the pre-NEP era). About 15–20 percent of the museum's budget itself was then spent on "popularization activities," which included public lectures, special exhibitions, and popular excursions.[56]

In 1921 the new director of the Iaroslavl' museum was B. E. Rozov, who believed Russia needed both central and provincial museums that educated the public. Rozov, who lobbied local and central officials for more funds for the museum, documented that close to fourteen thousand visitors came to the local museum between 1920 and 1921. The museum, according to Rozov, led all social classes on scientific excursions, including Red Army soldiers, local workers, and students, in addition to members of Soviet associations such as the "workers' clubs." Rozov knew that serving the Soviet Republic as a public institution was essential to the museum's existence. Members of the museum were also involved in such useful practices as studying local agricultural conditions, maintaining natural bogs and streams, and researching the uses of local plants for medicinal purposes. All of this was carefully logged by museum authorities and sent along to Glavnauka officials in yearly reports. These reports were constructed (by museum staff) to emphasize public utility of the museum and civic culture as key "Soviet attributes" of the society. The society and museum staff even set up a meteorological station in the area. The museum had ecological displays for the public but also put together reports for local officials on river pollution from local factories on the Volga.[57]

The Iaroslavl' Natural-History Museum expanded its exhibits and staff in 1923 and by early 1924 had a new director, N. I. Shakhanin, a botanist with a degree from Petrograd University. Shakhanin received a degree from the Physics-Mathematics faculty of Petrograd University, had taught in Iaroslavl' as a science instructor since 1918, and had worked in the museum since 1922. The chief curator of the museum was N. V. Kuznetsov, and the botanist of the collection was E. A. Garkavi, who had a degree from Donskoi University. Many of those affiliated with the society's museum staff were well-educated and highly experienced naturalists and biologists.[58]

Shakhanin noted that the museum offered exhibits in a wide range of areas, including sections on birds, mollusks, mineralogy, paleontology, and entomology. The museum had over three hundred varieties of stuffed birds on exhibit, as well as a new herbarium that featured brochures for viewers examining the diversity of plant life in the Iaroslavl' region. Between October 1924 and September 1925, over fifty-five hundred local people participated in nature excursions sponsored by the museum and led by its staff. Public lectures were held in its buildings, and it had supervision over the large auditorium that could seat approximately one hundred people. On average, the museum documented that approximately eighty to ninety people came to the more popular lectures, while numbers were much smaller (approximately twenty to thirty) for more sophisticated scientific presentations. Information about local flora and fauna and about agronomic and ecological topics dominated public lectures, but lectures on astronomy and air flight, as in the central cities of Russia, also seemed to bring in large numbers of visitors.[59] The director also noted that local citizens were keenly interested in the ecological conditions of the Northern Volga, and they flocked to lectures offering them practical information on pollution and disease in the area. Unlike the large central naturalist societies, local biologists and chemists could provide scientific information immediately relevant to provincial Russians. The provincial science society became a locus for natural historians, ecologists, biologists, and an array of individuals interested in regional studies.

Though these societies provided the Bolsheviks with an understanding of local cultural traditions, the Soviet state continued to bureaucratize these entities from the center, leading to center-periphery tensions. Beginning in 1924, the Iaroslavl' Natural-History Museum became an affiliate of the Museum Department of Glavnauka.[60] This was a mandatory reorganization based on central administrative dictates, and it meant that the museum itself, independently of the society, had to send questionnaires and financial budget reports back to Glavnauka. By July 1925 the Natural-History Museum had officially become part of the Iaroslavl' State Oblast Museum. Glavnauka's main Museum Department in Moscow, headed by N. Brotskaia, ordered these reorganizational changes throughout provincial Russia. This meant that although the Iaroslavl' museum was still attached institutionally to the Natural-History Society, it would be housed with all local museums in the Iaroslavl' region within a single building. For instance, this enlarged state museum, besides having a natural-history division, housed an ancient-historical and *zapovednik* (preservation) department.[61] Although N. I. Shakhanin remained head of the natural-history section, the well-known regional studies specialist *(kraevednik)* N. G. Pervukhin became the head of the newly enlarged oblast' museum in Iaroslavl'.[62]

The reorganization in the Museum Department of Glavnauka came as a result of a Council of People's Commissars (Sovnarkom) decree in early 1924 to centralize museum affairs in provincial areas. This decree ordered local

Narkompros branches to subsume natural-history museums, like the one in Iaroslavl', under more enlarged state museums for particular regions.[63] This reshuffling by Narkompros created a way for the Soviet authorities to centralize all museum affairs, bringing them literally under one roof. Soviet authorities could glorify the expanded museum as an epicenter of regional culture supported by central initiative and funding.

The Soviet centralization and reorganization of prerevolutionary cultural institutions typified the gradual process of Soviet bureaucratization in provincial areas. The process occurred slowly throughout the NEP, not suddenly after 1917. However, it was also an early indication of even further centralization of local cultural institutions that would lead to grave problems for provincial scientific societies while the NEP was drawing to a close around 1927 and the Stalinist cultural revolution was looming on the horizon. Although this bureaucratization of culture could be interpreted simply as Soviet methods of basic *kontrol'* (accounting), in reality it led to a gradual hegemonic struggle between the state and the local prerevolutionary cultural elite. For local intellectuals, more detailed inventory procedures became linked to long-term struggles with the new state. Although scientific societies were able to navigate safely through the new Soviet bureaucratic constraints under the NEP, perhaps even tolerating those methods as long as they received generous state funding, the tenuous relationship would be consistently more difficult to hold together after 1928.

Chapter 4

FORGING THE NEW WORLD

Scientific Print Culture and the Russian Reader in the 1920s

Professional educators and science popularizers, like Rubakin, survived the October Revolution of 1917 and continued to publish popular texts into the 1920s. These popularizers received funding from independent and state-run publishers. Bolshevik administrators in Gosizdat (the Soviet state publishing house) and Narkompros supported the printing of scientific texts by both Marxists and traditional popularizers alike. The Bolsheviks were keenly aware of the transformational role scientific texts could play in their envisaged cultural revolution of the following two decades. However, radical popularizers and leftist science educators opposed the Bolsheviks' initial support of the older generation of popularizers and educators. Marxists believed that studying the "interests" of the reader was worthless, since one needed to devise textual strategies that molded the reader instead. They envisaged a reader that accepted the preplanned, a priori, communicative discourse of revolutionary culture in post-1917 Soviet Russia.

SCIENCE, PUBLISHING, AND PRINT CULTURE IN SOVIET SOCIETY

The spread of popular science publications was the most significant factor in marketing scientific information in Russia at the turn of the twentieth century. The journal was an especially cheap and accessible source of scientific information for the Russian layman. In the era before the First World War, new popular scientific journals of all types offered the Russian reader excellent coverage of worldwide scientific developments. Publishers and editors geared these new journals to specific reading audiences, depending on the sophistication of the journal. On the one hand, for example, the natural-history journal *Priroda* (nature), started in 1912, attracted the educated layman and the more scientifically inclined. On the other hand, articles in the journal *Priroda i liudi* (nature and people, 1890–1918) outlined complex scientific developments in a more accessible fashion for the popular reader. Journals like *Priroda i liudi* included articles on popular themes such as air flight[1] and the exciting ideas of K. E. Tsiolkovskii on overcoming the Earth's gravitational forces by the use of futuristic jet-propelled rockets.[2] The journal was published by the Soikin publishing house in St. Petersburg, and it was dependent, like other popular journals, on advertisers as well as on a diverse group of subscribers.

In the late imperial tsarist era prior to 1917, Russian educators worked carefully to craft popular articles and texts that simplified difficult scientific theories. They labored to analyze the reader and how he would respond to new, scientific articles, books, and pamphlets. The pioneering work in this area in late tsarist Russia can be attributed to the bibliographer and science educator Nicholas Rubakin, whose work anticipated modern reader-response theory. Rubakin's work also points to the early ties between Russian reader-response theorists and science popularizers. In the late nineteenth century Rubakin had been part of various committees to combat illiteracy, especially in St. Petersburg. He was the author of hundreds of popular scientific and educational articles, pamphlets, and calendars at the end of the nineteenth and early twentieth century. He and his colleagues exemplified an older generation of prerevolutionary popularizers who were concerned with the reader's educational needs. Rubakin's cohort would come into conflict with Marxist scholars in the 1920s, who imbued their work with ideological overtones.

Rubakin's methodology for creating popular works revolved around his theory of biblio-psychology, which required consideration of the reader from a psycho-physiological and sociological point of view—that is, examining the effect of books on a reader of given social condition. Rubakin's philosophy emphasized the reader's receptivity and psyche[3] as fundamental points of analysis and the author who produced texts as secondary.[4] Rubakin's methodological approach conflicted with the perspective of Soviet Marxist scholars, who believed scientific popular texts had to have an ideological component. Marxists downplayed the importance of the reader as receptor, disregarding the significance of an individual's reading of a popular scientific text.

The early Bolshevik leadership—especially F. N. Petrov of Glavnauka, Commissar A. V. Lunacharskii of Narkompros, and others in Narkompros— saw the propagation of popular printed scientific texts as an integral part of their secular, cultural revolution. Just as it relied on preexisting scientific societies, Narkompros believed it had to support Gosizdat's publication of prerevolutionary popularizers and educators. Bolshevik state officials wanted texts that would challenge the public's religious preconceptions on a range of scientific issues, especially evolution and the creation of the universe. The state in the 1920s could not yet afford to unleash the young, radical Marxists against the older prerevolutionary generation of popularizers. Those science educators and editors were professionally embedded in their disciplines, and the state required their expertise for its enlightenment campaigns. Furthermore, old Bolsheviks such as Lunacharskii and Petrov patronized these prerevolutionary intellectuals and resisted any attempt to purge their societies.

The Soviet regime concurred with liberal and radical prerevolutionary intellectuals alike on the need to popularize scientific material, texts, and posters, regardless of the textual strategies pursued. The state fostered a climate wherein state, cooperative, and even some private publishing houses would create eclectic scientific material that did not necessarily mold a new Soviet scientized citizen in an a priori, Marxist fashion. This diverse climate was emblematic of the NEP era. The works of prerevolutionary popularizers like Rubakin continued to be popular among readers during the twenties, and Soviet state officials recognized this demand from below. Furthermore, editors, journalists, and scientists did not feel constrained, during the NEP, in writing on scientific topics. At least in the 1920s, scientific texts did not necessarily have to be filled with either class analysis or myopic utilitarian vision. Prerevolutionary science editors and publishers even tended to defy the radical Marxists and to show an editorial tendency to capture both the needs and the imaginative interests of the reader.

Although scientific publications appealed mostly to urban Russians, those readers came from a variety of professional and class backgrounds. The Russian urban readers of the 1920s not only had cosmopolitan tastes but were fascinated with the technological feats of other countries, seeing themselves as part of a European citizenry. The Soviet state itself fostered that sense of cosmopolitanism, especially the global significance of scientific and technological development. Increasingly, however, the isolationist tendencies slowly developing in Soviet Russia contradicted that view, making it difficult to reconcile the early Bolshevik technological cosmopolitanism with the new theory of "socialism in one country" that the Stalinist state would eventually support more substantially.

Popular literature in the natural sciences and technology had a special significance for Soviet power from the first days of the October Revolution in 1917. The popularization of natural scientific and technical knowledge was an important means by which the young Soviet regime believed it could struggle against religion, form a new ideology based on scientific principles, and attract the common man to scientific and technical knowledge. On August 16, 1918, a Sovnarkom decree created a Scientific-Technical Department (NTO) under Vesenkha. On October 9, 1918, NTO created a state scientific-technical publishing house (Gostekhizdat) based in Moscow with an affiliate in Petrograd. The head of the publishing house was A. G. Braun. Gostekhizdat was involved in publishing literature in all areas of technology and industrial production, except chemical technology and metallurgy. It published popular-technological guides for workers, foremen, and engineers, as well as textbooks for students in middle-level and higher technical schools.[5] By 1925 the average print-run of its publications was seven to eight thousand per title. Between 1921 and 1928 Gostekhizdat published 996 books with a print-run of over seven million copies.[6]

In March 1919, at the Eighth Congress of the Russian Communist Party, the Central Committee ratified a special decree on "The Party and the Soviet Press." The press was to be a powerful means of propaganda, agitation, and organization of information for the widest possible audience. On May 20, 1919, the All-Russian Central Executive Committee (VTsIK) issued a decree on "Government Publishing." All publishing activities of People's Commissariats, branches of VTsIK, and other Soviet establishments (as far as they related to sociopolitical and cultural questions) were subordinated to the new state publishing house (Gosizdat). The publishing activities of all scholarly and literary societies, and all other publishing houses, were also subject to the control and regulation of Gosizdat.[7]

Originally created under the auspices of Narkompros, Gosizdat's two principal tasks were to publish its own books and to regulate all publishing activities in the Russian Republic. It was headed by an editorial collegium: Sovnarkom named V. V. Vorovskii as its first chairman. The size of Gosizdat's publishing activities grew quickly. In 1919 it published 9.6 percent of all books in the country, and by 1920 it was already publishing 64 percent of all books.[8] In June of 1919 Gosizdat created a popular-scientific department. In the fall of 1920 the department planned a series of popular-scientific readers for workers. With these goals in mind, the department invited scholars and scientific specialists to write popular-scientific books and pamphlets, to be written in a style accessible to Soviet workers.[9]

After 1919, however, publishing activities and the quantity of books printed in the country dropped. A primary reason for the decline was the economic dislocation suffered during the Russian Civil War. Many printing houses stopped working or could not get electricity to run their presses. There was not enough ink or paper, due to the severe crises in the land. By the middle of 1921 the country was producing twenty-five times less paper than it was in 1914 before the First World War. At the Ninth Congress of the Russian Communist Party, various speakers noted that it was necessary to put all "productive strengths" into raising the quantity of paper production, improving its quality, and introducing some order into typesetting and press activities in the country.[10] Paper production did not reach prewar levels until

1928, although the regime spent substantially to import paper from abroad, especially after 1924.[11] The comparable problem in book production was officially raised at the party's Thirteenth Party Congress in 1924.[12] Delegates noted that during the NEP the number of presses and typesetting machines fell dramatically. The overall production of books did not reach prewar levels until 1925.[13]

The destruction of various prerevolutionary distribution networks after the revolution also made it difficult to deliver books to readers during the early Soviet era. During the Civil War, the distribution of books and newspapers was organized by Tsentropechat' (Central Press Agency). During the NEP, the Central Press Agency was replaced by *Kontragenstvo Pechati* (the Press Contracting Agency). This organization opened many book and newspaper kiosks in the major urban areas, especially at railway stations in the urban and outlying areas.[14] After the dislocation of the Russian Civil War, the distribution of printed publications developed and expanded, but at a slow pace. The number of Soviet bookstores rose dramatically between 1922 and 1924, but still only to half the prewar level.[15]

The relationship between government and private publishing houses after the revolution was also precarious. In 1917 government publishing houses produced only 11 percent of all titles published in Russia, but this figure doubled to 21.5 percent by 1918. Meanwhile, the share of private publishers fell from 80 percent of all titles in 1917 to 58 percent in 1918.[16] During the period of War Communism (1918–1920) economic hardships led to a gradual centralization of the publishing industry, as the printing sections of various commissariats were amalgamated into Gosizdat. However, by October of 1920 close to two hundred private firms still existed in Russia. That changed at the end of 1920 when the Soviet government moved against even the small private printing shops, but the number of private publishers would rise again during the NEP era.[17]

By late 1921 the situation shifted in favor of private firms. In November of 1921 Sovnarkom published a decree that allowed books to be printed and sold by private and cooperative publishers. The Sovnarkom decree enabled licensed private publishers to own printing equipment, sell their output at free-market prices, and (after obtaining special permission) import foreign books. All manuscripts had to be approved by the state, and Gosizdat reserved the right to buy, at wholesale prices, all or any number of copies of a book privately printed in Russia.[18] Although private companies printed close to 25 percent of all books in 1922, the number they produced began to drop gradually as the decade progressed towards 1928.[19] However, private publishers greatly expanded the variety of books and journals available for the Russian reader in the 1920s, and many authors sought out private publishers during the NEP to print their manuscripts. This publishing expansion especially included science popularizers, engineers, and technical specialists.[20] As the decade unfolded, a vast array of privately printed popular-scientific books and journals became available to a public eager to consume information on themes from astronomy to water pollution.

During the twenties cooperative publishers were especially involved in creating popular-scientific and technical literature for a broader audience. Cooperative associations like Nachatki znanii (basics of knowledge) published the works of prerevolutionary science popularizers, such as the biologist V. V. Lunkevich and the educator N. Rubakin. Like other authors, popularizers received royalties for their publications, and this was certainly an incentive for scholars and scientists to write popular pieces during the NEP. For example, the cooperative publisher Seiatel' (disseminator) produced a series of popular-scientific works on such themes as mathematics, physics, and astronomy. This series included works for popular consumption by both foreign and Russian authors, including Albert Einstein's *Osnovy teorii otnositel'nosti* (bases of the theory of relativity) or Ia. I. Perel'man's *Polet na lunu* (flight to the moon).

During the NEP, the Soviet state's publishing decrees gave private publishers temporary access to the market. This allowed older, prerevolutionary publishers to compete with the new Soviet publishing houses. For example, the expansive private, prerevolutionary St. Petersburg publishing house of P. P. Soikin once again became one of the more active firms involved in publishing popular-scientific works. Furthermore, it became financially solvent and incredibly successful in the early Soviet era. During the twenties Soikin produced several popular-scientific series as monthly supplements to the widely read journal *Vestnik znaniia* (herald of knowledge). One of these series was entitled Priroda i liudi (nature and people) and contained entries that described various geographical areas of the world and their flora, fauna, and indigenous peoples. An example is Elgin Lendt's *In the Virgin Forests of the Amazon* (1927). Readers were particularly interested in popular-scientific pieces on world geography and exotic places because they themselves would never be able to see them. And Soikin targeted those particular scientific interests of readers based on marketing studies and reader surveys.

During the NEP period, private and cooperative publishers printed popular material ranging from biographies of great scientists to translations of Western science-fiction novels. Specific editors and publishers paid especially close attention to this development. They included important prerevolutionary figures such as Maksim Gorky, P. P. Soikin, and various Moscow and Petersburg science professors. They continued their work after 1917, building important reputations as supporters of mass-scientific literature.

The content of the material produced by this array of state- and private-publishing sources included eclectic themes. Western scientists continued to publish articles in Russian journals, and their monographs were translated for new series for the lay reader's consumption. At least in the 1920s, the regime and various publishing houses were willing to offer the public a wide range of scientific information, including the work of foreign scientists from Western capitalist countries. Journals and science newspapers became the most widely read and accessible sources of popular-scientific information in Russia during the twenties. Journals were best at providing diverse social groups basic information on various aspects of the natural sciences and technology. Furthermore, they were the cheapest and most condensed form of information; and they were part of a larger genre of short publications the Soviet regime itself promoted in the 1920s to propagate information rapidly.

Popular-scientific journals began to spread throughout Russia and other republics of the Soviet Union during the twenties. For example, a popular-scientific journal entitled *Znanie* (knowledge) was published in the Ukraine in the Donets basin and was very popular especially among workers in coal and other resource-producing industries. Many popular-scientific journals geared toward workers were published as supplements to provincial newspapers. A popular-scientific supplement to the Sverdlovsk newspaper *Urals Worker* was entitled *Znanie i trud* (knowledge and labor). Another supplement to *Northern Worker,* published in Iaroslavl', was entitled *About Everything, Little by Little— Science, Technology, and Literature.*

Prior to the NEP most of the Soviet journals were associated with specific organizations and had small circulations. During the NEP the Communist Party and the Komsomol (Communist youth league) sponsored the publication of new literary and popular journals. This certainly allowed the party to emerge as a significant factor on the cultural scene during the twenties.[21] However, even those journals, which had large circulations, featured substantial sections devoted to popular-scientific themes. The editors of the journals felt compelled to compete with other privately published journals to meet the popular demand for clearly written articles on scientific discoveries, especially about new technology from Western Europe and America.

The Komsomol published a monthly journal in the 1920s entitled *Molodaia gvardiia* (young guard). The journal had a popular-scientific section that featured articles by Marxist science popularizers, like B. M. Zavadovskii, on a range of issues. However, by 1923 the journal contained a new subsection entitled "News of Technology," where new machines and technical devices from all over the world were analyzed and displayed in an apolitical manner. This section analyzed the benefits of new technological devices created in the West. Within the pages of this Komsomol journal, Western technological development was revered and portrayed as something that should be emulated by the new Soviet state. Instead of focusing on the dynamics of class struggle, the articles stressed important themes such as modernization and technological development, even if it meant borrowing Western models.

Varied popular-scientific journals and newspapers expanded rapidly in the 1920s and were geared to different social groups, not simply to Communists or educated laymen. The journals offered a variety of levels of sophistication based on their projected readership. For instance, the Leningrad Soviet published a popular-scientific journal during the twenties entitled *Nauka i tekhnika* (science and technology). *Nauka i tekhnika* was one of the most popular and widely read popular-scientific journals for workers during the twenties. It was a weekly and cost ten kopecks per issue. Besides being the most affordable popular journal, its format of short, one-page articles, written in a style that was accessible to most readers, made it attractive to a wide readership.

Beginning in 1923 with a weekly circulation of 128,000, *Nauka i tekhnika* had the goal of introducing the worker-reader to the latest movements in science and technology in Europe and America. Like other popular-scientific journals of this era, *Nauka i tekhnika* carried a section entitled "News of Science and Technology." This section described new scientific experiments, discoveries, and technological inventions in a more accessible language for readers. The concentrated emphasis on the feats of foreign technological developments in a journal published by a state organ was typical of the 1920s and would not be repeated in the following decade.

Many organizations (besides soviets) published popular-scientific journals during the twenties. The publishing house of the newspaper *Gudok* (siren), an organ of the All-Russian Central Council of Trade Unions (VTsSPS), published a monthly popular-scientific journal entitled *Iskra nauki* (the spark of science). The journal cost forty kopecks per month for subscribers to *Gudok,* and one ruble, fifty kopecks for nonsubscribers. The journal featured a "Question and Answer" section, where questions submitted to the editor by workers were answered by scientific specialists. Another section entitled "Soviet Industry and Technology" focused on applied technological developments. Another feature simplified the analysis of scientific topics written by prominent academic figures like S. F. Ol'denburg, secretary of the Soviet Academy of Sciences. The journal, supported by industrial trade unions, emphasized the dissemination of scientific information for the common worker as a form of extracurricular education. Well-known Russian academicians contributed to such newspapers and journals in an effort to connect the new Soviet Academy with a wider reading public.

More advanced discussion of scientific and technological development was promoted in Soviet Russia during the twenties in a similar fashion by a diverse body of journals representing various institutions and commercial publishing ventures, both Soviet state and private/cooperative. They all admired Western European and American technological development. Furthermore they attempted to capture the popular interest and imaginative impulse of cosmopolitan, urban readers. Astronomy, air flight, space travel, and world geography/travel captured the public's eye, as it concurrently did in most of the West. These published materials indicate the relative absence of isolation of the Soviet reading public in the 1920s in contrast to later times under Stalin. Even in the pages of Communist journals, it was difficult to discern the difference in scientific, thematic content when compared to non-party journals of the time. In the 1920s Russia's readers from diverse social groups were part of a broad European cultural milieu, and they were interested in the same scientific feats and developments that captured the imagination of Westerners.

Soviet scientific publications of the 1920s were offering the public an international, if not cosmopolitan, perspective on the changing nature of new technology. Diverse publishing ventures flourished during the Soviet 1920s. Lines of political activity were submerged, if not overlooked, in various publications in order to capture the reading public's interest in science and technology. Ultimately, the Soviet state's goal, which converged with that of popular educators (many of whom were not Communists), was to foster the desires of Russian urban readers in order to solidify their fascination with global scientific and technological activities. In the process the Soviet state during the NEP engaged non-Communist publishers and popularizers, such as Rubakin and Lunkevich, who were an integral part of that cultural movement.

ASSESSING POPULAR INTEREST IN SCIENCE

Assessing popular interest in science among the Russian mass readership in the 1920s is a difficult task. At best, one can provide a sketch of the themes that readers found most fascinating. Three types of sources are relevant to the gauging of popular themes: general readers' surveys and surveys geared toward a specific readership are essential; published and unpublished letters to editors and popularizers are valuable; and reports by officials of Gosizdat and Agit-Prop (Agitation and Propaganda Department of the Central Committee of the Communist Party) who analyzed popular reading interests during the twenties are also helpful.

Some of the most interesting sources for gauging reader response were reports sent back to Moscow by Communist Party activists in the Agit-Prop department of the Central Committee. These records provide frank assessment of conditions of libraries outside the capital cities and also how both urban and rural readers responded to printed material. Agit-Prop officials were most keenly interested in seeing whether the party's rhetorical constructs and propaganda were actually reaching and being absorbed by the masses. Many of these reports reveal the frustration on the part of these officials, especially in rural areas where many peasants paid little attention to scientific books.

The Soviets of the 1920s were intensely interested in the sociological analysis of society. The period was especially marked as a time of detailed Marxist analysis of various organizations and groups. Sociologists and statisticians collected data on the class composition of all types of organizations in Soviet society, including the ruling Communist Party. Investigators were interested in the social origins of various officials, students, blue-collar workers, and also white-collar workers *(sluzhashchie)*.[22] Soviet studies of the reader, which were carried out by a number of organizations, took on a similar orientation. Soviet investigators were particularly interested in the effect of certain types of media on specific groups or social categories of the population, for instance, worker or peasant readers.[23]

During the period 1917–1920, when the Soviet state had an almost complete monopoly on publishing, publishers did not have to worry much about competition or readers' demands, as had their counterparts in the prerevolutionary era. During the Civil War, many books and newspapers were distributed to the public without charge. With the introduction of the NEP, however, publishers were required to sell a portion of their product at a profit. Within the context of that mixed economy, profit-and-loss accounting was not a complete and effective indicator of a publisher's ability to satisfy reader demand. However, the need during the NEP to sell a portion of what was produced to individual readers certainly heightened official awareness of earlier economic failures.[24] The first Soviet reader investigations, conducted between 1923 and 1926, gathered some interesting material, mostly from people who willingly volunteered their thoughts on various questions posed to them. During the latter part of the 1920s this haphazard sampling of opinion from below was overshadowed by politicized studies of particular groups of readers, for example, party cadres or press correspondents.[25] However, the earlier studies are particularly valuable in gauging the public's interest in scientific and technological themes.[26]

In 1924 a special commission was directed to study the Russian reader and was created under the library department of Glavpolitprosvet. The commission was headed by the Soviet bibliographer L. N. Tropovskii. Also prominent participants in the activities of the commission were N. K. Krupskaia and M. A. Smushkova, who headed the library branch. The commission proposed to conduct a centralized sociological investigation of the reading interests of the public in the Soviet Union.[27]

On the initiative of the commission, research was conducted primarily in the following provinces: Moscow, Leningrad, Nizhegorod, and Cheliabinsk. Sociologists primarily studied readers' interests, but they also analyzed reasons for choosing certain books and goals that readers set themselves. These studies were conducted in large state libraries on the bases of observations, conversations with readers, and analyses of surveys of readers' opinions. The results of investigations in the Leningrad region were published by B. V. Bank and A. Ia. Vilenkin, two of the best-known sociologists studying the popular reader in the 1920s and 1930s in Russia.[28]

By 1924 Gosizdat also sponsored sociological research of this type, and scholars began to study the worker-reader by conducting reader surveys at various Moscow and Leningrad factories and institutions. One of the first serious studies was organized by E. Vinogradova in 1924.[29] Vinogradova wanted to assess the popularity of itinerant libraries at twenty-five factories and institutions (workplaces) in Moscow over a ten-month period. Itinerant libraries were a source for lower-class readers to obtain access to reading material by an easy method—the library came to their place of work. The workplaces where she conducted her survey included mills, shoe-factories, and fire brigades. The researchers counted how many times a book was read and how long readers spent on certain books. They classified belles lettres by author and scientific works by branch of knowledge and author. "Science" was a general category including social, political, economic, and popular-scientific works.

Vinogradova found that 40 percent of all books borrowed by readers were on scientific themes, while close to 60 percent were belles lettres. She found the popularity of works on religious themes to be much lower than those on natural-scientific topics. Of the natural-science books, the most popular were on the origin of the world, land, and mankind. Rubakin, Lunkevich, and Perel'man were found to be the most popular authors of books on natural-scientific and geographic themes. The study showed that prerevolutionary science educators were quite popular among readers in comparison to their Soviet and Marxist counterparts. Natural-scientific works were even more popular than fictional works by well-known authors like Maksim Gorky. Natural-scientific books were read by all age groups and by both men and women.[30]

The findings of this survey parallel some of the discoveries that the book scholar and popularizer Rubakin himself uncovered both before and after the revolution. In an intensive study of several thousand popular-scientific works published in the 1920s, Rubakin found that those written in a simpler fashion, taking into account the reader's abilities, were much more in demand than more technical works. He argued that more sophisticated works were less popular because they used scientific terms that were incomprehensible to the more underdeveloped Soviet reader.[31]

Popular-scientific journals conducted their own surveys of readers throughout the 1920s. Those surveys were concerned with which social groups were interested in popular science. Journals conducted such market surveys to increase their understanding of readers' interests and demands. They were also interested in generally categorizing their subscribers and clientele. Of course, some journals had political goals in mind, perhaps to show how their journals were read by workers to satisfy the populist tendencies of the Soviet regime. All the same, the surveys provide an interesting sociological profile of readers' tastes.

For example, in the autumn of 1925 the popular-scientific journal *Nauka i tekhnika* conducted an extensive survey of its readers, receiving twenty-one thousand completed questionnaires, which at the time represented approximately 17 percent of its circulation.[32] Ninety-five percent of those who filled out the questionnaire were subscribers to the journal. The editors assumed that the majority of their readers were urban dwellers, since subscription rates were rising in industrial and urban areas. Furthermore, popular-scientific journals and books had always been more heavily subscribed to by urban readers. Respondents to the survey were broken down into the following categories: blue-collar workers 36 percent, white-collar workers 31 percent, students 25 percent, peasants 5.5 percent, and others 2.5 percent. The editors argued that this was not exactly representative of the social breakdown of their readership because the journal received a number of questionnaires filled out by one worker on behalf of a number of less-literate workers. For instance, one metalworker from the Votkinskii factory in the Urals sent in his questionnaire for himself and ten of his fellow workers with the following comment: "We are all workers, and we read the journal collectively. Afterward, we discuss together what is most important for us to analyze more thoroughly, and what is of general interest." Of the workers who responded to the questionnaire, the largest group (48.5 percent) were metal workers, 22.8 percent electrotechnicians, 17.4 percent transport workers, 8.2 percent woodworkers, and 3.1 percent chemical industry workers. Forty-four percent of all respondents came from the Leningrad region, and 56 percent came from other regions in the Soviet Union. The number of female readers of the journal was low. Thirty-seven percent of the readers were between the ages of 26 and 35. Fifty percent of all readers had what was categorized as a middle education (professional school, technical courses, night courses, secondary school, etc.).

Thus, according to the editors, the majority of readers of the journal were workers, with an above-average education, primarily young and male.[33] Because editors of that period generally tried to inflate the percentage of worker-readers, one cannot state definitively that workers made up the clear majority of readers. Furthermore, the number of readers who were white-collar workers and students was significantly high. Together, those two sub-groups also represented a large percentage of those that read popular-scientific literature, based on this journal's statistical findings.

The specific scientific interests of readers were much harder to gauge. Almost 20 percent of the readers indicated that "News of Science and Technology," which consisted of short entries on new developments in science, was their favorite section. The same readers stated that they were interested in news of scientific feats in Western Europe and America. Another favorite section was that which discussed new developments in the medical sciences. Almost all respondents, regardless of occupation, asked that sections relating to their own work be expanded. A twenty-six-year-old machine-tool engineer from Leningrad wrote, "It would be good if you start a small section in your journal which would cover a broad range of special trades, such as glass-cutting or the tempering of metals." A forty-one-year-old teacher from Riazan had the following to add: "I wish that at the end of the year, the journal could give a short systematic overview of various important scientific movements in the USSR; this would be helpful to my students." A thirty-year-old female doctor from Kuban added, "I wish that you would publish articles on maternity and proper hygiene in child rearing." Lastly, a twenty-one-year-old peasant from Pskov province wrote: "You do not have a section on scientific developments in the agricultural area. There is nothing in the journal on new machines that can help those of us working in the countryside. For farmers, knowledge of new technology is important."[34]

Comments by those survey respondents point toward the consistent need of various readers of popular-scientific material for relevant information. Scientific articles of a utilitarian and practical nature, those capable of enhancing people's everyday work life, were in high demand. This need, however, did not preclude urban readers from interest in scientific themes not applicable to their jobs. Actually, public astronomy lectures and literature on astronomy, for example, were extremely popular among urban dwellers. The public had a genuine fascination for how the world around them was constructed. The survey shows that articles on air flight and space exploration were particularly noted as very popular among regular readers of journals. Nevertheless, the preponderance of responses concerning practical material suggests that readers primarily wanted to know how science and technology could benefit their lives and enhance their job performance.

As the survey indicates, white-collar employees and students were also avid readers of popular-scientific journals. In a 1927 survey conducted by the popular-scientific journal *Iskra,* students made up approximately 20 percent of all respondents, while employees made up approximately 30 percent. Furthermore, respondents once again indicated their interest in articles that related to their work. White-collar workers were especially interested in articles on topics such as the metric system and standardization or topics related to the economy. Students were specifically interested in articles on Darwinism, evolutionary theory, and Marxism. Doctors were interested in articles on biological and medical topics.[35]

Published and unpublished letters to the editor represent another tool for measuring reader response to popular-scientific themes. Many popular-scientific journals had sections entitled "Perepiska s chitateliami" (correspondence with readers). The editors of *Iskra* believed this provision was a means for readers to express their opinions about changes they wanted to see incorporated into the journal's format. Many of the letters to the editor of *Iskra* were on such subjects as the evolution of humans, the Earth, and planets in the solar system. These requests echoed the results of reader surveys conducted in urban areas by sociologists like Vinogradova. Many readers wrote in asking the editors to review more popular works on astronomy. They were especially interested in books on the stars and moon. Many readers expressed interest in how humans evolved and how the Earth developed. One reader wrote in a June 1923 letter to the journal: "Could you please review books in your journal that give readers a basic analysis of contemporary evolutionary theories on the development of man and the Earth? I am especially interested in learning more about hereditary influences and genetic variation."[36]

Iskra nauki, like other similar journals, had a section entitled "Questions and Answers," where readers' mailed-in questions were sometimes answered by science journalists but also by scientists, academics, and professors. Occasionally, well-known academics, such as Oldenburg or Perel'man, were hired by the journal to answer those letters with cogent replies. Letters to the editor covered a number of scientific topics from atomic structure to electric power. Many letters came from readers who had questions concerning their particular specialty and line of work. Sometimes readers had questions on medical advances relating to certain diseases. A forty-six-year-old female worker wrote explaining she suffered from goiter and was wondering whether a physician could explain to her what she should expect if the disease worsened.[37] Readers engaged experts working for these journals in a serious and personal manner regarding scientific or even medical problems with which they struggled.

Many workers wrote letters to the journal asking questions about their amateur scientific interests, like astronomical observations. Some wanted to know how one can observe certain stars and planets. One worker asked when and where one could observe the planets Jupiter and Mercury. With regard to Mercury, a scientific specialist explained that Mercury's position as the first of the interior planets makes it difficult to observe because it often gets lost in the suns rays, making it a challenge even for astronomy specialists to observe. A worker named Mel'nikov asked about the nature of cosmic rays falling down to Earth from interplanetary space. He wanted to know what effect these rays had on the earth's surface.[38]

One of the best-known popularizers of astronomical knowledge, Ia. Perel'-man, received many letters from his readers. Unpublished letters in Perel'-man's personal file in the Academy of Sciences archive evoke the expressive nature of popular science-reading interests among young Soviets in the 1920s. According to Perel'man, many of the letters he received from younger readers attested to an interest in rockets and the ability to travel into space. Almost all of these letters contained references to the ideas of Konstantin Tsiolkov-skii.[39] Even though a provincial schoolteacher of physics from Kaluga, Tsiol-kovskii was a visionary rocket specialist and is considered the grandfather of Soviet cosmonautics. According to Perel'man such letters displayed an utter fascination, if not obsession, that Russian readers had with the cosmos.

Perel'man wrote a number of popular-scientific books in the '20s and '30s in a series carrying the title "Zanimatel'naia nauka" (science for entertainment). These books were used as self-education texts by many people. They covered physics, mathematics, astronomy, and chemistry. A professor of physics at Moscow State University wrote Perel'man telling him that "your books interest not only my students, but also school children and common workers. In your books, you are able to provide the mass reader with new, interesting facts." A Leningrad worker wrote Perel'man saying that his popular books on physics were very interesting and were read by a number of his fellow workers. That worker was especially interested in physics and said he had learned a lot from Perel'man's book *Physics for Entertainment.* Workers found that Perel'man's books rendered complex scientific principles in a more accessible form for the layman.[40] Those works anticipated contemporary science texts and courses with titles like "Physics for Poets" that simplify disciplines for the layman.

On the fortieth anniversary of Perel'man's career as a science popularizer (1899–1939), three major academics—A. Ioffe, S. Bernshtein, and V. Smirnov—sent a letter to Perel'man's publisher commending him for his cultural work. Those scientists believed Perel'man's books helped spread science to a wide audience of Russian readers. In their letter they wrote: "Ia. I. Perel'man wrote books not for a small circle of enthusiasts of the natural sciences, but for the widest circle of readers. The basic idea of his work—'absorbing science'— captured the interest of an entire generation of Russian readers. Our young people especially liked the works of Perel'man. The general circulation of his books numbered in the millions of copies."[41]

The availability of popular-scientific material was more problematic in the Soviet countryside in the 1920s when compared to the situation in urban areas. In 1923 merely seven publishing houses published books for distribution in the countryside, and by 1924 that number had increased only to twelve. In 1924 the publication of books for rural readers was broken down into the following subject categories (including percentage of total books published): agricultural 37.5 percent, social-political 30 percent, literary/artistic 17 percent, scientific-popular 15.2 percent, and others .3 percent.[42]

Although popular-scientific books represented 15.2 percent of all books published for the peasant-reader, that does not accurately reflect the peasants' interest in scientific works. On the one hand, according to M. M. Slukhovskii, only 2.7 percent of peasant readers surveyed in the state sociological studies were interested in books on natural-scientific and medical topics. On the other hand, 20 percent were interested in books on agricultural themes, and 18 percent on crafts and industry.[43] The surveys reflected a tendency among peasant readers to demand books on practical themes and topics relating to their agricultural work.

In the 1920s I. Taradin conducted a study of rural book holdings in Voronezh province. He found on average that 35.3 percent of all books in peasants' personal collections were self-educational textbooks, 12.5 percent were non-fiction works on agricultural topics, and 36 percent were on religious topics. According to Taradin, though the figure of 36 percent for religious works had dropped from 50 percent since the revolution, that still indicated that religious books, published prior to 1917, were a high proportion of all books owned by peasants. Only 2.2 percent of books in peasant-home collections before 1917 were textbooks. That rise after the revolution in the percentage of textbooks owned by peasants to 35.3 percent was a direct result of the interest peasant farmers had in purchasing instructional texts and pamphlets dealing with agricultural and horticultural themes.[44]

Agit-Prop officials also monitored rural readers' interests during the twenties. The Central Committee's Agit-Prop Department trained various individuals to survey reading interests in Russia. Much of this concentrated on the countryside, where Soviet rule was rather tenuous before 1928. Government officials were especially concerned with what peasants were reading and with their ability to buy books during the NEP. In 1923 Gosizdat officials attempted to lower the taxes on small book stalls to give merchants incentives to lower book prices for peasants. They also provided peasants with free book catalogues at agricultural exhibitions in the countryside.[45]

One Agit-Prop worker surveyed book markets in the Orel region. He presented himself as an independent book trader and asked those purchasing books what they came to buy. He noticed that peasants were mostly interested in nonfiction books on the following subjects: pig-breeding, horticulture, and sheep-breeding. Most of their purchases were of scientific books on subjects that had practical use for their agricultural work. Many peasants told him that "we have very little money, except subsistence funds for food and provisions. We lose much of our surplus funds to taxes." He concluded that they could afford little for books. Furthermore, those who came to look at or buy books referred to them as *kuritel'nye* (smoking books). The peasants explained, "We buy them, read through them a bit, and then use the paper to smoke tobacco."[46]

The Agit-Prop researcher Levin noted that peasants in this region were very interested in scientific books containing basic medical information on infectious diseases. Levin believed this might have been due to the high rate of syphilis in the area and to the fact that farmers were interested in learning more about diseases affecting animals. He summed up his observations by noting:

> Concretely, scientific works are popular with peasant readers if these books can describe to them better and more efficient methods of breeding and planting. They are also important if they can help give scientific reasons for certain epidemics. However, in general, scientific books seem to have no present worth to the peasant. They stop and look at pictures in the books, but only give the rest a cursory glance. It is also absolutely imperative to immediately stop the appalling epidemic of peasants smoking the pages of books. Unfortunately, the peasants in this area cannot purchase and read books when they are more concerned with their dreary living conditions. They are poor and dirty. They have no meat to eat, and they only eat milk and potatoes.[47]

Another Agit-Prop researcher named Roga investigated readers' interests in the Petrograd region of Russia during July 1923. Roga's observations of peasants around Petrograd were quite similar to Levin's in Orel. Peasants were especially interested in scientific pamphlets on horticulture and animal husbandry. But Roga claimed that most peasants saw little worth in scientific books in general. Roga also noted that in this region a majority of books were bought at shops. According to Roga, book-peddlers had become a much more expensive source.[48]

Yet another Agit-Prop researcher, traveling in the Orel region of Russia, found several libraries in the area, but they were in dreadful condition. Many of the books just stayed on the shelves of the libraries. Most of the libraries contained either old Russian classics (like Turgenev) or Soviet polemical literature from the period of War Communism, with very little material that dealt with popular-scientific or practical-agricultural themes. The researcher believed that few peasants in that area could actually afford to purchase books. Peasants complained to him about their poverty and expressed a disinterest in official Soviet publications like newspapers. They reiterated their inability to afford books, which were seen as a luxury. One peasant said to him that "if we were living in the city or center, then things would be different."[49]

The researcher in Orel said that most villagers still lived by rumor, especially with regard to scientific inventions and new technology. One villager, in all seriousness, asked the researcher whether it was true that "in Moscow people saw a boat that could move along the streets by itself." The researcher noted that the peasant was only interested in nonfictional works that related to his vocation. He reported that most peasants only wanted to read books that could tell them more about breeding and planting, "how to breed a better pig, and plant better vegetables," as one peasant put the matter. He observed that it was rare to find villagers interested in popular-scientific or technological works that had no practical use.[50]

In contrast to the readership of rural Russia, readers in urban areas expressed an enormous interest in popular-scientific and technical books, journals, and pamphlets. In addition to a demand for articles relating to their work and for themes having practical application to their everyday life, the urban reading public had an appetite for a variety of fascinating themes such as astronomy, global exploration, and the cosmos beyond. These readers showed a genuine interest in understanding the world around them and had an imaginative impulse to understand the universe. They were forthright in the queries they posed to scientists through the venues of the journals' surveys and question-and-answer sections. The content of science in the public realm was not usually politicized or didactic, nor was it limited to glorifying Soviet Russia's accomplishments. In this way, most Soviet readers were exposed to technological information and the feats of Western technology, which were reported in laudatory articles and editorials by Communist and non-Communist journals alike. This popular demand from below for information on global technology had temporarily survived the October Revolution and had been cultivated by many Bolshevik leaders who were obsessed with Western scientific achievements.

Chapter 5

IMAGINING SCIENCE

Land, Air, and Space for the New Soviet Citizen of the 1920s

An important, overarching theme in the popular science media in the 1920s was the creation of the new scientific and modern world. In their work on the semiotics of Russian cultural history, Yuri Lotman and Boris Uspensky describe the dynamics of Russian growth in the 1920s as transformational and not as developmental, that is, a process essentially binary in nature that depicts a duality in Russian cultural history. The past can be painted in a dark frame to dramatize the brightness of the new world of the twentieth century, especially after the October Revolution.[1] The emblems of the new world would be the machine and modern technological advances.

TECHNOLOGY AND THE UTILITARIAN
APPLICATIONS OF SCIENCE

For the Bolsheviks, science popularization involved actively spreading technology to dispel the darkness of the masses by transforming their minds and instilling in laborers a rational mode of thought. It involved bringing the city (modern technology, education, and rational planning) to the countryside. There was an equation between light and knowledge. The Leninist electrification campaign was a symbol of technological progress and an integral part of a rational, scientific society.[2]

The pervasive theme of "science as enlightenment" in the popular-science media also encompassed the rationalization of production in industry and the countryside. One can find many articles in the popular journals concerning Soviet Taylorism.[3] The notion of a rationalized scientific agriculture was especially prevalent in the popular literature. Popular-scientific journals like *Priroda* (nature) carried articles entitled "Applied Botany." Many of the popular-science series published in the 1920s by Gosizdat and private publishers included pamphlets on the transformation of agriculture through science. The metaphor of the "invisible beings" was constantly evoked in pamphlets and journals explaining the basics of microbiology. Previously unknown diseases (among livestock and humans) were now found to be caused by various microscopic viruses and bacteria, which could be cured through applied scientific research. Many popular journals and pamphlets also stressed the importance of hygiene and health. Cleanliness and the use of disinfectants could fight disease, and emphasizing those themes had practical importance. Sanitation and hygiene were portrayed in the popular media as the accomplishments of modern industrial society. Science could transform Soviet society with a new ethos but also create the basis for a more productive industrial and agricultural economy.

In the popular-science media, technology was portrayed as a progressive force for society and industry. Popular-scientific journals carried sections on new technology and inventions and how they could be used in industry. Furthermore, Western technological developments were practically revered in the popular journals. This reinforced the portrayal of Western (especially American) technology in Soviet newspapers during the twenties.[4] Fordism and Taylorism blended in Soviet Russia during the twenties, emphasizing America as the giant emblem of modernity. Sometimes "America" was a symbol of how technology was transforming modern culture.[5]

In the Leningrad journal *Nauka i tekhnika,* many of the short entries on technology featured mostly new inventions or devices from America or Western Europe. One 1926 article described a new, grandiose hydroelectric station being built in Tennessee. The article described how magnificent this new station would be and how easily it could produce enough energy to run two factories. "The dam, blocking the river flow, will be 1,500 meters long, and the lake thus formed will have a surface area of 34 square kilometers. The power station, 375 meters long, will be part of the dam, and when it is completed will have eighteen turbines generating over 600,000 horsepower."[6] Another article described how a company in Spain (Oviedo) devised a technique to extract iron from ore without using a blast-furnace. The technique involved using compressed gas as a fuel and extracting the metal magnetically from the silicate mixture remaining after the burning process.[7] Both the advances and application of Western technology were emphasized for readers to digest. In these journals, borrowing from the feats of Western technology was portrayed as acceptable for an international citizenry. Furthermore, it situated Soviet Russia within a developing global technological revolution, not outside of it because of political, governmental divergences.

A 1923 article in *Iskra* was one of many in the journal that explicitly lauds the speed and technical performance of Ford's great American automobile assembly lines. During the twenties the Soviets became fixated on Western conveyor-belt assembly production. The article emphasized how the Soviets could learn from Ford's techniques in Detroit.[8] Even the Komsomol's thick journal *Molodaia gvardiia* continually invoked America as a symbol of modern technology. Short entries on American technology filled the section "News of Technology." These ranged from inventions that could be used for industry to those that could help agricultural productivity. One article entitled "Iron Horse" described a new tractor built in America that could replace any horse in its ability to plow the fields without stopping.[9] Young Communist readers were asked to consider how this new plowing device, once imported throughout Russia, could transform agricultural productivity. Remarkably, this Communist youth journal includes relatively few references to Soviet technological advances in the production of agricultural equipment. The articles focus instead on how underdeveloped countries like Russia could borrow from the advanced inventions of the West.

Although notes on Western technology occupied a large portion of these journals, as the 1920s progressed some began to carry sections on Soviet technology and inventions. For instance, *Iskra nauki* carried a section entitled "Soviet Industry and Technology." Until 1928 entries in these sections still discussed the application of Western technology to Soviet industry. One article in *Iskra nauki* described a huge freezer devised by a Danish professor that could keep large quantities of fish frozen. In 1927 a large freezer of this type was being imported and constructed in Baku near the Caspian Sea. The entry described how important this would be for the fishing industry in the Caucuses region.[10]

As the 1920s unfolded, more articles appeared that illuminated the new advances of Soviet science and technology. In 1927 *Iskra nauki* stressed the ties of science and Soviet industry in new sections such as "On the Path of Industrialization" and "Soviet Machine." The latter included articles emphasizing the advances in Soviet science and its application to machine production and technology. Articles also described the construction of large turbogenerators. Much of the section was devoted to describing technological advances like high powered steam turbines in Soviet industry during the first decade after the revolution.[11]

On the eve of Stalin's revolution from above, popular-scientific journals began to feature the work of Soviet inventors, anticipating the focus on national technological feats of the 1930s in Soviet Russia. Editors of popular journals encouraged amateur inventors and workers to send in descriptions of their new projects. Many journals formed sections devoted to Soviet inventions, including critiques of their potential by scientific specialists. Many of these project descriptions came from workers eager to display their own ideas. Projects varied from new barometers to various types of turbine engines. Scientists, although encouraging, were usually critical of these new inventions.[12] All the same, editors and scientists clearly sought to encourage technological innovation from amateurs.

In a later period, during the First-Five Year Plan (1928–32), the Soviet regime would commit an enormous amount of energy to sponsoring a mass movement of worker-inventors (the *rabochee izobretatel'stvo* movement). Kendall Bailes has argued that this movement actually did little to sponsor good inventive projects by workers.[13] One problem was that graduate technical specialists and engineers did not want to take time off from their work to evaluate the enormous number of amateur projects sent to them.[14] This is understandable considering the poor quality of most of the inventions. Many specialists, however, were not outspoken about this topic in public because they did not want to appear politically disloyal to the Stalinist regime, which insisted on support of the movement for political purposes. Some specialists boldly stated their opposition to the worker-inventor movement, arguing that it was not worth their time to spend energy on social projects that did not pay them extra money or had no real practical applications.[15] John Littlepage, an American engineer working in the Soviet gold-mining industry, was furious about the regime's demands on engineers in this regard: "One small and unimportant example will serve to show as well as anything else how the busiest and best-trained engineers are bogged down in routine and pestered by political control. I refer to the perpetual nuisance of so-called inventors, crack-brained persons who are convinced they have made some amazing mechanical discovery, a type that seems to be more numerous in Soviet Russia than elsewhere."[16]

The post-1928, state-sponsored worker-inventor movement differed dramatically from the initiative of editors and science-popularizers in the popular media of the NEP era. During the twenties the solicitation of workers' inventions by journals was geared toward establishing a form of discourse between scientist/educator and amateur. Sections in the popular journals did not emphasize the practical application of amateur inventions, nor did they focus on how Soviet workers could outpace inventors in the capitalist West. Instead, these sections stressed the importance of amateur inspiration in the conception of new technologies and devices. Even though specialists, who evaluated the projects sent in by amateurs, were typically doubtful about their potential application, responses never questioned the worth of inciting amateurs to invent contraptions and to think about how they could technically operate, based on certain scientific principles. The goals of the editors and scientists in the mid-1920s were, above all, educational.

The correspondences between scientists and readers in the 1920s did not emphasize the importance of worker-inventors as a superior class, nor did they exclude examples of Western technological ingenuity. Furthermore, in the early to mid-1920s (in contrast to the 1930s), editors never suggested that these inventors and their work represented something solely unique to Russia. Editorials stressed the need both to understand foreign technology and to improve on its foundations. Much of this editorial content would change in the late 1920s and early 1930s as the importance of "Soviet technology" was emphasized more in the popular media. By the mid-1930s, Stalinist culture would add a nationalistic component to the public discourse between scientists and laymen, attempting to break the cosmopolitan perspective that Soviet readers used as a framework for understanding global technology in the 1920s.

POPULAR AIR FLIGHT AND THE COSMOS BEYOND

Air flight was an especially popular theme in the mass-science media at the turn of the century. In cities throughout Russia, journals on airplanes and aviation were extremely popular with readers.[17] In the post-October period, many of the new journals were organs of various scientific and voluntary aviation societies. These journals focused on a range of topics, some concentrating on specific types of airships like dirigibles. Others were general popular-scientific journals on air flight, like the Moscow journal entitled *Vozdukhoplavanie* (air flight), founded in 1922. These journals arose in a wide range of Soviet cities in diverse areas such as Leningrad, Novgorod, and Novonikolaevsk. The Soviet regime also supported five key aviation institutes in the 1920s, which were extensively involved in publishing their proceedings for the public. Some of these institutes sponsored popular lectures and the publication of popular journals and pamphlets. Those particular institutes were in Voronezh, Kazan', Kiev, Moscow, and Khar'kov. Various air institutes were keenly aware of the practical importance of popularizing airflight but also of how fixated the Russian public was on this topic.

In the 1920s, air flight was not only popular but actually became a craze in Soviet Russia. Professors like N. A. Rynin in Leningrad were popularizers of air and space literature.[18] During the NEP, government and amateur societies popularized air study and travel in many ways. Certainly, both the Soviet state and voluntary organizations were interested in the development of aviation for the purposes of military defense,[19] and the building of a civilian air fleet during the NEP was important to the regime. An air transportation system could be used to integrate the Soviet Union and transport products and supplies to the far reaches of the empire. There was also a popular fascination with the air-flight development. Many articles in the scientific mass media were particularly devoted to popular analysis and conceptualization of new flying machines, and the public eagerly consumed journals devoted to air flight.

This air-flight craze was an integral part of a European and international phenomenon. In Europe the reporting of aeronautical feats became popular news items and were anticipated well ahead of time—much in the way that rocket flights by the United States and USSR in the 1960s were portrayed by television reporters. Before the First World War, popular air shows in the United States and Europe helped foster an international interest in how air flight technology could alter human relationships with the natural world. Feats of modern aviation were closely tied to nationalistic and patriotic sentiment. In his work on German aviation and popular culture, Peter Fritzsche has convincingly argued that in Germany, both before and after the First World War, technological change and nationalism intersected in the development of aviation. Many countries would subsequently become competitors in developing faster and larger airplanes.[20]

The case study of German aviation is a good example of the ubiquitous links connecting technological development, modernity, and the nation-state. However, after the Bolshevik Revolution in Soviet Russia, air flight did not acquire the nationalistic tendencies that Fritzsche sees in Germany. Because of the development of a different sociopolitical context, it was not until the 1930s that a nationalistic resurgence came to characterize Soviet aviation, with the emphasis of Russian cultural themes under Stalin. Part of this delay can be explained by the underdeveloped nature of Soviet aviation in the 1920s, which led to an emphasis on foreign models. But it mainly had to do with the Soviet public's fascination with foreign technology in general in the 1920s. Soviet Russia did not close itself off from Western technological development in the 1920s, and readers eagerly consumed news items on Western and international feats of flight.

One of the more popular Soviet journals on air flight during the twenties was *Samolet* (airplane). *Samolet* was a monthly popular-scientific journal devoted to aviation published by the "Society of the Friends of the Air Force" (ODVF), which in the 1920s claimed over 100,000 active members. The journal was founded in 1923 and had a print-run of over fifteen thousand copies per month. Articles in *Samolet* were quite diverse in subject matter. The editors of the journal strove to discuss a wide range of issues relating to aviation: "The goal of our journal is not only to discuss the building of airplanes or the Air Force itself. Ultimately we want to spread knowledge about aviation: construction of airplanes, their multifaceted use, their history and development in various countries."[21] Articles in the journal emphasized how important airplanes would be for civilian use. After the First World War, aviation factories all over the world became free of the burden of defense orders and could begin to prepare planes for peacetime use. Popular articles emphasized the use of airplanes internationally in a variety of areas: passenger service, postal transport, aerial photography, and observation of natural disasters from above.[22]

Another popular journal published in the 1920s was *Aviatsiia i khimiia* (aviation and chemistry), published by the Union of Societies of Aviation in the USSR. Some sections in this journal did concentrate on national defense and the air industry, but many of the articles emphasized the applications of airplanes to the civilian economy. Airplanes would be able to carry large numbers of passengers and parcels long distances throughout the Soviet Union. Many other articles in this popular journal described aerial photography and its practical uses for agriculture, forestry, and geology.[23] Aeronautical technology was generally shown as contributing to practical achievements that could benefit the Soviet public.

Although many of the popular-aviation journals of the 1920s were organs of various Soviet all-union or national societies, they still emphasized advances in foreign aviation. Both the feats of foreign pilots and the construction of new airplanes abroad filled these popular journals. This lauding of foreign achievement became one of the most fascinating aspects of these journals for the popular readers. Some articles discussed new flight paths and record distance runs that were completed in the West. In 1923 a 24,000-kilometer flight path was organized and completed over parts of Western Europe. *Samolet* even contained an entire section entitled "Aviation Abroad." Much of this section during the twenties was filled with articles about dirigibles (zeppelins). Some of this was a synopsis of Western press coverage. Articles in *Samolet* reproduced the American press stories on the flight of the German zeppelin ZR-3 from Berlin to America in 1924. Readers were fascinated as to the possibility of transatlantic flight in the new "airships."[24]

It was not until the 1930s that the feats of Soviet aviators would dominate the popular journals and media. By then, developments in Soviet aviation were portrayed as great feats for the nation. In the popular journals 1936 was characterized as a year of "Stakhanovite Socialist Aviation." In the summer of 1936, Chkalov, Baidukov, and Beliakov flew their historic nonstop flight in a Soviet ANT-25.[25] In 1936 Levanovskii and Levchenko flew from Los Angeles to Moscow,[26] and Molokov flew along the arctic seaboard of the USSR.[27] In the 1920s, however, international aeronautical feats were covered with the same frequency as equivalent Russian achievements. These events captivated a Russian audience not yet subjected to "blackouts" of information that would later characterize coverage of foreign technology, like the space race and U.S. rocket launches. Furthermore, the Stalinist 1930s would soon represent a departure point as the popular press began to cover aeronautical developments in an increasingly nationalistic, triumphal manner. Coverage of international air flight in the NEP era clearly distinguished the cultural arena in the first decade of Soviet power from the 1930s and beyond.

Air flight was not the only popular aeronautical craze in Soviet Russia during the nineteen twenties. The exploration of space was also a popular theme in the mass media. Some of that interest in Russia predated the 1917 Revolution and was tied to the philosophical ideas of Nikolai Fedorov. Fedorov's vague notions of space travel as a way to achieve immortality were at the crux of his mystical and scientific utopia, and his ideas were popular among many Russian intellectuals.

Fedorov worried that the Earth itself was overcrowded, and he believed fervently that the only way to relieve this Malthusian pressure was to explore and colonize space.[28] In the 1870s and 1880s, Fedorov helped a number of young scholars finance their studies. Many of these scholars had come to Moscow to study various scientific and philosophical topics. One of these disciples was K. E. Tsiolkovskii, a mathematics student from Kaluga, who would later become a visionary scientist and among the first to analyze the possibility of space flight using rocket-fuel propulsion.[29] According to V. L'vov, Tsiolkovskii learned about the possibility of space travel from his conversations with Fedorov, becoming his greatest disciple.[30] Victor Shklovskii also describes how Fedorov hoped the young mathematician would popularize the notion of space flight among the Russian public. Shklovskii quoted Fedorov as once telling Tsiolkovskii: "I'm going to do mathematics with you, and you'll help mankind build rockets so that we will finally be able to know more than earth and so that we can see our earth. People need a distant look, because only those people who are thinking about the future are real and present."[31]

In the Soviet period, the Biocosmists became devout disciples of Fedorov's basic visions, as their beliefs centered around interplanetary flight and immortality. Besides Tsiolkovskii, other followers of Fedorov in the Soviet period included Valerian Muraviev (the editor of Alexei Gastev's[32] journal at the Central Institute of Labor), Leonid Krasin, and even the renowned geochemist and science popularizer V. I. Vernadskii.[33] The Biocosmists spread Fedorov's and Tsiolkovskii's ideas in the popular media for an eager public willingly consuming articles on space travel.

Along with Tsiolkovskii and the Biocosmists, probably the best-known popularizer of space travel and astronomy in the 1920s was the physics professor Ia. I. Perel'man. In the 1910s, Perel'man was the editor of the popular-scientific journal *Priroda i liudi* (nature and people). After the revolution, he served in the Commissariat of Enlightenment working in the department on school reform. He also became editor of the popular journal *V masterskoi prirody* (in nature's workshop), in which he published many articles on rocket science and space travel.

Perel'man saw Tsiolkovskii, the inventor and teacher of physics in Kaluga, as the pioneer theoretician of space flight in Soviet Russia in the post-1917 era. Thanks to Perel'man's editorial initiative, Tsiolkovskii's theories and drawings about rockets were featured in the popular-scientific journals during the twenties. Drawings of his rocket ships appeared in his scientific tale "Beyond the Earth," which initially appeared in *Priroda i liudi* in 1918. Earlier in 1903 Tsiolkovskii had published an article in the journal *Nauchnoe obozrenie* (scientific review) entitled "The Research of Cosmic Space with the Help of Rocket Devices." In his article the theoretician proposed that flight in interplanetary space was possible with a rocket. He believed such a rocket could be propelled forward with enormous speed from the combustion of fuel. According to his calculations the rocket would have to be traveling at eleven kilometers per second to overcome the force of the Earth's gravity.[34]

In the 1920s Perel'man popularized Tsiolkovskii's theories in his book *Mezhplanetnoe puteshestvie* (interplanetary travel). Perel'man defended the notion of space flight against skeptics by noting that at one time people thought air flight itself was simply impossible. He offered the Russian reader a basic analysis of gravitational forces and how they could be overcome by a projectile traveling at high speeds.[35] For Perel'man, a technical solution to space flight had been worked out in theory by Tsiolkovskii and other European scientists, "and that which is worked on today in theory, can be brought to practical existence tomorrow."[36]

Tsiolkovskii himself was active in popularizing ideas about space travel. In the 1920s and 1930s he printed pamphlets out of his own publishing house in Kaluga, where he lived and taught. His private press became quite an unusual venture in Stalin's Russia of the 1930s. Russians were especially fascinated during this time with dirigibles, so much so that Tsiolkovskii spent as much time writing popular pamphlets on this topic as he did on rocket flight. He published a popular atlas on blimps and analyzed their design and function. He also published several popular pamphlets on his own inventions, which included diagrams of rockets and other contraptions.[37]

Rocket science and space travel were only part of a more general interest on the part of the Russian reader of popular science during the twenties in astronomy, the cosmos, and the exploration of the solar system. They also expressed special interest in research on planets and the solar system. Scientific societies sponsored public disputations in Leningrad and Moscow on the planet Mars, which drew huge audiences. There was also an upsurge in the number of amateur astronomical observers who joined various organizations in Russia's major cities. The study of the formation of the other planets in the solar system fascinated Russians of the early 1920s. Mars was an especially hot topic during this period. In 1921 at the Moscow Polytechnic Museum, A. A. Mikhailov delivered a series of popular lectures about Mars that were very well attended by Muscovites. He helped the Moscow Society for the Amateurs of Astronomy organize over twenty popular-scientific lectures at the Polytechnic Museum on astronomical themes in the first half of 1921 alone. These lectures packed the Polytechnical Museum's main auditorium, as eager citizens marveled and imagined planetary histories. Society members even noted how eager spectators waited patiently in long lines to get good seats in the museum's main hall on the day of a presentation that usually included awe-inspiring photographs of stellar configurations.[38]

K. L. Baev, a well-known Russian astronomer, wrote and edited an enormous quantity of popular articles on astronomy in the journals during the twenties. He gave several of the more popular lectures in Moscow at the Polytechnical Museum. His articles appeared both in Communist journals—*Molodaia gvardiia* (young guard), for instance—as well as non-party publications like *V masterskoi prirody*. Many of his articles concentrated on the formation and composition of planets in the solar system. Some of his articles were historical in nature, discussing the various scientific conceptions of how planets developed in the solar system.

In general, Russian astronomers wrote many articles in the popular media about the work of American researchers. Baev himself found the hypothesis of the geologist Thomas Chrowder Chamberlain and the astronomer Forest Ray Moulton, both professors at the University of Chicago, to be instrumental in understanding how the Earth formed. Their hypothesis on nebulas was part of well-known investigations conducted at the Likov Observatory in California at Mount Hamilton. Those studies systematically photographed large and small nebula-like objects that today we know as galaxies.[39] Baev and other Russian specialists eagerly transposed that research through the popular media for consumption by amateur astronomers in Soviet Russia. They editorialized on how Russian amateur astronomers needed to be connected to the findings of those in the West.

Practically every popular-scientific journal in the 1920s carried a section listing amateur observations of astronomical occurrences. *V masterskoi prirody* had a section entitled "Stellar Appearances." Readers could send in the date of their observation and a description of exactly what they thought they saw in layman's terms. These sections enabled amateur observers to begin a dialogue with scientific experts who would occasionally discuss the nature of these observances in the journals. This aeronautical and astronomical literature furthered the dialogue between amateurs and scientists and helped foster an active interest in science among nonspecialists. In turn, this literature reflected the imaginative potential of the urban Russian reader in envisioning the world and cosmos beyond. Readers relied on an international base of information regarding technological developments that included research outside the borders of socialist Russia.

GEOGRAPHY, GEOLOGY, AND THE EXPLORATION OF THE SOVIET LANDSCAPE

The popularization of geography was particularly important to prerevolutionary academics and Soviet scientists in the 1920s. Many science popularizers, beginning in late Imperial Russia, were trained as geologists or geochemists. They included the geologist V. Obruchev, the famous geochemist V. Vernadskii, and the well known mineralogist A. Fersman. These specialists were prominent, respected Russian academics, and their popular works and lectures were valued and appreciated by the public. They wrote about the vast mineral resources and natural wealth of the Russian empire. Their popular writings displayed a nationalistic sentiment and glorified the enormous resource potential of the Russian land. Many of the popular-scientific journals in the late nineteenth and early twentieth centuries were also filled with articles about world exploration. Those articles captured the popular imagination of Russian readers and inspired their desire to learn more about newly discovered areas and peoples all over the globe. Popular literature on geography, particularly, displays both an informative and imaginative component, especially since readers were fascinated by novels, Tolstoy's for instance, that described peripheral terrains of the Russian empire. Russian readers were keenly interested in the journeys of both Russian and foreign explorers, anthropologists, and geologists.

The popular media was filled with articles on geography that concentrated on two general themes. The first encompassed description of the natural resources and vast landscape of the Russian empire. That theme combined the scientific description of the immense potential of fossil resources and also glorified the Russian empire's natural wealth. The second theme looked at exploration of the Russian landscape and the globe. The focus on global exploration stressed the importance of world geography, while capturing the popular imagination with themes on distant lands and peoples. In the Russian popular journals of the late imperial period, descriptions of world exploration also emphasized superficial ethnographic analysis filled with Eurocentric descriptions of indigenous peoples.

Many of the popular geographic journals of the late imperial period offered mixed messages and signs. On the one hand, such articles provided Russian readers with sophisticated geological and geographical notes on and analysis of the world's more remote areas—the terrain of the island of Formosa or the jungles of parts of the African interior continent, for example. These descriptions grew from eclectic observations and analyses of plant and animal life, mineralogical formations, and topographical points. Within many of the popular journals, with the exception of the Academy of Sciences' *Priroda,* geological analysis was always intermixed with a type of pseudo-ethnography. Editors of these journals felt the need to include descriptions of the peoples of these areas in an exotic manner, defining them as different from civilized Europeans or Russians. In an article describing the geology and geography of the island of Formosa, the editors of *Vokrug sveta* (around the world) gave readers a detailed account of the terrain, flora and fauna, and mineralogical content of that area. However, they painted images of the people who inhabited the island as "wild natives" who were absolutely bewildered by Western dress and customs.[40]

Many of these articles focused on foreign explorers and their exploits, coloring the Eurocentric descriptions of remote global areas and peoples. The articles often described the scientific analysis of Russian naturalists and the travels of Russian tourists. A strange duality obtained with regard to these popular-geographic journals; while they educated, they also reinforced images of the "other," encouraging colonial and imperial responses to these encounters.[41] For example, in some of the first issues of the popular journal *Estestvoznanie i geografiia* (natural science and geography) in the 1890s, a series of articles appeared describing the geography and peoples of Siberia. Like the Russian North and the Caucasus, Siberia was a remote location and a popular topic for those readers living in the major urban centers of European Russia. Many of these articles were unsophisticated ethnographic treatises. In an article on the exploration of south-western Siberia, K. Nosilov described a boat expedition to Semipalatinsk, where his entourage came upon "wild tribes" of indigenous Siberians living along the waterways. His record of encounters with the local Kirghiz, an indigenous Mongol people of the area, describes their native political orientation as overtly despotic and hierarchical, even though they had had contacts with "other civilizations."[42]

An article in *Vokrug sveta* in 1895 described a Russian naturalist and his entourage on their trip to Sumatra. The article spent time describing the "savage Batak" people who had practiced cannibalism for ages. Interestingly enough, the author of this article had spent several months living near and among these peoples and, at the outset, described them as not so "uncivilized" as Europeans had typically thought. The author concluded his article by saying that after living for months among the Batak, he never once had any serious misunderstanding with them. Yet the tone of his article mimicked the nineteenth-century "civilized tourist" moving among a native people, whom he categorized for public consumption back in Russia. The author's frequent use of phrases like "savage natives" reinforced for the reader a culturally constructed distance between the "civilized" and "uncivilized" world.[43]

Thematic articles of the period often described global exploratory trips and expeditions to the periphery of Russia's vast empire. In contrast to articles like those in *Estestvoznanie i geografiia,* shaped by a colonial ethnographic perspective, many others presented a more sophisticated scientific and geographic analysis of places most Russian citizens would never venture to explore. By the turn of the century the Academy of Sciences' popular-scientific journal *Priroda* carried a specific subsection on geology and mineralogy. A. E. Fersman, one of the members of the journal's editorial board, always insisted that the public understood the importance of these new disciplines. The Academy's journal carried a more sophisticated section on "Geographical News" and ran commentary on exploration all over the globe.

Even prior to the 1917 Russian Revolution, Fersman, as an editor of articles on these topics, conjured up a nationalistic perspective about Russia's wealth and potential strength as a country. In an editorial in March of 1915 in *Priroda,* Fersman argued that the fossil wealth of a country could influence the industry, culture, and even military strength of its whole people. Many articles that he edited or wrote himself developed this general perspective in more detail. In an article in early 1915 describing the natural wealth of Galicia, recently seized by the Russian Army from the Austro-Hungarian Empire, Fersman tried to describe how the resources of this new possession could affect Russia's geopolitical importance. As the oil industry grew and advances in technology made extraction easier, Galicia had become a rich resource of oil by the turn of century. Fersman believed that Galicia, Bukovina, and the entire Carpathian region was infused not just with oil but other important natural resources and that the area had to be further developed by Russian industrial investors.[44]

As editor of geographical essays in *Priroda,* Fersman encouraged other geologists and explorers to write popular articles for the Russian layman, describing the exotic borderlands of the Russian empire. Just before the onset of World War I a Professor Mashasek, interested in the morphology of rock and mountain formation, contributed many popular articles to *Priroda* that described his trips and research as he traveled east of Tashkent in the Fergana region. His series of articles offered readers fantastic images and detailed descriptions of that area, along with scientific analysis of its geological construction.[45]

Many articles also described the expeditions of explorers and geographers to the north of Russia, especially to areas around Archangel. Professor L. L. Ivanova wrote a series of articles describing the expeditions of academics aboard the vessel *Ruirik* around the arctic north as they steamed from Archangel. Professor Ivanova's descriptions detailed the terrain, soil, and plant life. People were curious about these far reaches of the north and what type of fauna and flora characterized the area. Clearly, Ivanova took advantage of a natural sense of adventure among Russian readers following these expeditions, as she detailed news of the exploratory missions to these isolated areas. But her articles, at times, could also be quite specific, written in a dry, perfunctory scientific style. She described the terrain in a mundane manner by saying that "the severe climate of the area around *'Novaia Zemlia'* [new land] contained very little diversity of plant-life and we found an abundance of short grasses."[46] All in all, these series of articles represented excellent condensed versions of detailed scientific, exploratory trips for the Russian reader.

News and information on exploration certainly captivated the Russian reader in the late imperial period. Popular-scientific journals like *Estestvoznanie i geografiia* (the natural sciences and geography) carried articles on the terrain and cultures of the periphery of the vast Russian empire. *Vokrug sveta,* the most popular of Russian journals covering global exploration, carried descriptions of Russian and world expeditions, anthropological missions, geographic and geological analysis, and travel logs of Russians who visited distant lands. Both *Estestvoznanie i geografiia* and *Vokrug sveta* carried articles on regions that had recently been colonized by the Russian empire. Several articles in the 1860s appeared in *Vokrug sveta* describing expeditions to the Caucasus mountains and surrounding area. A particularly popular series of articles, which appeared in 1864, described the expeditions of Prince A. I. Bariatinskii and his entourage as they traversed the Caucasus range, analyzing both the terrain and indigenous peoples they encountered.[47] Serial entries of his expedition enticed readers and hooked subscribers who eagerly awaited news of the entourage in the next issue.

This fascination on the part of the popular reader with geographical expeditions continued after the First World War and across the revolutionary divide. Journals continued to meet the demand for news on exploration, for descriptions of the terrain of Russia's empire, as well as for fantastic stories of newly discovered lands. Soviet Geologists like Vladimir Obruchev, who originally went along with ethnologists in the late nineteenth century on trips to Central Asia, emphasized the importance of studying the geological deposits of the new Soviet empire and making this information known to a broad readership. As a propagandist of geology, he believed a minimum knowledge of geology and physical geography was necessary to every cultured person.

In the popular-scientific journals of the 1920s, geographic/geologic expeditions were always noted and highlighted in articles.

After the Bolshevik Revolution the stress shifted even more to studying the "little-known" geography of Soviet Russia's empire. The popular journals of the Soviet 1920s placed a more consistent emphasis on studying the vast mineral deposits of Russia for their potential utility. The Soviet state saw these geologists as orators of the glorification and natural geological wealth of new Soviet lands. The state's interests converged with the popularizers in spreading information about Soviet Russia's mineral wealth and natural resources.

Fersman was active once again in producing a series of popular-scientific books and articles on mineralogy and geochemistry. He was also secretary of the Commission for Studying the Natural Productive Forces of Russia (KEPS), a body of the Russian Academy of Sciences. The recurrent theme of "the productive strengths of the country" was part of the overarching Bolshevik public modernization campaign. The need to define the utility of the Russian landscape was inherently tied to post-1917 Bolshevik visions of the conquest of nature. Such national pride in the mineral wealth of Russia foreshadowed the more overtly nationalist portrayal of scientific feats in the Soviet press during the Stalinist 1930s.

The emphasis on utilitarianism and the resource potential of the Soviet landscape was also reflected in the focus on regional studies in the 1920s. Popular-scientific journals and newsletters in the 1920s, like Maksim Gorky's *Nauka i ee rabotniki* (science and its workers), periodically listed the various organizations for regional studies *(kraevedenie)* created during the revolutionary and Civil War periods that aided in the spread and popularization of science. Regional studies were publicized as part of a campaign to encourage the reading public to understand the geographical diversity of the USSR. Not only did the number of these societies grow tremendously (from 160 institutions in 1917 to 516 by 1923), but their emphasis shifted toward the study of natural productive resources and local demography and economy.[48] They popularized studies on the fauna, flora, and mineral wealth of the Russian periphery. Although these *kraeved* organizations were composed mainly of amateurs, the Academy of Sciences saw them as bases for the popularization of scientific research and a scientific world view.[49] During 1918–1920, the years of the Russian Civil War, large numbers of scientists were forced out of the major urban capitals and to provincial cities and towns such as Iaroslavl' or Ekaterinburg. This movement of scientists to provincial areas fostered new contacts between some major scholars and many organizations for regional studies.[50]

Editors of both private and state-published journals connected the themes of utilitarianism and resource potential with the overarching interests of the new Soviet state. The popular journal *Iskra* developed a series of articles on the regional mineral wealth of the country. They introduced this series with the following note: "The editors would like to meet our readers half way and foster their natural desire to broaden their horizons. In the following series of articles, we hope they will get a clearer representation of the natural wealth of the USSR. Therefore, on a regular basis, we hope to publish a series of articles that will inform our readers about our regional natural resources, and how we can exploit these resources for the benefit of our national economy."[51] This stated objective exemplifies an editorial process combining an interest in propagating solid scientific analysis with the nationalistic overtones reinforced by Bolshevik rhetoric from above.

A number of the articles featured in *Iskra* were written by such expert geologists as Obruchev. Many articles discussed mineral resources in the USSR and their practical economic use. The first article in the series by Obruchev was entitled "Fossil Wealth of Siberia: Its Contemporary Use and Meaning." Obruchev informed his readers of the immense quantities of valuable metals in the vast landscape of Siberia, noting the large quantities of gold, silver, zinc, and iron. He claimed in 1927 that preliminary estimates of coal deposits were significantly higher than deposits in the rest of the USSR. He also emphasized the enormous deposits of graphite in the Tungus Basin. According to Obruchev, that basin could fulfill the world demand for graphite for many years to come. Obruchev believed that, with the exception of gold, these resources had not been significantly mined.[52]

Maksim Gorky's journal *Nauka i ee rabotniki* featured articles on specific areas of the Soviet Union and the research conducted by various organizations on mineral deposits. Many of the articles described remote areas like the polar north, which was rich in coal, graphite, oil, and precious metals. Journals, like Gorky's, focused on particular Soviet research institutions and emphasized the extensive nature of their work in outlying areas. Research on the polar north was conducted after the revolution by three organizations of the Russian Academy of Sciences. KEPS conducted investigations on climate and waterways. The Russian Polar Commission organized expeditions to the Northern Urals by explorers like the Kunetsov brothers. The third organization was the Academy's Commission for the Study of the Tribal Composition of the Population of Russia (KIPS), which investigated and studied various peoples of the northern regions of Russia. Lastly, the Scientific-Technical Department of Vesenkha was interested in excavating the vast resources of the North for industrial use.[53] Gorky's journal was filled with articles and reports based on the activities of these commissions. As editor, Gorky insisted that these notes on state-sponsored research be written in a popular, accessible form for the average and educated Russian reader.

Along with this more utilitarian perspective came an imaginative, even fictional quality to many of the articles and popular books written on exploration and geography in the 1920s. Unlike glorified utilitarian themes, this imaginative component would vanish in the 1930s. Various popularizers wrote articles on fantastic voyages to fictitious and even actual lands in newspapers such as *Pionerskaia pravda* and *Komsomolskaia pravda* and in popular-scientific journals such as *Vokrug sveta, Pioner, Smena,* and *Tekhnika-molodezhi.* The fictionalized geographic stories were remarkably consistent in tone and appeal, whether in Communist or non-Communist publications that had survived the Revolution intact. That consistency attests to how journals backed by a variety of institutional sponsors attempted to compete for the interests of active Russian readers.

Obruchev's serialized science-fiction novels of the 1920s are the perfect example of those works that enticed many, especially younger, readers to understand better their geographic surroundings through imaginative writing. The first of these science-fiction novels, entitled *Plutoniia* (Plutonia),[54] describes the voyage to an unknown land, entered through a hole in the ice-fields of the Arctic to get to its underground void. The imaginary land was an underground world of rivers, lakes, volcanoes, and strange vegetation, a world with its own sun, Pluto, and inhabited by monstrous animals and primitive people. Another of Obruchev's popular science-fiction novels, *Zemli sannikova* (Sannikov's land), was actually based on historical incidents. In 1810 the industrialist Iakov Sannikov, who was investigating near the Arctic Ocean, noticed mountains of an unknown land far off on the horizon. In the following years he noticed various rising contours. In 1886, in the same area, the geologist E. Toll also saw an uncharted land on the horizon. Toll, in 1900 on the ship *Zaria,* organized an expedition to find and explore the land, but he and his ship perished in the Arctic Ocean.

The heroes of Obruchev's novels found islands, lived on them, and observed the existence and disposition of their inhabitants; in *Zemli sannikova* they are the Onkilons.[55] From serialized novels like these a reader could gain a sense of the many scientific problems that geographers encountered in places like northern Siberia. Later in the 1920s Obruchev published a series of popular articles on the exploration of the Arctic Ocean. He believed that this type of scientific-artistic story gave incentives to future generations to pursue research and help further geographic investigations. The utopian met the practical in this genre of popular-scientific novels, and it captured the imagination of young urban readers, especially as their minds ventured to uncharted waters and places. These novels added to the preexisting literature inviting readers to learn about lands in the distant reaches of the Soviet empire. Furthermore, this literature might have indirectly prepared Soviet youth for the voluntaristic and utopian 'storming'-of-nature campaigns of the Stalinist 1930s.

SCIENCE AND RELIGION IN THE POPULAR-SCIENCE MEDIA

The topic of science combating religious and superstitious behavior was a popular theme among editors of popular-scientific journals in Soviet Russia during the twenties. The idea of science struggling with religion was emblematic of the Bolshevik cultural revolution in the 1920s, and Lenin expressed that viewpoint quite fervently. Editors of popular journals believed that antireligious articles must go hand in hand with those that emphasized the importance of the natural sciences to readers. Popular-scientific journals served as a key medium in the broader effort to combat superstition in Soviet Russia with the spread of scientific achievements and progress.

A. V. Nemilov, editor of the popular journal *Chelovek i priroda* (man and nature), believed that if he was going to emphasize natural-scientific articles in his periodical, he also had to spread the importance of materialist philosophy: "Revolutionary work must be antireligious. It must underscore that the world is materialistic, that there is no spirit or secret mystical component to development. Furthermore, nature can be mastered by man."[56] Editors of journals like *Chelovek i priroda* believed that enlightenment in the 1920s meant making science accessible to the public. Editor Nemilov believed that the prerevolutionary Russian intelligentsia did not favor spreading antireligious propaganda and were far too idealistic in their notion of spreading "pure" science. However, in the 1920s a close correlation existed between, on the one hand, Bolshevik antireligious ideas and, on the other, the messianic notion of spreading *nauka* (science) propagated by the prerevolutionary elite in Russia. In a 1926 article in *Chelovek i priroda* I. Eliashevich argued that Lenin believed it was tactically permissible to use antireligious material written by bourgeois authors, even if it did not stress class struggle and only developed the importance of the sciences. According to the author, Lenin argued that scientific enlightenment was the way to combat religion and that Bolsheviks must use all available resources.[57] This line of Bolshevik reasoning asserted that editors did not necessarily need to propagandize materialism or antireligious themes overtly; it was sufficient to develop notions of basic scientific explanations for the origin of the Earth and mankind.

Editors of popular-scientific journals believed that articles on human evolution and on the evolution of the Earth could dissuade readers from religious explanations and offer evidence for natural, organic development. In a 1925 article in *Chelovek i priroda* S. M. Selivanov discussed the importance of explaining, with hard factual evidence, how the Earth was formed. He argued that the study of gaseous formations and volcanic development provided essential knowledge for readers upon which to build a solid, scientific understanding of evolution. Selivanov himself monitored the work of amateur science societies and was particularly interested in those involved in the study of astronomy. He fervently believed in public access to scientific information about new astronomical discoveries, hoping such knowledge would draw people closer to an understanding of the thoroughly natural processes behind the formation of stars, various planets, and the Earth.[58]

Other popular journals carried a series of articles throughout the course of the 1920s on the history of anthropological research and evidence for evolutionary development. Articles in *Iskra nauki,* the publishing house *Gudok*'s popular science journal, took readers back to turn-of-the-century discoveries of anthropologists in various parts of Africa and Europe. Articles were generally accompanied by photographs of craniums of various early human or simian ancestors. In many articles the work of American and Western European specialists was praised for its sophistication. In a 1925 article in *Iskra nauki* the American scholar Henry Fairfield Osborn was lauded for his discoveries and analysis of human fossil remains.[59] This was hard evidence against any creationist theory for the public, as it based itself on the authority of Western specialists.

In popular journals like *Iskra,* authors attempted to explain organic evolution from a gradualist perspective. G. Azimov gave readers a detailed explanation of how the Earth was first populated by single- and multicellular organisms that eventually evolved into more complicated living beings.[60] Authors not only provided explanations of the fossil record as proof of evolutionary change, but they also tried to show the concrete links between various animals on the evolutionary chain.[61] Some authors showed how professionals identify fossil remains to delineate specifically how various species evolved. Much of their analysis was filled with Darwinian concepts, even if they did not specifically refer to Darwin. Darwin's theories were generally submerged in their popular texts.[62] The use of various Darwinian terms, such as "survival of the fittest" and the "struggle for existence," was a common technique among popularizers; and these phrases became tropes for explaining the metaphoric and literal power of the modern concept of organic evolution.

Of all the potential methods for using scientific arguments against religion, evolutionary theory and evidence was perhaps the most persuasive weapon in the popular-science media. Bolshevik antireligious activists also astutely realized the potential of evolutionary theory in combating religious doctrine. Scientists of the late tsarist and early Soviet period, though for distinct purposes, worked with some success to bring science and Darwinism to the people. In the Bolsheviks mind-set, antireligious doctrine (and an assault on creationist theory) would therefore be a potent means of creating a secular, scientized culture.

ИЗДАТЕЛЬСТВО „**КРАСНАЯ НОВЬ**" *ПРИ ГЛАВПОЛИТПРОСВЕТЕ.*

№ 5. | Август 1923 г. | № 5.

Содержание № 5.

Iskra (The Spark), no. 5, August, 1923. Signature cover for the widely read 1920s-era popular science journal published by the Soviet Political Enlightenment Department.

НАУЧНО-ФАНТАСТИЧЕСКИЙ РОМАН **ВИНЬОЛЯ** и **НОКС.**

Перевод с англ. *Г. Ляндау.*

ГЛАВА ПЕРВАЯ.

Разговор завязался из-за мелкой медной монеты, найденной на одном из сидений железнодорожного купэ.

Лейк положил ее на ладонь, подбросил два или три раза и, посмотрев в открытое окно, перевел взгляд на незнакомого господина, прикурнувшего в противоположном углу.

Лейк невесело усмехнулся.

— Не много пользы для человека, не уверенного в ближайшем завтраке, сэр, — полувопросительно проговорил он.

— Как знать, — быстро откликнулся незнакомец, стряхивая сигарный пепел с отворота пальто. — Что там у вас такое? Полпенни?

— Французский су. Самая мизерная вещь, какую только можно себе представить. В особенности в Англии.

Незнакомец придвинулся.

— Эта мизерная вещь равноценна всего - на - всего восьмидесяти миллионам лошадиных сил, — заметил он с легкой улыбкой.

— Виноват, — сказал Лейк, выпуская из рук монету.

— По меньшей мере восьмидесяти, — повторил тот, уже без улыбки и пониженным голосом. — Чудесно, не правда ли? Впрочем, я, кажется, рискую завлечь вас в потемки. Задумывались ли вы когда-нибудь, что такое атомы, электроны и тому подобное.

Лейк почесал переносицу.

— Боюсь, что не особенно, — ответил он, сморщивая лоб. — Разве вот только раз, когда мне попалась однажды предлинная статья какого-то Джонни, который чуть ли не собирался оседлать атом. В одной лондонской газете, кажется. В общем, галиматья, для нормального человека прямо непроходимая. При этом словечки и выражения одно лучше другого: наружные отрицательные электроны, альфа-частицы, и все

в этом же роде. Недурно? Меня, во всяком случае, она пришибла основательно. Но, в общем, должен вам сказать, он — повидимому, очень мозговатый и ученый парень. Как только его настоящее имя... Да, Грент кажется.

— Грент — это я.

— Вы?

Лейк наполовину сполз с дивана.

— Ради бога простите. Я, кажется, вас нечаянно назвал Джонни.

— Пожалуйста, пожалуйста. Типичное английское имя, которого я, однако, уже давно не слышал. Тем более, что меня зовут как-раз Джоном — Джон Алек сандр Грент. Курите?

— Благодарю вас.

Лейк выбрал сигару и зажег спичку.

— Вы не англичанин? — с интересом спросил он.

— Англичанин. Я родился в Лондоне, но затем так долго жил в Нью-Йорке, что меня многие принимают теперь за американца. Приехал вчера... Итак, моя статья, повидимому, оставила вас холодным.

— Нет не совсем. Она была, правда, очень сложна и очень специальна, но в общем, признаться, меня заинтересовала. Вернее, она приоткрыла такие сногсшибательные горизонты, что я в первый раз в моей жизни зажмурил глаза, чтобы попробовать заглянуть

Lev B. Kamenev, "Rabochaia revoliutsiia i nauka" (Workers' Revolution and Science), cover of a 1925 pamphlet published by the Moscow City Soviet. In the 1920s it was not atypical of key Bolsheviks, such as Kamenev, to write basic politicized primers on popular scientific topics for a worker audience.

НОВОСТИ ВОЗДУХОПЛАВАНИЯ.

ПОСАДКА ВОЗДУШНЫХ КОРАБЛЕЙ НА ЗЕМЛЮ И ВОДУ.

Инженер Умберто Нобиле, известный итальянский конструктор воздушных кораблей, изобрел чрезвычайно простую и удобную систему посадки воздушных кораблей.

По системе Нобиле, воздушный корабль снабжается лебедкой, к барабану которой прикреплен один конец посадочного каната (рис. 2). Другой свободный конец каната снабжен специальным автоматическим якорем. В случае воздушного корабля небольшого объема, вроде итальянского

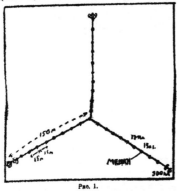

Рис. 1.

дирижабля мягкой системы «Мг», для приведения в действие лебедки достаточно силы одного или двух людей из команды. Обычно же на больших воздушных кораблях лебедка должна приводиться в действие при помощи небольшого двигателя.

На том месте, где воздушный корабль предполагает сесть на землю, располагаются под углом в 120 градусов три тормозных каната (рис. 1).

К канатам подвешиваются балластные мешки с песком. Эти мешки частью своего веса опираются на землю. Чтобы ослабить напряжение самих канатов, на концах их, в качестве противовеса, подвешивается группа балластных мешков.

На рис 1 приведены размеры установки для воздушного корабля, объем которого не превышает 5000 куб. метров.

Операция посадки производится следующим образом. Воздушный корабль, обладающий и большим изgiven подъемной силы, подлетает к тормозным канатам на небольшой высоте (около 100 метров), с очень замедленной скоростью. В этот момент посадочный канат быстро травится с лебедки, до тех пор, пока якорь не дотронется земли. Воздушный корабль медленно проплывает над тормозными канатами, влача за собой якорь, который, придя в соприкосновение с одним из тормозных канатов, цепляется за него.

С этого момента начинается торможение воздушного корабля. Торможение производится постепенно так как число волочимых мешков увеличивается, по мере того как

продвигается воздушный корабль. Благодаря торможению, воздушный корабль останавливается, пилот застопоривает двигатель и посредством лебедки выбирает посадочный канат, притягиваясь, таким образом, к земле на только, насколько это необходимо для погрузки и разгрузки люд й и груза. Автоматический якорь, спроектированный для этой цели, показан на рис. 3 (двурогий тип с рычагами, запирающими края якоря) и на рис. 4 (тип цепи, со звеньями, запирающимися рычагами, придерживаемыми пружиной).

Второй тип якоря более удобен в обращении, ибо не требует особой точности при зацеплении за «тормозной» канат.

Система Нобиле одинаково приложима и для посадки на воду. В этом случае балластные мешки заменяются мешками с водой, а подпорами служат поплавки (напр., про кие). Канаты могут лежать на воде или же быть погружены на не-

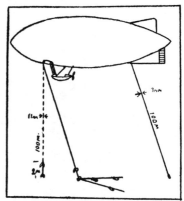

Рис. 2.

которую глубину в воду. Когда якорь схватывает канат, некоторые из мешков совершенно погружаются, а другие совсем или отчасти вылезают из воды.

Бывают случаи, когда воздушному кораблю необходимо держаться у поверхности воды и в то же время сохранять способность двигаться, с той целью, чтобы своими собственными силами добраться до какого-нибудь пункта, где он сможет взять запас горючего и балласта, разгрузить или нагрузить пассажиров и воды.

Для этой так называемой «свободной посадки» Нобиле придумал следующий маневр (рис. 5). На свободном конце посадочного каната прикрепляется вместо якоря мешок соответствующей формы и вместимости. Когда корабль снизится до такой степени, что мешок коснется поверхности воды и наполнится водой, пилот застопоривает двигатель и, оперируя лебедкой, подтягивает воздушный корабль вниз.

"Flight over Land and Water of Blimps/Zeppelins," *Nauka i tekhnika* (Science and Technology), no. 3, January, 1926. This journal frequently ran sections on news of scientific and technological developments. News of blimps and air flight were quite popular topics among Soviet readers of the 1920s.

Iskra, no. 6, June, 1928. By the late 1920s this journal was the organ of the All-Union Society "Technology for the Masses," and it was published under the auspices of *Gosizdat* (Soviet State Publishing House). This cover was an ominous yet ubiquitous symbol of Soviet technology reaching the masses. An emblem of scientific progress from Lenin's time, here electrification was more exemplary of the Stalinist industrialization drive.

This photo was taken in fall, 1939, at the central park in Kaluga, Russia, at the commemoration of Konstantin Tsiolkovskii's death in September, 1935. An anonymous painting held by participants shows a duplication of May Day, 1935, festivities in Red Square, the day Tsiolkovskii gave a taped radio address to the nation on the future of Soviet space flight. Tsiolkovskii was the great popularizer of space flight in Russia in the early twentieth century. *Arkhiv Rossiiskoi akademii nauk* (ARAN), fond 555, op. 2, d.161, 1.3.

Chapter 6

TRANSFORMING THE SPIRIT WITH SCIENCE

Evolution, Antireligion, and the Soviet State in the 1920s

A genuine appreciation for the revolutionary importance of evolutionary thought and Darwin's theories cut across ideological and generational lines in the Russian scientific community in both the tsarist and Soviet eras. Science popularizers of varied political and scientific backgrounds believed in the need to spread Darwin's ideas in the public realm. In the prerevolutionary era, scientists had to battle the church, censors, and the imperial regime in order to publish popular tracts on evolution and Darwinism. Conversely, there were those who popularized critiques of Darwin's theories and were apprehensive about the spread of evolutionary ideas beyond the walls of academe. In the Soviet era, however, diverse scientific thinkers used Darwin's ideas, and evolutionary theory in general, for a variety of political and apolitical purposes. Bolsheviks and non-Communist scientists alike used anticreationist thought and antireligious propaganda as tools against the persistence of superstition and nonscientific belief.

DARWINISM, SCIENCE EDUCATION, AND THE SPREAD OF EVOLUTIONARY THOUGHT

In the pre-Darwinian era in Russia, the idea of evolution received support from scholars representing a wide range of disciplines in the natural sciences.[1] During the 1840s and 1850s a number of professors at Moscow University became interested in studying the evolutionary development of the organic world. Professor Karl F. Rouillier was probably the first biologist-evolutionist in Russia to spread ideas about changes in various species over time. Rouillier and his colleagues laid the groundwork for the reception of more advanced Darwinian evolutionary theory in Russia.[2]

In 1845 Rouillier, chair of the zoology department at Moscow University, gave a series of public lectures on evolutionary theory and morphology and the habitual activity of animals. His lectures were quite popular and gave him a public reputation. Alexander Herzen, the Russian socialist, was taken by Rouillier's lectures and wrote an article publicizing them in the *Moskovskie vedomosti* (Moscow gazette).[3] Mikhail Katkov, the editor of *Moskovskie vedomosti,* published half of Rouillier's second lecture verbatim.[4] B. E. Raikov, the Petersburg science educator, argued that the lectures clearly stated that animals were in a continual historical process of change and evolutionary development. Although the outline for the lectures was approved in advance by the Ministry of Education, the public speech and published contents was alarming to Minister of Education Prince Shirinskii-Shikhmatov. The minister viewed the lectures as a direct affront to the teaching of the scriptures. Rouillier's lectures and book on this topic received permission for publication on the condition that he amend his conclusions to acknowledge that his scientific arguments "are of value only to the degree in which they accord to God's word."[5] Rouillier was very careful in his lecture notes, which he lithographed for his students, to state that humans were not derived from animals but separately from simian ancestors.[6]

During the intellectually progressive period of the 1860s, Russian scientists continued to develop and spread evolutionary ideas of organic development. I. I. Mechnikov and Alexander Kovalevskii belonged to a group of Russian scientists whose studies linked the comparative embryology of marine invertebrates with Darwin's theory of evolution. Kovalevskii was a pioneering evolutionary embryologist who was later praised by Darwin in *The Descent of Man and Selection in Relation to Sex* (1871).[7] Mechnikov, a microbiologist and immunologist, developed an explanation of how organisms defend against inflammation caused by destructive cells.[8]

Mechnikov was originally critical of Darwin's competitive theory of "survival of the fittest." He later became one of his most avid supporters in Russia. He was also involved in popularizing Darwin's theories and by the turn of the century had published a popular tract entitled *Izuchenii vrode cheloveka* (studies on the nature of man). The book was edited by N. A. Umov, a Moscow University physics professor, and was a popular explication of the organic development of humanoids from apes.[9]

During the 1860s news about Darwin's recently published *On the Origin of Species* was analyzed publicly in journals published by scientific societies like the Moscow Society of Naturalists. Darwin's theory was also mentioned in biology classes in Moscow and St. Petersburg. Professor S. S. Kutorga, at St. Petersburg University, advocated that students in his well-attended lectures should pay especially close attention to Darwin's groundbreaking theory. Furthermore, a number of young Russian scientists started an avid correspondence with Darwin. Those like V. O. Kovalevskii, the paleontologist, were interested in incorporating Darwin's theories into their specific branch of science.[10]

Alexander Vucinich has argued that during the 1870s Darwin's theories came under increased criticism. With the publication of Darwin's *Descent of Man* in 1871, the number of antievolutionists attacking transformist ideas increased in Russia. Attacks on Darwin's theories came from a wide range of intellectuals, such as defenders of the Russian autocracy, theologians, conservative scientists, and philosophers.[11] Anti-Darwinian arguments were popularized in Russia during the 1870s in the conservative journal *Russkii vestnik* (Russian herald). The editors translated contemporary English anti-evolutionist essays for popular consumption. Those essays included John Tyndall's attack on the theory of pangenesis and on the notion that all species derived from one primordial organism. Michael Pogodin, the conservative essayist and defender of the Russian autocracy, was critical of the materialistic basis of contemporary science.[12]

Although popular forms of antievolutionist criticism were on the rise during this period, this did not quell the countervailing popular interest in Darwin's theories among educated Russians. Popular tracts explicating Darwin's theories were printed in large numbers in Russia at the turn of the century. Those tracts were not written only by scientists interested in popularizing evolutionary thought. Some popularizers were involved in adult education and had no specific scientific training. In his own popular-scientific works, the library scholar Nicholas Rubakin concentrated much effort on popularizing Darwinian evolutionary theory. In the 1880s Rubakin lectured to workmen at his father's paper mill near St. Petersburg on scientific subjects like evolutionary theory, and in 1891 he became one of the leaders of the Committee for the Fight Against Illiteracy. Rubakin's *Istoriia russkoi zemli* (history of the Russian land) illustrates how he attempted to spread evolutionary theory on a popular level. In this book Rubakin discussed plant and animal life in the sea and introduced the concept of speciation. It is clear that he used distinctly Darwinian evolutionary concepts without specifically referring to them as such. Rubakin commented on how new species of crayfish, mussels, seaweed, and other marine life seemed to appear all at once. He thus posed the question to his readers: From where did these new species appear and how and why? According to Rubakin, the appearance of new species on the Earth did not occur instantly but over great spans of time—hundreds of thousands of years. He believed that no species of plant or animal just appeared suddenly out of nowhere but from an earlier known species through a very slow process of evolution.[13]

Another popularizer of biological thought at the turn of the century was the historian of science V. V. Lunkevich (1866–1941). Although Lunkevich originally held no academic position, in the last decade of his life he became head of the faculty of Darwinism at the Moscow Pedagogical Institute.[14] Many of his key biological articles appeared before the revolution in both popular and scholarly journals, like *Russkoe bogatstvo* (Russian wealth). His life's major work, *Osnova zhizni* (the basis of life), was originally published as a series of several entries in popular journals. Like Rubakin and others, Lunkevich believed that Darwinism explained some of the key factors in the transformation of species: adaptive mechanisms, natural selection, and the struggle for existence. However, Lunkevich argued publicly that Darwinism could not explain the complexity of living organisms. He advocated an evolutionary theory that was a synthesis of Darwin's concepts and new theories put forth by scholars in the experimental sciences.[15]

Between 1908 and 1910 a number of societies, scholars, and editors took part in the celebrations commemorating the fiftieth anniversary of the publication of Darwin's *On the Origin of Species.* These celebrations helped further popularize the ideas of Darwin and evolutionary theory in general in Russia. Many popular journals, such as *Natural Science and Geography,* published essays on Darwinian themes. The editors of *Vestnik znaniia* (herald of knowledge) dedicated an entire issue of the journal to the Darwin festivities. They published various essays that provided the lay-reader with an overview of Darwin's evolutionary theories.[16] In 1910 the journal published an inexpensive edition of *On the Origin of Species* and also part of the *Descent of Man.*[17]

Vucinich has shown how various learned societies paid tribute to Darwin's theories by sponsoring popular lectures by Russian scientists. In 1908 and 1909 both the Moscow and St. Petersburg naturalist societies sponsored public lectures and gatherings in honor of Darwin. Newspapers like *Russkie vedomosti* (Russian gazette) published commemorative articles on Darwin's evolutionary thought. In January of 1909, in an article in *Russkie vedomosti,* the plant physiologist K. A. Timiriazev described his visit with Darwin at the author's home in England. Timiriazev noted that Darwin acknowledged the important contribution to evolutionary theory made by Russian scholars such as Kovalevskii and Mechnikov.[18]

Timiriazev himself wrote voluminous popular tracts on the revolutionary importance of Charles Darwin's theories. He was one of the first to promote and spread Darwinism in Russia, especially in his public lectures at several Russian museums. He regarded Darwin's biological theory as one of the greatest achievements of nineteenth-century social thought. In his book *Darwin i ego teoriia* (Darwin and his theory, 1882), Timiriazev made Darwin's theories accessible to the educated Russian layman. He also published popular articles on Darwinism in the "thick" journal *Otechestvennye zapiski* (notes of the fatherland).

Timiriazev had translated into Russian Darwin's *On the Origin of Species* and introduced the book with an analysis of evolutionary theory. He believed that Darwin's key to understanding the basis of selection came from his reading of Malthus's work on population, especially Malthus's concept of the survival of a limited number of organisms from the stressed total. Timiriazev believed that it was the work of Malthus that brought Darwin and Alfred Russel Wallace independently to similar conclusions.[19]

Between 1908 and 1910, in celebration of the fiftieth anniversary of Darwin's publication of *On the Origin of Species,* Timiriazev published a series of articles in which he promoted Darwinism and defended it publicly against the attacks of more conservative natural scientists. A series of lectures by Timiriazev entitled "The Historical Method in Biology" were published. In these essays Timiriazev attempted to identify problems of morphology and physiology and suggested ways to solve them through the study of the historical process of the origin of form and function. Timiriazev continued to publicize evolutionary thought in postrevolutionary Russia.

The spread of evolutionary theory continued to be important to many scientists and educators in post-1917 Russia. In the Soviet era, scientists were especially interested in placing evolutionary theory in all secondary-school curricula as the basis for understanding animal and human development. Both liberal educators and Marxists alike during the twenties believed in the power of evolutionary theory as a progressive scientific force against religious explanations of creation. The Soviet state, particularly Narkompros's Glavnauka, supported this agenda and funded scientific organizations that promoted evolutionary thought and antireligion.

B. E. Raikov was one prominent science pedagogue and member of the Petrograd prerevolutionary intelligentsia involved in the popularization of evolutionary thought. Raikov worked on a four-volume series that analyzed biological-evolutionary theory in the pre-Darwinian era. According to Raikov, the growth of transformist ideas in Russia before Darwin had support from a diverse group of intellectuals in a variety of natural sciences.[20] Raikov was responsible for writing popular articles on the development of Lamarckian and Darwinian thought in Russia. He published several treatises critical of creationist theories.[21]

In 1907, ten years before the revolution, Raikov was one of the key founders of the Russian Society for the Spread of Natural-Historical Education. Raikov's organization survived the tumultuous Russian Revolution of 1917, as well as the Civil War, and continued to operate during the NEP era.

After 1917 Raikov and his society played an important role in the movement to insert evolutionary theory into secondary-school curricula.[22] Narkompros vigorously supported Raikov's organization and promoted the popularization of evolutionary ideas. Glavnauka had at times even saved Raikov's organization from the clutches of the NKVD, viewing it as a critical venue of public science education. The NKVD had hoped to subsume Raikov's organization under the rubric of newer Soviet scientific umbrella groups.

In post-1917 Russia, Raikov's Russian Society for the Spread of Natural-Historical Education continued to train natural-science teachers and to popularize knowledge of evolutionary theory. Raikov gave the opening address at the 1918 general meeting of the society in the post-October era. The meeting was held in Petrograd on December 20, 1918, and Raikov delivered a speech entitled "Evolutionary Theory and School Teaching: A Means to Struggle with Problems in Teaching the Biological Method." Raikov's message to teachers was a plea to introduce evolutionary theory into the secondary schools. He particularly stressed the importance of using logical examples to explain evolutionary theories to make them more naturally comprehensible to students.[23]

At a meeting of the society on January 24, 1919, Iu. P. Frolov, a research associate in the laboratory of I. P. Pavlov, delivered another argument in favor of teaching evolutionary theory in secondary schools. In his report Frolov argued that "the teaching of the natural sciences in the secondary schools should include an explication of how animal species undergo change over time: we must spread the idea of evolution." Frolov believed that evolutionary theory could also help explain to students the various structural and functional differences of organs in higher and lower animal species. He argued that teaching the basis of evolutionary thought was absolutely crucial to any diverse scientific curriculum and that the teaching of evolutionary theory would help break religion's hold over many students.[24]

Raikov's society was integrally involved in the adult-education movement, and here, too, the program fit well into Glavnauka's agenda to popularize evolutionary theory in an extracurricular arena. On December 20, 1918, Narkompros helped open the Institute for Adult Education in Petrograd. Members of the Russian Natural-History Society played a critical role in the lecture activities of the institute, and Narkompros allocated three million rubles in 1919 for the institute's budget. Raikov was mostly involved in the Scientific Excursion Department of the Adult-Education Section of Narkompros and, along with others in the society, believed that organized scientific excursions were the best way for adults to learn about the natural sciences. They set up excursion programs with the Petrograd Zoological and Geological Museum, and the Petrograd Botanical Gardens. These excursions placed much emphasis on demystifying occurrences in nature and on searching for natural and scientific explanations for evolutionary phenomena.[25] Raikov successfully lobbied Narkompros officials to fund all of these adult-education programs.

The society continued its educational activities in the 1920s. In 1922 Raikov traveled to various parts of Russia lecturing on evolution and the teaching of natural history in the schools. He stopped at various educational conferences attended by teachers, and his speeches and the proceedings of these meetings were generally covered in the popular press and major educational journals, like *Na putakh k novoi shkole* (on the path towards a new school), the organ of the scientific-pedagogical section of the State Academic Council of Narkompros. In March of 1922 Raikov attended the Moscow Conference of the Teachers of the Natural Sciences, where he gave the keynote address on the importance of using the biological method in the teaching of evolution. According to Raikov, teachers needed to use more concrete examples in the classroom and had to concentrate on the study of morphology when analyzing how animals change their structural composition over time. He believed this would make evolutionary concepts sound more plausible to skeptics.[26]

In 1923 Raikov and other members of the Russian Society for the Spread of Natural-Historical Education helped organize the first All-Russian Congress on Natural-Historical Education. The congress opened at Petrograd University on August 10, 1923, and close to fifteen hundred delegates from provinces all across Russia attended. This was the largest congregation of Russian naturalists and pedagogues ever assembled to discuss the spread of natural-scientific and evolutionary curricula in schools and in adult-education courses.[27]

Teaching methodology was once again stressed at this conference. The delegates believed that a course on natural science must include evolutionary theory as the basis for understanding organic change. They also unanimously stressed the need to use excursions and laboratory experiments in natural-scientific courses. At the congress, established scholars read a series of scientific reports explaining which popular-scientific texts were the best in various new fields, especially evolutionary theory.[28]

In the post-October period, Marxist popularizers, like B. M. Zavadovskii, were also eager to spread evolutionary theory and the ideas of Darwin. Zavadovskii was a key scientific propagandist in the Militant League of the Godless, and also wrote articles for the newspaper *Bezbozhnik* (the godless). Zavadovskii was a professor at the Sverdlov Communist University in Moscow between 1920 and 1930 and founder and director of the Timiriazev Biological Museum. During the twenties, the Timiriazev Scientific Research Institute became a haven for many Marxist science propagandists.[29]

For Marxists, Darwin's biological theories helped form a new social morality based on a materialist perspective. With Darwin's publication of *On the Origin of Species* in 1859, a radical change occurred in biological thought that complemented the transformations in sociology developed by Marx. However, some of the radical intellectuals of the late nineteenth century, like Peter Kropotkin, were highly critical of Darwin's theory of natural selection. They believed the Malthusian components of Darwin's theory were antithetical to any type of social theory based on altruistic notions. Kropotkin posited a theory of mutual aid in opposition to Darwin's struggle for existence. Leading Russian sociologists of the nineteenth century, such as M. M. Kovalevskii and N. K. Mikhailovskii, also expressed an extreme opposition to any type of social Darwinism. Many radical intellectuals believed that cooperation rather than competition was a better mechanism for transformation.[30]

Yet Marxists of the early twentieth century believed Darwin's theories of evolution underscored the causal, material factors of organic development. In popular pamphlets Marxists like Zavadovskii pointed out the parallels between Darwin's explanation of the biological process and Marx's scientific explanation of the social process. As Darwin found an explanation for the origin of organic forms in the material conditions of their development, so Marx opposed metaphysical explanations with his developmental theory of dialectical materialism.[31]

Various Communist educational journals of the 1920s carried articles on the importance of teaching evolutionary theory in order to combat religious superstition. Many articles were carried in the journal of the Central Bureau of Proletarian Students, entitled *Krasnoe studenchestvo* (red students). Marxist pedagogues argued in the pages of this journal that antireligious activists must be armed with better propaganda and that science and philosophy teachers must be at the forefront of providing activists with educational material. Marxists were especially concerned with arming antireligious propagandists with pamphlets on evolution and Darwinism.[32]

Within the pages of those educational journals, activists discussed various problems they incurred while spreading evolutionary doctrine in the universities. Marxist pedagogues complained about the lack of student antireligious cells in Soviet schools. A. Lukacheskii, a member of the Central Committee of the Militant League of the Godless, argued that many students in Soviet Russia looked down on antireligious activity, being more concerned with their potential careers, especially those who were taking courses in the sciences.[33] Others supporting Lukacheskii's viewpoint complained that "bourgeois" professors in the social sciences and humanities continued to spread idealistic philosophies among students in the higher schools, hampering students' ability to absorb evolutionary theory. N. Chelianov argued that many philosophy professors took a Kantian approach to explaining the history of ideas. Chelianov believed that supporting a theory of a priori knowledge was a potential threat to evolutionary theories and scientific materialist philosophy in general.[34]

Even the Komsomol journal *Molodaia gvardiia* continually carried articles on evolution and Darwinism. On occasion the journal provided bibliographic programs for the teaching of evolution in the schools and for readers to work through at home. The journal stressed programs of home study constructed by Zavadovskii, which covered various aspects of evolutionary thought. In his home-study courses, Zavadovskii included works by Timiriazev on Darwin, books on the development of the organic world, and the origins of humans from simian ancestors.[35]

Although Marxist educators placed Darwinism on the forefront of evolutionary theory, they were interested first and foremost in how various developmental biological theories could substantiate scientific materialist philosophy. Articles in general stressed how the natural sciences could buttress the theories of Marx regarding social change over time. On occasion Marxists argued that although Darwin had provided a sound theory for change in the organic world, other biological theorists, like Lamarck, could be enlisted to combat creationism. In a 1923 article in *Molodaia gvardiia,* Professor A. N. Bartenev argued that both Lamarck and Darwin had provided Marxists with the biological method of teaching people that the history of organic development must have a materialist foundation and that spiritual explanations of creation are ridiculous.[36] In essence, Lamarckian (witness Raikov's Lamarckianism) and Darwinian evolutionary conceptions coincided in the Soviet 1920s.

The Darwinian and Marxist conception of developmental change, therefore, did not always overlap. On the one hand, Darwin's conception of the mechanics of evolution focused on a gradual process of change over time. That concept had been partly borrowed from Newton's conception of change in mechanics as a continuous process. On the other hand, the Marxist or Hegelian theory assumed a discontinuous mechanism of change based on the concept of the dialectic.[37] Darwin's theories also did not contain any teleological component, only a mechanism for change and a description of how new organisms developed. He did not posit any doctrine of certain ends imminent in nature.

All the same, of all scientific concepts, evolutionary theory was able to unify all liberal and radical thinkers in Russia, especially in the 1920s. Even those as diverse politically and intellectually as Raikov and Zavadovskii could find consensus on the need to spread evolutionary theory, because the materialistic basis of evolutionary theories provided a critique of all transcendental causation and religious creationism. In this sense, for Russian thinkers, evolution was one of the most striking manifestations of natural-scientific materialist thought. For this reason, Russian conservative thinkers of the nineteenth century, such as Pobedonostsev and Pogodin, had worried over the popularization of Darwinian thought in Russia, seeing that it emphasized positivism, rationalism, and scientific materialism over dependence on religious faith. In contrast, both liberals and radicals believed Darwinism was a great triumph for scientific and secular thought. Marxists in the 1920s, like Zavadovskii, could support Raikov's movement to inject evolutionary teaching into the schools and, more importantly, into the public debate. At this intersection Marxists and liberals alike could temporarily converge on the battlefield in their quest to make evolutionary theory the crux of antireligious activity. However, this alliance would not last, as Stalin's revolution from above provided an arena for young radicals to criticize the moderate prerevolutionary scientific elite, the generation of Raikov, Lunkevich, and Rubakin.

SCIENTIFIC-ENLIGHTENMENT, ANTIRELIGIOUS PROPAGANDA, AND THE *BEZBOZHNIKI*

In the prerevolutionary period, two of the big components in the Social Democratic worker-education programs were antireligion and Darwinism. Intellectuals who led workers' circles *(rabochie kruzhki)* emphasized the importance of topics they themselves first became interested in: the "origin of the universe" and "the origin of species."[38] After the October Revolution the popularization of natural-scientific knowledge was an important means by which the young Soviet regime believed it could struggle with religious ideas and superstition. In the course of the 1920s, the Communist Party's antireligious campaign moved away from crude attacks on religion toward scientific enlightenment. The Communist Party and the Militant League of the Godless (whose members were called *bezbozhniki)*[39] came to support the spread of scientific information as one of the major elements in their antireligious programs. Science popularizers, like Zavadovskii, were active in the Militant League of the Godless, and vigorously supported a campaign to spread science among the Russian populace. These science specialists' role in antireligious campaigns has generally been overlooked. The party's failures in the arena of antireligious propaganda made it more dependent on science popularizers and more willing to take a secondary role in the process as it became more concerned with the outcome.

In the post-October and Civil War period, a coordinated propaganda program against religion was not succinctly outlined by the Bolshevik state. Instead, much of the struggle was concentrated on exposing the reactionary role of the church and implementing the January 1918 government decree on the separation of church from state, and school from church.[40] A commission, headed by Emelian Iaroslavskii and attached to the Central Committee, coordinated the execution of this decree during the Civil War.[41] The actual task of initiating an antireligious campaign in 1918 was originally in the hands of the Commissariat of Justice, which organized scientific lectures and debates and arranged for the preparation of posters and leaflets. It also published one of the early journals entitled *Revoliutsiia i tserkov'* (the revolution and the church), which contained propaganda articles by key Bolshevik luminaries, like A. Lunacharskii. The Red Army and the Commissariat of Enlightenment also took part in antireligious propaganda in the aftermath of the Bolshevik Revolution.[42]

The first official party position on antireligious propaganda was articulated in the program of the Eighth Party Congress in March 1919: "The party aims at the complete destruction of the link between the exploiting classes and the organization of religious propaganda, while assisting the actual liberation of the working masses from religious prejudices and organizing the widest possible *scientific-educational* antireligious propaganda."[43] It was not until after the Civil War that antireligious campaigns became more organized and systematic. By 1922 a few short-lived popular-scientific and antireligious journals appeared in Moscow and Petrograd, including *Nauka i religiia* (science and religiia), edited by Mikhail Gorev. This was the first Soviet-era publication to highlight the role of science in the antireligious campaign. Gorev prefaced the first issue in 1922 with a statement of purpose declaring that the journal would attempt to unite all social groups that decisively broke with the old world and grasped the importance of scientific progress. This first issue of *Nauka i religiia* in 1922 featured articles criticizing the Russian Orthodox Church for not offering its valuable collections of gold and silver to aid the starving peasantry during the famine. Gorev stressed that a significant reason for the famine was the peasants' reluctance to accept more scientific approaches to agriculture. Finally, he asked his readers: "Isn't it better, having been cast under the spell of the old religious order, to come forth and trust science?"[44]

At the end of 1922 the weekly newspaper *Bezbozhnik* appeared in Moscow replacing *Nauka i religiia*. Its editor was E. Iaroslavskii, and it played a crucial role in antireligious propaganda. One of Iaroslavskii's key editorial pronouncements emphasized the importance of a more long-term, scientific-enlightenment campaign to stamp out religion in Russia. In January of 1923

Bezbozhnik u stanka (the godless at the workbench), an antireligious journal edited by M. M. Kostelovskaia (a Moscow antireligious activist), started up in Moscow. It emphasized exposure of the class role of religion and criticized the scientific-educational approach for not having benefited from proper class analysis. According to Kostelovskaia science popularization was a "bourgeois" educational program and obstructed activists from showing how religious beliefs were constructed by elite social groups.[45]

That debate between rival journals highlighted an important issue: Should scientific enlightenment be brought into the antireligious campaign at all? Kostelovskaia argued that bringing science into the picture was dangerous because that would only help refine religious belief, enabling it to adapt to and accommodate scientific discoveries.[46] However, in Iaroslavskii's view, religion could only be eliminated by propaganda based on the achievements of science. Eventually, the party backed Iaroslavskii's position, stressing that activists should be found to promote antireligious and scientific-enlightenment work simultaneously.[47]

By 1923 a shift had occurred in the emphasis of the party's antireligious propaganda campaign, which moved away from crude attacks on religion and toward scientific-educational propaganda. The Communist Party began to criticize coarse antireligious methods, like the mockery of Christmas festivities conducted by the Komsomol in December of 1922. During the early twenties rural Komsomol groups sometimes staged such sarcastic antireligious festivals and carnivals, crudely mocking the Russian Orthodox Church and peasant religiosity, and angering many peasants who feared the Komsomol's aggressive intervention in the countryside.[48] According to party leaders like Iaroslavskii, these sardonic methods would only alienate true believers and ultimately lead to the failure of the antireligious movement. Supplanting these tactics with scientific educational methods, from Iaroslavskii's perspective, would be far more effective.

In 1923 the party's Central Committee issued a statement in support of moderating antireligious activity, while placing emphasis instead on scientific enlightenment: "Take all steps to avoid giving offense to religious feelings, shifting the weight of the work to a *scientific* explanation of the origin of religious holidays, especially of Easter."[49] At the Twelfth Party Congress of 1923, the party in a special resolution saw the need to emphasize that the antireligious campaign could be successful only by depending on science education to help stamp out both illiteracy and religious fervor: "But the party must not forget that all our antireligious agitation and propaganda will fail to affect the masses until long-term educational programs stressing natural-scientific knowledge are fully organized in the urban and rural areas."[50]

The head of the Central Committee's Agit-Prop Branch, Ia. Iakovlev, expressed this view in an earlier February 1922 circular to party organizations. Referring to the "General Directive on Antireligious Propaganda, Decree of the Tenth party Congress of the Central Committee," Iakovlev noted that antireligious propagandists must use scientific knowledge as their key tool, and that activists must be prepared to conduct a wide scientific-enlightenment campaign.[51] He urged that antireligious propagandists must concentrate on a science program that included the following two themes: the origins of the Earth and the solar system, and also the origins and development of organic life and humans. According to Iakovlev, antireligious propagandists must also be trained in circles and courses centering around the following two themes: natural sciences, including a short course on the study of the evolution of the organic and inorganic world, and the history of scientific materialism.[52]

At a September 1923 Agit-Prop meeting of the committee of antireligious propaganda, Iaroslavskii suggested that the program of antireligious propaganda should contain popular lectures on physics and other natural scientific disciplines.[53] The committee believed "antireligious propaganda should primarily spread elementary natural-scientific and agronomic knowledge in order to combat technical backwardness."[54] The Komsomol was now instructed to get involved in spreading scientific information in the countryside. After 1923 the youth organization pursued this task through science reading circles, where activists encouraged peasants to utilize scientific agricultural techniques with the help of agronomists. Komsomol activists mounted a lecture series on scientific topics, organized atheist reading circles, and created antireligious evenings featuring its natural-science circles.[55] These developments made the party and the Komsomol more dependent on science educators who could write cogent technical pamphlets on various topics that included basic evolutionary theories.

The Komsomol's scientific-education program included a series of lectures devoted to themes such as the evolution of the Earth and the origin of species. Komsomol lecturers were instructed to emphasize the inherent contradictions between scientific theories and religious teachings found in the Bible. Even this less-combative, long-term, scientific-educational approach often alienated peasants,[56] and some peasant communities reacted forcefully against Komsomol science lectures. Peasants maintained strong spiritual values and regularly practiced religious rites, sometimes reflecting eclectic beliefs. The Russian rural religious universe embraced different "subsystems"— Old Believer, Russian Orthodox, pagan, magical, miracle.[57] These religious subsystems survived despite the Communist Party and the Komsomol's concerted effort to wipe out religion with science.[58]

A study of popular values in Tver' province in the 1920s illustrates how

Christian and pagan customs merged in popular religiosity in the villages. The Bolshevik attack on religion in the Tver' newspaper, which often criticized Christian dogma, overlooked the central importance of popular faith. Certain peasant religious rites and customs were based on deeply embedded beliefs. Bolshevik attempts to combat religious values with scientific explanations of natural occurrences did not succeed in the Russian villages.[59]

Ethnographic reports of anthropologists like V. G. Bogoraz-Tan testify to the fact that folk religion was positively flourishing in Russia in the 1920s.[60] Alongside the tenacity of popular religion, historians have also noted a rise of Christian sectarian influence in the provinces and countryside during the twenties. A. Angarov estimated that the membership of Christian sects had increased almost four fold during the period 1917–27.[61] Within the general framework of peasant conservatism toward scientific and political propaganda, the climate in the village for reception of new religious ideas was quite favorable during the NEP.[62]

In areas like Iaroslavl' on the Northern Volga, Agit-Prop antireligious activists delivered lectures on utilitarian scientific themes along with general scientific material: for instance, "Evolution of the Organic World" and "The Origins of Plant Life on the Earth." The local Agit-Otdel (Agitational Department) of the Gubkom (Regional Party Committee) found that more practical science lectures, such as those on medical topics, were more popular with local people. A series of lectures, organized by the Iaroslavl' Agit-Prop Department, on the effects of cholera were well attended. People on the Northern Volga were worried about the spread of the epidemic in the 1920s. Lectures on disease that affected humans and animals, or practical topics on how to purify water, consistently attracted participants to Agit-Prop events.[63]

However, Agit-Prop officials consistently confronted more problems than success. The minutes of a July 1923 meeting of the Central Committee's Commission on Propaganda are quite revealing of the problems the party encountered with antireligious propaganda throughout Soviet Russia. Agit-Prop official Shainevich argued that in the Ukraine and in the Western Russian oblasti, antireligious propaganda was successful only among small segments of the population. In most cases activists alienated the majority of peasants with science lectures. Krasinov noted that the Communist Party's journals were weak and did not contain sufficient material concerning questions of scientific-enlightenment. Galkin spoke the longest at the meeting, and his speech is especially revealing: "The antireligious campaign is hardly being conducted at all in the localities; and where it is being conducted in the countryside, such as in Cherepovets, activists are using old, outdated texts. In Novgorod, for example, antireligious, propaganda material looks like the old, thick journals of the nineteenth century. In general the situation of antireligious propaganda in the provinces is very bad. We have no effective means to struggle against priests in the localities. It is necessary for the party to provide the provincial party committees with contemporary scientific literature."[64]

The reports that Agit-Prop's political and propaganda instructors in the provinces periodically sent to central authorities confirm these problems. In August of 1926 A. Saikin, a political instructor working in Smolensk province, noted that during agitational events and popular lectures, peasants and workers in Smolensk fervently and quite frequently castigated Communist activists with a variety of complaints regarding scientific propaganda.[65]

Large turnouts at Agit-Prop events did not necessarily reflect peasants' interest in natural-scientific propaganda lectures. On the contrary, in many instances peasants actually came to popular lectures to air their grievances with the party and to argue forcefully that science could not replace their religious rituals. In an October 1923 report on antireligious propaganda in various central provinces, activists acknowledged that in Riazan', Smolensk, and other areas intense interest centered on religious questions at popular lectures. In Riazan' public debates with peasants dragged on for hours, and peasants hurled hundreds of questions and criticisms at the propagandists. The report noted that in Kostroma province lengthy disputes arose between activists and participants at over thirty scientific and antireligious lectures.[66] Paradoxically, to the party's dismay, Agit-Prop science lectures became spheres for public protest, arenas for popular debate, platforms for the expression of religious fervor in a time when the state was openly squelching political disputation.

Activists complained about perpetual arguments between lecturers and priests who came to Agit-Prop's science lectures to complain in public about how they had been harassed and beaten by communist agitators. Priests generally opposed scientific explanations of the origin of the universe and man and tried to combat such arguments with expressions of creationist belief. At Agit-Prop lectures, particularly, priests fervently rebutted scientific criticism of church doctrine.[67]

In the 1920s local Agit-Prop departments began to evaluate their scientific propaganda, and the results were disconcerting to central officials. In 1927 and 1928, in Iaroslavl' province, the Agit-Prop branch of the local party organization evaluated its activity over the preceding few years. It found that Agit-Prop pamphlets on scientific themes were never sold in the markets or book kiosks. Night courses and lectures never attracted more than twenty individuals at a time, and most of those who came were already party members. Antireligious activists consistently tried to set up scientific lectures on various religious holidays, especially Easter, but found few participants. One of the lectures read on a regular basis by local activists was entitled "Is It Scientifically and Naturally Possible for a Dead Person (Namely Jesus) to Rise from the Dead?" This particular lecture, naturally, infuriated local clergy.[68]

At a July 1927 meeting of the Iaroslavl' Agit-Prop Collegium, several activists were dismayed by the problems they encountered with regard to scientific propaganda. Comrade Muratov argued that "for some time, I have been conducting lectures amongst seasonal workers in factories on antireligious themes. The general sentiment of most workers, however, is both negative and ubiquitous: 'anti-religious propaganda develops hooliganism.'" He optimistically (or naively) believed that "the masses still demand the demystifying of religion," but he candidly admitted that this would not be easily accomplished. He noted the very low numbers and quality of natural-science teachers in rural schools as a major problem in getting the public to trust scientific explanations. Comrade Kashnikov added that "our biggest obstacles in antireligious work seem to be our inattentiveness to using the widest scientific apparatuses in our struggle. All the time we are nudging forward, but we need to take more definitive action."[69]

The meeting in Iaroslavl' concluded with sharp and critical remarks by an Agit-Prop official named Egorov, who was in charge of the local antireligious sector. He argued that the party had been developing many cells of antireligious workers, yet they needed more *toloch'* or *tolky* (more punch). He suggested that perhaps antireligious workers could learn from voluntary scientific associations, such as the OSO-Aviakhim (Society of the Friends of Defense and Aviation-Chemical Construction),[70] and how they conducted their popular lectures. Antireligious activists wanted to emulate the activities of natural-science specialists, and co-opt them to join their struggle. They found it disconcerting that naturalists' lectures and science museums were popular in provincial areas, while Agit-Prop science lectures were viewed with disdain.[71]

Between July and October 1927, the Iaroslavl' Agit-Prop Otdel (section) in charge of antireligious and scientific propaganda began to meet after every lecture in the province to "evaluate" various problems. One basic problem was the alienation people felt in response to harsh ideological material. They continuously agreed that less dogmatic, more practical scientific lectures would be more palpable to the local public. The lack of well-trained leaders in the natural sciences working for the party was yet another problem addressed.[72]

Agit-Prop activists focused on the prospect that their "weak activism" could be resuscitated by uniting more with nonparty activists, such as members of the Militant League of the Godless and science educators. Comrade Kamenskii, an antireligious activist, argued that "we still know very little about antireligious propaganda. . . . We need to take account of the antireligious work of nonparty activists, like the League of the Godless, as well as scientific societies."[73] In closing, Comrade Egorov proposed that Agit-Prop officials coordinate their work in the locales with existing antireligious and scientific voluntary societies.[74]

At the national level, Iaroslavskii arrived at similar conclusions. In 1924, in coordination with his anti-religious newspaper, Iaroslavskii helped form the *Obshchestvo druzei gazety Bezbozhnik* (society of friends of the newspaper *Bezbozhnik*), the most important voluntary association of opponents of religion. The society was one of the key voluntary groups involved in spreading both scientific and antireligious propaganda in urban and rural Russia during the twenties. In June 1925 the organization became the League of the Godless[75] and in 1929, the Militant League of the Godless.[76]

Meeting for the first time in April of 1925 at Smolensk, the first All-Union Congress of Atheists heard a report stating that atheists must work in full contact with party and Komsomol organizations. Many delegates reiterated Iaroslavskii's position that voluntary atheist groups should work in close contact with party activists. Although only 18 percent of the delegates to that congress were party members, 34 percent were Komsomol members.[77]

At that first All-Union Congress of Atheists, T. Gagarin emphasized in his report the need to imbue antireligious propaganda with a natural-scientific, materialistic perspective. Like the party, the *Bezbozhniki* believed in creating a scientific-enlightenment program that would be the focus of a less combative antireligious campaign. Gagarin recommended that certain themes relating to the spread of science be included in all discussions in peasant antireligious circles: (1) a scientific, rational explanation of the development of life on the Earth and the origin of man; (2) science and technology in the service of mankind; (3) a belief in science and agronomy; and (4) a belief in science as key in the struggle against sickness.[78]

T. Varbanchika's report on disease stressed the need to instill in peasants the idea that science can be successful in combating sickness. Science could therefore offer some utilitarian benefits to agricultural communities. Her approach was to show delegates at the congress the need to explain to peasants that science had discovered the nature of, prevention of, and cure for many diseases, that the infection of malaria, for instance, is transmitted to humans by the bite of a particular mosquito living in stagnant waters.[79] The head of the Smolensk provincial education department, a teacher named Lebedeva, gave a report on antireligious work in the schools and in adult education courses. She believed that a special effort was needed to spread natural-scientific themes in the school curricula.[80] She emphasized that without basic science education the antireligious propaganda would "fall on deaf ears."

Various resolutions adopted at the January 1926 All-Union Congress of Atheists in Smolensk highlighted the need to popularize science as part of a broader educational antireligious campaign. Atheists requested, through Communist Party officials, the use of several rooms in the ethnographic and archaeological museum to create a standing antireligious exhibition. The exhibit would concentrate on combating superstition with scientific knowledge and included the following themes: (1) the struggle between science and faith in history, (2) scientific explanations of the origin of the Earth, (3) the use of the barometer and the lightning conductor in the scientific struggle with religious superstition, (4) the development of life on the planet: evolution of humans and animals, (5) science and agriculture, (6) the development of understanding of how microbes carry disease, and (7) the importance of chemistry and physics, especially regarding such practical matters as the phenomenon of boiling and the need to sterilize liquids and surfaces.[81]

During the twenties, cells of the League of the Godless had spread throughout Soviet Russia. On the Northern Volga, to the Northeast of Moscow, as in Smolensk in western Russia, atheists developed elaborate programs to spread science and antireligious doctrine. By the end of the decade in the Iaroslavl' region, they claimed they had over eleven thousand members, with seventy-five hundred in the cities of Iaroslavl' province alone. They particularly took pride in their collaborative work with party Agit-Prop activists.[82] The League of the Godless in Iaroslavl' helped organize detailed lecture series in such scientific areas as the evolution of inorganic and organic matter. On Orthodox holidays in particular, they attacked creationism with lectures describing the development of the universe and the evolution of animal and plant life-forms.[83]

Leaders of the atheists kept close contact with local gubkoms in provincial areas such as Iaroslavl'.[84] Furthermore, the Communist Party Agit-Otdel monitored antireligious activity in various provinces. In Iaroslavl' it noted that atheist-training seminars in October of 1927 contained many workshops on natural-scientific thought, and voluntary activists were in contact with Communist science popularizers. Party activists were concerned by the low number of those actually finishing the courses, as well as by the lower number of those who could eventually be used as leaders of antireligious cells (the ultimate goal). All the same, the atheists' natural-science programs gained praise from local party Agit-Prop leaders.[85]

One of the secretaries of the *Bezbozhniki* in Iaroslavl', identified only as Shalygin, persistently urged Communist Party Agit-Prop officials to use their resources to build exhibits, museums, and workshops to spread natural-scientific thought in the area. The atheists lobbied the local Gubkom to send them funds to support scientific lecture series, the building of herbariums and aquariums in local museums, and workshops to train activists. Most importantly, Shalygin emphasized that antireligious activists needed to coordinate their activities with local natural and physical scientists and to persuade geologists, naturalists, evolutionary biologists, and other scientists to give time voluntarily to their antireligious organizations. Shalygin believed it was both practical and economical to reach out to sympathetic scientists: "With the goal of economizing, it is only practical that at these exhibits one should use specialists from local universities and organizations in the sciences."[86]

The League of the Godless successfully attracted radical science specialists to their meetings but did not draw in the majority of less-politicized scientists in provincial areas. At these meetings Marxist science popularizers such as Zavadovskii (a professor of biology at the Sverdlov University) and I. D. Strashun emphasized that popularization of the natural sciences was the best method for wiping out superstition among the populace. At the All-Union Congress of Atheists in April 1925, Strashun delivered a lecture on how activists must be able to teach people how sickness in humans, animals, and plants derives from biological causes and not from any spiritual deprivation. He believed that popular-science lecturers, especially in the countryside, had to teach peasants about infectious diseases and how they are spread by microbial bacteria and viruses invisible to the human eye. Strashun also urged the connection between disease and social-living conditions, that tuberculosis, for instance, is a disease of the urban proletariat. Strashun also emphasized the importance of teaching practical scientific principles to rural Russians.[87]

At the same congress Zavadovskii delivered a speech entitled "The Natural Sciences and Religion." Zavadovskii was critical of Western scientists who still believed that the soul was the main motivator of human will. For example, Alfred Wallace, one of Darwin's better known associates, was ready to accept the idea that man evolved from simian ancestors but still believed that the soul came from God. Even more dumbfounding to Zavadovskii were popular-scientific articles in contemporary Western journals by scientists who saw no diametrical opposition between science and religious doctrines.[88]

As Marxists, Zavadovskii and Strashun agreed that science popularization must be imbued with the notion of class conflict and must stress dialectical, materialist theory. Zavadovskii would lead a virulent attack on the older generation of science popularizers both before and during Stalin's revolution from above. However, he and his colleagues still supported E. Iaroslavskii's view that the "scientific-educational approach" to antireligious propaganda was appropriate in the effort to wipe out superstition in the 1920s.

These Marxists also concurred with those in the League of the Godless who supported this approach to propaganda. As evidenced at their congresses, they actively pursued a program of science education as their main tool in the mid-1920s. Agit-Prop and voluntary atheists, however, found the Russian public in provincial areas unreceptive to propaganda lectures, regardless of the tactical approach. On the contrary, citizens instead frequented science lectures and museums that were not associated with the Communist Party or radical atheists and preferred to interact with scientists who could teach them practical methods. Even those radical atheists who chose to tone down political rhetoric, focusing on science education, still found they were competing to some extent with less politicized scientists and popularizers of the older generation. The Russian public, particularly those in provincial towns where most of the successful science popularization occurred, chose to attend popular lectures on astronomy, air flight, and exploration because they offered more imaginative approaches to understanding the world around them.

While the party's and the *Bezbozhniki*'s lectures seemed tainted with political overtones, local naturalists and scientists offered the public a means to understand their immediate surroundings with no doctrinal strings attached. This further infuriated Marxist science popularizers and antireligious activists alike. Though Zavadovksii's support of Iaroslavskii's gradualist antireligious campaign was in keeping with the limited tolerance of the NEP overall, that support did not signify a rapprochement between radicals and the older scientific intelligentsia. Indeed, the limited freedom the prerevolutionary educators enjoyed in the mid-1920s would soon become even more tenuous as activists stepped up their criticisms. That intensification of criticism became especially true after 1928, when the state from above and radicals from below placed prerevolutionary scientists in the grip of a politico-doctrinal vise.

Part III

PUBLIC SCIENCE ON THE DEFENSIVE

Stalinist Visions, Cultural Revolution,
and the Technological Future, 1928–34

Chapter 7

TECHNOLOGY SOLVES EVERYTHING

Science Popularization and the Stalinist Great Break, 1928–32

Changes in 1928, with Stalin's revolution from above, created a serious situation for Soviet science. During the Stalinist cultural revolution, liberal scientists and societies came under harsh attack by leftist professors and organizations. However, some of those radical forces had already established themselves in various Marxist institutes prior to 1928 and had attempted unsuccessfully to instigate both generational and ideological conflict. Many of the key Marxist science popularizers in that effort, like Zavadovskii, worked at the Timiriazev Institute in Moscow during the mid-1920s. During the post-1928 era, Marxists successfully put established science educators on the defensive, as the Stalinist cultural revolution created a tragic situation for Soviet science in general.

RADICAL CRITICS AND SCIENCE POPULARIZATION ON THE EVE OF THE GREAT BREAK

Though generally underemphasized in the historical literature, Moscow's Timiriazev Institute was the focal point for the radical assault on the older generation of science educators. The director of the institute was Academic S. G. Navashin, and the assistant director was A. K. Timiriazev (physicist, Marxist polemicist, and son of the famous K. A. Timiriazev who had died in 1920). Approximately one hundred associates at the institute received generous state salary subsidies and support per year.[1] This institute and its staff, along with other voluntary Communist associations, were influential in spearheading the assault on public science both before and during the cultural revolution.

The main goal of the institute was, ultimately, the propagation of the mechanistic view of dialectical materialism. The institute's experts consulted the Communist Party with regard to popularizing the latest developments in scientific research.[2] The institute helped the Moscow Raikom (district party committee) by conducting scientific lectures for party activists. Besides giving periodic lectures for party associations, members of the institute also conducted systematic scientific courses for party activists.[3]

Between 1924 and 1925 the institute continued its work of political and scientific enlightenment among party activists. Members of the institute published articles in popular-scientific journals and also some Communist newspapers. The newspaper *Komsomolskaia pravda* had a section entitled "Science and Technology." Science popularizers from the institute would regularly publish articles in the paper on popular natural-scientific themes such as Darwinism.[4] The institute's cooperation with the Communist Party offered it ideological sanctioning and political patronage during tumultuous times—the eve of Stalin's revolution from above in the late 1920s, for instance.

The institute's popularization branch included several Marxist science popularizers. They not only wrote popular-scientific works but also developed a methodology for Marxist science popularization. One of those individuals was the biologist B. M. Zavadovskii, who led the science popularization work of the institute. Another key staff worker, B. G. Andreev, edited and recommended popular-scientific works for publication, and also conducted popular-scientific lectures. Andreev helped edit the natural-scientific section of the periodical *Rabfak na domu* (workers' faculty in the home).[5] He also wrote short entries on chemistry and physics for Communist encyclopedias and anthologies, like the *Malaia sovetskaia entsiklopediia* (short soviet encyclopedia). Andreev participated in a natural-scientific lecture series on the radio, where he read lectures on chemistry and physics. He helped edit and write a number of popular-scientific works and pamphlets, including *Chemistry is a Friend of the Peasants* and *Physics at the Service of Mankind.*[6]

Another popularizer who worked on the institute's staff was M. A. Gremiatskii, the Moscow University professor of biological and natural sciences. Gremiatskii wrote popular-scientific books and pamphlets for many years. His works include books such as *Life: Its Nature and Origins* and also *How Did Man Appear on the Earth?* Gremiatskii read public lectures on popular-scientific themes and offered editorial advice to the institute with regard to popular-scientific publications. He was the editor for the section on the biological sciences in the periodical *Rabfak na domu.*[7] Gremiatskii and other popularizers also helped various publishing houses by reviewing popular-scientific books. These publishers included Gosizdat, Molodaia Gvardiia, and the bibliographic branch of Glavpolitprosvet.[8]

The institute's popularization and propaganda branch published several series of popular-scientific works. The series titles produced by the institute included "On the Path to Materialism (Tools for Self-Education)," and "Library of the Materialist." The print-run of these popular works averaged five thousand copies per title. The publications varied from works on Darwinism, like B. M. Kozo-Polianskii's *Darwinism and the Theory of Natural Selection,* to works on heredity, including M. S. Navashin's *The Repetition of Oneself in Offspring.*[9] Evolutionary themes and the theoretical elements and components of Darwinism were a critical component of the publishing goals of the editorial staff at the institute.

In the NEP period well-known prerevolutionary popularizers, such as N. A. Rubakin, V. V. Lunkevich, B. E. Raikov, and Ia. I. Perel'man, were attacked by Marxist propagandists centered at the institute. Those attacked were all prominent science educators who had worked hard to continue their activities after 1917. Radical popularizers believed that scientific popular works must be imbued with a dialectical, materialist perspective. Rubakin, particularly, came under increased criticism by more dogmatic Soviet science propagandists during the course of the twenties. The first of these attacks was written by a popularizer of unknown identity in a 1920 article in the journal *Kniga i revoliutsiia* (the book and revolution). Under the pseudonym Periskop (periscope), the author argued that the root deficiencies of Rubakin's brochures did not lie in mistakes of information or technical slips but in Rubakin's incurably flawed approach to the task of being a Soviet-era popularizer.[10]

Periskop believed that Rubakin's errors repeated the elementary mistakes of those "naive people who, speaking with children or foreigners, distort the language in the hope that it will be easier to understand." According to Periskop, this crudely constructed "falsification" of "people's language" sounded terrible in a popular-scientific work. (Periskop relied heavily on Soviet-era phraseology, like "people's language," in his attacks without clearly explaining what that loaded terminology meant.) Periskop believed that Rubakin's simplistic works were positively confusing if given to the "more advanced Soviet masses" of the 1920s.[11]

In his own analysis of popular texts, Rubakin criticized Periskop's and other radical Communists' overtly politicized constructions of public culture and the popular reader. He carried out his own analysis of the mass Soviet reader, observing readers' habits and conducting sociological surveys of the reception of popular science texts. He published the results of those studies in a series of articles in 1927. In a retort to Marxist analysts, Rubakin argued that word usage was an important factor in the creation of a popular-scientific text, arguing that at least 60 percent of the scientific terms used in the works of well-known science popularizers (both Russian and foreign), such as Timiriazev, Belshe, and Flammarion, could not be comprehended by the average Russian reader. He charged, therefore, that many of these Soviet-era popularizers, like Periskop, did no significant research into the psychology of the mass science-reading audience. After studying several thousand popular-scientific books that were published in the USSR during the twenties, Rubakin came to the conclusion that they were not giving the readers what they wanted. Again, he found too many words incomprehensible to the basic reader. Most works were written for educated people, not for the broader public.[12]

Professional public educators and scholars of reader receptivity, especially those who survived the upheavals of the 1917 Revolution, therefore began to engage Soviet-era popularizers in fundamental debates on broad issues that had educational and political ramifications for the average Russian. According to Rubakin and other prerevolutionary popularizers, the Soviet reader was changing, and as the reader changed, the content of the text itself could also change. According to this view, content exists only to the extent that it affects the reader; that is, the essence of a book is not in the book itself but in its functional dependence on the reader's receptivity.[13]

Communist popularizers in the Soviet Union during the twenties were unwilling to accept this notion of the reader's capabilities to decipher a popular-scientific text. They saw Rubakin's methodology as giving too much initiative to the individual reader, thus downplaying the authorial role and the content of the text (especially political content). This methodological argument had broad political ramifications beyond the debates of science popularizers. Rubakin and other prerevolutionary educators were actually contesting the Soviet Marxist belief that readers could be led by enlightened, politicized intellectuals or party bureaucrats. Rubakin believed that readers instead should be enticed, if not nurtured, to understand new scientific concepts on their own terms. Furthermore, Rubakin believed that this was a professional endeavor, not a political issue; in other words, the writing of popular educational and scientific tracts had to be conducted by those who had studied the reader and conducted scientific research in a particular discipline. Ultimately, this debate contested the intrusion into educational disciplines by those Marxists who seemed incapable of professionally understanding the educational and psychological problems of the under-developed reader.

Soviet-era popularizers, spearheaded by those in the Timiriazev Institute, continued their assault on Rubakin because he represented the most vocal of the prerevolutionary science popularizers. From his base in the institute, Zavadovskii probably articulated the strongest attack. In a series of articles on the principles of the popularization of the natural sciences (published in 1923), Zavadovskii included criticism of Rubakin's works. Although he admitted that Rubakin was one of the pioneers in this field, Zavadovskii claimed that Rubakin was not well versed in many of the scientific questions he wrote about.[14]

In a later piece entitled "Failures of a Popularizer," Zavadovskii argued that authors such as the biologist Lunkevich[15] and Rubakin, who were popular during the Civil War and the period just following, were of no use to the Soviet reader of the mid-twenties. He argued that Lunkevich remained on the level of the explicator of anecdotal facts and completely missed the viewpoint of the progressive or ideological side of science. He believed that Rubakin's explanations were a vulgarization of scientific facts, and he pointed to scientific mistakes in Rubakin's work. Finally, he believed that there was a perversion of language in Rubakin's popular works that tried to "falsify" the Russian language under the guise of a people's language.[16]

Lunkevich wrote over sixty popular-scientific works during his long, industrious career. His *Osnova zhizni* (basis of life) was a two-volume biological encyclopedia written for the common reader, which included various illustrations. Marxists argued that he had a tendency to use outdated material and an oversimplified language. In reality Lunkevich's work was well researched and aimed at those who had both elementary reading skills and basic scientific knowledge.

Soviet radicals were also critical of foreign authors of the older generation. Their criticisms were anchored in their ideological orientations but also reflected a subtle parochial, nationalistic tendency in their Marxist approach.[17] The works of V. Belshe, the German biologist and talented popularizer, were translated into Russian both before and after the October Revolution. Yet Marxists criticized his books—*Ernst Haeckel,* for instance—for not combining popular-scientific explication with a sociological analysis of the era. According to critics like Zavadovskii, Belshe was completely oblivious to social problems in Germany at the time and how they affected scientific development. Further, his critics charged Belshe with the ultimate sin of attempting to combine a belief in Darwinism with a faith in God. Indeed, in his *Religion of Our Time* Belshe defended Darwinism yet maintained his religious belief in God.

Supporters of Rubakin's generation argued that their popular-scientific works captivated the beginning reader and played an important role in introducing readers to basic scientific concepts. Librarians especially objected to Zavadovskii's criticism of Rubakin's works, asserting that in their popular libraries, Rubakin's works received the greatest demand among readers. These anecdotal responses by librarians were confirmed by sociological studies of the scientific tastes of readers in Soviet libraries. A survey published in the Soviet library journal *Krasnyi bibliotekar'* (red librarian), measuring the use of books in a Moscow lending library that served factory workers, found that between 1923 and 1924 there was a greater demand for Rubakin's popular works on nature and geography than for the work of any other single author, including literary figures such as Tolstoy and Gorky.[18] The survey also found that Rubakin's works were read by old and young, men and women and that Rubakin had a significant influence on new readers, some of whom read his books several times. The survey found that books written by Lunkevich and Perel'man were also popular among workers. The works of more politicized Soviet science popularizers, such as Zavadovskii, were barely mentioned by readers in that particular study.[19]

Zavadovskii argued that it was unfortunate that librarians and readers still valued the books of Rubakin, Lunkevich, and other prerevolutionary popularizers. He believed readers needed to look at works written by K. Timiriazev or E. Elachich,[20] writers who, in Zavadovskii's view, provided the reader with more contemporary, scientific argumentation.[21] Librarians, though, were some of the best judges of readers' tastes, since they interacted with them on a daily basis and advised them on books to read. Thus, Zavadovskii's assertions were directly contradicted by some reader surveys.[22]

The science popularizer M. Gremiatskii[23] was critical of the way Zavadovskii analyzed the works of Rubakin and others of the older generation. Gremiatskii, although a member of the Timiriazev Institute in Moscow, was a lone voice disputing Zavadovskii's claims at that radical institution. Gremiatskii argued that Zavadovskii's critique of Rubakin was one-sided and failed to point out the worthy aspects of Rubakin's popular-scientific works. Furthermore, he argued that Zavadovskii did not take into consideration the wide popularity of Rubakin's books and how the beginning reader was especially drawn to them. Gremiatskii pointed out that Rubakin and Lunkevich were the only popularizers serving the worker and peasant reader. Rubakin's works, according to Gremiatskii, contained interesting facts and good, solid conclusions that were comprehensible to the average reader. Gremiatskii believed criticizing prerevolutionary science popularizers for not understanding the ideological side of science was problematic if the reading public demanded their works. He added, however, that more carefully defined popular-scientific works, by Soviet scientists, would soon eclipse the older prerevolutionary writers. Unlike Zavadovskii, Gremiatskii believed that patience was a virtue and that time would show the positive tendencies of Soviet science popularization.[24]

During the twenties Marxist propagandists started to criticize openly those popularizers who did not infuse their published work with ideology. That campaign met with only limited success. Librarians, educators, and even other propagandists (like Gremiatskii) actually defended the work of the older generation. More importantly, as evidenced through reader surveys, workers were especially attracted to the popular works of Rubakin and Lunkevich and others of their generation. Some of those fundamental readers needed a popular work written in a simplified manner so that they could fully understand the scientific arguments put forth. The Marxist or politicized science activists could not yet displace the older prerevolutionary cohort involved in popular science education who were still professionally grounded and well liked by readers. However, propagandists like Zavadovskii would be critical players in radical organizations—for instance, VARNITSO (All Union Society of the Workers of Science and Technology for the Promotion of Socialist Construction)—which would be more successful after 1928 in crushing the prerevolutionary popularizers. Although the prerevolutionary scientific intelligentsia was temporarily successful under the NEP in fending off criticisms by Marxist popularizers, eventually a host of radical scientists, institutions, and societies, coordinated through the Stalinist cultural revolution, would inaugurate a barrage of successful professional attacks on Rubakin and his ilk. Furthermore, Zavadovskii and others would launch a public attack in the press, with devastating ramifications.

CULTURAL REVOLUTION AND SCIENCE EDUCATORS

The cultural revolution was a tragedy for Soviet science and science educators who had recently survived the upheavals of the first decade of Soviet power. Condemnation and arrests of scientists, which began in 1929, usually encouraged their opponents to declare whole branches of science to be "bourgeois" and "reactionary." Some of the condemned scientists had been the leaders of whole schools of science. In this social context the tragic events of the purges of the Soviet Academy of Sciences and similar upheavals occurred in 1929 and 1930.[25] During this first major purge of the Academy, scientists were criticized for being too concerned with "pure science." Any form of "academic individualism" was also condemned as a bourgeois holdover that needed to be expunged.[26] In 1930 a new charter for the academy was promulgated, stating that all scientific research would be appraised according to its usefulness to practical problems. The charter also stated that the Soviet Academy of Sciences must begin a program of strict centralized planning.[27]

The cultural revolution brought an increase in "specialist-baiting" of the older bourgeois technical intelligentsia.[28] During those years several show trials were held in which several thousand engineers were implicated. Most were accused of systematically sabotaging the Soviet economy in the interests of Western capitalist nations. Many of the specialists had received their education during the tsarist period and had held positions in tsarist ministries and educational institutions.[29] However, none of the trials received as much publicity as the Shakhty trial of 1928. That legal travesty focused on a number of engineers, who were dubbed "saboteurs and wreckers," and marked the beginning of a campaign directed not only against old specialists who may have been hostile to the Soviet regime but also against those who were merely politically neutral or indifferent.[30]

Radical science popularizers had already begun to draw battle lines during the mid-twenties but were unable to muster enough support to purge the older generation of popularizers. Because scientific societies, for example, were able to garner institutional and financial support from Glavnauka or other major Soviet patrons, they could fend off attacks by Marxist radicals prior to 1928. Additionally, those societies had formed complex symbiotic relationships with Soviet cultural and educational institutions, fulfilling, as required, important educational tasks for the state. During the cultural revolution, however, the political-cultural assault played out in the scientific realm would be amplified and spearheaded by new radical associations of technical specialists and scientists, including those members of VARNITSO, some of whom were less-than respected scholars in their fields.

The editorial boards of popular-scientific journals, for instance, were infiltrated and influenced by a variety of Marxists. In 1928 the popular scientific journal *Iskra* became the organ of the all-union voluntary society called TekhMass. The new editorial board consisted of Zavadovskii and V. Sverdlov (president of the All-Union Association of Engineers), who wanted to inculcate a scientific-materialist point of view in their readers. In a 1928 editorial Zavadovskii and Sverdlov wrote that the journal would cover a number of scientific and technological topics that were closely tied to the socialist reconstruction of industry and the economy. They noted that special attention would be paid to the resolutions of the Fifteenth Party Congress, which meant that issues of cultural enlightenment would be united with plans to develop the Soviet national economy.[31] Though Zavadovskii had previous institutional support at the Timiriazev Institute, he would soon form VARNITSO as a radical network to launch his assault against major scientific organizations.

Another example of how Marxists encroached on popular-scientific journals and societies involved the fate of amateur astronomy societies during the cultural revolution. Many prominent astronomers (for example, Nikolai Kozyrev, 1908–83) had started as amateurs, but Vartan T. Ter-Oganesov (1890–1963), who barely graduated with a scientific degree from Petrograd University in 1916, occupied posts after 1917 in Narkompros and was a delegate to the All-Union Central Executive Committee. Ter-Oganesov used his position to advance the amateur societies as promising routes for the *vyd-*

vizhenie (upwardly-mobile worker) movement[32] of young astronomy enthusiasts during the Stalinist cultural revolution. The older generation of professional and amateur astronomers found Ter-Oganesov's politicizing of astronomy repellent.[33] In 1930 Ter-Oganesov became the editor of the popular amateur astronomy journal *Mirovedenie,* which he made into a Marxist organ to criticize astronomers who did not conceptualize science through a political lens.[34]

Marxist science pedagogues during this period also criticized those educators who did not link science education to the practical tasks of the economy. A debate began that pitted Marxists against those accused of propagating only pure scientific material divorced from society's needs. As early as 1927 several distinguished Leningrad science pedagogues, centered around B. E. Raikov at the Leningrad Pedagogical Institute, were accused of holding this narrow bourgeois conception of education. Raikov had enjoyed the financial and institutional patronage of Narkompros earlier in the decade. Glavnauka officials had seen him as a key figure in spreading evolutionary concepts in the schools and supporting adult education in the natural sciences. They had even defended organizations he founded from attacks by the NKVD. Yet at a 1927 presidium of the Scientific-Pedagogical Section of Narkompros, N. K. Krupskaia openly criticized Raikov and the Leningrad contingent: "We have been struggling with the Leningrad natural scientists concerning the material on natural science in the secondary school program: the *Leningradtsy* have completely divorced natural science education from industry. Also, the teaching of evolutionary theory should not be seen as an end in itself in a course on the natural sciences."[35]

Krupskaia was especially virulent in her critique of those she termed "pure empiricists." Her criticisms also revealed the concern of some party members in Moscow regarding the independent stance of Raikov and his Leningrad cohort. This debate, which became known as the "Raikov Affair," was covered in a number of educational journals during the cultural revolution, especially in Narkompros's *Na putiakh k novoi shkole,* and was representative of broader assaults on the prerevolutionary scientific intelligentsia. Raikov was eventually arrested as a result of these criticisms in 1931. Fortunately, he was subsequently released by the Soviet authorities.[36]

Given the shifting political winds of 1928, Raikov and other scientific experts could no longer expect support if they continued to "divorce" science from practical ends. No longer would Narkompros be able to support individuals and societies who simply spread "science for science's sake." Some of the critiques against the old scientific intelligentsia would come from within Glavnauka itself, as patron began to dissociate from client during a militant period. However, the old prerevolutionary science educators and popularizers would not go down without a fight. They continued to devise complex rhetorical strategies to survive the changing political tides of Soviet politics, even under Stalin.

EDITING SCIENCE: THE POPULAR THEMATICS OF CULTURAL REVOLUTION

During the Stalinist cultural revolution (1928–31), editors of popular-scientific journals were quite explicit about stressing something much different from the previous goal of broad, popular enlightenment in the sciences. Militant editors and Marxist scientists believed in linking science education to the needs of an industrial developing economy. That emphasis became a critical focus throughout the period and culminated in the August 15, 1931, Central Committee decree that underscored the need for workers of the new Soviet state, in Stalin's words, to "master technology." Stalin's phrase was repeated in countless editorial statements, in virtually all newspapers, and on ubiquitous posters plastered throughout the nation.

Science in the broad sense became subsumed by the narrowly focused, yet more powerful and utilitarian, signifier of progress—applied technology. Though the Bolsheviks had stressed since 1917 the utility of technology, they had maintained an appreciation for the imaginative impulse of science. Journals had flourished that published scientific fantasies, revered feats of aeronautical heroism, documented the wonders of astronomical and planetary discoveries, and linked Russia to a global technological revolution. With the onset of Stalin's grandiose industrial revolution, however, popular science focused more on themes like the practical side of science—how science could benefit particular social groups, like workers, and how the Soviet Union was building a new economic system. The newer utilitarian and economic emphasis did not necessarily ruin the effort to popularize science; in fact, practical science was in popular demand as never before from a new generation of under-educated laborers from the countryside. But journals began to shed their more creative components, opting for articles and editorials that linked technological discoveries to the demands of an expanding, planned Communist economy.

For example, the popular-scientific journal, *Priroda i liudi* (nature and people), changed its name in October of 1931 to *Revoliutsiia i priroda* (revolution and nature). The editors made a long and polemical statement that the new task of the journal would be to begin a "war to popularize socialist technology." The task of socialist workers, according to these editors, was to master technology as Comrade Stalin had so clearly enunciated in his party speech. With the help of technological advances, the Soviet people would be able to conquer nature, as well as fulfill the industrial five-year plans. The technological struggle with nature thus also became a prominent theme in the popular journals of this early Stalinist period.[37]

The first issue of *Revoliutsiia i priroda,* with its new title and orientation, included a long editorial entitled "Technology for the Masses." The editors stressed Stalin's new propaganda phrase "technology in the period of reconstruction decides all." The earlier phrase "technology for the masses" became a catchword for linking the propaganda of science and technology with the industrialization drive of the First Five-Year Plan (FFYP). A new, pointed thrust of discourse was emerging from the party and directed at the people: technical literacy, not simply a general nebulous sense of scientific enlightenment, must be acquired by all. The *Revoliutsiia i priroda* editorial stressed this new orientation quite emphatically: "The growth of our new industries is dependent on the raising of the technical educational and literacy level of our working classes."[38] Empowering workers with the tools of science was a theme in most of the popular articles extolling the advances in Soviet technology. The emphasis of journal articles focused on science, in this sense, as both a democratic and utilitarian force and even as an alternative to the more academically oriented science of the capitalist West. This approach differed strongly from the more cosmopolitan content of and approach to science and technology in the early to mid-1920s.

During the cultural revolution radical Communists took over the editorial boards of numerous journals and in some cases dramatically altered their content. The popular journal *Mirovedenie,* under Ter-Oganesov's editorship, became a vehicle by 1930 to propagate not only dialectical materialist philosophy, but also the utilitarian applications of astronomy. Previously, the journal had maintained an independent stance for quite some time as a proponent of the importance of amateur astronomy. *Mirovedenie* had had an eclectic thematic approach, dedicated to the spread of knowledge on new astronomic discoveries by global specialists, while sponsoring the work of aspiring amateur scientists. It had provided its readers with sound but popular scientific analysis and information on astronomical sightings, meteorology, and stellar configurations. In contrast, the new editorial orientation caused problems and conflict between the radical editor and the older members of the amateur community.[39] Avid members of the Russian Amateur Astronomy Society fled in protest as the organization took on a politicized focus.

The popular journal *Iskra* also altered its direction, although not as dramatically as *Mirovedenie.* Like other journals after 1930, *Iskra* took up the call of the Communist Party and began to emphasize the importance of practical applications of technological discoveries. In a 1930 editorial entitled "Bolshevik Five-Year Plan in Four," the journal's editorial chief explained the importance of the intensification of industry and the tempo of development during this period of the FFYP. The journal's responsibility to Soviet society was therefore to focus on the industrialization of the country.[40] For the years 1930 and 1931, approximately 45 percent of all the journal's articles appeared under an expansive section entitled "Technology, Work, and Industry."

Other editors of popular journals, like *Revoliutsiia i priroda,* also began to extol articles focusing more on applied technological developments. Some discussed the importance of new metals and their production in various parts of the Soviet Union. One article looked at the development of aluminum production and the various industrial centers involved in this endeavor. The article described how, in Dnepopetrovsk and Leningrad, new industrial centers were able to produce and test the strength of aluminum components.[41] Some articles analyzed applications of scientific discoveries to the development of military technology. An article in *Revoliutsiia i priroda* focused on how Soviet artillery, aviation, and naval power would be advanced in the future as a result of investment in arms technology by the Soviet state.[42]

Popular journals devoted an enormous amount of print space to new Soviet technological discoveries and their immediate utility. The editors of *Iskra* donated much space in their journal to a large section entitled "Novosti nauki i tekhniki" (news of science and technology), which generally contained articles on a variety of topics from aero-technology to electro-technology. Basic technological advances were generally covered in full-page, highlighted articles—for instance, the christening of a new sugar refinery in Smolensk oblast in 1931.[43] New techniques for refining sugar were discussed in this article along with descriptions of various vacuum devices used in heating and drying sugar solutions. The iconography of photographs was generally clear and straight-forward: workers grasping the importance of technological advances alongside engineers and factory directors. In this case, workers were learning about the importance of new vacuum technology for sugar refinement at the Smolensk Sugar Factory in the Shevrenkovskii region. Direct hands-on technological education was the message of the article and its accompanying photographs.[44] Articles like these extolled Soviet industrial and technological advances and offered photos of workers together with engineers to depict visual images of how technology had broken down class barriers in the USSR. Compared to 1920s science literature, which clearly emphasized Western technology, Soviet technological advances during the FFYP were prominently displayed and shown to be the joint product of scientific specialists and workers alike.

Many of the popular-scientific journals of the FFYP era carried a section that dealt exclusively with inventions and their application to technological innovation. In the journal *Revoliutsiia i priroda* the section was entitled "The Value of Invention." During the FFYP this section carried articles mostly on Soviet inventors and stressed the importance of encouraging indigenous scientific invention. Such journal sections pushed the notion that workers should be the most daring of inventors. Unlike the popular-science media of twenties, the media of the thirties placed foreign technological advances in the back seat, behind Soviet discoveries. Invention seemed less a part of an educational process and more a venue for the laboring classes to excel in the process of discovery. Workers were shown in pictures, and described in editorials, eclipsing the former technical intelligentsia as the purveyors of scientific potential. Although Stalin issued his famous speech in July 1931 signaling an end to the distrust of so-called "bourgeois specialists," the new policy did not preclude science editors from emphasizing how workers could learn from specialists to build and reinvent a new type of engineer.

An article in *Revoliutsiia i priroda* extolled the importance of workshops sponsored by various Moscow factories to encourage workers on the shop floor to share their ideas for technological change with engineers and technical specialists. This particular article championed the Borets factory in Moscow for sponsoring talks and workshops organized to urge workers to display their inventions and to urge "specialists" to critique their work.[45] Many foreign technical specialists working in Russia, however, noted how this put enormous pressure on Soviet engineers during the early Stalinist years to critique an abundance of mediocre designs and blueprints by amateur worker-inventors.[46]

Many of the articles and short pieces in *Iskra*'s section on "News of Science and Technology" covered Soviet inventors and their projects. The emphasis in such articles was on amateur inventors who came from the shop floor and were, therefore, on the cutting edge of change, since they knew from hands-on experience what was actually needed in the factories. This editorial strategy fit into the Stalinist rhetoric of the period and emphasized "the mastering of technology by the working class." Unlike articles appearing in the 1920s, newer articles and editorials did not necessarily stress the importance of learning from the specialists. Instead, formally trained technical specialists were seen more as useful critics of a new class of *praktiki* (rapidly promoted specialists) who would eventually supplant the technical specialists once the cultural revolution had taken its due course.

Lastly, editors believed that journals should emphasize the importance of the natural wealth and resources of the country. The vast expanse of the Soviet empire was rich in everything from oil to precious metals. Articles emphasizing important national treasures were placed prominently at the beginning of issues. Furthermore, prominent academicians were urged and solicited to write articles with nationalistic thematic content. Stalinism placed great importance on extracting the maximum from the vast resources of the empire, emphasizing a need to command and conquer nature. In one lead article in *Revoliutsiia i priroda,* Academician A. E. Fersman wrote a tract entitled "All of Our Land," where he surveyed the metallic resources of the Urals. The thesis of such articles, consistently set out through the words and pictures, was anchored in the notion of utilizing the potential of Russian resources, not just in understanding their nature and worth.

These nationalistic tracts were not as introverted and exclusive as those to come in the middle through the late thirties. The scientific writing of era of the cultural revolution still contained peripheral commentary about Western technology and resources, but their value was not underscored as it had been in the mid-1920s. A reverence for the West and the felt need to learn from Western scientists and engineers are clearly missing in texts of popular journals published during the cultural revolution. That absence hints at what was to come, a rising tide of rhetorical and popular articles glorifying the wealth of the Soviet empire. That tide would utterly divide Russia of the mid-1930s from the international nexus so vital to building scientific and technological networks. In the period of the Stalinist cultural revolution, the emphasis on the feats of Soviet technology and invention had initiated a slow process of excluding commentary on the virtues of Western advances. Soon, discussion of the Western scientific and technical world would vanish from the pages of the public media for a long time to come.

Chapter 8

CULTURAL CONVEYOR BELTS

Public Science on the Retreat, 1928–32

During the period of the New Economic Policy (NEP), the Communist Party and Soviet state (specifically the Ministry of Education's Scientific Branch, Glavnauka) generously sponsored the popular-enlightenment efforts of many scientific societies, institutions, and publishers while avoiding any severe political interference in their work. With the end of the NEP in 1928, the Soviet state continued as the prime funding source for those societies and their enlightenment work. However, radical Communist factions and groups of intellectuals then launched an aggressive challenge to the authority of the prerevolutionary intelligentsia. While the initiative came from below, these groups lent support to party resolutions and directives from above, which demanded that all enlightenment activities buttress the socialist reconstruction of the economy.[1]

In the period of the Stalinist Great Break *(Velikii Perelom),* young militant Communists successfully infiltrated the editorial boards of popular-scientific journals, with the tacit support of more-militant Narkompros and central Agit-Prop officials. Their efforts mimicked similar developments across all disciplines, especially in some of the important central and regional educational journals. Larry Holmes has shown that after the autumn of 1928 at both the central and provincial levels, purges of editors and educators accompanied changes in the content of articles in educational journals. Furthermore, science and educational periodicals increasingly highlighted articles relevant to social and industrial tasks.[2]

Throughout the course of the cultural revolution, tensions grew between young militants and older professors in the sciences. In the scientific realm specific institutions, VARNITSO being the best example, helped to coalesce attacks against prerevolutionary societies and served as a spearhead for further criticism. The attacks against the prerevolutionary intellectuals greatly restricted the extent and nature of the public discussion of scientific issues during the 1930s. VARNITSO began to dictate to older established institutions the parameters of popular scientific and technical education.

The scientific intelligentsia's ordinary, daily survival tactics highlight the human drama of the era. Their struggles display and emphasize basic human emotions such as the new militants' jealousy of the old scientific elite and the radical Communists' contempt for how the Soviet regime patronized these specialists earlier in the decade. This contempt would drive young Communist militants, on their own accord, to undermine the symbiotic relationships created between the regime and the prerevolutionary scientific intelligentsia, complicating that very assault which had also been launched from above.

VARNITSO AND THE ASSAULT ON CENTRAL SCIENTIFIC SOCIETIES

During the Great Break, Bolshevik science pedagogues, grouped in VARNITSO and other organizations, criticized those educators who did not link science education to practical economic tasks. Even within Glavnauka, an earlier patron of scientific societies, these pedagogues openly challenged their associates who were accused of propagating material and a point of view divorced from immediate economic and industrial needs. VARNITSO overtly extinguished the process of public debate and discussion of science education during this period. Once Stalin unleashed the rhetorical constructs of practicality, various science educators used those models to serve their own purposes, simultaneously fulfilling the Stalinist state's dictates.

Through the period of the cultural revolution VARNITSO led a campaign against liberal, prerevolutionary scientists, educators, and scientific societies.[3] The history of this agency reflects, in some ways, a history of science education in general, over the course of the late 1920s and 1930s in the USSR. From the outset of the new nation, Communist organizations interacted and collided with preexisting voluntary and learned societies, fostering institutional and ideological conflict. Back on April 27, 1927, a group of leftist professors met to draft the outlines of what would soon become VARNITSO. Those Communists, with particularly high connections within the Bolshevik party, were specifically insistent on linking all science education and popularization to practical economic tasks of the FFYP. Their number included B. M. Zavadovskii, V. M. Sverdlov, M. M. Zavadovskii (head of the Biology Department at Moscow State University), and also A. N. Bakh (director of the Karpov Chemical Institute). On September 26, 1927, they and their like-minded colleagues signed a declaration creating a new organization to promote science education at production sites and to propagate technical knowledge among the masses. The declaration also stated that one of the main functions of the group was to unite and organize socialist thinking among scientific and technical workers of the Soviet Union. The Bolsheviks gave direct support to their efforts, and a Council of People's Commissars (Sovnarkom) resolution of February 13, 1928, endorsed the declarations and formation of the organization that came to be known as VARNITSO.[4]

VARNITSO's initial founders and supporters included members of the scientific and technical intelligentsia who held particularly high positions in educational and industrial institutions. More-radical professors at the Timiriazev Institute, like B. M. Zavadovskii, had been critical of prerevolutionary societies and popularizers in the debates of the 1920s. The radicals' intended purpose was to win over specialists to a mechanistic, Marxist worldview, to cooperate with the Soviet government and Communist Party in building socialism, and to propagate scientific and technical information among the Soviet masses. VARNITSO and its members thereby helped create several Communist voluntary technical societies, TekhMass for one, offering workers with limited skills politicized classes in the sciences in factories after work hours.

From its inception VARNITSO used the revolutionary rhetoric of class war and international struggle to set itself apart from other mass scientific organizations. Its organizing group argued that science and technology were instruments in a struggle between two world systems—capitalism and socialism. As part of that effort, the society also encouraged graduate students in the sciences to join their group and take part in proselytizing for the organization. In a letter to People's Commissar of Enlightenment Lunacharskii in December of 1927, a group of young Communist graduate students declared that Glavnauka must support the funding of VARNITSO to unite scientific enlightenment with industrial tasks. The students complained that "we have had a series of good scientific research institutes with decent facilities, yet we lack scientists engaged in applied research. We must focus the work of our educational departments and research institutes on the needs of agriculture, industry, national health, and sanitation."[5] These students wanted to refocus the emphasis of science enlightenment on the utilitarian needs of a developing economy.[6] The students were also taking advantage of the growing trend to criticize Glavnauka's previous support of prerevolutionary "bourgeois" societies.

The issue of the practicality of scientific research and education was stressed in Bolshevik rhetoric of the Stalinist Great Break era.[7] Although it may have rung hollow at times, many organizations felt they needed either to pay lip service to the Bolshevized term *practicality* or to use it as a means to focus attention on their particular organization. In the NEP era, these societies had to justify their funding requests to Glavnauka officials by underscoring their "cultural-enlightenment" efforts. Now, during the cultural revolution, they felt pressured to convince state officials that their societies could also fulfill the more utilitarian purpose of aiding the development of the Stalinist industrial complex.

VARNITSO spearheaded an attack against the institutional power of the Academy of Sciences as a bastion of the old bourgeois order and as an institution with privileged backing from Glavnauka.[8] In appeals sent to Glavnauka in 1927 and 1928, VARNITSO officials argued that the academy monopolized international contacts and funding for scientific conferences and expeditions within the Soviet Union. In April 1927 founding members of VARNITSO drafted letters that were sent to F. N. Petrov, head of Glavnauka, insisting that "the Academy of Sciences was a right-leaning organization, concentrating too much power in its own hands." VARNITSO warned Petrov and Glavnauka that the academy opposed "Sovietization" and would develop contacts only with those Western scientists who supported alternative socioeconomic systems of power.[9] The overall tone of the April 1927 meetings indicated a vindictive attitude toward the privileged academy and the sense that new Communist organizations should end the academy's dominance over scientific institutions in the USSR.[10]

VARNITSO slowly gained some support from moderate Narkompros officials like Petrov who had been open to diversified opinions. VARNITSO's campaign gained practical ground as it targeted those Narkompros officials who had control over funding, as well as the direction of science-education policy. Petrov was also present at some of the initial organizational meetings of VARNITSO in the Spring of 1927, and he, too, echoed similar criticisms of the academy as a privileged organization of the old bourgeois elite.[11] Whether Petrov, a supporter of less-ideological science education in the NEP era, was rethinking his position or merely pandering to the young radicals is difficult to assess. However, VARNITSO was successfully putting pressure on Glavnauka and its leaders, who believed they needed to respond to the growing ideological debates on the horizon.

VARNITSO's aggressive competition with other institutions for limited funds and support reflected not only the younger radical generation's ideological distaste for the standards of the prerevolutionary bourgeois scientific establishment but also the radicals' jealousy of the older generation's academic privileges.[12] Moreover, VARNITSO lobbied for its members' own professional interests. That was especially important for chemists and other scientists within several distinct disciplines who were members of VARNITSO.[13] These subgroups of scientists acted as ideological combatants both against other disciplines in the sciences and as political agents protecting and advancing the needs and interests of their members against non-Communist scientists. For instance, chemists in VARNITSO argued that their research had practical applications to the developing Stalinist industrial economy, over against the work of theoretical physicists, whom they criticized for receding into their insular laboratories. Although by 1928 VARNITSO still had fewer than a thousand members, that number included many prominent applied scientists, engineers, and Marxist scholars. Over the next two years, the organization rapidly expanded to three thousand members. By the end of 1932 it boasted a membership exceeding eleven thousand members.[14]

As it advanced the political interests of its members, the society infused its scientific propaganda with the "practical economic" rhetoric of the Stalinist FFYP. VARNITSO members urged all individuals and organizations to contribute to the USSR's industrial reconstruction. In pursuit of this goal VARNITSO, at its very inception, sought to assist Agit-Prop. The close ties that developed between the two agencies aided VARNITSO in fulfilling the party's requisite tasks, while enabling it to use the party's initiatives for its own ends. In 1928 Agit-Prop requested that VARNITSO produce materials propagating the utilitarian and economic relevance of science and technology. A. I. Krinitskii, head of Agit-Prop, urged VARNITSO members to stress the links between scientific knowledge and socialist ideology, and he asked VARNITSO to help set up technical circles and stations in factories to educate workers. Krinitskii specifically wanted to involve the organization in training under-skilled workers in basic science education on the shop floor and in producing practical pamphlets for various courses. The program fit in well with plans by Communist educators to unite all educational efforts with the remedial technical needs of under-skilled factory workers.[15]

VARNITSO launched a campaign in the popular press against mainline, "bourgeois" scientific societies and their popular-enlightenment work. That effort climaxed at a March 1931 meeting in Moscow of VARNITSO's Central Bureau, to which most of the major pre- and post-revolutionary scientific and voluntary societies in Moscow and Petrograd were invited to send representatives. VARNITSO hoped to use the meeting to condemn non-Communist educators and scientists while promoting the interests of its own members and the Communist Party's agenda. However, most of these non-Marxist organizations—including the Society of the Amateurs of Natural Sciences, the Society of the Investigators of Nature, Raikov's Leningrad Society for the Spread of Natural-Historical Education, among others—refused to fall into the trap and declined to send anyone to the gathering.

At the meeting VARNITSO's Zavadovskii gave a critical report on "The Restructuring of Work of Scientific Societies."[16] With few exceptions most scientific societies, he claimed, were still "citadels of bourgeois intellectuals." Furthermore, their major purpose remained the pursuit of pure scientific research. Zavadovskii insisted that such societies now demonstrate their relevance to Russia's industrial and overall economic development.[17] Following the meeting, Zavadovskii and his colleagues continued their attack in various periodicals and in the daily press. In an article in *Za kommunisticheskoe prosveshchenie,* Zavadovskii argued that societies like the Society of the Investigators of Nature had forfeited their right to funds from the Soviet government, even their right to exist, because of their preoccupation with theoretical work at the expense of tasks associated with popular education, economic utility, and industrial development.[18] In addition he pointedly declared that few of their members came from worker or peasant origins. Finally, he urged the revolutionary intelligentsia to restructure scientific organizations, opening them to the masses and dedicating them to the cause of "socialist reconstruction."[19] His proposal echoed suggestions from other VARNITSO members to consolidate many of the uncooperative societies into new organizations, thereby depriving them of their independent status and threatening them all with eventual extinction. VARNITSO wanted to upset the delicate balance between patron (Glavnauka/Narkompros) and client (prerevolutionary societies), which had been symbiotically structured in such a delicate manner during the NEP era. Ultimately, this destabilizing effort initiated a battle between Communist militants and the old prerevolutionary intelligentsia, who had previously enjoyed institutional support among Soviet state leaders during the NEP. VARNITSO members used the Communist Party's rhetorical constructs against their rivals, urging them to create voluntary societies that had utilitarian platforms and workers as members.

Zavadovskii, A. N. Bakh (Director of the Karpov Chemical Institute), and other members of VARNITSO continuously sent letters to Stalin and other Politburo members regarding the issue of "older bourgeois scientific" educators. In a 1931 letter to Stalin, these Communist professors argued that while VARNITSO was helping to build socialism, "Menshevik enemies of the state and older intelligenty" still lurked in older bourgeois scientific societies.[20] Their appeals for financial aid always stressed how VARNITSO was promoting science and technology that would support both workers and the Soviet state's industrial needs.[21] They vigorously protested the continued funding of many of the older societies by Glavnauka.

VARNITSO officials also lobbied Narkompros to put pressure on the prerevolutionary scientific societies. They were especially concerned that the societies actively recruit workers and peasants[22] and show evidence of direct and immediate contributions to the transformation of the nation's economy. At the same time, the Stalinist state and the Communist Party officially issued a similar requirement that all voluntary scientific and technical societies contribute in a practical way to economic development. At the first All-Union Conference of the Workers of Socialist Industry (February 1931), Communist Party representatives proclaimed: "The Bolsheviks should master technology. . . . Technology in the period of reconstruction decides all." VARNITSO became the leading agent of the new line to pressure voluntary scientific societies to take up utilitarian goals.[23]

Many of the old, established societies responded by training workers and new specialists and by conducting science short courses on the shop floor in factories. They then submitted to VARNITSO accounts of their attempts to aid "socialist construction." Their reports were testimony to VARNITSO's direct pressure on these organizations and to VARNITSO's ability to associate itself with the party's public policy and rhetorical constructs handed down from above. For the prerevolutionary scientific societies and educators, VARNITSO was an ideological threat, a competitor for funds from Glavnauka, and a carrier of the party's anti-pure-science line. During the 1920s Narkompros officials, like Lunacharskii, intervened directly and personally to buttress the budgetary needs and claims of prerevolutionary societies. After 1928 that budgetary policy became difficult for Glavnauka to continue, especially since Glavnauka itself was being pressured from two sides, by Communist Party departments like Agit-Prop and by new Communist voluntary organizations like VARNITSO.

A number of prerevolutionary societies responded to VARNITSO with an effort to improve their standing with the agency by demonstrating efforts at cooperation. For example, in 1931 the Moscow Society of the Investigators of Nature wrote VARNITSO a letter explaining that "since 1929 it has been involved in a number of science educational activities which have utilitarian economic goals."[24] Its members had successfully disseminated scientific information among the populace and had participated in a variety of public educational lectures and courses analyzing the mineral wealth of the country. Another organization, the Russian Association of Physicists, responded in a similar fashion to VARNITSO's attacks. In April 1931 the physics association's vice president, Professor V. Romanov, insisted that his organization was not solely preoccupied with theoretical problems: "At the last congress we addressed issues focusing physics on industrial development and the preparation of Communist cadres in the physical sciences."[25] Romanov argued moreover that A. F. Ioffe, president of the association, had undertaken a thorough reorganization in order to correct what VARNITSO characterized as the physicists' insular orientation and lack of applied research. There is no direct archival evidence to confirm Romanov's assertion that Ioffe had indeed carried out such a "thorough investigation," but both Romanov and Ioffe knew that they had to position the association in this way to deflect criticism by VARNITSO and other Communist organizations. Many other societies argued that they actively engaged in cultural-enlightenment work by consulting workers at Moscow factories on the practical applications of new theoretical work. Nevertheless, many other scientific societies, including the Moscow Society of the Investigators of Nature, protested to VARNITSO that involving workers and peasants in the organization's work was a more complex matter than VARNITSO was willing to admit.[26]

During the period of the Stalinist Great Break scientific societies, with few exceptions, eagerly showed that they were not insular bastions of the older scientific intelligentsia and supporters of merely pure scientific research. They well understood how crucial their effort was to continued state funding. They were highly sensitive to VARNITSO's openly public criticisms, given the fact that those criticisms might be representative of the shifting political trends in the Soviet regime above. Scientific societies with a long tradition dating from the prerevolutionary era of societal independence now found legitimizing their existence especially difficult. They were overwhelmed by the flurry of criticisms hurled at them during the era of the Stalinist cultural revolution and Great Break. Furthermore, they now had to compete with new Communist voluntary societies that emphasized popular education for workers and stressed utilitarian goals linked to the expansion of the Soviet industrial complex. Ultimately, Communist organizations such as VARNITSO worked the party and state bureaucracy in pursuit of their own budgetary needs in direct competition with preexisting scientific societies. VARNITSO successfully combined the ideological weaponry of the cultural revolution with their political skills at in-fighting to pursue their quest for funding and resources.

In the light of these complex internecine wars, the cultural revolution becomes a more nuanced and complicated process involving state dictums from above, militancy from below, and aggressive struggle for institutional hegemony and control over funding and limited resources. VARNITSO effectively used the Soviet state's rhetorical statements regarding "practicality" to its advantage, as it aggressively attacked prerevolutionary "bourgeois" scientific societies. On some level, VARNITSO's critique of the agendas of the old societies, with respect to practicality, rang hollow, given that the old societies had been linked to public educational goals and civic service during the 1920s. Yet, as VARNITSO argued, those societies were still run by *intelligenty* and not sufficiently engaged in providing technical advice to industrial workers. As their alternative, VARNITSO spawned many technical associations, TekhMass for instance, which more assiduously taught workers in factories remedial science education. VARNITSO's societies were still mainly run by intellectuals—though true Communists—but were more directed toward Stalin's insistence on specifically tying scientific enlightenment to industrial productivity.

Even toward the end of the cultural revolution in late 1931, Communist Party leaders continued to emphasize the popularization of technological information for Soviet workers. Party leaders like Nikolai Bukharin were seriously distressed over technical illiteracy, especially among the working class, and stressed the need for more technological education outside of formal institutions.[27] VARNITSO's call for "practicality" in adult education was therefore echoed by Communist Party leaders as the thirties began. The militants effectively placed the issue of utilitarianism in technical and science education firmly within the technological agenda of party leaders. In short, VARNITSO had taken up the call from above and skillfully used it both to solidify its own position vis-à-vis the government and to reinforce the party's rhetorical strategies. Despite the efforts of older societies to adjust rhetorically to criticism by radicals, the real repercussions of this trend for public science education were devastating for prerevolutionary societies but simultaneously transformative for the new radicals.

REGIONAL STUDIES, PUBLIC SCIENCE, AND STALINIST DISCONTENTS

As VARNITSO concentrated its attacks on the urban mainline institutions, a similar conflict played out more gradually in the provinces. Although perhaps not with the same ideological intensity, that conflict's final effects were equally devastating to science educators outside the urban mainstream. Provincial scientific societies had also maintained a precarious existence during the NEP era, as they, too, lobbied Glavnauka for funding while maintaining some sense of relative independence. Iaroslavl' naturalist societies had been particularly successful in advocating their cause, especially since they made up some of the oldest and best organized prerevolutionary voluntary scientific societies in the Russian provinces. Their liquidation during the cultural revolution reflected how the political tensions of that era had a lethal effect on scientific organizations outside the urban capitals.

The Iaroslavl' provincial natural-history societies were well funded during the NEP era, and they developed strong branches in cities such as Rostov, Rybinsk, and Kostroma. However, Glavnauka demanded more and more meticulous documentation from these organizations as the twenties came to an end. Furthermore, the encroaching state was involved in reorganizing such societies to fit them into new centralized bureaucratic structures. Although relatively independent, the scientific societies were subjected to the Soviet state's bureaucratic reshuffling throughout the 1920s. Additionally, every piece of equipment was inventoried, all budgets meticulously analyzed by Glavnauka, and all members required to fill out yearly reports on their activities. This centralizing process would become even more accentuated during the period 1928–31. As Stalin's revolution from above grew, other overlapping Soviet institutions, both within and outside Narkompros, began to place more and more demands on the provincial societies. The Stalinist institutions interfered in the societies' ability to make independent decisions and ultimately infringed on their viability as independent purveyors of civic culture in Russia. Furthermore, incremental Soviet *kontrol'* evolved into a hegemonic power struggle between the central state and scientific organizations on the periphery.

In the summer of 1918 the Soviet Ministry of Enlightenment (Narkompros) created the Central Kraevedcheskoe Obshchestvo (Regional Studies Society). The purpose of this organization, and its many local affiliates, was to unite scholars interested in regional issues, entice them to educate local communities, and further study the resource potential of various geographic areas. The *kraeved* (regional studies) movement intersected with the science-popularization trend in the Soviet state's effort to engage regional specialists in the spread of science widely among the populace. As the twenties progressed, the kraeved movement became overwhelmed by demands, especially from such institutions as Vesenkha, to concentrate its work on local resource analysis for more utilitarian and industrial purposes.

Three simultaneously occurring factors placed pressure on provincial naturalist societies in the Northern Volga region, finally culminating in their liquidation in 1931. One factor was the requirement to place more emphasis on regional-resource development and study. The Iaroslavl' Natural-History Society's name was officially changed in 1924 (approved by Narkompros's Glavnauka) to the Iaroslavl' Natural-Historical and Regional Studies (Kraevedcheskoe) Society. In November 1930 the age-old function and designation of the society, natural history, was deleted, and it was renamed the Iaroslavl' City-Oblast Regional Studies Society. It continued to exist under that designation until April of 1931, when the society was officially dissolved by the Central Bureau of Regional Studies under the authority of Narkompros.[28] A second, and equally ruinous, factor affecting the Iaroslavl' society was the pressure exerted by local and central "productive forces" associations. These organizations, with strong ties to Vesenkha, pressured local scientific societies to place more emphasis on natural-resource utilization and applied-science research. Lastly, a third pressuring factor emerged because Glavnauka representatives themselves felt the pressure to force provincial societies to conform more explicitly to centralized dictates. Glavnauka demanded that these voluntary scientific organizations take part in utilitarian endeavors having clearly direct links to the developing economy.

By the late 1920s local associations for the study of the productive forces sprouted up all over provincial Russia. The most active along the northern Volga, *Assotsiatsiia po izucheniiu proizvoditel'nykh sil Iaroslavskoi gubernii* (Association for the Study of the Productive Strength of Iaroslavl' Province) had been involved in regional studies beginning in 1923. Yet as the decade progressed, these local associations competed for funds and legitimacy alongside the Iaroslavl' Natural-History Society. The "productive forces" organizations appealed to local executive committees by arguing that they were uncovering information that would be valuable to local and central industrial institutions in ways that purely scientific investigations could not be. The Iaroslavl' Society for the Study of Productive Forces was especially involved in hydro-biological analysis of the Northern Volga River Basin. Between 1924 and 1926 one investigator for the society, V. I. Koshelev, launched a study that looked at the history of industries that developed along the river and how they used the waterway as a practical resource and foundation for economic development.[29] Natural-resource potential was critical to these organizations, as they extensively surveyed rock, fossil fuels, and indigenous deposits in the area. By 1927 local engineers and professors (who were associated with the organization) lobbied for local-government funds to continue studying the "productivity" of the area. Professor B. C. Greze of Iaroslavl' University began a study in 1927 to look at the fishing industries on the northern Volga. He was especially interested in how sustainable those fisheries would be over time. Records show that this organization particularly appealed to the Regional Central Executive Committee for funding, as well as the Regional Party Section (Gubkommunistotdel), arguing with the needed rhetorical skill that this organization was more beneficial to the state's industrial needs than older naturalist societies.[30]

These "productive forces" organizations created local agendas designed to compete with broader voluntary scientific societies for funding from regional Soviet-state and Communist Party institutions. Furthermore, they wrapped themselves in the rhetorical cloak of the Stalinist themes of utilization and resource potential of a given region. Between 1928 to 1932 local scientific societies, like the Iaroslavl' Natural-History Society, were pressured to engage more directly in the Stalinist industrialization and collectivization programs. Central dictates from above made the need to study the "productivity" of a Russian provincial region the most critical element of any society's agenda if it was to survive as a public institution.

Beginning in early 1929 the Iaroslavl' Natural-History Society started sending letters to Glavnauka and local authorities, like the *gubispolkomi,* informing

them that they were now giving lectures and workshops on scientific topics having relevance to the national and local economic plans. These letters
contained appeals similar to those that the scientific societies of the major
cities had sent along to VARNITSO, to show that they were cooperating
with the state's economic goals. In 1929 the Iaroslavl' naturalists held a series
of lectures in the area for local engineers and farm administrators on the
importance of chemical fertilizers and pesticides for agriculture. They developed a series of technical and scientific lectures for local factory workers.
Most of the lectures for workers in the past had been designed to supplement
their basic scientific grounding—broad workshops on math, physics, and
even astronomy (still a popular topic among laborers).[31] After 1928, however,
the old-line societies tried to adapt to the changing tides and to lobby state
institutions using the new rhetoric of economic utility and industrial productivity.

By late 1930 a steady stream of central dictates from officials of the Glavnauka department of Narkompros laid out a practical agenda of activities in
which the societies needed to engage if they were to remain afloat. Their
once benevolent patron, Glavnauka, also capitulated to the driving forces
from above and below to link science education with economic productivity.
By the winter of 1931 Glavnauka had launched a campaign to make sure the
scientific societies conformed to a program of strict requirements. In February of 1931 the agency sent out a circular to all provincial scientific societies
and regional museums in the USSR requesting a detailed survey and account
of their activities by March 1, 1931. Glavnauka demanded that voluntary scientific organizations educate the local public on the importance of the Soviet
military-industrial complex during the FFYP, the role of the Red Army in the
collectivization drive, and the fight against class enemies in local regions.[32]
Approximately one week later M. P. Potemkin, head of the Central Regional
Studies Bureau in Moscow, sent a directive to all local regional studies organizations with an even more utilitarian, and equally coercive, demand.
Potemkin insisted that regional study societies and naturalists develop exhibits and workshops lauding recent industrial achievements in the USSR.
They were particularly instructed to focus their attention on exhibits that
would look at the industrial capacities, as well as natural-resource potential,
of the local region.[33] On February 20, 1931, the Glavnauka department of
Narkompros sent to regional scientific and kraeved organizations directives
addressing the need to campaign for the party on local collective farms.
Narkompros argued that those groups had to conduct technical seminars and
lectures on the introduction of machinery and chemical fertilizers.[34]

With their backs to the wall, societies responded promptly to criticisms by
setting up popular seminars and scientific lectures geared to those social

groups that the regime supported. The organization of Iaroslavl' naturalists went to great lengths to describe to Glavnauka officials their lectures for Soviet workers and the short courses they organized for Red Army soldiers in the area. Although the actual topics did not always develop from utilitarian, industrial themes, the society nevertheless offered short courses to particular social groups targeted by Narkompros. Since the society had always popularized astronomy at its observatory, it set up particular nights exclusively for workers to observe stellar sightings and to consult with local astronomy specialists.[35]

But their previous patron, Glavnauka, could no longer come to their rescue, especially financially. Budget records show a steady stream of complaints from provincial scientific organizations to Glavnauka's financial department beginning in 1929 and ending with their liquidation in 1931. The records indicate that these societies were hanging on by a thread during the period of the cultural revolution.

A January 25, 1929, letter from the Iaroslavl' society to Glavnauka complains about the lack of funding to pay wages. The letter states that if the government were to discontinue its subsidy for the society, the society would lose not just scientists but also basic necessities for its facilities. Society officials argued that for the three months following October 1, 1928, the society received only twenty-eight rubles of its budgetary request sent to Glavnauka.[36] Clearly, this was not just a time of ideological change but also of financial privation. The 1929–1930 *smeta* (estimate) sent to Glavnauka included an attached memo protesting the lack of funds distributed to local scientific societies on the northern Volga. They especially berated government officials for the condition into which the society had fallen because of a lack of funding: wages were not being paid to employees of the museum, exhibits were suffering, and lectures were becoming more sparsely attended. The societies had to rely more on their voluntary scientific staff, which was supposed to concentrate mostly on educational activity, not basic upkeep of facilities.[37]

By mid-1930 financial tensions would be the least of the Iaroslavl' society's worries. The first frontal assault came from the Central Bureau of Regional Studies in Moscow. Claiming, as a Narkompros organization, it had jurisdiction over the Iaroslavl' society, the bureau asserted that the society should be dissolved and its membership subsumed under a more centralized subsection based in Ivanovo (a larger industrial center to the east).[38] The central Ivanovo organization agreed with the bureau's assessment, adding that the Iaroslavl society was oriented toward narrow, myopic studies of flora and fauna that were irrelevant to the broader economic and industrial topics of the entire Northern Volga area.[39] The stinging critique fit well with the rhetorical fervor of the FFYP era regarding economic utility and with the Stalinist trend toward more-centralized organizations.

The destruction of some provincial societies was also linked to general bureaucratic reorganization after 1929. Between 1929 and 1936 Iaroslavl' became part of the Ivanovo Industrial Oblast Obkom (or Regional Party Headquarters), during a time when the older *gubkomi* (or Gubernaia Communist Party Organizations) were being subsumed under *obkomi* (Regional/Oblast Communist Party Structures). Cultural, scientific, and regional reshuffling might have been replicating broader geopolitical reorganizations occurring in the party itself. These reorganizations were critical in an era when the party in Moscow was becoming more suspicious of local independence.

The local regional society attempted to strike back by holding a membership meeting in early August. On August 8, 1930, it sent a memorandum to the Ivanovo Regional Studies Headquarters in its own defense. The members who signed the memorandum argued that the society was never "organized on a very narrow basis" and that it had a regional and economic scope to its work that focused on research in areas beyond the town of Iaroslavl'.[40] Unfortunately, the Ivanovo Central Bureau refused to listen to these entreaties pleading that the Iaroslavl' society remain independent and did not approve the request.[41]

On November 3, 1930, the Ivanovo Central Bureau changed the name of the Iaroslavl' naturalist society to the Iaroslavl' City-Oblast Regional Studies Society.[42] The naturalist section of the newly named society appealed, in January 1931, to the All-Union Society of the Lovers of Nature in Moscow for help and affiliation. The local naturalists argued that although they had always been interested in "regional studies" they were actually more associated with all Russian naturalists who study their various locales.[43] The records, however, show no response to this appeal. Increasingly, provincial naturalists were having difficulty fending off regional studies groups and trying to affiliate themselves with other major naturalist organizations in Moscow that continued to enjoy state sanctioning. Glavnauka, once the supporter of amateur scientific societies, seemed to have completely abandoned provincial naturalists and scientific societies to the whims of the centralized regional-studies organizations within Narkompros.

In November 1930, Glavnauka itself sent a circular to all regional scientific societies in the provinces warning them that they should try to affiliate themselves with central organizations based in Moscow or risk complete liquidation. Signed and presumably written by I. Kancheev, an assistant director of Glavnauka, it argued that provincial scientific organizations must realize that "the present movement, to centralize all scientific and cultural organizations in Soviet Russia, will serve the purpose of maximizing our scientific workers to take part in the greater goal of the socialist reconstruction of the industrial sector."[44] This statement, probably more than any other, speaks clearly to the extent to which Glavnauka, itself under great pressure, would go to support centralizing tendencies by the end of the cultural revolution. The statement was a far cry from the days when Glavnauka intervened in the earlier 1920s to help these societies to maintain their local independence.

With no central or local patrons left to turn to for help, the oldest provincial scientific organization in Russia was finally dissolved on April 25, 1931, by a decree from Narkompros's central office, which was effected by the local Iaroslavl' Branch of the Commissariat of Enlightenment. The liquidation order, which affected all naturalist branches on the northern Volga, ended with a demand that all property of the organization (and its remaining budgetary funds) be transferred to the local Narkompros bureau.[45] The society made a final appeal to Narkompros itself at the end of April, but it was of no avail since the society was officially extinguished.[46]

After 1929 when Communist Party political organizations were being reorganized from the center, provincial scientific societies found themselves subsumed under larger oblast organizations by Narkompros. This grand reorganization reflected the scope of the center's hold over peripheral organizations during that period. At an earlier point in time, local science and public culture in the Russian provinces had been an important component of a developing civil society. However, by the early thirties these communities of provincial science educators had all but dried up, with their civic tasks forcibly linked to utilitarian ventures. As conveyor belts for the Communist Party's propaganda campaigns, the scientific societies no longer represented the vestiges of independent civic activity, a role they had defended in the twenties.

SCIENCE, MASS-AGITATIONAL PROPAGANDA, AND THE COMMUNIST PARTY'S PERILS IN THE PROVINCES

As VARNITSO and the Soviet state were attacking central scientific societies, local societies were simultaneously under pressure to link their public activities to economic and utilitarian goals. Meanwhile, during the cultural revolution, the Agitational-Propaganda Sector of the Communist Party resuscitated its own scientific-enlightenment campaign in the provinces, even attempting at times to use the facilities of these local scientific societies for its own radicalized and more politicized ends. In the provinces this became especially pronounced, and Agit-Prop's local cells stressed not only utilitarian goals but also antireligion as a key weapon in its assault on the public's so-called "antiquated and superstitious values." Mass-agitational activity along these lines would fail miserably in local areas, as party cells sent back frank accounts of critical problems to the central and regional headquarters. Those failures reveal the party's ineffectiveness in scientific propaganda in outlying regions and explain why the Communist Party would become so dependent on Communist voluntary societies in the period 1928–34 to carry out public science education.

Beginning in late 1928 the Iaroslavl' Gubkom (Regional Party Committee), in collaboration with the provincial League of the Godless, began to draft plans for joint antireligious activity and the construction of a substantial, local antireligion museum. The gubkom was especially interested in this aspect of scientific enlightenment, hoping that if successful the museum could hold agitational-propaganda lectures on scientific themes. Gubkom members believed that two large scientific departments were needed in the museum. One department would deal exclusively with inorganic sciences, such as geography, geology, and the evolution of the earth. The other department would deal with the organic world and focus on the evolution of animals, plants, and, of course, Homo sapiens. The first department's emphasis would debunk religious and superstitious representation of the inorganic world and focus on the replacement of superstition with developmental geological and evolutionary theories. The second department's thrust would be on spreading evolutionary theories of the organic world, especially Darwinism, to inculcate a materialist perspective among the local peoples.[47]

All of these plans were based on two premises: that the local party activists in the gubkom could successfully put together a good "scientific" museum, lecture series, and public exhibits to serve as antireligious propaganda; that they could independently train new party activists to successfully conduct scientific lectures on basic topics for the public. As evidenced in party records, both failed miserably. To begin, the local party activists, alongside antireligious groups, began to collect technical and medical diagrams, posters, and equipment (such as skeletal replicas and microscopes) to teach various scientific disciplines in public workshops. They hoped to construct herbariums and aquariums in order to create public exhibitions. However, due to lack of funds and qualified scientific personnel, the local gubkom began in November and December of 1928 to instruct Communist Party activists to rely instead on local naturalists, as well as on the use of part of the state's natural-history museum department for agitational purposes. In essence, even local League of the Godless members were suggesting to the regional party heads that they should rely on existing science-museum staff and lecturers and that setting up new facilities might be difficult.[48] The funds did not exist, nor did the scientific personnel or momentum within local Agit-Prop cells, to conduct that kind of widespread science-educational activity. Furthermore, the whole effort seemed redundant if the State Museum, reorganized in 1924 in Iaroslavl', already had these detailed scientific exhibits.

According to local party activists, all that was needed was to give the preexisting scientific exhibits more of an ideological, politicized thrust when explaining various natural occurrences. One of the first-developed antireligious museums funded by the Communist Party itself opened in Iaroslavl', but not until much later, in October 1938 at the height of the Stalinist purges, when one was built on the premises of the old church Il'i Prorok.[49] However, the local *bezbozhniki* (members of the League of the Godless) began a small atheist museum in April 1930. Although the *bezbozhniki* claimed to have elaborate exhibits on natural science and the history of atheism in the USSR, this and others of their small, hastily constructed museums could not compare to the regional natural history museum that had attracted loyal visitors for decades.[50] The original naturalist science-museum exhibitions, of course, were never stifled with political rhetoric.

Not long before the *bezbozhniki* opened their small museum on Iaroslavl', the local Agit-Prop department of the gubkom began a campaign to train local natural-scientific activists who could take part in antireligious activity for the party. In late 1928 and early 1929, they set up scientific workshops for older and new party recruits in the Iaroslavl' and Ivanovo regions. The courses, for the few who attended, were rigorous. Out of a total of 288 hours of class work, close to 140 were devoted strictly to themes in the natural sciences, lecture subjects ranging from astronomy to general biology.[51] The training program for local party activists was designed to train leaders in the provinces through a course sequence focused heavily on inorganic and organic evolutionary themes. Part 1 dealt with the foundations of physical-chemical laws of nature, atmospheric phenomena, and the construction and evolution of the universe. Part 2 of the workshops, generally taught by Communist Party activists with little advanced training in the sciences, dealt with the evolution of animal, plant, and human life forms on earth. The workshops used short, popular texts and pamphlets, accessible to the average layman, for example, Azimov's "O proiskhozhdenii zhizni na zemli" (on the origin of life on earth). The instructors usually helped participants through the readings of short scientific pamphlets and served more as guides than teachers of natural science.[52] They sometimes tried to enlist the more advanced students from the Iaroslavl' Higher Party School to teach courses in mathematics, geography, and physics, as a way to entice workers and others to attend party activist courses.[53]

Problems were rife in these so-called "natural-scientific training courses." Party activists complained of a lack of reading materials for all participants;

attendants were under-educated; retention of key material was abysmally low. Participants came only from the towns, as it was difficult to attract those from rural areas who might then be sent back to the countryside to conduct propaganda. Activists stated that attendance rates never exceeded 60 percent of enrollment because most of the courses were held at night, and most participants could not get out of work early enough to attend all sessions. They were tired after work and therefore could not pay close attention, often dozing off during lectures.[54] Agit-Prop members complained that few women came to the workshops, and classes generally never exceeded enrollments of thirty individuals. In addition, few actually completed the training. Even the workshop leaders themselves admitted that they were not trained science teachers and could only serve superficially as instructors on topics they found overly technical, given their educational background. Sometimes the Agit-Prop officials serving as teachers were engaged in other local activities for the party; the training workshops were therefore intermittently interrupted.[55] In spite of a Communist Party announcing itself the herald of a "scientized culture" for the future, few involved activists could claim they were well versed in their subjects or even in basic scientific analysis.

Beginning in 1930 the Agit-Prop Sector of the Iaroslavl' Okruzhkom (Area Party Committee) tried to focus its attention on the cities and factories in the region. They set up cells and scientific seminars in textile factories and other industries in the Upper Volga River Basin. Many of the night lectures and courses were aimed at uniting science and antireligious theory. Some dealt with more utilitarian subjects focusing on the economics of the FFYP, but those types of scientific lectures were rare.[56] At a cultural-enlightenment meeting of the Iaroslavl' Party Committee in September 1930, one activist admitted that "worker disillusionment with scientific agitational programs can be attributed to high rates of illiteracy in textile factories on the Volga."[57] Another argued that "we organize these workshops on science and religion, but few workers actually come, since they have no direct relevance to their occupation or leisurely interests."[58] In response, a committee member argued that the Communist Party must mix agitational lecture material with activities in the worker clubs to attract workers' interest more effectively. Otherwise, he believed, the party's attempt to create scientific, antireligious activists would fail in the locales.[59]

In the early winter months of 1931, local party activists and leaders, distressed by the poor results of agitational lectures, began to organize self-studies of Agit-Prop work. The reports from those studies reveal the failure of Agit-Prop activists to convert workers in factories scattered throughout the Northern Volga region. Agit-Prop workers candidly criticized their own failures, even admitting problems in attracting new members to the Communist Party itself. In the week of February 3–9, 1931, the local Agit-Prop Sector conducted a survey of its activities in various factories around Iaroslavl'. Activists stated that their work was largely ineffective, especially among workers. They were especially distressed over the lack of qualified leaders and instructors for workshops on political, scientific, and antireligious themes.[60] The head of the Agit-Prop Sector in Iaroslavl', Comrade Grigor'ev, argued: "Our Agit-Prop Sector work is so weak in the provinces, and it has no direction or leadership. Mobilization of broader networks does not exist, and we are not paying ample attention to voluntary scientific organizations which could help us."

In April 1931 the Iaroslavl' Party Committee instructed its Agitational-Mass Sector to explore the results of scientific propaganda in specific factories and to report back to local party leaders. At the Red Hammer textile factory in Iaroslavl', activists had to concede that workers were not attending science propaganda lectures and that efforts to attract workers to lead antireligious cells had failed. Agit-Prop activists were particularly frustrated by the fact that engineers and scientists constituted only a small percentage of the party's antireligious propaganda sector and did not volunteer regularly as instructors in their workshops.[61]

These self-studies are vivid testimony that the Communist Party had to rely on independent voluntary associations for scientific, technical education, especially in the factories. The tragic irony is that these self-studies were being carried out in the Spring of 1931, at the same time that the local prerevolutionary scientific societies were being attacked and dissolved as "bourgeois vestiges" of the past. With the dissolution of old-line scientific societies combining with the party's inability to attract workers and others to their agitational work, Agit-Prop officials began to rely on radical technical voluntary societies that had been formed by Communist-oriented engineers and technical specialists. The success, attributes, and problems of those radical groups is the epilogue to the long history of scientific and technical popularization in Russia as it began to dissipate in the early Stalinist era. New workers, who streamed into the cities during the FFYP, would be interested in utilitarian technical lectures that benefited their chances of social mobility. They were still taken by the imaginative impulses of scientific topics but had little patience with Agit-Prop's science lectures, which, in their minds, improperly mixed education with political rhetoric.

Chapter 9

TECHNOLOGY FOR THE MASSES

Technical Societies, Stalinist Culture, and Soviet Labor, 1928–34

During the Stalinist Great Break, Communist science educators demanded that scientists not only increase their voluntary, enlightenment work but also get more thoroughly involved in aiding industrial development in the USSR. The state believed that popular-scientific enlightenment had to coalesce with the Communist Party's utilitarian needs to construct the industrial sector of the economy. Initially, radical scientists and propagandists attacked older prerevolutionary voluntary societies for not aiding the socialist construction of the economy. Eventually, however, they organized their own mass organizations, outside the purview of Agit-Prop, to aid the economy and to fulfill other tasks, among them educating workers. TekhMass was organized in 1928 as a new Communist voluntary organization designed to promote the education of workers to integrate them more effectively into the factory environment of the FFYP. This organization would compete with prerevolutionary science societies in its attempt to educate the masses in technological matters. It would also promote the Party's mass-cultural rhetoric of advanced technology as the ubiquitous signifier of Soviet modernization.

TekhMass, like other radical organizations of the cultural-revolutionary era, skillfully placed the discussion of public scientific and technical education within a larger struggle to refocus enlightenment toward the more utilitarian needs of the developing industrial economy. TekhMass engaged the popular educational slogans rhetorically stressed by Communist Party leaders, namely, terms linking scientific and technical education to practical ends. Some organizations felt the need to pay lip service to the Bolshevized term "practicality," but TekhMass members not only wholeheartedly believed in serving the public in utilitarian ways but also used that platform as a means to focus attention on their particular organization. Key members of both VARNITSO and TekhMass, especially N. Krupskaia, had supported the more radical pedagogues in the 1920s who trumpeted this movement of the "practicality of education." Then, a decision in 1930 by the Congress of Polytechnic Education began an effort to link some primary schools with neighboring factories and *kolkhozi* (collective farms). TekhMass activities became part of a general movement in technical education, a project especially supported by the regime.[1]

Although they originally fostered the party's mass propagandistic, educational, and economic agendas, Communist voluntary societies, like TekhMass, also provided basic needs for those laborers who wanted more guidance in areas in which they never received formal educational training. Unlike workers' aversion to the impractical Agit-Prop lectures, laborers were keenly interested in courses and workshops that could help benefit their careers and offer them technical education. Workers actually attended the classes, lectures, and events offered by Communist voluntary organizations. They honestly discussed their needs in written responses to questionnaires, and their aspirations were captured in the archival records of these new organizations. Their responses attest to the fact that workers had their own agendas to fulfill.[2] They found individual spaces even within the institutional and cultural arenas constructed for them by the Stalinist state and Communist intellectuals where they could articulate their needs.[3] They even found ways to criticize Soviet propaganda, while clearly articulating their own educational needs to Communist specialists.

Workers not only maneuvered their way through the Stalinist system; they also contested the cultural constraints placed on them by activists and Soviet officials alike[4] and found ways to express their complaints in direct ways to authorities through letters or through their responses to TekhMass questionnaires.[5] Workers strongly vocalized the inconsistencies of Soviet educational policy and technical propaganda. The new Communist technical societies even had to rethink and reshape their educational programs and tactics continually to meet the demands of workers.

However, the dialogue worked both ways, as the state eventually changed the name of TekhMass to Obshchestva Za Ovladenie Tekhnikoi, or ZOT (all-union society for the mastering of technology) in order to harness its resources for use in its mass propaganda campaign, "The Party and Workers Should Master Technology . . . Technology Decides All." With the demise of many prerevolutionary scientific societies and the failure of Agit-Prop work, the Soviet state realized the potential of the radical voluntary organizations to aid its own scientific popularization campaign. After 1932 even the Communist science educators who were militant members of those organizations had come under the firm control of the party. Societies like TekhMass were reorganized, given new names, and became conveyor belts for Stalinist cultural campaigns in the 1930s.

Ultimately, a series of convergences bringing together the Soviet state, activists, and society occurred in the arena of mass-technical education and Stalinist culture. Workers, who did not have any formal training in specific areas, received needed scientific advice and technical courses at night to improve their qualifications during a tumultuous period. The modernist, technological program and vision of various Communists in the voluntary organizations was supported by their targeted audience from below and reinforced by the regime from above. Finally, the Stalinist state harnessed young Communist scientific activists to fulfill its utilitarian goals of practical technical education, while promoting its own cultural vision of the new modernized, futuristic society. This Stalinist vision emphasized applied science and how the Soviet Union would become a technologically advanced society. It was a futuristic cultural vision of technology shaping and supporting Soviet society. Stalinist mass culture can be understood through the prism of converging agendas that reflect the development of both state and society. The science-popularization movement was shaped and transformed both from above and below during the early Stalinist era when vestiges of prerevolutionary scientific organizations were being extinguished.

TECHNOLOGY FOR THE MASSES, 1928–31

Key members of the VARNITSO supported the formation of voluntary technical-education societies like TekhMass. VARNITSO subsequently encouraged various science professors to take an active part in the voluntary work of this new society. These professors included M. M. Zavadovskii (Biology Department, Moscow State University), A. N. Bakh (Director of the Karpov Chemical Institute), and also A. I. Oparin (Moscow State University). They encouraged the growth of Communist science societies as vehicles to spread Marxist propaganda and to inculcate a scientific weltanshauung in the minds of the Soviet people. TekhMass was indeed a logical outgrowth of VARNITSO's broader plans and visions to restructure scientific and popular enlightenment in Soviet Russia. As VARNITSO attempted to extinguish prerevolutionary scientific organizations, it was simultaneously cultivating the development of new Communist, technically oriented voluntary groups. The birth of these new scientific and technical societies in the Stalinist era signaled a dramatic turn in the history of the science-popularization movement in Russia.

During the First Five-Year Plan the Communist Party itself emphasized the popularization of technological information. Bukharin and Stalin, among other Communist Party officials, wrote a number of articles on the topic during the period. In a 1931 piece in *Za industrializatsiiu* (for industrialization), Bukharin described the Central Committee's distress over technical illiteracy, especially among workers. He argued that a lack of understanding of basic scientific concepts among the working class would prevent any growth in the industrial sector. As a solution Bukharin suggested more technological education be made available outside of formal institutions, an effort to include more correspondence courses, and the publication of technological information in the popular press.[6]

Like Bukharin, many members of the Communist Party during the late twenties and early thirties had called for the need to fund organizations that would better satisfy the technical-educational needs of workers on the shop floor. Furthermore, they argued that the party needed to support the efforts of those science popularizers who focused on the technical needs of the new working class. N. Krupskaia and V. Sverdlov were two important Communist Party members involved in mass-technical enlightenment during this period. They were part of the organizational group that formed the voluntary society TekhMass. At a November 1927 meeting of the organizational committee of the society, Krupskaia argued that a national organization like TekhMass was needed in order to spread the latest movements in technology to the widest audience possible throughout the USSR. She argued that Soviet scientists and engineers had an obligation to write popular-technical works and serve as consultants at factories to answer workers' questions.[7] She echoed others in the party who believed that scientists must serve the working class by providing practical technical advice to laborers.

The initial plan of the society included organizing popular-science reading circles, lectures, and consultations in factories on all technical subjects. The society also organized an editorial board to create close ties with publishers in order to produce popular-scientific works. The board especially worked toward creation of technological sections in existing popular journals, particularly those aimed at workers.[8]

TekhMass was organized as an all-union voluntary society to spread and popularize technological and scientific information, and cells of the society were primarily organized within factories. Though the organization was based in Moscow, it had an important early branch located in Leningrad. The society would eventually have branches in republics all over the former Soviet Union, including Khar'kov, Minsk, Tbilisi, and Ashkhabad. Since key members of VARNITSO had helped organize TekhMass, they held most of the important central posts at the society's headquarters in Moscow. The chairman of the organization was V. M. Sverdlov, president of the All-Union Association of Engineers. Other prominent members of the society included biologists M. M. and B. M. Zavadovskii, A. N. Bakh, and N. Krupskaia.[9] According to a 1928 survey, most of the leading members of the group were Communist Party members and had joined the party either before or just after the 1917 revolution during the Civil War era. They also held significant positions in the Soviet trade-union structure or in Narkompros, or they were directors of technical institutes.[10]

From its inception, TekhMass had been involved in popularizing scientific and technical information. In 1928 the Moscow branch of the society organized a series of lectures in factories by various scientists including the Zavadovskiis. The title of the series of popular-scientific lectures was "The Meaning of Science in the Period of Construction," reflecting the orientation of the society (and the Communist Party) in this era of hyper-industrialization.[11] A cycle of lectures prepared for various Moscow factories emphasized the practical applications of technological and scientific theory. The lectures focused on the technological applications in various industrial efforts, including the chemical, food, metal, and textile industries.[12]

The society worked closely with the Moscow provincial political-enlightenment department on a program of scientific courses for workers in people's universities. These were general courses in the evenings on natural-scientific and physical-mathematical topics. The society worked with the Moscow Komsomol on spreading scientific information among the youth of the city. The society also networked among other voluntary enlightenment organizations in the city to develop science-education programs.[13]

The Leningrad oblast section of TekhMass became one of the largest branches of the society. It had been quite active during the course of 1928 and 1929, and by 1930 it had over fifty thousand members. The Leningrad oblast branch emphasized enhancing workers' qualifications and the training of new cadres in various polytechnic courses sponsored by the society. Between late 1930 and early 1931 alone, over eleven thousand new, first-time TekhMass students studied in these courses. Workers at over 183 Leningrad factories took part in various scientific and technical courses conducted by TekhMass, including the factories of Krasnyi Putilovets and also Krasnyi Treugol'nik.[14]

In the TekhMass circles at factories in Leningrad, instructors encountered a variety of telling problems. Sometimes workers were not prepared for a given level of scientific instruction. Because courses were taught mostly at production sites, the classes sometimes met irregularly, and good textbooks were in short supply.[15] Despite such problems, the Leningrad Oblast and City Party Committee maintained that by late 1931, TekhMass had registered over forty-three thousand students in their courses.[16] That number, of course, does not take into account the large numbers who attended organized lectures, technical evenings, and film showings.

At TekhMass national conventions held in Moscow, open discussion occurred among delegates concerning various problems regarding technical education in Stalin's Russia. The delegates included both Communist leaders of the organization, including Sverdlov, as well as those directors and factory foremen who had more hands-on experience with problems on the shop floor. At a February 28, 1928, convention of the organization in Moscow, Sverdlov argued that raising the level of Soviet economic production was only part of the problem the USSR had to face. According to Sverdlov, economic organizations and institutions in the past paid little attention to technical education and issues of the popularization of science at the shop-floor level.[17] I. Berman, the general secretary of TekhMass, took this concern one step further by fervently arguing that production was completely detached from the technical level of workers and peasants in the country. He mentioned as an example that tractors and other new farm equipment would be pouring into the countryside without anyone there who had the ability to repair or properly run this machinery.[18]

Other delegates to the conference, especially teachers, managers, and collective farm administrators, were less abstract in their comments and urged delegates to understand the basic needs of workers and peasants. One delegate read letters sent to him from peasants and workers expressing what they believed was needed in the area of Soviet mass-technical education outside of formal institutions. Several of the letters pointed to an inability to follow complicated books on technology and even basic manuals for repair of machinery.[19] Another delegate—named Timokhov, a foreman in a metalworkers factory—argued that technical books and pamphlets in the workers'-clubs libraries in the factories were generally not written in a colloquial or accessible language. Timokhov believed that books for metalworkers were geared to the most highly skilled masters and not to the semiskilled workers who were then flooding into the factories.[20] He based his criticisms on discussions with metalworkers, as well as on the complaints they wrote down and passed to him and factory directors. He argued that even when workers' clubs organized courses, only the apprentices of masters would come. *Stazhery* (trainees), according to Timokhov, felt intimidated at these settings, which only contributed to the lack of communication between the masters and new workers.[21]

Workers, and even some peasants on collective farms, literally bombarded local authorities and TekhMass leaders with complaints and advice on better ways to construct technical educational material for the public. At the February 1928 conference in Moscow, many delegates read to participants countless letters sent to them. One of the delegates exclaimed that workers and peasants had been writing TekhMass representatives complaining about the lack of accessible textbooks on general topics in the natural sciences and technology. The delegate reiterated earlier statements at the conference bemoaning the lack of specific manuals on the maintenance of machinery in urban and rural areas. Some of the letters were anonymous, but others were signed. One TekhMass delegate read a series of anonymous letters he had received from peasants. One typical letter from a peasant read as follows: "Scientists and educators need to make books and pamphlets which have practical use and purpose. For example, you could write pamphlets instructing us on how to construct better and more efficient water wells and shafts."[22] Another peasant sent a letter with the following observation and request: "We are interested in articles and even pamphlets explaining how we can accurately build well shafts and then connect them together in sequence—please write in your journals about practical matters such as this, which affect our daily lives. Engineers need to show how basic mathematics and geometry classes can apply to practical construction needs."[23]

To address the educational needs of workers more effectively, the organization decided to introduce a system whereby participants in Tekh-Mass night classes, lectures, and seminars would fill out questionnaires, which asked for basic information such as age, skill, and educational level. The questionnaire included ample room at the end for participants to explain why they attended sessions and what their educational goals were. The responses to this questionnaire reveal workers' aspirations during this tumultuous time of rapid migration of semiskilled laborers into the urban work force.

Most of the respondents had finished, on average, approximately five to six years of schooling, and the level of writing and grammatical structure of their responses is generally low. Many who came to the classes—the age varied from the late teens through the early thirties—were working temporarily in heavy industries, like the metalworks. All respondents were forthright in their demands and needs, many wanting to be masters or skilled metalworkers and some expressing interest in training for positions in new electrical-power stations. Many indicated that seasonal work in the factories was inadequate for them financially and that they wanted to better their qualifications for permanent positions in specific industries. Their responses expressed a desire to settle into a permanent trade, instead of moving from job to job. Many answered that they would not be satisfied with simply fulfilling their qualifications for jobs, but would like to continue in night courses once they found permanent jobs.[24] These workers were not shortsighted in the least and realized the potential for social mobility if they chose to further their education consistently. However, they also displayed a vivacious drive to expand their scientific and technical knowledge base.

Because some participants were only semiliterate, a single worker sometimes filled out a questionnaire in the name of several of his coworkers. One such response came indirectly in this way from M. K. Nikolovich, a seasonal cabinet maker with only four years of schooling. He answered that many workers "wanted to learn an industrial specialty such as metal work because the job would be yearlong and interesting, while most of our work is seasonal." He went on to say that "if I can get the qualifications to work in a metal factory, I would still want to continue my technical studies at night, especially if they were at or near the factory."[25]

Many respondents certainly wanted to receive enough practical instruction to gain the necessary qualifications that were prerequisites for the permanent job of their choice. A. I. Kolobaev, a sixteen-year-old *stazher*, had no real specialty training and only four years of formal education when he enrolled in the TekhMass night courses. Kolobaev wanted to learn how to improve his skill at operating a metal lathe, his father being a lathe operator with the requisite qualifications. He responded in his questionnaire that "I want to know as much as I can about operating a lathe, and receive the qualifications so that I can perform this trade for some time to come."[26] Many of the respondents, although eager to learn, were certainly obsessed and focused on acquiring their requisite qualifications, either to advance in the factory or to move off the shop floor into the new universities and technical schools for workers.

Victor M. Kulikovskii, a twenty-eight-year-old metal worker with nine years of formal education, wanted to learn a more specialized part of his trade. However, he was not particularly satisfied with the limited knowledge he had of metalwork, and he came to the TekhMass classes to learn more scientific theory, perhaps even to get into an advanced technical school or university. On his questionnaire, he wrote: "I want to continue further in my part-time studies and even get the necessary qualifications to enter a higher technical school or university."[27] Kulikovskii reflected on how workers, though exhausted, were still driven to study at night in science classes that could offer them the basic theory they missed because they had not completed their primary or secondary education. His enthusiasm echoed the strivings of other workers who also came to these courses to learn not just practical applied science, but also to take classes on leisure topics like "the technical aspects of photography," which integrated chemical and physical principles into the study of photographic technique. Courses in photography provided workers with an understanding of how light spectra and ionization of chemical elements affected photographic paper and images. In this way, Tekhmass instructors could promote a type of utilitarian physics and chemistry through the medium of a leisure activity.

The variety of short courses and technical aid that TekhMass members offered to workers throughout Soviet Russia was impressive. The curricula varied from courses focusing on basic scientific educational themes, such as algebra or calculus, to more vocational, technical courses like electro-welding technique. They met in a variety of venues including factories after hours, local school houses at night, and buildings procured by the society. Detailed lesson plans and curricula, unfortunately, have not survived in the archival record, but records do exist that suggest broad programs of study, as well as the extensive nature of course offerings.

TekhMass cells were set up all over industrial Russia, not just in the major capital cities of Moscow and Leningrad. For example, by April of 1928 an active cell was set up in the city of Penza. On the one hand, this cell broke up its course offerings into basic extension learning: courses in algebra, geometry, physics, and basic arithmetic. However, on the other hand, it also ran an extensive technical, vocational program of courses, including electro-welding, properties of metals, and elementary principles of electrical engineering. Hobby courses, including photography, proved popular in Penza, and the society's courses built technological concepts into that part of the curriculum as well. According to the Penza cell's records, a course taught in the Spring of 1928 on amateur photo-developing proved particularly popular among local workers with little access to expensive photographic equipment or darkrooms, and the course frequently had a waiting list. At the Revolution Factory in Penza, a workers' inventors *kruzhok* (circle) was also well attended. Local engineers (in this case volunteer members of TekhMass) were encouraged by Soviet officials to evaluate the amateur inventions of workers during the early Stalin era. The workshop setting at the Revolution Factory was particularly valuable to workers who could get expert advice on the technical drawbacks of their inventions and proposals. Even though it met at night, the inventors workshop was well attended and fostered lively interaction between amateurs and technical specialists.[28]

On the middle Volga and centered in Samara, TekhMass formed a branch of its society in August of 1928. By January of 1930 it had 258 cells in various surrounding towns and registered over twenty-one thousand members. In the course of the years 1929 to 1930, it provided formal technology lectures, technical workshops, and short courses. They registered over 123,000 students and visitors combined to these varied events. Members of the organization were especially helpful in setting up a *Dom Tekhniki* (House of Technology) in Samara to serve as both a headquarters for TekhMass cells and as a central place to hold night classes and lectures. The House of Technology, sponsored voluntarily by TekhMass members, had a darkroom (with photographic equipment), a medium-sized auditorium, and rooms for workshops and classes.[29]

In outlying areas in Russia and in the industrial regions of other Soviet Republics, TekhMass circles developed more slowly than in the central industrial capital cities. Sometimes problems in leadership and organization, as well as with the membership, created stumbling blocks for activists. For instance, in a TekhMass branch in the Ukraine formed in 1929–30 and centered in Khar'kov, several visiting central members found in 1930 that the branch lacked any clear organizational leadership. TekhMass was quite extensively established in that part of the Ukraine, registering almost 150,000 members spread out over 300 cells. However, members complained that leaders of cells were generally party officials who were burdened with other tasks and found little time to organize workshops and lectures for local factory workers.[30]

TekhMass cells were organized even in industrial areas of the Urals, such as the city of Sverdlovsk, where the first cell was established in April of 1930. In 1930 and 1931 membership recruitment was quite low compared to other industrial centers in Soviet Russia, with totals for the Sverdlovsk center registering less than ten thousand individuals. There were also complaints from new members that administrative direction of the cells was weak in the Urals.[31]

As in the case of the Ukraine, central TekhMass officials were dispatched from Moscow to various "troubled" areas to deal with problems between rank-and-file members and local leadership. In 1931 central-administrative members were sent to the Ural branch headquarters in Sverdlovsk. Their advice was to develop better networks among the TekhMass cells of other large industrial centers in the Urals. In this case they argued for the need to coordinate activity between Magnitogorsk and Sverdlovsk cells. They also suggested that in areas such as the Urals, where the various cells could be spread out along great distances, the need was acute to get local Communist Party and Komsomol officials to help TekhMass financially and administratively.[32]

Regardless of the geographic position of these cells, dispersed throughout Soviet Russia in the early 1930s, TekhMass classes were well attended by workers and fulfilled a niche to aid laborers with limited educational training. This was especially true in outlying areas where cells were set up in disparate towns over a large geographic area. Many workers at the time saw these courses as a route out of the factory; and TekhMass could provide them with specific qualifications, much like the earlier Rabfak (worker preparatory school) had done. The TekhMass night courses were very attractive to those workers who were eager to continue, even after they received ample training to pass qualification standards.

M. V. Vasilievich, an eighteen-year-old, part-time laborer, echoed the intentions of many participants when he wrote on his questionnaire at a Moscow night-course, "I have already sat through the course to prepare for the metalworks, yet I definitely want to continue my studies."[33] Vasilievich, with only four years of formal education, was just one of many participants who needed the training that a voluntary organization like TekhMass could offer. He found even basic remedial courses in chemistry, physics, and mathematics to be essential building blocks in furthering his education. Vasilievich found the routine difficult, especially going to class after work; he pointed out, however, that this was the only way nontraditional, working students could get access to quality education.[34]

Whatever the problems and difficulties, such workers were willing, at least temporarily, to sit through the night courses to better their chances for continual employment and improved future prospects. Nevertheless, workers had explicit and practical criticisms for the way the classes and sessions were organized, and they conveyed those concerns in countless letters directed to officials of the voluntary scientific societies and, in some cases, in their responses to questionnaires concerning their experiences in the courses. Workers were hoping to find valuable educational resources that would benefit their jobs directly and functionally and, by and large, supported the courses offered by these societies. Yet the party eventually saw these voluntary societies as conveyors of both practical knowledge and propagandistic messages of the virtues of Soviet socialist industrialization. The Stalinist state was going to support movements that encouraged utilitarian, technological enlightenment for the working class. The Communist Party was also looking to these groups to spread and embrace a new vision of a society that was offering technology for all within the context of a rapidly industrializing economy. In this sense, popular technology was blazing a new Stalinist vision for Soviet society.

THE STALINIST STATE AND THE MASTERING OF TECHNOLOGY, 1931–34

As the FFYP progressed, the advancement of workers' qualifications and the training of industrial cadres became a central task of the Communist Party and the Soviet state. This shift in responsibility became especially important because of the massive migration of unskilled peasants into cities and industry. Though elementary and secondary schooling had spread tremendously during the early Stalinist era, older peasants and workers did not benefit from those formal educational initiatives. In 1931, to combat technical illiteracy, Stalin and the party unleashed the propaganda slogan "The Bolsheviks Should Master Technology." Workers (and specialists) were told to deepen their knowledge of science and technology to aid the country in its massive industrialization plan. In 1931, especially in Moscow and Leningrad, many institutions including TekhMass and VARNITSO became involved in the new movement to spread technical education.[35]

In accordance with this campaign for mass-technical education, the party devised a new propaganda slogan: *Za Ovladenie Tekhnikoi* (for the mastering of technology). The slogan heralded a national effort throughout the USSR that was widely editorialized in the press. In 1932, therefore, TekhMass changed its name to Obshchestva Za Ovladenie Tekhnikoi. ZOT continued the work of TekhMass but now carried out more specific requests of the party. Their assignments included the formation of technical circles at factories, the purpose of which was to introduce new technology to workers. The party also insisted that the teaching of workers stress how new technology could be applied to various branches of industry. By 1931–32 the party had begun the process of harnessing these voluntary societies to work toward increasing the number of qualified workers and specialists in industry. In many respects, from that time onward, educating and training workers and specialists became the principal task of the voluntary societies.[36]

In Leningrad the oblast and city party committees instructed Communist Party members to volunteer their time to help ZOT form cells in a variety of factories throughout the city. With the help of the party, by May 1932 the Leningrad Branch of ZOT claimed it had over sixty-eight thousand members. ZOT organized, in that year alone, over sixty-eight new circles in factories, registering thousands of students. The Leningrad branch of ZOT estimated that during the second half of 1932 alone over thirty thousand people had participated in ZOT lectures, film evenings, technical courses and a variety of other mass-educational activities. Although fulfilling similar functions as the earlier TekhMass had done, ZOT was now much more infused with party cadres and with initiatives from above.[37]

Like its predecessor TekhMass, ZOT attempted to use more-traditional means for spreading new technical information among Soviet laborers. The society worked with party and state publishing houses to produce pamphlets, books, and handouts on varied technological processes, trying to target particular sectors of the work force in different ways. For instance, it set up a cooperative venture with the Komsomol's publishing house Molodaia Gvardia to create a series of technical encyclopedias, which became popular among young apprentices in certain trades and industries. The volumes published in late 1932 focused on an array of practical technical topics such as metallurgy, machine-tool building, transportation industries, energy, and basic chemical processes. These encyclopedias generally related basic science-educational topics to practical branches of industry, stressing how productive, technical knowledge could be applied to the Soviet economy.[38]

What distinguished ZOT's activities from its predecessor TekhMass was the emphasis on propagating popular images of how Soviet technology would soon advance beyond the capitalist West's capabilities. ZOT had a particularly well organized subsection, its "Agit-Mass" sector, which by 1932 had links with the Communist Party's Central Committee Agit-Prop department. To engage the public's interest, ZOT's Agit-Prop sector organized technology-film and discussion nights.

ZOT's Agit-Prop department was particularly interested in expanding its film section to create films on an array of technical themes. For ZOT film was a medium by which Soviet technology could be glorified in the early Stalinist era. The department worked with other Soviet institutions creating specific types of technical films relating to various sectors of the economy. Indeed, all the films involved the application of technology to sectors of the Soviet economy. Early on, for example, the ZOT department worked in conjunction with Narkomzem (Ministry of Agriculture) to produce a series of films on the application of new technology to agricultural production. Over time, ZOT produced films on a variety of technical topics such as "Aviation and Air Flight," "Paper and Polygraph Industry," "Hydrotechnics," and "Electrification and the USSR." The films were Agit-Technical productions, and from ZOT's standpoint they had both a propagandistic and educational importance.[39]

By February of 1933 ZOT worked jointly with the Tekhfilm (technical film) section of Mosfilm. They produced new, short documentary-style educational films of Soviet technological feats. ZOT, in turn, formed its own film section, with members of Tekhfilm joining the ranks of ZOT on a voluntary basis.[40] Tekhfilm representatives advised ZOT on creating films with wide appeal that could capture topics in which the Soviet government had invested huge capital resources. ZOT members immediately chose to focus on electro-welding, in which millions of rubles had been invested during the FFYP alone, noting that higher educational and technical school curricula had included electro-welding technique and theory for only a year or two. Topics emphasized during the just-completed FFYP, such as machine-tool building and natural-resource potential, were especially appealing to ZOT members who believed that such themes were easily transferable to documentary film and accessible to the average worker interested in learning new techniques.[41]

ZOT films were generally followed by discussion sessions at a local factory, where workers were invited to air their views on the importance of the topic or elaborate on their critique of the films. Much like the TekhMass questionnaires, the transcripts from the discussions are a penetrating source for gauging workers' interests and opinions regarding the popularization of technology. Some workers found the films of great instructional value, while others were concerned that they were not educational in their orientation at all. Those participants complained that the films only espoused the virtues of Soviet industrialization instead of focusing on educational development.

Transcripts of one particular discussion night on July 25, 1933, in the Moscow Stalin Factory No. 1, are instructive. Six hundred workers from three factories who had already seen the film entitled "Electrical Welding" packed into the auditorium for the discussion event. TekhMass volunteers were pleased by the attendance but concerned about the critical and combative interplay between participants and teachers. Eager workers attended both the film and discussion nights; however, they were mainly interested in those portions relating to their daily jobs, not cinematic praise of Soviet industrial accomplishment. Practical technological films appealed to new workers eager to supplement their spotty educational background. A worker from Stalin Factory No. 1 said, "I am a beginner to this trade, and the film showed in a detailed fashion how other factories operate beyond my own. After watching this film, it has been easier for me to continue learning new welding techniques."[42]

Other welders, though, were highly critical of the film's educational value. One electro-welder commented, "I study the welding of non-ferrous and imperfect metals. I came here to the films and night classes to learn more about this technique. The film did not tell me anything about that technique, and I learned nothing in general."[43] An engineer who saw the film argued that the factual information regarding the technical process of welding was simply insufficient. He suggested the production of films that were more instructive and that might be accompanied by handouts or manuals when explaining the use of new machines. Other skilled engineers also participated in the criticism of ZOT's efforts. Several expressed the view that ZOT films were not generated as educational material but designed more as newsreels extolling new Soviet industrial developments.[44] A new member of the ZOT film department ended the discussion with a summary of what he saw as the film's problems and a list of workers' complaints concerning ZOT's activities in general. He said that it "is obvious to many here today that these films are generally too "popular." It is necessary to view a film that will really increase our workers' qualifications. We don't need to hear about the "advantages" of electro-welding in the Soviet Union, but need a film that is capable of giving workers a technical understanding of the process they are interested in learning more about."[45]

At other discussion evenings following ZOT instructional films, similar complaints were heard time and time again. On December 9, 1933, at the "Red Proletariat" machine-tool factory in Moscow, over one hundred workers critically discussed the film shown earlier entitled "Machine Tool Industry in the USSR." Before the discussion began, a Communist Party member gave a short introductory lecture on the importance of film in technical instruction. Neither the lecture nor the film, for that matter, was well received by the attending workers. One worker argued fervently "that this film did not really explain anything very carefully. These ZOT films insufficiently describe how to properly work new machines, and most of us get very little out of them."[46] Another worker argued that "we demand instructional films that will educate us properly. Many of the machines you show us do not even exist yet in our machine-tool factory. Therefore none of this can be applied to our everyday job routine."[47] Workers who were more skilled and seasoned expressed the view that such films would leave the misleading impression on new workers that the level of Soviet machine-tool manufacture was far more advanced than it, in fact, was. All the same, workers consistently showed enthusiasm for lectures, films, and discussion nights—a remarkable fact given their exhaustion at the end of long days at their factory jobs. Equally remarkable is the freedom they felt in boldly criticizing what they saw as any attempt to use technical classes to valorize Soviet technology at the expense of workers' education.

Although workers' responses to ZOT films and lectures varied, on the whole they consistently expressed complaints regarding the applicability of the films to their job environment. Many found the films too extolling of Soviet industry instead of practically instructional of fundamental processes regarding new technology that might affect their lives more directly. Others complained that the films were not organized well and should be accompanied with handouts and pamphlets describing machines more carefully. Even Communist Party and ZOT members themselves expressed the view that the films needed to be more educational and instructional on a practical level. Party members were frank and openly critical in suggesting how institutions could learn from the criticisms of workers, while engineers openly criticized the vacuous nature of propaganda films and pamphlets that were not well suited to technical, educational seminars.

Nevertheless, even after the miserable failure of its own scientific and antireligious campaigns, Agit-Prop saw in ZOT a window of opportunity to purvey Soviet technical propaganda. What might have produced another failure in that regard actually achieved some degree of success, from Agit-Prop's point of view. To this degree, the Soviet state and the Communist Party showed adept flexibility in harnessing the efforts of voluntary groups as in the NEP era. The difference in this case was that TekhMass and ZOT members were typically associated, not at odds, with the state's goals and usually Communist in their political orientation. Even though they technically represented independent radical voluntary associations, their agendas converged with those of the state.

Something else had happened that was not anticipated by either the Soviet state or mass propagandists. The new technical associations attracted many semiskilled workers who found the societies useful as apolitical means to acquire technical education outside of formal institutions, to better their qualifications, and to integrate themselves permanently into factory life. Furthermore, many of these workers found the new Stalinist "technical vision" to be overlapping with their practical educational needs. To some extent there was a convergence of party vision with practical needs on the shop floor.

In retrospect one can view these Communist voluntary societies from a number of perspectives. They can be seen either as transmission belts for the industrial propaganda of the era of the FFYP or, alternatively, as arenas in which workers could engage specialists and gain technical qualifications they lacked. In this way the workers interacted with these organizations in their own utilitarian and "productive" fashion. Furthermore, workers' responses and initiatives from below encouraged both party and nonparty specialists to question their educational methods, even during a time when the imposition of Stalinist cultural norms from above was overbearing. Indeed, that open dialogue attests not only to the remarkable ability of workers to define their own interests during the early Stalinist era, but also indicates their ability to engage authorities outside the state bureaucracy in a limited fashion. When ZOT's film nights started to look more and more like stagnant Agit-Prop evenings, workers emphatically told ZOT members that the approach was unproductive, and they were heard.

Ultimately, on the one hand, the educational goals of Communist organizers in these societies were fulfilled to a limited extent. They offered technical advice and education to needy individuals who fell through the cracks of the educational system for a variety of reasons. On the other hand, they served the ideological goals of the Stalinist state by eventually providing the message to the masses that Stalinist culture would be defined not just by economic progress, but by the "technological advancement" of the class providing the regime its base of support since the Revolution of 1917. Stalinist culture was driven to create an industrialized society enveloped in a modernistic technological future. TekhMass, Technology for the Masses, therefore, carried this double meaning: practical technological education for the people and the propagandistic vision of a technologically advanced USSR.

CONCLUSION

The Shop Floor as the Temple of Science

The science-popularization movement began in Russia in the eighteenth century when scholars in the Academy of Sciences saw the importance of spreading scientific ideas among the public. Enlightened publishers, like Nikolai Novikov, then followed in the traditions of their European intellectual counterparts and spread progressive scientific ideas and information through their newly established presses. Much of the early publishing of popular-scientific works was sponsored by groups like the Russian Freemasons, who shared a common vision about the importance of science, progress, and popular education.

In the nineteenth century the science-popularization movement became closely tied to the development of adult education in Russia. People from all walks of Russian life became involved in the movement, including educators, publishers, journalists, and of course scientists themselves. The broadly based participation indicated the multifaceted aspects of the movement, but also how popularizers did not represent a single cohort, corporate identity, or political orientation. Scientific societies became an integral part of the movement and helped spread scientific ideas through the journals they formed and museums they opened in both the central and provincial cities of Russia. By the turn of the twentieth century, the popular-scientific journal, particularly, became a potent means of popularizing scientific ideas. It was a cheap and accessible source of scientific information for a variety of social groups.

In the prerevolutionary era, the Russian intelligentsia believed in the importance of spreading scientific ideas beyond the walls of academe. Well-known Russian scientists, such as V. Obruchev and V. Vernadskii, took much time away from their academic work to participate in the movement. They enthusiastically wrote popular-scientific articles for journals and newspapers and edited popular-scientific books and series. Vernadskii and others imparted the importance of popularization to their students, A. E. Fersman for one, who carried on the tradition of popular education in the sciences. Russian scientists dating back to the era of Peter the Great had pursued extroverted, civic agendas.

In the pre-1917 period, Russian readers were eager to purchase popular-scientific books and journals. A significant demand developed among the reading public for scientific information, and popular journals proliferated in the late tsarist era offering readers information on astronomy, air flight, new technology, and world geography. Russian workers were keenly interested in expanding their elementary technical and scientific education, while Russian professionals in a variety of fields wanted information that could supplement their expertise.

After the October Revolution, the Soviet Commissariat of Enlightenment generously sponsored the popular-enlightenment activities of scientific societies, museums, and editorial boards. Although there were across-the-board cutbacks in state subsidies during the NEP era, the state managed to provide scientific societies with the majority of their working budgets. Policies of the NEP did not dictate a wholesale abandonment of funding for voluntary and public scientific organizations, and scientific societies successfully lobbied Glavnauka, the Scientific Department of the Ministry of Enlightenment, called Narkompros, for funding. In doing so, they used the very rhetorical catch-phrases that the Soviet state itself emphasized in its own cultural-enlightenment campaigns. This politically correct dialogue created an interesting symbiosis between Soviet state institutions and the remnants of the prerevolutionary scientific intelligentsia. As the twenties progressed, however, the relationship between Glavnauka and scientific societies (especially in the provinces) grew more complicated as Narkompros imposed more bureaucratic constraints on these institutions. Bolshevik methods of state *kontrol'* led eventually to a hegemonic power struggle between local scientists and the political center in the early Stalinist era. Paradoxically, however, prerevolutionary organizations for most of the NEP period benefited greatly from this precarious, yet relatively stable, relationship.

Furthermore, key individual Bolshevik leaders, such as Lenin, Lunacharskii, and Petrov, supported the concept of science popularization and of initiating programs at the federal level. Lunacharskii himself personally intervened on numerous occasions on behalf of distinguished prerevolutionary intellectuals, like B. Raikov, and for the sake of a whole array of scientific organizations. The tensions between local societies, on the one hand, and the bureaus of central government, on the other, even produced institutional conflict within the Soviet state itself. Different Bolshevik administrators had varying perspectives on cultural change, and they used the institutions they controlled to combat rival proposals. Perhaps the best example of this internecine bureaucratic warfare developed between Narkompros's

Lunacharskii and Glavnauka's Petrov, on one side, and the Supreme Council of the National Economy (Vesenkha), on the other. However, the Soviet state as a whole saw the importance of maintaining nongovernmental institutions to spread science in society, as well as the significance of that form of education for economic and industrial utility. The Bolsheviks envisaged science popularization as an essential element in their cultural revolution and transformation of Russian society. Making science accessible to the masses became part of the great modernizing paradigm that Bolsheviks would stress well into the Stalinist era: the tsarist past as scientifically backward, the socialist future as radiant and technologically advanced.

The Soviet central government supported an antireligious campaign during the 1920s that was less combative toward believers and more oriented toward spreading scientific information and evolutionary thought as means of progressive education. Agit-Prop's antireligious activists, as well as the voluntary *bezbozhniki,* understood the importance of tempering the ideological side of antireligion and injecting that effort instead with basic scientific education. They envied the success of private scientific societies and urged their own activists to emulate those prerevolutionary scientific groups who were captivating the attention of Russian citizens. Although the Communist Party failed miserably in its effort to convert the societies into vehicles of political propaganda, it nevertheless proved resilient and adaptive. A part of that resilience was manifested in its willingness to work with supposed "bourgeois" scientific intellectuals in the 1920s. Indeed, during the NEP, the regime urged non-Communist Russian intellectuals, particularly, to promote popular-scientific information.

As it had in Western Europe, popular science caught the imagination of the general public in Russia during the early years of Soviet power throughout the 1920s, and, as a result, popular-scientific journals flourished. As the journals continued to offer the reader a broad spectrum of themes and trends in science, a convergence developed between a cosmopolitan reading public in the 1920s and a Soviet state eager to popularize scientific and technical information on global developments, even if it meant laudatory commentary on capitalist technological ingenuity. Even the Communist Party journals were filled with the same type of information as that appearing in the non-party journals. Both contained material on Western technology and inventions, and both seemed to compete for the interest of the reader. Readers from varied social groups bought these journals for different reasons. Professionals sought out information about their fields, students looked for material they could not always find in traditional curricula, and workers sought out information for understanding new technologies at their workplace. Members of all of these social groups shared a sincere fascination with learning more about a variety of scientific themes: the cosmos, air flight, geography. Journals, museums, and books served as conduits through which this information reached the public.

Scientists after 1917 took part in civic organizations that continued to foster public engagement with science education, and those educators were active in developing public enlightenment outside the Soviet state's control. Though many of these organizations were registered with the Soviet state, they continued to develop public discussion of scientific ideas in an independent fashion. This scientific public sphere would be even more hotly contested in Stalin's Russia, though unfortunately dramatically curtailed by the mid-1930s. Open discussion of scientific topics was indicative of how vibrant that scientific public sphere was after the Bolshevik Revolution of 1917 and throughout the NEP era. Though institutionally and financially dependent on Glavnauka, scientific societies were able to maintain independent programs and foster their own plan of civic action, at least in the 1920s.

With the advent of the Stalinist cultural revolution after 1928, however, the focus of science popularization underwent a radical change. The cultural signifiers or scientific tropes that the regime stressed after 1928 were more oriented toward utilitarian technological feats of the Soviet state. Technology had to serve the laboring masses and the Soviet state's class-oriented economic and sociological agendas. In addition technology had to be inextricably linked to the developing economy and expanding industrial infrastructure. All of these cultural symbols had equivalent institutional campaigns designed to isolate and ostracize the older generation of enlightened intellectuals.

Radical organizations such as VARNITSO threw traditional scientific societies and institutions on the defensive. Editors of journals and science newsletters refashioned and purged their editorial boards, offering new cohorts of authors the chance to write articles valorizing Soviet technology and its application to industry and planned economics. Provincial scientific societies came under pressure to conform to more standardized norms, and many were subsumed under larger regional and central administrative structures. New Communist organizations, TekhMass being the outstanding example, competed with older scientific groups while offering the Soviet laborer night classes on the shop floor.

The Communist Party's Stalinist platform of workers "should master technology" was an inherent part of many of the lengthy editorial remarks by the editors of many science journals. Furthermore, editors stressed articles that invoked the importance not just of Soviet, indigenous inventors, but those who specifically came from working-class backgrounds. Workers and the new *praktiki* would be leading the Soviet technological revolution; they received encouragement from central regime agencies above and were supported from below by young Communist engineers and scientific specialists during the FFYP.

The face and the mind of Bolshevism had taken on a new cultural mask. Stalinism was offering the public new technological temples to ponder: the shop floor and the practical, technical knowledge embedded in its walls. The application of science and technology to industry, and especially its use by the new factory labor force, defined the parameters under which science educators were instructed to operate. Furthermore, Stalinism was slowly, from the period 1928 up to 1934, becoming more myopic, isolationist, and certainly less cosmopolitan, in the European sense of the word. Even though during the cultural revolution, editorials still peripherally mentioned Western technology and inventions, they focused primarily on Soviet technological feats and achievements. On the eve of the Kirov Affair in 1934, Russia was slowly closing itself off from the outside world, particularly with respect to the dissemination of scientific information to the public.

The nationalistic cultural themes of the Stalinist thirties affected the writing of popular-scientific articles. This was particularly evident in the glorification of Soviet aviation in the popular journals of the 1930s. Soviet science, technological prowess, and popular nationalism provided a potent nexus for understanding the culture of the Stalinist era. The regime favored supporting an advanced, technological revolution that would simultaneously open up the doors of the scientific temple to all who chose to enter. Before 1934 TekhMass and other similar organizations maintained a dynamic presence in the system while bringing complicated technological education in a simplified manner to the masses on the shop floor. Furthermore, the new Stalinist working class had a strong interest in popular technological information that could help them at their work. They were keenly interested in promoting their own self-education and progress up the social ladder. Although they were critical of the pedagogical methods of propagandistic organizations, as well as the propaganda of the regime itself, workers still expressed a vivacious interest in technological information. From that perspective, workers acted similarly across the 1928 divide, as they continued to search out non-institutional educational means to develop their base of technical knowledge, just as they had done before 1917 and then under the NEP.

The Stalinist regime, however, imposed constrained limits on popular science and technological education from 1928 onward. That very regime tried to control TekhMass and similar radical technological organizations after 1931, attaching them to broad Stalinist cultural conveyor belts. Public science, in the early Stalinist era, indeed went on the defensive as it was attacked from above and below. Central and provincial scientific societies and organizations were particularly criticized for not linking their institutions to campaigns to help the developing industrial economy. Communist Party Agit-Prop activists tried to infiltrate voluntary organizations like ZOT, using them for their own purpose and agenda. This had real consequences for editorial boards, volunteer organizations, and public science in general.

Nevertheless, the new Communist organizations and their associated activists believed broadly in the Stalinist regime's vision of making technology accessible to the widest possible audience. Technological film nights and agitational lectures bred a revolutionary dynamism, though at times a dynamism born of worker frustration and criticism. The work of these organizations remained inclusive, as they reached out to Soviet laborers in an effort to encourage them to take part in technological change. The technological revolution still had a vision of science and technology as the ultimate transformers of modern culture. Though thematically more prescribed and constrained than in the earlier period of the 1920s, the technical information the new Communist organizations propagated was not always filled with empty platitudes. Actually, many of the films and lectures they presented discussed practical scientific issues that workers devoured voraciously, even after a long day of work. Although workers shunned, and sometimes slept through, the party's Agit-Prop lectures after work, they nevertheless approached Tekh-Mass activities with a keen interest sensing the value of technical education for their future.

The new Communist technological popularization after 1928 maintained a semblance of the prerevolutionary missionary zeal to spread *nauka* to the people. However, the vision after 1928 varied in its approach toward enlightened principles and inclusive thematics in comparison to the pre-Stalinist era. Stalinism and its industrialism bred a "technological future" that certainly gazed forward, yet left out parts of science that the broader public found interesting and imaginative. The more utilitarian thematics of the early Stalinist era, linking science to industrial productivity, marginalized more imaginative scientific themes. The diverse Russian readers of the 1920s had been cosmopolitan in their tastes, as they mimicked the interests of readers across continental Europe. Russian readers were particularly interested in news and information about foreign technology, air flight, astronomy, and global exploration. They consumed endless articles on daring feats of explorers, airplane pilots, and ethnographers from a variety of countries, including their own. At least in the twenties, the Bolsheviks supported this interest in international scientific and technological news and did not constrain its development as they did in the 1930s. Furthermore, the thematic content of science journals in the 1920s resembled the material in periodicals before

1917. Readers viewed such scientific information as practical, in the sense of advancing their knowledge, but also found the material engaging, lively, and part of their leisurely reading.

Stalinist industrial utilitarianism suppressed laudatory commentary on international, particularly Western, technological developments. Soviet intellectual introversion dissociated a vibrant, active science readership from its European counterpart. However, science popularization in the early Stalinist era continued to maintain the modernizing agenda it had developed immediately after the revolution. Furthermore, newly minted workers from the countryside streaming into the urban arenas found adult education in the sciences vital to their future. Early Stalinist culture, from the perspective of the changing tides of science enlightenment, was inherently paradoxical and seemed backward and constrained, yet also futuristic and visionary; myopic and anticosmopolitan, yet utilitarian and functional; directed and shaped by central bureaus from above, yet also supported and contested by the masses from below.

NOTES

For full bibliographical data, see the bibliography. Unless otherwise indicated, all translations of Russian records in the notes are by the author.

INTRODUCTION

1. Kendall Bailes in his biography of V. I. Vernadsky analyzes the interaction of science, politics, and culture in Revolutionary Russia, while focusing on Vernadsky's individual, scientific worldview and how it stood out as an alternative to Stalinist dogmatism. See Kendall E. Bailes, *Science and Russian Culture in an Age of Revolutions: V. I. Vernadsky and His Scientific School, 1863–1945* (1990).
2. Alexander Vucinich has looked at the importance of some early nineteenth-century professional scientific societies in his work but without primarily focusing on their contribution to public culture. See Alexander Vucinich, "Politics, Universities, and Science," in *Russia Under the Last Tsar*, ed. Theofanis George Stavrou (1969).
3. Loren Graham has edited a collection of essays (*Science and the Soviet Social Order*, ed. Loren R. Graham [1990]) that includes chapters on the relationship of science to Russian society and culture in the Soviet era. The essays by Katerina Clark and Richard Stites look at scientific thought in literature, including science fiction. Though they analyze the changing images of science and technology in Soviet literature, as well as the world outlook of Soviet science fiction, they do not comment on the public reception of science. For a broad analysis of science and Russian society, one can also refer to Graham's *Science in Russia and the Soviet Union* (1993), a voluminous overview of Russian science. In *Health and Society in Revolutionary Russia*, ed. Susan Gross Solomon and John F. Hutchinson (1990), Susan Solomon has looked at the relationship between Soviet social hygiene and public health in recent work.
4. Jeffrey P. Brooks, in his study of the literacy and tastes of Russian readers in the late tsarist era (*When Russia Learned to Read, Literacy and Popular Literature, 1861–1917* [1985]), briefly considers the relationship between science and superstition. Brooks, however, deals mostly with the chapbook publications influenced by Russian *lubok* (popular prints) and their influence on readers, not with the broader popularization of scientific thought.
5. See Richard Stites, *Revolutionary Dreams: Utopian Vision and Experimental Life in the Russian Revolution* (1989). For an analysis of the relationship between Bolshevik culture and Russian science fiction as a specific genre, see Richard Stites, "Fantasy and Revolution: Alexander Bogdanov and the Origins of Bolshevik Science Fiction" in Alexander Bogdanov, *Red Star: The First Bolshevik Utopia* (1984).
6. On occasion, and after much prodding by the Soviet state, they attempted to conduct mass-voluntary activity; however, according to Weiner (*A Little Corner of Freedom: Russian Nature Protection from Stalin to Gorbachev* [1999]) this was done mainly to convince the regime that they could take part in such Communist

activities. Nevertheless, Nathan Brooks ("Chemistry in War, Revolution, and Upheaval: Russia and the Soviet Union, 1900–1929" *Centaurus* [November 1997]) has shown convincingly that instead of fighting to maintain their "pure scientific pursuits," chemists, unlike ecologists and biologists, threw themselves wholeheartedly into the development of rapid industrialization of the economy during the early Stalinist era. Thus, one might need to look at histories of Russian scientific disciplines on a case-by-case basis.

7. For his broad analysis on science and the state in the late Imperial and early Soviet period, see chapter one of Nikolai Krementsov, *Stalinist Science* (1997).

8. For an insightful, analytical overview of the transitional qualities of the NEP period in Soviet Russia, see William Rosenberg, "Introduction: NEP Russia as a 'Transitional' Society," in *Russia in the Era of NEP,* ed. Sheila Fitzpatrick et al. (1991), 1–12.

9. Sheila Fitzpatrick argues that much of the revolutionary challenge in the cultural professions came "from below" or, more specifically, from militant atheists, Komsomol members, and Communist proletarian writers' groups ("The 'Soft' Line on Culture and its Enemies: Soviet Cultural Policy, 1922–1927," *Slavic Review* [June 1974]: 269).

10. Krementsov, *Stalinist Science,* 23–24.

11. For an analysis of the development of the Communist Academy and the Institute of Red Professors, see Michael David-Fox, *Revolution of the Mind: Higher Learning Amongst the Bolsheviks* (1997). In a recent article, however, David-Fox explores the premise that a new academic order only coalesced in Soviet Russia after a slow evolutionary process between 1917 and 1927 as "a result of a still incompletely understood historical conjuncture in scholarly, scientific, and educational life." See Michael David-Fox, "The Emergence of a 1920s Academic Order in Soviet Russia," *East-West Education* 18, no. 2 (fall 1997): 106–42.

12. See David Joravsky, *Soviet Marxism and Natural Science, 1917–1932.* (1961), 70–71. Joravsky argues that this period of gradual cultural revolution from 1917 until 1929 (before the Great Break) had its contradictory characteristics. For example, concessions to bourgeois specialists simultaneously accompanied a gradual drive against them (63–67).

13. For a pioneering study that focuses more on the relationship between the technical intelligentsia (especially engineers and technical specialists) and society during the inter-war era, see Kendall E. Bailes, *Technology and Society Under Lenin and Stalin: Origins of the Soviet Technical Intelligentsia, 1917–1941* (1978).

14. For a recent look at dissonant public opinion during the purge era of the Stalinist 1930s, see Sarah Davies, *Popular Opinion in Stalin's Russia: Terror, Propaganda and Dissent, 1934–1941* (1997). Also see Sheila Fitzpatrick, *Everyday Stalinism, Ordinary Life in Extraordinary Times: Soviet Russia in the 1930s* (1999).

CHAPTER 1

1. See Mario Biagioli, *Galileo, Courtier: The Practice of Science in the Culture of Absolutism* (1993). Throughout the 1630s Galileo embarked on a mass-publicist campaign and published one of the first European popular-scientific prose pieces entitled *Dialogues Concerning the Two Chief World Systems* (1632). He sent this to

bishops, cardinals, and intellectuals in an effort to convert those in the church and those residing within the walls of academia. For an analyis of Galileo as an artisan who represented the progressive forces of science and modernism see Bertolt Brecht, *Galileo* (1966). For a biography of the early years of Galileo's life one can refer to Stillman Drake, *Galileo at Work* (1978).

2. This treatise outlined a precise mathematical approach to the laws of mechanics and showed that all phenomena could be explained on the basis of simple, universal laws of motion and the law of gravitation. See Sir Isaac Newton, *Mathematical Principles of Natural Philosophy,* trans. and ed. Andrew Motte (1729). For a social history of Newtonian philosophy see Margaret C. Jacob, *The Newtonians and the English Revolution 1689–1720* (1976).

3. See Roger Cotes, "Preface to the Second Edition (1713)," in Sir Isaac Newton, *Mathematical Principles of Natural Philosophy* (1938). Cotes's preface was important in the further popularization of Newtonian mechanics.

4. Anthony M. Alioto, *A History of Western Science* (1993), 226–27.

5. Scientific academies also took shape in Italy during the time of Galileo and served as a starting point for the spread of scientific ideas. Galileo was a member of the Academy of the Lynx, one of the first scientific academies in Rome. For an analysis of the nexus connecting naturalists, academies, and science museums in seventeenth century Italy, see Paula Findlen, *Possessing Nature: Musuems, Collecting, and Scientific Culture in Early Modern Italy* (1994). In France during the seventeenth century, governmental sponsorship and supervision of the arts and letters became more institutionalized. For an analysis of how academies in France switched from a patronage system based on direct participation to the remote nature of Royal patronage, see David Lux, *Patrongage and Royal Science in Seventeenth-Century France* (1989).

6. Lorenzo Magalotti, *Essays Concerning the Experiments of the Academy* (1667). One member of this group of Galilean scientific thinkers, Francesco Redi, published numerous works aimed at debunking earlier accepted theories. See Paula Findlen, "Controlling the Experiment: Rhetoric, Court Patronage and the Experimental Method of Francesco Redi (1626–1697)," *History of Science* 31 (1993): 35–64.

7. Diderot expounded on his theory of the purpose of an encyclopedia in his "Definition of an Encyclopedia" in *Rameau's Nephew and Other Works,* trans. Jacques Barzan and Ralph Bowen (1956), 280–310. For a more comprehensive analysis of science during the Enlightenment, see Thomas L. Hankins, *Science and the Enlightenment* (1985) and Charles C. Gillespie, *Science and Polity in France at the End of the Old Regime* (1980).

8. See R. K. Webb, *The British Working Class Reader, 1790–1848: Literacy and Social Tension* (1955), 113–18.

9. The founder of the London Mechanics' Institution in Great Britain was a professor of Medicine in Glasgow, George Birkbeck. In 1800 he delivered a course of lectures to laborers in Glasgow on natural philosophy. They became a success, and eventually such institutes spread to Edinburgh and other cities. See Robert Stewart, *Henry Brougham, 1778–1868: His Public Career* (London), 183–85.

10. Brougham was responsible for starting and expanding the Society for the Diffusion of Useful Knowledge in 1826. This society grew out of a plan by Brougham and others to produce cheap scientific and educational books and

texts for workers. The society published cheap penny magazines and encyclo-pedic newspapers offering educational material to working-class Britons. Brougham published popular scientific pamphlets on mathematics and the physical sciences. Although he was criticized for his lack of scientific and theo-retical grounding, Brougham, like other amateur science popularizers in Eu-rope, believed it was significant to develop more accessible scientific texts for the common person (Stewart, *Henry Brougham,* 188–91).

11. In an essay drawing on the writings of the French sociologist Pierre Bourdieu, R. Chartier focuses on the relationship between the text as conceived by the author and printed by the publisher, on the one hand, and as read and pro-cessed by the reader, on the other. See "Texts, Printing, and Readings," in *The New Cultural History,* ed. Lynn Hunt (1989).

12. One book addressing this problem by analyzing popularized scientific ideas is a work on the spread of phrenology in nineteenth-century Britain. The author, Roger Cooter, analyzes how popularizers of the famous phrenologist Franz Joseph Gall spread his ideas among the new and varied reading public. See Roger Cooter, *The Cultural Meaning of Popular Science: Phrenology and the Organi-zation of Consent in Nineteenth-Century Britain* (1984), 2–8, 11–17. For another monograph analyzing the popular images of science, see Alfred Kelley's *The Descent of Darwinism: The Popularization of Darwinism in Germany, 1860–1914* (1984). Also see *The Popularization of Medicine, 1650–1850,* ed. Roy Porter (1994).

13. See Susan Faye Cannon, *Science in Culture: The Early Victorian Period* (1978), 2–8, 13–20.

14. *Geographiia, ili kratkoe zemnogo kruga opisanie* (1710).

15. B. Fontenel', *Razgovory o mnozhestve mirov* (1740).

16. E. A. Lazarevich, *Popularizatsiia nauki v Rossii* (1981), 13.

17. These articles include titles such as "Kratkoe iz"iasnenie o planete Saturne" (short explanation of the planet Saturn) (1735) and "O lune i o lunnykh piat-nakh" (on the moon and on the lunar spots) (1740–41). Geography and astron-omy were very popular themes with the Russian reader in the late imperial and early Soviet periods.

18. Aleksei Pokrovskii, "Kalendari v Rossii" in *Kalendari i sviattsy* (1911), lxi–lxii.

19. A. V. Zapadov, *Russkaia zhurnalistika 30-kh-60-kh godov XVIII v.* (1957), 9–11. Also see S. P. Luppov, *Kniga v Rossii v poslepetrovskoe vremia* (1976), 63–64.

20. Lomonosov was also a proponent of the popularization of science in eigh-teenth-century Russia. He gave speeches at the public meetings of the Acad-emy of Sciences in which he discussed the role of science as aiding Russia's in-dustrial development. Those speeches included his 1751 lecture entitled "Slovo o pol'ze khimii" (words on the use of chemistry). See D. D. Blagoi, "Poet uchenyi," in *Izvestiia akademii nauk SSSR, otdelenie literatury i iazyka* 1940, no. 1: 75–78.

21. The journal started out with a circulation of two thousand copies (a sizable print run for the time), but its distribution slowly came down over the next couple of years. See Petr Pekarskii, *Istoriia imperatorskoi akademii nauk v Peter-burge, tom 1* (1870), 308–10.

22. Lazarevich, *Popularizatsii,* 25.

23. See *Svodnyi katalog russkoi knigi grazhdanskoi pechatii XVIII veka, 1725–1800: Dopolneniia razyskivaemye izdaniia utochneniia* (1975).

24. See Gary Marker, *Publishing, Printing, and the Origins of Intellectual Life in Russia, 1700–1800* (1985), 58–59.
25. Luppov, *Kniga v Rossii,* 50–51.
26. Lazarevich, *Populiarizatsii,* 30–31.
27. Ferri de Sen-Konstan Zhan, *Dukh Biuffona* (1783), 10.
28. Lazarevich, *Populiarizatsii,* 33–34.
29. V. G. Berezina, *Russkaia zhurnalistika pervoi chetverti XIX veka* (1965), 5.
30. See I. F. Kruzzenshterna, *Puteshestvie vokrug sveta v 1803–1806 godax na korable Nadezhde i Nebe* (1809).
31. See Kelley, *Descent of Darwinism,* 10–14.
32. See Nicholas V. Riasanovsky, *A Parting of Ways: Government and the Educated Public in Russia, 1801–1855* (1976), 248–97.
33. N. Pisarevskii, *Obshcheponiataia fizika* (1852).
34. See also I. Danilevskii and A. Osovskii, *Esli li gde konets svetu?* (1849), which discusses the form of the plant and animal world and includes a discussion of the work of Copernicus and Galileo.
35. Nikolai Polevoi, *Materialy po istorii russkoi literatury i zhurnalistiki tridtsatykh godov* (1934), 332.
36. Ibid., 332–33.
37. *Ukazatel' statei sereznogo soderzhaniia, pomeshchennykh v russkikh zhurnalakh prezhnykh let.* Vypusk' 2: *Biblioteka dlia chteniia, 1834–1854,* comp. V. Kolenov (1858), 1–3.
38. The 1860s and 1870s saw an increase in the number of publications in the natural sciences. Natural scientific books made up 12.8 percent of all publications in 1876, and the average print-run of those works was twenty-five hundred copies. See M. V. Muratov, *Knizhnoe delo v Rossii v XIX i XX vv., ocherk istorii knigoizdatel'stva i knigotorgovli 1800–1917 gody* (1931), 106.
39. V. Bazanov, *Vol'noe obshchestvo liubitelei rossiiskoi slovesnosti* (1949), 14–15.
40. Berezina, *Russkaia zhurnalistika,* 74. Also see A. Bestuzhev, "Vzgliad na russkuiu slovesnost' v techenie 1824 i nachalo 1825 godov," in *Poliarnaia zvezda, izdannaia A. Bestuzhevym i K. Ryleevym* (1960).
41. E. A. Lazarevich, *S vekom naravne, populiarizatsiia nauka v rossii. Kniga. Gazeta: Zhurnal* (1984), 53–54.

CHAPTER 2

1. For overviews of the prerevolutionary adult-education movement see S. Elkina, *Ocherki po agitatsii, propagande i vneshkol'noi rabote v dorevoliutsionnoi Rossii* (1930) and V. P. Vakhterov, *Vneskhol'noe obrazovanie naroda* (1917).
2. T. I. Vzdorpov, *Istoriia otkrytiia i izucheniia russkoi srednevekovoi zhivopisi XIXv.* (1986), 139–40. The popularization activities of scientific societies in Russia, like their counterparts in Western Europe, can be seen as part of a broader movement to develop voluntary organizations by the educated, middle classes of Russian society in the late nineteenth and early twentieth centuries. Joseph Bradley ("Voluntary Associations, Civic Culture, and *Obshchestvennost'* in Moscow," in *Between Tsar and People: Educated Society and the Quest for Public Identity in Late Imperial Russia,* ed. Edith Clowes et al. [1991], 146–47) suggests that volun-

tary associations contributed significantly to the development of Russian civil society (*obshchestvennost'*). Furthermore, Bradley argues that professionals in Russia claimed stewardship over the workers and peasants and engendered notions of self-improvement through their adult-education programs.

3. Geoffrey Eley and David Blackbourn, *The Peculiarities of German History* (1984), 194–96. In his "Nations, Publics, and Political Cultures: Placing Habermas in the Nineteenth Century," in *Culture/Power/History: A Reader in Contemporary Social Theory,* ed. Nicholas B. Dirks et al. (1994), 303–304, Eley asserts that voluntary association in general was a main indicator of social progress as the nineteenth century unfolded in Europe. Reading, educational, and literary societies were important to the development of new public aspirations. According to Eley, voluntary association was the main context through which bourgeois society displayed its goals and aspirations as it staked out leadership within respective nations.

4. Samuel D. Kassow, "Russia's Unrealized Civil Society," in *Between Tsar and People,* 367–68. Louise McReynolds, in her study of the late-imperial Russian press (*The News Under Russia's Old Regime* [1991]), shows that by catering to the broadly inclusive tastes of daily street traffic, newspaper publishers challenged the dominance that the government and intellectuals in society previously enjoyed over print communication. For McReynolds, "The collection and distribution of reader-oriented information had far-reaching political implications; newspapers opened up the "public sphere" (3–5).

5. Jurgen Habermas, *On Society and Politics: A Reader,* ed. Steven Seidman (1989), 231–32. See also Jurgen Habermas, "The Public Sphere: An Encyclopedia Article," *New German Critique* 1 (1974): 49–54.

6. Jurgen Habermas, *The Structural Transformation of the Public Sphere,* trans. Thomas Burger (1992), 51. Habermas claimed in his writings that he has reconstructed Marxist thought by deconstructing it and then putting it back together with a developed analysis of the communicative evolution of societies. See Jurgen Habermas, *Communication and the Evolution of Society,* trans. Thomas McCarthy (1979), 95–96.

7. Eley, "Nations, Publics, and Political Cultures," 310. As a feminist theorist, Sylia Benhabib sees women and their interests ignored in public-sphere debate and theory. For her critique of Habermas and public sphere theory, see S. Benhabib, "Models of Public Space: Hannah Arendt, the Liberal Tradition, and Jurgen Habermas," in *Habermas and the Public Sphere,* ed. Craig Calhoun (1992), 73–95.

8. Eileen Yeo, "Culture and Constraint in Working-Class Movements, 1830–1855," in *Popular Culture and Class Conflictm 1590–1914: Explorations in the History of Labour and Leisure,* ed. Eileen and Stephen Yeo (1981), 160–61.

9. *Otchet deiatel'nosti S. Peterburgskogo obshchestva estestvoispytatelei za pervoe dvadtsatipiatiletie ego sushchestvovanii: 1868–1893* (1893), 14–17.

10. Many scientific societies were actually entitled amateurs of the natural sciences (*liubiteli estestvoznanii*). See S. M. Selivanov, "O nauchnoi tsennosti liubitel'skikh nabliudenii," *Mirovedenie* 1921, no. 2 (November): 113.

11. Alexander Vucinich, "Politics, Universities, and Science," in *Russia under the Last Tsar,* ed. Theofanis George Stavrou (1969), 166.

12. Ibid., 167–68, 171.

13. The zemstvos were created as elected, local councils in the 1860s during the

reign of Alexander II and were also involved in expanding local infrastructure, schools, and public institutions.

14. See *Otchet deiatel'nosti S. Peterburgskogo,* 15–17.
15. Vucinich, "Politics, Universities, and Science," 166–67, 171.
16. Ibid.
17. "Ustavy S.Peterburgskago obshchestva estestvoispytatelei," Tsentral'nyi gosudarstvennyi arkhiv RSFSR (hereafter GARF), f.2307, op.2, d.358, l.36.
18. Ibid., l.37.
19. See "Ustav obshchestva," in Gosudarstvennyi arkhiv Iaroslavskoi oblasti (hereafter cited as GAIaO), f. 1541, op.1, d.1, ll.1–3.
20. GAIaO, f. 1541, op.1, d.1, ll.4–8. The society, officially named the Society for the Study of the Iaroslavl' Guberniia from a Natural-Historical Perspective, sent its list of by-laws to the ministry on October 31, 1864, and was sanctioned as an independent voluntary naturalist society on Nov. 21, 1864. Between 1902 and 1924 the organization was renamed the Iaroslavl' Natural-History Society, and it sought funding from a wide variety of sources.
21. GAIaO, f. 1541, op.1, d.1, l.3.
22. A type of higher school came into existence in Iaroslavl' on April 29, 1805. It was named after its sponsor, the Russian nobleman Pavel G. Demidov. This was unique for the time and probably only one of four of its type, the others in Moscow, Petersburg, and Vilna. In 1834 it was transformed into a lyceum, and later in 1868 into a law lycee, which it remained until 1918, when by Lenin's decree it became a university. See Imeni Demidova, *Iaroslavskii Universistet v ego proshlom i natoyaschem* (1995).
23. GAIaO, f. 221, op.1, d.116, ll.1–2. Records from the 1917 budget show the zemstvos donating even more (combined total of 1,950 rubles) than the Ministry of Education (1,500 rubles).
24. See *Trudy Iaroslavskogo Estestvenno-istoricheskogo Obshchestvo, Tom 1,* ed. A. I. Iakovleva (1902), x–xiii. L. P. Sabaneev (1844–1898), an active naturalist and zoologist and a founding member of the society, was also known for his studies of fishing and fauna. His popular texts on fishing were known and loved by Russians throughout the empire.
25. For an overview of the history of the Iaroslavl' Natural-History Society, see, N. I. Shakhanin, *K 70-letiiu Iaroslavskogo estestvenno-istoricheskogo obshchestva* (1952).
26. GARF, f.2306, op.19, d.52, l.4.
27. See N. N. Pozdniakov, "Politekhnicheskii muzei i ego nauchno-prosvetitel'noi deiatel'nosti 1872–1917 gg.," in *Istoriia muzeinogo dela v SSSR* (1957), 130–45.
28. For more information on scientific and technical exhibits in late imperial Russia and especially the 1872 science and industry exhibit, see *Obshchee obozrenie Moskovskoi politeknicheskoi vystavki* (1872).
29. S. G. Lepneva, "O rasshirenii muzeiia iarosl. est.-ist. obshchestva v tseliakh populiarizatsii nauchnykh znanii," GARF, f.2306, op.19, d.52, ll.10–11.
30. Ibid., l.15.
31. Ibid., ll.20–21.
32. N. V. Bagrova, "Iz istorii pervykh muzeev Iaroslavlia," in *Kraevcheskie zapiski, vp. V, VI* (1984), 41–43.
33. Selivanov, "O nauchnoi tsennosti," 113–14.

34. "Zapiska o deiatel'nosti obshchestva liubitelei estestvoznaniia, antropologii i etnografii i ego material'nykh sredstvakh," GARF, f.2306, op.19, d.38, ll.4–5.
35. Ibid., ll.5–6.
36. GARF, f.2306, op.19, d.128, ll.47–47ob.
37. Ibid., ll.48–48ob.
38. "Otchet, russkoe obshchestvo liubitelei mirovendeniia 1909–1916," GARF, f.2307, op.2, d.365, ll.15–15ob.
39. Ibid., l.23ob.
40. For an analysis of the adult-education movement and popular enlightenment during World War I, see Scott J. Seregny, "Zemstvos, Peasants, and Citizenship: The Russian Adult Education Movement and World War I," *Slavic Review* 59, no. 2 (summer 2000): 290–315.

CHAPTER 3

1. Though Narkompros would generally register societies promptly, it required the necessary budgetary information before releasing state funds to various organizations. For instance, in a 1918 Narkompros memorandum to the director of the respected, well-established Russian Society for the Spread of Natural-Historical Education, G. Grinberg stated that although the organization was officially registered with Narkompros, without a yearly budget estimate the ministry could not extend proper funding to the society. See "Komissariat narodnogo prosveshcheniia 15 iiunia 1918, predsedateliu russkogo obshchestva," GARF, f.2307, op.2, d.362, l.2.
2. "Otchet russkogo obshchestva liubitelei mirovedeniia za 1919 god," GARF, f.2307, op.2, d.365, l.67.
3. Ibid.
4. GARF, f.2307, op.2, d.365, l.11.
5. "Predsedatel' obshchestva k narodnomu komissaru po prosveshcheniiu A. V. Lunarcharskomu," GARF, f.2307, op.2, d.365, l.208.
6. For a short overview of the Russian Technical Society see Harley Balzer, "The Russian Technical Society," in *Modern Encyclopedia of Russian and Soviet History,* vol. 32, 176–80. One of the best monographs in Russian on the topic of technical societies in prerevolutionary Russia is N. G. Fillipov, *Nauchno-tekhnicheskie obshchestva Rossii, 1866–1917* (1976). For a more detailed analysis of engineers and technical training in general in tsarist Russia, see Harley Balzer, "Educating the Engineers: Economics, Politics, and Technical Training in Tsarist Russia" (Ph.D. diss., University of Pennsylvania, 1980).
7. GARF, f.2307, op.2, d.382, ll.5–6.
8. Ibid., l.11.
9. "Poiasnitel'naia zapiska k sokrashchennoi smete russkogo tekhnicheskogo obshchestva na ianvar'-iiun' 1919 g.," GARF, f.2307, op.2, d.382, ll.27ob.–28ob.
10. The government funds budgeted for scientific institutions dropped from 11.5 percent of the total Narkompros budget for the 1922/23 fiscal year to 9.7 percent for the 1923/24 fiscal year. As the decade continued, this share showed a steady decline. See *Narodnoe prosveshchenie v RSFSR k 1924/25 uchebnomu godu (Otchet Narkomprosa RSFSR)* (1925), 31. The sum allotted for scientific institu-

tions dropped from 8.4 percent of Narkompros's budget for the 1924/25 fiscal year to 7.9 percent for the 1925/26 fiscal year. During the same time period the amount of the Narkompros budget allotted to adult education dropped from 19.3 percent to 15.5 percent. See *Narodnoe prosveshchenie v RSFSR k 1926/27 uchebnomu godu (Otchet Narkomprosa RSFSR)* (1927), 9–14.

11. GARF, f.2307, op.2, d.358, l.41.

12. "Otchet po petrogradskomu obshchestvu estestvoispytatelei za I polugodie 1922 goda," GARF, f.2307, op.2, d.358, ll.42–43ob.

13. "Ot russkogo liubitelei mirovedeniia k vsem chlenam obshchestva, soobshchenie soveta," *Mirovedenie* 1921, no. 2 (November): 235–36.

14. N. Morozov (Predsedatel'), "Ob"iasnitel'naia zapiska k finansomu ochetu R.O.L.M. za 1923 god," *Mirovedenie* 1924, no. 1 (July): 129.

15. "Otchet o deiatel'nosti R.O.L.M. za 1924," *Mirovedenie* 1925, no. 1 (August): 139.

16. GARF, f.2307, op.2, d.365, ll.88–91, 96–96ob.

17. A growing struggle between the Communist Party's institutions and Soviet state scientific organizations after 1929 would complicate this institutional dynamic even more. According to Nikolai Krementsov, VSNKh's Scientific-Technical Administration (NTU or NTO) was reorganized a year later in 1929. When its role was diminished, a number of its scientific institutions were further subordinated to appropriate agencies supervising various branches of industry. After the cultural revolution, its role diminished even more, as "in 1932, the VSNKh was liquidated and replaced by a number of new commissariats that supervised various branches of industry and assumed responsibility for the relevant scientific institutions" (Krementsov, *Stalinist Science,* 33).

18. See Paul R. Josephson, *Physics and Politics in Revolutionary Russia* (1991), 64–65.

19. "Ot president ob. 5-3-1920 k tov. Lunacharskomu," GARF, f.2306, op.19, d.128, ll.20–21.

20. "Zaveduiushchii glavnaukoi narodnomu komissariatu vnutrennikh del, 26 iiulia 1923," GARF, f.2307, op.2, d.365, l.181.

21. Ibid., ll.181–82.

22. After the Bolshevik Revolution of 1917 the Marxist historian M. N. Pokrovskii became Deputy People's Commissar of Enlightenment and chairman of Narkompros's State Academic Council. He was also chairman of the Presidium of the Communist Academy and rector of the Institute of Red Professors (George M. Enteen, *The Soviet Scholar-Bureaucrat: M. N. Pokrovskii and the Society of Marxist Historians* [1978].

23. "V narkompros zav. tov. Pokrovskomu, ot NKVDa zav. tov. Zaitseva, 31-1-1923," GARF, f.2307, op.2, d.362, l.1.

24. Ibid., ll.3–4.

25. GAIaO, f. 221, op.1, d.116, l.5.

26. GARF, f.2306, op.19, d.27, ll.14–14ob.

27. GARF, f.2306, op.19, d.128, ll.78, 88.

28. GARF, f.2307, op.2, d.365, l.1.

29. People's universities emerged in Russia at the beginning of the twentieth century. They were organized by professionals such as lawyers, doctors, and, of course, teachers. These institutions offered lectures and short courses in a variety of cultural, scientific, and technical subject areas. Soon after the Bolshevik Revolution of 1917 they were replaced by workers' schools *(rabfaki)* or by other

analogous state-sponsored institutions. See L. V. Dubrovina, *Narodnye univer-sitety* (1963); Anatoli Darinsky, "People's Universities in the USSR," *Convergence* 7, no. 1 (1974): 51–54.

30. "Otchet o deiatel'nosti Ia.E-I.O za 1917 god," GARF, f.2306, op.19, d.52, ll.31–32. For a further analysis of people's universities see Iu. S. Vorob'eva, "Moskovskii gorodskoi narodnyi universitet im. Shaniavskogo," in *Gosudarstvennoe rukovodstvo vysshei shkoloi v dorevoliutsionnoi Rossii i v SSSR* (1979), 180–89. See also O. Kaidanova, *Ocherki po istorii narodnogo obrazovaniia v Rossii i v SSSR* (1939).

31. See GAIaO, f. 221, op.1, d.113, ll. 24 and 37.

32. GAIaO, f. 221, op.1, d.116, ll. 13–15ob.

33. GAIaO, f. 221, op.1, d.116, ll. 22 and 24.

34. GARF, f.2306, op.19, d.52, ll.5ob–6.

35. "Ia.E-I.O. 1-3-1921, v nauchnyi otdel narkomprosa ot predsedateli ob.," GARF, f.2307, op.2, d.356, ll.7–8.

36. See Anketa po nauchnym obshchestvam, dokumenti, GAIaO, f. 221, op.1, d.190, ll. 20–20ob. On July 4, 1924, a key member of Glavnauka's collegium, I. Valkov, sent out a circular specifically indicating that all Soviet regional scientific societies had to list all members' names, their party affiliation, their education, and the nature of their organizational involvement.

37. See a circular sent by A. Pinkevich of Glavnauka to the Iaroslavl' Gubispolkom, dated August, 28, 1924. GAIaO, f. 221, op.1, d.190, ll. 58–61.

38. See V. Srochno Tsirkuliarno, R.S.F.S.R. Narkompros Glavnauka, F. Petrov Vsem Podvedomstvennym uchrezhdeniam, December 2, 1924, GAIaO, f. 221, op.1, d.189, ll. 34–35. Reports sent by societies to Glavnauka encompassed: (1) detailed documentation of yearly activities; (2) lists of members and their backgrounds; (3) detailed justifications for budgetary requests; (4) an inventory of all equipment, furniture, and possessions of the scientific societies, including their affiliated museums and libraries.

39. GAIaO, f. 221, op.1, d.232, l.21.

40. GAIaO, f. 221, op.1, d.232, l.45. *Severnyi rabochii* was a daily newspaper. Its predecessor *Severnyi krai* was the Iaroslavl' region's first provincial newspaper of any real journalistic substance. After the Bolshevik revolution, it became the organ of the Gubispolkom and Gubkomitet of the R.K.P. (Russian Communist Party). *Severnyi krai,* however, did compete between 1909 and 1917 with another local newspaper entitled *Golos* (the voice or herald).

41. GAIaO, f. 221, op.1, d.232, ll.49–54ob.

42. For announcements of local science clubs, see *Vlast' Truda,* no. 45, March 2, 1918. But many issues beginning in 1918 covered local science topics and events.

43. GAIaO, f. 221, op.1, d.232, ll.49–54ob.

44. GAIaO, f. 221, op.1, d.189, ll.10–12.

45. Ibid., ll. 114–115.

46. GAIaO, f. 221, op.1, d.217, l.53.

47. GAIaO, f. 221, op.1, d.217, l.64.

48. March 3, 1926, Glavnauka Doveritel'no-Tsirkuliarno Vsem mestnym nauchnym uchrezhdeniiam pod vedomstvennym Glavnauke, in GAIaO, f. 221, op.1, d.217, l.53.

49. GAIaO, f. 221, op.1, d.217, l.65.
50. GAIaO, f. 221, op.1, d.215, ll.1–5.
51. In 1923 the faculty of the university's Law School, the most prestigious of its schools or departments, was terminated, as were some law schools elsewhere in Soviet Russia. Deprived of its law faculty, as well as Lenin's patronage, the university was closed in 1924, only to be reopened in 1970. Temporarily, the university was replaced by the opening of a pedagogical institute in Iaroslavl' in the late 1920s. However, archival and secondary sources provide no evidence for why the university in this provincial town might have been singled out for termination by central Narkompros officials. For a complete review of these matters see *Imeni Demidova: Iaroslavskii Universitet v ego proshlom i nastoiashchem* (1995).
52. Ankety Iaroslavskogo est-istori. obshchestva, in GAIaO, f. 221, op.1, d.198, l.64.
53. Ibid., l.58.
54. See Kendall E. Bailes, "Natural Scientists and the Soviet System," in *Party, State, and Society in the Russian Civil War,* ed. Diane P. Koenker et.al. (1989), 267–95.
55. Beginning in 1921, local scientists and naturalists also gave lectures at the night courses and workshops of the rabfaki on the Northern Volga. For a recent discussion of local rabfaki and of problems with adult education in the Iaroslavl' area, see Iu. G. Salova, *Kul'turnoe razvitie Iaroslavlia, 1917–27* (1994), 24–28.
56. GAIaO, f. 221, op.1, d.159, ll. 16–18.
57. Ibid., ll.15–17.
58. See *Kul'turnaia zhizn' Iaroslavskogo kraia 20–30-x gg., dokumenti i materialy,* ed. A. M. Selivanova (1995), 185–88.
59. GAIaO, f. 221, op.1, d.189, ll. 6–11.
60. For a recent analysis of historical changes in museum administrative matters in the provinces, see N. P. Riazantsev, "Muzeinoe stroitel'stvo i okhrana pamiatnikov istorii i kul'tury v Iaroslavskom krae v 1920–1930-e gody," in *Muzei verkhnei volgi: problemy, issledovaniia, publikatsii,* ed. E. V. Ianovskaia (1997), 270–74.
61. GAIaO, f. 221, op.1, d.189, ll.128, 142–44. The official letter from N. Brotskaia (Zav. Museinym Otdelom Glavnauki) to the Iaroslavl' Natural-History Society and Museum Staff went out on July 4, 1925.
62. N. V. Bagrova, "Iz istorii pervykh muzeev Iaroslavlia," in *Kraevedcheskie zapiski, vypuskii V, VI* (1984), 45–46.
63. Ibid.

CHAPTER 4

1. For an analysis of aeronautics and the construction of national identity in imperial Russia, see Scott W. Palmer, "On Wings of Courage: Public 'Air-mindedness' and National Identity in Late Imperial Russia," *Russian Review* 54 (April 1995).
2. *Desiat' let kul'turnoi,* 3–4.
3. N. A. Rubakin, *Chto takoe bibliologicheskaia psikhologiia?* (1924), 17–22. Jeffrey Brooks has argued that popular enlightenment developed in Russia, in part, because popular culture was successfully linked to mainstream educated culture

by defining a common cultural heritage for all Russians ("Russian National-ism and Russian Literature," in *Nation and Ideology: Essays in Honor of Wayne S. Vucinich,* ed. Ivo Banac, John G. Ackerman, and Roman Szporluk [1981], 315–34). Stephen Moeller-Sally ("Parallel Lives: Gogol's Biography and Mass Readership in Late Imperial Russia," *Slavic Review* 45, no. 1 [spring 1995]: 62–64) has recently attempted to analyze the interplay between the educated elite and popular reader in Russia through the genre of popular biography. Also see Greg Carleton, "The Figure of the Mass Reader in Early Soviet Literature: Artificial Interpretive Communities and Critical Practice," *Critical Studies in Mass Communication* 12, no. 1 (March 1995): 1–22.

4. Rubakin, *Chto takoe bibliologicheskaia psikhologiia?* 24.

5. NTO was headed originally by N. P. Gorbunov and later by Prof. N. M. Fedorovskii, who, along with A. A. Eikhenval'd, was sent to Berlin in August of 1920 by VSNKh to meet with foreign scientists such as Albert Einstein. On March 29, 1921, Sovnarkom RSFSR created the Bureau of Foreign Science and Technology (BINT). Its task was to form ties with foreign scientific organizations, publish scientific and technical information, and also exchange scientific literature with groups abroad. See A. Ia. Cherniak, *Istoriia tekhnicheskoi knigi, chast' II sovetskii period* (1973), 15, 45–46. At this time a number of publishers of scientific information were under VSNKh's control, including BINT's publishing house, Gostekhizdat, and the scientific chemical-technical publishers. See *Kratkii otchet o deiatel'nosti BINTa 1921–1924* (1924), 10–11.

6. RGAE, f. 3429, op. 61, d. 985, l.58.

7. *O partiinoi i sovetskoi pechati, radioveshchanii i televideniem* (1972), 65–66.

8. A. Ia. Cherniak, *Tekhnicheskaia kniga v period velikoi oktiabr'skoi sotsialisticheskoi revoliutsii i grazhdanskoi voiny 1917–1920 gg.* (1973), 7.

9. Tsentral'nyi gosudarstvennyi arkhiv oktiabr'skoi revoliutsii i sotsialisticheskogo stroitel'stva SSSR (Gosudarstvennyi arkhiv Rossiiskoi Federatsii, or GARF), f. 395, op. 9, d. 313, ll.39–40. By the middle of the decade the popular-scientific branch of Gosizdat had expanded its production of works considerably. During 1926 this branch produced 116 new works with a total print-run of 696,000 copies. This was a considerable increase over the previous year. In 1925 the popular-scientific branch of Gosizdat produced a total of 77 new titles with a total print-run of 549,000 (GARF, f.395, op.14, d.15, ll.46, 69). The 1926 figures represented 3.0 percent of all titles produced that year by Gosizdat, and 1.4 percent of the total print-run of books. For 1925 the figures were 2.95 percent and .8 percent, respectively (GARF, f.395, op.14, d.13, ll.17–18).

10. Cherniak, *Tekhnicheskaia kniga v period,* 7–8. During the civil war, book trading decreased to a minimum. Books, however, were freely distributed by centralized means under Tsentropechat', the central agency for the spread of printed publications.

11. Jeffrey Brooks, "The Breakdown in Production and Distribution of Printed Material, 1917–1927," in *Bolshevik Culture: Experiment and Order in the Russian Revolution,* ed. Abbott Gleason et al. (1985), 154.

12. Ibid., 152–53. Brooks argues that much of the printed material at this time was only reaching the urban reader; rural areas were not receiving publications due especially to the breakdown in distribution. Statistically, however, much of the "literate" reading public lived in the rural areas. According to the 1926 census

figures, over 70 percent of the nearly sixty million literate people lived in the countryside (*Vsesoiuznaia perepis' naseleniia 1926 goda* [1929] 17: 48–50).

13. Specific figures and data for book production in the pre- and post-World War I era can be found in a detailed study by G. I. Proshnev, *Etiudy po knizhnomu delu* (1924), 30–36. See also *Kniga v 1924 g. v SSSR,* ed. N. F. Ianitskii (1925).

14. A. I. Nazarov, *Oktiabr' i kniga* (1968), 227–28.

15. See *Kniga v 1924,* 210–11.

16. V. Slavskaia, "Kniga i revoliutsiia," *Kniga i revoliutsiia* 1920, nos. 3–4: 4–5.

17. A. I. Nazarov, *Kniga v sovetskom obshchestve* (1964), 176–77.

18. *Zakony o chastnom kapitale. Sbornik zakonov, instruktsii, prikazov i raz"iasnenii,* comp. B. S. Mal'tsman and B. E. Ratner (1928), 247–48. For a general overview of private and cooperative book publishing under the NEP, see Alan M. Ball, *Russia's Last Capitalists: The Nepmen, 1921–29* (1987), 146–48.

19. *Pechat SSSR za 1924 i 1925 gg.,* ed. I. M. Vareikis (1926), 127; and N. F. Ianitskii, *Knizhnaia statistika sovetskoi Rossii, 1918–1923* (1924), 15–16. By 1923 the number of titles privately published (not including works published by cooperatives) reached 25 percent of the total number of titles published. That percentage sharply declined, however, in the period between 1928 and 1931 during the Stalinist cultural revolution (down to 0.1 percent in 1931). See A. I. Nazarov, *Oktiabr' i kniga* (1968), 254–55, as well as E. I. Shamurin, *Sovetskaia kniga za 15 let v tsifrakh* (1968), 25–26.

20. Peter Kenez, *The Birth of the Propaganda* (1985), 240–41.

21. See Katerina Clark, "The Quiet Revolution in Intellectual Life," in *Russia in the Era of NEP,* ed. Sheila Fitzpatrick, Alexander Rabinowitch, and Richard Stites (1991), 216–17.

22. Sheila Fitzpatrick, "The Problem of Class Identity in NEP Society," in *Russia in the Era of NEP,* 12–14.

23. See Jeffrey Brooks, "Studies of the Reader in the 1920s," *Russian History/Histoire Russe* 9, nos. 2–3 (1982): 187–88. Also see O. E. Vol'tsenburg and A. N. Shloberg, *Kak ustroit' i vesti malenkuiu biblioteku* (1921), 35–36.

24. See Jeffrey Brooks, "Discontinuity in the Spread of Popular Print Culture, 1917–1927," Occasional Paper of the Kennan Institute for Advanced Russian Studies, May 1981. See also Brooks, "The Breakdown in Production and Distribution of Printed Material," 153–55.

25. See Brooks, "Studies of the Reader in the 1920s," 201.

26. For a general analysis of some of the early studies of the Soviet reader, see *Massovyi chitatel' i kniga,* ed. N. A. Rybnikov, S. Vvedeniem, and E. Khlebtsevich (1925). Also see E. I. Khlebtsevich, *Izuchenie chitatel'skikh interesov: Massovyi chitatel'* (1927).

27. B. V. Bank, "Iz istorii izucheniia chitatelei v SSSR," in *Sovetskii chitatel'* (1968), 21.

28. B. Bank and A. Vilenkin, *Krest'ianskaia molodezh' i kniga (opyt issledovaniia chitatel'skikh interesov)* (1929); B. Bank and A. Vilenkin, *Derevenskaia bednota i biblioteka* (1927). Scholars such as Bank and Vilenkin continued to work in the 1930s, but found it increasingly difficult to produce less politicized sociological analysis.

29. E. Vinogradova, "K izucheniiu chitatelia," *Krasnyi bibliotekar'* 1925, no. 4 (April): 9–13.

30. Ibid.
31. Nicholas A. Rubakin, "Kak pisat' nauchnye knizhki dlia massovogo chitatelia," *Kniga i profsoiuzy* 1927, no. 2: 3.
32. M. Rappeport, "Chto dala nasha anketa?" *Nauka i tekhnika,* January 13, 1926.
33. Ibid., 2.
34. Ibid., 3.
35. "Nasha anketa," *Iskra* 1927, no. 6 (June): 38.
36. *Iskra,* no. 3 (June 1923): 50.
37. *Iskra nauki,* no. 11 (November 1927): 448.
38. *Iskra nauki,* no. 6 (July 1928): 238.
39. Leningradskoe otdelenie Arkhiva Akademii nauk SSSR (Sanktpeterburgskii filial Arkhiva RAN [hereafter SF ARAN]), f. 796, op. 1, d. 85., ll.1–1ob.
40. SF ARAN, f.796, op.2, d.2., ll.11, 23.
41. SF ARAN, f.796, op.2, d.2., l.60.
42. I. A. Shomrakova, "Krest'ianskii chitatel' 20-godov (1920–1930)," in *Istoriia russkogo chitatelia, sbornik statei,* vypusk 2, ed. I. E. Barenbaum (1976), 116.
43. M. N. Slukhovskii, *Kniga i derevniia.* (1928).
44. I. Taradin, *Sloboda roven'ki: Voronezh* (1926), 129. According to Taradin's statistics, by 1924 41.5 percent of all peasant households in this province owned books. He also notes that literacy rates rose in this province from 15.8 percent in 1900 to 38.46 percent in 1924.
45. "Torgovyi sector gosizdata, 1923–1929," in GARF, f.395, op.9, d.310, ll.11–12.
46. "TsK RKP Agit. prop sector, 7–19–1923, otchet t. Levina," in GARF, f.395, op.9, d.310, l.25.
47. Ibid.
48. "Otchet T. Roga, komandirovannogo dlia obsledovaniia chitatel'skikh interesov v Petrogradskom Oblasti, 7–27–1923," in GARF, f.395, op.9, d.310, ll.29–30.
49. GARF, f.395, op.9, d.310, l.71.
50. Ibid. ll.71–72.

CHAPTER 5

1. Iurii M. Lotman and Boris A. Uspensky, "Binary Models in the Dynamics of Russian Culture," in *Semiotics of Russian Cultural History,* trans. Boris Gasparov, ed. Alexander D. Nakhimovsky and Alice Stone Nakhimovsky (1985), 31–35.
2. For a discussion of both the metaphoric and practical aspects of the Bolshevik electrification campaign after 1917, see Jonathan Coopersmith, *The Electrification of Russia, 1880–1926* (1992).
3. Frederick W. Taylor was an engineer from Philadelphia who compared industry to the military order and mapped out steps for an economy of movement in the factory. After the revolution Lenin was interested in adopting Taylor's methods of labor organization. See Richard Stites, *Revolutionary Dreams, Utopian Vision and Experimental Life in the Russian Revolution* (1989), 146–47. See also Samuel Haber, *Efficiency and Uplift: Scientific Management in the Progressive Era, 1890–1920* (1964).
4. Jeffrey Brooks, "The Press and Its Message: Images of America in the 1920s and 1930s," in *Russia in the Era of NEP,* 235. Also see Jeffrey Brooks, "Official Xeno-

phobia and Popular Cosmopolitanism in Early Soviet Russia," *American Historical Review* 97, no. 5 (December 1992): 1446–47; Hans Rogger, "America in the Russian Mind," *Pacific Historical Review* 47 (February 1978): 27–51.

5. Richard Stites, *Revolutionary Dreams,* 148.

6. "Novosti nauka i tekhniki," *Nauka i tekhnika,* May 26, 1926, p. 21.

7. *Nauka i tekhnika,* February 3, 1926, p. 22.

8. Z. Papernov, "4000 avtomobilei v den'(zavod Forda)," *Iskra* 1923, no. 5 (August): 28–31.

9. *Molodaia gvardiia* 1923, no. 2 (February–March): 231.

10. *Iskra nauki* 1927, no. 11 (November): 431.

11. Ibid., 420–28.

12. For examples of these inventions see *Iskra* 1924, no. 8 (August): 39–41.

13. Kendall E. Bailes, *Technology and Society under Lenin and Stalin* (1978), 362–64.

14. See *Izobretatel'stvo i ratsionalizatsiia v SSSR* (1962).

15. One uniquely outspoken engineer was quoted in a journal as opposing this movement, even requesting additional pay for devoting time to evaluating worker-generated projects (*Inzhenernyi trud* 1931, no. 8, 193).

16. Demaree Bess and John D. Littlepage, *In Search of Soviet Gold* (1938), 211–13.

17. *Periodicheskaia pechat' SSSR* notes that nineteen new journals on aviation began publication in the period 1917–32. See *Periodicheskaia pechat' SSSR 1917–49,* no. 4 (1955), 52–58.

18. See N. A. Rynin, *Mechty, legendy, i pervye fantasii* (1930); Nicholas Daniloff, *The Kremlin and the Cosmos* (1972).

19. In an article on rural Russia and air flight in the 1920s, Scott W. Palmer focused on Soviet flight as a struggle against rural backwardness and a militaristic ideological war of dominance against the nation. However, in my view, scientists saw this not just as combating backwardness but also as engaging and catering to the public's own interest in feats of modern technology. See Palmer's article, "Peasants into Pilots: Soviet Air-Mindedness As an Ideology of Dominance," *Technology and Culture* 41 (January 2000): 1–26.

20. Peter Fritzsche, *A Nation of Fliers: German Aviation and the Popular Imagination* (1992), 5–8.

21. "K druz'iam vozdushnogo flota," *Samolet* 1923, no. 1, p. 2.

22. I. Pereterskii, "Aviatsiia v kul'turnoi zhizn' strany," *Samolet* 1923, no. 1, p. 17.

23. Ia. Shatukovskii, "Aviatsiia v narodnom khoziaistve," *Aviatsiia i khimiia* 1926, no. 1 (August): 4.

24. *Samolet* 1924, no. 11 (November): 40–41.

25. See L. Khvat, *Besprimernyi perelet* (1936). Also see "Po stalinskomu marshrutu," *Chto chitat'* 1936, no. 2, pp. 45–47; Georgyi Baidukov, *Russian Lindbergh: The Life of Valery Chkalov,* ed. Von Hardesty (1991). Baidukov was the copilot on Chkalov's most well-known and publicized flights.

26. See *Istoricheskii perelet Levanevskogo* (1936).

27. See *Zamechatel'naia rabota Molokova* (1936); "Tri istoricheskikh pereleta," *Chto chitat'* 1937, no. 1: 76–78.

28. Peter Wiles, "On Physical Immortality," *Survey* 1965, nos. 56/57, pp. 132–34. See also Svetlana Semenova, *Nikolai Fedorov* (1990). According to N. P. Peterson, a Russian historian of philosophy, as early as the 1860s Fedorov had already incorporated the idea of space travel into his bizarre philosophies of resurrection.

See "Pis'mo N. Petersona k N. A. Chaevu o N. F. Fedorove," *Russki arkhiv* 1915, no. 5: 78–81; N. F. Fedorov, *Filosofia obshchego dela,* ed. V. A. Kozhevnikov and N. P. Peterson (1913).

29. George M. Young, Jr., *Nikolai F. Fedorov: An Introduction* (1979), 31–32.
30. V. L'vov, "Priamoe Voskhozhdenie," *Neva* 1966, no. 2: 130.
31. Viktor Shklovskii, "Kosmonavtika ot A do Ia," *Literaturnaia gazeta,* April 7, 1971, p. 13. In 1876, after studying in Moscow for three years, Tsiolkovskii returned to provincial Kaluga and began to teach physics and mathematics. In 1879, at the young age of twenty-two, he became one of the first scholars to work out a plan for an artifical earth satelite (Young, *Nikolai F. Fedorov,* 34).
32. Alexei Gastev was involved in time-labor studies and founded the Central Institute of Labor in Moscow in the 1920s. He was also instrumental in developing Soviet studies of the scientific organization of labor and technology (known by its Russian acronym the "NOT" movement).
33. Stites, *Revolutionary Dreams,* 170. The Bolsheviks were particularly attracted by Fedorov's idea of melting of the polar ice caps to provide needed water for certain drought-stricken areas in Russia (S. V. Utechin, "Bolsheviks and Their Allies after 1917: The Ideological Pattern," *Soviet Studies* 10 (1958/59): 113–35.
34. "O vozmozhnosti poletov v mezhplanetnoe prostranstvo," *Chto chitat'* 1937, no. 1: 80–81.
35. See Ia. Perel'man, *Mezhplanetnoe puteshestvie* (1923).
36. Ia. Perel'man, "Za predely atmosfery," *V masterskoi prirody* 1919, nos. 5–6: 32.
37. See K. Tsiolkovskii, *Atlas dirizhablia iz volnistoi stali* (1931).
38. "Otchet M.O.L.A. na pervoe polugodie 1921 goda," GARF, f.2307, op.2, d.371, l.69
39. K. L. Baev, "Rozhdenie i smert' planet," *V masterskoi prirody* 1919, no. 1: 1–4.
40. See "Ostrov Formosa—geograficheskii ocherk," *Vokurg sveta,* July 23, 1895.
41. Cultural critics of imperialism, such as Edward Said, have argued that this notion of cultural hegemony is at the root of European narratives depicting "the other" as inferior people. See Edward Said, *Orientalism* (1978), 6–8, 19–21. Homi K. Bhabha and other critics believe that these nationalistic or glorifying geographic narratives leave little room for the voice of the subaltern being described. See Homi K. Bhabha, "Introduction: Narrating the Nation," in *Nation and Narration,* ed. Homi K. Bhabha (1990), 3.
42. K. Nosilov, "Po iugo-zapadnoi sibiri," *Estestvoznanie i geografiia* 1896, no. 6 (August): 670–96.
43. See "Vstrecha s liudami," *Vokrug sveta,* March 19, 1895, pp. 178–79.
44. A. E. Fersman, "Iskopaemyia bogatstva Galitsii i Bykoviny," *Priroda* 1915 (March): 386–99.
45. Prof. Mashasek, "Noveishiia uzsledovaniia Tian'-Shania," *Priroda* 1912 (December): 1495–96.
46. Prof. L. L. Ivanova, "Na novoi zemle," *Priroda* 1913 (January): 87–94.
47. "Pereezd' cherez kavkaz," *Vokrug sveta* 1864: 70–77.
48. Members of this movement helped establish museums throughout provincial Russia and encouraged local residents to gather data and artifacts about their locales (Utechin, "Bolsheviks and their Allies," 130–35).
49. Kendall Bailes, "Natural Scientists and the Soviet System," in *Party, State, and Society in the Russian Civil War* (1989), 290–91.

50. S. F. Ol'denburg, "Nauka v SSSR," *Iskra nauki* 1927, no. 11 (November): 406–407.
51. *Iskra* 1927, no. 1 (January): 15.
52. V. A. Obruchev, "Iskopaemye bogatstva Sibiri, ikh sovremennoe ispol'zovanie i znachenie," *Iskra* 1927, no. 1 (January): 15–18.
53. M. Zhdanko, "Issledovanie nashikh severnykh bogatstv," *Nauka i ee rabotniki* 1921, no. 2: 12–17.
54. See V. A. Obruchev, *Plutoniia* (1924).
55. See V. A. Obruchev, *Zemli sannikova* (1926).
56. See *Chelovek i priroda* 1925, no. 1 (January): 1.
57. I. Eliashevich, "Lenin i religiia," *Chelovek i priroda* 1926, no. 1 (January): 13–18.
58. S. M. Selivanov, "Proiskhozhdenie mira," *Chelovek i priroda* 1925, no. 2 (February): 35–36.
59. "Proshloe i budushe cheloveka," *Iskra nauki* 1925, no. 4 (October): 27–29.
60. G. Azimov, "Proiskhozhdenie zhizni na zemle," *Iskra* 1924, no. 4 (April): 5–10.
61. M. Gremiatskii, "Proiskhozdenie cheloveka," *Iskra* 1925, no. 5 (May): 10–11.
62. For an example of this kind of analysis in a popular scientific article, see A. - Bystrov, "Proiskhozhdenie loshadi," *Iskra* 1924, no. 11 (November): 12–14.

CHAPTER 6

1. See B. E. Raikov, *Russkie biologi-evoliutsionisty do Darvina* (1951–59). Raikov also discusses the importance of M. G. Pavlov (1793–1840), one of the more popular professors in scientific studies at Moscow University in the 1820s and 1830s.
2. S. R. Mikulinskii, *Karl Frantsovich Rul'e, Uchenyi, chelovek, i uchitel' 1814–1858 gg.* (1979), 5–6.
3. See Alexander Herzen's article in *Moskovskie vedomosti*, December 8, 1845.
4. See Karl Rouillier's article in *Moskovskie vedomosti* 1852, no. 4.
5. Raikov, *Russkie biologi-evoliutsionisty* 3, 193–200.
6. James Allen Rogers, "The Reception of Darwin's *Origin of Species* by Russian Scientists," *ISIS* 64, no. 224 (1973): 494–95. Rouillier, however, had no definite answer on the process and means of evolution. Like other pre-Darwinists in Russia, he believed that changes in heredity were influenced by surrounding conditions and by the Lamarkian notion of the inheritance of acquired characteristics. See Karl Rul'e, "O vliianii naruzhnykh uslovii na zhizn' zhivotnykh," in *Izbrannye biologicheskie proizvedeniia* (1954), 36–50.
7. Darwin had been in correspondence with Alexander's brother Vladimir, the paleontologist. In May of 1873 Darwin sent a letter to Vladimir noting how interesting and important his brother Alexander's doctoral dissertation was from an evolutionary standpoint. Alexander Kovalevskii's work on small marine organisms was important to some of the arguments in Darwin's *The Descent of Man*. See Charles Darwin to Vladimir Kovalevsky, May 21, 1873, in Charles Darwin, *Izbrannye Pis'ma* (1950), 237.
8. See M. A. Gremiatskii, *Il'ia Il'ich Mechnikov. Ego zhizn' i rabota* (1945).
9. *Borba za nauka v tsarskoi rossi* (1931), 183–84.
10. James A. Rogers, "Charles Darwin and Russian Scientists," *Russian Review* 19 (1960): 378–79.

11. Alexander Vucinich, *Darwin in Russian Thought* (1988), 99.
12. Mikhail Pogodin, *Prostaia rech' o mudrenykh veshchakh* (1873), 447.
13. N. A. Rubakin, *Istoriia russkoi zemli* (1919), 18–19.
14. See I. I. Puzanov, "Pamiati V. V. Lunkevich," *Biulleten' moskovskogo ob-va ispytatelei prirody: Otdel biologicheskii,* vyp. 6, 1947.
15. See V. V. Lunkevich, *Osnovy zhizni* (1910) and "Staroe i novoe v evoliutsionnoi teorii," *Russkoe bogatsvo* 1910, no. 1: 133–56.
16. *Vestnik znaniia* 1909, no. 2, pp. 168–72, 209–50.
17. Vucinich, *Darwin in Russian Thought,* 313–14.
18. Ibid., 315.
19. K. A. Timiriazev, "Znachenie perevorota, proizvedennogo v sovremennom estestvoznanii Darvinom," in Charles Darwin, *Proiskhozhdenie vidov,* perevod i vvodnaia stat'ia K. A. Timiriazeva (1952), 23–24.
20. See B. E. Raikov, *Russkie biologi-evoliutsionisty do Darvina* (1951–59).
21. B. E. Raikov, "Iz istorii darvinizma v Rossii" (part 1), *Trudy instituta istorii estestvoznaniia i tekhniki* 16 (1957): 3–30.
22. Along with its central organization, the society had five hundred members and twenty affiliates in other cities. The society was unique in the Russian Republic for its ability to unite pedagogues, natural scientists, and teachers in higher institutions. Raikov and V. A. Vagner edited the society's journal, *The Natural Sciences in the School.* See GARF, f.2307, op.2, d.362, ll. 1, 3–4.
23. "Otchet zasedanii 20 dekabriia," *Estesvoznanie v shkole* 1919, no. 1: 52.
24. "Otchet zasedanii 24 ianvaria 1919 goda," *Estesvoznanie v shkole* 1919, no. 1: 53.
25. Ibid., 60.
26. "Khronika—Moskovskaia konferenstsiia prepodavatelei estestvoznaniia," *Na putakh k novoi shkole* 1922, no. 1 (July): 78.
27. "Itogi I vserossiiskogo s"ezda po estestvenno-istoricheskomu obrazovaniiu," *Estestvoznanie v shkole* 1924, no. 1: 1.
28. N. K. Krupskaia discussed the program of various pedagogues who met at the first All-Russian Congress of Natural-Historical Education in Petrograd. She argued that for the most part the congress was against the various pedagogical schemata of GUS programs. See N. K. Krupskaia, "Novye programmy v otsenke s'ezda po estestvenno-istoricheskomu obrazovaniiu," *Estestvoznanie v shkole* 1923, no. 9 (November): 78–80.
29. Zavadovskii had graduated from Moscow University in 1919 and thus started his active scientific career under Soviet rule. He was director of the laboratory of experimental biology at the Sverdlov Communist University, but left in 1931 to join the faculty of the All-Union Institute of Animal Husbandry. In 1932 he became a member of the Communist Party (B. M. Zavadovskii, *Ocherki vnutrennei sekretsii* [1928]).
30. See Daniel P. Todes. *Darwin without Malthus: The Struggle for Existence in Russian Evolutionary Thought* (1989).
31. See B. M. Zavadovskii, *Darvinizm i marksizm* (1926).
32. See A. F. Manelonskii, "Po Bogoslovam—ikh te orudiem," *Krasnoe studenchestvo* 1927, no. 3 (October): 50–51.
33. A. Lukachevskii, "Antireligioznaia propaganda i studenchestvo," *Krasnoe studenchestvo* 1927, no. 3 (October): 51.

34. N. Chelianov, "Iz istorii bor'by za materialisticheskoe mirovozzrenie v vuzakh," *Krasnoe studenchestvo* 1927, nos. 4–5 (November): 58–59.

35. See "Obsheobrazovatel'nyi minimum v oblasti estestvennykh nauk," *Molodaia gvardiia* 1922, nos. 1–2 (February–March): 204–205.

36. A. N. Bartenev, "Lamark i Darvin," *Molodaia gvardiia* 1923 nos. 7–8: 143–44.

37. See J. G. Crowther, *Soviet Science* (1936), 3–6.

38. See Allan K. Wildman, *The Making of a Workers' Revolution: Russian Social Democracy* (1967), 33–35. Richard Pipes claims that some of the workers' *kruzhki* also studied difficult works of an advanced nature. Especially popular in this category were the writings of Darwin and Spencer. Various theories on the origin of the earth and universe were also stressed in these groups. See Richard Pipes, *Social Democracy and the St. Petersburg Labor Movement 1885–1897* (1963), 5, 29.

39. The League of the Godless was a voluntary society founded by Emelian Iaroslavskii and was associated with the newspaper *Bezbozhnik* (the godless). The organization had cells in factories, rural areas, and educational institutions. See Daniel Peris, *Storming the Heavens: The Soviet League of the Militant Godless* (1998). During the 1920s the Central Committee's Agit-Prop department had its own commission for antireligious activity. See B. N. Konovalov, *K massovomu ateizmu* (1974); Dimitry V. Pospielovsky, *A History of Soviet Atheism in Theory and Practice* (1988).

40. See James Thrower, *Marxist-Leninist "Scientific-Atheism" and the Study of Religion and Atheism in the USSR* (1983).

41. Joan Delaney, "Origins of Antireligious Organizations," in *Aspects of Religion in the Soviet Union 1917–1967,* ed. Richard H. Marshall, Jr. (1971), 104–105.

42. See G. Vorontsov, *O propagande ateizma* (1959).

43. *Kommunisticheskaia partiia sovetskogo soiuza v rezolutsiiakh i resheniiakh s"ezdov, konferentsii i plenumov TsK,* 8th ed. (1970), 2:37–38.

44. See *Nauka i religiia* 1922, no. 1, p. 10.

45. See Delaney, "Origins of Antireligious Organizations," 110–15.

46. In the 1920s, Marxist propagandists were especially critical of scientists who maintained strong religious beliefs. They believed espousing science and religion would send mixed signals to the common reader and also encourage a type of scientific thinking that could coexist with religion. See E. A. Lazarevich, *Populiarizatsiia nauki v Rossii* (1981), 162.

47. For a discussion of Iaroslavskii's position on antireligious propaganda during NEP and the period of the First Five-Year Plan, see George L. Kline, *Religious and Anti-Religious Thought in Russia* (1968), 150–51.

48. A. M. Bol'shakov, *Derevnia, 1917–1927* (1927), 331–32.

49. *Kommunisticheskaia partiia i sovetskoe pravitelstvo o religii i tserkvi* (1959), 76.

50. *Komm. partiia sovetskogo soiuza,* 471.

51. "Tsirkuliarno, 8 fevralia 1922, vsem obkomam, oblbiuro i gubkomam RKP, o postanovke antireligioznoi propagandy, zam. zaved. agit-prop otdel TsK RKP (b), Ia. Iakovlev," Tsentral'nyi partiinyi arkhiv Instituta Marksizma-Leninizma pri Tsentral'nom komitete KPSS (Rossiiskii tsentr khraneniia i izucheniia dokumentov noveishei istorii—hereafter RTsKhIDNI), f. 17, op. 60, d. 146, l.50.

52. Ibid., ll.51–52.

53. "Zasedaniia podkomissii po antireligioznoi propagande v derevne pri p-otdele

propagandy TsK RKP, ot 12-go sentiabria 1923 g.," RTsKhIDNI, f.17, op.60, d.438, l.1.

54. "Protokol, soveshchaniia p-otdela propagandy agitpropa TsKRKP po antireligioznoi propagande v derevne, 5-go oktiabria 1923," RTsKhIDNI, f.17, op.60, d.438, ll.9–10.

55. *Komsomol'skaia paskha* (1924), 94–97. For a discussion of the spread of scientific techniques in agriculture by the Komsomol, see I. Liubimov, *Komsomol v sovetskom stroitel'stve, 1917–1927* (1928), 153–54.

56. Peter Kenez, *The Birth of the Propaganda State: Soviet Methods of Mass Mobilization, 1917–1929* (1985), 183–85.

57. Moshe Lewin, *The Making of the Soviet System* (1985), 61–71.

58. Lynne Viola, "The Peasant Nightmare: Visions of Apocalypse in the Soviet Countryside," *Journal of Modern History,* no. 62 (December 1990): 754–55. For an analysis of religious activists in the villages and their relationship to the developing Soviet state under the NEP, see Glennys Young, *Power and the Sacred in Revolutionary Russia: Religious Activists in the Village* (1997).

59. Helmut Altrichter, "Insoluble Conflicts: Village Life between Revolution and Collectivization," in *Russia in the Era of NEP,* ed. Sheila Fitzpatrick, Alexander Rabinowitch, and Richard Stites (1991), 204–205.

60. For further analysis see Vladimir G. Bogoraz-Tan, *Khristanstvo v svete etnografii* (1928).

61. See A. Angarov, *Klassovaia bor'ba v sovetskoi derevne* (1929), 32.

62. See V. A. Kumanev, *Sotsializm i vsenarodnaia gramotnost'* (1967).

63. See Report by Iaroslavl' Gubkom Agitprop Otdel sent to Narkompros, May 9, 1922, in local Iaroslavl' Communist Party archive, Tsentr Dokumentatsii Noveishei Istorii Iaroslavskoi Oblasti, hereafter cited as TsDNIIaO (formerly, Partarkhiv Iaroslavskogo Obkoma KPSS), TsDNIIaO, f. 1, op. 27, d.961, l.100.

64. "Protokol zasedanii komissii pri II/otdele propagandy TsK RKP po voprosu ob anti-religioznoi propagandy za iiulia mesiats 1923 g.," RTsKhIDNI, f.17, op.60, d.4, ll.42–42ob.

65. "Otchet politinstruktora A. Saikina za iiulia mesiats 1926 g., nastroeniia i zaprosy krest'ianstva," RTsKhIDNI, f.17, op.60, d.405, l.162.

66. RTsKhIDNI, f.17, op.60, d.438, l.35.

67. Ibid.

68. See "Itogi raboty kursov Antireligioznikov pri APO GK, Iaroslavl', VKP (b)," 1927–28, in TsDNIIaO, f. 1, op. 27, d. 3409, ll. 1–2, 38–39.

69. See "Zasedaniia Agitkollegii Pri APO GK OT 20-7-1927 goda," in TsDNIIaO, f. 1, op. 27, d. 3088, l.50.

70. Founded in 1927, the Society of Friends of Defense and Aviation-Chemical Construction, Osoaviakhim, was one of the largest mass voluntary associations in the USSR before WWII. Many Communist propagandists and organizers therefore looked to it as an example of successful mass mobilization. See William E. Odom, *The Soviet Volunteers: Modernization and Bureaucracy in a Public Mass Organization* (1973).

71. Ibid., l.51.

72. TsDNIIaO, f. 1, op. 27, d. 3088, ll. 46–47.

73. Ibid., l.47.

74. TsDNIIaO, f. 1, op. 27, d. 3088, ll. 46–48, 98–99. Many of these evaluations

dealt with antireligious and scientific propaganda in Iaroslavl' between June and October of 1927.

75. See Delaney, "Origins of Antireligious Organizations," 114–17.

76. For a detailed account of the Militant League see Daniel Peris, "The 1929 Congress of the Godless," *Soviet Studies* 1991, no. 4. Peris's article concentrates on the period after 1929. Like Delaney, he generally argues that during the period 1923–1929 a broader educational approach to antireligious activity was sponsored by the Bolshevik state. Though his work in general focuses on the bureaucracy of the league and the failures of its antireligious work, he seems to treat the scientific debates regarding religion in a more inconsequential manner.

77. T. Gagarin, "Tezisy doklada: Itogi i perspektivy antireligioznoi raboty," Report Given at the First All-Union Congress of Atheists in Smolensk (April 1925), in Archive of the Smolensk Oblast All-Union Communist Party SSSR 1917–41 (hereafter cited as Smolensk Archive), National Archives and Records, Washington, D.C., WKP 458, 1.

78. T. Gagarin, "Tezisy doklada: Itogi i perspektivy antireligioznoi raboty," Smolensk Archive, WKP 458, 2.

79. T. Varbanchika, "Kak meshat' bolezni veroi i naukoi," Report Given at April 1925 All-Union Congress of Atheists in Smolensk, Smolensk Archive, WKP 458, 1925, 1–4.

80. T. Lebedeva, predsed. Gubprosa, "Tezisy doklada: Antireligioznaia rabota uchitelia v shkole i vne shkoly," Smolensk Archive, WKP 458, 1925.

81. Protokol no. 1, Zasedaniia prezidiuma smolenskogo gubernskogo soveta soiuza bezbozhnikov SSSR, ot 9 ianvaria, 1926 g., January 9, 1926, All-Union Congress of Atheists in Smolensk, Smolensk Archive, WKP 458, 1926.

82. TsDNIIaO, f. 229, op. 9, d. 95, ll. 108–109.

83. Ibid.

84. See "V Gubkom BKP (b) ot Gubsoveta Soiuza Bezbozhnikov," Nov. 22, 1928, in TsDNIIaO, f. 1, op. 27, d. 3414, l.12.

85. See "O sostoianii antireligioznoi raboti v 3-I raione g. Iaroslavlia," analysis of antireligious work in three regions of Iaroslavl' from mid-1927 to early 1928, in TsDNIIaO, f. 1, op. 27, d. 3088, l.75.

86. See Shalygin's letters in the local party archives sent to Gubkom leaders on the topic of agitation-propaganda and antireligion throughout 1928, in TsDNIIaO, f. 1, op. 27, d. 3414, ll. 13–22.

87. I. D. Strashun, *Bor'ba za zdorov'e—bor'ba s religiei* [Trudy pervogo vsesoiznogo s"ezda bezbozhnikov, vypusk 7] (1925), 3–5.

88. Prof. B. M. Zavadovskii, *Estestvoznanie i religiia* [Lektsiia, prochitannaia 24 aprelia 1925 g. dlia delegatov vsesoiuznogo s"ezda bezbozhnikov stenograficheskii otchet, vypusk 6] (1925), 3–4, 6–10. In this speech to delegates, Zavadovskii discussed an article in the English science journal *Nature* entitled "On the Prohibition of Darwinism."

CHAPTER 7

1. "Imennoi spisok nauchnykh i administrativno-tekhnicheskogo personala G.N-I.I. im. Timiriazeva," GARF, f.406, op.12, d.1920, ll.129–130.

2. G. Bosse, *Protokoly soveta instituta im. Timiriazeva* (1925), 9–11. The Institute, though based in Moscow, published pamphlets and distributed these through-out parts of the former USSR.

3. "Kratkii otchet o deiatel'nosti G.T.N-I.I. za 1925/26 god.," GARF, f.406, op.12, d.1920, l.27.

4. "Nauchno-populiarizatsionnaia deiatel'nost' instituta im. Timiriazeva," GARF, f.406, op.12, d.1920, ll.58–59.

5. The rabfak, or workers' school, was a type of educational institution estab-lished during the first years of the Russian Revolution to prepare workers and peasants for higher education.

6. GARF, f.406, op.12, d.1920, l.78.

7. Ibid., l.80.

8. Ibid., ll.87–88.

9. "Godovoi otchet o deiatel'nosti G.T.N-I.I. za 1924/25 god.," GARF, f.406, op.12, d.1920, ll.19–20.

10. Periskop, "Populiarizatsiia ili vul'garizatsiia? (O narodnykh knizhkakh N. A. Rubakina)," *Kniga i revoliutsiia* 1920, nos. 3–4: 69–70.

11. Ibid., 71.

12. N. A. Rubakin, "Kak pisat' nauchnye knizhki dlia massovogo chitatelia," *Kniga i profsoiuzy* 1927, no. 2: 3–5.

13. N. A. Rubakin, *Chto takoe bibliologicheskaia psikhologiia?* (1924), 9–10.

14. B. M. Zavadovskii, *Sbornik statei po voprosam populiarizatsii estestvoznaniia* (1923), 21.

15. V. V. Lunkevich was a biologist, science popularizer, and historian of the natu-ral sciences. Born in 1866, he studied at Petersburg and Khar'kov Universities. From 1925 to 1933 he was in the biology faculty at Crimean University. From 1933 onward he taught biology at the Moscow Pedagogical Institute.

16. B. M. Zavadovskii, "Provaly populiarizatora," in *O populiarizatsii estestvoznaniia, sbornik statei* (1926), 54.

17. Katerina Clark, in a study of intellectual life in Soviet Russia, has argued that during the "quiet revolution" of the NEP a new generation of nonparty cultural leaders with a nonacademic background displaced the cultural leaders of War Communism. Simultaneously, at the beginning of the twenties, a new genera-tion of party-oriented writers made its entry into Soviet culture with a militant brand of parochialism. See Katerina Clark, "The Quiet Revolution in Intellec-tual Life," in *Russia in the Era of NEP,* ed. Sheila Fitzpatrick, A. Rabinowitch, and R. Stites (1991), 224–26.

18. E. Vinogradova, "K izucheniiu chitatelia," *Krasnyi bibliotekar'* 1925, no. 4 (April): 9–13.

19. Ibid.

20. Evgenii Elachich was a science popularizer who was highly regarded by Zavadovskii. Elachich was known especially for his short popular pieces on paleontology.

21. Zavadovskii, *Sbornik statei,* 79–81.

22. E. Vinogradova, "K izucheniiu chitatelia," 9–13.

23. M. Gremiatskii was a doctor of the biological sciences and after 1935 was a professor at Moscow University. He worked on anatomy, anthropology, and the history of the natural sciences. Gremiatskii wrote popular-science pam-

phlets that appeared in the series *Nachatki nauki* (rudiments of science). In one of his more popular works, the author explained the pioneering work of the Austrian monk Gregor Mendel in the study of heredity (M. Gremiatskii, *Chto takoe nasledstvennost' i kak ona proiavliaetsia u cheloveka?* (1927), 32–34.

24. M. Gremiatskii, "K voprosu o populiarizatsii estestvoznaniia," *Knigonosha* 1926, no. 40: 7–8.

25. Considerable variation occurs among the statistics of the purge, perhaps because it was an ongoing process throughout 1929 and 1930. Academician A. E. Fersman commented on this in one of the first official reports on the purge, which was published in January 1930. See A. E. Fersman, "Khronika," *Nauchnyi rabotnik* 1930 (January). See also "Chistka apparata akademii nauk," *Izvestiia,* September 4, 1929, p. 3; Loren R. Graham, *The Soviet Academy of Sciences and the Communist Party 1927–1932* (1967), 128–29.

26. The purges in the natural sciences during the Cultural Revolution had an adverse effect on the development of new technology and scientific progress in general in Soviet Russia. See Medvedev, *Soviet Science* (1978), 25–33.

27. Vucinich, *The Soviet Academy,* 9–11. An earlier 1927 charter, which replaced the 1836 charter, made the academy a truly Soviet institution with powerful secretaries, direct channels of government interference, and covert party control.

28. During this period the technical intelligentsia witnessed its own purges. Younger technicians moved upward into positions vacated by the older generation. The "practicals" or "self-taught" (*praktiki* or *samouchki*) were a group of the technical intelligentsia who performed the work of technologists without having obtained a degree (Kendall E. Bailes, *Technology and Society Under Lenin and Stalin: Origins of the Soviet Technical Intelligentsia, 1917–1941* (1978), 30–31.

29. Ibid., 69–70.

30. Ibid., 71–72.

31. "Ot redaktsiia," *Iskra* 1928, no. 6 (June): 1.

32. The *vydvizhenie* was the movement (during the Stalinist Cultural Revolution) for proletarian advancement.

33. Robert A. McCutcheon, "The 1936–1937 Purge of Soviet Astronomers," *Slavic Review* 50, no. 1 (spring 1991): 101–103.

34. V. T. Ter-Oganesov, "Na perelome," *Mirovedenie* 1930, no. 19 (May–August): 5–16.

35. F. F. Korolev, T. D. Korneichik, and Z. I. Ravkin, *Ocherki po istorii sovetskoi shkoly i pedagogiki* (1961), 449.

36. See David Joravsky, *The Lysenko Affair* (1970), 325.

37. *Priroda i liudi,* October 15, 1931, pp. 64–65.

38. *Revoliutsiia i priroda,* October 30, 1931, pp. 3–4.

39. See Ter-Oganesov, "Na perelome," *Mirovedenie* 1930, no. 19.

40. *Iskra* 1930, no. 12 (December): pp. 1, 30–31.

41. A. Vladimirov, "Perspektivy aliuminievogo rosta," *Revoliutsiia i priroda,* October 30, 1931, pp. 4–5.

42. F. Balabin, "Kharakter budushchei voiny," *Revoliutsiia i priroda,* October 30, 1931, p. 26.

43. L. Girich, "Sakharovarenie i ego ratsionalizatsiia," *Iskra* 1930, no. 11 (November).

44. Ibid, 1–2.

45. *Revoliutsiia i priroda,* October 30, 1931, pp. 35–36.
46. See Bess and Littlepage's commentary on this problem in *In Search of Soviet Gold.*

CHAPTER 8

1. See Sheila Fitzpatrick, "The 'Soft' Line on Culture and Its Enemies: Soviet Cultural Policy, 1922–1927," *Slavic Review* (June 1974): 269.
2. See Larry E. Holmes, *The Kremlin and the SchoolHouse: Reforming Education in Soviet Russia, 1917–1931* (1991), 116–17.
3. For the first substantial work on VARNITSO by a Soviet author, based on solid archival documentation, see L. M. Zak, "Sozdanie i deiatel'nost' VARNITSO v 1927–1932 godakh," *Istoriia SSSR* 1959, no. 6: 94–107. Zak's work concentrated on the political activity of the organization and how it mobilized forces to support socialism. For a more updated and critical analysis of the organization, see I. A. Tugarinov, "VARNITSO i akademiia nauk SSSR, 1927–1937," *Voprosy istorii estestvoznaniia i tekhniki* 1989 no. 4: 46–54.
4. Rossiiskii gosudarstvennyi arkhiv ekonomiki (hereafter cited as RGAE), f.4394, op.1, d.1, ll.4–5.
5. Letter from I. Iskol'dskii to A. Lunacharskii dated December 17, 1927, in RGAE, f.4394, op.1, d.1, ll.44–48.
6. On the debates within Narkompros and the debate over technical education during the mid-twenties, see Holmes, *The Kremlin and the Schoolhouse,* 83–92.
7. The movement of the "practicality" of education was especially trumpeted by the young radical militant pedagogue V. N. Shulgin, who had entered Narkompros in the 1920s on the invitation of Krupskaia (an initial member of VARNITSO). Shulgin's ideas were put into practice in 1930 by a decision of the Congress on Polytechnical Education to link primary schools with neighbouring factories and kolkhozi. See Sheila Fitzpatrick, *Education and Social Mobility in the Soviet Union, 1921–1934* (1979), 136–52.
8. On the Academy's relationship with the Communist Party during the period of Cultural Revolution, see Loren R. Graham, *The Soviet Academy of Sciences and the Communist Party, 1927–32* (1967). Also see David Joravsky, *Soviet Marxism and Natural Science, 1917–1932* (1961).
9. RGAE, f.4394, op.1, d.1, ll.109–10.
10. Much to the dismay of VARNITSO members, however, by the mid-1930s, the Soviet Academy of Sciences would acquire a leading position amongst all Soviet scientific institutions. The academy would even begin to absorb laboratories and institutes previously subordinate to various commissariats after the 1917 Revolution, eventually even subsuming its major competitor, the Communist Academy (Krementsov, *Stalinist Science,* 37–39.
11. RGAE, f.4394, op.1, d.1, ll.109–10.
12. The Communist Party during the cultural revolution would ultimately support the centralized nature of the academy, with some important changes, and not support radical plans of restructuring. When an assault on the Academy of Sciences came after 1929, the young militants, realizing the party's support for the academy, demanded not so much a reorganization of the institution as access

to the privileges it provided its members. See Loren Graham, *Science in Russia and the Soviet Union, A Short History* (1993), 97. Also see V. D. Esakov, *Sovetskaia nauka v gody pervoi piatiletki: osnovnye napravleniia gosudarstvennogo rukovodstva naukoi* (1971).

13. Kendall Bailes has noted that the leadership of VARNITSO contained a number of important chemistry specialists, and the society was thus particularly active in promoting the chemical industry. In March of 1928, the Soviet government responded favorably to a petition written by prominent VARNITSO members and created a Soviet Committee for Chemicalization headed by a Politburo member (*Technology and Society Under Lenin and Stalin* (1978), 164.

14. L. M. Zak, "Sozdanie i deiatel'nost' VARNITSO v 1927–1932 gg.," *Istoriia SSSR* 1958, no. 6: 104–107.

15. RGAE, f.4394, op.1, d.13, ll.5–6.

16. "Protokol no. 83/4 zasedaniia TsB VARNITSO," RGAE, f.4394, op.1, d.41, l.15.

17. RGAE, f.4394, op.1, d.41, l.16.

18. B. M. Zavadovskii, "Nauchnoe obshchestvo v epokhu sotsialisticheskoi rekon-struktsii," *Za kommunisticheskoe prosveshchenie,* March 19, 1931, p. 3.

19. K. K'iatkovskii, "Iskopaemye ot nauki," *Za kommunisticheskoe prosveshchenie,* March 19, 1931, p. 3.

20. "Obrashchenie gruppy akademikov i professorov k tovarishchu Stalinu, 1931 g." (undated). RGAE, f.4394, op.1, d.41, l.5.

21. See "Tovarishchu Stalinu, ot predsedatel' VARNITSO, Akademik Bakh, December 26, 1929," RGAE, f.4394, op.1, d.13, l.1. No letters exist in the available archival records regarding any response by Stalin to Academician A. N. Bakh's letters. Letters were also sent by VARNITSO to many members of the Communist Party's Central Committee.

22. The distinctly "proletarian" aspect of the period of cultural revolution involved the promotion of workers into more responsible positions and also their recruitment into higher educational institutions. This period also witnessed an enormous increase in the overall number of administrative and professional positions. See Sheila Fitzpatrick, "Cultural Revolution as Class War," in *Cultural Revolution,* ed. Sheila Fitzpatrick, 32–33.

23. *Pervaia vsesoiuznaia konferentsiia rabotnikov sotsialisticheskoi promyshlennosti: stenograficheskii otchet* (1931), 195.

24. "V VARNITSO 20 aprelia 1931, ot prez. ob-va Mosk. obshch. isp. prirody," RGAE, f.4394, op.1, d.57, l.36.

25. "V VARNITSO 15 aprelia 1931, ot zam. prez. Ross. assots. fizikov V. Romanov" RGAE, f.4394, op.1, d.57, l.54.

26. RGAE, f.4394, op.1, d.57, ll.36ob., 45. In their letters to VARNITSO and other state organizations, some voluntary scientific societies emphatically declared that recruiting working class individuals into their organizations was a complicated matter. They believed that any policy of recruiting and promoting such individuals would be difficult to maintain without affecting the entire nature of their scientific societies.

27. As an example of party concern depicted in the popular press at this time, see N. Bukharin, "O tekhnicheskom propagande i ee organizatsii," *Za industrializatsiiu,* August 9, 1931, p. 2.

28. GAIaO, f. 221, op.1, d. 1., l.4.

29. "Perechen' nauchno-issledovatel'skikh rabot," in GAIaO, f. 221, op. 1, d. 242, ll. 8–9.
30. "Otchet o deiatel'nosti Komiteta Assostiatsii po izucheniiu proizvoditel'nykh sil Iaroslavskoi gub. za vremia s 1926–1927 gg.," in GAIaO, f. 221, op. 1, d. 242, ll. 210–13.
31. GAIaO, f. 221, op. 1, d. 296, ll. 20–34.
32. See February 9, 1931, "Circular to all Scientific-Research, Museums, and Regional Studies Groups from Narkompros's Zav. Sektorom Nauki (Luppov)," in GAIaO, f. 221, op. 1, d. 316, l.5.
33. GAIaO, f. 221, op. 1, d. 316, l.6.
34. See February 20, 1931, Narkompros "Circular to Provincial Scientific Societies and Orgnanizations," in GAIaO, f. 221, op. 1, d. 316, l.15.
35. GAIaO, f. 221, op. 1, d.296, ll.19–20, and refer to d.285, l.24.
36. Letter dated January 25, 1929, sent to Central Glavnauka officials via the Iaroslavl' Gubernaia Department of Narkompros, in GAIaO, f. 221, op. 1, d. 304, l.38.
37. Smeta 1929–30gg, GAIaO, f. 221, op. 1, d.304, ll. 104–104ob.
38. GAIaO, f. 221, op. 1, d.310, l.1.
39. GAIaO, f. 221, op. 1, d.310, l.2.
40. GAIaO, f. 221, op. 1, d.310, l.13.
41. GAIaO, f. 221, op. 1, d.310, l.16. This denial by the Central Bureau of the Ivanovo Regional Studies Sector occurred as a result of an August 27, 1930, meeting in Ivanovo.
42. GAIaO, f. 221, op. 1, d.310, l.18.
43. GAIaO, f. 221, op. 1, d.315, l.13.
44. GAIaO, f. 221, op. 1, d.310, l.25. This was a circular sent by Narkompros's Scientific Sector in Moscow (Glavnauka) to all provincial and local scientific organizations on November 15, 1930.
45. GAIaO, f. 221, op. 1, d.318, l.22. "V Iaroslavskoe Ob., Perepiska po likvidatsii obshchestva 25 aprelia 1931g."
46. GAIaO, f. 221, op. 1, d.318, l.9.
47. Tsentr Dokumentatsii Noveishei Istorii Iaroslavskoi Oblasti, hereafter cited as TsDNIIaO (formerly, Partarkhiv Iaroslavskogo Obkoma KPSS), f. 1, op. 27, d. 3414, ll. 12, 13, 14–22. (Material from Iaroslavskii Gubkom VKP (b), 1917–29, Agitpropotdel).
48. TsDNIIaO, f. 1, op. 27, d. 3414, ll.21–23.
49. See *Severnyi rabochii,* January 27, 1940. In 1939 antireligious activists claimed that nearly ninety public lectures were conducted at the museum, attracting close to eight thousand participants from the local public. The museum offered photography exhibits with pictures of the solar system and various planets, as well as a special department for children. See also *Severnyi rabochii,* March 22, 1940.
50. See TsDNIIaO, f. 229, op. 9, d. 95, ll.108–109.
51. TsDNIIaO, f. 1, op. 27, d. 3409, l.1.
52. TsDNIIaO, f. 1, op. 27, d. 3150, ll. 8–10.
53. TsDNIIaO, f. 1, op. 27, d. 1691, ll.1–3. (Raspisanie zaniatiia kursakh rabotnikov pri Gubsovpartskole, Ia. Gubkom VKP [b] Agitpropotdel)
54. TsDNIIaO, f. 1, op. 27, d. 3409, ll. 1–4.

55. TsDNIIaO, f. 1, op. 27, d. 3088, ll. 38–46, 47–48, 98–99.
56. TsDNIIaO, f. 273, op. 68, d.49, ll. 1–5 (material from Iaroslavskii Okruzhkom VKP [b] Ivanovskoi Promyshlennoi Oblasti Agit-Prop Otdel Propagandy i Kul'tury).
57. TsDNIIaO, f. 273, op. 68, d.49, l.1ob.
58. Ibid., l.2.
59. Ibid. ll. 2–2ob.
60. TsDNIIaO, f. 273, op. 68, d. 97, ll. 1ob., 5ob., 48–49.
61. TsDNIIaO, f. 229, op. 9, d. 95, ll. 12–14.

CHAPTER 9

1. For an in-depth analysis of radical militant pedagogues of the 1920s and early 1930s, see Sheila Fitzpatrick, *Education and Social Mobility in the Soviet Union*, 136–52.
2. Donald Filtzer's 1986 book on workers under Stalin (*Soviet Workers and Stalinist Industrialization: The Formation of Modern Soviet Production Relations, 1928–1941* ([1986]) directly addresses this issue of how workers found effective means to circumvent the draconian pressures placed upon them by managers and the regime. Solomon Schwartz (*Labor in the Soviet Union* [New York: Praeger, 1952]) has also documented draconian labor laws under Stalin, as well as the violations and circumventions of those laws. Lewis Siegelbaum and Ronald Suny have also argued that there was a tragic irony to the early Soviet era in the labor arena: namely in an ostensibly Marxist state, workers had very little collective means to create their own agendas ("Class Backwards? In Search of the Soviet Working Class," in *Making Workers Soviet: Power, Class, and Identity*, ed. Lewis H. Siegelbaum and Ronald Grigor Suny [1994], 1–26).
3. Stephen Kotkin has criticized Filtzer and others for not analyzing the terms on which workers actually became part of the greater Stalinist enterprise. Kotkin's perspective, grounded in a Foucaultian construct, is to analyze the dynamic relations of power between workers and the regime. See Stephen Kotkin, "Coercion and Identity: Workers' Lives in Stalin's Showcase City," in *Making Workers Soviet: Power, Class, and Identity*, 274–78. For a more elaborate analysis of this perspective, see Stephen Kotkin, *Magnetic Mountain: Stalinism as Civilization* (1994).
4. In a recent monograph on Soviet labor in Stalin's Russia, Kenneth Strauss has attempted to describe workers not as passive resistors but as class-conscious actors during Stalin's regime. For an analysis of how workers looked upon Soviet factories during the early Stalin era as security networks, cultural providers, as well as community organizers, see Kenneth M. Strauss, *Factory and Community in Stalin's Russia: The Making of an Industrial Working Class* (1997).
5. Witness how Sarah Davies and Sheila Fitzpatrick have analyzed the tenacity of alternative discourses to the regime's propaganda in their work on the Stalinist 1930s. Davies argues that Soviet propaganda has a multivalent nature to it since ordinary citizens invested state dictums with their own interpretive meanings. See Sarah Davies, *Popular Opinion in Stalin's Russia: Terror, Propaganda, and Dissent, 1934–41* (1997). For a recent look at dissonant public opinion during the

purge era of the Stalinist 1930s, one can also refer to Sheila Fitzpatrick, *Everyday Stalinism, Ordinary Life in Extraordinary Times: Soviet Russia in the 1930s* (1999).

6. N. Bukharin, "O tekhnicheskom propagande i ee organizatsii," *Za industrializatsiiu,* August 9, 1931, p. 2.

7. "Zasedanie obshchestva tekhnika massam ot 22-go noiabria 1927 g.," Tsentral'nyi gosudarstvennyi arkhiv oktiabr'skoi revoliutsii i sotsialisticheskogo stroitel'stva SSSR (Gosudarstvennyi arkhiv Rossiiskoi Federatsii, hereafter cited as GARF), f. 5576, op.1, d.1, ll.22–24.

8. "Protokol no. 2, zasedaniia initsiativnoi gruppy po uchrezhdeniiu obshchestva tekhnika massam 12-ogo noiabria 1927 goda," GARF, f. 5576, op.1, d.1, ll.11–13.

9. See *Ankety chlenov Soveta obshchestva 1928* (Questionnaires of the Members of the Soviet of the Organization TekhMass in 1928), GARF, f. 5576, op.1, d.7, ll.1–50.

10. GARF, f. 5576, op.1, d.1, l.14.

11. At a February 1928 meeting of the society, Sverdlov reiterated certain points discussed at the 15th Congress of the Communist Party. He argued that the increase of technical grammar and the spread and popularization of technical knowledge was one of the more important elements for the construction of a socialist economy. See "Stenogramma 28 fevralia 1928 goda," GARF, f. 5576, op.1, d.12, ll.1–2.

12. The leaders of TekhMass were impressed by the fact that in Western Europe and America, large factories and industries organized scientific courses for their workers. Sverdlov argued that the Soviets must be able to learn from organizations such as US Steel, which passed out scientific literature in more comprehensible forms to both their qualified and less-qualified workers (ibid. l.4).

13. "Plan raboti po Moskve: massovaia rabota—populiarizatsiia nauchnotekhnicheskikh znanii," Tsentral'nyi gosudarstvennyi arkhiv RSFSR (hereafter cited as GARF), f.406, op.12, d.2455, l.37.

14. *Iskry nauki* 1931, nos. 5–6, 172. Also see *Otchet Leningradskogo oblastnogo i gorodskogo komiteta VKP (b) IV oblastnoi i gorodskoi partiinoi konferentsii* (1932), 127.

15. N. B. Vasil'eva, "Deiatel'nost' Leningradskikh dobrovol'nykh obshchestv *Tekhika-Massam, Za Ovladenie Tekhnikoi, 1928–1935 gg,*" in *Dobrovol'nye obshchestva v Petrograde-Leningrade v 1917–1937 gg. sbornik statei* (1989), 92.

16. *Otchet Leningradskogo oblastnogo i gorodskogo komiteta VKP (b) IV oblastnoi i gorodskoi partiinoi konferentsii,* 127.

17. GARF, f.5576, op.1, d.12, l.3.

18. Ibid., l.14.

19. Ibid., l.27

20. Ibid. , ll.36–37

21. Ibid.

22. Ibid., ll.26–27.

23. Ibid., l.27

24. The author sampled approximately two hundred cases from the participants of night courses at the Central Technical Station of the All-Union Society TekhMass. The surveys were conducted in July of 1928 in Moscow. See GARF, f. 5576, op.1, d.17.

25. Ibid., l.125.

26. Ibid., l.89.

27. Ibid., l.93.
28. GARF, f. 5576, op.1, d.52, ll.3–4.
29. Ibid., ll.91–92.
30. See "Otchet o prodelannoi rabote na Ukraine po ukrepleniiu Otdeleniia Tekhmass, 1930 goda," GARF, f. 5576, op.1, d.52, l.130.
31. See "Otchet o prodelannoi rabote v gorode Sverdlovske Ural'skoi Oblaste ot aprelia 1930 do 1931 g.," written by a TekhMass instructor named Grashchenkova, GARF, f. 5576, op.1, d.52, l.147.
32. Ibid., l.153.
33. GARF, f. 5576, op.1, d.17, l.130.
34. Ibid.
35. *Pervaia vsesoiuznaia konferentsiia rabotnikov sotsialisticheskoi,* 195–96.
36. GARF, f.5576, op.1, d.108, l.26.
37. Vasil'eva, "Deiatel'nost' Leningradskikh dobrovol'nykh obshchestv," 94–95.
38. GARF, f.5576, op.1, d.111, l.2.
39. GARF, f.5576, op.1, d.142, ll.132–36.
40. Ibid., l.1
41. Ibid., l.115
42. Ibid., l.119.
43. Ibid.
44. Ibid., l.121.
45. Ibid. l.120–21.
46. Ibid. l.124.
47. Ibid.

GLOSSARY

Selected List of Russian Terms and Abbreviations

Agit-Prop: The Administration of Agitation and Propaganda of the Central Committee of the Communist Party

Cheka: security police (during Civil War Period)

FFYP: First Five-Year Industrial Plan (1928–32)

Gosplan: Government Planning Organization

Glavnauka: Scientific Department of the Ministry of Enlightenment

Gosbiudzhet: Government Budget Organization

GPU: State Political Administration

Gubnarodobraz: Provincial People's Ministry of Enlightenment Branch

ispolkom: executive committee (of the soviet)

KEPS: the Commission for Studying the Natural Productive Forces of Russia

khozraschet: commercial cost-accounting (programmatic under NEP)

kolkhoz: collective farm

Komsomol: Communist youth league

kraeved movement: the regional studies movement

kulak: a rich peasant, in Soviet rhetorical terms someone who exploits the labor of other peasants

Narkomvnudel (NKVD): People's Commissariat of Internal Affairs

Narkompros: Soviet Commissariat (or Ministry) of Enlightenment (Ministry of Education)

NEP: the New Economic Policy, introduced March of 1921

NOT: Scientific Organization of Labor

obkomi: oblast (regional) Communist Party structures

Proletkult: Proletarian Cultural Movement

rabfaki: workers' preparatory faculties, to prepare young workers to enter higher schools

Sovnarkom: Council of People's Commissars, highest governmental agency, renamed the Council of Ministers in 1946

stakhanovite: workers and peasants rewarded for overfulfillment of work norms

VARNITSO: All Union Society of the Workers of Science and Technology for the Promotion of Socialist Construction

Vesenkha (VSNKh): Supreme Council of the National Economy

VTsIK: All-Russian Central Executive Committee of the Soviet of People's Deputies

VTsSPS: All-Russian/Union Central Council of Trade Unions
vydvizhentsy: workers and peasants promoted to managerial work, white-collar, or professional positions, as well as those selected for higher educational institutions during the Stalinist Cultural Revolution (1928–1931)
TekhMass: Technology for the Masses
zemstvas: regional and local councils created under Alexander II in the 1860s
ZOT: All-Union Society for the Mastering of Technology

BIBLIOGRAPHY

PRIMARY SOURCES

Archival Sources

RUSSIAN FEDERATION (FORMERLY USSR)

Moscow:

Soviet Communist Party Archives:

Rossiiskii tsentr khraneniia i izucheniia dokumentov noveishei istorii
(RTsKhIDNI) (formerly, Tsentral'nyi partiinyi arkhiv instituta Marksizma-
Leninizma pri Tsentral'nom Komitete KPSS [TsPA IML]).

Soviet Central and Russian Federation State Archives:

Gosudarstvennyi arkhiv Rossiiskoi Federatsii (GARF) (formerly, Tsentral'nyi
gosudarstvennyi arkhiv oktiabr'skoi revoliutsii i sotsialisticheskogo
stroitel'stva SSSR, vysshikh organov gosudarstvennoi vlasti i organov
gosudarstvennogo upravleniia SSSR [TsGAOR SSSR]).
Rossiiskii gosudarstvennyi arkhiv ekonomiki (RGAE) (formerly, Tsentral'nyi
gosudarstvennyi arkhiv narodnogo khoziaistva SSSR [TsGANKh SSSR]).
Tsentral'nyi gosudarstvennyi arkhiv RSFSR (TsGA RSFSR) (presently housed
under the archival administration of GARF).

Soviet/Russian Academy of Sciences Archives:

Arkhiv Rossiiskoi akademii nauk (Arkhiv RAN) (formerly, Arkhiv akademii
nauk SSSR [AAN]).

Manuscript Repositories and State Museum Archives:

Gosudarstvennyi biologicheskii muzei im. K.A. Timir'iazeva (GBMT)
Rossiiskaia gosudarstvennaia biblioteka, otdel rukopisei (RGB) (formerly
Gosudarstvennaia ordena Lenina biblioteka SSSR imeni V. I. Lenina [GBL]).

St. Petersburg (formerly Leningrad):

Soviet and Russian Academy of Sciences Archives:

Sanktpeterburgskii filial Arkhiva (RAN) (formerly Leningradskoe otdelenie
Arkhiva akademii nauk SSSR [LO AAN]).

Iaroslavl':

Soviet/Russian Communist Party Archives:

Tsentr Dokumentatsii Noveishei Istorii Iaroslavskoi Oblasti (TsDNIIaO) (formerly, Partarkhiv Iaroslavskogo Obkoma KPSS).

Former Soviet and Russian State Archives:

Gosudarstvennyi arkhiv Iaroslavskoi oblasti (GAIaO).

UNITED STATES:

Washington, D. C.:

Smolensk Archives. Records of the Smolensk Oblast of the All-Union Communist Party of the Soviet Union, 1917–41. Washington, D.C.: National Archives and Records.

Selected Published Document Collections

Gor'kii i nauka, stat'i, rechi, pis'ma, vospominaniia. Moscow, 1964.
Kommunisticheskaia partiia i sovetskoe pravitelstvo o religii i tserkvi. Moscow, 1959.
KPSS v rezoliutsiiakh i resheniiakh s"ezdov, konferentsii i plenumov TsK. 10 vols. Moscow, 8-e izd., 1970.
Materialy sobrannye osoboiu kommisiiei dlia peresmotra deistvuiushchikh postanovlenii o tsensuri pechati. Chast' vtoraia: administrativnyia rasporiazheniia. St. Petersburg, 1870.
O partiinoi i sovetskoi pechati, radioveshchanii i televidenii. Moscow, 1972.
Otchet Leningradskogo oblastnogo i gorodskogo komiteta VKP (b) IV oblastnoi i gorodskoi partiinoi konferentsii. Leningrad. 1932.
Pervaia vsesoiuznaia konferentsiia rabotnikov sotsialisticheskoi promyshlennosti: stenograficheskii otchet. Moscow, 1931.

Special Collections in the U.S.A.

Harper Manuscipt and Popular Pamphlet Collection. University of Chicago Rare Books Depository Library. Chigago: Regenstein Library, University of Chicago.
Library of Congress Popular Pamphlet Collection. European Division. Washington, D.C.: Library of Congress.
Russian Mass-Education Pamphlet Collection. Hoover Institution on War, Peace, and Revolution Library and Archives. Stanford, Calif.: Stanford University.

Periodicals, Popular Journals, and Newspapers

Antireligioznik (1926–41)
Aviatsiia i khimiia (1926–31)
Bezbozhnik (1925–41)
Bezbozhnik u stanka (1923–31)
Chelovek i priroda (1920–26)
Estestvoznanie i marksizm (1929–32)
Estestvoznanie v shkole (1918–29)
Front nauki i tekhniki (1929–38)
Inzhenernyi rabotnik (1924–32)
Inzhenernyi trud (1924–35)
Iskra (1923–30)
Khochu vse znat' (1923–32)
Kniga i profsoiuzy (1924–29)
Kniga i revoliutsiya (1920–23)
Kniganosha (1924–26)
Krasnyi bibliotekar' (1923–)
Mir prikliuchenia (1910–30)
Mirovedenie (1918–37)
Nashi dostizheniia (1929–37)
Molodaia gvardiia (1922–41)
Narodnyi uchitel' (1924–35)
Nauchnyi rabotnik (1925–30)
Nauchnoe slovo (1928–31)
Nauka i ee rabotniki (1920–22)
Nauka i nauchnye rabotniki (1926–34)
Nauka i religiia (1920–22)
Nauka i tekhnika (1923–)
Nauka i zhizn' (1934–)
Pechat' i revoliutsiia (1921–30)
Pedagogicheskie kursy na domu (1924–)
Pod znaniem marxizm (1922–44)
Priroda (1912–)
Rabotnik prosveshcheniia (1920–30)
Samolet (1923–)
V masterskoi prirody (1919–29)
Vestnik znaniia (1925–41)
Vokrug sveta (1861–)
Vozdukhoplavanie (1922–25)

SELECTED SECONDARY SOURCES (BOOKS AND ARTICLES IN ENGLISH AND RUSSIAN)

Adams, Marc, ed. *The Well-Born Science: Eugenics in Germany, France, Brazil, and Russia.* New York: Oxford University Press, 1990.

Alexandrov, Daniel A. "The Politics of Scientific 'Kruzhok': Study Circles in Russian Science and their Transformation in the 1920s." In *Na perelom, sovetskaia biologia v 20-x-30-x godakh,* edited by E. I. Kolchinskii. St. Petersburg, 1997.

Alioto, Anthony M. *A History of Western Science.* Englewood Cliffs, N.J.: Prentice Hall, 1993.

Amaiarova, V. C. and L. N. Kogan. *Nauchnaia populiarizatsiia i sotsialisticheskaia kul'tura.* Moscow, 1977.

Andrews, James T. "Another Side of Maksim Gor'kii: Gor'kii, Science, and Mass-Enlightenment in Revolutionary Russia," *The Soviet and Post-Soviet Review* 22. no. 1 (1995).

———. "Local Science and Public Enlightenment: Iaroslavl Naturalists and the Soviet State, 1917–31." In *Provincial Landscapes: The Local Dimensions of Soviet Power, 1917–53,* edited by Donald J. Raleigh. Pittsburgh: University of Pittsburgh Press, 2001.

———."Maksim Gor'kii, Science, and the Scholarly Community in Revolutionary Russia," *The Soviet and Post-Soviet Review* 22. no. 1 (1995).

———. "N. A. Rubakin and the Popularization of Science in the Post-October Period," *Russian History/Histoire Russe* 16, no. 1 (spring 1989).

———."VARNITSO, the Stalinist State, and Public Scientific Enlightenment in Soviet Russia: Cultural Revolution as Competition, 1927–32," *East-West Education* 18, no. 2, (fall 1997).

Andrews, James T., ed. *Maksim Gor'kii Reexamined.* Special Issue in *The Soviet and Post-Soviet Review* 22. no. 1 (1995).

Angarov, A. *Klassovaia bor'ba v sovetskoi derevne.* Moscow, 1929.

Arendt, Hannah. *The Human Condition.* Chicago: University of Chicago Press, 1958.

Baidukov, Georgyi. *Russian Lindbergh: The Life of Valery Chkalov,* edited by Von Hardesty. Washington, D.C.: Smithsonian Institution Press, 1991.

Bailes, Kendall E. "Natural Scientists and the Soviet System," In *Party, State, and Society in the Russian Civil War,* edited by Diane Koenker, et.al. Bloomington: Indiana University Press, 1989.

———. *Science and Russian Culture in an Age of Revolutions: V. I. Vernadsky and His Scientific School, 1863–1945.* Bloomington: Indiana University Press, 1990.

————. *Technology and Society Under Lenin and Stalin*. Princeton: Princeton University Press, 1978.

Ball, Alan M. *Russia's Last Capitalists: The Nepmen, 1921–29*. Berkeley: University of California Press, 1987.

Balmuth, Daniel. *Censorship in Russia, 1865–1905*. Washington, D.C.: University Press of America, 1979.

Bank, B. and A. Vilenkin. *Derevenskaia bednota i biblioteka*. Moscow, 1927.

————. *Krest'ianskaia molodezh' i kniga (opyt issledovaniia chitatel'skikh interesov)*. Moscow, 1929.

Bank, B. V. "Iz istorii izucheniia chitatelei v SSSR." In *Sovetskii chitatel'*. Moscow, 1968.

Bazanov, V. *Vol'noe obshchestvo liubitelei rossiiskoi slovesnosti*. Petrozavodsk, 1949.

Berezina, V. G. *Russkaia zhurnalistika pervoi chetverti XIX veka*. Leningrad, 1965.

Bess, Demaree and John D. Littlepage. *In Search of Soviet Gold*. New York: Harcourt, Brace & Company, 1938.

Bhabha, Homi K., ed. *Nation and Narration*. London: Routledge, 1990.

Biagioli, Mario. *Galileo, Courtier: The Practice of Science in the Culture of Absolutism*. Chicago: University of Chicago Press, 1993.

Blackbourn, David and Geoffrey Eley. *The Peculiarities of German History*. Oxford: Oxford University Press, 1984.

Bogoraz-Tan, Vladimir G. *Khristanstvo v svete etnografii*. Moscow, 1928.

Bol'shakov, A. M. *Derevnia, 1917–1927*. Moscow, 1927.

Borba za nauka v tsarskoi rossi. Moscow, 1931.

Bradley, Joseph. "Voluntary Associations, Civic Culture, and Obshchestvennost' in Moscow." In *Between Tsar and People: Educated Society and the Quest for Public Identity in Late Imperial Russia*, edited by Edith Clowes et al. Princeton: Princeton University Press, 1991.

Brooks, Jeffrey. "The Breakdown in Production and Distribution of Printed Material, 1917–1927." In *Bolshevik Culture: Experiment and Order in the Russian Revolution*, edited by Abbott Gleason et.al. Bloomington: Indiana University Press, 1985.

————. "Official Xenophobia and Popular Cosmopolitanism in Early Soviet Russia," *American Historical Review*, Volume 97, no. 5 (December 1992).

————. "The Press and Its Message: Images of America in the 1920s and 1930s." In *Russia in the Era of NEP*, edited by Sheila Fitzpatrick, Alexander Rabinowitch, and Richard Stites. Bloomington: Indiana University Press, 1991.

————. "Studies of the Reader in the 1920s," *Russian History/Histoire Russe*, 9, no. 2–3(1982).

————. *When Russia Learned to Read.* Princeton: Princeton University Press, 1985.

Brooks, Nathan. "Chemistry in War, Revolution, and Upheaval: Russia and the Soviet Union, 1900–1929," *Centaurus* (November 1997).

Calhoun, Craig, ed. *Habermas and the Public Sphere.* Cambridge, Mass.: MIT Press, 1994.

Cannon, Susan Faye. *Science in Culture: The Early Victorian Period.* New York: Science History Publications, 1978.

Chartier, Roger, ed. *The Culture of Print.* Princeton: Princeton University Press, 1989.

Cherniak, A. Ia. *Istoriia tekhnicheskoi knigi, chast' II sovetskii period.* Moscow, 1973.

————. *Tekhnicheskaia kniga v period velikoi oktiabr'skoi sotsialisticheskoi revo-liutsii i grazhdanskoi voiny 1917–1920 gg.* Moscow, 1973.

Clark, Katerina. "The Quiet Revolution in Intellectual Life." In *Russia in the Era of NEP,* edited by Sheila Fitzpatrick, Alexander Rabinowitch, and Richard Stites. Bloomington: Indiana University Press, 1991.

Coopersmith, Jonathan. *The Electrification of Russia, 1880–1926.* Ithaca, N.Y.: Cornell University Press, 1992.

Cooter, Roger. *The Cultural Meaning of Popular Science: Phrenology and the Orga-nization of Consent in Nineteenth-Century Britain.* Cambridge: Cambridge University Press, 1984.

Crowther, J. G. *Soviet Science.* London: Williams & Norgate, Ltd. 1930.

Darinsky, Anatoli. "People's Universities in the USSR," *Convergence 7*, no. 1. (1974).

David-Fox, Michael. *Revolution of the Mind: Higher Learning Among the Bolshe-viks.* Ithaca, N.Y.: Cornell University Press, 1997.

Davies, Sarah. *Popular Opinion in Stalin's Russia: Terror, Propaganda and Dissent, 1934–1941.* Cambridge: Cambridge University Press, 1997.

Delaney, Joan. "The Origins of Soviet Antireligious Organizations." In *Aspects of Religion in the Soviet Union 1917–1967,* edited by Richard H. Marshall, Jr. Chicago: University of Chicago Press, 1971.

Dinershtein, E. A. *Stanovlenie izdatel'skoi sistemy v RSFSR* Moscow, 1969.

Dirks, Nicholas B., Geoff Eley, and Sherry B. Ortner, eds. *Culture/Power/History: A Reader in Contemporary Social Theory.* Princeton: Princeton Univer-sity Press, 1994.

Dobrovol'skii, L. M. *Zapreshchennaia kniga v Rossii 1825–1904.* Moscow, 1962.

Eisenstein, Elizabeth L. *The Printing Revolution in Early Modern Europe.* Cam-bridge: Cambridge University Press, 1983.

Elkina, S. *Ocherki po agitatsii, propagande i vneshkol'noi rabote v dorevoliutsionnoi Rossii.* Moscow, 1930.

Esin, B. I. *Russkaia dorevoliutsionnaia gazeta 1702–1917 gg., kratkii ocherk*. Moscow, 1971.

Fillipov, N. G. *Nauchno-tekhnicheskie obshchestva Rossii, 1866–1917*. Moscow, 1976.

Filtzer, Donald. *Soviet Workers and Stalinist Industrialization: The Formation of Modern Soviet Production Relations, 1928–1941*. Armonk, N.Y.: M. E. Sharpe, 1986.

Fischer, George, ed. *Science and Ideology in Soviet Society*. New York: Atherton Press, 1967.

Fitzpatrick, Sheila. *The Commissariat of Enlightenment: Soviet Organization of Education and Arts Under Lunacharskii, October 1917–1921*. Cambridge: Cambridge University Press, 1970.

———. *The Cultural Front*. Ithaca, N.Y.: Cornell University Press, 1992.

———. *Education and Social Mobility in the Soviet Union, 1921–1934*. Cambridge: Cambridge University Press, 1979.

———. *Everyday Stalinism, Ordinary Life in Extraordinary Times: Soviet Russia in the 1930s*. New York: Oxford University Press, 1999.

———. "The Problem of Class Identity in NEP Society." In *Russia in the Era of NEP*, edited by Sheila Fitzpatrick, Alexander Rabinowitch, and Richard Stites. Bloomington: Indiana University Press, 1991.

———. "The Soft Line on Culture and Its Enemies: Soviet Cultural Policy, 1922–1927," *Slavic Review* 33 (June 1974): 267–87.

Fitzpatrick, Sheila, ed. *Cultural Revolution in Russia, 1928–1931*. Bloomington: Indiana University Press, 1978.

Fontenel', B. *Razgovory o mnozhestve mirov*. St. Petersburg, 1740.

Findlen, Paula. *Possessing Nature: Musuems, Collecting, and Scientific Culture in Early Modern Italy*. Berkeley: University of California Press, 1994.

Fritzsche, Peter. *A Nation of Fliers: German Aviation and the Popular Imagination*. Cambridge, Mass.: Harvard University Press, 1992.

Galilei, Galileo. *Il Saggiatore*. Milan, 1965.

Gillespie, Charles C. *Science and Polity in France at the End of the Old Regime*. Princeton: Princeton University Press, 1980.

Golubeva, O. D. *Gor'kii—izdatel'*. Moscow, 1968.

Gorky, Maksim. *Literaturno-kriticheskie stat'i*. Moscow 1937.

———. *Sobranie sochineniia v tritsati tt., t.29*. Moscow, 1955.

Graham, Loren R. *Science and Philosophy in the Soviet Union*. New York: Knopf, 1972.

———. *Science in Russia and the Soviet Union: A Short History*. Cambridge: Cambridge University Press, 1993.

———. *The Soviet Academy of Sciences and the Communist Party, 1927–1932*. Princeton: Princeton University Press, 1967.

Gremiatskii, M. A. *Chto takoe nasledstvennost' i kak ona proiavliaetsia u chelovekaʔ* Moscow, 1927.

———. *Il'ia Il'ich Mechnikov. Ego zhizn' i rabota.* Moscow, 1945.

Haber, Samuel. *Efficiency and Uplift: Scientific Management in the Progressive Era, 1890–1920.* Chicago: University of Chicago Press, 1964.

Habermas, Jurgen. *Communication and the Evolution of Society,* translated by Thomas McCarthy. Boston: Beacon Press, 1979.

———. *On Society and Politics: A Reader,* edited by Steven Seidman. Boston: Beacon, 1989.

———. "The Public Sphere: An Encyclopedia Article," *New German Critique* 1 (1974).

———. *The Structural Transformation of the Public Sphere,* translated by Thomas Burger. Cambridge, Mass.: MIT Press, 1992.

Hankins, Thomas L. *Science and the Enlightenment.* Cambridge: Cambridge University Press, 1985.

Hare, Richard. *Maxim Gorky, Romantic Realist and Conservative Revolutionary.* London: Oxford University Press, 1962.

Hunt, Lynn, ed. *The New Cultural History.* Berkeley: University of California Press, 1989.

Ianitskii, N. F., ed. *Kniga v 1924 g. v SSSR.* Moscow, 1925.

———. *Knizhnaia statistika sovetskoi Rossii, 1918–1923.* Moscow, 1924.

Jacob, Margaret C. *The Newtonians and the English Revolution 1689–1720.* Ithaca, N.Y.: Cornell University Press, 1976.

Jones, W. Gareth. "The Morning Light Charity Schools, 1777–1780," *Slavonic and East European Review* 56 (January 1978): 49–60.

Joravsky, David. *Soviet Marxism and Natural Science 1917–1932.* New York: Columbia University Press, 1961.

———. *The Lysenko Affair.* Cambridge, Mass.: Harvard University Press, 1970.

Josephson, Paul R. *Physics and Politics in Revolutionary Russia.* Berkeley: University of California Press, 1991.

Kaidanova, O. *Ocherki po istorii narodnogo obrazovaniia v Rossii i v SSSR.* Berlin, 1939.

Kelley, Allen. *The Descent of Darwinism: The Popularization of Darwinism in Germany, 1860–1914.* Chapel Hill: University of North Carolina Press, 1984.

Kenez, Peter. *The Birth of the Propaganda State: Soviet Methods of Mass Mobilization, 1917–29.* Cambridge, Cambridge University Press, 1985.

Khlebtsevich, E. I. *Izuchenie chitatel'skikh interesov. Massovyi chitatel'.* Moscow and Leningrad, 1927.

Kline, George L. *Religious and Anti-Religious Thought in Russia.* Chicago: University of Chicago Press, 1968.

Kol'tsov, A. K. *Lenin i stanovlenie akademii nauk kak tsentra sovetskoi nauki.* Moscow, 1969.

Komkov, G. M. *Akademiia nauk SSSR tom.1 1724–1917: Kratkii istoricheskii ocherk.* Moscow, 1977.

Konovalov, B. N. *K massovomu ateizmu.* Moscow, 1974.

Korchagin, A. I. *K. A. Timiriazev, zhizn' i tvorchestvo.* Moscow, 1943.

Korneichik, T. D., F. F. Korolev, and Z. I. Ravkin. *Ocherki po istorii sovetskoi shkoly i pedagogiki.* Moscow, 1961

Korol, Alexander G. *Soviet Education for Science and Technology.* Cambridge, Mass.: MIT Press, 1957.

Kotkin, Stephen. *Magnetic Mountain: Stalinism as a Civlization.* Berkeley: University of California Press, 1995.

Kotkov, G. D., B. V. Levshin, and L. K. Semenov, *Akademiia nauk SSSR, kratkii istoricheskii ocherk (v dvukh tomakh), tom pervyi 1724–1917.* Moscow, 1977.

KPSS v rezoliutsiiakh i resheniiakh s"ezdov, konferentsii i plenumov TsK. 10 vols. Moscow, 1970.

Krementsov, Nikolai, *Stalinist Science.* Princeton: Princeton University Press, 1997.

Krupskaia, N. K. *O bibliotechnoi dele—sbornik.* Moscow, 1957.

———. *Pedagogicheskoe sochineniia v desiati tomakh.* Vol. 8. Moscow, 1960.

Kumanev, V. A. *Sotsializm i vsenarodnaia gramotnost'.* Moscow, 1967.

Lazarevich, E. A. *Iskusstvo populiarizatsii nauki.* Moscow, 1978.

———. *Populiarizatsiia nauki v rossii.* Moscow, 1981.

———. *S vekom naravne, populiarizatsiia nauka v rossii. Kniga. Gazeta. Zhurnal.* Moscow, 1984.

Lemke, Mikhail. *Ocherki po istorii russkoi tsenzury i zhurnalistiki XIX stoletiia.* St. Petersburg, 1904.

Lewin, Moshe. *The Making of the Soviet System.* New York: Pantheon, 1985.

Liubimov, I. *Komsomol v sovetskom stroitel'stvo, 1917–1927.* Moscow and Leningrad, 1928.

Lotman, Iurii M. and Boris A. Uspensky. "Binary Models in the Dynamics of Russian Culture." In *Semiotics of Russian Cultural History,* translated by Boris Gasparov, edited by Alexander D. Nakhimovsky and Alice Stone Nakhimovsky. Ithaca, N.Y.: Cornell University Press, 1985.

Lunkevich, V. V. *Osnovy zhizni.* St. Petersburg, 1910.

Lupov, S. P. *Kniga v Rossii v poslepetrovskoe vremia.* Leningrad, 1976.

Lux, David. *Patronage and Royal Science in Seventeenth-Century France.* Ithaca, N.Y.: Cornell University Press, 1989.

McCutcheon, Robert A. "The 1936–1937 Purge of Soviet Astronomers," *Slavic Review* 50, no. 1 (spring 1991).

McReynolds, Louise. *The News Under Russia's Old Regime.* Princeton: Princeton University Press, 1991.

Makogonenko, G. P. *Nikolai Novikov i russkoe prosveshchenie XVIII veka.* Moscow, 1952.

Malykhin, N. G. *Ocherki po istorii knigo-izdatel'skogo dela v SSSR.* Moscow, 1965.

Marker, Gary. *Publishing, Printing, and the Origins of Intellectual Life in Russia, 1700–1800.* Princeton: Princeton University Press, 1985.

Mikulinskii, S. R. *Karl Frantsovich Rul'e, uchenyi, chelovek, i uchitel' 1814–1858 gg.* Moscow, 1979.

Medvedev, Zhores. *The Rise and Fall of T.D. Lysenko.* New York: Columbia University Press, 1969.

———. *Soviet Science.* New York: Norton, 1978.

Murzaev, E. M. *Vladimir A. Obruchev 1863–1956, zhizn' i deiatel'nost'.* Moscow, 1959.

Nazarov, A. I. *Kniga v sovetskom obshchestve.* Moscow, 1964.

———. *Oktiabr' i kniga.* Moscow, 1968.

Odom, William E. *The Soviet Volunteers: Modernization and Bureaucracy in a Public Mass Organization.* Princeton: Princeton University Press, 1973.

Otchet Leningradskogo oblastnogo i gorodskogo komiteta VKP (b) IV oblastnoi i gorodskoi partiinoi konferentsii. Leningrad, 1932.

Peris, Daniel. "Commissars in Red Cassocks: Former Priests in the League of the Militant Godless," *Slavic Review* 54, no. 2 (summer 1995).

———. "The 1929 Congress of the Godless," *Soviet Studies* 1991, no. 4.

———. *Storming the Heavens: The Soviet League of the Militant Godless.* Ithaca, N.Y.: 1998.

Pipes, Richard. *Social Democracy and the St. Petersburg Labor Movement 1885–1897.* Cambridge, Mass.: Harvard University Press, 1963.

Pisarzhevskii, O. *A. E. Fersman 1883–1945.* Moscow, 1955.

Pogodin, Mikhail. *Prostaia rech' o mudrenykh veshchakh.* Moscow, 1873.

Polevoi, Nikolai. *Materialy po istorii russkoi literatury i zhurnalistiki tridtsatykh godov.* Leningrad, 1934.

Porter, Roy, ed. *The Popularization of Medicine, 1650–1850.* London: Routledge, 1994.

Pospielovsky, Dimitry V. *A History of Soviet Atheism in Theory and Practice.* London: Macmillan, 1988.

Pozdniakov, N. N. "Politekhnicheskii muzei i ego nauchno-prosvetitel'noi deiatel'nosti 1872–1917 gg." In *Istoriia muzeinogo dela v SSSR.* Moscow, 1957.

Proshnev, G. I. *Etiudy po knizhnomu delu.* Moscow and Leningrad, 1924.

Raeff, Marc. *The Origins of the Russian Intelligentsia: The Eighteenth-Century Nobility.* New York: Harcourt, Brace & World, 1966.

Raikov, B. E. *Russkie biologi-evoliutsionisty do Darvina.* 4 vols. Moscow and Leningrad, 1951–59.

Ravkii, Z. I. *Sovetskaia shkola v period vosstanovleniia narodnogo khoziaistva, 1921–25 gg.* Moscow, 1959.

Reiber, Alfred J. *Merchants and Entrepreneurs in Imperial Russia.* Chapel Hill: University of North Carolina Press, 1982.

Remizova, T. A. *Kul'turno-prosvetitel'naia rabota v RSFSR (1921–1925 gg.).* Moscow, 1962.

Rogers, James A. "Charles Darwin and Russian Scientists," *Russian Review* 19 (1960).

———. "The Reception of Darwin's Origin of Species by Russian Scientists," *ISIS* 64, no. 224 (1973).

Rogger, Hans. "America in the Russian Mind," *Pacific Historical Review* 47 (February 1978): 27–51.

Rubakin, N. A. *Chto takoe bibliologicheskaia psikhologiia?* Leningrad, 1924.

———. *Istoriia russkoi zemli.* Moscow, 1919.

———. *Iz temy vremen v svetloe budushchee. Rasskazy iz istorii chelovecheskoi kul'tury.* Kazan', 1920.

Ruud, Charles A. *Fighting Words: Imperial Censorship and the Russian Press, 1804–1906.* Toronto: University of Toronto Press, 1982.

Said, Edward. *Culture and Imperialism.* New York: Knopf, 1993.

———. *Orientalism.* New York: Pantheon, 1978.

Sankov, V. E. *U istokov aviatsii, vozdukhoplavaniia i aviatsiia v russkoi zhurnalistike.* Moscow, 1976.

Schwartz, Solomon. *Labor in the Soviet Union.* New York: Praeger, 1952.

Semenova, Svetlana. *Nikolai Fedorov.* Moscow, 1990.

Shamurin, E. I. *Sovetskaia kniga za 15 let v tsifrakh.* Moscow, 1968.

Shloberg, A. N. and O. E. Vol'tsenburg. *Kak ustroit' i vesti malenkuiu biblioteku.* Petrograd, 1921.

Shomrakova, I. A. "Krest'ianskii chitatel' 20-godov (1920–1930)." In *Istoriia russkogo chitatelia, sbornik statei, vypusk 2,* edited by I. E. Barenbaum. Leningrad, 1976.

Siegelbaum, Lewis H., and Ronald Grigor Suny, eds. *Making Workers Soviet: Power, Class, and Identity.* Ithaca, N.Y.: Cornell University Press, 1994.

Slukhovskii, M. N. *Kniga i derevniia.* Moscow, 1928.

Solomon, Susan Gross. "Rural Scholars and the Cultural Revolution." In *Cultural Revolution in Russia, 1928–1931.* Bloomington: Indiana University Press, 1978.

Solomon, Susan Gross, and John F. Hutchinson, eds. *Health and Society in Revolutionary Russia.* Bloomington: Indiana University Press, 1990.

Stewart, Robert. *Henry Brougham, 1778–1868: His Public Career.* London: Bodley Head, 1986.

Stites, Richard. *Revolutionary Dreams, Utopian Vision and Experimental Life in the Russian Revolution.* Oxford: Oxford University Press, 1989.

———. *Russian Popular Culture.* Cambridge: Cambridge University Press, 1992.

Sytin, N. D. *Zhizn' dlia knigi.* Moscow, 1960.

Timiriazev, K. A. *Zhizn' rasteniia.* Moscow, 1920.

Timirizev, A. K. *Chem zanimaetsia fizika i kakuiu pol'zu prinosiat fizicheskie instrumenty.* Petrograd, 1918.

Todes, Daniel P. *Darwin without Malthus: The Struggle for Existence in Russian Evolutionary Thought.* New York: Oxford University Press, 1989.

Utechin, S. V. "Bolsheviks and their Allies After 1917: The Ideological Pattern," *Soviet Studies* 10 (1958/59): 113–35.

Vakhterova, V. P. *Vneskhol'noe obrazovanie naroda.* Moscow, 1917.

Van Keuren, D. K. "Museums and Ideology: Augustus Pitt-Rivers, Anthropology Museums and Social Change in Later Victorian Britain," *Victorian Studies* 28 (1984): 171–79.

Vareikis, I. M., ed. *Pechat SSSR za 1924 i 1925 gg.* Moscow, 1926.

Vasil'eva, N. B. "Deiatel'nost' Leningradskikh dobrovol'nykh obshchestv Tekhika-Massam, Za Ovladenie Tekhnikoi, 1928–1935 gg." In *Dobrovol'nye obshchestva v Petrograde-Leningrade v 1917–1937 gg. sbornik statei.* Leningrad, 1989.

Viola, Lynn. "The Peasant Nightmare: Visions of Apocalypse in the Soviet Countryside," *Journal of Modern History* 1990, no. 62 (December).

Vorob'eva, Iu. S. "Moskovskii gorodskoi narodnyi universitet im. Shaniavskogo." In *Gosudarstvennoe rukovodstvo vysshei shkoloi v dorevoliutsionnoi Rossii i v SSSR.* Moscow, 1979.

Vucinich, Alexander. *Darwin in Russian Thought.* Berkeley: University of California Press, 1988.

———. "Politics, Universities, and Science." In *Russia Under the Last Tsar,* edited by Theofanis George Stavrou. Minneapolis: University of Minnesota Press, 1969.

———. *The Soviet Academy of Sciences.* Stanford, Calif.: Stanford University Press, 1956.

Vvedenskii, Alexander I. *Tserkov' i gosudarstvo.* Moscow, 1924.

Vzdorpov, T. I. *Istoriia otkrytiia i izucheniia russkoi srednevekovoi zhivopisi XIXv.* Moscow, 1986.

Webb, R. K. *The British Working Class Reader, 1790–1848: Literacy and Social Tension.* London: G. Allen & Unwin, 1955.

Weiner, Douglas. *Models of Nature: Conservation and Ecology in the Soviet Union, 1917–1935.* Bloomington: Indiana University Press, 1987.

———. *A Little Corner of Freedom: Russian Nature Protection from Stalin to Gorbachev.* Berkeley: University of California Press, 1999.

Westfall, Richard S. *Science and Religion in Seventeenth-Century England.* New Haven, Conn.: Yale University Press, 1958.

Wildman, Allan K. *The Making of a Workers' Revolution: Russian Social Democracy.* Chicago: University of Chicago Press, 1967.

Wiles, Peter. "On Physical Immortality," *Survey* 56/57 (1965).

Yeo, Eileen and Stephen, eds. *Popular Culture and Class Conflict, 1590–1914: Explorations in the History of Labour and Leisure.* Sussex: Harvester, 1981.

Young, George M., Jr. *Nikolai F. Fedorov: An Introduction.* Belmont, Mass.: 1979.

Young, Glennys. *Power and the Sacred in Revolutionary Russia: Religious Activists in the Village.* University Park: Pennsylvania University Press, 1997.

Zak, L. M. "Sozdanie i deiatel'nost' VARNITSO v 1927–1932 gg.," *Istoriia SSSR* 1959, no. 6.

Zapadov, A. V. *Russkaia zhurnalistika 30-kh-60-kh godov XVIIIv.* Moscow, 1957.

Zaret, David. *The Heavenly Contract: Ideology and Organization in Pre-Revolutionary Puritanism.* Chicago: University of Chicago Press, 1985.

Zavadovskii, B. M. *Darvinizm i marksizm.* Moscow, 1926.

———. *Ocherki vnutrennei sekretsii.* Leningrad, 1928.

———. "Provaly populiarizatora." In *O populiarizatsii estestvoznaniia, sbornik statei.* Moscow, 1926.

———. *Sbornik statei po voprosam populiarizatsii estestvoznaniia.* Moscow, 1923.

Surveying for Archaeologists and
Other Fieldworkers

SURVEYING FOR ARCHAEOLOGISTS AND OTHER FIELDWORKERS

A. H. A. Hogg

"There is a marvel in the region which is called Ercing. There is in that place a sepulchre . . . And men come to measure the tumulus. In length it has sometimes seven feet, sometimes fifteen, sometimes twelve, sometimes nine. In whatsoever measure you measure it once, you will not find the same measurement a second time; and I have tested it myself." — from *The Marvels of Britain*, attributed to Nennius (ninth century)

St. Martin's Press New York

Library of Congress Cataloging in Publication Data

Hogg, Alexander Hubert Arthur
  Surveying for archaeologists and other fieldworkers

  Includes index.
  1. Archaeological surveying. I. Title.
CC76.3.H63   930.1′028   80-10396
ISBN 0-312-77727-2

To my former colleagues of RCAM Wales

Contents

Tables

Figures

General Editor's Introduction

The original intention of the Croom Helm Studies in Archaeology was to provide a comprehensive survey of the archaeology of Britain and Ireland, at a level that would be of use and interest both to university students and to informed laymen. A series of period studies was therefore commissioned, and the first volumes are now well advanced.

It was soon realised, however, that there are a number of topics, of equal interest and importance to archaeologists working in these islands, which transcend the conventional period boundaries. These might include ancient technology, archaeological techniques, and the ancillary sciences. As opportunity arises, therefore, the period series will be supplemented by other studies.

I am glad to welcome A. H. A. Hogg's *Surveying for Archaeologists* as the first of these supplementary volumes. As the author rightly stresses, the making of plans to an appropriate level of accuracy is the central discipline of field archaeology. But it is a discipline which is often sadly neglected by practising field workers, and no wholly satisfactory manual of survey principles and practice has previously appeared.

No one could be better fitted than Dr Hogg to write such a manual. He brought the skills of a trained civil engineer, as well as the enthusiasm of an archaeological amateur, to the post of Secretary of the Royal Commission on Ancient Monuments in Wales. The fruits of the practices set out in this book are to be seen in the Commission's three *Inventory* volumes for Caernarvonshire, and in the first volume for Glamorgan.

What Dr Hogg preaches here, on the basis of a quarter of a century of practice, is not free from controversy. Some experienced field workers may consider, for instance, that he undervalues the plane table. But they will find that he always presents a reasoned case for his preferred methods, as well as a sufficient account of the techniques of which he disapproves.

Above all, Dr Hogg gives fully worked-out and illustrated examples of the widest possible range of techniques, from the simplest sketch-plan to surveys demanding costly equipment and mathematical calculations. It would be difficult to find a problem in field surveying for which his book does not furnish a solution.

Leslie Alcock

Preface

The study of Archaeology is addictive, but many of those affected cannot hope to get a paid appointment in the subject of their choice. After twenty years as a professional civil engineer and an amateur archaeologist, I had the good fortune to obtain such a post.

Part of my earlier work had involved surveying, either practically or as a lecturer, and it had always seemed to me self-evident that an *accurate* plan was an essential part of any definitive description of a field monument. I was therefore rather shocked to discover that many professional archaeologists had a less than rudimentary understanding of the basic principles of surveying; but my new colleagues proved anxious, and fully competent, to learn the necessary and essentially simple techniques.

The object of this book is to enable any archaeologist, whether amateur or professional, to attain any desired degree of competence so far as necessary for his work, without any instruction beyond that given here. Obviously practical tuition is desirable, but it cannot always be obtained. To attain this object I have had to give verbal descriptions of techniques which can be demonstrated far better and more quickly in the field (for example, Para. 7.3), and to include much material which is essential for reference in case of need but which many archaeologists may never require, such as Part V on numerical work.

You may consider that I have placed excessive emphasis on accuracy. There are several reasons for this. First, that the moderate degree of accuracy aimed at here does not add in any way to the work involved. Second, that errors may accumulate, so that a collection of careless measurements, each only slightly wrong, can build up to cause an appreciable distortion of the final plan.

1

And third, that even if for some reason you decide that rough work is acceptable you ought to understand what its effects will be.

No attempt has been made to cover the whole field of surveying. Precise geodetic work is not discussed, and at the other extreme important practical matters such as curve ranging are omitted, for they are not relevant to archaeology. Nevertheless, surveyors concerned with other disciplines may well find much that is useful in this work.

Part I
INTRODUCTION

1 General Discussion

1.1 *Surveying and Archaeology.* Field Archaeology and Excavation
are the foundations upon which the whole structure of archaeological knowledge is built, and of the various techniques which
make up these methods of investigation surveying is probably the
most important. The need for *accurate* plans is surely self-evident,
whether to accompany an excavation report or as part of the
definitive description of any field monument.

Nevertheless, of these techniques surveying is also the most
neglected. There is an illusion that it is difficult, and as a result
works which are otherwise excellent describe idiosyncratic methods
which are both unduly laborious and potentially inaccurate; the
difficulties which these methods try to avoid are mostly imaginary.
In fact, many thousands of field monuments can be surveyed
accurately without using any more abstruse mathematical
knowledge than the recognition of a triangle combined with the
ability to make and record measurements correctly and systematically. This latter requirement is not as easy as it sounds, but anyone
who is really incapable of fulfilling it, and not merely too lazy to do
so, should be diverted to some other field of research; for if he (or
she) *cannot* observe and record accurately, how can any of his
results be trusted, especially in far more difficult problems such as
disentangling complex stratification?

One point of view, which arises out of this neglect of surveying,
must be most strongly condemned. Some archaeologists consider
that the preparation of plans can be safely entrusted to technicians
with no archaeological knowledge; the 'experts' will then sketch in
archaeological detail which the technicians have missed, and will
interpret the results. My own experience, supported by that of
others, leaves no doubt at all that for even a moderately complex
structure actual participation in the detailed work of measurement

5

is essential if the full harvest of potential information is to be gathered.

1.2 *The Purpose of the Book.* Like most techniques, surveying is best learnt by a prolonged practical apprenticeship, but few practising field archaeologists can spare the time to give the necessary instruction, and moreover they have all too often been wrongly taught themselves. Even in those University Departments which do arrange for instruction in surveying, the course is usually provided by lecturers from some other department, and though extremely valuable it is not directed primarily towards archaeology, and seldom discusses the difficulties which are likely to arise in the field.

In writing this book my aim has been to describe all surveying techniques likely to be needed by any archaeologist working on land, and to explain them in such detail that anyone can apply them competently, even if no experienced adviser is available. I have paid particular regard to the needs of the full-time archaeologist, but I have also kept in mind my own difficulties as a beginner, strongly addicted to field archaeology as a part-time activity but handicapped by the lack of advice on recording. The last chapter (28) is dedicated to those who find themselves similarly placed.

I have taken as the upper limit of sophistication the type of equipment which might reasonably be hoped for in an adequately equipped School of Archaeology, or at least might be lent without too great reluctance by another Department: that is, a dumpy level and a theodolite capable of reading to one minute of arc. These are amply accurate enough for the sort of work envisaged and more precise instruments, besides being more expensive, can in some circumstances actually add to the surveyor's difficulties.

The only important restraint imposed by this limitation is that reliable astronomical observations are not possible.

1.3 *The Functions of Surveying.* In an archaeological context, the functions of surveying can best be defined in relation to an ideal scheme of research; 'ideal' is here used in its primary sense; the scheme, though strictly logical, would require several lifetimes to complete, apart from various other objections. Nevertheless, it provides a useful background against which to organise one's ideas. For convenience, to avoid abstractions, the scheme will be outlined in relation to 'hill-forts', but with slight modifications it is applicable to any type of structure.

Logically then, the first step is the recognition of a distinct class of defended enclosure. These enclosures need to be placed in their topographical context by locating them on the map. One aspect of surveying, therefore, is the accurate location of sites.

The individual members of the general class of hill-forts will be found to differ from each other in many details. Clearly some form of typological analysis is desirable, so an accurate objective plan and description of each hill-fort is needed. The distribution-map will assist typological classification by allowing the separation of the 3,000 or so hill-forts of Britain into groups of manageable size. This problem, of typological classification, is discussed further below.

Finally, so far as this particular class of structure is concerned, excavation of apparently representative types should provide material which may or may not support the supposed typology and which may relate the type to other structures and place it in its correct chronological context. Surveying is necessary to provide an accurate description of the site and of any features revealed during the excavation, and to assist in analysing and recording the stratification.

In practice, all those stages of investigation are in progress at the same time and generally without relation to each other. On an excavation, accurate surveying is of primary importance, more so than the correct identification of the objects found; for the latter will normally be preserved for future study, whereas structural features are inevitably destroyed. Nevertheless, it is probably by the detailed recording of surface features that surveying can make its most valuable contribution.

The study of hill-forts can again be taken as an example. Until the last decade or so, with a few honourable exceptions, archaeologists could attain far-reaching conclusions from the examination of a brooch or of the decoration on a potsherd but regarded hill-forts as a single type, whether they enclosed 0·5 or 50 ha and whatever the details of their plan (hut groups were approached with similar insensitivity). Yet hill-forts are just as much artifacts as potsherds, and even though some may have taken a millennium to reach their present form they should, at least in principle, be equally open to typological analysis. Since adequate excavation of a hill-fort may take up to a decade, only a few of our 3,000 or so examples can be examined, and the information so obtained can only be extended to other sites on the evidence of their typology. Similar reasoning applies to most types of field monument.

Most archaeologists who have tried, with some success, to classify such remains have been compelled to rely on subjective criteria, but recently attempts have been made to develop objective methods; the chief problem seems to be that the techniques used have been designed for items which may have fifty or more recognisable and distinct characteristics, whereas few field monuments have as many as ten. It would be inappropriate to discuss methods of classification in detail, but the subject has been mentioned in order to emphasise the need for reliable plans, from which the characteristics can be determined with certainty.

1.4 *The Arrangement of the Book.* Advice as to how to use this book is given in the next section, but some account of the principles governing its arrangement may be helpful. It is divided into several parts, the first two being mostly essential information for anyone intending to make a survey; the remainder are for reference if needed.

Part I forms an introduction. The current chapter (1) explains the general scheme of the work, and Chapter 2 deals with basic principles which are common to almost all aspects of surveying.

Part II covers chain surveying. It is, appropriately, the longest part, for this is the method of choice for practically all archaeological survey work. More than nine sites out of ten require no additional apparatus, and even on those where the survey network can be more easily fixed by a theodolite or other instrument chaining still remains the best and simplest way of measuring detail in almost every case.

The technique is of great antiquity. Something very similar is shown in Egyptian tomb-paintings, and it had been fully developed in Britain by the seventeenth century, primarily for the survey of estates, which requires accuracy similar to that needed for archaeological plans. As a result of this long evolution, the equipment needed has been reduced to a fairly compact and standardised form, while probable difficulties and sources of mistakes have been recognised and ways found to overcome them. As indicated earlier, the belief that the technique is 'difficult' is mistaken, and attempts to evade the imagined difficulties are misdirected.

Chapter 3, the first of this section, describes the equipment needed, Chapter 4 explains the elementary principles on which the technique is based, and Chapter 5 shows how these principles would apply in practice by a detailed account of a simple (imaginary) survey. Chapter 6 deals with plotting the survey and preparing the plan for publication.

So far, the discussion has assumed, for simplicity, that no problems arise, and no mistakes are likely to be made. Chapter 7 gives fairly simple ways of overcoming the defects of the real world, so far as they affect surveying. It also describes how to set out a rectangle when a chain only is available, and explains the modifications of technique necessary when dealing with buildings. The title of Chapter 8 is self-explanatory.

Part III (Chapters 9, 10 and 11) discusses the use of the level, which is the most commonly available instrument, and Part IV (Chapters 12 to 15) treats similarly of the theodolite or tacheometer.

Part V (Chapters 16 to 20) describes methods of numerical calculation. Some readers will turn away from this in horror. They will not find themselves intolerably handicapped if they do, for as indicated earlier most sites can be surveyed using nothing more than the simplest and most elementary geometry. Nevertheless, they will find it worth while to try to overcome their distaste, for just as a theodolite is sometimes useful, so occasionally a calculation will greatly simplify a difficult piece of surveying, and improve its accuracy. To understand a numerical method it is essential to work through a representative example, and the resulting blocks of arithmetic are admittedly heavy and repulsive; but anyone who is capable of looking up a number in a telephone directory and dialling the result will find himself numerate enough to work through them. Perhaps at this point an apology should be offered to those other readers who may feel insulted at being given an explicit definition of a cosine or of a 3–4–5 triangle; but it is hoped that they will understand the reasons for so doing.

In Part V, therefore, I have included an example of what I believe to be the simplest method of solving any problem likely to arise in archaeological surveying. Problems are mostly solved by the laborious use of logarithms, for that approach is necessary in order to understand what is being done; but since electronic hand-calculators are now widely available and save an enormous amount of work duplicate methods of solution using these are also given.

Among the Miscellaneous Techniques (Part VI), Chapter 21 describes various methods, none requiring a computer, for plotting from oblique aerial photographs. Chapter 22 deals with other uses of photography, including the use (but not the preparation) of photogrammetric surveys, and a simple emergency method of following a feature such as a ditch exposed in the face of a working quarry. Chapter 23, included reluctantly for reasons there given, deals with the plane-table. Chapter 24, alone among the contents of this book, is derivative, for I have had the good fortune never to have been involved in underground surveying. Nevertheless, I think that I have gleaned from various sources enough useful items to justify its inclusion. That would not be true about underwater surveying, which is why I have excluded it.

Much fieldwork is only concerned with locating a site on a map. On occasion, also, circumstances may prevent preparation of anything more than a sketch plan. In Part VII, Chapters 25 and 26 are relevant to this type of work. They have been left to the end of the book because the work involved is usually rather rough and accuracy should be sacrificed only if you know what you are doing. The contents of Chapters 27 and 28 have all been covered earlier, but are recapitulated here for convenience, with the relevant cross-references. Chapter 27 deals with excavation, which for many archaeologists is the main application they are likely to make of survey techniques. Chapter 28 is intended for those who are deeply interested in archaeology and who would like to make their own contribution to the subject but whose available time is restricted.

Finally, there are four appendices. The first concerns the use of units. Throughout this book, I have used metric linear measurements and the Babylonian system of degrees, minutes and seconds for angles, not because I like them but because they are now official. Nevertheless, the accuracy of a survey does not depend on the units used, and you may find that you have or wish to use equipment differently graduated.

Appendix I therefore lists other common systems of measurement. Appendix II lists the approximate (1978) prices of items of equipment, arranged by chapters, with the names of some suppliers. Appendix III assembles the data used in the numerical examples in Part V, and Appendix IV contains short tables of some useful quantities.

1.5 *How to Use the Book.* My object has been to give all the information needed even if you cannot get other instruction, but obviously if you can manage to do so you should attend a course in surveying and especially get some practice in using the equipment, working with an experienced surveyor. At the same time though, you should work through the relevant sections of this book, for most courses of instruction are not directed primarily towards archaeological fieldwork, and a really experienced man may well rashly take the risk of scamping precautions which you, as a beginner, should follow slavishly.

If you are trying to learn surveying by yourself, without any experienced guide, the best procedure will be to choose a fairly small and easily accessible site for which a published plan exists. Then, without further reference to that published plan, survey the site yourself, and draw out your own draft plan quite independently. After you have done that, compare your draft in detail with the published plan, measuring identifiable distances. If the two plans agree, you can reasonably feel confident that your technique is fairly reliable. What, though, if they do not agree? You are not necessarily the one who is wrong, so select one or two easily identifiable and appreciably different measurements, preferably *not* actually part of your network and check them in the field; and if you find that you are at fault, try to work out what went wrong.

I have been concerned throughout with the needs of a fieldworker. If though, your primary objective is to pass an examination, you will probably find some of the material unnecessary, as for example Chapter 7; you should check your requirements by a study of papers set in the past.

For actual fieldwork, Parts I and II are essential reading. The others are for reference, depending on the work which you are undertaking. If you wish to supplement and extend your knowledge by additional reading, there are many text books of varying quality. Those originally written by David Clark, and by R. E. Middleton and O. Chadwick, have passed through several editions, any of which would be of value; but all contain much more material than is necessary for archaeological work. Similarly, the *Manual of Topographical Surveying* (HMSO, latest edition 1965, anonymous; earlier editions by Sir Charles Close) is concerned with the type of accuracy needed for national maps; but it includes incidentally comments and other material of interest to a field archaeologist.

1.6 *Sources*. This book is based for the most part on surveying practice that has been current for a century or more, which I have slightly modified where appropriate as a result of experience in the field. A few items are original, and others have been assimilated from colleagues and from reading during half a century, mostly more than 25 years ago. I have therefore included no formal references, but occasionally the source is indicated in parenthesis. Should anyone feel that I have used their work without giving due credit, I offer my apologies for this oversight.

2 The Basic Principles

2.1 Accuracy; 2.2 Choice of Network; 2.3 Booking; 2.4 General Remarks.

2.1 *Accuracy*. There is one essential difference between a trained and an untrained surveyor. The former recognises that all measurements inevitably contain errors, and plans his survey so that these tend, so far as possible, to cancel out, not to accumulate. The sort of overall accuracy which may be expected using the methods described in this book is generally about one part in five hundred or a thousand, perhaps rising to one part in two thousand if special care is taken. Having regard to the nature of archaeological sites, this degree of accuracy is acceptable. Greater precision requires a quite disproportionately greater amount of work.

In this context, it is useful to have some idea of the sort of precision obtainable by different methods of measurement, assuming even ground, good visibility, and little wind. These are tabulated below; the figures are of course only rough indications, and are very dependent on circumstances.

Linear Measurements:

Steel band, in catenary	1 in 10,000
Steel band, on specially prepared ground	1 in 2,500
Chaining	1 in 800
'Linen' tape	1 in 200
Tacheometry (rapidly diminished by bad conditions, and limited to about 150 m)	1 in 100
Pacing between known points	1 in 50
Pacing only	1 in 20

Angular Measurement:

Theodolite (simple type, reading to one minute)	02' = 1 in 1,700	approx.
Prismatic Compass	1° = 1 in 60	approx.

13

In a survey which aims at accuracy, therefore, the prismatic compass is only useful for fixing the approximate north point, though it can provide a check on possible mistakes.

The point has been made that the trained surveyor recognises that 'errors' will occur in his measurements, but he also recognises that he will sometimes make 'mistakes'. It is useful to distinguish between these two types of inaccuracy. An 'error' is small and unavoidable; for example two measurements of the same length might differ by 0·03 m, or of the same angle by half a minute. A 'mistake', on the other hand, is an actual misreading; perhaps of 9 m on a chain instead of 11 m, or of 1° in an angle.

2.2 *Choice of Network*. Surveying a site falls into two main parts. The first is to establish a network of lines covering the whole area. Detail is then recorded by measurement from those lines, or sometimes from the stations at which they meet. This section is concerned with the arrangement of the network. The traverse, which is an alternative way of fixing a system of lines, is described in Chapter 19.

The network must obviously be 'rigid', that is, the measurements which are taken must fix the shape of the network exactly and unambiguously. The simplest arrangement of this kind is the triangle, the shape of which is (theoretically) determined exactly by measuring all three sides, two sides and the included angle, or one side and two angles. Most accurate surveys, therefore, are based on networks built up of triangles.

At first glance, it would seem that nothing more is needed than to add one triangle to another until the whole site is covered; but in practice some precautions have to be observed, for unfortunately all measurements contain errors, even if mistakes are avoided. Single triangles should be 'well-conditioned', that is, their angles should not be very different from 60°. The effect of using an ill-conditioned triangle is shown, exaggerated, in Figure 2.1. The radii of the arcs drawn from two known points are supposed to differ from the correct distances by errors e; the diagram shows how the displacement of the point of intersection from the correct point becomes appreciably greater than e for triangles of this shape. An ill-conditioned triangle is never desirable, but may sometimes be tolerated if you are measuring angles as well as distances.

The cumulative effect of errors in a network of triangles can be envisaged if you imagine it to be built up of Meccano-like strips,

2.1 Ill-conditioned Triangles

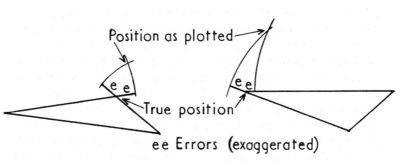

ee Errors (exaggerated)

with a little slackness at every joint, corresponding to the error. You will appreciate that the relative movement of two widely separated points in the network is likely to be much greater than the movement at each separate joint, and that it will also increase as the number of intermediate joints increases. Your object, therefore, should be to enclose the site with a large rigid network comprising relatively few triangles, which is then subdivided as necessary. In brief, you work from large to small. The detailed arrangement will depend on the nature of the site, but will usually consist of several triangles forming a polygon, or of two, three, or more polygons interlocking (see Chapters 4, 5 and 20).

As a basic principle in designing a network, the inevitable presence of errors must always be allowed for; but the near certainty of an occasional mistake must also be kept in mind. Some apparently unnecessary lines should always be included, so that except in the rare event of two mistakes balancing each other the network becomes geometrically impossible to draw unless all the lengths have been correctly recorded. The errors may introduce *small* discrepancies in the drawing, but these will normally be evened out by eye. Thus a quadrilateral can be drawn, though incorrectly, if the four sides and one diagonal have been measured, even if one measurement is wrong; but if the other diagonal is also recorded the presence of a mistake will become obvious as soon as you try to draw the outline.

If a mistake is present, you will have to check measurements on the site. For that reason, a small-scale plot of all measured lines, without detail, should if possible be made before leaving the district. The location of the mistake will be simplified if magnetic bearings have been taken along all measured lines.

2.3 *Booking.* Normally, though not invariably, the field measurements are 'booked', and the plotting is done at home or in an office; the reasons are explained below. From this there follows a third very important principle, to which there should be no exceptions: the booking must be such that an accurate plan of the site can be drawn by someone who has never seen it. This applies even if you are absolutely certain that you will draw out the draft plan yourself, for memory is never completely reliable, especially if the plotting is not done immediately after the survey. In fact, you will certainly find it necessary to rely on your memory sometimes, but whenever you do you should mentally count a small black mark against your technical competence.

One of the main indications of the poor standards of much archaeological field survey is the widely held belief that before a plan is accepted as finished it must be 'taken out into the field for checking'. If your field notes are such that this so-called 'checking' really seems necessary, your technique is very defective indeed, and the final plan cannot be accepted as fully reliable. It is surely self-evident that detailed point by point measurements of visible features will give a more reliable plan than if the same features are sketched in by eye; but this does not preclude sketching natural detail which is not structurally significant, where this will give a better impression of the nature of the ground.

A less obvious danger is that the archaeologist 'checking' the plan will 'correct' it to fit his preconceived, and possibly mistaken, interpretation of the site. This is not a hypothetical risk; I have come across at least half a dozen examples, but it would probably be libellous and certainly unkind to specify them.

This is not to say that all subjective interpretation must be rigidly excluded from your field notes. The first aim should be always to make a record which is so far as possible completely objective, but subjective comment can be included in your notes, and even added to the finished plan. For example, it would be perfectly legitimate to mark two overlapping ramparts 'Period I?' and 'Period II?'; but archaeologically it would be a mortal sin to disregard your field measurements and 'correct' your plan to make this interpretation look more probable.

2.4 *General Remarks.* As noted earlier, measurements and other details are normally booked in the field as more or less rough notes, and the final plan is plotted in the office (which does not exclude work at home). The main reasons for this are economy and convenience. The time available for work out of doors is limited; to make a survey after dark is difficult, and over much of Britain bracken or other vegetation inhibits fieldwork from June to November. Moreover, even an unpaid amateur will probably have extra expenses when in the field, while a professional's work will be costing his employer some subsistence payments. Whenever possible, therefore, work should be done in the office merely for reasons of economy. Further, conditions out of doors are seldom ideal for accurate drawing, especially if the plan is large.

Apart from these considerations, it does not matter whether a plan is drawn out in the field or office. On an excavation, the needs of the work almost always compel the surveyor to plot in the field, despite the accompanying inconveniences; for there is usually a lot of close-set detail which could not easily be booked by conventional methods, and which often has to be recorded as quickly as possible so that further levels can be uncovered.

One further point needs to be emphasised. The suggestion is sometimes made that a learner gains by seeing the plan develop in front of him as he works on the site. This is a mistaken approach. If a student learns to work in this way he will probably be completely at a loss when weather conditions are unsuitable, or when he has to deal with a large site, where the framework has to be 'balanced' (that is, the errors have to be distributed fairly evenly) before plotting can start.

One other general rule remains to be noted. Calculations, however simple, are more likely to be done incorrectly in the field than in the office. The actual observations, therefore, should always be booked. Examples appear in Paras. 5.6 and 13.2.

Finally, mention should be made of the 'rituals' which form part of surveying technique, such as the repetition of a reading which has been given to you. At first, some of these seem meaningless, but they are all directed towards reducing the risk of mistakes. They should therefore be performed with special care whenever fatigue and foul weather tempt you to scamp them, for it is under those conditions that mistakes are most likely to occur.

Part II
Chain Surveying

3 Equipment

3.1 *Basic Requirements.* Chain surveying is a technique of considerable age (see Para. 1.4). It is the most useful method of recording detail, even when the main network has been established in some other way; and for the majority of sites a straightforward chain survey is all that is needed. The principle is very simple. A network of interlocking triangles is marked out by 'ranging-rods' or 'poles' at their vertices ('stations') and the sides ('chain-lines') are measured; details are fixed by measurement from these chainlines.

The equipment is equally simple. It comprises poles, the chain, 'arrows' used as temporary markers during measurement, and a tape for measuring distances from the chain. These are the essentials. A means of measuring the slope of chain lines and one for fixing the north point are very desirable. On a survey which will last more than one day you will need pegs (which are expendable), a hammer to drive them in and preferably a saw to make them. 'Wands', also expendable, are sometimes useful. Material for pegs and wands can almost always be found near the site.

You will also need a field book ('chain book' Para. 4.6), an 'HB' or 'H' pencil and probably a good eraser.

3.2 *Detailed list* (Figure 3.1.) The *chain* is of steel, with main links nearly 0·2 m long, joined by two or three smaller links. The reason for using this, rather than a tape, is that it will lie in position and thus forms in effect a graduated ruled line on the ground, from which measurements can be made; save under quite exceptionally favourable conditions a tape will blow about.

A 20 m chain is to be preferred. Do not get a 30 m one, under the impression that because you will not have to move it so often you will save work. It is very inconvenient indeed to fold up and to handle when folded, and measurements can easily be misread.

3.1 Equipment for Chain Survey

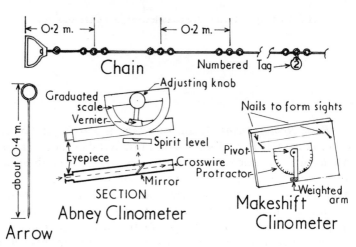

A linen or plastic *tape* (in case) 20 m or 30 m long; in this case, 30 m is preferable.

'*Arrows*' in a set of five or ten. These are narrow steel rods, 30 to 40 cm long pointed at one end and formed into a loop at the other. They should each be fitted with a tag of broad bright-coloured tape, preferably four red and one yellow or five of each. You will almost certainly have to buy a set of ten, but five is enough for most fieldwork. Since they are easily lost, keep the other five in reserve; and they may often be useful as anchorages for chain or tape.

Six (at least) 2 m *poles* or *ranging-rods*. These may be of wood or metal. They have a steel-shod point at one end, and are painted alternately red and white (or sometimes red, black and white) in 0·5 m or 0·2 m lengths. The latter are preferable; they are more clearly visible at a distance, and can be used for measurement.

By far the most useful type of pole, very well worth the extra expense, is the sectional type, of metre lengths with screwed ends. They are very much easier to carry (in a suitable shoulder-bag) than the full 2 metres (which are often too long to fit in a car), and can be screwed together to build up longer poles, which are often invaluable.

A set of six poles is the minimum requirement, but if you have only that number you will often be inconvenienced, so if at all possible get a dozen or more.

Simple ranging-rods and arrows could be made at home, but in general the saving by using 'home-made' equipment is so small, in proportion to the total cost, that the work involved is not worth while, especially since the result is seldom very satisfactory.

In addition to the above essentials, it is an advantage to have:

A Prismatic Compass (for description see Para. 25.5). In chain surveying, this is only needed to get the approximate north point; but it is almost indispensable for rough reconnaissance fieldwork.

An Abney Clinometer (or substitute) (Figure 3.1). This is essentially a sighting-tube (not usually telescopic) pivoted to a protractor with a spirit-level. A small opening with a mirror at 45° halfway along the tube allows the bubble to be observed at the same time as the line of sight, so that the spirit-level can be brought horizontal, and thus the slope of the line of sight measured. In chain surveying it is useful for correcting the measured length of a line to allow for slope; but rougher methods (Para. 4.5) may be adequate. It is also useful for measuring profiles of earthworks, if a level is not available (Para. 26.8).

If you intend to use the clinometer for slope-corrections *and for no other purpose*, an inexpensive makeshift can be good enough (Figure 3.1). In its crudest form two nails driven into a roughly shaped board form the line of sight. A school 180° protractor is then fixed to the board with its base parallel to the line joining the nails (this order of work is easier than trying to get the nails on the sight line after fixing the protractor). A weighted arm, recessed as shown, is pivoted at the centre of the protractor. In use, the nails are sighted along the correct slope and the arm is gripped in position with the thumb. Two or three readings should be averaged. With care, this device could also be used to measure a profile provided no great accuracy is required.

Pegs can almost always be made on or near the site, by sawing through a 3 to 5 cm diameter branch and pointing one end. The length required depends on the nature of the ground; 10 to 20 cm is usually adequate. It is hardly ever necessary or even desirable to get commercially cut pegs of squared timber. Invariably, though, the pegs should be sawn, not broken. A sawn end can always be recognised as artificial, whereas a broken end can easily be mistaken for a natural object.

Wands are merely straight twigs, used as temporary marks and treated as expendable. They can be made more recognisable by peeling off the bark. Given an adequate supply of poles, they are not often needed on ordinary chain survey.

3.3 *Care and Use.* For most of the equipment, the main hazard is loss rather than damage. Sectional poles should have their joints kept lightly oiled, and should not be left screwed together for a long time as they can seize up. Poles should *never* be used as javelins, despite the temptation, for this loosens the attachment of the shoes and may bend or even break the pole.

The *chain* (see also Para. 4.4) must *always* be unfolded and folded according to a strict ritual. **Never** take the two handles and pull them apart, since this will certainly strain the links and may cause breakage. The correct procedure is as follows: one of the party, A, keeps hold of both handles and throws the rest of the chain away from him as hard as possible. The other, B, finds the 10 m tag and moves away, A still holding *both* handles, until the doubled chain lies straight. A then releases one handle, and B backs away running the chain through his hands until it is fully extended; if folded properly, it will slide over itself without getting tangled. It is then inspected to get rid of any kinks or interlocked links. The chain should be left extended until the end of the day's work, and transported merely by pulling the leading end.

If you are working single-handed, after throwing out the chain anchor one handle firmly and the other lightly, so that when you have straightened out the doubled chain you can easily release one end by pulling harder.

To fold up the chain, take the 10 m mark and walk away with it until the chain is nearly doubled. Then hold together the first pair of links (that is, those which meet at 10 m) and fold the second pair against them. Then fold the third pair in the opposite direction, and so on folding the pairs backwards and forwards alternately until the handles are reached, and tie firmly with a cord or strap passing through the handles.

If the chain is wet or dirty it should be dried and wiped fairly clean, but unless it is to be left unused for a very long time there is no need to oil it; a day's work in grass or heather will remove most rust.

Although a chain is very durable it is liable to stretch slightly over years of use. If you are only concerned with small sites, the necessary correction is likely to be negligible. If you survey large sites or require special accuracy, or indeed if you just want the satisfaction of knowing that your chain really is right, you should check it occasionally, perhaps once a year, or at the beginning of any major survey. You may have access to some institution which owns a steel band or other sufficiently reliable standard of length; a University Geographical or Civil Engineering Department may well have something suitable. Lacking this, soon after you have bought the chain you can chisel marks on a concrete path, or drive two very substantial pegs (preferably of oak and set in concrete) which you can mark with brass nails. Your new chain can be used as standard. For choice, this 'standard length' should be in an area under your own control, since there is always a risk that a bit of kerbing by a public road, which might otherwise be suitable, may be disturbed. The marks need not be exactly 20 m apart; you could, for example, keep a record that '20 m = standard plus 122 mm', the extra 12·2 cm being measured by a tape or scale.

There are three ways of dealing with a stretched chain. The most rational is to keep a log-book, in which the actual length of the chain is recorded at regular intervals, say a fixed date every year, plus any time the chain has suffered an accident, such as being run over by a lorry. This method has the advantage that the correction at every given date can be estimated with fair accuracy. If for example, the chain was 12 mm too long on 1 September 1976 and 18 mm too long a year later, then to apply a correction of 16 mm for a survey done in May 1977 would not be far wrong. Take care not to forget, when applying such a correction, that if the chain is too long the true length of a line will be *greater* than the apparent length as measured.

The second method, which can be very laborious and is therefore seldom used, is to shorten a number of the small oval links by hammering, until the stretch is eliminated. This has the merit that no correction is needed and that the strength of the chain is little affected.

The third, most widely used, method is to remove the necessary number of small oval links. It is essential that those removed should be distributed evenly along the chain. This method also removes the need for any correction, but has the disadvantage that the chain is weakened.

It is good practice to keep a record of the history of the chain, for you may sometimes need to estimate a correction when no check has been possible. In an organisation owning several chains, these can be numbered by file-cuts on the handles.

4 The Elements of Chain Survey

4.1 *General.* This chapter discusses the principles on which chain surveying is based. An imaginary survey, illustrating the practical applications of those principles, is described in the next chapter. Both these assume ideal conditions; the ways of overcoming various practical difficulties are explained in Chapter 6.

4.2 *Choice of Network.* The principles which should govern the arrangement of a network have been described in Para. 2.2, but its actual form must depend on the site. Various types which are widely applicable are illustrated in Figure 4.1.

The simplest of all is the quadrilateral (a). The diagonals may well pick up no detail, but one must be measured to make the network rigid. One diagonal alone, though, provides no way of balancing errors or of detecting mistakes, so both diagonals should always be measured. There is no need to book the chainages at their intersection.

This emphasises an important point: *To measure a chain line without booking any detail does not take very long, so it is often worth while to include lines simply to secure a rigid network.* Detail is picked up from subsidiary lines.

Most common, perhaps, are oval enclosures. Networks such as (b) are suitable for these, but are greatly improved if two radial lines can be collinear (c) or better still several (d). When the enclosure has substantial ramparts, it may be useful to have a double ring of chain lines, one set following the inside of the defences, the other the outside (e). This is also a very good rigid network.

Large sites may require networks of two or more interlocking polygons (f, g). An effort should be made to get one or more continuous alignments running right across the site, or at least to note the intersection points of some lines produced (as x, x in f, g).

27

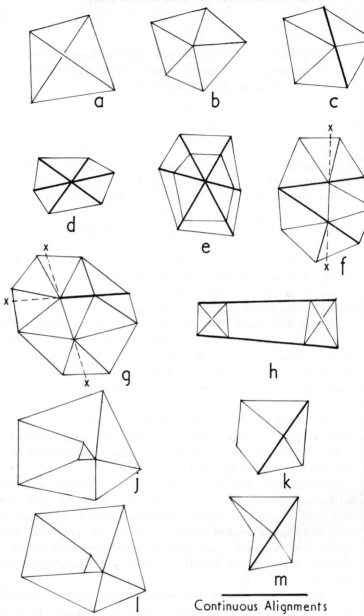

Continuous Alignments

Sometimes the feature to be surveyed may be itself an obstacle to accurate measurement. A possible example of a suitable network (appropriate to a long cairn) is given in (h).

Finally, beware of traps. For example, (j) and (k) look at first glance like quite good networks; but they are not in fact rigid, for the same measurements can give the shapes (l) and (m).

It may be worth while to emphasise again that these are all merely examples of the main network. Additional subsidiary lines can be inserted as desired to pick up detail.

If you have no compass available, you should preferably aim at least one of your chain lines towards some landmark identifiable on the OS map, so as to establish the north point.

Unless it is absolutely certain that the work can be finished in one day the stations must be marked by pegs; but the actual stations are at the poles, which should therefore be replaced in the same holes each day. In fact, for chain surveying, the difference in positions between pole and peg will be insignificant, but it can affect your calculations in theodolite work.

4.3 *Preliminary Booking.* Before starting the detailed survey, a sketch of the framework must be drawn in your fieldbook, each station being designated by a letter (or number, Arabic or Roman). Usually, in practice, you will also record each station's position (Para. 7.2).

It is an advantage, also, to take any necessary compass bearings, and where relevant to note the slope of the ground. You are less likely to forget these things if you do them at this stage.

It is also very good practice simply to measure all chain lines once without booking detail (which of course requires a repetition of that measurement). The risk of a mistake is almost eliminated. Whether you in fact follow this good practice often involves a difficult choice (see Para. 5.5).

4.4 *Chaining.* Measurement of the chain lines follows a ritual which has developed over many years; it should be adhered to, as it is the most efficient method. The ideal team comprises three people, a leader, L and a follower, F, who handles the chain, and the surveyor who books the records. The third man is a luxury, and usually F is also the surveyor. The party is assumed to have a chain, five arrows, and one or two poles (optional), and to be measuring from A to B.

The first step is, rather obviously, to unfold the chain (Para. 3.3). When that has been done, if you are using one for the first time, you should make yourself familiar with its graduation. It is made up of 100 major links each nearly 0·2 m long, connected by smaller links. The system of numbering on metric chains is not rigidly standardised, but usually every metre is marked by a yellow tag, with red tags, numbered 5 or 10 as appropriate, at the 5-metre points; the distance given is always from the *nearer* end, and zero is the outer face of the handle. You will be wise to practise a little by taking points at random, noting their chainage (to 0·01 m) and then checking it with the tape.

For measurement, L has initially the five arrows and a pole. F holds the end of the chain at A, and 'lines in' L's pole so that it is on the line AB, about 20 m from A. L stands to one side of the line facing towards it, and is directed by F who may say, for example, 'To you half a metre; from you 10 centimetres; to you in the head', (the top of the pole is leaning away from L); 'to you two centimetres; right!' L fixes the pole in the ground, and having established the right directions he then pulls the chain *tight*, applying a fairly strong tension; it can be brought to the required straight line by a flick of the wrist. F is holding the handle against the pole at A, and L puts a red-tagged arrow firmly in the ground against the outer face of the handle at his end.

Leaving the arrow in the ground, L and F both move on for 20 m along line AB, L pulling the leading handle of the chain. Time will be saved if F gives a count-down as his end of the chain moves past the arrow. 'Five' ('metres' implied), 'four, three, two, one, STOP'.

The procedure is then repeated, F at the arrow lining in L's pole, and L then putting in a second 'red' arrow, 40 m from A.

When they move on to the third 20 m section, F lifts the first arrow and carries it with him (and similarly at each successive stage), so the number of red arrows which he is carrying shows how many multiples of 20 m he has moved. At the 100 m point, L puts in the yellow-tagged arrow, and F hands back to him the stock of four 'red' arrows. The same ritual continues, F returning the 'yellow' arrow to L when convenient. F then knows that if he is carrying a 'yellow' arrow he has moved some multiple of 100 m, if he is carrying (say) 3 'red' arrows he has moved some multiple of 100 m plus 60 m.

An alternative, perhaps preferable, is for L to start with six arrows; their colours do not matter. When measuring the 100 to

120 m length, F has five arrows, which he transfers to L, and the sixth arrow is marking 120 m, and similarly on passing each multiple of 100 m.

The follower F will find a pole helpful for 'lining in' L, but it often proves a tiresome extra burden especially if F is taking notes, and it is not essential.

The last 20 m or so of the line can, if desired, be taped.

4.5 *Allowance for Slope.* A plan represents a projection on to a horizontal plane at sea level. For our type of work, the effect of height is negligible, but chain lines are often far from horizontal and a correction is needed. The corrected distance is always less than the measured distance. As a rough guide, if the slope is less than 1 in 20 no correction is needed, and if more than 1 in 10 measurement 'by steps' is best. The standard method of dealing with this problem is to work out the correction for each 20 m length, and then to insert the arrow not at the end of the chain but the appropriate distance beyond it. The objection to this is that numerous calculations have to be made in the field, with consequent delay and increased risk of mistake. It is preferable, except on very steep slopes, to measure along the ground, record the relevant slope, and correct in the office. The corrections are almost always small, so the work can be a bit rough. Three methods are available.

(a) *With Clinometer.* The slope is measured and recorded, either during the chaining or as a preliminary. The latter is preferable, as having too many jobs to do at once leads to confusion and thus to mistakes. Generally, the slope from one station to another is uniform enough for a single measurement to be adequate. If there is a marked break in the ground, it can be recorded as, for example, 'Line AB, fall 5° 10' for 63 paces, 2° 20' for the remaining 92 paces'; as the correction is small, controlled pacing between fixed points is accurate enough.

If theodolite observations are being made slopes can be measured with that instrument.

(b) *With Dumpy Level.* If a level is available, probably the quickest way of correcting for slope is to take the necessary spot levels. At a break in slope between stations, a mark must be left where the level was taken. The level book will contain the note 'between A and B; see chain book', and the chain book will record, against the appropriate chainage 'see level book'.

(c) *'By Eye'.* This is a very rough method for use in an emergency, but as the correction is usually small it is often adequate. All measurements are along the chain line.

Lay down a pole or some other obvious mark on the ground. Walk about 30 paces downhill. Turn round and hold your arm out horizontally to give a (very roughly) level line of sight. Walk uphill until that line of sight passes through the mark. Then pace the remaining distance.

Tables relevant to methods (a) and (c) are given in Appendix IV.

If the slope is steep, it is always less trouble, and compared to method (c) more accurate, to measure in steps (Para. 5.4). When this is done the actual measurements should be recorded, not merely the total chainages. This reduces the risk of mistakes associated with arithmetical calculations in the field.

4.6 *Allowance for Sag.* The chain line has sometimes to be carried across a deep hollow. For choice, a tape should be used to measure the unsupported distance, for it can be pulled tight so little or no error will be introduced. The measurement should be made between marks where ordinary chaining is interrupted. Sometimes, as for example in a high wind, a chain may be more convenient. In that case, sufficient accuracy can be obtained by estimating the sag by eye, and deducting the correction for sag, as given in Appendix IV.

4.7 *Booking Detail, Introductory Notes.* When detail is to be recorded near a chain line, measurements along the line are made as above, but after F has lifted the arrow at his end the chain, and of course the other arrow, are left in position until all the features near that 20 m length of chain line have been recorded. This is usually done by measurement of 'offsets', horizontal distances taken perpendicular to the line of the chain; a fuller description is given below.

For the tape, 30 m rather than 20 m is to be preferred. The case is held by L, who usually remains at the chain and reads off chainage and offset or other measurements. F holds the free end of the tape, and does the booking. Two general points should be noted. First, F should *always* repeat L's statements of distance and L will correct him if he is wrong. It may seem absurd to do this when L and F are only separated by a few metres, but even at that short distance mistakes can occur, and in rough weather and perhaps 20 m apart the risk is considerable. For the same reason in 'fi*v*e' and 'ni*n*e' the *v* or *n* must be overemphasised, and 'oh' or 'zero' is preferable to

4.2 Conventions for Booking Detail

Top of Scarp

Occasional hachures may be added if desired, but are not essential.

Toe of Scarp

Estimated vertical height of scarp, to assist in final drawing.

Centre-line or Contour. Examples:

Centre-line of crest of bank, 1·2 metres wide.

240 metre contour.
The level is always written on the upper side.

Circular feature, here top of scarp, 1·4 metres radius. The position booked is that of the centre.

Revetment or wall-face, visible.

Revetment or wall-face, probable line.

Fence.

Gateway (1·8 metres wide).

Hedge.

Top of cliff or crags.

Other lines (preferred symbol); the feature should always be described verbally.

may be used if desired.

Building. The outline should be roughly correct, but need not be ruled or drawn to scale. Cross-hatching may be added for emphasis, but is not essential.

'nought', which can be confused with 'four'. Second, since there is apparently no standard convention as to whether chainage or offset should be stated first, it will be found useful to adopt the following practice: the figure for the chainage is always preceded either by 'at', if the other measurement is an offset perpendicular to the chain line, or 'to', if the other measurement is not at right angles. Which measurement is which then remains clear, whether stated as 'at 5·25, 4·91' or '4·91 at 5·25'. Examples are given in the next section.

Details are recorded in a 'chain book'. This is about 20 × 10 cm or larger, strongly bound along a short side. A pair of red lines about 1 cm apart run perpendicular to the short sides, along the middle of each page. Some types have only one line, but this is less convenient to use. Ordinary note books are seldom strong enough for the rigours of fieldwork, so the extra cost of a proper chain book is worthwhile.

Before using a new chain book it will be found helpful to give it a (consecutive) reference letter or number, and to number alternate pages. A page or two should be left blank at the beginning for indexing.

Most of the detail which has to be recorded in archaeological field survey can be classified under a very few headings. It is convenient to use standardised conventions for these. A possible set of such conventions is set out in Figure 4.2. Note, though, that these are merely suggested as useful; they are not in fact 'standard', and to use other symbols is not 'wrong', provided your colleagues use the same.

5 An Imaginary Survey

5.1 Conditions Assumed; 5.2 Choice of Network; 5.3 Measuring and Booking, Preliminary Remarks; 5.4 Booking Detail; 5.5 Completing the Survey; 5.6 Supplementary Notes on Accuracy, Booking, and Squaring Off.

5.1 *Conditions Assumed.* The procedure for an actual survey can best be followed by describing in some detail how the work would be approached in practice. To introduce all the difficulties which may sometimes be encountered would be confusing at this stage, so they are discussed in Chapter 7; but to emphasise the advantage of having plenty of poles, even on such a small site, we will assume that you only have a set of six 2 m sectional ranging-rods.

The site to be surveyed is a small enclosure, roughly semi-circular in plan, on slightly sloping ground at the edge of a steep natural scarp (Figure 5.1). On the north and east is a modern wall, too high to measure or to see across, with a gateway at the north-east corner. The party comprises L (the leader) and F (the follower) who is organising the work.

5.2 *Choice of Network.* After obtaining the tenant's permission, the first step is to fix the stations. There are two good clear lines: from the scarp edge through the gateway, and along the east side of the modern wall; so stations A and B are fairly easy to select. You find, to your relief, that a 4 m pole (that is, four sections screwed together) at C is visible from A and B (though not conversely) so after a little to-ing and fro-ing you decide on that station. You will obviously need a line on the north side of the wall, so you line in stations D (on AC) and E (on AB). Given a set of six poles, you will only have 1 m sections available for these. If possible, you would also have fixed the line from E through the entrance by another station on line AC, but you have run out of poles. It is by now obvious that you will not finish the job in a day, so L goes round driving pegs at A, B, C, D and E while F makes a freehand sketch of the site and network (Figure 5.2) (including stations which will obviously be needed but are not yet marked), and takes magnetic

5.1 Draft Plan

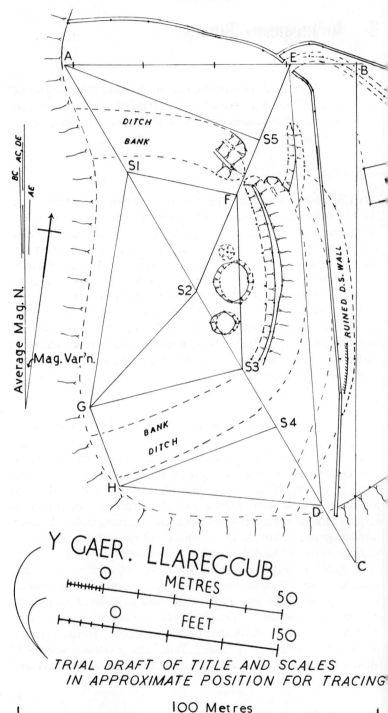

Y GAER. LLAREGGUB

METRES

50

FEET

150

TRIAL DRAFT OF TITLE AND SCALES
IN APPROXIMATE POSITION FOR TRACING

100 Metres

REFERENCE SCALE USED DURING PLOTTING

5.2 Field Notes, Chain Survey

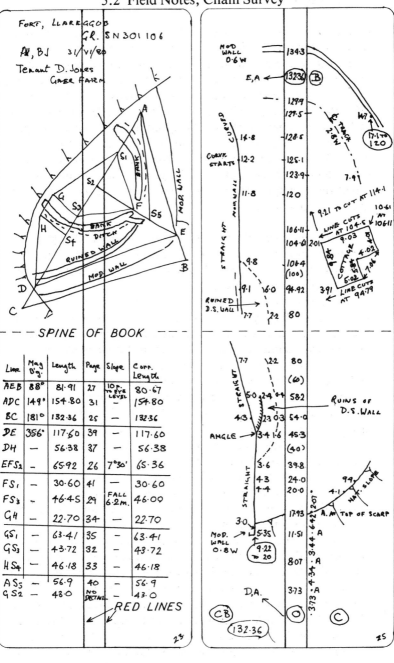

FORT, LLAREGGUB
GR. SN 301 106
AW, BJ   31/VI/80
Tenant D. Jones
GAER FARM

SPINE OF BOOK

Line	Mag B'g	Length	Page	Slope	Corr. Length
AEB	88°	81·91	27	10 ft to Eye Level	80·67
ADC	149°	154·80	31	—	154·80
BC	181°	132·36	25	—	132·36
DE	356°	117·60	39	—	117·60
DH	—	56·38	37	—	56·38
EFS₂	—	65·92	26	7°30'	65·36
FS₁	—	30·60	41	—	30·60
FS₃	—	46·45	29	FALL 6·2m.	46·00
GH	—	22·70	34	—	22·70
GS₁	—	63·41	35	—	63·41
GS₃	—	43·72	32	—	43·72
HS₄	—	46·18	33	—	46·18
AS₅	—	56·9	40	—	56·9
GS₂	—	43·0	NO DETAIL	—	43·0

RED LINES

23

25

bearings along the main chain lines, or at very least along two of them. On the sketch S indicates a subsidiary station which will not be marked by a peg. The site is named, with grid reference and any other relevant details such as the name and address of the tenant; the date of the survey and the names (or initials) of L and F noted. After this, another page if necessary is used for a list of chain lines, with space for columns to record magnetic bearing, length and page reference at least; columns for slope and corrected length are also useful. You may consider this an unduly meticulous waste of time; but it does not in fact take very long, and I have found (all too often) that scamping these notes almost always adds a lot of un-necessary work later.

5.3 *Measuring and Booking, Preliminary Remarks.* Suppose that you decide to start at C and measure the line CB, in that direction. Since you cannot see B from C, you will need to line in a temporary pole, sighting from B towards C.

The chain book is held with the spine away from you and zero is at the foot of the page nearest to you, so that when you are facing in the direction of measurement the detail on the right-hand half of the page corresponds to that to the right of the chain line, and *vice versa*. In windy weather two rubber bands will help keep the pages under control, but in ordinary conditions they tend to be a nuisance, for they seem almost invariably to lie over the point one wishes to plot. In good conditions an HB pencil is best for booking (carry a spare, for they vanish without trace if dropped in long grass), but when the pages are wet a black ball-point pen is better; numbers and details should then be drawn extra large.

One point, though obvious from the field notes reproduced, nevertheless needs emphasis. The over-riding essential is legibility. The fieldbook is handheld, and notes are often taken in adverse conditions, so prize-winning calligraphy is not to be expected; the ideal is something which will still be clear even after the book has been dropped in a muddy puddle. A beginner will often make a careful and fairly accurate sketch for the whole length of a chain line, and then, using small neat numerals, will try to fit the records of measurement into that plan. This is an entirely mistaken approach. The sketch in the field notes is solely a convenient way of recording measurements; for example, a featureless straight wall 100 m long may require less space than a complicated feature only 10 m across. This will become obvious in the explanation which follows.

5.4 *Booking Detail* (Figures 5.2, 5.3). Suppose that you are chaining line CB (Figure 5.2) including detail. Put the name of the line, ringed, at the bottom of the page, with a space for the total length when measured. Station C is at chainage 0; *chainage of stations on the measured line, and their names, are always ringed.* It is helpful to indicate the directions of adjacent lines (for example, DA here), but this is often neglected. Some methods of fixing important detail are illustrated between chainages 80 and 120 on line CB (Figure 5.2), and separately in Figure 5.4 (see Para. 5.6).

To start with, you are ascending a steep slope, so you will measure in steps, measuring the horizontal distances with the tape to the nearest centimetre. Do not try to get these to some pre-selected length, but record the steps alongside the central pair of lines and add them up to get the actual chainages. Thus the first four horizontal distances between the points marked by arrows (A) are 3·73, 4·34, 3·44, and 6·42 m, giving the corresponding chainages of 3·73, 8·07, 11·51, 17·93. Fortunately there is not much detail to record. The third arrow (11·51) is put in to get an offset (5·35) to the corner of the modern wall, but as it is difficult to square off accurately on a slope, this is also fixed (after the 20 m arrow has been put in) by a diagonal of 9·22 to 20. Because of the awkwardness of working on a steep slope, the point where the top of scarp cuts the wall is fixed by measurement from that corner. The fourth arrow (17·93) has been put at the top of the natural scarp. *Remember, when you are booking this, that the pair of red lines in the chain book corresponds to the single line of the chain on the ground, so the line representing the top of scarp leaves the pair of lines on the right exactly opposite where it enters on the left.* (For an example of what not to do, see Para. 7.4, Figure 7.3.)

You have now reached fairly level ground, so you can start following the proper routine for chaining. If your arithmetic is right, the 20 m mark should be 2·07 from your last arrow, so measure this distance and put in a red arrow; return all the rest to L. Record the 2·07 distance; it happens to be right, but it is surprisingly easy in the field to make a mistake such as 20·00 − 17·93 = 3·07. If the distance is booked, such a mistake can be put right without returning to the site.

L now takes his end of the chain to the 40 m point, and having been lined in by F marks it with a red arrow, as described earlier. When released, the ends of the tightly-stretched chain will move a few centimetres towards each other owing to the roughness of the ground. The aim should be to allow the same movement at each end.

The chain is left lying on the ground, and forms in effect a ruled line from which measurements can be taken. It is heavy enough to be unaffected by wind (which is one reason why it is used rather than a tape), and is unlikely to be disturbed except by one of the surveying party tripping over it.

To measure offsets, F takes the zero end of the tape and goes to the point to be recorded, L stays at the chain. If F has a loop of string through the ring of the tape, he can keep it hooked round a finger, leaving his hands free. Depending on the nature of the site, it may be an advantage for L and for F to carry a pole for plumbing to the relevant points, but in general any extra burden is to be avoided.

F holds the end of the tape at the point with which he is concerned. L estimates the point at which the tape is perpendicular to the chain (see below), and reads off the offset and chainage, for example, '3·6 at 19·8' or 'at 19·8, 3·6'. F repeats this and records it, and L says 'Right' (if it is). F, however, is carrying one arrow, so he knows that he must add 20, which makes the chainage 39·8. It is very advisable not to rely entirely on this system, but to book every 20 m point, putting the figure in brackets if there is no offset at that chainage, as at 40, 60, and 100.

The offsets are always measured from the chain line (not built up in steps). Thus at '54' the readings might be 'at 14·0, 4·3', 'Same chainage, 2·3', 'Same chainage, 0·3', the face of the modern wall and the ancient wall being 4·3 and 2·3 m respectively *from the chain line*.

The first page of the booking continues to chainage 80. Plotting is simplified, and the risk of mistakes reduced, if the final measurements at the top of one page are repeated at the bottom of the next; but it is not essential to do this. The main feature which needs comment on this page (Figure 5.2) is the cottage. It is assumed here that only the outline is needed. Complicated buildings are discussed more fully in Para. 7.7.

Since it is a sharply defined structure, measurements can be made to a centimetre. All sides are measured, and a diagonal is taken across the re-entrant angle to determine whether it is a right angle. The points where the sides produced cut the chain line are noted, and where appropriate the distance of the corner to the chain ('9·21 to cut at 114·1'). The faces which cut at 94·79 and 104·50 are too nearly perpendicular to the chain line for it to be worth taking these distances as well as the offsets. Only three corners are accessible for offset measurements, and the most distant ('10·61 at 106·11') is annotated to avoid confusion. A diagonal (say '17·4 to 120') would have been quite useful as a check on this point.

Few other comments are needed on this chain line. The modern track has been booked by recording its centre line and its width, and the continuation of the modern wall by an offset, which is long and therefore also fixed by a diagonal; the resulting triangle is not very 'well-conditioned', but the feature itself is not important. Note that the name of the station and its chainage are ringed.

As soon as you have completed this line, 'index' it by noting at the beginning of the survey 'BC 132·36; p. 25. This only takes a moment, and will save a lot of bother when you start plotting.

There is no need to go through all the chain lines of this imaginary survey in such detail, but three of them, BA, EF, and F to subsidiary S3 will illustrate some points which deserve note.

Three occur on line BA (Figure 5.3). The distance measured 'backwards' from B to the shorter modern wall is booked as '−4·5'; it would be legitimate to take zero at the wall, when B would be booked at 4·50, E and A at 23·35 and 86·41, but if you use that method you will almost certainly some time find yourself trying to plot the network with BA = 86·41 m. The other points are: the width of the gateway (or any similar feature) is booked, not left to be inferred from the offsets; and the junction of the two walls (which cannot be fixed directly by an offset because the main wall is too high) is located by measurement along the wall face.

The line EF exemplifies three fairly important principles or techniques. The first is that a feature such as a hill-fort entrance should, so far as possible, be surveyed from a single line. The end of the inner rampart to the right of EF could theoretically be fixed by an offset from BA and the other side of the entrance by one from ED; but if these offsets are rotated only slightly in opposite directions, quite a large falsification of the plan will result.

Second, the use of a subsidiary station (S on plan) is to be noted. The rampart north of EF can be measured much more conveniently from a line 'Subsid. 5 at 21·82 on EF to A' than it could be from BEA, for the offsets are much shorter. A subsidiary is (normally) only marked temporarily, not pegged.

Finally, so far as EF is concerned, attention needs to be drawn to the method of booking. Standard practice is to take offsets on both

5.3 Field Notes, Chain Survey

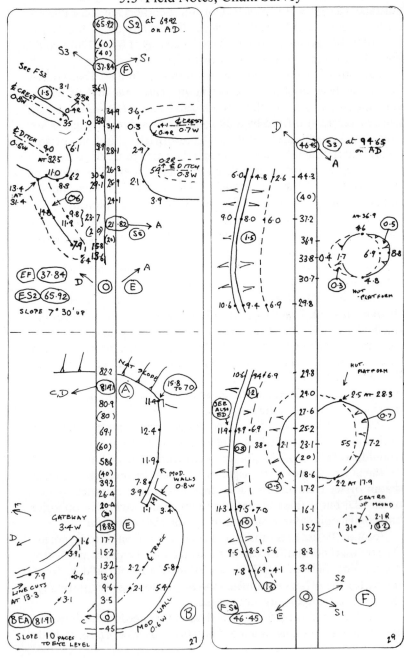

sides of the line as they are reached, and to record the corresponding chainages in order; line CB has been recorded in this way. In many archaeological surveys, though, it is a nuisance to have to keep on moving from one side of the chain line to the other and back again; it is much less trouble to finish off all the work on one side, and then to deal with the other. The chainages at which offsets are booked will not be the same for both sides. There are two ways of indicating this: either a mark can be made on the appropriate red line to show on which side the offset was taken (as for FS3), or the central column can be divided by a line along its middle, and the two sides booked quite independently (as for EF). The former arrangement is probably the more convenient when only a few chainages are involved, the latter if they are numerous.

The line FS3, from F to the subsidiary on AD, is for the most part self-explanatory if considered in conjunction with the conventions (Figure 4.2). Alternative methods for booking a hut-platform or similar feature are shown; but make sure it *is* nearly circular before you record it as such, for a square with rounded corners can be very deceptive.

A mark is supposed to be left at '11·9 at 25·2'. It is a good precaution to duplicate a few measurements off nearly parallel chain lines, either to the same feature such as a line of bank, or as implied here to some quite temporary mark such as a stick.

5.5 *Completing the Survey.* As noted earlier, a site of this size may well take more than one day. It will be instructive to go briefly through an imaginary account of two days' work, but without describing the measurement of each line in detail. To exemplify the extra work caused by a shortage of poles, it will be assumed that only six are available.

During the first day's work already discussed, the general shape of the network has been fixed, the stations A, B, C, D and E chosen and marked, and lines CB and BA measured. Returning on the second day, you will inevitably be unable to leave poles at all the stations, so you bring half a dozen or so 'wands' — fairly straight twigs preferably peeled to make them conspicuous — which will serve as expendable markers. You can *start* a line from a wand, but generally they are neither straight enough nor easily enough visible to run a line *towards* them.

Of the remaining stations, F, G and H, F might be worth a peg, if there is any prospect of further work on the site, but provided the work can be finished on the second day, G and H could merely be marked by poles.

Poles are needed at A, D, E and F. A sensible first step might be to chain ADC booking detail. In default of poles, wands must be left at the four subsidiary stations. In placing S_2, L would line his pole on EF produced, while the follower would keep him on the line AD. In this particular case the distance to F is less than 30 m and could be taped and booked, but in general a link of this kind would be chained as a continuation of EF. The other subsidiaries are chosen so that chain lines can be run close to the back and front of the defences. If this can be done conveniently, it gives a better result than trying to measure right across the bank and ditch.

H and G are then marked with poles, the pole from F is 'borrowed' temporarily for use in chaining (unless conditions permit the use of L's arrow for lining in) and HS_4, GS_3, S_1G and HD, all booked, with detail. Wands are left at G and H; there are now enough poles available to mark out all the remaining stations including S_5, so the order in which the remaining lines are measured does not make much difference. A convenient run would be DE, EFS_2, FS_3, and AS_5, perhaps with GS_2 as an afterthought, which requires no detail but is a useful extra check.

Ideally, if you have not already done so, you should now check the measurements of all chain lines, though without detail. What you would do in fact would depend on many circumstances, such as the time of day, the weather, and how quick you are at chaining. Obviously it would not, in general, be sensible to come back the next day merely to do this checking, since the object of the check is to make sure that you do not need to come back another day. Probably the next best compromise is for L to mark with pegs as many stations as possible, including subsidiaries, and for F to take the magnetic bearings of all lines measured. This at least permits the identification, with fair certainty, of any line which contains a mistake.

5.6 *Supplementary Notes on Accuracy, Booking, and Squaring Off.* Most earthworks or ruined dry-stone structures cannot be measured more accurately than to the nearest 0·1 m at best, and it is simplest to book measurements to that accuracy rather than to worry about whether such a length can be represented on the final plan. Buildings can be measured much more accurately, but if say the final plan is to be at a scale of 1/2,500 it may seem rather absurd to record lengths to 0·01 m. Nevertheless, it is usually more sensible to do this than to spend time deciding what is the nearest 0·1 m.

As noted earlier, it is tempting to sketch the whole plan in advance, and then to add the measurements as they are taken; but it is a mistake. If you do this, you will almost certainly find in places that you have not enough room for the entries. In practice, the sketch-plan should only be drawn a little way ahead of the measurement.

Although the offsets are defined as perpendicular to the chain line, nothing has been said so far as to how this is ensured. The method depends on circumstances. Usually, quite an accurate right angle can be estimated by looking down at the tape, and judging whether the two angles it makes with the chain are equal. Moreover, provided that the feature being recorded is linear, and at an acute angle to the chain line, quite a large departure from perpendicularity has little effect (Figure 5.4). The method of fixing an important point by a diagonal has already been noted (Para. 5.4). If, though, the position of the truly perpendicular offset is needed very accurately, it can be fixed by swinging the tape in an arc, and noting the points at which a radius rather greater than the offset cuts the line. The average gives the correct chainage (Figure 5.4). It is advisable to record all the measurements, rather than to rely on the average chainage being worked out correctly.

5.4 Offsets to Chain Line

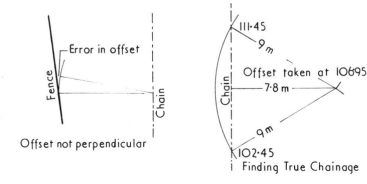

Offset not perpendicular

Finding True Chainage

This discussion of an imaginary chain survey has implied the assumption that no serious problems have arisen. What may happen in practice, and the necessary precautions which result, are discussed in Chapter 7, but first an explanation will be given of the work needed to arrive at the finished plan.

6 Plotting and Finishing the Plan

6.1 General Remarks; 6.2 Equipment for Plotting; 6.3 Plotting the Network: 6.4 Plotting Detail; 6.5 The Finished Drawing: the Materials; 6.6 The Finished Drawing: Tracing; 6.7 Publication; 6.8 Rational Scales

6.1 *General Remarks*. Preparation from the field notes of a finished plan for publication falls into two parts: a pencil draft is plotted; and this is traced in ink for reproduction. It is convenient to consider these two procedures separately.

6.2 *Equipment for Plotting*. The following items are either essential or desirable.

Accurate scales, 30 cm (or more) long, one graduated in millimetres (that is, a metric 1/1,000 scale); and preferably a metric 1/2,500 scale. Similar scales graduated in 1/500 and 1/1,250 are useful, and perhaps 1/2,000 also, but these are not essential for one can easily divide or multiply by two mentally. The sort of ruler available in stationery shops is not adequate; and note, incidentally, that the edge of a scale should be treated carefully and can be damaged by use as a ruler.

Corresponding to each of these scales an 'offset scale' is needed (for its use see Para. 6.4). This is a short length of scale, usually 5 or 7·5 cm long, similar to the longer scale but cut off truly square at each end. The graduations start from these cut ends.

It is *absolutely essential* that both main and offset scales are trapezoidal (that is, flat-faced) in section. Scales of oval section are no use for this type of work.

You will also need: a 60° and a 45° set square, of transparent material. The size is not crucial, but 17 cm shortest side is convenient. It is often useful, but not essential, to have a smaller (10 cm shortest side) 60° set square.

A 15 cm diameter protractor (transparent). The full circle type is marginally more useful than the half circle, but preferably get both.

A metre straight-edge (of rustless steel) is necessary unless all your drawings are going to be very small. Graduation in centimetres is useful, but not essential. If you get a T-square (see below) you can manage without a straight-edge.

A drawing-board is not essential, for any flat surface will serve as base, but it is very useful indeed. Size is a matter of choice, depending on the dimensions of the plans you are likely to make. Probably the most generally useful, without becoming excessively cumbrous, is the Imperial size (80 × 58 cm).

If you have a drawing-board, it is well worth while to get a corresponding T-square (which can serve in place of the metre straight-edge). You will not use the T-square much for plotting an ordinary chain survey, but it can be very useful when finishing the final tracing.

If you need to fix the paper in place, drafting tape is usually preferable to drawing pins; but if you prefer the latter those with very large heads are worth the slight extra cost. Pins should only be used near the edges of a drawing-board; the centre should be kept undamaged.

Finally you will require pencil and paper and an eraser. The pencils should be 'drawing' quality, and either H or HB. My own preference is for HB, but experts usually prefer H. For almost all purposes, good quality white cartridge paper is adequate for the pencil draft; thin card has a better drawing surface, but is more expensive, and cannot be used with a tracing table if you have that equipment. There is, though, one difficulty in using either of these materials. Paper, and to a lesser degree card, is not dimensionally stable. That does not usually matter for a small drawing, say up to 50 cm across, but for a larger one precautions have to be taken. If, as on the excavation of a site with complex stratification, you need to be able to superimpose successive plans of the same area, dimensionally stable transparent material is needed. If tracing plastic is used, a very hard pencil (4H, 5H) may be required.

6.3 *Plotting the Network.* The first step should always be to plot this on a small scale say 1/1,000 or 1/2,500 for the example given here; lengths need not be corrected for slope. This plot should be on tracing-paper, for a reason which will appear subsequently. Any gross mistake should be revealed by this plot, so it is a good idea to do it before you leave the area where you are working, if you are away from home. Sketch on this plot, very roughly, the outermost features which will appear on the plan; and mark the true north point. The margin of the relevant 1/50,000 map gives the magnetic variation (Para. 25.3).

Next, you need to decide on the size and scale of your plan. Two factors have to be taken into account. First assuming that you accept the desirability of keeping to a set of rational scales (Para. 6.8) what is the smallest of these which will allow you to represent clearly the significant features of the site? And second, what is the page size of the periodical in which you hope to publish? Most of the major publications include 'Notes to Contributors' which give details of this kind. 'Throwouts' (folding plans) are expensive and should be avoided if possible.

Consider Figure 5.1. Note incidentally that this represents not a finished plan but a stage in plotting the pencil draft; the hachures, for example, are merely sketched roughly as a guide to the eye when tracing. It is size and scale, though, which are being discussed here. As plotted, at 1/500, with title and scales as shown, it can be enclosed in a rectangle 34 × 21 cm with the longer sides north-south. On a page measuring 17·5 × 13·5 cm, which is fairly typical, it could comfortably be reproduced at 1/1,000 with the north point 'upright'. Some periodicals are smaller, perhaps 15 × 10 cm. In that case, by setting the north point at about 10° to the page edge, reproduction at 1/1,000 is still possible, though the title and scales would need to be rearranged and crowded together. In my view this is in every way preferable to using an odd scale such as 1/1,300 to keep the north point 'upright'; but this problem is discussed in more detail in Para. 6.8. The exact arrangement does not have to be decided until the plan is ready to be traced.

A linear reduction to one half the original size is probably the most favoured for block making; you can go as far as one quarter, but rather special care is then needed to make sure that thin lines do not vanish in reproduction. You will therefore need to plot at 1/500, so if you have not got a scale with that graduation use a 1/1,000 scale and mentally double all your measured distances.

First, work out the corrected lengths of all the chain lines. If you have indexed them in your chain book, as suggested earlier (Para. 5.2) you can write the corrected figures there. Three different methods are given in the specimen bookings. Reference should be made to the tables in Appendix IV.

For the line EFS_2 the slope was measured with a clinometer, and found to be 7° 30'. Each 20 m step, therefore, is 20 − 0·17 m or 19·83 m. The deductions for 37·84 and 65·82 will be 0·33 and 0·57 respectively, making the corrected lengths 37·51 and 65·25.

Line FS_3 had its correction found by levelling. The difference in level between the two ends was 6·2 m and the measured length

46·45 m, corresponding to a fall of 2·66 m in each 20 m. The approximate correction for 20 m is therefore

$$\frac{(2·66)^2}{2 \times 20} = 0·18$$

or 0·41 in the whole length. The exact corrected length is

$$\sqrt{46·45^2 - 6·2^2} = \sqrt{2119·2} = 46·03$$

Finally, the correction for BEA was found using the rough 'by eye' method. The second table in Appendix IV gives a correction of 0·36 per 20 m for a slope of ten paces to eye level. Thus BE is 18·85 − 0·34 = 18·51, and BA = 81·91 − 1·47 = 80·44.

You can now start to draw the network, but if the plan is large and you are working on cartridge paper or other dimensionally unstable material you should either draw on the paper a scale rather longer than the longest chain line or better draw a faint grid, of sides of 20 cm or as convenient, covering the whole sheet (Para. 18.1). This will allow any dimensional change to be detected and allowed for in later drawing or in tracing. If the drawing of the network is not finished in a day, the plotted lengths of chain lines should be determined from this drawn scale, not from the boxwood scale. For small plans, up to about 30 or 40 cm square as drawn, these precautions will seldom be needed; but a background grid is always desirable if co-ordinates are being used for plotting.

Now mark the positions of B and C at the corrected distance apart; you then have to fix A, by measurements from these two points. AB = 80·67 m and AC = 154·82 m. If you have a beam compass you can strike these off directly, but it is just as easy to use the following method, which has the further advantages that you do not have to buy an otherwise unnecessary compass and you do not make holes in the paper at B and C.

By superimposing your small-scale tracing on the main plan with, say, C on both coincident, you can get a fairly accurate indication of the direction of CA (Figure 6.1). With the straight-edge draw three or four lines in about that direction and measure 154·82 m to scale along each; there is of course no limit to the distance. You then have three dots, indicating the arc of radius 154·82 m. Repeating this from B gives the position of A, though in this case, as BA is less than the length of your scale, you can measure direct.

Check all three lengths, and if they are correct stations A, B and

6.1 Plotting Intersection of Chain Lines

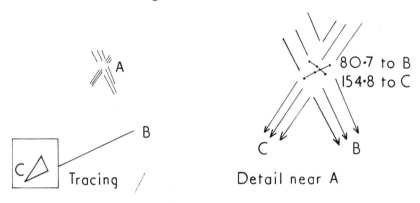

Tracing   Detail near A

C are presumably fixed, but you have several other lines which should fit the network. Do not try to use too many of these at once, but choose those which seem likely to give the best check, perhaps DE and S_2E in this case. These lengths, as measured on the plan, ought of course to be exactly the same as on the ground, when corrected for slope; but in practice there may well be a *small* difference. (If the difference is large, something is wrong.) In chain surveys the errors are usually balanced out subjectively, though systematic methods can be used (Para. 17.9). In this example, it might be found that DE on plan was a little too short, while S_2E was exactly right; you could then assume that DE, only, needed adjustment. Alternatively, both DE and S_2E might be too long on the plan, in which case it would be more reasonable to move B as plotted a little towards C, so that the plan-lengths of DE and S_2E are still too long but not by so much, while BC is now a little too short. It is essential to realise that this sort of adjustment, which is of rather doubtful legitimacy anyway, must *only* be applied to 'errors'. If for example S_2E and DE both turned out to be about 8 m too long as plotted, you would not 'adjust' the line AB so that those two lines were 4·5 m too long and CB 4·5 m too short, but you would search for a 'mistake' either in measurement or in plotting.

Having fixed ABCDE and S_2 to your satisfaction, the rest of the network can be completed. Before plotting detail, choose a part of the paper well outside the plan and mark on it the north point.

If you are using a board with a T-square, then for each line for which you have a magnetic bearing measure the angle it makes with the T-square edge. You can then average the corresponding bearing of the T-square relative to magnetic north, and by deducting the magnetic variation the true north can be drawn. Alternatively, through a single point draw parallels to all the relevant lines, and measure from each of them to get the magnetic north. This will usually differ slightly according to which line is used, so take an average.

6.4 *Plotting Detail* (Figure 5.1). The 30 cm scale is placed along the plotted chain line, and the offset slid along it, the booked points being marked with a faint dot (Figure 6.2). The dots are then joined up to give the plan, using the same conventions as for booking, but drawing accurately instead of sketching. Explanatory notes can be added to help with the final tracing. It is easier to plot one side of the chain line at a time, and if you have several features running roughly parallel, as perhaps in a multiple-rampart system, you will often find it less confusing to dot out and complete two or three lines at a time, rather than to try to plot all at once. The modifications needed when you have to deal with a feature such as the building near BC are obvious.

If the line has required correction for slope, no attempt is made

6.2 Use of Offset Scale

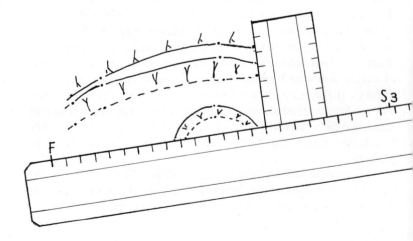

to work out the adjusted length for every chainage. Taking BA as an example, the corrected length was 1·24 m less than the measured length, but each 20 m section is only 0·3 m less. Marks are therefore put at points corresponding to 19·69, 39·38, 59·07, 78·76 m from B; detail from 30 to 50 m is plotted with the 40 m point on the scale against the 39·38 metre mark, and similarly for other sections of the survey. If greater accuracy is needed, the points corresponding to every 10 m can be marked.

6.5 *The Finished Drawing: The Materials.* This section requires some introductory comment. Everything described elsewhere in this book is within the competence of anyone who can measure a length and write down the result; but to produce a really attractive finished plan requires a natural gift which not everyone has been fortunate enough to receive. Nevertheless, even if you are (like me) thoroughly ham-handed, you may need or wish to finish your own plan rather than to rely on a draughtsman; this section is intended to help you to do so. The result will not be as decorative as you may hope, but should at least be workmanlike and inoffensive. If, on the other hand, your pen tends to obey your wishes, you will probably be able to reject much of what is said here; but do not skip it entirely, as it may contain some points worth your consideration.

Your choice of drawing equipment will depend on how often you are likely to need it, and perhaps also to some extent on whether you have to buy it yourself or can order it through the organisation which employs you. You will require a set of pens and either pen-stencils or adhesive sheets for lettering.

You will require a mapping pen, and a pen with a fine but soft nib, with some spare nibs for both of these. A ruling pen (resembling a pair of tweezers) is useful but not essential.

You will also need a range of stylo-type drawing pens of the type used with pen-stencils. This is where choice becomes difficult. There are several different brands, but essentially they fall into two types: an open or lightly covered reservoir, holding a small amount of ink, the writing point being a tube with an accessible sliding rod; and a more elaborate device resembling a fountain-pen, with a much larger reservoir, both it and the sliding rod being enclosed. The latter types are beautiful examples of precision engineering but have the disadvantage that they need to be treated as such. If allowed to clog, for example, they can be very difficult to clean; but a special stand is available to minimise this risk.

If you are going to do a lot of drawings, and if expense is unimportant, then a full range of the more elaborate pens, with the stand and other accessories, is certainly desirable; they give about ten line thicknesses. If on the other hand, you only produce half a dozen or so drawings a year, then three or four of the simpler type will be adequate.

Lettering, again, offers a choice. The first decision has to be whether to use pen-stencils or adhesive lettering. Most professional draughtsmen now prefer the latter, which offers a very wide range of letter forms and is easy to apply (it is important to remember that most types require a fixing spray, to prevent them from coming unstuck). Nevertheless, my own preference is for pen-stencils; they are more versatile, and there is no risk that just as you finish a drawing you find that you have run out of an essential letter. An adequate set, to start with, would be a range of four sizes, the largest with capitals about 10 mm high; in the smallest two, at least, you need numerals. The necessary pens will serve also for drawing.

There are now several different makes of stencil, and availability is as good a reason as any for choosing one rather than another; but keep in mind that when you choose your first half-dozen you are almost committed to go on using that make for ever, since the appropriate pens cannot be used with another make.

Finally, rather obviously, you will need ink and tracing material. The ink should be a really good quality black drawing ink; the small saving on a cheaper type is more than counterbalanced by its defects.

There is now an embarrassingly wide choice of tracing material. Tracing-paper is not durable enough for a final drawing. Tracing linen is now out of fashion, but has many good qualities. It is durable, erasures (by careful use of a razor-blade) are easy, and if creased it can be flattened with a domestic iron (also a hopelessly botched drawing, if washed and boiled, can be made into a very high quality handkerchief). Its chief defect is that it is dimensionally very unstable. Drawing is done on the matte side.

Synthetic tracing films are mostly dimensionally stable (a few which claim to be are not) but do not stand up to rough treatment as well as tracing linen, being more liable to tear or crack, and if creased they cannot easily be flattened. Erasure cannot be done with a razor-blade, but requires special erasing fluid. Some makes will give almost as clear a line with pencil as with ink; this property, combined with dimensional stability, makes them the obvious choice for use on an excavation where several successive strata have to be compared.

Alternatively, the finished drawing can be traced on to ordinary thin cartridge paper. Save for its lack of dimensional stability, this is in many ways the most convenient material to use; but it requires a tracing table. Essentially, this is merely a sheet of hard heat-proof translucent material supported over a light source. Commercially built tracing tables are (unduly?) expensive, and are unlikely to be available except in a fairly well equipped drawing office, but a perfectly adequate makeshift for small drawings can be constructed using a sheet of thick plastic from a derelict television set supported above a couple of electric lamps; household aluminium foil will serve as a reflector. Fluorescent tubes are to be preferred, as they give out less heat; if ordinary lightbulbs are used they should be of low wattage and only switched on when actually in use to avoid overheating the plastic sheet. The surface *below* the bulbs will also need protection from heat.

The question of dimensional stability has been rather over-emphasised above, because it is so often forgotten; but apart from the particular case of a multi-stratum excavation it does not cause much practical difficulty. The effect is negligible for a small plan, and even for a large plan it will usually be unimportant, *provided the scale is drawn at the same time as the basic network and is traced*, not redrawn on the tracing to the nominal scale. This will obviously correct automatically for most of the dimensional change, though not completely since the effect is not always exactly the same along and across the sheet. In any case, your attempt at scientific accuracy is quite likely to be frustrated by the block-maker. Some are careful to avoid any distortion, but surprisingly often, even in publications of a very high standard, what was presumably drawn as a rectangular frame turns out in reproduction to have opposite sides of slightly different lengths. This is perhaps one reason why frames are now unfashionable.

6.6 *The Finished Drawing: Tracing.* Continuing with the assumption that you are a complete novice, your first step must be to decide on a style. The best way of doing this is to look through several volumes of recent national periodicals, such as *Archaeological Journal, Antiquaries Journal, Britannia, Archaeologia,* and *Medieval Archaeology,* or perhaps better still the *recent* volumes of the three Royal Commissions on Ancient Monuments. Local periodicals may be useful, but are not of such high quality though some are very good indeed. Having picked out some examples which you think look pleasant and not too difficult, examine them carefully under a magnifying glass (for they will have been reduced at least to one-half for reproduction, possibly to one-third or one-quarter). Then when you have a fairly clear idea of the technique used, practice reproducing bits of the 'model' to their supposed original size, and invent some imaginary earthworks to draw.

Most earthwork plans depend almost entirely on the use of hachures, even on a closely contoured site. It is difficult to understand why this curious convention gives an immediate impression of banks and ditches, but no really satisfactory alternative has been devised so the labour it involves has to be tolerated.

The form most commonly used resembles an emaciated tadpole (Figure 6.3). This can, with practice, be drawn quite quickly using the fine but soft nib. If depressed heavily this gives a broad line (the head) and as the pressure is reduced the line thins out to form the tail. In this as in all hachuring, the thicker end represents the top of the slope. Slightly less common, and slower to draw, but rather easier to give a neat result without a lot of practice, is the thin wedge, with a flat or slightly concave top and slightly concave sides. Other types can be devised. These can be outlined with a mapping pen, and then blacked in. The thicker the heads of the hachures and the more closely set they are, the steeper and higher the scarp represented; but there is no standard formula relating the two. Some sort of consistency is desirable, and although you can get a fairly good result by relying on your subjective estimate of what is needed you may find it useful to draw out three or four imaginary scarps of different (but uniform) horizontal width in which the hachures steadily increase in intensity. You can then assign an arbitrary vertical height to correspond to each point on the 'scarp', which taken in conjunction with your field notes will serve as a rough guide to how heavy the hachures should be at various points on the plan. The variation of vertical height along the 'scarp' need not be linear but should follow a smooth curve, and need not be the same for all plans unless they form a set.

Next to hachuring, the most useful convention is stipple, used mainly to represent rubble. This can be bought in the same material as adhesive letters, and will give a much more uniform result, but that unfortunately can be a disadvantage, as the variation in the

6.3 Simple Conventions for Finished Plans

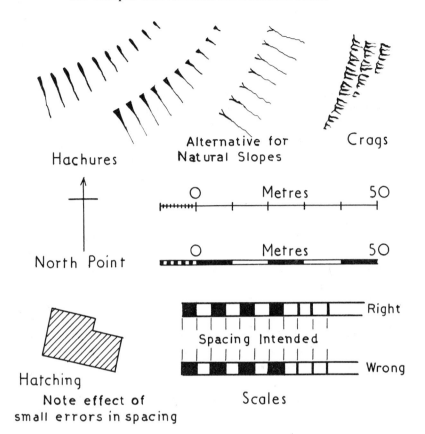

Hachures   Alternative for   Crags
                Natural Slopes

North Point   O   Metres   50

                O   Metres   50

Hatching   Right
                Spacing Intended
                                                Wrong
Note effect of   Scales
small errors in spacing

height of the surviving ruins of a wall, for example, cannot be represented, nor can the way in which the stones may fade out into the surrounding turf be shown. It is preferable therefore, though laborious, to do the stippling by hand.

Hatching is very difficult to do neatly, for a single mistake in spacing shows up glaringly. Cross-hatching is even worse. It is helpful to put up a sheet of squared graph paper under the tracing, and to use that to give uniform spacing to the lines.

Continuous or broken lines are conveniently drawn with one of the stencil pens, though a sharper and more uniform result can be got with the ruling pen. If you are ruling a line, the set square should be raised by resting it on a sheet of card or another set square so that the edge in use does not touch the paper. Otherwise there is always a risk that the ink will run under the set square, even though you may be using a pen designed to prevent that happening.

Lettering, scales and north point are best left until the plan itself is finished.

Before starting to trace, linen and some tracing films need to be dusted over with french chalk, to remove minute traces of grease which prevent the ink from adhering uniformly. The ink bottle should be stood on a tray where it cannot easily be knocked accidentally, and should *always* be kept corked except when actually filling your pen. Not only does it become clotted if much exposed to the air, but a bottle of drawing-ink displays to a very high degree the universal malevolence of inanimate objects, at any rate if being used by an amateur draughtsman.

Bear in mind constantly that the ink takes some time to dry, and plan your work so that there is no risk of smearing it. Several minutes wait is always necessary before you can work over a recently inked area, and even then it is very advisable carefully to blot the drawing although you may feel sure that it is completely dry, and although no professional draughtsman would sink to the use of blotting-paper.

It may be helpful to outline the scarps of banks and ditches *very* faintly in pencil, and to avoid irregularity in spacing faint pencil lines can be drawn indicating the position of every third or fifth hachure.

Having completed the plan, the direction of the north point should be traced lightly in pencil, and the original draft removed from beneath the tracing. The draft and tracing are then very carefully compared to make sure that nothing has been missed or incorrectly represented.

North point, scales and lettering should be kept as simple as possible (Figure 6.3). For the north point (which should of course show true north) a simple arrowed cross is perfectly adequate. The easiest scale to draw is the upper one, but the lower, with alternate black and white divisions, perhaps looks better. Note when drawing this that the lines dividing the sections before they are inked in must be completely within the black section, or the divisions will be of unequal length. It is customary to include one unit (say 10 m) of the main scale drawn to the left of zero and subdivided into smaller units (metres). This allows measurements to be made to one metre without the need to subdivide the main scale; but it is only needed if someone is likely to require these more accurate measurements, and it would obviously be out of place on a sketch-plan. Two scales should be given, one metric and the other in feet, to simplify comparison with plans published before metrication. It is now becoming fashionable to include a simple areal scale, a square equivalent to one acre or one hectare in area; my own view is that there is little or no advantage in this, for direct visual comparison of areas is difficult, and the linear scale gives all the information necessary. The area of an enclosure is better given in the descriptive text. Finally, so far as scales are concerned, always give a drawn scale; *never* rely on a simple statement such as 'Scale 1/250' or '1 cm to 5 m' for that will appear without alteration when the plan is reduced for publication.

If stencils are being used for lettering, all titles and other details should be first stencilled on a spare piece of paper, to the size chosen but without bothering too much about such matters as evenness of line. These can be inspected, and pencil notes made of desirable improvements such as changes in spacing. This draft can then be placed under the finished tracing, and moved until it seems to be in a satisfactory position; it can then be used as a guide to the finished lettering. Some editors prefer to put the actual name of the site in type, and it can then be omitted from the plan; but this is undesirable, for the drawing or the line-block has then nothing to identify it if it is needed for future use. In an organisation where several staff are engaged in similar work it is advisable to note, outside the area to be published, the division of responsibility, for example, S.AH 1973 Bk 5 D WG 10 vi 74 T DR 12 viii 74; S, D and T indicating Surveyed, Drawn, Traced, with initials of those responsible and dates of work.

The final tracing should always be carefully compared with the pencil draft, the scale should be checked by using it to measure some distance which is known from the *original record in the chain book* (to make sure there was no mistake in plotting), and the drawn metric and Imperial scales should be compared.

When lettering a drawing using a T-square as guide, keep in mind the probable orientation of the drawing as it will be published. Good quality drawing-boards have a hard edge along one of the shorter sides, and for geometrically accurate work the T-square should only be used with this; but for lettering the other edges can be used.

6.7 *Publication.* Usually, your plan will be intended for publication. If, as assumed above, you have prepared the drawing with regard to the page size of the periodical concerned and with the intention that it shall be reproduced at a rational scale (Para. 6.8) you will need to specify the reduction as appropriate, for example, 'Reduce to ½'; alternatively you can make two marks below the drawing at (say) 20 cm apart and mark on a line between them 'Reduce to 10 cm'. Editors and block-makers (provided they take any notice of your instructions) will tolerate reductions such as 1/2.5, ⅓ or ¼. They can be persuaded, reluctantly, to use others; for example, you might draw a plan at 50 ft to 1 inch (1/600) and wish it to be published at 1/1,000, so you place the marks 33.33 cm apart (= 200 m at 1/600) and state 'Reduce to 20 cm'. This will probably be done less accurately than for one of the integral reductions such as ½ or ¼.

Some editors, printers, and publishers interpret their functions rather too widely and may ignore instructions of this kind, believing that some different size of plan will look prettier on the page, and never mind whether the scale is rational. A few may even alter the drawing itself. If you feel strongly about these possibilities, you should put in the margin of each drawing, 'Do not depart from these instructions or alter this drawing in any way without the author's permission'. These dangers are not imaginary: in a recent excellent book the publishers decided, without consultation, to 'improve' the appearance of the drawn scales; their art department not only believed that a metre was exactly equivalent to a yard, but saw nothing surprising in a child burial where the skeleton measured 24 ft from head to toe. The discredit for this, of course, fell upon the innocent author.

Some editors prefer to have the whole plan redrawn. In that case, they will sometimes accept a pencil draft. Whatever arrangement is made, though, the final drawing will need to be checked very carefully against your original, by you.

6.8 *Rational Scales.* Archaeological opinion in Britain is moving slowly towards acceptance of the view that plans should be reproduced to a standard series of scales. Of the three Royal Commissions on Ancient and Historical Monuments, the English Commission now uses a scale of 1/5,000 for all hill-forts, the Scottish has for some time aimed at 1/1,000 for earthworks and 1/250 for houses, and the Welsh, which has a larger size range to cover, uses the largest appropriate scale from the sequence 1/10,000, 1/2,500, 1/1,000, and so on, with a preference for 1/2,500 for earthworks and 1/250 for most buildings. It is arguable that 1/2,000 and 1/200 should be included, but on the whole that seems unnecessary.

The advantages of this system seem obvious, especially in simplifying comparison of plans of similar structures. To those accustomed to such a rational scheme the appearance of a volume with a random selection of scales dictated merely by convenience or by misguided aestheticism is as offensive as the presence of mis-spellings and grammatical mistakes, and is much more of an impediment to the use of the work. Nevertheless, there are still many archaeologists who do not hold the views expressed here, and you will not be regarded as having committed a gross solecism if the scales of your plans as published are not rational. Indeed, there is a strong possibility that many people will not notice even if they are obviously wrong; the eight-metre child mentioned above escaped the attention of most reviewers.

7 Problems and Precautions

7.1 *Hazards*. The description of the imaginary survey in Chapter 5 assumed that nothing went wrong and no particular difficulties arose. For any site that takes more than one day to survey, you will be exceptionally fortunate if that is true. This chapter goes through the difficulties which are likely to be experienced in a real survey, and the ways of overcoming them. The special problems, of setting out a rectangle with a chain, and of surveying buildings, are also discussed. Until you have worked in the field, you will think some of the risks envisaged are so improbable that they can be ignored, but every recommendation made here is based 'on personal experience.

Apart from difficulties of terrain, the main hazards to surveying are children, other humans, and cattle. Children can hardly be blamed for finding that ranging-rods make admirable javelins, but after a day's work on even a lightly infested site you will feel that there was much to be said in King Herod's favour. Farmers and farm workers too may claim some justification, in that pegs can injure animals' feet and that as a matter of principle any apparently official activity ought to be frustrated; but it is hard to understand why, as happens quite often, an apparently sane adult should lift a pole, look at its point, and then replace it upright in the wrong position. Cattle merely knock poles down by rubbing.

So far as daily work is concerned, all that can be done is to try to keep all poles where they can be under constant observation, and preferably within shouting range. At stations, they can be supplemented by wands, which are less likely to attract attention and may remain even if the pole is shifted. It should be your invariable practice, at least if there is the slightest chance of disturbance but preferably always, to check that the pole to which you have chained is in fact at the station peg. If it is not, record the position of the station relative to the chain line (as Para. 7.3, Figure 7.6d) and correct when plotting.

Poles and arrows which are not in use should *always* be stuck *sloping* into the ground. It is annoying, when working towards a station, to be faced with a choice of three or four upright poles, any of which may be the one required.

As routine, always note what equipment you have taken on to a site and make sure that you collect it when you leave. A fallen pole can easily be forgotten. Similarly, when moving from one chain line to the next, always check that you have the full set of arrows.

7.2 Locating Stations. As noted, pegs are very liable to be removed, and the loss of a station before a survey is finished can be a major disaster, possibly making several days' work valueless. All pegs used to mark stations should therefore be driven down slightly below ground level and their tops smeared with dirt. The pegs can usually be made on site (Para. 3.2).

On most sites this precaution is absolutely essential; but having made the peg almost invisible you have to provide for its redis-covery, either by yourself *or by someone who takes over the work from you.* A wand may with luck remain in place for a few days, and this can sometimes be supplemented with a small heap of stones, but these latter should not be used where there is any risk of damage to farm machinery. These temporary marks, though, cannot be relied upon, and some more permanent method of recovery is needed.

The simplest solution is to drive the peg at some recognisable corner of a conspicuous boulder, or some other obvious and immovable feature. Incidentally, do not use an anthill, however easily recognisable; after a week or so the peg will be buried some centimetres deep, and the inhabitants resent disturbance.

More commonly, the peg will be within 20 m or so of two (or better three) landmarks. Examples of the sort of sketches recording such locations are given in Figure 7.1. Every station ought to be recorded in this way. In stony country, a thick red or yellow wax crayon can be used to make long-lasting marks. This will help to save time in identification, but should not be relied on exclusively. Measurement should be made along the ground, to the nearest centimetre.

To recover a station, as for example station M in Figure 7.1, two or three arrows are put in at 1·84 m from the corner of one gatepost

7.1 Field Notes to Locate Stations

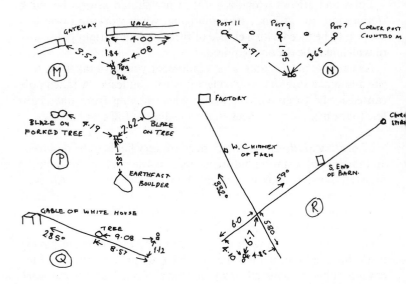

to indicate the line of an arc passing over the peg. Then 3·52 m from the other gatepost should give the exact position of the peg; the third measurement is a safeguard against mistakes, and will probably not be needed. In practice, the peg will usually be a few centimetres away, but can be discovered by slicing the turf with a blade held nearly horizontal.

Sometimes quite elaborate constructions may be needed to locate the peg (Figure 7.1, Q and R). These will not usually fix it as accurately as direct measurements from adjacent points, and a bigger area will need to be searched to recover the peg. At such stations, it is helpful to use a peg of large diameter.

Occasionally, no amount of ingenuity will guarantee the peg's recovery. In that case, every effort should be made to record *all* chain lines which involve that station on the first day, even if this requires a departure from the simplest programme of work.

It is useful, whenever possible, to run chain lines towards some conspicuous landmark well away from the site, such as a church spire, a factory chimney, the gable of some building, or even the junction of hedges or a line of roadway. Provided one peg on that line survives, the whole can be recovered. This is particularly useful on a 'salvage' site, where a sudden change in programme of earth-moving may destroy pegs without warning.

7.3 *Difficulties in Chaining.* The most usual obstruction in chain survey is a wall or hedge which does not prevent sighting but stops the chain from lying flat. This is easily dealt with, in a way essentially the same as chaining up a steep slope 'by steps'. Two poles are set up on the chain line, one on each side of the obstacle (Figure 7.2a). The first is chained in and booked. The horizontal distance from the first to the second is measured, with a tape or if more convenient with a pole, *and booked*, so that it is on record in case of an arithmetical mistake caused by working in the field. The chainage of the second pole is found by addition and the chaining is then continued, starting with the appropriate point on the chain at the second pole. This simplifies plotting, as the chainage runs on without interruption.

This type of obstruction is simple, and the way to deal with it is obvious, but some of the problems which arise are more difficult to solve. Standard works on chain surveying give various ingenious constructions for carrying a line past or across obstacles without breaking the continuity of measurement. This latter requirement does not apply to the type of work considered here, and almost all the difficulties these constructions are intended to overcome can be evaded by a suitable arrangement of the network. For example, Figure 7.2b shows how a survey could be linked up across a wide river. The broken lines, supposed to be too long to measure, enable a new starting-point to be fixed by lining in across the water.

Nevertheless, there is one method which is often useful. It provides a way of 'lining in' between two poles which are not intervisible.

The procedure is illustrated in Figure 7.2c. Stations A and B are not intervisible. The leader L, say, takes a pole to point 1a, from which B is visible, and F takes one to 2a from which A is visible; 1a and 2a should be as far apart as possible. L then lines F in towards B, so that 1a, 2b and B are in line. F then lines L in to A, so that 2b, 1b, A are in line. The procedure is repeated, L and F lining each other in with the appropriate station alternately. Poles 1 and 2 rapidly arrive at the line AB. You will find it worth while to carry out this procedure once on fairly level ground where A and B *are* intervisible; you will then accept that it really works.

The same procedure is possible with any even number of

7.2 Difficulties in Chain Survey

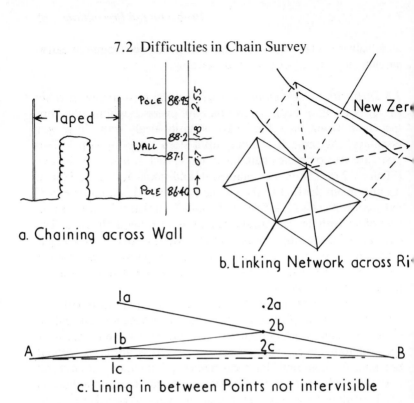

a. Chaining across Wall

b. Linking Network across Ri

c. Lining in between Points not intervisible

Station

d. Line terminating near Station

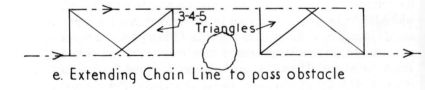

3-4-5
Triangles

e. Extending Chain Line to pass obstacle

intermediate poles; odd poles line in even, then even line in odd. In practice though, this is very seldom necessary, and as there is a possibility of a small divergence at every pole the line may not be quite straight.

Occasionally, you may know the general direction of a station but the pole has been displaced. Preferably of course it should be re-erected, but this is not essential. Run the chain line towards some obvious feature which is in about the right direction, and fix the station relative to this chain line by an offset and two equal diagonals of rather more than one-and-a-half times the offset in length (Figure 7.2d). The true distance station to station can easily be worked out, so that the network can be plotted; and the actual chain line used can be drawn in without difficulty to provide the detail.

Sometimes part of the site may be obstructed by a thicket. You can often run a straight line into and through this by sighting back on the way you have come step by step without knowing where you are going to emerge. For preference of course, the end of the line which you finally reach should be made a station, but if that is not convenient it can be marked, and surveyed in relation to the rest of the framework. This way of working is often convenient to use in conjunction with a closed traverse enclosing a wooded site.

The catch with this sort of randomly-oriented straight line is that after penetrating some way into the thicket it runs up against a tree. This can be got round by setting out a subsidiary line, or preferably two, parallel to the main line and a short distance from it. After passing the obstruction, the main line can be recovered (Figure 7.2e).

Another possibility is that woodland is penetrated by a path which is almost straight but does not provide a line of sight. A prismatic compass traverse (as Para. 25.7, but with the distances chained) will give the *distance* between points at each end quite accurately, so a line of that kind can be used to connect two stations and thus to fix a network, provided no detail is needed.

Sometimes it may be necessary to anchor the end of a chain or tape. The marker arrow should *never* be used as such an anchorage, for if it is displaced the measurements along the chain line up to that point have to be repeated. A satisfactory anchorage can generally be obtained by a spare arrow passing through the loop at the end of the chain and with its head inclined away from the direction of pull and a second arrow stuck vertically through the loop of the first.

Both should be pushed as far into the ground as possible. If available, a heavy rock resting on the chain and against the anchorage may be helpful.

A final problem which sometimes arises during a chain survey is breakage of the chain. This is a nuisance, but not disastrous. Join the broken ends firmly with several turns of string or wire (most field boundaries contain loose strands, if nothing better is available), and remeasure one line (without detail) to determine the new length. Note this, and note on every page of the remainder of the survey 'broken chain'. If the break is small, involving the loss of one or two of the small intermediate links, nothing else is needed. If several of the main 0·2 m links are lost, as may result from damage by farm machinery, the position of the loss should be indicated on each 20 m length of booking; there can be no certainty that it is always on the same side of the 10 m point.

7.4 *Booking.* Two types of difficulty may arise in booking. The first, by far the more common, is the result of carelessness; the second is caused by the need to record exceptionally complex detail.

If conditions are good, a single minor mistake can be rubbed out; but often the paper will be damp or dirty and any attempt at erasure will produce a smear surrounding a hole. Normally therefore, it may be better to cross out the mistake. A very common example, particularly among beginners, is to draw a line which crosses the chain line obliquely as in Figure 7.3 chainage 10·45. If you have done this, you should devise some way to indicate that the lines are really the same, either by arrows or by writing the chainage obliquely. Note that any such method is 'wrong' and would lose marks in an examination but it will serve to ensure that the detail is plotted correctly despite the mistake in booking.

This mistake is not very harmful in practice, and will not be repeated after a little experience. A much more usual difficulty is to discover that you have made a sketch of the detail to be recorded and when you come to book the necessary measurements there is no room to put them in. Examination of line EF (Figure 5.3) will show how easily that could happen. When it does, do not try to fit the information in by using very small figures, and do not rub out your sketch and redraw it. Merely draw bold lines across the page at each end of the botched section and start afresh with a new and larger sketch. If there is room for this on the same page no other information is needed, but sometimes you may need to write over

7.3 Dealing with Botched Entries in Chain Book

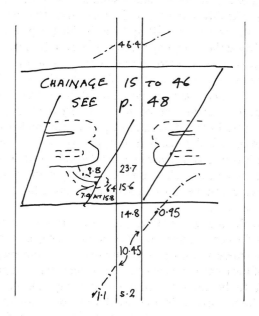

the abandoned section between the two cross-lines something such as 'Chainage 15 to 40 see p. 48' (as Figure 7.3). The separated section could refer only to one side of the chain line, or to a particular feature such as the building near line CB if that had been more complicated. There will be no difficulty in devising expedients of this kind once you have fully understood that the function of a chain book is solely to give an unambiguous record of measurements and other data from which the plan can be drawn. It is *not* a sketch roughly to scale to which dimensions have been added.

Sometimes there is so much detail to record that with no amount of care or skill can it be booked legibly using conventional methods. When there are merely a lot of linear features running roughly parallel to the chain line, the offset measurements can be kept to an adequate size by using two lines, indicating by a bracket that they refer to a single chainage (Figure 5.3, at 23·7 on ES_2). It is always better to do this than to use very small figures.

When the detail is really complicated, as for example with a group of numerous contiguous irregular stone-built huts, recording can be done more conveniently by plotting direct on to squared paper. A4 size is convenient, and a similar sized backing board of plywood, preferably waterproof, is necessary. The paper is best attached to the board by drafting-tape. Bulldog clips can be used, but in windy weather you may need an almost unbroken run round the whole perimeter. If there is risk of rain a flap of transparent plastic may be useful protection. Alternatively, if only a few sections of the survey are complex enough to require this method of booking, the drawing can be made on a sheet of tracing plastic sealed over a background of squared paper. This makes the whole arrangement practically weatherproof, but whether the appreciable extra work involved is worth while will depend on what conditions are to be expected, as well as on the number of sheets needed. If you use this method, be sure to mark on the plastic the details noted in the next paragraph.

A line is ruled along one of the graduations of the squared paper, not necessarily central, and the 10 or 20 m chainages marked, also the stations where necessary. Records are made of the 'name' of the line, and of the total chainage when measurement is completed; this is not left to be inferred from the drawing. Details are then measured in by offsets in the usual way, but instead of being recorded as numbers in the chain book they are plotted direct. There is of course no need to do the whole of a chain line by this method. It would be quite possible to book most of 'line xx' in the ordinary way, with a note in the relevant place such as '40-80, see squared paper sheet 3'.

No attempt need be made to cover the whole of the complicated area from a single chain line, but where the parts covered from adjacent lines overlap it is useful to record a few points from both. Where possible, as for example on stone-built huts, these points can be marked and numbered in crayon on the actual remains.

The scale to be used for the squared-paper plot needs to be considered. Ideally, it should be larger than that of the final pencil draft, and should be replotted in the office to the required scale. This is almost unavoidable if the pencil draft is to be to a scale of 1/250, for example, for paper with 4 mm squares (= 1 m) is difficult to obtain, if indeed it exists. For scales such as 1/100, 1/500, or 1/1,000 circumstances may sometimes justify yielding to the temptation to make the field plot the same scale as the pencil draft, so that it can be traced directly; but it is important to remember that drawing in the field is never likely to be as accurate as it can be in the office.

For most work, paper with only centimetre divisions permits accurate enough plotting, and it is easier to use than that showing millimetres. The fine graduations tend to be confusing. If you intend to replot you can of course use squares of any size.

7.5 *Setting out a Rectangle with a Chain* (Figure 7.4). It is very much easier to make an accurate plan of existing points than to set out points in specified positions. Nevertheless, it is sometimes necessary to set out a true rectangle, as for example in preparation for an excavation. A theodolite should be used if at all possible, but if one is not available the job can be done with a chain. A prismatic compass is far too inaccurate for the work, but if the site is not too large and the ground is fairly level the little horizontal circle fitted to some levels may be adequate; accuracy to at least 5 minutes is needed, which corresponds to a possible error of about 1 m in 700.

Whatever method is used to set out the right angle, the accuracy of the result cannot be better than the accuracy of the linear measurements. So the first essential is that the chain used must be correct; if available, a steel band may be better. Further, the ground must be free of irregularities, and every chain length should be corrected for slope. Finally, all lines should be measured at least three times and averaged. These preconditions are assumed in what follows; they can of course be relaxed if the resulting inaccuracy is acceptable.

To avoid algebraic symbols, assume that you wish to set out a rectangle of 200 by 100 m. The same principles apply to any size and shape, save that a long narrow rectangle will involve 'ill-conditioned' triangles with the resulting risk of error. It should therefore be dealt with as two shorter rectangles.

The line AB, 200 m long, is supposed to have been chosen as base and established.

The next step is to set out *approximate* right angles at A and B. Anchor the end of the tape at A, and measure 12 m along the line AB. One surveyor then holds 24 m on the tape at that 12 m mark, and the other puts a pole at 9 m from A. Since 9.12.15 is a 3-4-5 triangle (Para. 16.5), the angle at A is a right angle and the pole is on the line AD. So at least it ought to be, but in practice the inevitable presence of errors means that it is not, exactly. Nevertheless, as a first approximation to the required point, measure 100 m in that direction, and put in a mark at D_1.

Repeat the process for B to fix C_1. Now measure AC_1, C_1D_1, and D_1B.

AD$_1$ and BC$_1$ are very nearly perpendicular to AB, so C$_1$D$_1$ is almost exactly parallel to and at the correct distance from AB; but the true positions of C and D are not yet known. <u>If the rectangle were 'true'</u>, then AC and BD would each measure $\sqrt{100^2 + 200^2} = \sqrt{50000} = 223\cdot61$ m (or using excessive accuracy 223·607). Suppose in fact AC proves to be 223·32, that is 0·29 m too short.

Put in a mark at C$_2$ on the line AC$_1$ and 0·29 m from C$_1$, that is at the correct distance from A, and set out a perpendicular to AC$_1$C$_2$ to cut C$_1$D$_1$ at C$_3$. This is equivalent to drawing an arc of radius AC$_2$, centre A; the angle involved is so small that the straight tangent C$_2$C$_3$ is practically indistinguishable from the curve. C$_3$ should therefore coincide with C as required.

As a check, or as an alternative way of fixing C$_3$, similar triangles show that C$_1$C$_3$/C$_1$C$_2$ = AC/AB. In this case, C$_1$C$_3$ = 0·29 × 223·61 ÷ 200 = 0·32 m. If you are making the corrections by calculation alone, careful regard must be paid to sign. If the diagonal as measured is too short, as in this case, the corrected point is outside the first approximation; and conversely.

Having fixed C$_3$, and D$_3$ similarly, all measurements are made again. If any appreciable error should remain (which is unlikely) the whole procedure is repeated, taking C$_3$ and D$_3$ as the second approximation to C and D.

7.4 Setting Out Rectangle with Chain

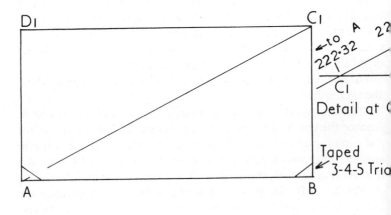

As a check, C_1C_3 plus D_1D_3 should, when allowance is made for sign, equal the 'error' in C_1D_1.

7.6 *Buildings*. For a surveyor with a professional conscience, standing buildings offer a particularly difficult problem. It is hardly ever possible to follow the fundamental principle of breaking down a large rigid network into smaller elements. Fortunately most houses are basically rectangular with walls of uniform thickness, and the plans of these can be worked out without much disquiet as to the validity of the result. For mansions and castles of irregular plan and incorporating alterations which may have taken place piecemeal over five centuries or more, a really accurate plan may be impossible without the use of a theodolite, to run traverses through the winding corridors with single lines of sight penetrating otherwise inaccessible rooms; and it is in this type of structure that accurate knowledge of details such as wall thicknesses may be crucial to a proper interpretation of its history. When, as often, the necessary equipment is lacking or circumstances prevent its use, one can only stifle one's conscience and fit the available incomplete jigsaw together as well as possible, partly comforted by the high probability that one's professional sins will never be discovered.

For an extensive establishment, such as a castle or abbey, the main outline should be surveyed as for an earthwork, but with all measurements taken to a centimetre; a theodolite is always a great advantage in this type of work, and is often essential, but sometimes, perhaps thanks to a single convenient putlog-hole, a satisfactory network for a chain survey can be laid out. In addition to fixing all corners and other exterior features with particular care it is often useful or even necessary to run lines of sight into rooms, linking them to the chained framework by a taped quadrilateral. The individual buildings, surveyed separately, will be fitted to this framework.

Since the plan of a building is usually built up from measurements of the individual compartments, these have to be recorded with particular care, and in this case, in contrast to the records of a chain survey, the sketch-plans should aim at being a reasonably correct representation of the structure, so far as that can be done before measurement.

7.7 *A Building Survey* (Figures 7.5 – 7.8). A fairly typical building survey follows, which exemplifies the general approach. Since most of the measurements are noted directly on to sketch-plans, a field book rather larger than a chain book and containing blank paper is to be preferred; double lines can be ruled as required for the few chain lines needed (Figure 7.6). In a building, a firm support is often available, so the outlines of many of the sketches can be ruled, but they are still to be regarded as diagrams to which dimensions are added, not as anything approaching accurate plans. Most of the detail and measurements, though, will have to be recorded in a hand-held book, and legibility rather than neatness remains the primary aim.

The first step, before starting any measurements, must be to make a complete sketch-plan of the whole building (Figure 7.5), showing all obvious features such as doors (D) and windows (W), but merely as square-sided openings, with no attempt to indicate shape. All rooms or other compartments are outlined, and identified by numbers, letters, or names; but fine details, such as fireplaces or recesses, are omitted. It is customary to draw house-plans with the main entrance towards the bottom of the page, but the approximate direction of north should be shown.

Next, when possible, a controlling framework should be established. In this example two lines, EG and JG, can be laid out touching projecting corners of the building, and E and J can be lined in along the east gable-end of the main block. Although direct measurement there is impossible, the external length of the gable-end can be estimated fairly accurately from internal measurements, so the triangle EGJ is quite reliable. The line CD gives an additional check.

In less favourable cases a theodolite traverse such as EFHJ might be used, either closed by measurement through room 3 or even left open, relying on the accuracy of the angular measurements. A theodolite can also be used to fix the position of otherwise inaccessible points, by triangulation. The magnetic bearings merely give the direction of north; they are not reliable enough to establish the outline.

A framework of this kind, if accepted as reliable, is taken as fixed, and subsequent measurements are adjusted 'by eye' to fit into it.

In addition to the external frame, some long internal lines are desirable. In an occupied building permanent marks can seldom be made, and the lines are linked to each other by recording shared features. Thus AB is connected to the running measurements on the

7.5 Field Notes, Survey of Building: Sketch Plan

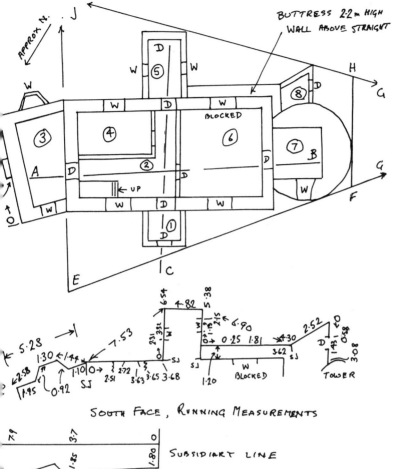

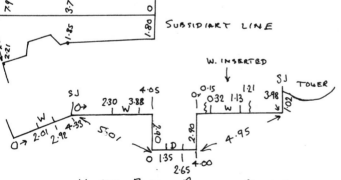

SOUTH FACE, RUNNING MEASUREMENTS

SUBSIDIARY LINE

NORTH FACE, RUNNING MEASUREMENTS

TOWER HOUSE   OWNER-OCCUPIER   J. JONES

AH; J.S 10.VI.79

7.6 Field Notes, Survey of Building: Chained Control

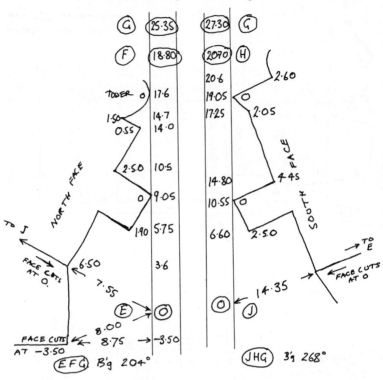

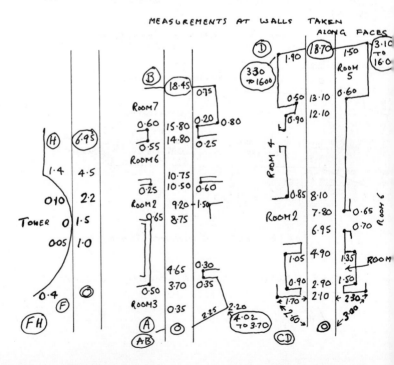

MEASUREMENTS AT WALLS TAKEN ALONG FACES

north face and hence to EFG by measuring the positions of windows and wall thicknesses; CD is linked to EFG by the external angles of the porch (room 1), to AD by detail of room 2, and to GHJ by the wall thicknesses, positions of windows, and external running measurements of room 5. Subject to the external frame, these internal lines form overriding controls to which the remaining detail must be fitted.

Note that along these controlling chain lines only the main features of the building are booked (Figure 7.6). External detail, which would be plotted next, is recorded by measurements noted against sketches of the relevant walls. These can either refer to single facets, as on the south side of room 3, or they can be running measurements. The latter are indicated by a small arrow beside the zero, showing the direction in which they have been taken. Subsidiary lines can be used if they are likely to be helpful, such as that which gives the direction of the south wall of room 3; this was not accessible from line GHJ. The tower would be recorded by a running measurement round its outer face (not reproduced), noting the points of contact with EF and FH which would have been marked with chalk or crayon.

Finally, the detail for each internal compartment is recorded as a separate sketch (as Figure 7.7). These should be drawn as large as conveniently possible, and all walls and diagonals recorded; a diagonal may sometimes have to be measured to a point near but not at an angle. Corners and other important points should be lettered (independently of the main control lines, otherwise the alphabet will prove too short), and measurements which have no associated detail can be listed. The letters can also be used to separate out information which would overcrowd the sketch-plan, as for DC in room 2. Important features can be recorded as separate dimensioned sketches, as for the window in room 2, or they can be described verbally, like the stair. Note that the sketch-plans of all compartments should be continued into the adjacent rooms, which should be numbered. The wall thicknesses must be recorded. As stated earlier, the inevitable small discrepancy which will be found in plotting should be distributed among the internal measurements; the shape established by the controlling chain lines should be kept fixed.

A complete 'snapshot' cover of the exterior of a building can be very useful both in interpreting it and in drawing the plan, and despite possible opposition from professional photographers can

7.7 Field Notes, Survey of Building: Internal Detail

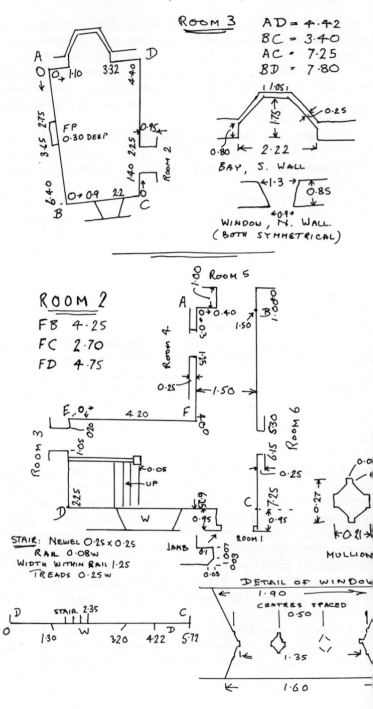

ROOM 3

AD = 4·42
BC = 3·40
AC = 7·25
BD = 7·80

A — D

0→ 1·10   3·32   4·40

3·65 2·75

FP 0·30 DEEP

0·95

2·25 1·40

Room 2

6·40

0→ 0·9   2·2   0→ C

B

1·05

1·75   0·25

0·80   2·22

BAY, S. WALL

1·3   0·85

0·9

WINDOW, N. WALL.
(BOTH SYMMETRICAL)

ROOM 2

FB 4·25
FC 2·70
FD 4·75

ROOM 5

A   1·00

0→ 0·40   B 1·00

0·3   1·50

Room 4

1·25

0·25   1·50

E, 0→   4·20   F

Room 3

1·05 0·20

2·25   UP   ←0·05

D   W

0·95

4·00

Room 6

6·15   5·30

0·25

7·25

C   0·95

0·27

0·0

STAIR: NEWEL 0·25 × 0·25
RAIL 0·08W
WIDTH WITHIN RAIL 1·25
TREADS 0·25W

JAMB   0·1   0·007   0·03   0·05

ROOM 1

0·21

MULLION

DETAIL OF WINDOW

1·90

CENTRES SPACED
0·50

D   STAIR 2·35   C

0   1·30   W   3·20   4·22   D   5·72

1·35

1·60

properly be regarded as an extension of the surveyor's note taking. As its purpose is to save time, a separate visit by specialists seems unjustified.

Upper floors are usually linked to the ground floor by assuming the walls to be vertical, unless there is good reason to suppose otherwise. On particularly difficult sites a theodolite may be needed.

Some types of building, notably churches, tend to be much longer than they are broad. In such a case, the interior should be subdivided into several shorter quadrilaterals (as Figure 7.8) to avoid the use of ill conditioned triangles.

7.8 Long Narrow Building: Network for Interior

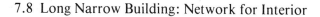
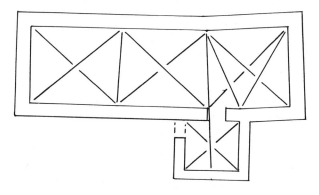

If the building is known to be rectangular, some time can be saved by omitting the diagonal measurements. For some purposes, such as recording vernacular house-plans, the builder may reasonably be supposed to have aimed at a rectangular plan even if he did not achieve it. The house can therefore be drawn as if it were rectangular, even where it may not be. If this is done, it should be stated in a note ('house treated as if rectangular', or 'angles assumed to be right angles'); for someone might wish to use your plan to examine one aspect of the competence of vernacular builders, and he could be misled.

7.8 *Sites on Chaotic Terrain.* Sometimes, perhaps on no more than a dozen sites in Britain, the terrain on which a structure has been built makes an objective survey almost impossible. Rough Tor, in Cornwall, is one such, and can be taken as typical. I am greatly indebted to Mrs Henrietta Miles for the following suggestions as to how a place of this kind might be treated.

The Tor may be visualised as a huge loose dump of granite boulders, ranging in size from a football to a small house; they tend to be slabs rather than spheroids. Round the top of this dump are lines of rough walling. Two are certain, but as both were formed by tilting slabs on end to form a double row of orthostats, many of which have now fallen, details of their exact lines and limits, and especially of the entrances through them, are doubtful. Archaeologists of equal competence disagree as to whether the third apparent rampart is artificial or natural.

On a site of this size it would in practice be impossible to survey every stone, or even to sketch them against a surveyed framework. Moreover, even if such a task were possible, the result would be of little value, for it would include so much 'background noise' — the natural scatter of rocks — that the 'information' — the plan of the remains — could not be distinguished.

The simplest solution would be for the surveyor to make a plan which would show his own subjective interpretation of the site; but that would be unsatisfactory, for as indicated very wide differences of opinion are possible.

If ground survey is the only method available, an approach to objectivity could be obtained by surveying every stone which seems at all likely to have been artificially placed, and indicating by different shading, ranging from solid black through heavy and light stipple to outline only, an estimate of the likelihood that they were so placed; the remaining purely natural rock scatter would be represented by some mechanical stipple or other appropriate pattern.

The best system would be to use a photogrammetric survey as base, to which the actual aerial photographs would be fitted as a mosaic. Stones likely to have been artificially placed would then be shown in heavy outline, with differential stippling as suggested above. The finished plan, reproduced as a half tone plate, would probably give as good a representation of the site as could be hoped for in practice; but it would be a laborious and expensive procedure, difficult to justify except for a structure of major importance.

8 Single-handed Chain Surveying

8.1 General; 8.2 Chaining; 8.3 Lining in; 8.4 Measuring Detail;
8.5 Arrangement of the Network.

8.1 *General.* Sometimes you may need to make a survey single-handed. This is quite easy, especially for a small site, and is not as laborious as might be feared. Using the tricks described here, the time required is only likely to be increased by a quarter to a half.

8.2 *Chaining.* The main source of delay is in chaining. The procedure is as follows: assume that you have put in a marker-arrow and wish to move the chain on for the next 20 m. Take the leading end of the chain and pull it on for rather *more* than that distance (say 25 paces). The method of keeping in line is described below.

Return to the following end, and pull it back to the marker-arrow. Anchor it there, firmly, but *do not* use the marker as part of the anchorage; if that is displaced, the disaster is considerably greater than for normal chaining, with an assistant, for to re-establish the point takes much longer single-handed. Do not remove the marker.

Then return to the leading end, pull the chain tight and straight, and put in the marker-arrow on line.

8.3 *Lining in* (Figure 8.1). The other main modification is to place an intermediate pole about mid way on each chain line (if longer than one chain length). Suppose that you are chaining from A to B, I being the intermediate pole. If you are between A and I, you line yourself in by sighting forwards along the line IB, if past I by sighting back along IA. The ways in which the necessary inter-mediate poles can be fixed are explained in Para. 8.5.

8.4 *Measuring Detail.* Detail is booked in the ordinary way. Short offsets, up to perhaps 6 m depending on the feature being recorded, can be measured step by step with a 2 m pole, preferably one with 0·2 m divisions. Larger offsets, and diagonals, must be taped, the end of the tape being anchored *at the feature*, not at the chain.

The other modification of normal practice required when working single-handed is merely that, to save time, detail on one side of the chain is booked working backwards from the leading end. On reaching the following end the position of the chain relative to that marker-arrow is checked. If, as sometimes happens, it has moved, the distance is recorded in the chain book. The record of this should be made conspicuous, for example, by enclosing the figure in a square 'box'. There is then no need to remeasure the line; those corrections can be inserted when plotting.

The end of the chain is then freed, the marker-arrow lifted, and the remaining detail booked. The process is then repeated for the next chain length.

8.5 *Arrangement of the Network* (Figure 8.1). For a simple and small enclosure, especially one without much internal detail, a polygon is the obvious choice. A description of marking out such a network for a single-handed survey will make the basic principles clear.

Choose a roughly central station O, and another A on or just outside the enclosing bank. Put Intermediate I_1, to give a convenient direction for your chain line AB, and then choose

8.1 Networks for Single-handed Chain Surveys

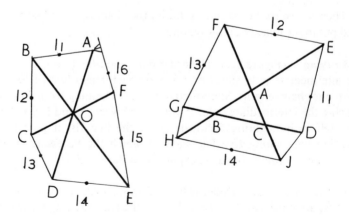

station B, lining in on AI_1 produced. Proceed similarly with I_2 and C, and I_3 and D, but for D, if you are working with a hexagonal grid, you have to line in with OA as well as I_3C. E and F are fixed similarly, and you will have a network in which you can line yourself in along any line except FA.

If FA is short, the necessary intermediate can be located by putting up two poles roughly on line near the mid point, going to A (say), sighting towards F and estimating relative to them where the intermediate should be. A pole is then put up in the estimated position, and checked from A, repeating the procedure if necessary. If a recumbent pole near the mid point is not hidden by grass the correct position can be read off against its graduations.

Alternatively, the first 20 m length could be run from F in roughly the right direction, a pole put up at its end, and the line continued by sighting back. Station A is then fixed by an offset with diagonals as in Para. 7.3.

For a larger site, the central point can be replaced by a triangle (Figure 8.1). A side of less than 60 m can often be measured with the tape anchored near the mid point, provided no detail is needed; this is quicker than chaining from one angle to the other. It is very important, if this construction is used, to make sure that the radial lines are collinear with the sides of the triangle (cf Figure 4.1, j - m).

Part III
THE LEVEL

9 The Level: General Description

9.1 Essential Features; 9.2 Choice of Instrument; 9.3 The Staff;
9.4 Setting Up; 9.5 Checking the Level; 9.6 Adjustments;
9.7 Precautions.

9.1 *Essential Features.* Telescopic levels are widely used, especially on excavations. All have the same primary function, to provide a horizontal line of sight (also termed line of collimation). The intersections of this line with a levelling staff held vertically allow the relative heights of different points to be determined.

Much ingenuity has been employed in constructing devices for this purpose. A useful account has been published by M. A. R. Cooper (*Modern Theodolites and Levels*, Crosby Lockwood and Son, 1971); it is perhaps a little too technical for the archaeologist who merely wishes to use the instrument.

There are many variants, but levels fall into three main types. The simplest is illustrated diagrammatically in Figure 9.1; it comprises:

(a) The telescope (see also Para. 9.4). This is fixed through semi-permanent adjusting screws (S) to

(b) A sensitive spirit-level and

(c) The stage, which is integral with the spindle (Sp); this rotates in a bearing in the upper parallel plate (u.p.p.) or tribrach, which is connected by the levelling screws (l.s.) to the lower parallel plate (l.p.p.) which screws onto the tripod head (g).

The levelling screws now almost always number three, but old instruments may have four.

In the telescope, the line of sight is indicated by cross-hairs (now almost always engraved on glass) just inside the eyepiece end. The eyepiece can be moved to focus on the cross-hairs, either on a screw thread or in older instruments by sliding (see Para. 9.4). The spirit-level is parallel to the line of sight, and both are perpendicular to the spindle and its bearing. These last can be set vertical by the levelling screws; the detailed technique is described in Para. 9.4. It is assumed here that the instrument is in adjustment; checking and correction are described in Para. 9.5.

9.1 The Level: Diagram of Essential Features

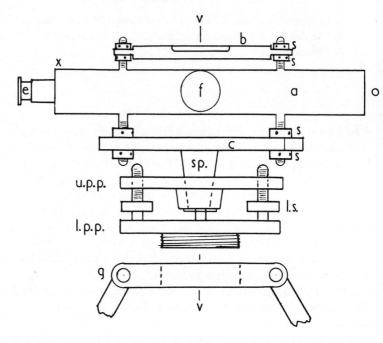

In many dumpy levels the lower semi-permanent adjusting screws are eliminated, and the telescope is fixed rigidly to the spindle.

The tilting level is essentially the same in principle, but the lower semi-permanent adjusting screws are replaced by a pivot and screw with which the telescope is levelled for each reading.

The automatic level works on a radically different system. It contains a freely-pivoted mirror, prism or lens (the compensator), which is acted upon by gravity so that the line of sight is always horizontal. Tilting and automatic levels both have to be levelled roughly before use; this is done either by three levelling screws or by a ball-and-socket tripod head.

In modern levels the essential features are often concealed by a casing, and prisms or mirrors are used to simplify reading the spirit-levels.

9.2 *Choice of Instrument.* You will probably have to take what you can get, but if you have any choice the following notes may be of use.

My own choice is a standard dumpy level. I am no doubt biased through having learnt surveying fifty years ago, but this type has the advantages that you can see whether it is working properly, adjustment is easy, and provided that the lenses, cross-hairs, and spirit-level are intact it can always be used, even if it has suffered other damage.

The automatic level is slightly easier to use, but much more expensive, and if anything does go wrong (admittedly unlikely) a professional overhaul is unavoidable.

The tilting level suffers from the great disadvantage that the telescope has to be relevelled before every reading (see below). If you cannot avoid using one, then provided it has three levelling screws the best thing to do is to fix the tilting screw with a piece of adhesive tape so that it cannot be moved accidentally, and then to use the instrument as if it were a dumpy. Before fixing the screw it must be used as if it were a semi-permanent adjustment to make the telescope perpendicular to the spindle (see Para. 9.5).

Cooper (*Modern Theodolites*, p. 81) cites rates of progress for running a line of levels, comparing an automatic with a tilting level. Allowing a walking speed of 5 km/hr, the figures show that to set up and take two readings consistently takes two minutes longer using the tilting level; for sights up to 60 m in length, the automatic required one-and-a-half minutes. Unfortunately the time taken in setting up, as distinct from taking readings, is not given, but a quarter of a minute would seem reasonable, as against the half-minute needed to set up a dumpy.

In archaeological work, to take twenty or more readings from a single setting-up is much more usual than to run a long line of change points. Using the above figures, to set up and take twenty readings should require twelve and three-quarter minutes with an automatic level, thirteen with a dumpy, and thirty-two and three-quarters with a tilting level; obviously the quarter-minute precision is absurd, but these figures show very clearly the great delay caused in this type of work by the need to relevel for each sight.

To sum up, the automatic level is preferable, provided someone else is paying for it; but it costs roughly twice as much as a dumpy, and the advantage is very small. Further, since the dumpy is now regarded as obsolescent (Cooper, *Modern Theodolites*) reconditioned instruments tend to be rather cheaper than other types.

Of the various optional extras, the only one which shows any real advantage is a tripod with telescopic legs. This is helpful when setting up on rough ground, but that is less important with a level than with a theodolite. The main advantage is that transport is much easier.

There are other extras which at best offer no benefits to the user.

(a) A graduated horizontal circle permits measurement of the angles between sights, but for the type of work envisaged here the lack of movement in a vertical plane makes this almost useless; if you need these angles, you need a theodolite.

(b) Tacheometric cross-hairs (Para. 14.2). These are occasionally useful, but generally if you need distances it is quicker and more accurate to measure them with a tape or chain. Moreover, if conditions are bad you may read against the wrong line. Unless the alternatives are easily available, though, it is not worth a fuss to alter whatever is fitted as standard.

(c) A ball-and-socket tripod head. The supposed advantage of this is that you do not have to bother about getting the tripod head even roughly horizontal. In practice it tends either to work loose during use or to jam immovably, whichever is likely to cause the greater inconvenience.

(d) An erect image. Most levels, and nearly all theodolites, show an inverted image. Very little practice is needed to get used to reading this, so the supposed advantage of an erect image is imaginary. Moreover, there is the considerable disadvantage that if you have to use the more usual type, or if someone accustomed to that has to use your level, work will be slowed down and the risk of mistaken readings greatly increased. The same objection applies to levelling staffs numbered upside-down.

A new instrument, or a reconditioned one bought from a reputable firm, should be in correct adjustment when bought. Casual purchase is a gamble, though for a level the risk is less than for a theodolite. Apart from obvious defects such as broken lenses, cross-hairs, or spirit-levels, the most likely faults are worn spindles or levelling screws. If the instrument can be set up properly, the focusing screw works smoothly, the spindle does not stick and there is no relative rotation between the upper and lower parallel plates, it is probably capable of giving adequate results. If there are small defects, the level will only be worth consideration if you can repair them yourself, for the cost of a professional overhaul is now very high indeed. Spare spirit-level tubes can be bought, but are not always easy to fit.

9.3 *The Staff.* Besides the level itself, a levelling staff is essential. These are now graduated (Figure 9.2) in metres, decimetres and centimetres (but see Appendix I). The telescope inverts the image, but you will get used to this after a few readings. *Do not* get a staff which is graduated upside-down (they are obtainable) for if you learn on one of that kind you will make numerous mistakes when you use the normal type; and the apparent advantage is illusory.

The choice of staff is unavoidably a compromise. It has to be transported to the site, and carried about when there, which makes

9.2   Graduation of Levelling Staff

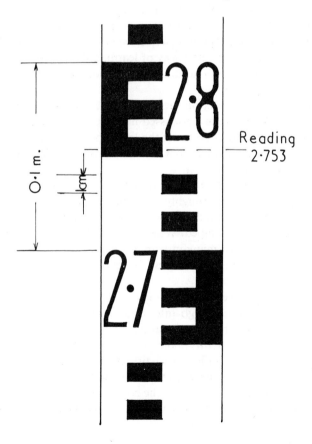

Reading
2·753

a light, short staff desirable; but the longer it is the less often will your line of sight run a few centimetres above its end. Four metres is about the shortest acceptable. The most convenient type now is probably that made in detachable sections of light metal alloy; these are not affected by damp or corrosion, but care must be taken to make sure they do not get bent. A small attached spirit-level is useful for tacheometric work, but is not needed for levelling. Handles are quite unnecessary. In general, the choice of a staff is very much a matter of personal preference.

Before you do any actual levelling, you should familiarise yourself with the graduation and numbering of the staff, always looking at it upside-down. Note that some numbers are in Roman figures to reduce the risk of confusion, and that some small numerals indicate the metre with which you are dealing. It will be useful, also, to get a colleague to indicate points on the staff (preferably with most of the face concealed), which you will read and then verify with a tape to discover whether you have got the reading correct. This is a better way of learning than by starting at once with the level, for your accuracy can be checked.

9.4 *Setting up.* Observation and booking, and the various applications of levelling, are discussed in succeeding chapters, but the first step must always be to set the level up ready for use. The following description assumes that you are starting the day's work, by setting up at the first station.

Set the tripod firmly on the ground, with its feet pressed into the surface and with the head roughly level. Make sure that the fixing screws between the head and legs are not slack and that the sliding legs (if any) are firmly clamped. When taking the level from its box note how it is arranged; many instruments have only one position in which they can be replaced. Screw the level firmly to the tripod head.

Before using the level, the cross-hairs need to be brought into focus. There is no need to go into great detail as to the optics involved, but in brief the main focusing screw is used to bring the image of the staff into the plane of the cross-hairs; so if the eyepiece is focused on to the cross-hairs there will be no apparent relative motion (parallax) between the staff and the cross-hairs even if the eye is moved a little. To bring the cross-hairs into focus, point the telescope towards the sky or some featureless blank surface and move the eyepiece gently in and out.

This setting is specific to one observer, but two different persons often have eyes sufficiently alike for one to be able to check the other's readings without refocusing. In theory, the setting of the eyepiece will remain right indefinitely, but in practice the characteristics of one's eye change during a day's observation, so occasional refocusing may be needed, preferably when the level is moved to a new position.

The instrument is then levelled.

The telescope, with its attached spirit-level, is placed parallel to a pair of levelling screws, and these are turned in opposite directions until the bubble is central. The rule as to which way to turn the screws is 'the bubble follows the left thumb', which may seem obscure in print but which will reveal its meaning unequivocally the first time you try to set up a level. The telescope is then turned through a right angle and levelling repeated, using *only* the third, previously untouched, levelling screw. (With four screws, opposite pairs are used together, and must be kept just tight.) The telescope is then turned back to its first position and relevelled if necessary, and the process is repeated until the bubble remains central. Provided the instrument is in adjustment, the axis of the spindle is now truly vertical, and the line of sight of the telescope, which is parallel to the spirit-level, will be horizontal in whatever direction it is pointed.

This reads as a slow and laborious procedure, but in fact it takes far less time to do it that to read about it. After a day's practice, or less, the average time for setting up a level on reasonably good ground will be about half a minute; so there is no reason to worry about the need to move the instrument during a series of readings (Chapter 10).

9.5 *Checking the Level.* There is no obvious reason why levels should ever go out of adjustment, unless brutally ill-treated; but they do. The most usual indication is that the instrument cannot be levelled so that the bubble of the spirit level remains central; but apparently inexplicable mistakes in reduced levels may also suggest faulty adjustment.

To check the accuracy is simple. Two firmly driven pegs or other suitably immovable stations are established, on fairly level ground, as far apart as conveniently possible up to 100 m or so. The level is then set up as accurately as its condition permits *exactly* midway between the two pegs; two of the levelling screws should be on that line. Sight on the staff on one peg (A, say), and using those two screws turned in opposite directions (and thus not altering the height of instrument) bring the bubble to the centre of its run and read the staff. Sight towards the other peg B, and repeat, having centred the bubble again. The difference between these readings gives the true difference in level between A and B, even if the instrument is not in adjustment (see Figure 9.3); so if A is taken as at 100·000, B's level can be worked out.

9.3 Checking Level

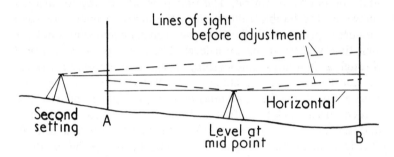

The level is then set up on BA produced, as near to A as possible consistent with clear focusing. The bubble is centred as before, and the staff reading taken for A. Provided, as almost always happens, the inaccuracy of adjustment is small, this will give the height of instrument above A, so the correct reading at B is easily worked out. The staff is held at B, and using the levelling screws but paying no attention to the spirit-level, the cross-hairs are brought to that reading. The reading for A is checked, and if it has altered from its first value the procedure will have to be repeated. When finally the readings at A and B give the correct difference, the line of sight is horizontal.

If the level is out of adjustment, the bubble will no longer be central, but this does not mean that further work must be abandoned until time has been found to make the adjustment needed. If for example the bubble is displaced from the centre towards the eyepiece by 5 mm, then so long as it is in that position the line of sight will be horizontal. If the bubble-tube is graduated, the readings of the ends of the bubble can be noted; alternatively, pieces of adhesive tape can be fixed to the sides of the tube, and the ends of the bubble marked on them.

The second check is whether the axis of the spindle is perpendicular to the line of sight. This is tested by setting up in the ordinary way (Para. 9.4 above). Make sure the bubble is central or that it is between the appropriate marks as explained in the last paragraph; that is that the line of sight is horizontal. Then turn the telescope through 180° about its vertical axis. If it is in adjustment, the line of sight will remain horizontal.

If this adjustment is wrong, again the level can still be used, but will have to be relevelled with a levelling screw for each sight, which is a nuisance. This would not be legitimate in really accurate work, for moving one levelling screw changes the height of instrument a little, but the effect is very small and can be neglected for the type of surveying considered here.

9.6 *Adjustments.* Before attempting any adjustment make sure that you understand exactly what needs to be done, and work through the whole procedure in imagination before you touch any of the adjusting nuts. If you have the slightest doubt about your ability to do the work, do not attempt it; as explained above the level can be used without being exactly adjusted. Nevertheless, the method is simple.

The first step is to set the telescope truly horizontal, as described above. The spirit-level can then be moved by means of the adjusting screws between it and the telescope. These screws are usually capstan-type nuts, turned with a small tommy-bar. They should be moved smoothly and if possible gently; only a small movement will be needed. It is important that these nuts are left tight when the adjustment is finished, but avoid excessive force.

To adjust so that the line of sight (and thus, now, the spirit-level) is perpendicular to the spindle, the instrument is set up as well as possible and the bubble centred. The telescope is then rotated through 180°. Any displacement of the bubble which results is *half* got rid of by the levelling screws, and the adjusting screws between the stage and the telescope are used to make the bubble central again.

After adjustments, the level should again be checked, as before.

In some levels, the spirit-level is attached to the stage instead of directly to the telescope. In that case, adjustment is in the reverse order: the spirit-level is first brought perpendicular to the axis of the spindle, and afterwards the level is adjusted relative to the stage so that when the line of sight is horizontal so is the spirit-level.

Occasionally, though very seldom, the spirit-level has no adjustment relative to the telescope. In that case the line of sight is brought parallel to the spirit-level by adjusting screws which move the diaphragm carrying the cross-hairs; but in general these screws should be left alone.

9.7 *Precautions*. In principle, when the level is screwed to its tripod it should be carried upright, so that the spindle is roughly vertical; this avoids strain on the levelling screws. In practice, levels suitable for the sort of work envisaged here are robust enough to stand being carried over one's shoulder. If you are passing through openings, have the instrument in front of you, and if you are working amongst traffic always carry it upright, for if it is over your shoulder there is an even chance that impact with a moving vehicle will break your neck as well as the level.

When the level is in use, you should try to avoid any contact with it at all when you are taking a reading. Never try to steady it (or yourself) by holding the tripod.

In some conditions, typically a sunny day with a cold wind, you will find that the level drifts slowly out of adjustment, owing to differential expansion of the levelling screws and tripod legs. This effect can be reduced by always setting up with the same leg towards the sun. The movement of the bubble will be small, and for the type of work envisaged here it is legitimate to correct it by means of the levelling screws. A large movement is an almost certain indication that the level has been knocked out of position, and it should be relevelled and a check taken back to the last change point (Para. 10.1).

10 The Level: Observation and Booking

10.1 Booking; 10.2 Reducing Levels; 10.3 Adjustment of Errors.

10.1 *Booking*. There are several purposes for which levelling may be used, and these are discussed in the next chapter; but the methods of observation and booking are always the same. To fix our ideas, assume that we are starting from a 'bench mark' having a known level, and determining a run of levels at points 1 to 8 (Figure 10.1). The bench mark (BM) may either be related to ordnance datum (OD) or may be given some arbitrary value relative to site datum (SD) as for an excavation; abbreviations for these are OBM or SBM.

Observations are recorded in a level book, preferably purpose-made though you can laboriously rule your own. This is similar in

10.1 Run of Levels

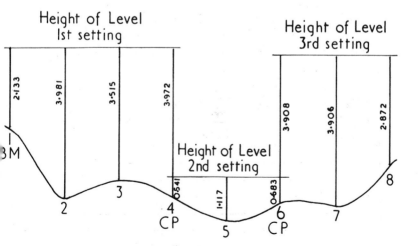

10.2 Booking and Reducing Levels
(a) Height of Instrument Method (b) Rise and Fall Method

B.S.	I.S.	F.S.	H.O.I.	R.L.	Remarks. Point
2·133			125·393	123·260	1. Site B.M.
	3·981			121·412	2
	3·515			121·878	3
0·541		3·972	121·962	121·421	4 C P
	1·117			120·745	5
3·908		0·683	125·187	121·279	6 C P
	3·906			121·281	7
		2·872		122·315	8
6·582		7·527		− 123·260	
−7·527				0·945 ✓	
−0·945 ✓					

(a)

SPINE

B.S.	I.S.	F.S.	Rise	Fall	R.L.	Remarks Point
2·133					123·260	1 Site B.M.
	3·981			1·848	121·412	2
	3·515		0·466		121·878	3
0·541		3·972		0·457	121·421	4 C P
	1·117			0·676 ~~0·576~~	120·845	5
3·908		0·683	0·434		121·279	6 C P
	3·906		0·002		121·281	7
		2·872	1·034		122·3~~15~~15	8
6·582		7·527	1·936	2·981	−123·260	
−7·527			−2·981 ~~·881~~	2·881	−0·955 ✗	
−0·945			−1·045 ✗		−0·945 ✓	
			−0·945 ✓			

(b)

size to a chain survey book but bound along the longer edge. The pages, ruled horizontally, are also divided into columns, usually by red lines. The abbreviations in Figure 10.2a stand for backsight, intermediate sight, foresight, height of instrument, reduced level. These occur on the left page; the right-hand page, only partly indicated in the figure, may carry additional columns but these are not necessary. In some books two columns, headed Rise and Fall, may replace the HOI column (see Figure 10.2b and Para. 10.2).

The observations are imagined to start from a firmly driven peg which forms the site bench mark, 123·26 m above site datum. You set up (Para. 9.4) at any convenient point and look *back* to the staff held on this, so this is a 'backsight'; the reading is 2·133. In fact, you could seldom be sure of the last figure, but it is much less bother and rather more accurate to make a rough estimate of the third decimal place than it would be to try to make up your mind as to whether it is really nearer 2·14 or 2·13. The reduced level of site BM is therefore recorded as 123·260, although the third decimal place is in fact unknown. The line of sight (or line of collimation) cuts the staff at 2·133 m above the BM. Similarly, points 2 and 3 are 3·981 m and 3·515 m below the line of sight. These can be observed without moving the instrument, and are booked as intermediate sights.

It is important that the staff should be vertical when read. Even when a spirit-level is fitted, there will almost always be slight movement, so a much better way of achieving this is to sway the staff slowly backwards and forwards well past the vertical; the *lowest* reading is then booked. This method cannot be used, though, if the readings for three (tacheometric) cross-hairs are needed.

There is no automatic check to detect mistakes; it is easy at the end of a day's work to misread a metre, or even, surprisingly, having *read* a number such as 3·081 correctly to *book* it as 3·801. As a precaution, having read the staff *and booked the reading*, you should always verify it by a second look. If you have a helper to do the booking, he should read the number back to you after he has booked it, for checking. Even when you are alone, you may find it helps to say the figures to yourself out loud.

Point 4 is the last visible from the instrument as now set up, so it will be used as a change point (CP). A 'foresight' is taken to it (3·972, say) preparatory to moving the instrument *forward*. The level is then set up again, a backsight taken back to point 4, and levelling continued. Note that each line in the level book corresponds to a single point (*not* to a single *observation*), so both backsight and foresight to point 4 are entered on the same line.

A CP need not be part of the run of levels which is being surveyed. In choosing a CP, it is important that it should be firm and well-defined, for if the staff is not resting at exactly the same level for both backsight and foresight a mistake is introduced which is carried forward throughout the rest of the run. In really bad ground it may be worth while to carry a metal plate, preferably with a knob on top and with spikes which can be forced into the earth.

For a reason explained later, the last reading in a run is recorded as a foresight (also, you should record the last reading on a page as a foresight and repeat it as a backsight at the beginning of the next page). The booking and reduced levels might then appear as in Figure 10.2.

10.2   *Reducing Levels.* Having taken the necessary readings the 'reduced' levels have to be worked out. There are two methods. Of these, the 'height of instrument' method is more easily understood and is quicker to use than the theoretically preferable 'rise and fall' method.

Referring to Figure 10.2, the level as first set up is 2·133 m above the BM, which is itself 123·260 m above site datum (SD); so the line of sight ('height of instrument') is 125·393 m above SD. Point 2 is 3·981 m below the instrument, so it is at $125·393 - 3·981 = 121·412$ m above SD, and similarly for the remaining points. Point 4, used as a change point, is at 121·421, and for its second setting up the level is 0·541 above this. 'HOI' is thus 121·962; and so on.

With the rise and fall method, the difference between each successive staff reading is worked out, and the levels found from those differences. Thus the staff reading on the site BM is 2·133, on point 2 3·981. So point 2 is lower than the BM (a fall) of $3·981 - 2·133 = 1·848$. The BM is at 123·260, so (2) is at 121·412. At (3), the staff reads 3·575, so the rise from (2) to (3) is 0·466 and (3) is at 121·878.

The advantage of the rise and fall method is that it provides a check on the arithmetical accuracy of every level calculated:

(sum of backsights − sum of foresights)

= (sum of rises − sum of falls)

= (last reduced level − first reduced level); it is to permit these checks that the last reading on a page is entered as a 'foresight'. With the height of instrument method only the levels of the change points can be checked in this way. This advantage though, is counterbalanced by the disadvantage that 'rise and fall' requires twice as much arithmetic as 'height of instrument'. Much will depend on how quickly you can do arithmetic, but my own preference is for the theoretically inferior method; I find that I am almost always able to work out the reduced level while the staff is being moved from one point to the next, so that the levels are all worked out as soon as the fieldwork is finished. The arithmetic can be made almost as reliable as in 'rise and fall' by a second check in which each reduced level is added to the relevant reading, to make sure that the total gives the height of instrument; this is better than repeating the original subtraction, for if any calculation is repeated exactly, the risk of repeating a mistake is increased.

It is very important to realise that 'rise and fall' does not and cannot detect a misreading, only a mistake in arithmetic.

Examples of the two modes of booking are given in Figure 10.2. Arithmetical mistakes have been included in each.

Note that with 'height of instrument' the mistake at point 5 goes undetected. The two mistakes in the rise and fall example are more likely to be made, but all are identified. Some time is saved if the rise and fall columns are worked out and checked before the reduced levels are filled in.

10.3 *Adjustment of Errors.* For accurate work, any run of levels should start *and finish* on a known level, but even when no mistakes have been made there will almost always be a small error to distribute. In the last example, suppose that point 8 is known to be at 122·30 m above OD; the closing error is therefore 0·015 m. This is built up from errors in the backsights and foresights; the intermediate sights make no contribution. There are six backsights and foresights and each is equally likely to be wrong, so the adjustment to each should be 0·0025 m, but since half a millimetre is insignificant 0·002 and 0·003 are used alternately. The backsights need to be decreased, to 2·131, 0·538, and 3·906, and the foresights increased, to 3·975, 0·685, and 2·875. The corresponding HOI values are 125·391, 121·954, and 125·175. The adjusted intermediate levels are worked out from these without altering the intermediate sights.

11 The Level: Applications

11.1 *Establishing a Site Bench Mark.* The main applications of a
level in archaeological fieldwork are for drawing profiles and
sections and for contouring, but as a preliminary it is often
necessary to establish a site bench mark.

The accuracy with which that needs to be tied in to ordnance
datum depends on the circumstances. To do this is always an
advantage, but is sometimes not worth the work involved, as, for
example, when a site is to be completely destroyed. Otherwise, in
order to ensure that present and possible future work can be related
accurately, site levels should either be based on ordnance datum or
on a *permanent* site datum. If the SD is really permanent, a rough
link with OD may be acceptable, such as the intersection of a
contour with a road, but the value assigned to the SD and the way in
which it has been fixed should always be recorded. The merit of OD
is that it is an accepted standard, though even when that is used the
basis should be defined (see Para. 27.5).

The nearest OBM is often quite a long way from the site, and
special care is needed to establish the site BM. The main precaution
is rather obvious: the line of levels is run from the OBM to site BM
and back again. If done correctly, the closing error will obviously
be small. In order to locate mistakes, the change points used should
be the same (so far as possible) for both outward and return runs;
to work out the reduced levels as you go may save time. Two other
points are perhaps less obvious. An OBM is normally the crossbar of
a broad arrow cut on a vertical surface. The staff cannot easily be
supported at the right level, so rest it on the ground and take the
reading against the crossbar (0·224 say). Then the first entry is
made as 0·000 backsight against the OBM and the second as 0·244
foresight against 'CP1. Ground below OBM'. The second point to
remember is that after reading the staff held on the SBM *the level*

should be lifted, moved a little way, and reset. If you do not do
this, and you have made a mistake in reading the staff held on the
SBM, you are likely to repeat the mistake, so despite the long run of
levels you have no real check on your accuracy. An example of a
short run of this kind is given in Figure 11.1; the rise and fall
method is slightly preferable for this sort of work.

This exemplifies a general rule, that any run of levels should start
and finish on a point for which the height above datum is known.
Thus if you were taking levels at stations A to F in a polygon,
starting at A, you would not stop at F but would continue back to
A, to make fairly sure that you had made no mistakes. You can
only hope that you have not made two which cancel out. Note that
these precautions only check the CPs, not the intermediate points.

11.1 Establishing Site Bench Mark

B.S.	I.S.	F.S.	Rise	Fall	R.L.	Remarks.
0.000					201.450	O BM
3.821		0.224		0.224	201.226	CP1 Ground Below BM
3.903		0.107	3.714		204.940	CP2
3.622		0.081	3.822		208.762	CP3
0.048		0.147	3.475		212.237	Site BM
0.066		3.517		3.469	208.768	CP3
0.124		3.889		3.823	204.945	CP2
0.225		3.832		3.708	201.237	CP1 Below OBM
		0.000	0.225		201.462	O BM
11.809	11.797	11.236	11.224		− 201.450	
−11.797		−11.224			0.012	
0.012 ✓		0.012 ✓			Rise OBM to SBM	10.787, 10.775
					Average 10.781	
					Accept SBM as	212.23

11.2 *Profiles.* A profile (to be distinguished from a section) is the
trace of the intersection of the ground surface with a vertical plane.
A line is chosen, and a zero point on it fixed; spot levels are then
taken at measured distances from zero along the line. The points,
on a scale drawing, are joined up usually with a smooth curve.

Linear measurements for preference should be horizontal, but they can be taken along the ground and either measured thus in plotting or corrected for slope. If all levels can be taken from one setting of the instrument, there is often no need to reduce them; they can be plotted as measurements down from the line of sight (see also Paras. 13.4 and 27.6).

11.3 *Sections.* The strata exposed in the side of an excavation will normally be plotted in the field, the vertical measurements being taken from a horizontal string at some defined level. This application is described in more detail in Para. 27.6.

11.4 *Direct Contouring.* The easiest method is to mark out the contours directly on the ground, using 'wands'; these are then recorded by chain surveying. Two or three contours can be run at a time. Different types of wand (for example, peeled, unpeeled, and with a tuft of leaves) can be used to distinguish the contours, but these are usually widely enough spaced not to get confused. Contours should be booked separately from other detail. The wands are put in by the staff man, who is directed 'up' or 'down' by the man at the level. Thus, with HOI = 125·393, points on the 125 m contour would be found by moving the staff to obtain a reading of 0·39. Time is saved if a broad rubber band is put round the appropriate reading. When you have finished chaining a run, the last wand in each contour line should be left in place, and checked when marking out the next stretch. This method is appropriate when the slope of the ground is fairly gentle.

11.5 *Contouring with Profiles.* This method is useful for fairly small features of marked relief, such as hill-fort entrances or burial-mounds. Lines for profiles are chosen, running mostly at right angles to the contours. These are surveyed, care being taken to record the positions of the 'zeros'. The diagram (Figure 11.2) shows the sort of arrangement which might be used, but in practice about three times as many profiles would be taken, and to measure in the tops and toes of scarps is often useful.

The profiles are drawn on a separate sheet of squared paper, using the same horizontal scale as the plan, but an exaggerated vertical scale; paper can be saved by overlapping the profiles, taking a different zero datum for each, as in the diagram. The points at which the contours cut each profile can then be marked,

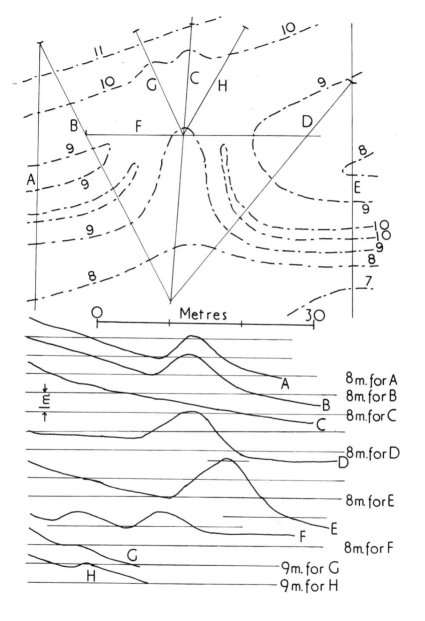

and joined up to give the plan; in a real case, the vertical interval would probably be much smaller than one metre. The profiles themselves, and the lines along which they have been taken, are not reproduced on the final drawing.

The same method is applicable when the profiles follow the lines of a regular grid which has been set out as a preliminary to excavation.

11.6 *Contouring with Random Spot Levels.* Contours can also be interpolated among a scatter of spot levels distributed irregularly, provided they have been placed with some regard to the form of the ground. Usually, the levels are fixed by tacheometry (Paras. 14.3 – 6), but ordinary levelling may be more convenient if, as in a town, a large-scale plan is available with plentiful detail, so that the positions of the spots can easily be fixed. Incidentally, the value of contouring in a town survey is often not realised; compare for example the plans of Conway in the *History of the King's Works* (I, Figure 35) and in the *Caernarvonshire Inventory* (I, Figure 58). As a piece of draughtsmanship, the latter is the less elegant of the two; but it is of far greater value, as it carries contours, which show clearly how the defences were arranged to take advantage of the form of the ground.

11.7 *Single-handed Levelling.* In an extreme emergency, levels can be taken single-handed; but the procedure is very laborious, and would be quite unsuitable for a lot of observations.

Since no one is available to hold the staff, it is tied upright, either to some support such as a fence post or using a makeshift tripod of poles. The *level* is then moved around, and set up first as nearly as possible over the bench mark and then over the points at which the spot levels are needed. At each point the staff is observed and the height of instrument above ground level measured. A 'change point' is provided for by observing the staff in its old and new positions without moving the level. Naturally there is no standard method of booking for this eccentric procedure, and if you are unlucky enough to have to use it you will need to record in detail exactly what you have done, step by step.

Part IV
THE THEODOLITE OR TACHEOMETER

12 The Theodolite: Essential Details

12.1 Description; 12.2 Modifications and Accessories; 12.3 The Vernier Scale; 12.4 Setting up; 12.5 Transport and Adjustments.

12.1 *Description* (Figure 12.1). The Theodolite, though a very versatile instrument, is essentially simple. A telescope (or in the most elementary forms a sighting tube) is attached to a graduated circle and supported so that it can rotate about a horizontal axis, thus permitting measurement of vertical angles. The supports of the telescope stand on a plate which can rotate about a vertical axis, so horizontal angles can be measured on another graduated circle. By providing three cross-hairs at the eyepiece end, distances can be measured directly by readings on a levelling staff, and the instrument becomes a tacheometer or tachymeter. Since almost all theodolites now have tacheometric cross-hairs the terms are effectively interchangeable.

From this simple basic idea, instruments of great accuracy and of corresponding complexity have evolved. Some can be read to one-fifth of a second of arc, roughly one centimetre at 10 km distance. For our purpose, one minute of arc is quite accurate enough. This gives an accuracy of about three parts in ten thousand, without any difficulty; to obtain half that precision in linear measurements quite laborious precautions are needed. Astro-archaeology is the only research handicapped by this limitation. For all other archaeological work instruments of greater precision can be a positive disadvantage, for the measurements take much longer.

There are many different makes and types of theodolite, and some recent modifications are very useful, but the nature of all such instruments is essentially the same, and can best be understood by describing a simple type (Figure 12.1). Some features are the same as for a level, and to avoid repetition reference back should be made to these.

The telescope (a) is essentially the same as for a level (Para. 9.1) but should, for choice, have three cross-hairs, converting the instrument into a tacheometer (Chapter 14).

12.1 The Theodolite: Diagram of Essential Features

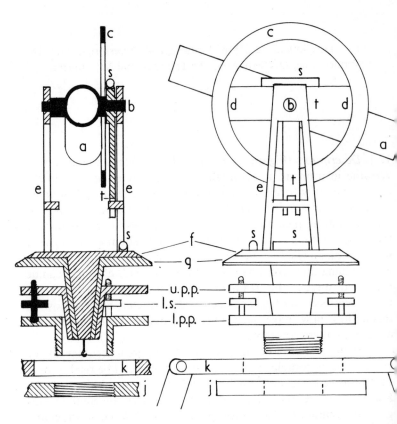

Fixed to the telescope, and rotating with it about the horizontal (or trunnion) axis (b) is the graduated vertical circle (c). Sometimes, but very rarely in modern instruments, the telescope has an attached spirit-level, which simplifies the use of the instrument as a level.

The horizontal axis passes through a T-piece (t) with an attached spirit-level (s). The arms of the T carry vernier scales (d) (Para. 12.3 below) which read against the vertical circle. When the instrument is properly set up and the line of sight is horizontal the vernier may read 90° and 270° (by far the best), 0° and 180°, or 0° and 0° (worst). Make sure what system is used on your instrument.

The T can be clamped to the vertical circle, and there will be a fine adjustment of some kind (usually a tangent screw) which allows fine controlled movements. There are several alternative arrangements, and for simplicity they are omitted in Figure 12.1.

The ends of the horizontal axis rest in bearings in the A-frames or standards (e). The upright of the T is slotted, and fits over a projection on one A-frame. The slot is clamped to this projection, either by capstan screw or by a tangent screw, so that relative adjustment is possible.

The A-frames are rigidly fixed to the vernier plate (f), also known as the upper limb or upper plate. This plate carries a spirit-level (S) with axis parallel to the horizontal axis, and sometimes a second spirit-level at right angles to it. The plate is fixed to a slightly tapered spindle, the inner axis, corresponding to the vertical axis of the instrument.

The vernier plate rests on the lower plate (or limb), (g) which has a graduated circle round its circumference, and is attached to a hollow spindle, the outer axis, within which the inner axis can rotate.

The outer axis rotates in a bearing in the upper parallel plate (u.p.p.) The upper and lower plates can be clamped together, and the lower plate can be clasped to the upper parallel plate; both clamps have tangent screws for fine adjustment.

The lower parallel plate (l.p.p.) is not screwed direct to the tripod head (k) but to a sliding plate (j) which can move relative to the tripod head and can be clamped to it.

The tripod head and the sliding plate are pierced so that a plumb-bob can be suspended from the lower end of the inner axis.

The vernier scales are provided with small magnifiers to assist reading them, not shown in Figure 12.1.

12.2 *Modifications and Accessories.* All theodolites incorporate the features described above, but in most modern instruments they are more or less masked by a protective casing. In general, for the type of work envisaged here, complications should be avoided, but there are some modifications or accessories which, at least in some circumstances, are really useful.

The most valuable of all, which should be obtained if at all possible, is the modification which replaces the vernier scales. The graduated scales are engraved on glass and totally enclosed, and a system of prisms brings their images to one or two eyepieces, where they can be read through small magnifiers which are focused in the same way as the telescope eyepiece. This device cuts down the time needed to read angles to about a quarter of that taken when working with verniers.

Theodolites can also be obtained with automatic levelling devices connected to the vertical circle. These save some time and improve accuracy in tacheometric work, but for the sort of surveying envisaged here the gain is not very great, and the considerable extra cost would be hard to justify.

For most field surveying, the limited vertical range of an ordinary theodolite (some 30° or 40° above or below horizontal) is no disadvantage. If, though, you are working inside a tall building, such as a ruined castle keep, a prismatic eyepiece is almost essential. With it, observations can be made to elevations up to about 80°.

If you are working a lot in very bad light, as for example underground, a properly made device to illuminate the cross-hairs will be useful; but this is not essential if the need only arises occasionally (Para. 24.4).

If you need magnetic bearings more accurately than can be read on a prismatic compass, you can get a compass to attach to the theodolite; this will usually allow readings to about 15 minutes or better. Again, the need for this is only likely to arise in underground work, where you need all the checks you can get.

The optical plummet, which replaces the plumb-bob and string, is seldom available except for instruments which would be excessively accurate for the type of work envisaged here.

As noted earlier (Para. 9.2) the purchase of a second-hand theodolite, except from a reputable dealer, is a gamble. In addition to the checks described there you can see whether the tangent screws work smoothly, and measure the horizontal angle between two well-defined marks using different parts of the horizontal circle; but a much used instrument can often conceal faults which could only be detected by an expert instrument technician.

12.3 *The Vernier Scale*. Most readers will be familiar with this, but it is described here for reference. In the diagram (Figure 12.2) the main scale is divided into half degrees. The vernier scale has 30 divisions, corresponding in total length to 29 of the main divisions, so when the 17th vernier graduation, say, coincides exactly with a division of the main scale, zero on the vernier scale has moved $^{17}/_{30}$ ths of half a degree, that is, 17 minutes, from the adjacent

12.2 Vernier Scale

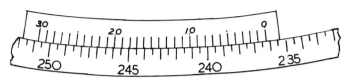

preceding graduation on the main scale. The same principle applies to any system of subdivision; those most commonly found are 1', 30'' or 20''.

12.4 *Setting Up.* A theodolite takes rather longer to set up than does a level, for it has to be set vertically over the station. In reasonably good conditions, after a little practice, setting up should take about one-and-a-half minutes.

Remember that the stations are at the poles, not at the pegs; so a pole must always be replaced in the same position relative to the corresponding peg, and in setting up you plumb down to the hole in which the pole stood. Where grass or vegetation is long, a short length of rod to make a temporary mark is useful. The distinction between peg and pole will make no measurable difference on the finished plan, but can introduce inconveniently large closing errors when the angles are checked.

To set up, the plumb-bob is brought as nearly as possible into the right position by moving the tripod legs, at the same time trying to keep the tripod head roughly level. Using the sliding plate, the plumb-bob is then centred exactly over the required point, and the sliding plate is clamped. The instrument is then levelled, as for the level (Para. 9.4).

You will sometimes find that the tripod head is so far off level that there is not enough travel available in the levelling screws. The slope of the tripod head can be altered *without much movement of the plumb-bob* by moving the end of the appropriate leg *along the circumference* of the circle passing through the three tripod feet; *not* radially to that circle.

12.5 *Transport and Adjustments.* The extra weight of a theodolite puts more strain on its attachment to the tripod than occurs with a level, but most instruments are fairly robust. Nevertheless, there is an additional risk, in that in some types fixings such as the clamp of the sliding plate or the upper bearings of the horizontal axis may come unscrewed; so get into the habit of making sure, as routine, that everything is safe before lifting the instrument. Also, make sure when putting it into its case that it is correctly arranged; never exert any force to close the lid.

The adjustment most often needed is to ensure that the spirit-level on the vernier plate is perpendicular to the vertical axis. This is done in the same way as the second adjustment of the level (Para. 9.6). The same warnings apply.

The accuracy of the vertical readings can be checked as for the first adjustment of the level (Para. 9.6), the vernier being set at zero. In the older type, the spirit-level on the T-piece can be adjusted, but in modern instruments all that can usually be done is to note the zero-error; they are, however, very unlikely indeed to go wrong.

Apart from these simple adjustments, it is almost always unwise to attempt to rectify faults in a theodolite, especially in a modern one.

13 The Theodolite: Observation and Booking

13.1 General Remarks; 13.2 Horizontal Angles; 13.3 Vertical Angles; 13.4 Profiles with a Theodolite.

13.1 *General Remarks.* The primary function of a theodolite is to measure angles, both horizontal and vertical. These measurements are much more accurate than most others in the type of survey considered here, and usually, though not always, form the basis for a numerical calculation; the various types of these are discussed in the next Part (V).

There are several different rulings for angle books, but probably the most common is that shown in Figures 13.1 and 14.2. Although this is designed for tacheometry, it can be used equally well for any angular measurements; as will be obvious from the examples, you are not obliged to keep rigidly to the headings as given. Except in one case, I have assumed throughout that the instrument reads to minutes, and that an estimate has been made of tenths. When booking minutes or seconds note that a single figure must *always* be preceded by zero, and where appropriate the zero after the decimal point must also be given. Thus 4 minutes exactly should be booked as 04·0, not as 4 or 4·0; if blurred by rain these could be misread. The same convention for degrees (for example, 082° rather than 82°) is good practice, but not essential.

A modern theodolite which has been well looked after will probably be in adjustment, so the procedure described later, designed to detect 'mistakes', is a sufficient precaution. If you suspect that the instrument is not in adjustment, errors can be eliminated by taking readings according to the following programme: 'right face' (rf) means that the vertical circle is on the right of the telescope, 'right twist' (rt), or alternatively 'swing right' means that the instrument is rotated clockwise as viewed from above, while lf and lt have corresponding 'left' meanings. Thus left face left twist (lflt) means that the vertical circle is on the left of the telescope and the instrument is rotated anticlockwise;

when the telescope is turned about its horizontal axis so that the vertical circle moves from one side to the other, the instrument is said to have 'changed face'. If four sets of readings are taken (rfrt, rflt, lfrt, and lflt), averaging the resulting angles will eliminate errors caused by slight maladjustment of the spirit levels and slight slackness of the supports. Even if you feel confident that the instrument is in adjustment you should do a full run of this kind occasionally as a check, and see whether there is any appreciable difference in the resulting angles. It is particularly desirable to 'change face' when you are taking vertical angles, for those depend on the vernier arm or its equivalent being truly horizontal. The change in 'twist' is usually less important.

13.2 *Horizontal Angles.* Many applications of the theodolite require horizontal angles only. The station at which the instrument is set up must obviously be noted, and it is sometimes useful to record bad weather conditions, as a guide to the reliability of the readings.

Three precautions should be invariable:

(a) A run of readings should *always* start and finish on the same point, for it is very easy indeed to move the wrong tangent screw. If the final reading does not check to sufficient accuracy (say less than 01 minute), the whole run should be disregarded and repeated.

(b) The run should start at some random reading; for if the first figure is near a simple value such as 0° or 90°, there is a tendency to book it at exactly that. Moreover, such a figure is easy to remember, so if a mistake has been made it is likely to be repeated at the end of the run.

(c) All runs should be taken at least twice, starting with different random angles.

Figure 13.1 exemplifies a round of bookings, and shows how a standard tacheometry angle book can be adapted when only angular measurements are needed; almost always, to keep one book for all theodolite and tacheometer observations is preferable to using separate books, even though many of the column headings will often be found to be irrelevant.

If only horizontal angles are being observed (Figure 13.1, top) everything except 'Angles; horiz.' can be crossed out in the first four column headings, giving ample room to book two runs of readings. The first run starts with the reading 319° 07·0' to the spire, and is taken clockwise (right twist), as indicated by the

13.1 Booking Angles

Station ___B___
Height of Instrument ___/___

No. of Point.	Angles Horiz.	Vert.	Reading of Wires	Reading of Axial	Rise	Fall	Reduced Level	Dist.	Horiz. Dist.	Remarks
319°	070'	74°	30·3'✓							SPIRE
105°	24·5'	220°	47·7'	↑						A
135°	258°EST	250°	49·0 EST		3m POLE ① TOP 135° 27·6'	DOWN 27·0' ① ② 250°	51·1' 50·4'			E
230°	10·6'	345°	33·8'							F
319°	06·4'	74°	30·1'							SPIRE

Station ___B___
Height of Instrument ___1·33___

Unless noted, all poles 2m., with 0·1m in ground. All sights to top of pole.

No. of Point.	Angles Horiz.	Vert.	Reading of Wires	Reading of Axial	Rise	Fall	Reduced Level	Dist.	Horiz. Dist.	Remarks
Vernier A	B	A	B							
319°01'00"	07'00"	—	—							SPIRE
105°24'00"	24'30"	88°3d00	30'00"							A
135°26'00"	25'30"	94°05'30"	05'00"							E(3m.)
230°10'30"	11'00"	102°30'30"	3d 30"							F
319°06'30"	06'00"	✓								SPIRE

arrow, closing with 319° 06·4' to the spire again. The second run can be booked in the remaining two columns, and is taken left twist, so the entries start at the bottom.

If horizontal and vertical angles are being taken, 'Angles horiz. and vert.' are kept as headings, and the readings are allowed to overflow into adjacent columns. There is no possibility of confusion. With a vernier theodolite, one vernier is booked in full, giving degrees, minutes, and seconds; only minutes and seconds are booked for the other.

If someone else is booking, he should compare the readings on the second run with those on the first before the observer sights another point. Thus in Figure 13.1 top, suppose that the second reading for A were given as 220° 37·7', then deducting from the reading to E, 250° 49·0' would make the angle ABE 30° 11·3', instead of 01·3' as previously. The booker would then say 'Check'. He would not say what he thought the reading ought to be, for that might cause the observer to repeat the mistake.

It is sometimes useful to take the first reading not to a station but to some permanent landmark, such as a church spire or the gable end of a distinctive building. This is advisable if your station poles are liable to displacement by humans, cattle, or wind. It is also useful if you are going to return for tacheometry, for you can then simply set up at each station in turn without the need to put up poles at the others.

You will often find that the pole on to which you are sighting is not vertical, and that the bottom is invisible. There is no need to go to the pole and reset it plumb. Observe the horizontal reading for the top and (say) halfway down; clearly the corrected reading at the bottom can easily be deduced. Both actual readings should be booked, so that the estimated correction can be checked in the office. An example is given in Figure 13.1, assuming a 3 m pole.

13.3 *Vertical Angles* (Figure 13.1 bottom). These are usually taken either to allow the chain measurements to be corrected for slope or to establish the levels of the stations; tacheometry is discussed below (Chapter 14). They can also be used to find the heights of inaccessible features in buildings.

The method of booking is similar to that for horizontal angles. The measurement involves the assumption that when the reading is 90° (or sometimes 0°) the telescope is horizontal, but quite a small maladjustment can have a considerable effect on the result; so if the levels to be determined are important, the readings should be taken right face and left face.

If all that is required is a correction for slope, measure the height of the horizontal axis above ground level (with the pole which marked the station) and then sight on the same height above ground on the pole at the station being observed. Since you will be making a corresponding observation from that station the final average will be accurate enough for the required purpose.

If more precise values are needed for the levels of the stations, two methods are available. Neither is quite as reliable as normal levelling, and indeed if the time spent in calculations in the office is taken into account theodolite observations show little advantage; but they save time in the field.

The simpler of the two methods is to observe the tops (or a known subdivision) of the poles marking the stations. A record must be made of the total height of each pole and of the length inserted in the ground. Since the distances between stations are known the differences in level can easily be calculated. The average difference found by observations taken in both directions will be accurate enough for subsequent contouring, but is not really precise. The method has the advantage that only one (of the assumed party of two) is needed; the second can be engaged in other work, assuming that the stations are already marked with poles.

Levels of greater precision, good enough for most purposes, can be obtained by sighting on the levelling staff, and recording also the vertical angle. If the height of instrument is also measured carefully observations may be made from every alternate station; but this is not good practice as the risk of an undetected mistake is increased.

The example given in Figure 13.1 bottom assumes the use of an instrument with vernier scales, nominally reading to 30 seconds. Once again, it is convenient to disregard most of the column headings.

13.4 *Profiles with a Theodolite.* Unless special care is taken, levels calculated by measuring vertical angles will be less accurate than those found by levelling; nevertheless they are adequate for most profiles (cf. Paras. 11.2, 26.9).

The theodolite is set up at 'zero' on the line of the profile, usually on the main rampart; its height above ground level is noted. The telescope is set to some convenient vertical angle, which is booked. If aimed at the ground just beyond the far end of the profile, all the necessary readings can often be taken with one setting, but the angle can be changed if desirable. The staff is then held up at suitable points and readings taken. Distances can be measured horizontally, using a tape anchored at zero, or they can be taken from the telescope to the relevant staff reading. An alternative, which makes measurement easier but needs some mental arithmetic, is to take the distance from ground level at zero to a point on the staff corresponding to 'staff reading minus height of instrument'.

The readings can be plotted as measurements down from the line of sight, and the distances can also be marked off directly, either horizontally or along the line of sight; no calculation is needed.

For most defensive earthworks a single setting-up as above is enough; but if the ditches are very deep points can be established on intermediate ramparts and parts of the profile observed from them.

14 Tacheometry

14.1 The Instrument; 14.2 Basic Principles; 14.3 Contouring;
14.4 Booking and Precautions; 14.5 Reducing Readings;
14.6 Plotting.

14.1 *The Instrument.* As usually available, a tacheometer (or tachymeter) is simply a theodolite with 'tacheometric' cross-hairs (Figure 14.1), which can therefore be used in conjunction with an ordinary levelling staff to measure distances. Almost all theodolites now have such cross-hairs, so in colloquial use the terms theodolite and tacheometer are practically interchangeable. The existence of variant types needs to be noted, but they are seldom encountered in archaeological work, so will not be described in detail here. If one should become available, the accompanying instructions must be studied. I have no personal experience of these instruments, apart from a very brief examination of the second type.

In the simplest variant, sighting is to a horizontal staff, instead of to a vertical one. The cost is similar to that for ordinary tacheometric equipment. The advantage is that swaying in the staff has relatively little effect on the readings; the disadvantage is that the ordinary levelling staff cannot be used.

Recently, a very ingenious (and correspondingly expensive) 'self-reducing' theodolite has been devised, in which the cross-hairs move to compensate automatically for the change in vertical angle. The distance is invariably 100 times the intercept between two cross-hairs and the 'rise' or 'fall' is a simple factor such as two or five times another intercept. Work in the field is about twice as fast as with an ordinary tacheometer, and work in the office is greatly reduced.

Finally, although it is not really the same type of instrument, mention must be made of electronic distance measurement. In very oversimplified terms, this can be regarded as a theodolite which measures distances directly, and with great accuracy, either by a form of radar or by interferometry. Such instruments are very expensive indeed, and require some experience in use. They would

121

be of value in establishing a large network, but details would have to be filled in by other methods.

14.2 *Basic Principles* (Figure 14.1). For the ordinary tacheometer, the only one which will be discussed in detail here, the principle is simple. The lines of sight through the upper and lower cross-hairs diverge at one hundredth of a radian, so if the telescope is horizontal the distance from the telescope to the staff is 100 times the intercept on the staff. This is a slight oversimplification, for in some older instruments an additive constant is needed, and very rarely indeed the multiplier is not 100. These quantities can be checked by a few horizontal sights to the staff held at measured distances. The explanation which follows can easily be modified if necessary, but in practice, for this type of work, any additive constant is likely to

14.1 Tacheometry

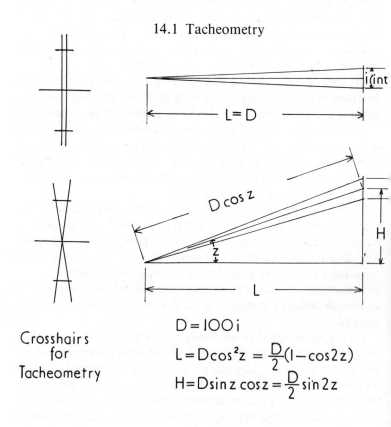

Crosshairs
for
Tacheometry

$$D = 100\,i$$
$$L = D\cos^2 z = \frac{D}{2}(1 - \cos 2z)$$
$$H = D\sin z \cos z = \frac{D}{2}\sin 2z$$

be negligible having regard to the inevitable inaccuracy of the measurements.

The relevant formulae are set out in Figure 14.1. Fortunately, tacheometric slide-rules and tables are available to simplify the calculations. Alternatively, they can be done very quickly with an electronic calculator; a programme is given in Para. 17.2, table 17.1.

For measurement, an ordinary levelling staff is used, but it must be held vertically and should therefore be fitted with a spirit-level. Unfortunately, in practice the staff-man is only able to hold the staff really steady under absolutely ideal conditions; this fact is the major source of inaccuracy in tacheometry, for as will be obvious everything depends on the precision with which the intercept between the upper and lower cross-hairs is known; any movement of the staff between taking those two readings will cause a disproportionate error in the final result. Even under ideal conditions, the distance measurement will usually be rather rough, for one can seldom read the staff to an accuracy of better than about 2 mm. Since there will be that sort of uncertainty in the readings for both upper and lower cross-hairs, the calculated distance may be nearly half a metre wrong.

The most useful application of tacheometry, therefore, is to fix spot levels for contouring. For accessible detail, the method is not only much less accurate than chain surveying but is also much slower. Nevertheless it can be of value in fixing isolated features around the perimeter of a survey, particularly, for example, as when a scatter of isolated huts spreads down a craggy hillside. Preferably in such a case two or more points should be taken on the feature to be recorded, and their distance apart noted by the staff-man. Otherwise, the precautions to be observed are the same as for spot levels.

14.3 *Contouring*. A possible method of contouring with a tacheometer is to keep the telescope horizontal and use it as a level; the distance and direction are fixed tacheometrically. This is considerably slower and less accurate than the alternative method, of marking out the contour with wands which are then located by chain surveying (Para. 11.4).

The real value of a tacheometer appears in dealing with a site, such as a hill-fort, where the variation in level may be considerable. The instrument is used to fix spot levels, and the contours are drawn by interpolation between these. Several hundred spot levels may be needed on a large site.

A survey of this kind will often be based on a trigonometrical network, and the observations will take more than one day. In that case, it will almost always be preferable to complete measurement of the angles for the network first, and to establish the levels of the stations, either by levelling or by measurement of vertical angles. The tacheometric survey of the spot levels is then treated as a separate operation. In what follows it is assumed that this programme is being followed, and that a 'landmark' (which may be another station) has been included among the angular observations. Alternative methods of booking are explained in Para. 14.4.

The instrument is set up over a station, and its height above that level is recorded, as well as the 'name' of the station (Figure 14.2).

The lower plate of the tacheometer is kept locked throughout the work.

A reading is taken to the 'landmark' or to a known and fairly distant station. This, which should be a random angle, is booked. Observations are then taken to the staff (desirable precautions are noted below). The reading to the 'landmark' should invariably be checked before leaving the station, and preferably at intervals during the round of levels. If it has altered appreciably, any observations since the last check will have to be scrapped and repeated.

Each position of the staff is given a number in the angle book. The staff-man also carries a note book, in which he records each number, together with any relevant notes, such as '20 top of scarp', 21E end of line of crags', '22 centre of doorway 1 m wide, of round hut, inner face, wall 0·9 m thick', '23 hut, inner face opposite doorway, 6·3 m to 22', and so on. The observer and staff-man can very easily get out of step, so at least at every tenth spot (for example, 90 in Figure 14.2) the staff-man should shout the number and the observer should confirm that he agrees. If he does not, observations on previous spots must be repeated until the mistake is found and eliminated. This regular check is essential.

Apart from keeping this record, the staff-man has only two responsibilities: to choose the spots so that interpolation will be easy and accurate; and to hold the staff vertical and stationary. This last is very difficult indeed, especially in any sort of wind.

The observer has to record the horizontal and vertical angles and the readings of the three cross-hairs. The angles present no problems, save that it is obviously important that the instrument should be level; otherwise an error is introduced into the vertical angle. In the type of work considered here, an occasional *small* adjustment by the levelling screws is permissible.

The main difficulty arises in reading the cross-hairs, for in practice the staff is almost always in movement, so that you need to observe two four-figure readings simultaneously. I have found the following approach fairly satisfactory, but I do not claim it as ideal. Much depends on how quickly you can read the staff and how many figures you can carry in your head long enough to record them accurately.

Having sighted on the staff, and clamped both the horizontal and the vertical scales, I try to read the *decimal* parts against the upper and lower cross-hairs to three decimal places, neglecting the whole metres. When I am satisfied that I have, in effect, got both readings simultaneously, I book them. Then I book the whole-metre readings for all three cross-hairs. I look again and verify whether the *intercept* between the upper and lower readings agrees with what I have recorded (the actual readings will almost certainly have altered). If that is correct, I read the decimals for the upper and *middle* cross-hairs; if the upper reading has increased by (say) 0·013 m I reduce the middle reading by that amount, and book it. If it is a particularly important point I may make a further check, by reading again the last two decimal places for all three cross-hairs, to make sure that the new readings all differ from those booked by the same amount; but usually I am content with the final, *essential*, check that the average of the two outer readings equals the reading against the central cross-hairs. Provided this check is satisfactory, I then signal to the staff-man to move to the next spot. While he is doing so, I read and book the horizontal and vertical angles, being particularly careful not to move the telescope before doing this. All this is not, in fact, anything like as laborious as it sounds.

14.4 *Booking and Precautions.* The columns in most angle books provide for recording as in Figure 14.2 top. I prefer to allow more space by putting the number of point in the 'remarks' column and using the 'rise' column to book one of the outer cross-hairs readings (Figure 14.2 bottom). No risk of confusion is caused.

As noted above, sights should be made occasionally to the starting station or landmark, as time permits, and this reading must

14.2 Booking for Tacheometry

Station __B__　Level 292.63 OD
Height of Instrument __1.28(GL)__ = 293.91 OD

No. of Point.	Angles Horiz.	Vert.	Reading of Wires	Reading of Axial	Rise	Fall	Reduced Level	Dist.	Horiz. Dist.	Remar
SPIRE	319°07'	—	—							
88	197°16'	74°30'	3.352 / 1.274	2.314	5351	—	345.11	207.8	192.86	
89	148°13'	110°40'	3.160 / 2.119	2.638	—	3438	256.90	104.1	91.13	
90✓	135°25'	98°35'	1.935 / 0.240	1.087	—	2501	267.81	169.5	165.72	
91	113°28'	88°45'	1.881 / 0.105	0.994	1922	—	312.14	177.6	175.50	
92	111°35'	90°00'	2.702 / 1.465	2.083	0	0	291.83	123.7	123.70	
SPIRE	319°06'	—	—							

Station __B__　　Level 292.63 OD
Height of Instrument __1.28(GL)__ = 293.91 OD

No. of Point.	Angles Horiz.	Vert.	Reading of Wires	Reading of Axial	Rise	Rise Fall	Reduced Level	Dist.	Horiz. Dist.	Remar Point
319°	07'	—	—							SPIR
197°	16'	74°30'	3.352	2.314	1.274	R 53.51	345.11	207.8	192.96	88
148°	13'	110°40'	3.160	2.638	2.119	F 34.38	256.90	104.1	91.13	89
135°	25'	98°35'	1.935	1.087	0.240	F 25.01	267.81	169.5	165.72	90✓
113°	28'	83°45'	1.881	0.994	0.105	R 19.22	312.14	177.6	175.50	91
111°	35'	90°00'	2.702	2.083	1.465	L	291.83	123.7	123.70	92
319°	06'✓									SPIR

always be checked at the end of a round of observations. The spirit-levels should also be checked fairly frequently.

When taking spot levels, to diminish the large errors arising from the uncertainty of distance measurements, you should try to get the line of sight roughly parallel to the ground surface. Also, keep in mind that the effect of sway in the staff is less when the readings are low, and that it is easier for the staff-man to hold the staff steady if he is only using two sections instead of three. If readings near the top of the staff cannot be avoided, a useful check is to take two (or better three) sets of readings, with different vertical angles. As a special case, if the staff is not too far away, it is almost always worth while to have the telescope horizontal if possible, for it greatly decreases the subsequent work of reducing the observations.

On the outskirts of the survey, especially if these include a steep hillside, contouring can often be extended accurately enough if the staff-man measures the slope with a fairly accurate clinometer, and records it against the relevant point number in his notes.

14.5 *Reducing Readings.* Unless a suitable electronic calculator is available, the first step in reducing the readings is to fill in the 'Distance' column. This is simply 100 times the difference in readings between the outer cross-hairs. Then, if you have used up the Rise column for one of the readings, write R or F as appropriate down the edge of the Fall column. If, for example, 90° on the vertical circle is 'horizontal', angles less than 90° correspond to 'R', and similarly those over 90° to 'F'. This is the rise or fall relative to the telescope, not as in levelling relative to the previous point.

Calculation of the horizontal distance and of the rise or fall is facilitated by using either 'tacheometric tables', or a tacheometric slide-rule, which may either be the normal ruler type or circular. The slide-rules are almost always accurate enough, and are much quicker to use than the tables. Tables and slide-rules are always accompanied by instructions, so there is no need to describe them here.

Rarely, usually if the vertical angle is approaching 40° or more, the formula has to be used. The necessary calculations are described in Para. 17.2.

Having filled in the rise or fall, the reduced level is given by height of instrument above datum minus the axial reading plus rise (or minus fall).

If an electronic calculator is available all the calculations can be done as quickly as with a slide-rule, and more accurately (Para. 17.2).

14.6 *Plotting.* This can almost always be done using a 25 or 30 cm diameter circular protractor, and a scale. The protractor is placed so that the appropriate reading lies on the line joining the station to the 'landmark' or starter station, and the angles corresponding to the points are marked and numbered. The positions of the various spot levels can then be scaled off. The corresponding level should be marked against each spot.

Contours are filled in by interpolation, either by eye (if no great

14.3 Contouring with Spot Levels

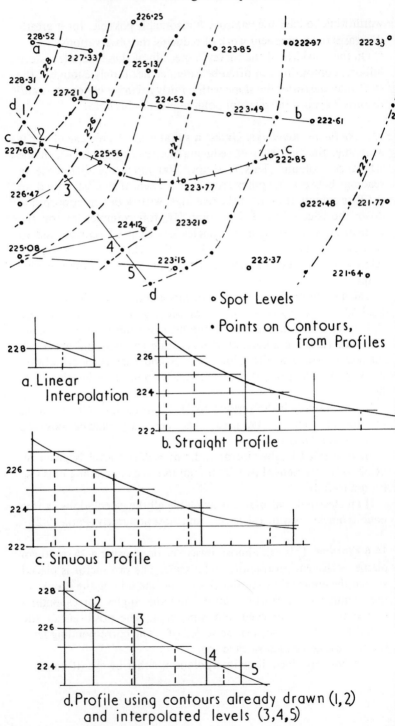

○ Spot Levels

• Points on Contours, from Profiles

a. Linear Interpolation

b. Straight Profile

c. Sinuous Profile

d. Profile using contours already drawn (1,2) and interpolated levels (3,4,5)

accuracy is needed), by slide-rule, or by sketching profiles on squared paper. The last is probably the simplest method; note that a contour which has already been drawn can be used in sketching the profile, also that a profile can be drawn following a gently sinuous line in plan; in this last case, measurements must be taken step by step along the curve. Examples are given in Figure 14.3.

Although rather more work is involved, you will probably find it best to complete one contour at a time. This avoids the risk of straying on to the wrong line of dots. Also, if there is much detail on the main plan, confusion can be avoided by plotting the spot levels and resulting contours on a separate sheet, the two plans being combined in the final tracing.

Except on very large-scale plans, as for example of a burial-mound, it is probably better to reserve contours to represent the form of the natural ground surface, using a convention such as hachuring or stippling to indicate artificial structures; but there is no general rule about this.

15 Setting Out a Rectangle

15.1 *General Remarks*. Many excavators now use a rectangular co-ordinate system as a basis for their records. Although a theodolite is not absolutely essential (see Para. 7.5), it greatly simplifies setting out the necessary frame. One minute of arc corresponds to 3 parts in 10,000, and if used with care a theodolite, reading direct to one minute, can give an accuracy of 1 in 10,000 without much trouble. To get the same accuracy in linear measurement is laborious, so the first thing to decide is what sort of precision you need. Working over smooth ground cleared of irregularities, taking levels at every change of slope, and averaging at least two measurements, the accuracy of ordinary chaining can be raised to about 1 in 1,000, assuming of course that the chain itself is accurate. With a steel tape under similar conditions, and using pegs as described below but driven flush with the ground, this can be improved to about 1 in 5,000. If that is not good enough, the measurements must be made 'in catenary', that is with the tape raised free of ground and its irregularities.

This method is described in detail below. It is not quite as laborious as it sounds, but is obviously to be avoided if lesser accuracy is acceptable. If measurement in catenary is replaced by measurement along the ground the necessary modifications are obvious. For really precise work corrections would also be needed to allow for comparison with a standard tape, height above sea level, the stretch of the tape under tension, and its temperature; but the corrections for sag and slope are adequate to give 1 in 10,000 accuracy.

15.2 *Equipment and Materials.* For measurement of angles and slopes, the theodolite and the levelling staff are necessary. The level is useful, but not essential.

For linear measurement, a *50 m steel band*, graduated throughout in millimetres, is to be preferred (not a studded band chain, which is not closely graduated). One of 100 m is rather inconveniently long, but a 30 m steel tape can be used. This band should be reserved exclusively for accurate work. To accompany this, you will need a *tension handle* reading to 10 kg, and a *roller grip* which allows a handle to be attached at any point on the band.

If not measuring in catenary the tension handle and the roller grip are not necessary, but the band should be of heavier section.

Other equipment required is a heavy hammer to drive pegs, and a light claw-hammer to drive and extract nails. A pair of pliers is also useful.

Another very useful accessory is a builder's level, sometimes called a bricklayer's level or simply a long spirit-level. This is essentially a solidly made straight-edge about a metre long, fitted with spirit-levels so that it can be held either horizontal or vertical. It should be painted along *one angle only* with alternate red (or black) and white strips on the broad face and contrasting strips on the adjacent narrow face; this is far easier than a plumb-line to sight on and to manipulate. It is not mentioned specifically in what follows, but should be used for any distant sight and wherever a measurement needs to be plumbed upwards or downwards.

Finally, an ample supply is needed of properly made pegs of about 5 cm square and 40 cm long, also some 3 or 4 cm (1½ inch) nails.

If not working in catenary, the pegs should be shorter, so that they can be driven flush with the ground surface.

Most of the necessary corrections can be worked out longhand, but time will be saved if a table of logarithms or (preferably) an electronic calculator is available on site.

15.3 *Corrections.* The expressions for these are given in Appendix IV. Assuming that a high degree of accuracy is desired, exact or closely approximate formulae should be used. The correction for slope needs no further discussion. That for sag is probably best determined in the field, though it can be worked out provided the weight of the band per metre is known, as well as the applied tension. Once found it does not alter, provided the tension is kept the same.

As part of your preparation for measurement you have pegs nos. 2, 3, and 4, say, equally spaced at 24·9 m (see Para. 15.4); the level of the top of peg 3 is the mean of those for pegs 2 and 4. Preferably they should all be at the same level, but this is not essential. Temporary pegs are driven nearly to ground level midway between 2 and 3, and between 3 and 4, and levels taken on them.

One end of the steel band is anchored on the nail on peg 2 (do not use peg 0); the other end passes over the top of peg 4, and the middle over peg 3. The same tension is applied as will be used when measuring the line (probably 5 or 10 kg), and the sags are found by measuring up from the intermediate temporary pegs. Then the correction in each half length is $\frac{8}{3} \times$ (Sag)^2 ÷ length; for a numerical example see Para. 15.5. Note that if the tension or length is altered, the correction will vary inversely as the tension, or directly as the cube of the length.

In this work the nails on the pegs should not normally be used as anchorages, for the pull may displace the pegs. The sag correction should therefore be determined before the main measurement is started. It is for this reason, also, that peg 0 is not used in determining this correction.

15.4 *Setting out.* Whether or not you are aiming at a high degree of precision, the corner points should be established first, the intermediate pegs being put in later.

To fix our ideas, suppose that a rectangle ABCD 300 × 200 m is to be marked out, using a graduated 50 m steel band; in practice the area is usually likely to be much less, but the principles remain the same. Initially, you have one corner (A) fixed, and the direction of one side AB; the corner A is marked by a nail driven into the top of a peg.

Having set up the theodolite over A and sighted along AB with the horizontal angle reading zero, pegs must be driven at intervals of about 24·95 m along this line; the *exact* distances are not at this stage crucial, but they should be kept nearly equal. For convenience call these pegs 1, 2, etc, the corner A being at peg 0 and peg 12 being about a metre short of the required position of B.

The even numbered pegs are lined in and then driven firmly into the ground leaving 20 or 30 cm standing above the surface. Note that, because the image in the telescope is inverted, if you want the image of the peg to move to the right you must signal for the peg to be moved to the left. Note also that if the peg starts to lean sideways while being driven it must be corrected by *hitting the earth close to the base of the peg* (perhaps with a stone rammed in to give extra effect). The peg itself should never be knocked sideways, as this loosens it. Having got a peg in line, a nail is lined in and driven into the top, thus marking the alignment; enough should be left projecting to allow it to be withdrawn, for these pegs can be reused. The odd numbered pegs are lined in, but are only driven in lightly at this stage; their function, as will be seen, is merely to reduce the correction for sag. In windy weather, additional pegs may be useful to help keep the tape on line, but such conditions should be avoided if possible.

Levels are taken on the even numbered pegs, and the odd numbered pegs are driven down so that when the staff is held on (say) peg 3 the reading is the average of that for pegs 2 and 4. The theodolite can be used for this, and may if convenient be set to some definite vertical angle.

Measurements are made between the nails on the even pegs, with the steel tape under some definite tension (say 5 kg) and passing over the top of the intermediate odd peg (two nails in its top may serve as a guide). *No attempt is made to get either end of the tape to read zero against the nail*, but readings on the tape are taken simultaneously at each end, and recorded. Three sets of such readings should be taken, or more if these do not all agree.

If measurement is being made along the ground, only the even numbered pegs are used, and they are driven flush with the ground. There is of course no correction for sag.

The distance from A (peg 0) to peg 12 must now be worked out (see Para. 15.5); the difference between this and the total distance (300 m) gives the remaining length to the corner peg B. That peg is carefully lined in with the theodolite, and driven at the appropriate measurement from peg 12. Mark three points in line on the top, and then mark three others at the right distance from peg 12. A nail is driven where these two lines cross. This method is easier than trying to measure and line in at the same time, and is rather more accurate. If peg 12 has been driven flush, but the station peg is to project above ground level, the builder's level may be used for plumbing.

To fix AD, the horizontal angle is set at zero (with the theodolite still at A), and using the lower plate adjustment the telescope is sighted on B. Keeping the lower plate clamped, the angle is turned to 90° (or 270°) and a peg driven on that line a little beyond the intended position of D. The top is then marked. The telescope is transited (turned through about 180° vertical angle) so as to 'change face', and the procedure is repeated. Provided the two marked lines on the peg are almost coincident, their average is accepted as giving the required line for AD, which can then be marked out and measured.

The theodolite is then moved to B, and BC is set out; and finally, with the instrument at C or D, line CD is marked out.

Assuming the distance CD proves correct, the accuracy of the setting out can be fairly safely accepted. Nevertheless, if any doubt is felt, all angles can be remeasured and the whole rectangle worked out as a quadrilateral (Para. 20.2). If this shows that the corner pegs are not quite correctly placed, the procedure for moving them (described in Para. 15.7) should be followed.

15.5 *Examples of Measurement.* To illustrate the procedure, a numerical example for measuring a 200 m line is given:

Line AD. Required length 200 m.

Tape 50 m steel band.

Pegs at average spacing of 24·95 m.

Sag under 5 kg, with 24·95 m span,
                  found to be 0·11 m whence

Sag correction (per 24·95 m) $= 8 \times (0{\cdot}11)^2 \div (3 \times 24{\cdot}95)$
                                 $= 0{\cdot}0013$ m
         or for 50 m tape $= 0{\cdot}0026$ m

Theodolite set at 88° vertical angle (2° elevation) giving a rise of $49{\cdot}9 \times \sin 2° = 1{\cdot}742$ m in each 49·9 m length.

The correction is then worked out as below. Since the differences in level are relatively small, the formula $h^2/2L$ gives results which are never more than a tenth of a millimetre wrong.

Peg	Staff Reading	Rise or Fall relative to Line of Sight	Rise of Line of Sight	Total Rise	Correction for 49·9 m.
0	1·321				
		0·018 R	1·742	1·760	0·031
2	1·303				
		0·243 R	1·742	1·985	0·039
4	1·060				
		0·076 R	1·742	1·818	0·033
6	0·984				
		0·772 R	1·742	2·514	0·063
8	0·212				

For each 50 m span three pairs of measurements (in mm) are taken from the ends of the band; in span 2 to 4 one pair was found to be apparently inconsistent with the other two, so a fourth pair was measured, and the doubtful pair (marked XX) rejected.

Peg 0	62	48	45		
Peg 2	34	45	51		
Total	96	93	96		Average: 95
Peg 2	52	61	51	50	
Peg 4	51	49	50	52	
Total	103	X110X	101	102	Average: 102
Peg 4	43	40	43		
Peg 6	41	42	43		
Total	84	82	86		Average: 84
Peg 6	77	29	53		
Peg 8	74	121	96		
Total	151	150	149		Average: 150

All corrections are then deducted from 50 metres.

Peg	End readings	Sag	Slope	Corrected Span	Cumulative Distance
0					0
2	0·095	0·003	0·031	49·871	49·871
4	0·102	0·003	0·039	49·856	99·727
6	0·084	0·003	0·033	49·880	149·607
8	0·150	0·003	0·063	49·784	119·391

Peg D, therefore, should be 0·609 m from peg 8.

The nails on the intermediate pegs 2, 4, and 6 are at 49·871, 99·727, and 149·607 m from A, so the intermediate 10 m pegs can be set out by measurement from them, using the theodolite for alignment. Finally, all the odd and even pegs are removed to avoid confusion.

15.6 *Detached Base Lines.* Suppose that the corner A of a rectangle has been fixed, and the directions of the sides AB, AD, but that the ground is too irregular for accurate linear measurement; points b and d, however, can be set out on those lines and close to the required points. It is often possible to set out a base XY near by on ground which does allow measurement to be made precisely. The points A, b, and d can then be connected to this base by a careful theodolite triangulation from which the lengths Ab, Ad can be worked out. B and D can then be fixed by short measurements, as in the last section. A pair of transfer pegs (Para. 15.7) can be driven on the line BC, using the theodolite set up at B to establish the direction; and a pair can be set out similarly on the line DC. The intersection of the two lines gives the point C.

Two possible arrangements out of many are indicated in Figure 15.1. In one, the network can be solved as a polygon centred on A (Para. 20.2); the directions Xb and Yd would be observed but would not be utilised in the calculations, though they might serve later as checks. Alternatively this network could be solved as two quadrilaterals XYbA, AYbD (Para. 20.6). Similarly, the other example can be treated as two quadrilaterals AXYd, AXbY; provided the angular measurements were made carefully, there should be no appreciable difference between the two calculated lengths found for AY.

15.1 Detached Base Lines

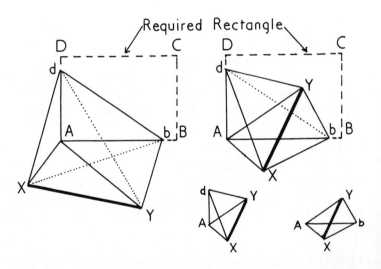

There are a great many other possible arrangements of this kind, and there is no need to list them all. For example, a single side AB could be the measured base.

A detached base line for measurement may be useful even where maximum precision is not needed, and indeed on very rough ground where measurement is difficult an ordinary chain-and-theodolite survey may be made more accurate by deducing all main measurements from a single carefully chained base.

15.7 *Transfer Pegs.* The correct and approximate positions for a station may be so near each other that the new peg cannot be driven without disturbing the old; or you may wish to dig round a correctly placed peg so as to embed it in concrete. Transfer pegs are used in those circumstances. These are merely four pegs preferably in a cruciform arrangement, driven at a safe distance from the peg to be disturbed; and marked with nails, so that string lines joining opposite pairs of nails cross at the mark which has to be displaced. The exact position can thus easily be recovered after disturbance.

Alternatively, two pegs on opposite sides of the mark can be used, their distances to the mark being recorded.

After use the transfer pegs are removed, to avoid confusion.

Part V
NUMERICAL AND
SEMI-GRAPHICAL METHODS

16 Introduction and Basic Formulae

16.1 *Introduction.* Few printed pages are drearier than those which set out long numerical calculations, and since at least nine sites out of ten can be easily and accurately surveyed using only the very simplest geometry you may, with luck, never need to refer to this Part at all. Nevertheless, provided that you do not allow them to frighten you, numerical methods can often save time and labour, and there are a few structures which would be very laborious to survey without using them.

I have therefore given an example of every problem which is likely to arise in practice; where two or more methods are available, that which seems simplest has been chosen. I suggest that you should skim through this section, so that you are aware of its contents; but do not try to struggle through the numerical work. If you are faced with a particular problem, first work through the relevant example so that you understand what you are doing, and then apply exactly the same procedure to your own data. Do not allow the appearance of these calculations to discourage you; taken step by step you will find that they are quite simple.

16.2 *Arrangement.* Survey calculations are based on a very few trigonometrical formulae. These, accompanied by numerical examples, are set out in this chapter, after the introductory material. The next gives a miscellaneous collection of methods which are sometimes useful. Chapter 18 deals with problems which can arise when plotting the results, or subsequently. Finally, because of their importance, the solutions of traverses and of triangulated networks are treated separately in Chapters 19 and 20.

Six-figure logarithms are used, with positive characteristics; that is, 10 is added to log sin, log cos, etc, so that for example 9 appears before the decimal point instead of $\overline{1}$. No confusion can arise. For small sites five figures may be just adequate, but four-figure tables are not.

Save for a few obvious exceptions, all calculations are based on the network described in Appendix III. This will help in understanding how 'errors' and methods of 'balancing' affect the final results.

16.3 *Electronic Calculators*. For brevity, these are often called 'hand calculators'. The invention of these semi-magical devices has enormously simplified all types of surveying calculations. New and more versatile types are constantly being developed, so only general advice can be given here. The following facilities are desirable:

Seven- or eight-figure display.

Normal notation, with Scientific Notation available if needed; for example $131 \cdot 22$ and $0 \cdot 0043$ are 'Normal', $1 \cdot 3122 + 02$ and $4 \cdot 3 - 03$ are in 'Scientific Notation'.

Trigonometrical and Inverse Trigonometric functions.

Two memories at least. Four would sometimes be useful, but if you have too many you may forget what is stored in them.

Polar conversions are not essential, but are very well worth having, and can save a lot of time in some calculations. Several examples of their application are therefore given.

Finally, you will almost certainly find a calculator using algebraic notation preferable; it is indicated by the presence of an = key, and entries are mostly made as you would write them. The alternative, Reversed Polish notation (with a key marked ENT) is likely to be confusing unless you have been educated in its use.

Unfortunately, calculators have not yet evolved a standard key pattern, and their great variety and rapid development make it impossible to give programmes for all types. I have therefore not attempted to generalise the notation, but have kept to that of one calculator. The explanations which follow should enable you to translate the programmes to suit another calculator, if studied in conjunction with its instruction manual.

In the calculator used here, most of the keys will perform two alternative operations, one of which is given directly and the other by first pressing the F. key. For example, one key is marked x^2 in black, and has above it (in green) the symbol $\sqrt{x}$. Suppose we are operating on the number 16; then if the programme reads Figures x^2. the result will be 256, whereas if it reads Figures $F.\sqrt{x}$. the result will be 4.

The F. key is used here to obtain inverse trigonometrical functions; thus entering 0·5 followed by F. $\sin^{-1}$. will give 30 (degrees). Some calculators would use an Inv. key followed by the sin. key; others have a separate key for arc.sin.

There are also several different ways of referring to Memories. That used here has STO1 and RCL1, implying STOre in memory 1 and ReCalL from memory 1. Once understood, this is easily interpreted into another notation.

Finally, an explanation of Polar Co-ordinates may be useful to those not familiar with them. In these, the position of a point is defined by a radial distance measured from the origin at a stated angle to the x-axis. Thus the co-ordinates $\sqrt{3}$, 1 can also be written as 2, 30°. Using the programmes given, the P. key converts x, y co-ordinates to polars, the R. key Reduces polars to x and y. The potential advantages in survey calculations are obvious, but at least in the calculator used here the (. key must be pressed before any further work is done; otherwise nonsense figures are produced.

For programmes which are in frequent use, the ingenious arrangement devised by A. L. Allan may be useful (Program Cards for the Small Hand Calculator, *Survey Review* XXIV (1978) p. 233). The programme is written out step by step on a circular disc, which is rotated behind a cover with a single 'window' through which each step is seen in turn.

Two warnings must be given. In working through a long programme, the wrong key can very easily be pressed. This is by far the most usual cause of a mistake, but very occasionally (and very disconcertingly) the hypothetical little green men who operate within the device may go mad and start producing nonsense results. The course of a calculation, therefore, must be kept under review, with the possibility of a mistake in mind. A useful precaution is to copy down some crucial figures which appear during the course of calculation, even though they are not needed in the final result; this will save you from having to return to the beginning after a mistake.

Two programmes (Paras. 16.8 and 18.4) are explained verbally step by step. These will enable the others to be followed.

Addendum. During the preparation of this book, electronic calculators have fallen considerably in price, and many new models have been developed. In particular, programmable calculators have become relatively inexpensive; but to make really full use of these requires rather higher numerical ability than merely to tap out a programme step by step. Moreover, although in some types the programme can be preserved on a detachable card and is thus always available when needed, in most of the cheaper models it is lost when the calculator is switched off. In the sort of work envisaged here, therefore, the programming facility would probably not be used very often.

16.4 *Definitions*. Calculations are almost always used to find the co-ordinates of stations, which are normally measured East and North relative to some defined axes. For brevity, the co-ordinates of station P can be written E(P), N(P). If the axes chosen are not truly oriented, but are taken relative to 'site north', the risk of confusion is reduced if lower case letters are used, as e(p), n(p) or x(p), y(p).

A line, PQ say, has length and direction. The length can be written as PQ or as L (PQ). The Bearing, Bg (PQ), is measured clockwise from the meridian. It can also be expressed as the Reduced Bearing (RB or RBg), measured the nearest way from the meridian. Thus the bearings 32°, 117°, 206°, and 293° can also be written as N32°E, S63°E, S26°W, and N67°W. Note that the order in which P and Q are written is important. If Bg (PQ) is 109°, or S71°E, Bg (QP), is 289°, or N71°W.

A line can also be specified in terms of the difference between the co-ordinates of its ends. If P is at 120E, 275N, and Q at 360E, 350N, then the 'Easting' of PQ, (EPQ), is 240 and the 'Northing', N(PQ) is 75. Again, the order is important; E(QP) = −240, N(QP) = −75. To avoid negative signs these are usually called Westings and Southings, for example, W(PQ) = 240. Eastings and Westings are also termed 'Departures', Northings and Southings 'latitudes'.

16.5 *Trigonometrical Functions*. Most readers will be insulted by the suggestion that they do not know what follows; but a few may have forgotten these expressions, so they are given here. All refer to a triangle with sides a, b, and c, and the opposite angles A, B, and C; C is a right angle (Figure 16.1).

16.1 Notation of Triangles and Signs of Trigonometric Functions

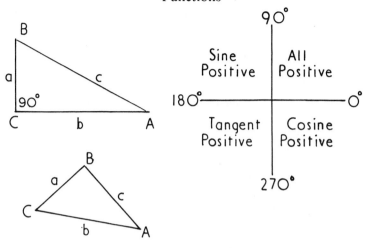

The Theorem of Pythagoras states that:
$$a^2 + b^2 = c^2$$
If a, b, and c are whole numbers, the triangle is called a 'Pythagorean Triangle'. Of these, the '3–4–5' triangle is the simplest, and is of considerable use in surveying.

The trigonometrical functions are:

sine A = a/c; cosine A = b/c; and tangent A = a/b.

These are abbreviated to sin A, cos A, and tan A; their reciprocals (cosecant, secant, and cotangent) will not be used.

The inverse functions can be written either as $\sin^{-1}$, $\cos^{-1}$, $\tan^{-1}$, as inv sin, or as arc sin, etc.

$$\text{inv sin (a/c) or } \sin^{-1}(a/c) = A$$
$$\cos^{-1}(b/c) = A$$
$$\text{and } \tan^{-1}(a/b) = A.$$

The signs of the functions are important. In the first quadrant, with A between 0° and 90°, all are positive. Between 90° and 180° only the sine is positive, 180° to 270° only the tangent, and 270° to 360° only the cosine. A useful nonsense–mnemonic which I learnt at school is '*s*ome *t*all *c*aterpillars'.

16.6 *Trigonometrical Formulae.* The following are sufficient to solve all surveying problems. The notation is the same as above, but C is not necessarily 90° (Figure 16.1).

The most useful is the sine formula

$$\frac{a}{\sin A} = \frac{b}{\sin B} = \frac{c}{\sin C} \tag{16.6.1}$$

Angles can be found from

$$a^2 = b^2 + c^2 - 2bc \cos A \tag{16.6.2}$$

which is useful when using a hand calculator; but if using logarithms,

$$\tan \frac{A}{2} = \sqrt{\frac{(s\text{-}b)\,(s\text{-}c)}{s\,(s\text{-}a)}} = \frac{r}{s\text{-}a} \tag{16.6.3}$$

where $r = \sqrt{\dfrac{(s\text{-}a)(s\text{-}b)(s\text{-}c)}{s}}$

and $s = (a + b + c) \div 2$

This is preferable to the alternatives $\sin \dfrac{A}{2} = \sqrt{\dfrac{(s\text{-}b)(s\text{-}c)}{bc}}$

and $\cos \dfrac{A}{2} = \sqrt{\dfrac{s(s\text{-}a)}{bc}}$

for all three angles can be found using the same four logarithms.

Calculations using these formulae are the elements which are combined to give the solutions of surveying problems. Examples follow.

16.7 *Conversion of Minutes and Seconds to Decimals of a Degree.*
Most hand calculators require angles to be entered in degrees and decimals. Usually, to convert all the angles as a single operation is quicker than doing each as required. The programme is simple. Enter 60 and transfer it to STO 1. Enter seconds, and press keys ÷, RCL 1, +. Then enter minutes and press ÷, RCL 1, =. The result gives the minutes and seconds in decimals of a degree. The 60 is retained in STO 1 until all the angles have been converted.

The calculator gives results to eight figures, but unless you are working to exceptional accuracy there is no need to go beyond the fourth decimal place, for $0 \cdot 0001°$ corresponds to $03 \cdot 6$ seconds, less than 00.1 minutes. Similarly, in linear quantities, the third decimal place, corresponding to 1 mm, is accurate enough. In long calculations, where errors may build up, another decimal place may sometimes be worth while, for there is then no need to worry about discrepancies in the last figure. Sometimes, if one number in a sequence of calculations is small, it should not be abbreviated, for the *proportional* effect of cutting off the last few decimal places may be unacceptably large; but this difficulty ought not to arise in a properly planned survey.

In all examples which follow, where the hand calculator is used, the angles are assumed to have been already converted to degrees and decimals of a degree.

16.8 *Co-ordinates, given Length and Bearing of a Line.* The formulae used are

E(AF) = AF sin Bg(AF)

N(AF) = AF cos Bg(AF)

The calculations are arranged as table 16.1, the necessary information being noted first, after which the logarithms are copied down, and the necessary arithmetic follows. The apparently unconventional arrangement saves writing down the log of the length twice, which is a worth-while saving if a lot of calculations have to be made.

With the calculator, the R key is used, which reduces polar co-ordinates to Cartesians. With polar co-ordinates, the angle is measured from the x-axis, and the R key gives x first, so we shall get the northing first. The procedure will be described in detail, since it illustrates clearly how the calculator is used; but the description takes much longer than the calculation.

As in any such calculation, the work can best be arranged in columns. That on the left sets out the programme, which is the same for any calculation of this kind. The others are specific to this particular problem, the second giving the data, the third the results, and the fourth the significance of the various quantities.

For any given problem the first and fourth columns are written out; the modification needed if one were dealing with a line PQ instead of AF is obvious. Then the data are entered, AF = 160·12 m, Bg (AF) = 150·6017°, and so on. Note that there is no need to work out the reduced bearing.

'Figs' in the Programme column indicates that the data are to be keyed in, 160·12 in this case. The F and x/y keys transfer this to the invisible y register. The bearing, 150·6017, is then keyed in.

Pressing the R key gives, directly, the x-co-ordinate of the Polars, which in this case is the Northing of AF, − 139·501; there is no need to record this, but it may be useful as a check.

Table 16.1 Co-ordinates Given Length and Bearing

```
Data: Length of AF  160·12 metres.
      Bearing  150° 36·1'  (150·6017°)
             = S 29° 23·9' E
      Coordinates of A: 169·10 E; 779·25 N.
Required: Coordinates of F.
```

(a) <u>Solution using logarithms.</u>

			E(A)	169·100
	1·895 420 whence		E(AF)	78·600
log sin 29° 23·9'	9·690 974		E(F)	247·700
log 160·12	2·204 446			
log cos 29° 23·9'	9·940 132		N(A)	779·250
	2·144 578 whence		N(·AF)	-139·501
			N(F)	639·749

(b) <u>Solution using calculator.</u>

Programme	Data	Results	Notes
Figs.	160·12		AF
F. x/y.			
Figs.	150·6017		Bg.(AF)
R.		(-139·501)	N(AF)
(. +.			
Figs.	779·25		N(A)
).		639·749	N(F)
F. x/y		(78·599)	E(AF)
(. +.			
Figs.	169·1		E(A)
).		247·699	E(F)

Care is now necessary. If you try to add the north co-ordinate of A directly, you get a mysterious and meaningless number, so it is essential to use the (.key. Indeed, whenever you are doing any supplementary calculations on the results obtained with either the R or P key, the brackets should always be used. So the sequence is (, +, then key in the figures for N(A), and then). This gives the Northing for point F (which has nothing to do with the F key).

Pressing the F and x/y keys then extracts the y-co-ordinate, that is E (AF), from where it has been lurking in the y-register, and the same procedure as before gives E(F).

16.9 *Length and Bearing, Given Co-ordinates* (Table 16.2). This, the converse of the previous calculation, is used less often. The P

Table 16.2 Length and Bearing Given Co-ordinates

```
Data: Coordinates of A: 169·10 E, 779·25 N.
      Coordinates of F: 247·70 E, 639·75 N.
Required: Length and Bearing of AF.

(a) Solution using logarithms.
E(F)-E(A)= 78·60 E; log.= 1·895 423
N(F)-N(A)=139·50 S; log.= 2·144 574
  whence log tan (R.Bg)  = 9·750 849

So Reduced Bearing of AF = S 29° 23·9' E
    True Bearing         = 150° 36·1'

The Northing is larger than the Easting;
Log 139·50  =  2·144 574
- log cos R.Bg.9·940 132
So log AF   =  2·204 442   whence AF= 160·119

(b) Solution using calculator.
```

Programme	Data	Results	Notes
Figs.	639·75		N(F)
-.			
Figs.	779·25		N(A)
=. F. x/y.			
(.			
Figs.	247·7		E(F)
-.			
Figs.	169·1		E(A)
).			
P.		160·119	AF
F. x/y.		150·6013	Bg.(AF)

key on the calculator gives the result almost at once, but if logarithms are used the formulae are

$$\tan \text{(reduced bearing)} = \frac{\text{Easting or Westing}}{\text{Northing or Southing}}$$

and Length = either (Easting or Westing)
                          ÷ sin (RBg)
        or   (Northing or Southing)
                          ÷ cos (RBg)

Provided that the Easting and Northing are about the same it does not matter which is used, but if one is appreciably larger that should be taken as basis, for the *proportionate* error will be smaller. If only the length is needed, to add the squares and take the square root of the total (Pythagoras) is perhaps a little quicker, if the necessary tables are to hand.

With the calculator, the P key converts (x,y) co-ordinates to Polars. The only points to note are that the north co-ordinates must be dealt with first, and as previously a nonsense result is obtained unless the (. and). keys are used.

Table 16.3 Triangle with All Three Sides given

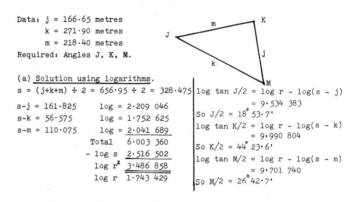

Data: j = 166·65 metres
k = 271·90 metres
m = 218·40 metres
Required: Angles J, K, M.

(a) <u>Solution using logarithms.</u>
s = (j+k+m) ÷ 2 = 656·95 ÷ 2 = 328·475

s-j = 161·825	log = 2·209 046	
s-k = 56·575	log = 1·752 625	
s-m = 110·075	log = 2·041 689	
	Total	6·003 360
	- log s	2·516 502
	log r²	3·486 858
	log r	1·743 429

log tan J/2 = log r - log(s - j)
= 9·534 383
So J/2 = 18° 53·7'
log tan K/2 = log r - log(s - k)
= 9·990 804
So K/2 = 44° 23·6'
log tan M/2 = log r - log(s - m)
= 9·701 740
So M/2 = 26° 42·7'

(b) <u>Solution using calculator</u>

Programme	Data	Results	Notes
Figs.	218·4		Side m
÷ . Figs. STO 1.	166·65		Side j
=. F. STO 2		(1·31053)	(m/j in Memory 2)
Figs.	271·9		Side k
÷.RCL 1.=.STO 1.		(1·63156)	(k/j in Memory 1)
x². +. F. RCL 2.			
x². -. 1.			$(k/j)^2 + (m/j)^2 - 1$
÷ . 2. ÷ . RCL 1.			
÷ . F. RCL 2.			÷ 2 (k/j) (m/j)
=. F. cos⁻¹.		37·7902	Angle J
RCL 1. x². +. 1.			$(k/j)^2 + 1 - (m/j)^2$
-. F. RCL 2. x².			
÷ . 2.÷. RCL 1.			÷ 2 (k/j)
=. F. cos⁻¹.		53·4230	Angle M
F. RCL 2 . x². +.			
1. -. RCL 1. x².			$(m/j)^2 + 1 - (k/j)^2$
÷. 2 ÷ . F. RCL 2.			÷ 2 (m/j)
=. F. cos⁻¹.		88·7868	Angle K

16.10 *Solution of Triangle, Three Sides Given* (table 16.3). This problem seldom arises, and is given primarily for completeness. Nevertheless, it can sometimes be used, with a hand calculator, as a quick check in the field, as for example on the central angles in a chained polygon, to see whether they total 360°; but it will not always locate small mistakes.

If logarithms are used, the most convenient formula is (16.6.3).

This is preferable to the sine or cosine formulae of the same type, as only four logarithms are needed to give all three angles.

This formula can also be used with a hand calculator, but unless four memories are available at least two of the quantities involved will have to be written down and re-entered as required; but as the whole calculation takes less than five minutes, this is counterbalanced by the advantage that there is no need to remember a special programme. The formula $\cos A = (b^2 + c^2 - a^2)/2bc$ is only slightly quicker, in that form.

The quickest method, for which a programme is given, is to use the same formula, but rearranged thus:

$$\cos A = \left(\frac{b}{a}\right)^2 + \left(\frac{c}{a}\right)^2 - 1 - 2\left(\frac{b}{a}\right)\left(\frac{c}{a}\right)$$

$$\cos B = \left(\frac{b}{a}\right)^2 + 1 - \left(\frac{c}{a}\right)^2 - 2 \cdot \frac{b}{a}$$

$$\cos C = \left(\frac{c}{a}\right)^2 + 1 - \left(\frac{b}{a}\right)^2 - 2 \cdot \frac{c}{a}$$

This takes about half as long to work out as the first method, so can be useful if the programme is to hand.

In any calculation of this kind, all three angles should be worked independently, and the total checked.

16.11 *Solution of Triangle, Two Sides and One Angle Given* (table 16.4). This problem may take two forms, which require different methods of solution. That considered in this section deals with an angle included between the two given sides. When the angle is not so included, the method is closely similar to that when one side and two angles are given (Para. 16.12) and indeed requires no separate explanation.

Table 16.4 Triangle with Two Sides and Included Angle Given, Using Calculator

Data: j=166·65 metres
      k=271·90 metres
      M= 53·423
Required: Side m.

(a) Programme for Cosine formula.

Programme	Data	Results	Notes
Figs. cos. x. 2. x.	53·423		Angle M
Figs. STO 1. x.	166·65		Side j
Figs. F. STO 2. +/-. +. RCL 1. x^2. +. F.	271·9		Side k
RCL 2. x^2. =. F. $\sqrt{x}$.		218·400	Side m

(b) Programme using Polar keys.

Programme	Data	Results	Notes
Figs. F. x/y.	166·65		Side j
Figs. R. (. -.	53·423	(99·307)	Angle M (gives MX)
Figs.). F. x/y. P. F. x/y	271·9	(-172·593) 218·400 142·2098	Side k (gives JX) Side m External angle at J

With two sides and the included angle, the natural formula to use is (16.6.2)

$$a^2 = b^2 + c^2 - 2bc \cos A$$

The calculations, using logarithms and tables of squares, are obvious, and to set out an example seems unnecessary. Two programmes for a hand calculator are given. The first uses the above formula, altering the order of terms to reduce the number of entries. The second uses the Polar keys; it is slightly shorter, and gives the angles as well as the unknown side, but has the disadvantage that the programme must be at hand for reference.

16.12 *Solution of Triangle, One Side and All Angles Given* (table 16.5). Problems of this type arise very frequently (see for example, Chapter 20, on Polygonal Networks). The formula used is (16.6.1).

$$\frac{a}{\sin A} = \frac{b}{\sin B} = \frac{c}{\sin C}$$

Table 16.5 Triangle with One Side and All Angles Given

```
Data:  j = 166·65 metres.
       J = 37° 47·4'
         = 37·7900°
       K = 88° 47·2'
         = 88·7867°
       M = 53° 25·4'
         = 53·4233°
Required: Sides k and m.
```

(a) <u>Solution using logarithms.</u>

```
                              log k 2·434 411 whence k = 271·901
        log j     - log sin J log sin K  9·999 903
        2·221 805 - 9·787 297     =      2·434 508
                              log sin M  9·904 748
                              log m 2·339 256 whence m = 218·402
```

```
Alternative arrangement:
              log j 2·221 805
            - log sin J 9·787 297
                    2·434 508                    2·434 508
          + log sin K 9·999 903    + log sin M 9·904 748
              log k 2·434 411          log m 2·339 256
            whence k 271·901        whence m 218·402
```

(b) <u>Solution using calculator.</u>

Programme	Data	Results	Notes
Figs. ÷.	166·65		Side j
Figs. sin. =. STO 1. x.	37·79		Angle J (j/sin J stored in memory)
Figs. sin. =. RCL 1. x.	88·7867	271·901	Angle K Side k
Figs. sin. =.	53·4233	21ᶠ·402	Angle M Side m

This is equally applicable to the case where two sides and an angle not included between them are given, as noted earlier; the necessary modifications are obvious.

In the table, two alternative arrangements are given for the calculation with logarithms. The arithmetic is the same in both. The second is slightly longer, but is perhaps easier to follow.

17 Applications, Including Semi-Graphical Methods

17.1 Introduction; 17.2 Tacheometry; 17.3 Satellite Stations; 17.4 Horizontal Angles with Sextant and Clinometer; 17.5 Intersections: Plotting Angles; 17.6 Intersection of Two Rays: Numerical Solution; 17.7 Intersection of Three or More Rays; 17.8 Intersection of Chained Rays; 17.9 Balancing a Chained Quadrilateral; 17.10 Resection: The Three-point Problem.

17.1 *Introduction*. Usually, ingenuity in surveying is misdirected; the more straightforward the observations and calculations, the better will be the results. Nevertheless, there are occasional exceptions to this rule; satellite stations (Para. 17.3) are an example. This chapter assembles a miscellaneous collection of methods which are sometimes valuable as stages in reducing the raw data to information which can be plotted. The semi-graphical approach (Paras. 7–10) is particularly useful.

17.2 *Tacheometry*. The tacheometer has been described in Chapter 14, and the formulae for height and distance were discussed in Para. 14.2, where reference was made to the availability of tacheometric tables and slide-rules. If a hand calculator is available, these can be dispensed with.

In the previous discussion, the vertical angle was measured from horizontal as zero, but most theodolites now measure from vertically upwards as zero, so that 'horizontal' corresponds to 90°. If so, the calculator gives the 'rise' or 'fall' automatically. The appropriate programme is given in table 17.1 (which also gives the full calculation using logarithms).

Necessary preliminaries are that the vertical angles have been expressed as degrees and decimals (as Para. 16.7), and the 'distances' (that is, $100 \times$ the intercepts) have been worked out. At the same time, the middle reading should again be checked to see that it is in fact the average of the other two; if not, the sight should be rejected. The calculator could be used for these calculations, but normally they would be done mentally, for the risk of a mistake in such simple arithmetic is not much greater than that of keying the wrong number. Note that the height of instrument

Table 17.1 Reducing Tacheometric Observation

Data: (extract from fig. 32)   Height of Instrument: 293·91 OD.

Vert. Angle	Cross-hairs			Rise or Fall	R.L.	Dist.	Horiz. Dist.	Point No.
74° 30'	3·352	2·314	1·274	R 53·51	345·11	207·8	192·96	88
110° 40'	3·160	2·638	2·119	F 34·38	256·90	104·1	91·13	89

(a) <u>Full calculation using logarithms</u>.

Dist./2 = 103·9	log	2·016 616		2·016 616
90° - 74° 30' = 15° 30'	log sin 2z	9·711·839	log cos 2z	9·933 066
		1·728 455		1·949·682
	antilogs	53·51		89·06
				+ 103·9 = 192·96
Dist./2 = 52·05	log	1·716 421		1·716 421
110° 40' - 90° = 20° 40'	log sin 2z	9·819 832	log cos 2z	9·875 571
		1·536 253		1·591 992
	antilogs	34·38		39·08
				+ 52·05 = 91·13

In practice, a tacheometric slide-rule will almost always give results of sufficient accuracy.

(b) <u>Using calculator</u>.

Programme	Data	Results	Notes
Figs. F. STO 2. _ _ _	293·91	_ _ _	H. O. I. _ _ _
Figs.	207·8		Dist. (Point 88)
x.			
Figs. STO 1.	74·5		Vert. Angle
sin. x². =.		192·96	Horiz. Dist.
÷. RCL 1. tan. -.			
Figs.	2·314		Axial Reading
+. F. RCL 2. =. _ _ _		345·11	Reduced Level _ _
(programme repeated)			
Figs.	104·1		Dist. (Point 89)
x.			
Figs. STO 1.	110·6667		Vert. Angle
sin. x². =.		91·13	Horiz. Dist.
÷. RCL 1. tan. -.			
Figs.	2·638		Axial Reading
+. F. RCL 2. =.		256·90	Reduced Level

above datum is retained in memory 2 for all calculations at a given station.

After the horizontal distance and level have been found for point 88, the programme is repeated for point 89, and so on as required. The repetitive part is indicated by broken lines. As will be realised, there is no need laboriously to write out the 'programme' and 'Notes' columns over and over again. They can be written on a mask with part cut out, and moved down the page; only the Data,

Results, and Point Number need to be filled in.

17.3 *Satellite Stations.* Sometimes a feature such as the angle of a
building or a telegraph-pole may be located in a good position for a
station. It has the great advantages of being vertical and
permanent, but you cannot set up a theodolite over it.
Nevertheless, at the expense of a little extra office calculation, it
can be used.

The instrument is set up near the station, at a convenient point S
'the satellite station', and observations are taken in the usual way.
The necessary adjustments to give the corresponding angles for
measurements taken from the true stations can be worked out using
the sine formula. The network can then be balanced, treating the
adjusted angles as if they had been observed at the true station.

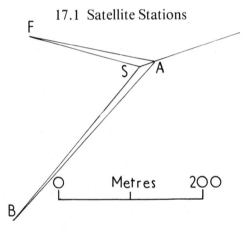

17.1 Satellite Stations

If A and S are the true and satellite stations (Figure 17.1), and
sights are taken to B and F, then angles ABS (added) and AFS
(deducted) are the adjustments needed to the observed readings.
From the sine formula:

$\sin ABS = AS \sin ASB/AB$.

The percentage error in the adjustment is proportional to the
percentage errors in AS and AB, so since the adjustment is
normally small AB can usually be measured from a careful small-
scale plot. AS, of course, must be measured accurately on the site.
This can be done when the theodolite is set up; S need not be
marked by a peg.

The calculations are so simple that there is no need to give a worked example, but the following numerical results will enable you to make sure that you understand the method: AS = 1·16 m, circuit of readings from station S:
B 220° 42'; F 286° 15'; A 72° 14'.
AB = 273 m; AF = 159 m (measured from draft plan).

By subtraction, the angle ASB = 148° 28', so by the sine formula angle ABS = 07·6'; and similarly the angle AFS = 14·0'. So if the readings had been taken from A they would have been:
to B, 220° 49·6'; to F, 286° 01·1'.

The most likely mistake is to add the correction when it should be subtracted, or conversely. The risk is less when a calculator is used, as it automatically gives the right sign, but nevertheless a diagram should always be drawn (as in Figure 17.1) with the length SA exaggerated. If working with logarithms the angles must be reduced to the appropriate values smaller than 90°, in this case 180° − 148° 28' for ASB and 214° 01' − 180° for ASF.

17.4 *Horizontal Angles with Sextant and Clinometer.* The sextant is so seldom used in ordinary surveying that a detailed description would be unjustified. Essentially, one object A is observed directly, the other B via its reflection in a mirror attached to an arm which moves against a graduated arc. When the image of B is brought into coincidence with A, the reading on the arc gives the angle between them. In the box sextant the mirrors are enclosed in a cylindrical box, in the naval sextant (which is capable of greater accuracy) the whole construction is visible.

For surveying, the instrument has two disadvantages. One, minor, is that the angle measured cannot exceed 120° so a complete circuit has to be measured in steps, with intermediate marks. More seriously, the angle measured is the true angle; to obtain the horizontal angle, this must be corrected using observations made with a clinometer.

Nevertheless, even the box sextant can give results to within 05', roughly 1 part in 700, so it is much more accurate than the prismatic compass; and since a sextant is sometimes available when a theodolite is not, the necessary formula for correction is given here (but without a worked example and without detailed explanation).

The standard formula is
cos H = (cos M − sin a sin b)/cos a cos b

where M is the measured angle, a and b the elevations of the two points observed, and H the required horizontal angle.

For a useful range of moderate altitudes, an alignment chart (Figure 17.2) can be used. I have described its construction in *Civil Engineering*, xxxvi no. 420, (June) 1941 pp. 484–90.

To use it, a transparent straight-edge is set to pass through the measured angle and the intersection of the curves corresponding to the elevations or depressions of the two points observed. The straight edge is then tangential to the curve giving the appropriate correction, the point of contact being shown by the radial guidelines. Two examples which will make the use of the diagram clear are indicated by fine lines.

With a measured angle of 56°, and altitudes of the same sign and both equal to 9°, the chart shows the correction as 48' to be added, and the same correction is indicated for altitudes of 15° and 8°, or of 20° and 8·5°; the calculated values, to the nearest minute, are 46', 50', and 49'.

With a measured angle of 70°, and both altitudes 8° but of opposite sign, the correction is found to be 1° 35' to be deducted, which should also apply for 17° and −2°; the calculated value for both is 1° 38'.

It will be evident that determination of horizontal angles with a sextant is laborious, and should be regarded as an emergency procedure, only applicable when not many angles are needed.

17.5 *Intersections: Plotting Angles.* A simple survey involving angular measurements can often be plotted directly without loss of accuracy. Consider as illustration triangle ABF (Figure 17.3) to be drawn to a scale of 1/500. The side AB is given as 273·00 m, and the angles A and B as 55° 11', 35° 14' respectively. A small-scale plot will show that AF and BF are roughly 160 and 220 m. An ordinary protractor, of say 10 cm radius, will not be adequate; for BF (to 1/500) will measure about 44 cm, so that any error is multiplied four times or more.

The method adopted, therefore, is to measure some length BP along BA, set up a perpendicular at P and mark off PQ = BP × tan B. Then QBA is the required angle. In this case a convenient length for BP would be 50 cm, and PQ would then be 50 × tan 35° 14' = 35·31 cm. The length BP is chosen to give a simple multiplier. Clearly any desired degree of accuracy can be attained, at least in principle.

If the angle to be drawn much exceeds 45°, the perpendicular

17.2 Alignment Chart for use with Sextant and Clinometer

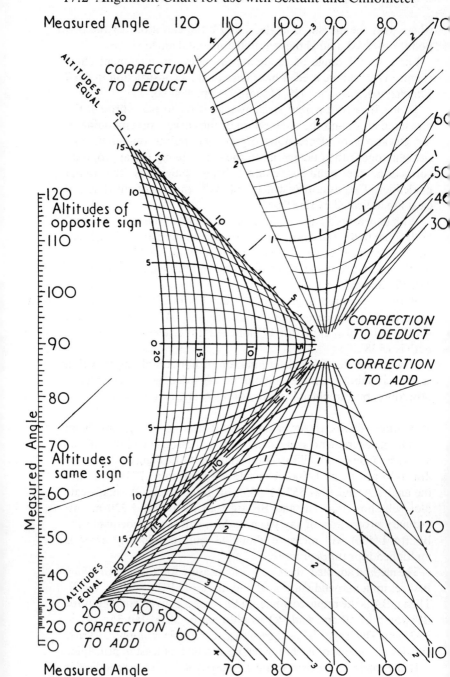

17.3 Plotting Intersection

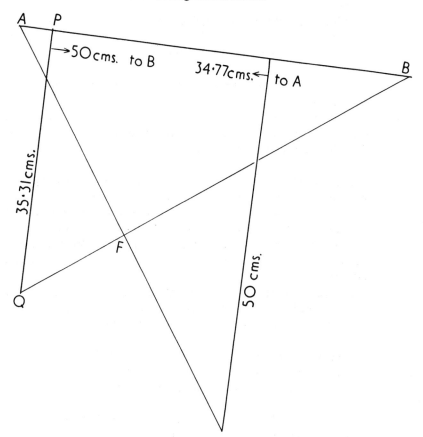

becomes unduly long; for 55° 11' it would be 71·90 cm at 50 cm from A. In such a case, therefore, the length of the perpendicular is chosen, and is divided by the tangent of the angle to find where it should be drawn. In the example, 50 cm divided by tan 55° 11' = 34·77 cm so a 50 cm perpendicular set up at 34·77 cm from A will give the required angle.

Angles drawn in this way should always be checked with a protractor, to detect possible mistakes. The same method is applicable when bearings are given.

17.6 *Intersection of Two Rays: Numerical Solution.* Two rays, which intersect at F, are observed from G and H, and have known bearings. The co-ordinates of F are to be found (see Figure 17.4, neglecting JF).

This is a straightforward application of solutions already given.

(a) If GH and Bg (GH) are not known, they must be worked out as Para. 16.9. The angles G and H in the triangle are then determined.

(b) The sides GF, HF are then found as Para. 16.12; their bearings are known.

(c) Then, as in Para. 16.8, the co-ordinates of C are calculated using line GF. Also, as a check, they are calculated using line HF. This should be invariable practice; a mistake is easy to make.

17.7 *Intersection of Three or More Rays.* Since errors are always present, three rays which should intersect at a point will in fact form a small triangle, so three calculations will need to be made if the previous method is used. If four observations are available, this number will increase to six. The following semi-graphical method offers an easier solution, and as will be seen it has other incidental advantages.

F is to be located using observations from G, H, and J. The 'true' co-ordinates are taken, but the bearings are worked out from the 'measured' angles (Appendix III) so the data are:

G at 114·75E, 622·75N, Bearing GF 82° 42·8'
H at 136·75E, 332·35N, Bearing HF 19° 49·5'
J at 470·00E, 455·00N, Bearing JF 309° 44·3'

These lines are plotted at a small scale (Figure 17.4); as drawn, the scale used was 1/2,500. To save space in reproduction, the two diagrams have been overlapped, so the point H appears close to the larger-scale plot; there would be no need for this economy in practice. This plot shows that F is near 250E, 642N; so a square enclosing that point is examined on a larger scale. The limits 245 to 255E, 635 to 645N seem suitable.

The distance from G to 245E is 130·75 m, and GF has a bearing 82° 42·8'. So the line GF cuts 245E at 130·75 ÷ tan 82° 42·8' + 622·75 (the N coordinate of G). This gives 16·719 + 622·75 = 639·47 m N. Similarly, it cuts 255E at 140·75 ÷ tan 82° 42·8' + 622·75 = 640·75N.

For HF, the line runs nearer N–S than E–W, so the intersections with 635 and 645N are used, giving 302·65 tan 19° 49·5' + 136·75

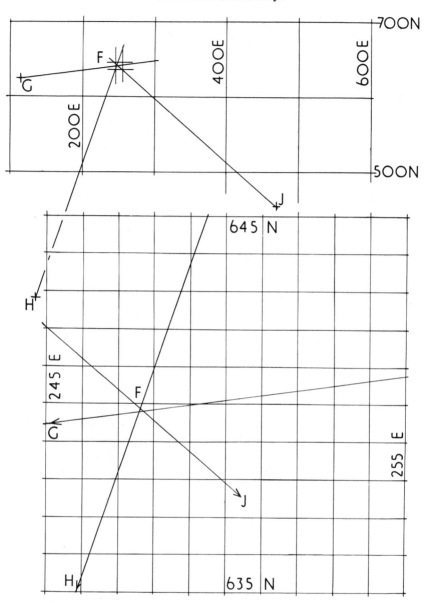

and 312·65 tan 19° 49·5' + 136·75, or 245·86 and 249·47 E.

For JF, the intersections with 245 and 255E are again calculated, bearing in mind that F is west of J. The results are therefore 225·00 tan 39° 44·3' + 455·00, 215·00 tan 39° 44·3' + 455·00, giving 642·05 and 633·74N.

Plotting these three lines, to an original scale of 1/50, gives a triangle of error with sides of less than 0·2 m, and by inspection the co-ordinates of F are about 247·6E, 639·8N; these seem unlikely to be much more than 0·1 m in error. In fact, the 'true' co-ordinates of F are 247·70E, 639·75N.

If greater accuracy were considered desirable, there would be no difficulty in applying the same method to examine the square 247–8E, 639–640N, which could be plotted to 1/10th. Logically, the point chosen should be placed so that its distances from the rays through G, H, and J are proportional to GF, HF, and JF, thus giving the same angular error for each.

Apart from its simplicity, and the ease with which it can be adapted to any number of rays, the great merit of this method is that it can display, to any scale desired, the actual magnitude of the uncertainty caused by the errors involved.

17.8 *Intersection of Chained Rays.* A straightforward chain survey is almost always plotted by direct measurement. Occasionally, though, to determine co-ordinates for the stations may be useful, as for example when the scale used is so large that the work extends to more than one sheet. This also is most simply done by a semi-graphical method similar to the last. The stations used in this example are the same, but the 'measured' distances are given instead of the bearings. GF = 134·05 m; HF = 327·15 m; JF = 288·75 m. As before, a small scale plot (not shown) indicates that F lies within the square 245–255E, 635–645N, so this is examined in detail (Figure 17.5).

The line 635N is 12·25N of G, so an arc of 134·05 m radius, centre G, will cut that line at $\sqrt{(134·05)^2 - (12·25)^2} = 133·49$ m E of G, that is, at $133·49 + 114·75 = 248·24$. Similarly, the arc will cut 645N at $\sqrt{(134·05)^2 - (22·25)^2}$E of G, at 246·94. The short length of arc joining these two points is very nearly a straight line, and can be treated as such to a first approximation. For this centre only, a short length of the true arc is shown in the diagram. It cuts 640N at 247·69E, whereas the straight line cuts at 247·59.

Similarly, an arc of radius 327·15, centre H, cuts 245E at

17.5 Intersection of Chained Rays

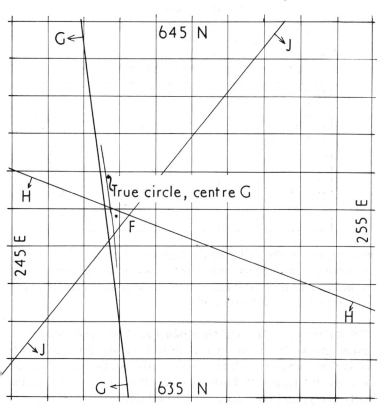

641·07N and 255E at 637·38N; and one of radius 288·75, centre J, cuts 635N at 244·22E and 645N at 252·57N. Since the radii are larger, these will approximate still more closely to straight lines. A programme for a hand calculator, which speeds the work considerably, is given in table 17.2.

Plotting these to scale 1/50, the triangle of error is appreciably larger than for angular measurements, as might be expected. Selecting by eye a point whose distances from the arcs centred on G are proportional to 134, 327, and 272, or roughly 1:2½:2, the likely position for F is at about 247·9E, 639·8N.

Again, the one-metre square 247–248E, 639–640N, could be examined to a larger scale, and the point F could be chosen so that the distance from each side of the triangle of error would be

Table 17.2 Intersection of Arc with Co-ordinate Line, Using Calculator

Data: Length GF = 134·05 metres.

Coordinates of G: 114·75 E; 622·75 N.

Required: The E. coordinates at which an arc of radius 134·05 metres with centre G cuts the lines 635 N and 645 N.

Programme	Data	Results	Notes
Figs.	134·05		Length GF.
x². STO 1. −.			
Figs. x².	12·25		635 N. − N. coord. of G
=. F. √x. +.			
Figs. F. STO 2.	114·75		E. coord. of G
=.		248·24	E. coord. of intersection with 635 N.
RCL 1. −.			
Figs. x².	22·25		645 N. − N. coord. of G
=. F. √x. +.			
F. RCL 2. =.		246·94	E. coord. of intersection with 645 N.

proportional to the radius of the corresponding arc, thus making the percentage adjustment the same for each line; but having regard to the inherent possible inaccuracy of the measurements, the extra work would not seem worth while.

17.9 *Balancing a Chained Quadrilateral.* A chained network is almost always 'balanced' by eye: there is no standardised simple method of doing it by calculation. Nevertheless, the particular case of a quadrilateral with both diagonals measured can be treated fairly easily, and may occasionally be useful, as for example in preparation for an excavation. The corresponding problem with measured angles is discussed in Para. 20.6. It is important to remember that 'balancing' does not eliminate errors (still less mistakes); it merely distributes them so that the network becomes geometrically possible (see Para. 19.2).

The quadrilateral to be balanced is BEJF. The data are set out in table 17.3, together with the main calculations involved, and the necessary graphical work is shown in Figure 17.6. To allow comparison with the 'true' lengths and co-ordinates, the 'measured' lengths have been reduced proportionately so that their total is the same as that for the 'true' lengths; even so, the 'errors' included are larger than would be acceptable if the work were important enough to justify the work of balancing.

The principle involved is simple. The measurements are geometri-

Table 17.3 Balancing Chained Quadrilateral

Data:

Line	Length	0·5 % strain
BE	197·5	+ 0·99
BF	251·8	+ 1·26
BJ	348·3	- 1·74
EF	333·7	- 1·67
EJ	232·8	+ 1·16
FJ	288·3	+ 1·44

Coordinates of J: 470·0 E; 455·0 N.
Bearing of JF: 309·7294°
whence
Coordinates of F: 248·277 E;
639·271 N.

Programme	For FE and FB. Data	Results	Notes	For JE and JB Data	Results	Notes
Figs. x^2. STO 1. -.	333·7		Length FE	232·8		Length JE
Figs. x^2. =. F. √x. +.	19·729		659 N - N(F)	109·00		579 E - E(J)
Figs. F. STO 2.	248·277		E(F)	455·00		N(J)
=. RCL 1. -.		581·39	FE cuts 659N		660·71	JE cuts 579E
Figs. x^2. =. F. √x. +.	22·729		662 N - N(F)	112·00		582 E - E(J)
F. RCL 2. =.		581 20	FE cuts 662N		659·09	JE cuts 582E
Figs. x^2. STO 1. -.	251·8		Length FB	348·3		Length JB
Figs. x^2. =. F. √x. +. F. RCL 2.	160·729		800 N - N(F)	-30·00		440 E - E(J)
=. RCL 1. -.		442·10	FB cuts 800N		802·01	JB cuts 440E
Figs. x^2. =. F. √x. +. F. RCL 2. =.	163·729		803 N - N(F)	-27·00		443 E - E(J)
		439·58	FB cuts 803N		802·25	JB cuts 443E

Point	Coords. before strain	Coords. after 0·5% strain	Coords. after 0·19%
B	E: 440·39 N: 802·04	442·96 800·52	441·37 801·46
E	E: 581·37 N: 659·43	578·46 662·31	580·26 660·52
F	E: 248·28 N: 639·27	247·17 640·19	247·86 639·62

cally incompatible, so we strain them (that is, increase or decrease them) all in the same proportion so that they can be fitted together. To find what strain is needed, one of the lines, BE in this case, is left out, and the network solved. The gap BE is found, in this case, to be longer than the line BE which should close it. A small strain is then imposed on all the lines, and the gap and line BE again compared. From this it is easy to work out the strain which would make the fit exact.

The calculations, essentially the same as those in table 17.2, are set out in table 17.3, the squares examined being 440–443E, 800–803N for B and 579–582E, 659–662N for E. In practice rather

17.6 Balancing a Chained Quadrilateral

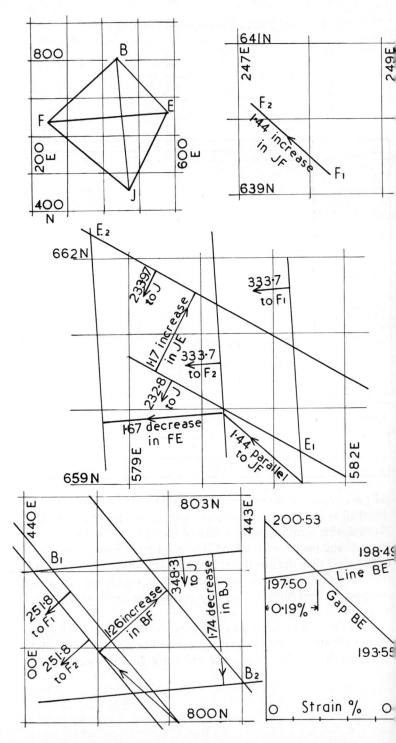

larger squares would probably be more convenient. The resulting co-ordinates (of B_1 and E_1 in the diagram) give a gap of 200·53 m, as against the measured length for BE of 197·5 m, a difference of about 1·5 per cent. So a strain of 0·5 per cent in each line, chosen so as to decrease the gap, seems likely to be of about the right magnitude.

The necessary changes in most of the lines are obvious, and a rough plot giving JF a large change in length shows that an increase in that line will decrease the gap BE, so the effect of increasing JF, BF, and EJ, and of decreasing BJ and EF, all by 0·5 per cent, is examined.

All the remaining work can be done graphically, and although at first glance the diagrams look complicated they are in fact simple if considered step by step.

The radius JE is supposed to have been increased by 1·17 m, so the new straight line, which approximates to the short length of arc through E_2, will be 1·17 m from the line through E_1 and parallel to it. Similarly, the new 'arc' through B_2 will be 1·74 m nearer J.

Two steps are needed to find the new positions of the 'arcs' centred on F. The line JF is to be increased, so F_2 moves 1·44 m away from J, in a direction parallel to JF. If the radii FB and FE were not altered, the new arcs would be represented by lines parallel to the original 'arcs' but distant from them by 1·44 m *measured parallel to JF*; these intermediate lines are shown on the diagram. In fact though, FE has decreased in length, so to get the correct position of the new 'arc' the line must be moved a further 1·67 m towards F. The intersection of this 'arc' with the new 'arc' centred on J gives E_2, the new position of E. BF has increased by 1·26 m, and a similar construction gives B_2.

The co-ordinates of B_2, E_2, and F_2 can all be read directly from the large-scale plots. The gap B_2E_2 proves to be 193·55 m, while the line BE, if increased by 0·5 per cent, becomes 198·49 m. Plotting these shows that the gap and line will be equal when the strain is 0·19 per cent. The corresponding co-ordinates can be found graphically, for example by dividing the line E_1E_2 in the ratio 19 to 50; but it is just as easy to calculate them. Thus, with no strain E(B) is 440·39, and with 0·5 per cent strain it is 442·96, an increase of 2·57; so 0·19 per cent will correspond to an increase of 0·98, making the value of E(B) after 'balancing' the network 441·37. As a final check, the lengths corresponding to the final co-ordinates should be worked out, to make sure that the strain in each line is acceptably close to 0·19 per cent.

17.10 *Resection: The Three-point Problem.* Sometimes, especially perhaps during a 'salvage' excavation, it may be very useful indeed to be able to fix the position of a point by observations from it to stations which are visible but inaccessible. Suppose that F is the required point, and G and H are known stations; then if the angle GFH is known, it defines a circle, passing through G and H, on which F must lie. Similarly, if J is another known station, angle HFJ defines another such circle through H and J, and F will be where the two circles cut.

In practice, this construction is not used, or only in a very modified form, but it makes one very important point clear: the problem cannot be solved if F lies on (or very near) the circle which passes through G, H, and J. Since this cannot easily be detected in the field, a fourth station should always be observed if at all possible. Ideally, one station should be distant, and two close; provided the station co-ordinates are known relative to the site grid, they need not lie within the area represented by the plan.

There are several different methods of solution, all rather laborious; the semi-graphical method described here is the least so.

The data are set out in table 17.4.

Initially, the approximate co-ordinates of F are found by drawing rays at the appropriate angles on a sheet of tracing-paper. Stations A, G, H and J are plotted on a separate drawing to a suitable scale, and the tracing is moved over it until the rays pass through the relevant points. The position of F can then be pricked through. For some purposes, as for example when working on a chain survey on which A, G, H and J are shown, this solution is adequate, but if the co-ordinates of F are needed accurately more calculations are needed. We will assume that by this 'tracing-paper' method they have been found to be about 250E, 640N. As previously, a suitable square is examined. In this case 248–252E, 638–642N seem appropriate; as the diagram becomes rather crowded, a large scale is desirable, and the original plot was drawn to 1/25.

The longest ray is HF, so the uncertainty in the co-ordinates of F will have least effect on the bearing of that line. As a first approximation that is found to be 20·2093°, from which the corresponding bearings of AF, GF, and JF can be found. The intersections of those rays with the grid lines which form the sides of the square can then be worked out. The results are set out in table 17.4, but the calculations are not given in detail as the method

Table 17.4 Resection

Data: Coordinates   A 169·10 E; 779·25 N.
                    G 114·75 E; 622·75 N.
                    H 136·75 E; 332·35 N.
                    J 470·00 E; 455·00 N.

    Angles   AFG 67·8833°
                GFH 62·8967°
                HFJ 70·0967°

Required: Coordinates of F.

A calculator has been used for convenience, but the same method is applicable with logarithms.

First approximation: F taken as at 250 E; 640 N.

Tan (Bg. HF) = (250·00 - 136·75) ÷ (640·00 - 332·35)

             = 0·368113

Whence Bg. HF = 20·2093°

From this the bearings of the other lines can be found, and thus their intersections with the relevant grid lines.

Line	Bearing	E. coords. of intersections with		
		638 N	642 N	640 N
AF	150·9893°	247·43	245·21	246·32
HF	20·2093°	249·26	250·74	
		N. coords. of intersections with		
		248 E	252 E	250 E
GF	83·1060°	638·86	639·34	
JF	310·1126°	642·02	638·65	

Second approximation: F taken as at 248 E; 640 N.

Tan (Bg. HF) = (248·00 - 136·75) ÷ (640·00 - 332·35)

Whence Bg. HF = 19·8806°

Line	Bearing	E. coords. of intersections with		
		638 N	642 N	640 N
AF	150·6606°	248·49	246·25	247·37
HF	19·8806°	247·28	248·72	
		N. coords. of intersections with		
		248 E	252 E	250 E
GF	82·7773°	639·64	640·14	
JF	309·7839°	639·86	636·53	638·20

has already been described in Para. 17.7. In arranging the table, space is left in case more values are needed; thus, the line AF cuts 642N inconveniently far west of the square being examined, so the intercept with 640N is found by interpolation.

When plotting these (Figure 17.7, indicated by suffix 1) it is helpful to use coloured (fine) ball-point pens, as the number of lines involved can lead to confusion; in the diagram different styles of line are used. Examination of this first plot suggests that 248·0E, 640·0N would be a rather better approximation for F. This gives the second set of approximations in the table (suffix 2 on plot).

Now consider the rays from A and G. The intersections AG$_1$ and

17.7 Resection

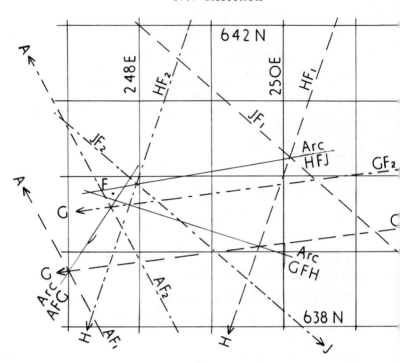

AG$_2$ both correspond to points on the circle through A and G, on some point of which F must lie; so the line joining those points represents accurately at this scale, a short length of the circumference of that circle. Similar reasoning applies to all other intersections. If the angles observed from F had all been exactly right, the three circles, and therefore the three equivalent straight lines would all meet in a point, but since the angles contain errors the lines form a small triangle. A first estimate for the co-ordinates of F is found by bisecting the angles of the triangle of error, giving 247·65E, 639·77N (the 'true' values are 247·70, 639·75).

As always, a final check should be made, by working out the bearings corresponding to this point. The calculated angles prove to be: AFG, 67·9113° (0·0230° too big); GFH, 62·8655° (0·0312° too small); and HFJ, 70·1105° (0·0138° too big). If these discrepancies are considered unacceptably large, the calculations can be repeated, using the co-ordinates 247·65E, 639·77N as a third approximation to the co-ordinates of F and examining square 247-248 E, 639–640 N at a larger scale. This should get rid of inaccuracies caused by representing the arcs by straight lines, but the effect of errors in angular measurements will remain.

18 Miscellaneous Calculations

18.1 Drawing a Grid; 18.2 Tracing a Gridded Plan; 18.3 Plotting Intermediate Points on Chain Lines; 18.4 Rotation of Co-ordinate Axes; 18.5 Linkage to National Grid; 18.6 True Bearing from National Grid; 18.7 Calculation of Areas; 18.8 Calculation of Volumes.

18.1 *Drawing a Grid.* If stations are to be plotted using their co-ordinates, the accuracy of the background grid is important. Even for a chain survey a grid is useful, if the plan is large, for the original drawing can then be done on cartridge paper and the dimensional changes corrected, when tracing, as described in Para. 18.2.

The grid must be constructed by drawing a rectangle of the full size required and then dividing it; it must not be built up from smaller squares. The construction is essentially the same as for setting out a rectangle with a chain (Para. 7.5). It is illustrated in Figure 18.1, where the inaccuracies have been exaggerated; but working with a set square of ordinary size the verticals are always liable to be slightly wrong.

As an example, suppose that we wish to draw a rectangle ABCD, 100 cm long and 80 cm high. Only the construction for C will be given; that for D is exactly similar.

AB is drawn with the straight-edge, and lines at right angles to AB are marked off at B (and A) with the set square. These lines are produced to make BC_1 (and AD_1) 80 cm. Since the set square is probably of only 15 or 20 cm side, BC_1 and AD_1 will not be exactly perpendicular to AB, but they will nearly be so, and therefore C_1D_1 will be parallel to AB and at the required distance from it.

If ABC were exactly 90°, then AC_1 would equal $\sqrt{100^2 + 80^2}$ = 128·06 cm.

Draw the straight line AX aiming to pass through C_1. It does not matter if you miss by a short distance, which may easily happen as AX is rather longer than the (assumed) metre straight-edge. Make AX the required 128·06 cm and draw XC perpendicular to AX_1 to cut the line D_1C_1 at C. In practice, the length XC will be relatively very small, so this is almost exactly equivalent to drawing an arc of

18.1 Drawing a Rectangular Grid

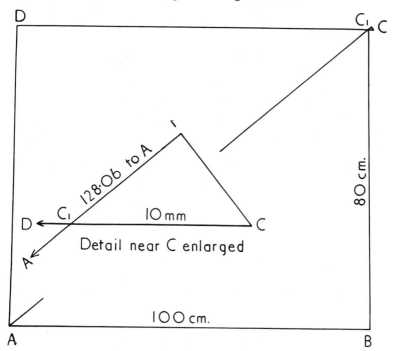

radius 128·06 cm with centre A. D is then fixed by the same method, and finally both diagonals and all four sides are checked.

To give an idea of the accuracy which may be expected, suppose that a very imperfect set square has been used, so that C_1 came 10 mm to the left of C (as in the diagram). Then if all the other works were done with complete accuracy, the line DC would be 0·06 mm too close to AB, and 0·12 mm too long; such errors would be imperceptible.

Provided the rectangle is not unduly long and narrow any proportions can be used. Other things being equal, a 3–4–5 triangle is to be preferred, since the calculation needed to fix the diagonal is then very simple.

18.2 *Tracing a Gridded Plan.* If the pencil draft of a large plan has been drawn on cartridge paper it will often prove to have altered slightly in its overall dimensions before it is ready for tracing. This can easily be corrected when the tracing is made; it is assumed that that will be on dimensionally stable material.

Suppose the original grid was in squares of 20 cm side (the same method applies to any sized grid). Draw in pencil a true 20 cm grid on the tracing material.

Now consider a single square; for convenience, points in it are specified by their co-ordinates relative to the south-west corner (0,0); thus (20,10) is the middle of the east side.

Superimpose (0,0) on the tracing and on the draft and trace the detail within a 10 cm square centred on that point. Then move the tracing so that the (0,10) points on tracing and draft coincide, and trace the adjacent detail; and so on moving the co-ordinates which are made to coincide by 10 cm at a time until the whole draft has been traced. The discrepancies at the boundaries of the 10 cm squares will be inappreciable. There is of course no need to adhere to the measurements given, but the principle will be clear.

18.3 *Plotting Intermediate Points on Chain Lines.* Large plans can sometimes be plotted more conveniently on several small sheets rather than on one very large one. A chain line may then join two stations which are on different sheets; but points on the line can easily be determined.

As an example, consider the line BE; B is at 441·2E, 801·1N, E at 580·3E, 659·9N. The measured chainage from B to E is 197·8 (as compared to the true distance between those co-ordinates which is 198·21), so small adjustments will need to be made when plotting detail (see Para. 6.4).

The midpoint is easily fixed, at $(441·2 + 580·3) \div 2 = 510·75$ and $(810·1 + 659·9) \div 2 = 730·5N$, and its chainage will be $197·8 \div 2 = 98·9$. The quarter-points can be obtained similarly, lying midway between the ends and the midpoint, and hence if desired the eighth-points. Often no more is needed, but sometimes the intersection with a specified grid-line is useful. Suppose that 500E is the line at which two sheets join. Call the intersection of BE with 500E the point P.

The easting of BP is $500 - 441·2 = 58·8$ m, while that of BE is 139·1 m. The southing of BE is 141·2 m, so the southing of BP is $141·2 \times 58·8 \div 139·1 = 59·688$. Since B is at 801·1N, P is at $801·1 - 59·688 = 741·421N$. Similarly the chainage of P, measured from B, is $197·8 \times 58·8 \div 139·1 = 83·61$ m.

As a check, it is advisable to plot also the half- and quarter-points to make sure that they lie on BP, PE.

18.4 *Rotation of Co-ordinate Axes.* Occasionally, it may be desirable to alter the co-ordinate axes; the most usual reason, to relate your survey to the National Grid, is discussed in the next section.

Suppose you have a point P, with co-ordinates x, y in your co-ordinates, and that your y-axis has a bearing z relative to true N. Then the straightforward formulae are

$$E = x \cos z + y \sin z$$
$$N = -x \sin z + y \cos z$$

If the origins are different, the E and N co-ordinates of the (x,y) origin must be added.

Calculation by logarithms is laborious. A programme for a calculator is given in table 18.1, and will be described in some detail as it is a good illustration of the use of the Polar keys.

The calculation is supposed to be the first of a sequence of points (Q, S, etc), so the N co-ordinate of the (x, y) origin is stored in the second memory; if only a single point were involved it could be entered later (see below). Unfortunately, with two memories, no store is available for the corresponding E co-ordinate, and the full figures will have to be keyed in for each calculation. The bearing of the y-axis relative to the N-axis is then stored in memory 1; for a single calculation, this also could be entered later.

Now the main calculation starts. The y co-ordinate of Q is entered, and by using the F. and x/y. keys is transferred to the (invisible) y register. The x co-ordinate is then entered, and pressing the P. key yields the Polar co-ordinate of the point Q, that is, the length OQ. The F. and x/y keys transfer that to the y register, replacing the y co-ordinate, and yield the bearing of OQ relative to the y axis. The sequence (. +. RCL 1. and). brings the bearing of the y axis out of memory 1 and adds it to the last figure, giving the true bearing of OQ. If this were a single calculation, the figures for the bearing of OQ relative to the y axis could be entered instead of RCL 1. Since you are using the Polar keys, take care not to forget the brackets.

Since you have the length OQ in the y register and the true bearing in the visible x register, the R. key gives the Northing of

Table 18.1 Rotation of Axes, Using Calculator with Polar Keys

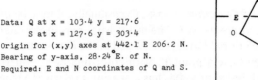

Data: Q at x = 103·4 y = 217·6
      S at x = 127·6 y = 303·4
Origin for (x,y) axes at 442·1 E 206·2 N.
Bearing of y-axis, 28·24° E. of N.
Required: E and N coordinates of Q and S.

Programme	Data	Results	Notes
(a) Figs.	206·2		N. coord. of O.
(a) F. STO 2.			
Figs. STO 1.	28·24		Bearing of y-axis
Figs.	217·6		y (for Q)
F. x/y			
Figs.	103·4		x (for Q)
P.		(240·9177)	(length OQ)
F. x/y.		(25·4163)	(Bearing of OQ from y-axis)
(. +. RCL 1.).		(53·6563)	(Bearing of OQ from N.)
R.		(142·7744)	(Northing of OQ)
(a) (. +. F.			
(a) RCL 2.).		348·9744	N. coord. of Q
F. x/y.		(194·0535)	(Easting of OQ)
(a) (.+.Figs.	442·1		E. coord. of O.
(a)).		636·1535	E. coord. of Q
Programme repeats:			
Figs.	303·4		y (for S)
F. x/y.			
Figs.	127·6		x (for S)
P.		(329·1403)	(length OS)
F. x/y.		(22·8100)	(Bearing of OS from y-axis)
(. +. RCL 1.).		(51·0500)	(Bearing of OS from N.)
R.		(206·9113)	(Northing of OS)
(a) (. +. F.			
(a) RCL 2.).		413·1113	N. coord. of S
F. x/y.		(255·9707)	(Easting of OS)
(a) (.+.Figs.	442·1		E. coord. of O.
(a)).		698·0707	E. coord. of S

(a)...(a): These are not needed if the two coordinate systems
have the same origin.

OQ, and (by using brackets) the N co-ordinate of the origin can be
recalled, or entered direct, and added. That gives the N co-ordinate
of Q. The F. and x/y. keys then give the Easting of OQ, and adding
the E co-ordinte of the origin gives the E co-ordinate of Q.

18.5 *Linkage to National Grid.* Save in exceptional cases, the Grid,
unlike ordnance datum for levels, cannot be fixed precisely on the
ground, so there is no real advantage in showing it on a plan if the
scale much exceeds 1/2,500. Some people do not realise this

Table 18.2 Linking Surveys to National Grid

Data:	National Grid		Survey	
	E	N	x	y
A	(1)021	208	129·90	1·10
B	980	358	124·25	156·15
C	(1)063	416	217·75	194·14
D	901	213	13·90	33·95

Points A and C are in square 59 80, B and D in 58 80.

Line	National Grid Coord. Diffs.			Survey Coord. Diffs.			Diff. in Bearings
	E	N	Bearing	x	y	Bearing	
AB	-41	+150	344·7126	- 5·65	+155·05	357·9131	13·2005
AC	+42	+208	11·4158	+87·85	+193·04	24·4697	13·0539
AD	-120	+5	272·3859	-116·00	+32·85	285·8116	13·4257
BC	+83	+58	55·0543	+93·50	+37·99	67·8876	12·8333
BD	-79	-145	208·5828	-110·35	-122·20	222·0829	13·5001
CD	-162	-203	218·5909	-203·85	-160·19	231·8389	13·2480
						Average:	13·2102

Coordinates of points relative to Survey origin, after rotating axes 13·2102 degrees anticlockwise:

	E	N	Differences from National Grid	
			E	N
A	126·211	30·756	894·789	177·244
B	85·278	180·412	894·722	177·588
C	167·622	238·764	895·378	177·236
D	5·774	36·228	895·226	176·772
	Averages:		895·029	177·210

Hence the coordinates of the points relative to the National Grid are:

	E	N
A	59 021·24	80 207·97
B	58 980·31	80 357·62
C	59 062·65	80 415·97
D	58 900·80	80 213·44

though, and the result can look impressive. Table 18.2 sets out in summary the method which can be used.

Four points are supposed to be identified on the national grid and on your survey (but see further comments below). Their grid co-ordinates are known to the nearest metre (0·4 mm on the 1/2,500 map); perhaps an estimate to half a metre could be made, but the method is unaffected.

These four points define six lines, and the bearings of these are worked out relative to the national grid and to the survey grid. If the national grid co-ordinates were exact, the difference for any pair of bearings would give the angle between the survey and the national grids, but in fact there is a range of uncertainty, so an average is taken.

The axes of the survey grid are then rotated (as in Table 18.1, but without moving the origin), and the differences between these new co-ordinates and the national grid co-ordinates found and averaged. From these, the co-ordinates of the points relative to the national grid are found by addition, and the grid can easily be superimposed on the plan.

Four points is a convenient number; two, at least, are essential. With more than four, the number of lines increases rapidly; six points define fifteen lines. In such circumstances it would be reasonable to select the longest half dozen or so.

If your survey can be linked to an OS Trigonometrical Station, then in principle you should be able to make an exact connection with the grid; but the policy of the Ordnance Survey over revealing such information varies, and in any case, save in the unlikely event that such accuracy is really essential, it would be difficult to justify taking up an inevitably overworked Officer's time with such an enquiry.

The scale of the OS maps does in fact vary slightly as you move from east to west across the country, owing to the projection used; but the variation is not appreciable, so if you find the 'metres' of your plan differ from those of the 1/2,500 map, your survey is wrong.

18.6 *True Bearing from National Grid.* If the accurate direction of true north is needed, as for example in examining the possible function of a stone alignment, it can be found either by astronomical observations or from the National Grid. The former is difficult, and will not be discussed here. The latter is, in principle, simple, but also requires tiresome calculations if accuracy better than about 01' or 02' is needed. In that case, reference should be made to *Projection Tables for the Transverse Mercator Projection of Great Britain* (Ordnance Survey, published by HMSO, 1950), which give all the necessary information. In any case, three difficulties arise.

(a) Assume that the required direction is found by estimating the relative bearing of two points, located by their grid references on the 1/2,500 map; then both positions are liable to an uncertainty of at least 0·5 m (0·2 mm on the map), giving a total uncertainty of a metre at least, which requires a line of sight 3·5 km long to give the bearing relative to the grid correct to within 01'. With the 1/10,000 map, owing to its great generalisation, the corresponding distance may be as much as 70 km. This applies whatever method is used to convert grid bearing to true bearing.

(b) As will be apparent to any user of 'one-inch' or 1/50,000 maps, grid north may diverge by as much as 3° from true north, and the amount alters according to longitude. On the 1/50,000 maps the value is given, to the nearest minute, for each corner, so the required correction can easily be interpolated for the point at which the observation is made; but the accuracy will only be to about one minute. If greater precision is needed the 'Convergence' must be calculated using the *Projection Tables*.

(c) A third, less obvious, source of error arises because the map has to represent a spherical surface on a plane. Straight lines on the ground may therefore appear slightly sinuous on the map. Even for a 100 km sight the divergence is seldom as much as 01·5 minutes, but for really accurate work it also should be calculated from the Projection Tables. The effect is zero for an east-west grid line, greatest for one running north-south.

Fortunately, for most purposes, an accuracy within two minutes is good enough; it will at least allow a decision as to whether an alignment is likely to be of astronomical significance. Nevertheless, when stating a significant bearing obtained only by measurements on the 1/2,500 map and interpolation from the 1/50,000, the basis for the calculation should be given, so that anyone who wishes to do so can appreciate what accuracy is to be expected.

18.7 *Calculation of Areas*. In describing an enclosure, the area usually needs to be stated. For many purposes, a rough value is good enough, and can be found by sketching by eye the outline of a simple figure which appears to be of about the same area. In Figure 18.2, part of the outline of the sketched oval is shown, as well as the estimated equivalent trapezium. For the oval, the area is given by

$\frac{\pi}{4}$ × length × breadth (the same will apply to a D-shaped figure),

and for the trapezium, the mean of the lengths of the two parallel sides × the distance between them. The results are given in table 18.3. Even when a more accurate estimate is to be made, a rough estimate of this kind should always be worked out as a check.

If the area is needed more precisely, the figure is divided up into strips of equal width; there will usually be a small segment unaccounted for at each end; these will be considered later.

18.2 Estimation of Areas

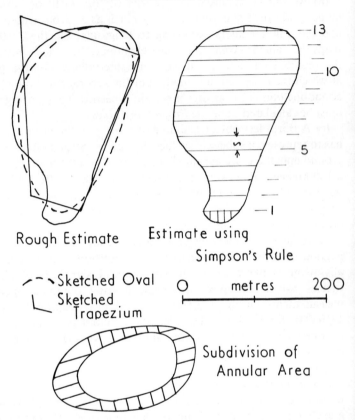

Rough Estimate

Estimate using
Simpson's Rule

Sketched Oval
Sketched
Trapezium

O   metres   200

Subdivision of
Annular Area

Suppose the strips are all of width S, and the sides, taken in order, measure a, b, c, d, . . . m, n, p. Two formulae (out of many) are commonly used.

The simplest is the Trapezoidal Rule. Each strip is treated as a trapezium, so their areas are s(a + b) ÷ 2, s(b + c) ÷ 2 and so on. The total area thus becomes

$$s(\frac{a}{2} + b + c \ldots + m + n + \frac{p}{2}).$$

If the outline is convex, a little is lost in each strip. The number used may be odd or even.

Table 18.3 Estimating Areas

<u>Rough Estimates</u>:

Equivalent Oval (sketched): 257 x 146 x π/4
=29470 square metres
= 2·95 hectares.

Equivalent Trapezium: 224 x $\dfrac{173 + 74}{2}$

= 2·77 ha.

<u>Estimate using Simpson's Rule</u>:
One-third of Spacing times (Sum of ends + 4 x Sum of 'evens'
+ 2 x Sum of 'odds')

Section	Ends	Evens	Odds		
1	50				
2		53			
3			62		
4		77			
5			106		
6		128			
7			142		
8		152			
9			158		
10		161			
11			156		
12		139	624	x 2 =	1248
13	90	710		x 4 =	2840
	140		140		140

Spacing: 20 m.x $\frac{1}{3}$ x 4228 = 2·82 ha.
N. Segment: 90 x 6 x 2/3 = 0·04 ha.
S. Segment: 50 x 16 x 2/3 = 0·05 ha.

TOTAL   2·91 ha.

Simpson's Rule is more accurate. The value found is exact, providing the boundary curves are cubics. The strips are considered

in pairs, and the areas are $\dfrac{s}{3}(a + 4b + c)$, $\dfrac{s}{3}(c + 4d + e)$, etc, so that

the total is $\dfrac{s}{3}(a + 4b + 2c + 4d + \ldots + 2m + 4n + p)$

or $\dfrac{s}{3}$(sum of first and last measurements plus

4 × sum of even measurements plus 2 × sum of odd measurements excluding first and last). As will be seen in table 18.3, this lends itself to a simple arrangement for calculation.

To apply Simpson's Rule, the number of strips must be even, so that the number of measurements is odd; but if for any reason the number of strips is odd, one can be treated as a trapezium, Simpson's Rule being used for the rest. It is often convenient to take a simple measurement for the spacing (20 m in Figure 18.2), and to treat separately the little segments left over. Simpson's Rule, for these, gives the formula Area = base × height × ⅔.

For an area such as the water surface in a moat (see Figure 18.2), to calculate the total and the internal areas and to take the difference is not very accurate, for each will include an error, and these will be combined and may be quite large relative to the much smaller area of the 'moat'. A better result is obtained by dividing it up into several lengths for which the areas can be calculated by Simpson's Rule, the wedge-shaped pieces joining them being worked out separately treating each as built up from a triangle plus a segment. The wedges, of course, need not be right-angled.

Areas can also be found using a planimeter. This ingenious application of the calculus comprises two arms pivoted together, one supported on a pivot, the other carrying a pointer. Near their junction a small wheel measures, by its rotation, the area traced out by the pointer. There are two objections to this instrument, apart from its cost. To get an accurate result requires very great care in following the perimeter *exactly*, and movement must be slow and careful to ensure that the small wheel rotates as it should, and does not slip. Also, unless you use the device frequently, it will take you far longer to remember how to apply it than to work out the required area numerically. Nevertheless, if you have a lot of areas to measure, and do not require great accuracy, a planimeter may be useful.

18.8 *Calculation of Volumes.* Except for very simple cases, volumes are more laborious to calculate than areas. Moreover, there is no approximate check comparable to sketching the apparent equivalent oval. For a mound circular in plan and having a profile which is symmetrically parabolic, the volume is half the height times the area of the base, and this can be extended fairly accurately to any low oval mound.

Accurate calculations, though essentially simple, can be laborious. Save for one special case, considered later, the method is to take equally spaced parallel sections, work out their areas, and then work out the volume either using the Trapezoidal or Simpson's Rule; the latter is very much to be preferred if a fair degree of accuracy is needed.

The sections can be parallel to any plane, but will usually be either vertical or horizontal. The former, which would be the method of choice for a length of rampart, is so obvious as to need no explanation. The latter, which is to be preferred for mounds of limited extent, can involve some minor difficulties, so an example is given. The volume of material is to be estimated, given a contoured

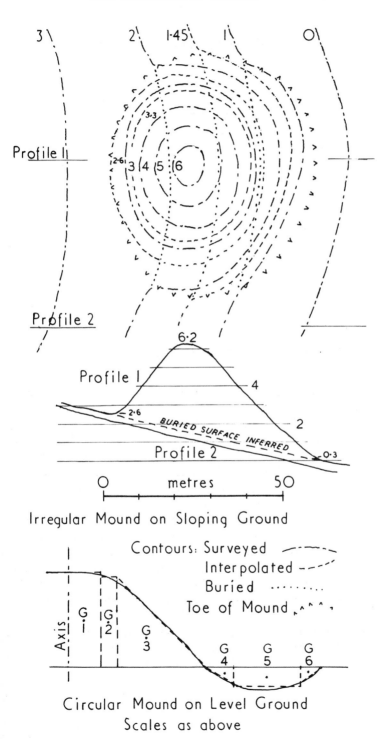

Profile I

Profile 2

Profile I

6·2

4

2·6

BURIED SURFACE INFERRED

2

Profile 2

0·3

O   metres   5O

Irregular Mound on Sloping Ground

Contours: Surveyed —·—·—
          Interpolated - - - -
          Buried · · · · · · ·
          Toe of Mound ʌʌʌ

Axis

G
1

G
2

G
3

G
4

G
5

G
6

Circular Mound on Level Ground
Scales as above

Table 18.4 Estimating Volumes

(a) Contoured **Mound**.

Contour Level	Area enclosed	Vertical Spacing	Volume (cu. m.)
0·3	0		
1·45	809·6	1·15	1883·0
2·6	1673·8		
2·6	1673·8		
3·3	1068·1	0·7	1548·7
4·0	691·2		
4·0	691·2		
5·0	296·9	1·0	650·7
6·0	73·4		
6·0	73·4		
6·2	0		7·3

(volume of 'cap' equals half area of base times height)

$$| \quad 4089·7$$

Volume of Mound: 4090 cubic metres.

(b) Circular Mound on Level Ground.

Radius from Axis to C.G.	Width	Height	Area times Radius
4·5	9·0	5·0	202·5
11·25	4·5	4·8	243·0
21·83	25·0	4·8 (triangle)	1309·8
			1755·3
		x 2π =	11028·9
43·5	7·5	0·8 (triangle)	130·5
55·0	18·0	1·05	1039·5
66·0	6·0	0·8 (triangle)	158·4
			1328·4
		x 2π =	8346·6

Estimated volumes in cubic metres: Mound, 11030; Ditch, 8350.

plan of a mound resting on sloping ground (Figure 18.3 and table 18.4).

The first step is to draw a profile of the mound. By drawing one or more further profiles adjacent to its base, the probable contours of the natural ground surface beneath the mound can be drawn.

Examination of the profile indicates that at 2·6 m above site datum, the level of the toe on the upper side, there will be a discontinuity in the shape of the curve relating area enclosed to contour level, so that part of the mound needs to be examined separately. A fairly accurate result will be obtained by considering the areas enclosed by contours at 0·3 (the lowest part on the toe) 1·45, that is, (2·6 + 0·3) ÷ 2, and 2·6 (the upper edge), though a better result would be given by using 0·725 and 2·175 also. The 1·45 contour is interpolated on the mound and as one of the 'buried' contours. This encloses a crescentic space, corresponding to the made up material cut by a plane at level 1·45 above site datum. The area is found by using Simpson's Rule, and is 809·6 square metres. Value for 0·725 and 2·175 would be found similarly if required.

The 2.6 contour is also found by interpolation; it is an oval, corresponding to the surface of the mound, and is treated here as having the area of an ellipse of the same overall dimensions, as are all higher contours.

Above 2·6 m, and leaving aside the rounded summit above 6·0 m, there is a height of 3·4 m. This could be divided into an even number of parts, but it is less bother simply to interpolate the 3·3 contour midway between 2·6 and 4·0, and to work out that part and the part from 4·0 to 6·0 separately. The calculations are set out in table 18.4.

It will be observed that the check, height times area of base divided by two, gives a very much larger result, roughly 7,000 cubic metres. The reason for this is that the sides of the mound are concave in profile, not convex as assumed in the above formula.

If a bank, mound or ditch is truly circular in plan, and of uniform cross section, the volume is given by the cross-sectional area times the length of arc traced by its centre of gravity (not its mid point, unless the profile is symmetrical). The centre of gravity can be located by dividing the section into vertical strips, not necessarily all of the same width, and multiplying the area of each by its distance from some convenient zero line; the total is divided by the total area. Usually, though, a satisfactory approximation to the true profile can be built up out of rectangles and triangles, as in Figure 18.3, where G_1, G_2 etc. indicate the positions of their centres of gravity. The calculations necessary to find the volume are also given in table 18.4. The multiplication by 2π, to give the lengths of the arcs traced out by the centres of gravity, can be left until last. The only rule which has to be remembered is that the centre of gravity of a triangle is at one-third of its height; if for example, a strip has a steeply sloping top, it can be treated as made up from a triangle and a rectangle, each part being worked out separately.

The same approach is applicable to any bank or ditch of uniform profile: the volume is given by the cross-sectional area times the length of the line corresponding to the centre of gravity of the cross section. In practice, this seldom differs appreciably from the length of the centre-line.

If the cross section is not uniform, there is no simple exact solution, but provided it does not vary much, reasonable accuracy can be obtained by plotting the line corresponding in plan to the centre of gravity, taking cross sections equally spaced along that line, and finding the volume by Simpson's Rule.

19 The Traverse

19.1 General; 19.2 Distribution of Errors; 19.3 Closed Traverse using Logarithms; 19.4 Closed Traverse using Hand Calculator; 19.5 Open Traverses; 19.6 Linked Traverses.

19.1 *General.* One of the most useful applications of the theodolite is surveying by means of a traverse. This is essentially a series of straight lines, the direction of each being fixed by measurement of the angle it makes with the adjacent ones; its nature will become obvious from the examples which follow. A traverse may be 'closed' in which case it starts and finishes at the same station, or 'open'; an open traverse may link two known points, but need not necessarily do so.

Traversing is the only possible method for most underground surveying. On the surface, its main application is on wooded ground, as for example following the ramparts of an enclosure where the central area is planted. It is a wise precaution when traversing to supplement the theodolite observations with magnetic bearings: unless this is done a mistake can only be located by remeasuring all the angles. The check on the total of the internal angles (Para. 19.3) should always be made before leaving the site.

Although a polygon with a central station (Chapter 20) requires rather more angular measurements than a simple closed traverse, it is always preferable, for it allows a very much better distribution of any errors which occur, as well as reducing the risk of mistakes escaping unnoticed. The techniques of calculation for traverses and polygons with central stations include particular attention to methods of distributing errors, so the principles governing such distribution can usefully be discussed here.

19.2 *Distribution of Errors.* Some examples of this have already been given without discussion (Paras. 17.7–10), but the principles need to be explained in more detail.

The most important is to emphasise that distribution (also termed 'balancing') may only be applied to 'errors' (Para. 2.1).

'Mistakes' must be found and eliminated before any calculation is started. This can be understood from a simple example. Suppose you had three stations forming a triangle of which the true angles (if you could determine them) were 65° 12', 35° 14', and 79° 34'. Estimating your measured angles to 0·1', you might get these to be 65° 11·6', 35° 13·6' and 79° 33·3', adding up to 179° 58·5'. Since the real total *must* be 180° and you are equally likely to make an 'error' in each measurement, you would add 0·5' to each reading, giving 'adjusted' angles 65° 12·1', 35° 14·1', and 79° 33·8'. 'Adjusted' is a better term than 'corrected', for you have no way of knowing what is 'correct', you only know what the total angles of a triangle must be.

Suppose, though, that your records read 65° 11·6', 35°13·6', and 89° 33·3', adding up to 189° 58·5'. Obviously you have made a 'mistake', probably by misreading 10° in one of the angles. If you 'balance' them by deducting 3° 19·5' from each you finish up with all three angles badly wrong.

The first principle, then, is that the quantity you wish to distribute must be small enough to arise from 'errors' only. The distinction depends on the nature of the work being done, and unless defined by specific rules must be a matter of subjective judgement; for most archaeological work 01·5' closing error, or in bad conditions even 05', would be reasonable, but for a geodetic survey it would imply a 'mistake'.

The second principle is that all measurements of the same kind are equally liable to error, unless of course you have valid reasons to suppose one is worse than the others. So in the triangle just considered you adjust all angles equally, by 0·5'. The purist would maintain that you must not introduce any subjective element, but my own view is that if, say, the first two angles had been measured under ideal conditions and the third from a very windy hill top one might legitimately argue 'the last angle is likely to be much less accurate than the other two; let us allow it 3 units of "error", as against one each for them'. The unit then comes out to 1·5' ÷ 5 = 0·3', making the adjusted angles 65° 11·9', 35° 13·9', and 79° 34·2'.

For a linear measurement, the error which may occur is likely to depend on the length of the line; some assumption has to be made about this. One possibility is that the error may be expected to vary with the length; another, for which there is perhaps rather more theoretical justification, is that it should vary according to the square root of the length. To illustrate what these alternatives mean, imagine that you have five pegs, successive measurements between them being recorded as 100, 200, 300 and 400 m, but the total length being known from other evidence to be 1001 m. Then according to the first assumption, the best values for the adjusted lengths would be 100·1, 200·2, 300·3 and 400·4 m, but according to the second 100·16, 200·23, 300·28 and 400·33 m.

Without additional evidence, there is no way of deciding which set of adjusted measurements is the better. I have discussed them at some length in order to emphasise this, for the object of distributing errors is simply to ensure that at every stage you are dealing with a geometrically possible problem and that you have got the errors evenly distributed. It is reasonable to hope that by doing this you will be getting a fairly good approximation to whatever the 'true' shape of the network may be. Bearing in mind that the errors are by definition relatively small, then in the type of survey considered here you can legitimately depart a little from the theoretically ideal method of balancing them in order to simplify your calculations. This argument would not be valid for really precise work.

Essentially then, the method followed is that the calculations fall into successive stages, at each of which the errors which cause geometrical impossibilities, such as a triangle with angles not totalling 180°, are distributed as evenly as possible according to some simple rule. These adjustments are then incorporated in the data and forgotten, and the adjusted measurements are used in all subsequent calculations, being subjected to further adjustment if necessary.

19.3 *Closed Traverse using Logarithms.* Because of the importance of the traverse as a survey method, a full solution is given both by the use of logarithms (in this section) and using the hand calculator (in the next). The principles are exactly the same, but the arrangement differs.

The first step should be to draw out a table (as table 19.1), preferably on a wide sheet of paper, though if necessary, as here, the table can be arranged in two parts, separating the 'Departure' to 'Co-ordinates' from the rest. The data, underlined in table 19.1, are then entered. Note that the entries run anticlockwise.

The next step before doing anything else is to draw out carefully, to any convenient small scale, an outline of the traverse, using a protractor for the angles (Figure 19.1). This will detect any

Table 19.1 Closed Traverse, Using Logarithms

Data underlined.

Station	Line	Angle	Adjusted	True Bearing	Reduced Bearing	Length
	JF			309° 43.8'		
F						
	FG	132° 59.6'	59.0'	262° 42.8'	S 82° 42.8' W	134.05
G						
	GH	92° 57.3'	56.6'	175° 39.4'	S 04° 20.6' E	290.95
H						
	HN	110° 06.5'	05.8'	105° 45.2'	S 74° 14.8' E	357.35
N						
	NJ	71° 38.5'	37.8'	357° 23.0'	N 02° 37.0' W	219.90
J						
	JF	132° 21.5'	20.8'	309° 43.8' ✓	N 50° 16.2' W	288.75
Total		540° 03.4'	00.0'			

Station and Line	Departures E	W	Latitudes N	S	Adjustments E	W	N	S	Coordinates E	N
F									247.70	639.75
FG	—	132.967	—	17.002	—	+.175	—	+.022		
G									114.558	622.726
GH	22.034	—	—	290.114	+.012	—	—	+.153		
H									136.604	332.459
HN	343.928	—	—	97.019	-.452	—	—	-.128		
N									480.080	235.568
NJ	—	10.039	219.671	—	—	-.013	-.289	—		
J									470.054	454.950
JF	—	222.067	184.561	—	—	+.292	+.243	—		
F									247.695	639.754
Totals	365.962	365.073	404.232	404.135						

Diffs. E - W = 0.889   N - S = 0.097

Calculations. Set out in full:

	2·123 745 Dep. = 132·967	1·343 103 Dep. = 22·034
log sin 82° 42.8'	9·996 478	log sin 04° 20.6' 8·879 285
FG log 134.05	2·127 267	GH log 290.95 2·463 818
log cos 82° 42.8'	9·103 235	log cos 04° 20.6' 9·998 751
	1·230 502 Lat. = 17·002	2·462 569 Lat. = 290·114

Usual arrangement; antilogarithms are entered directly in the table.

	2·536 467		1·001 700		2·346 485
l.s.	9·983 373	l.s.	8·659 475	l.s.	9·885 963
HN	2·553 094	NJ	2·342 225	JF	2·460 522
l.c.	9·433 764	l.c.	9·999 547	l.c.	9·805 617
	1·986 858		2·341 772		2·266 139

Distribution of Closing Error by Method 1.

Closing Error = 0·894 metres. Parallel through station J, JX = 340 metres.
So all except GH are adjusted in the ratio 0·447 to 340; JF and FG are increased, HN and NJ are decreased.

For GH, the length GX (204 m.) has to be increased, while XH (87 m.) has to be decreased. So although GH is 291 metres long, the corresponding Departure and Latitude are only increased as if it were 117 metres; that is, they are increased in the ratio $\frac{117}{291} \times \frac{0·447}{340}$.

19.1 Closed Traverse

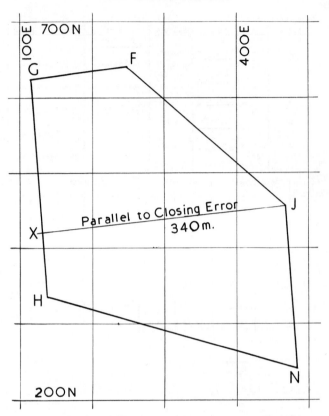

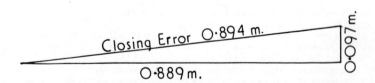

gross mistakes, and is useful subsequently.

The sum of the internal angles is then checked. If there are n sides, the total must be $(n - 2) \times 180°$. In the example there are five sides and H can be joined to J and F, showing that the angles must add up to $(5 - 2) \times 180° = 540°$. In fact, the angles as measured total 03·4 minutes too much, so we have to deduct 0·7 minutes from four of them and 0·6 from one; as the effect of 0·1 minute is insignificant, it does not matter which. The total of the adjusted angles is checked.

The true bearings are then worked out. That of JF is given. The next is found by adding the internal angle at F and subtracting 180°; if , as at N, the total is less than 180°, that amount is added. If you have inadvertently arranged your data in clockwise order, the internal angle has to be subtracted, which most people find slightly more difficult to do mentally.

From the true bearings, the reduced bearings are found; the quadrant in which a line lies is obvious from the small-scale plot.

The next step, which is the most laborious part of the work, is to calculate the departures and latitudes (as Para. 16.8). These calculations should be arranged systematically and before any logarithms are looked up the quantities needed should be indicated. In the table these have been shown in full, as for example, "FG 134·05" and "log sin 82° 42·8' ", "log cos 82° 42·8' " but in practice it is usually sufficient to write simply 'FG' 'ls' and 'lc', and to look up the required lengths and angles in the table above. You will find it advisable to put a / through the unadjusted 'minutes' figure, to reduce the risk of using that when looking up the logarithms, instead of the 'adjusted' value. Also, unless you are quite exceptionally good at avoiding mistakes, you should make the first entries for the logarithms in pencil, and check through the whole set a second time. This sounds horribly laborious, but in total will save time, for the effect of an unnoticed mistake is cumulative.

Then go through the Departure and Latitude columns, first putting a / in those you will not be using and then copying the figures automatically into the others.

Since it is a closed polygon, the total Eastings must equal the total Westings, and similarly for Northings and Southings. In fact, the Eastings add up to 365·962 m, and the Westings to 365·073, a difference of 0·889 which has to be distributed. There are several ways in which this can be done, two of which will be given here; remember that you are merely distributing the error evenly, not getting rid of it.

In method 1, the closing error is drawn to the largest convenient scale (Figure 19.1). From this its magnitude (0·894 m) and direction can be found. A line is drawn parallel to that direction and passing through a station chosen to give the longest possible line across the traverse. In this case it passes through J, cutting GH at X; this is slightly longer than a parallel line through H would have been.

The calculated circuit started at F and finished 0·889 m to the east and 0·097 m to the north, a total distance of 0·894 m, but the same closing error would have been found if the calculations had started at J. It follows that if all the lengths JF, FG, and GX were increased in the proportion 0·447 ÷ JX, and XH, HN and NJ decreased similarly, the closing error would be eliminated. By making JX the longest possible line, the adjustments are kept as small as possible. In practice, since the work is graphical, a small residual closing error remains.

The second method, set out in table 19.2, distributes the error in Departures in proportion to their magnitude, and similarly for the Latitudes. For both methods, since the adjustments are small, a slide-rule gives sufficient accuracy.

Table 19.2 Closed Traverse: Adjustment of Closing Error by Method 2

Station and Line	Departures E	Departures W	Latitudes N	Latitudes S	Adjustments E	Adjustments W	Adjustments N	Adjustments S	Coordinates E	Coordinates N
F									247·70	639·75
FG	—	132·967	—	17·002	—	+·162	—	+·002		
G									114·571	622·74(
GH	22·034	—	—	290·114	-·027	—	—	+·035		
H									136·578	332·59?
HN	343·928	—	—	97·019	-·418	—	—	+·011		
N									480·088	235·56?
NJ	—	10·039	219·671	—	—	+·012	-·026	—		
J									470·037	455·212
JF	—	222·067	184·561	—	—	+·270	-·022	—		
F									247·700	639·75?

Totals 365·962 365·073 404·232 404·135
Diffs.   E - W = 0·889   N - S = 0·097

In this method the Departures and Latitudes are dealt with separately. The sum of all the Departures is 731 metres, and the Eastings exceed the Westings by 0·889 metres. So all Eastings are decreased, and all Westings increased, in the proportion 0.889 to 731. Similarly, all Northings are decreased, and all Southings increased, in the proportion 0·097 to 808.

The theoretical merit of the first method is that it does not alter the bearings of the lines, and thus does not alter the angles between them; this is logical for a theodolite traverse, since the angles are measured much more accurately than the lengths. The second method is more automatic, but has the disadvantage that it alters the angles appreciably. For example, that at J becomes 132° 18·7' as against 132° 20·8' after adjustment. Since the whole closing error for the angles was only 3·4', the angle at J is unlikely to require 2' further adjustment. The second method is more appropriate when the angles are not very accurately known, as for example with magnetic bearings; but its convenience will sometimes outweigh its theoretical defects.

Both these methods apply when the angles, and hence the bearings of the lines, are known accurately. When the bearings are known much less accurately than the linear measurements, as for example in a traverse where nothing better than a prismatic compass is available for angular measurements, there is some justification for distributing the closing error in the Departures in proportion to the lengths of the Latitudes, and conversely. In practice though, the potential accuracy of such a survey is seldom great enough to justify the labour of calculation.

19.4 *Closed Traverse using Hand Calculator*. The data are the same as for the last section. The differences of a few millimetres between the results arise from different accuracies in 'rounding-off' the adjustments.

The programme (table 19.3) is rather more complicated than those given hitherto, because of the need first to get results and then to distribute the closing errors. The angles are supposed to have been balanced, and the true (adjusted) bearings worked out; but there is no need to set out the very simple programmes involved. Similarly, at the end of the work, no programme is given for calculating the adjustments needed to eliminate the closing error.

If space permits, separate columns can be used for the Results and Adjustments relating to Departures and for those relating to Latitudes; but if that is done, then before any calculations start dashes should be put in the spaces which will not be used. A few other points deserve note.

First, the programmes are repetitive, so in the main programme only the six lines would need to be written out, on a separate sheet, and this would be moved down the page as required. Second, there is no need to 'reduce' the bearings; the calculator will give the correct figures if the 'true bearings' are entered. In calculating the adjustments, method 1 has been used. The entries cannot be made completely automatically, for it is necessary to note that for the sides of the polygon which have to be increased the adjustment is of the same sign as the Northing or Easting (and conversely), so 'inc' and 'dec' should be entered in the appropriate columns before the

Table 19.3 Closed Traverse, Using Calculator

Only the main programme is given. The angles are assumed to have been balanced, and the bearings worked out from them.

Programme	Data	Results	Adjustments	Coords.	Remarks
Figs. STO 1.	639·75				N(F)
Figs. F. STO 2.	247·70				E(F)
Figs. F. x/y.	134·05		inc.		FG
Figs.	262·7120				Bg(FG)
R.		(- 17·005)	(-·022)		N(FG)
(. +. RCL 1.). STO 1.		622·745	-·022	622·723	N(G)
F. x/y.		(-132·967)	(-·176)		E(FG)
(. +. F. RCL 2.).		114·733	-·176	114·557	E(G)
F. STO 2.					
Figs. F. x/y.	290·95		inc.		GH
Figs.	175·6557				Bg(GH)
R.		(-290·114)	(-·158)		N(GH)
(. +. RCL 1.). STO 1.		332·631	-·180	332·451	N(H)
F. x/y.		(22·040)	(+·012)		E(GH)
(. +. F. RCL 2.).		136·773	-·164	136·609	E(H)
F. STO 2.					
Figs. F. x/y.	357·35		dec.		HN
Figs.	105·7527				Bg(HN)
R.		(- 97·015)	(+·128)		N(HN)
(. +. RCL 1.). STO 1.		235·616	-·052	235·564	N(N)
F. x/y.		(343·929)	(-·455)		E(HN)
(. +. F..RCL 2.).		480·701	-·619	480·082	E(N)
F. STO 2.					
Figs. F. x/y.	219.90		dec.		NJ
Figs.	357·3830				Bg(NJ)
R.		(219·671)	(-·290)		N(NJ)
(. +. RCL 1.). STO 1.		455·286	-·342	454·944	N(J)
F. x/y.		(- 10·040)	(+·013)		E(NJ)
(. +. F. RCL 2.).		470·661	-·606	470·055	E(J)
F. STO 2.					
Figs. F. x/y.	288.75		inc.		JF
Figs.	309·7300				Bg(JF)
R.		(184·561)	(+·244)		N(JF)
(. +. RCL 1.). STO 1.		639·847	+·098	639·749	N(F)
F. x/y.		(-222·068)	(-·294)		E(JF)
(. +. F. RCL 2.).		248·593	-·900	247·693	E(F)
F. STO 2.					
Figs.	639.75				N(F) at start
-. RCL 1. =.		- 0·097			N Closing Error
Figs.	247.70				E(F) at start
-. F. RCL 2. =.		- 0·893			E Closing Error

Note the repetitive character of the Programme. The abbreviations in the Remarks column are those given in Section 16.4.

The Adjustments are worked out by Method 1; there is no need to describe the appropriate Programme. "Inc. " or "dec." is first entered against the Line, to indicate whether it should be increased or decreased; that is, whether the sign of the adjustment is the same as that of the Departure or Latitude, or the opposite. The effect of the adjustments is cumulative. Thus the adjustments to the Northings of FG, GH, and HN are -·022, -·158, and +·128 respectively; the adjustment to the North Coordinate of N is the sum of these, -·052.

numerical values are worked out; these differ slightly from those in the previous section, for the reason explained above.

Note also that the effect of these corrections is cumulative, and note also that if the first entry is negative, as here, the $^+/-$ key must be used. As in the last section, a negligibly small residual closing error remains, because of the inherent slight inaccuracy in semi-graphical methods of distributing errors.

19.5 *Open Traverses.* An open traverse, strictly, is only linked to the main survey at one end. Particular care is needed in the field in such a case, for a small angular error can cause quite a large displacement in all the points beyond it, and there is no way of distributing, or even of detecting, any of the errors which are likely to occur. This is, therefore, a rather unsatisfactory type of survey, but is sometimes unavoidable, as for example in underground work.

More often, an 'open' traverse in fact closes on some fixed point at each end, with angles taken to some known direction. This is solved in exactly the same way as a closed traverse. The closing error is distributed by method 2; since the ends of the traverse are reliably fixed, the slight theoretical defect of that method is more than outweighed by its simplicity.

19.6 *Linked Traverses.* It is often convenient to use traverses which have one or more sides in common. Unfortunately there is no logically satisfactory way of distributing the closing errors without introducing the complications of the Theory of Least Squares.

The simplest method is to solve the complete outer circuit as a closed traverse, and to take the co-ordinates so found as established; the traverse links are then treated as open traverses running between known points. Thus in Figure 19.2 (assuming JK is not measured) there are the two linked traversers FGHNJ and FJNMKE. The traverse FGHNMKE would be solved first, and then NJF treated as a subsidiary traverse connecting N and F. If the two angles at N as measured do not add up to the adjusted value of angle HNF, each is adjusted by half the error in order to work out the initial bearing of NJ; and similarly at F.

If the second traverse had been divided into FJKE and JNMK, the simplest solution would be to find three pairs of co-ordinates for J, working from F, K, and N independently. J is then taken as being located at the average of these.

19.2 Linked Traverses

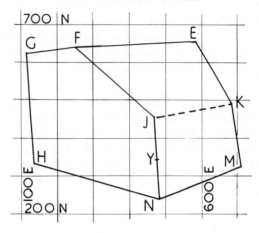

Both these methods give undue weight to the outer circuit, but this can be tolerated if the cross-links are fairly long. Suppose though, that there is only a single cross-link, as would occur if the two traverses linked were FGHNJ and JNMK. Clearly the direct measurement JN is likely to be rather more reliable than the distance between J and N calculated as part of the traverse FGHNMKJ. So where there is a single link, the least unsatisfactory treatment is to solve the two traverses separately, making the co-ordinates of the mid point of the link the same for both. The co-ordinates of the ends of the link are then averaged, the others being left unaltered.

There is no need to go into full detail, but with the example given the following results are obtained.

As already calculated (table 19.2) the co-ordinates of J are 470·055E, 454·944N; and for N, 480·082E, 235·564N. So if Y is the mid point, its co-ordinates are 475·069E, 345·252N.

Taking this as the starting point for YNMKJ, and retaining the same bearing (177° 23·0') for NJ gives the following co-ordinates, using data from Appendix III.

    N 480·092E, 235·343N
    M 711·936E, 330·421N
    K 684·865E, 494·744N
    J 470·046E, 455·163N

These values are accepted for M and K, but for N and J the

averages from the two traverses are used, giving
   J 470·050E, 455·054N
   N 480·087E, 235·453N
This involves accepting small changes in some of the measured angles. It may be worth while to emphasise, once again, that all such methods are merely intended to distribute the errors evenly throughout the network; they do not eliminate them.

20 The Polygonal Network

20.1 *Use of the Network.* Very few archaeological sites require the
elaboration of a theodolite survey to fix their plan; in a quarter of a
century, I have probably used the method, on average, less than
once a year, and about a third of those sites could have been done
entirely by chain survey, though less easily and less accurately.
Nevertheless, when the theodolite is needed it is very useful indeed.
The applicability of the traverse to wooded sites and to
underground work has already been discussed, but some types of
open site can also offer difficulties.

The main criterion in deciding whether or not to use a theodolite-
controlled network is the ease of chaining. On open ground, and
with the type of accuracy envisaged here, that will always be the
method of choice, even if several lines have to be measured which
pick up no detail and are required merely to fix the shape of the
network. The theodolite becomes of value on craggy sites where
direct measurements of some necessary lines may be difficult or
impossible, or in dealing with enclosures where substantial rampart
systems prevent any easy link across them. Nevertheless, since there
is perhaps some personal satisfaction in the feeling that a plan
is really accurate, the theodolite may sometimes be used to measure
angles when these are not essential; an obvious occasion would
be when the instrument is to be used as a tacheometer to provide
spot levels for contouring. As will be seen from the examples
below, the greater accuracy of angular measurements tends to
balance out the linear errors.

20.2 *Numerical Examples: General Discussion.* The typical basic
network for this type of work is a polygon, usually five- or six-
sided, with a central station. Geometrically this is a very satisfactory rigid arrangement, and it becomes even better when several

such polygons are linked together (Paras. 20.7, 20.8). Unhappily, the calculations involved in reducing the actual observations to the co-ordinates of the stations are laborious; but they are not inherently difficult, involving merely addition and subtraction and the use of tables or a calculator. Since a survey of this kind may well take two people a week or more in the field, it is surely unreasonable to grudge less than half a man-day spent on working out the results.

In the two sections which follow, complete solutions, including the calculation of co-ordinates, are given for a typical single polygon; partial solutions for interlocking polygons are given in Paras. 20.7 and 20.8. The single polygon is solved first using logarithms and second with a hand calculator, using identical data. The first solution, though rather longer, is more easily followed and will simplify the understanding of the second. Both provide a programme of work which is applicable to any problem of this kind.

The main difficulty in solving such a problem lies not in understanding what has to be done, but in doing it right. Each calculation involves well over 500 digits, and my own experience indicates that the chance of writing one down incorrectly is high. The calculations are designed to detect a mistake, but only when the work is finished. You are therefore very strongly advised to make all entries in pencil, and to follow the advice given as to checking, wearisome though it may be.

20.3 *Reduction of Polygonal Network by Logarithms.* All the angles of the network have been measured, as well as the chain lines corresponding to the circumference, but not the radial lines. The co-ordinates of station B are known, and the bearing of EB. These are entered in the appropriate tables below.

The first step, as when working out a traverse, is to draw the network carefully to a suitable scale (Figure 20.1). Squared paper may make a convenient background. As with any type of survey, this small-scale plot not only makes it easier to envisage what is being done, but will detect any large mistake. To simplify the notation imagine that you are looking outwards from the centre along each radial line and name the two angles at the circumference 'Right Hand' and 'Left Hand' (RH and LH); for example ∠AGF is ∠GR, ∠FGH is ∠GL.

Most of the laborious routine of calculation is made necessary by

20.1 Polygon Network

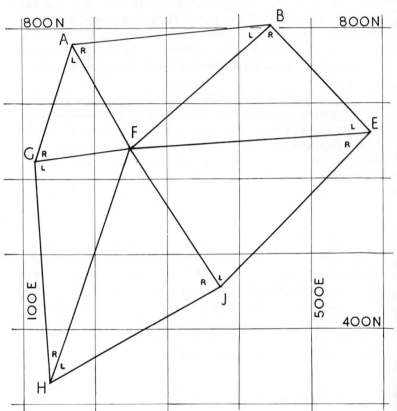

the presence of errors. As explained in Para. 19.2, the objective at each stage is to have a geometrically possible diagram as basis for your calculations. Only the relevant errors are distributed at each step and the figures which result are used in the next stage. Logically, this is rather unsatisfactory; why, for example, should the central angles, once balanced, be immune from further adjustment, in contrast to those at the circumference? The main reason is simply convenience for although a system of step by step calculation could be devised to give almost the same adjustment to every angle, the work involved (unless a computer were available) would be excessive, and the final result would be only a little more accurate, for the errors which have to be distributed are small.

The calculation should proceed by the following stages:

(i) After drawing the small-scale plan, draw out a table (as table 20.1), first setting out the whole scheme of calculation symbolically, then entering the known numerical values.

(ii) Next, the measured angles are adjusted to satisfy the elementary requirements of geometry. First, the angles of each triangle are brought up to total 180°. The measured angles of GFH, for example, add up to 180° 02·4', so each is reduced by 0·80', similarly for BFA each is increased by 0·23' or 0·24'. My own preference is to work to the absurd 'accuracy' of 0·01', rather than to worry about where to put an odd 0·1'; but this is purely a matter of individual choice.

When the triangles have been 'balanced', the total of the central angles will usually require further adjustment, to bring them to the necessary total of 360°. In this case, the sum is 0·17' too small, so five get an additional 0·03', one 0·02'. The central angles are given no further adjustment, but the other two angles of each triangle have to be decreased, by 0·01' or 0·02', to bring the totals back to 180° again.

When this stage has been reached, a / is drawn through each previous 'minutes' figure, to eliminate the risk of using it by mistake.

Although it is good practice to use this rather meticulous double adjustment of the angles, it would be acceptable to miss out the first stage, so that you start by balancing the central angles to give 360°, and then balance each triangle by adjusting only the other two angles.

(iii) You now have six geometrically possible triangles which fit together at their vertices to give a total of 360°, so at first glance you may hope that all the inconvenient demands of geometry are satisfied; but one remains.

If you start with an assumed length for one radial (say AF) and work all round the circuit using the $a/\sin A = b/\sin B$ formula until you get back to AF, you will find that the final value differs from that with which you started.

Suppose that it is smaller, and you have gone anticlockwise. Then the diagram (Figure 20.2) shows that this would occur if some right-hand angles were too large and the corresponding left-hand angles too small. Since we do not know where the errors are likely to be, we 'shift' the same adjustment from each RH angle to each LH angle, thus leaving the total for each triangle unaltered. This is

Table 20.1 Polygonal Network, Using Logarithms
(a) Adjustment of Sides and Angles

Angles: preliminary balancing.

Triangle	Left-hand Angles Measured	Adjusted 2	Central Angles Measured	Adjusted 1	Right-hand Angles Measured	Adjusted 2	Initial Total
GFH	92° 57·3'	56·50' 56·48'	62° 53·8'	53·00' 53·03'	24° 11·3'	10·50' 10·49'	180° 02·4'
HFJ	49° 58·1'	57·90' 57·89'	70° 05·8'	05·60' 05·63'	59° 56·7'	56·50' 56·48'	180° 00·6'
JFE	78° 33·3'	33·70' 33·68'	43° 11·8'	12·20' 12·23'	58° 13·7'	14·10' 14·09'	179° 58·8'
EFB	48° 53·8'	53·80' 53·79'	36° 20·8'	20·80' 20·83'	94° 45·4'	45·40' 45·38'	180° 00·0'
BFA	35° 13·9'	14·13' 14·12'	79° 34·5'	34·73' 34·75'	65° 10·9'	11·13' 11·12'	179° 59·3'
AFG	48° 73·6'	33·80' 33·79'	67° 53·3'	53·50' 53·53'	63° 32·5'	32·70' 32·68'	179° 59·4'

359 59·83'

Angles: calculation of Shift.

Triangle	Left-hand Angle	log. sin.	Diff. 01'		Right-hand Angle	log. sin.	Diff. 01'
GFH	GL	92° 56·48'	9·999 427	006	HR	24° 10·49'	9·612 278	281
HFJ	HL	49° 57·89'	9·884 030	106	JR	59° 56·48'	9·937 274	073
JFE	JL	78° 33·68'	9·991 287	026	ER	58° 14·09'	9·929 528	078
EFB	EL	48° 53·79'	9·877 097	110	BR	94° 45·38'	9·998 502	011
BFA	BL	35° 14·12'	9·761 128	179	AR	65° 11·12'	9·957 928	058
AFG	AL	48° 33·79'	9·874 879	112	GR	63° 32·68'	9·951 960	063
Totals			9·387 848	527			9·387 470	542

Sum for L.H. Angles exceeds that for R.H. Angles by 378; so Shift required
equals 378 divided by 1069, equals 00·35' from L.H. to R.H. Angles.

Adjusted Angles and Bearings.

GH 175° 40·10' (given) S 04° 19·90' E
HR   24° 10·84'
FH 199° 50·94'   S 19° 50·94' W
HL   49° 57·54' - 180°
HJ   69° 48·48'   N 69° 48·48' E
JR   59° 56·83'
FJ 129° 45·31'   S 50° 14·69' E
JL   78° 33·33' - 180°
JE   28° 18·64'   N 28° 18·64' E
ER   58° 14·44'
FE   86° 33·08'   N 86° 33·08' E
EL   48° 53·44' + 180°
EB 315° 26·52'   N 44° 33·48' W
BR   94° 45·73'
FB   50° 12·25'   N 50° 12·25' E
BL   35° 13·77' + 180°
BA 265° 26·02'   S 85° 26·02' W
AR   65° 11·47'
FA 330° 37·49'   N 29° 22·51' W
AL   48° 33·44' - 180°
AG 199° 10·93'   S 19° 10·93' W
GR   63° 33·03'
FG 262° 43·96'   S 82° 43·96' W
GL   92° 56·13' - 180°
GH 175° 40·09'

Calculation of Sides (GH taken as 290·95).

```
log FG 2·126 763
+ 1s. HR 9·612 376
       2·514 387          ←         2·514 387
- 1s. GL 9·999 430  - 1s. GFH 9·949 431
  log FH 2·513 817        log GH 2·463 818
- 1s. JR 9·937 299
       2·576 518          →         2·576 518
+ 1s. HL 9·883 993  + 1s. HFJ 9·973 244
  log FJ 2·460 511        log HJ 2·549 762
- 1s. ER 9·929 555
       2·530 956          →         2·530 956
+ 1s. JL 9·991 278  + 1s. JFE 9·835 434
  log FE 2·522 234        log JE 2·366 390
- 1s. BR 9·998 498
       2·523 736          →         2·523 736
+ 1s. EL 9·877 058  + 1s. EFB 9·772 818
  log FB 2·400 794        log EB 2·296 554
- 1s. AR 9·957 948
       2·442 846          →         2·442 846
+ 1s. BL 9·761 065  + 1s. BFA 9·992 777
  log FA 2·203 911        log BA 2·435 623
- 1s. GR 9·951 982
       2·251 929          →         2·251 929
+ 1s. AL 9·874 840  + 1s. AFG 9·966 835
  log FG 2·126 769        log AG 2·218 764
```

	Measured	Calculated as above
GH	290·95	290·950
HJ	355·45	354·619
JE	233·15	232·482
EB	197·80	197·950
BA	273·00	272·661
AG	165·65	165·487
Totals	1516·00	1514·149
logs	3·180 699	3·180 169 Diff. = 530

So 530 must be added to all the calculated logs

Table 20.1 Polygonal Network, Using Logarithms
(b) Calculation of Co-ordinates

Traverse round circumference:

Line	Station	Departures E	W	Latitudes N	S	Coordinates E	N
	G given					114·750	622·750
GH		22·002	—	—	290·473		
	H					136·752	332·277
HJ		333·231	—	122·552	—·		
	J					469·983	454·829
JE		110·390	—	204·925	—		
	E					580·373	659·754
EB		—	139·057	141·219	—		
	B					441·316	800·973
BA		—	272·127	—	21·734		
	A					169·189	779·239
AG		—	54·441	—	156·490		
	G					114·748	622·749

Radial lines:

Line	Station	Departures E	W	Latitudes N	S	Coordinates E	N
	G given					114·750	622·750
GF		132·981	—	16·958	—		
	F					247·731	639·708
FH		—	110·979	—	307·431		
	H					136·752	332·277
FJ		222·252	—	—	184·879		
	J					469·983	454·829
FE		332·642	—	20·046	—		
	E					580·373	659·754
FB		193·585	—	161·265	—		
	B					441·316	800·973
FA		—	78·542	139·531	—		
	A					169·189	779·239

Calculations:

```
         1·342 467            2·522 745            2·042 929            2·143 193
ls.      8·878 119     ls.    9·972 453    ls.     9·676 009    ls.    9·846 109
log GH   2·464 348     log HJ 2·550 292    log JE  2·366 920    log EB 2·297 084
lc.      9·998 758     lc.    9·538 029    lc.     9·944 675    lc.    9·852 810
         2·463 106            2·088 321            2·311 595            2·149 894

         2·434 772            1·735 925            2·123 790            2·045 241
ls.      9·998 619     ls.    9·516 631    ls.     9·996 497    ls.    9·530 894
log BA   2·436 153     log AG 2·219 294    log FG  2·127 293    log FH 2·514 347
lc.      8·900 985     lc.    9·975 192    lc.     9·102 087    lc.    9·973 401
         1·337 138            2·194 486            1·229 380            2·487 748

         2·346 845            2·521 977            2·286 872            1·895 103
ls.      9·885 804     ls.    9·999 213    ls.     9·885 548    ls.    9·690 662
log FJ   2·461 041     log FE 2·522 764    log FB  2·401 324    log FA 2·204 441
lc.      9·805 846     lc.    8·779 266    lc.     9·806 217    lc.    9·940 231
         2·266 887            1·302 030            2·207 541            2·144 672
```

20.2 Effect of Shifts in Circumferential Angles

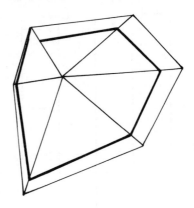

called 'the Method of Equal Shifts'.

To understand the method of calculation, write down the a/sin A = b/sin B equation for each triangle as follows, using logarithms.

log BF − log sin ∠AR = log AF − log sin ∠BL
log AF − log sin ∠GR = log GF − log sin ∠AL
log GF − log sin ∠HR = log HF − log sin ∠GL
log HF − log sin ∠JR = log JF − log sin ∠HL
log JF − log sin ∠ER = log EF − log sin ∠JL
log EF − log sin ∠BR = log BF − log sin ∠EL

∠AR and ∠AL are the 'right-hand' and 'left-hand' angles at A, and similarly throughout.

Adding, you will see that the 'log sines' sum is the same on each side of the equation. The geometrical requirement, therefore, is that the sum of the 'log sines' of the LH angles equals that of the RH angles.

Now enter the logarithms, to six figures, of the sines of the *balanced* angles, in the appropriate columns of table 19.3. For those not familiar with the convention, the use of 9 rather than 1 or 8 instead of 2 is merely for simplicity in addition; in this context there is no possibility of confusion. You also enter, in the Diff 01' column the amounts by which the last three figures of the 'log sines' increase if the angle is increased by 01'. Note that if the angle exceeds 90° as in ∠GL and ∠BR, the effect is negative, so ring these quantities to avoid confusion. Using wide paper, this and the previous part of the table can be combined.

Now, having laboriously looked up and noted twelve six-figure logarithms you will, if you are sensible, look them all up again. The reason for this barely tolerable penance is that if you do make a mistake at this stage you will not detect it until you have done a lot more calculation, all of which will be wasted.

Adding the columns, the sum of the 'log sines' for the LH angles proves to be 374 greater than that for the RH angles, and a shift of one minute from the LH to the RH angles will decrease the LH total by 527 and increase the RH by 542. The shift needed is therefore $374 \div 1069 = 0.35'$.

(iv) Now, assuming your arithmetic is right, you have a network of triangles which is geometrically consistent. You have now to calculate the sides, and from them the station co-ordinates, but there ought to be no more closing errors to distribute; if any greater than a few millimetres appear, a mistake has been made somewhere.

The bearings will be needed later, and if they are worked out at this stage they will give an automatic check on the accuracy of the list of adjusted angles. Note, when making out this part of the table, that the type of entry recurs every fourth line; so the easiest way of preparing it is to list first of all the circumferential lines, GH, HJ, etc. at the appropriate spacing, then the right-hand angles, $\angle HR$, $\angle JR$ etc. and so on. The adjusted angles, and the given bearing of GH are then entered, and the calculation proceeds automatically.

(v) The lengths of the lines must now be worked out. Arrange a table, in symbolic form with space for logarithms, corresponding to the $a/\sin A = b/\sin B$ formula applied round the circuit. It is desirable always to keep to the same arangement, with radial lines on the left, and circumferential lines on the right. If FG were known, then Log FG $-$ log sin $\angle GHF$ (abbreviated to l.s. $\angle HR$) $+$ log sin $\angle HGF = $ log FH; log FH $-$ log sin $\angle HJF + $ log sin $\angle JHF = $ log FJ; and so on until FG is reached again. For the circumferential lines, log FG $-$ l.s. $\angle HR + $ log sin $\angle GFH = $ log GH; log FH $-$ l.s. $\angle JR + $ l.s. HFJ $= $ log HJ etc. Note again, that the type of quantity entered recurs regularly; this simplifies the preparation of the table.

When the symbolic framework for this calculation is complete, enter the log sines of the adjusted angles; but to calculate the lengths of the sides we need to assume some known lengths to start with.

As in the next section, we could start by assuming FG $= 100$ m, but for a reason given below it is better to get the lengths nearly right. Only the circumferential lines have been reliably measured, so we start with GH (any other measured line would serve), and the actual procedure of calculation is log GH − l.s. ∠GFH (= 2·514387) + l.s. ∠HR = log FG and log GH − l.s. ∠GFH + l.s. ∠GL = log FH, after which the calculation proceeds as before. Two points should be noted: first, that the 'radial-line' column starts with the line immediately before the measured circumferential line; and second that special care is needed to be sure that you do not *add* log GH and l.s. ∠GFH. Indeed, you would be well advised to check as you proceed that the measurements on your small-scale plan do agree reasonably well with the calculated logarithms. To do this is tiresome, but less so than finding a mistake after you have completed all the arithmetic. Assuming everything has been done correctly, the final value of log FG will agree very closely with the initial value; a small difference in the last figure is to be expected.

(vii) Unfortunately, the calculation had to be started using a single measurement. In this example, we have assumed that all the circumferential lines were measured with equal care, so they ought all to be taken into account, and their total is presumably more reliable proportionately than the length of GH only. The measured total is 1516 m, while that calculated from GH is 1514·149 m; the logarithms of these numbers differ by 0·000530, so that amount must be added to all the calculated logarithms of the lengths. As we started with a measured line, the adjustment is small and the addition can easily be done mentally.

(viii) The remaining work requires no special comment. The departure and latitude are calculated in the standard way for all lines, and set out in tabular form. Note that every station is fixed in two ways, as part of the traverse round the circumference and by radials from F. Do not yield to the temptation to rest content with one of these calculations, for the duplication provides a valuable final check on the accuracy of your work.

20.4 *Reduction of Polygonal Network Using Calculator* (Table 20.2). The principles involved are exactly the same as in the last section, to which reference should be made for explanation of the reasoning. What follows describes the differences in approach required with a calculator, although much of it is almost identical with table 20.1.

Stages (i) and (ii) are the same as when using logarithms, though the arrangement of the table is different and the angles are expressed as decimals of a degree.

Stage (iii), calculation of the required 'Shift', proceeds differently. Rather than looking up 'log sins', it is quicker to start with some assumed value for a radial line, and work round the circuit back to it. In this case FG is taken as 100 and the value on returning to it is 100·088. Examination of the programme shows that if the LH angles are too big the final result is too big; that is, a change in the last datum produces a similar change in the result, which is a fairly easy rule to remember. This assumes that you have worked anticlockwise. A second calculation is therefore made with a shift of 0·01° from LH to RH angles, giving a final result of 99·940 for FG. So the actual Shift needed will be 0·01 × 0·88 ÷ 0·148 = 0·00595° from LH to RH angles; this can be applied as 0·0059° and 0·0060° alternately.

For stages (iv) and (v), using the adjusted angles plus or minus the shift as appropriate, a similar programme gives all the lines starting with the assumption that FG is 100. As previously, the total of the lengths of the reliable measured lines is compared with the total as calculated, but as the necessary multiplication can be done rapidly by putting the required factor into a memory, there is no advantage now in getting the calculated lengths nearly right.

The remaining work, stage (viii), again requires little comment. The two sets of calculations, for the circuit and for the radial lines, are arranged for easy comparison of the results. Note that in working out the bearings, there is no need either to reduce them or to express them as positive angles.

The mathematically minded reader will observe that the method of calculating 'shifts' is not really identical with that used for logarithms, but the difference is completely negligible. He will also see that the tables could have been arranged rather more compactly: for example, the bearings could have been entered directly in the calculation of co-ordinates. This has not been attempted, because too elaborate a scheme can tend to cause mistakes.

20.5 *Different Applications of Single Polygonal Networks.* There are two modifications of the polygonal network which are sometimes useful. One is, paradoxically, to have the 'central' station outside the circuit (Figure 20.3). The RH and LH angles are assigned as before; the slight confusion at V and Y in the figure is easily resolved. In balancing the 'central' angles the numerical

Table 20.2 Polygonal Network, Using Calculator
(a) Adjustment of Sides and Angles

Except that decimals of a degree are used instead of minutes, the preliminary balancing of the angles proceeds exactly as in Table 20.1a. The balanced angles are used in the table below.

Calculation of Shift:

Programme	With angles as balanced Data	Results	After 0 01° shift, LH to RH Data	Results	Notes
Figs. ÷ .	100·00		100·00		FG taken as 100
Figs. sin. x.	24·1747		24·1847		H͡R
Figs. sin.	92·9415		92·9315		G͡L
÷ .		(243·867)		(243·774)	(FH)
Figs. sin. x.	59·9415		59·9515		J͡R
Figs. sin.	49·9647		49·9547		H͡L
÷ .		(215·728)		(215·593)	(FJ)
Figs. sin. x.	58·2347		58·2447		E͡R
Figs. sin.	78·5615		78·5515		J͡L
÷ .		(248·695)		(248·504)	(FE)
Figs. sin. x.	94·7565		94·7665		B͡R
Figs. sin.	48·8964		48·8864		E͡L
÷ .		(188·045)		(187·874)	(FB)
Figs. sin. x.	65·1853		65·1953		A͡R
Figs. sin.	35·2354		35·2254		B͡L
÷ .		(119·526)		(119·378)	(FA)
Figs. sin. x.	63·5448		63·5548		G͡R
Figs. sin.	48·5630		48·5530		A͡L
= .		100·088		99·940	FG

Shift required = 0·00595. This has been included in the angles entered below.

Adjusted Angles and Bearings | Calculation of sides after Shift with FG taken as 100.

Programme	Data	Results	Notes	Programme	Data	Results	Notes
Figs. STO 1.	180			Figs. ÷ .	100·00		'FG'
Figs. + .	175·6683		Bg(GH)	Figs. sin. x. STO 1.	24·1806		H͡R
Figs.	24·1806		H͡R	Figs. sin.	62·8838		G͡FH
+ .		199·8489	Bg(FH)	= .		217·298	GH
Figs. - . RCL 1.	49·9587		H͡L	RCL 1. x. Figs. sin.	92·9356		G͡L
+ .		69·8076	Bg(HJ)	÷ .		243·812	FH
Figs.	59·9475		J͡R	Figs. sin. x. STO 1.	59·9475		J͡R
+ .		129·7551	Bg(FJ)	Figs. sin.	70·0938		H͡FJ
Figs. - . RCL 1.	78·5556		J͡L	= .		264·849	HJ
+ .		28·3107	Bg(JE)	RCL 1. x. Figs. sin.	49·9587		H͡L
Figs.	58·2406		E͡R	÷		215·648	FJ
+ .		86·5513	Bg(FE)	Figs. sin. x. STO 1.	58·2406		E͡R
Figs. - . RCL 1.	48·8904		E͡L	Figs. sin.	43·2038		J͡FE
+ .		-44·5583	Bg(EB)	= .		173·630	JE
Figs.	94·7625		B͡R	RCL 1. x. Figs. sin.	78·5556		J͡L
+ .		50·2042	Bg(FB)	÷ .		248·582	FE
Figs. - . RCL 1.	35·2295		B͡L	Figs. sin. x. STO 1.	94·7625		B͡R
+ .		-94·5663	Bg(BA)	Figs. sin.	36·3471		E͡PB
Figs.	65·1912		A͡R	= .		147·839	EB
+ .		-29·3751	Bg(FA)	RCL 1. x. Figs. sin.	48·8904		E͡L
Figs. - . RCL 1.	48·5570		A͡L	÷		187·943	FB
+ .		-160·8181	Bg(AG)	Figs. sin. x. STO 1.	65·1912		A͡R
Figs.	63·5508		G͡R	Figs. sin.	79·5793		B͡FA
+ .		-97·2673	Bg(FG)	= .		203·637	BA
Figs. - . RCL 1.	92·9356		G͡L	RCL 1. x. Figs. sin.	35·2295		B͡L
= .		-184·3317	Bg(GH) ✓	÷ .		119·438	PA
				Figs. sin. x. STO 1.	63·5508		G͡R
				Figs. sin.	67·8922		A͡FG
				= .		123·593	AG
				RCL 1. x. Figs. sin.	48·5570		A͡L
				= .		100·000	FG ✓

Table 20.2 Polygonal Network, Using Calculator
(b) Calculation of Co-ordinates

```
Total for GH, HJ, JE, EB, BA, and AG, as measured = 1516·00
Total with FG taken as 100                         = 1130·847
                                      Ratio        =    1·34059
```

The lengths used below in calculating the coordinates are therefore 1·34059
times the value found with FG taken as 100.

Traverse round circumference

Programme	Data	Results	Notes
Figs. STO 1.	622·75		N(G)
Figs. F. STO 2.	114·75		E(G)
Figs. F. x/y.	291·307		GH
Figs.	175·6683		Bg(GH)
R.			
(. +. RCL 1.).		332·275	N(H)
STO 1. F. x/y.			
(. +. F. RCL 2.).		136·753	E(H)
F. STO 2.			
Figs. F. x/y.	355·053		HJ
Figs.	69·8076		Bg(HJ)
R.			
(. +. RCL 1.).		454·830	N(J)
STO 1. F. x/y.			
(. +. F. RCL 2.).		469·984	E(J)
F. STO 2.			
Figs. F. x/y.	232·766		JE
Figs.	28·3107		Bg(JE)
R.			
(. +. RCL 1.).		659·755	N(E)
STO 1. F. x/y.			
(. +. F. RCL 2.).		580·373	E(E)
F. STO 2.			
Figs. F. x/y.	198·191		EB
Figs. +/-.	-44·5583		Bg(EB)
R.			
(. +. RCL 1.).		800·973	N(B)
STO 1. F. x/y.			
(. +. F. RCL 2.).		441·315	E(B)
F. STO 2.			
Figs. F. x/y.	272·993		BA
Figs. +/-.	-94·5663		Bg(BA)
R.			
(. +. RCL 1.).		779·240	N(A)
STO 1. F. x/y.			
(. +. F. RCL 2.).		169·189	E(A)
F. STO 2.			
Figs. F. x/y.	165·687		AG
Figs. +/-.	-160·8181		Bg(AG)
R.			
(. +. RCL 1.).		622·752	N(G)
F. x/y.			
(. +. F. RCL 2.).		114·749	E(G)

Radial lines

Programme	Data	Results	Notes
Figs. STO 1.	622·75		N(G)
Figs. F. STO 2.	114·75		E(G)
Figs. F. x/y.	134·059		FG
Figs. +/-.	-277·2673		Bg(GF)
R.			
(. +. RCL 1.).		639·708	N(F)
STO 1.			
F. x/y.			
(+. F. RCL 2.).		247·732	E(F)
F. STO 2.			
Figs. F. x/y.	326·851		FH
Figs.	199·8489		Bg(FH)
R.			
(. +. RCL 1.).		332·275	N(H)
F. x/y			
(. +. F. RCL 2.).		136·753	E(H)
Figs. F. x/y.	289·095		FJ
Figs.	129·7551		Bg(FJ)
R.			
(. +. RCL 1.).		454·830	N(J)
F. x/y.			
(. +. F. RCL 2.).		469·984	E(J)
Figs. F. x/y.	333·246		FE
Figs.	86·5513		Bg(FE)
R.			
(. +. RCL 1.).		659·755	N(E)
F. x/y.			
(. +. F. RCL 2.).		580·375	E(E)
Figs. F. x/y.	251·954		FB
Figs.	50·2042		Bg(FB)
R.			
(. +. RCL 1.).		800·972	N(B)
F. x/y.			
(. +. F. RCL 2.).		441·316	E(B)
Figs. F. x/y.	160·117		FA
Figs. +/-.	-29·3751		Bg(FA)
R.			
(. +. RCL 1.).		779·239	N(A)
F. x/y.			
(. +. F. RCL 2.).		169·191	E(A)

20.3 Polygon with Centre outside Circuit

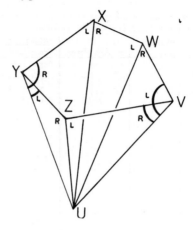

values of some (for example, $\angle$YUZ and $\angle$ZUV) will need to be increased by the average adjustment, and others ($\angle$VUW, $\angle$WUX, $\angle$XUY) to be decreased.

The second application is when a closed traverse has a central feature (such as a church spire) which is visible but not accessible. The accuracy of the traverse can be greatly improved by including this feature in the points observed from each station of the circuit. The central angles can easily be found, as 180° less the two relevant angles at the circumference, and the calculation then follows the procedure for a polygon with a central station, with the gain in accuracy given by the use of angular rather than mainly linear measurements.

20.6 *Balancing a Quadrilateral.* The quadrilateral is important enough to deserve special mention. Besides being a convenient network for many types of structure, it is useful when the ground is generally irregular. A short base line, preferably one diagonal, is located on good ground and measured with particular care; then, again taking particular care with measurement of the angles, it can be extended to give an accurate length for the other diagonal which can be three or four times as long, with its ends so placed as to be part of the main network, although accurate direct measurement between them would be difficult. Another special case is the final check on accuracy in setting out a rectangle (Chapter 15).

Table 20.3 Quadrilateral with Angles Measured

'Balancing Angles:

	Measured	Adjusted		Measured	Adjusted
B̂R	39·8033	39·8058	ĴR	45·5033	45·5058
ÊL	48·8967	48·8992	F̂L	43·1967	43·1992
	88·7000	88·7050		88·7000	88·7050
ÊR	58·2283	58·2358	F̂R	36·3467	36·3442
ĴL	33·0517	33·0592	B̂L	54·9533	54·9508
	91·2800	91·2950		91·3000	91·2950

Measured sides:
BE = 197·80
EJ = 233·15
JF = 288·75
FB = 252·20

Average angle at X = 90° +/- 1·2950

Calculation of Shift:

Programme	With angles as balanced Data	Results	With 0·01' shift, LH to RH Data	Results	Notes
Figs. ÷.	100 00		100·00		XB taken as 100
Figs. sin. x.	36·3442		36·3542		F̂R
Figs. sin.	54·9508		54·9408		B̂L
÷.					gives XF
Figs. sin. x.	45·5058		45·5158		ĴR
Figs. sin.	43·1992		43·1892		F̂L
÷.					gives XJ
Figs. sin. x.	58·2358		58·2458		ÊR
Figs. sin.	33·0592		33·0492		ĴL
÷.					gives XE
Figs. sin. x.	39·8058		39·8158		B̂R
Figs. sin.	48·8992		48·8892		ÊL
=.		100·116		99·970	XB

So required Shift = 0·01' x 116 ÷ 146 = 0·0079'

Calculation of sides after shift:

Programme	Data	Results with XB = 100	Final Results	Notes
Figs. ÷.	100·00		149·373	XB
Figs. sin. x. STO 1.	36·3521			F̂R
Figs. sin. F. STO 2.	88·7050			X̂
=.		168·663	251·938	BF
RCL 1. x. Figs. sin. ÷.	54·9429			B̂L
Figs. sin. x. STO 1.	45·5137			ĴR
F. RCL 2. =.		193·525	289·075	FJ
RCL 1. x. Figs. sin. ÷.	43·1913			F̂L
Figs..sin. x. STO 1.	58·2437			ÊR
F. RCL 2. =.		155·776	232·688	JE
RCL 1. x. Figs. sin. ÷.	33·0513			ĴL
Figs. sin. x. STO 1.	39·8137			B̂R
F. RCL 2. =.		132·687	198·199	EB
RCL 1. x. Figs. sin.	48·8913			ÊL
=.		100·0006 ✓		XB

Total excluding XB = 650·651 and Measured Total = 971·9.
So Ratio 1·49373

In a four-sided traverse also, when diagonal observations are possible, solution as a quadrilateral network will give a more accurate adjustment of the errors than the usual method; and it is sometimes possible, even in a polygonal traverse, to treat four stations as the corners of a quadrilateral.

The only difficulty which arises is how best to 'balance' the measured angles. One alternative is to treat the quadrilateral as a triangular 'polygon' (EBF in the example which follows) with an external 'centre' (J); but this is open to the objection that the angles at J receive different treatment from the others. The method set out in table 20.3 seems preferable. The calculations are only carried as far as the determination of the lengths of the lines.

Little comment is needed. The point X, the intersection of the two diagonals, is not marked on the ground, but is introduced as part of the calculations; there is no need to work out its co-ordinates. The procedure is to work out the four possible angles at X from the angles at the circumference, and to average the results. The right-hand and left-hand angles are then adjusted so that the triangles total 180°, and the calculation proceeds in the usual way. Note that since the sine of an angle is the same as the sine of 180° minus that angle, one of the calculator's memories can be used to save re-entering the central angle at each repetition.

20.7 *Two Linked Polygons.* For a large irregular site it is often impossible to find a single 'central' station from which all those on the perimeter can be observed. Such a site can be covered by two or more interlocking polygons; this arrangement gives a very good rigid network.

Two such polygons are shown in Figure 20.4, and the calculations, including the data (the measured angles) are set out in table 20.4; they are carried as far as determining the shifts needed. The first step, as always, is to 'balance' the triangles, essentially as in Para. 20.3, stage (ii). The first adjustments, 1, bring each triangle to 180°. The central angles, though, now total 0·0083° too much around E and 0·0030° too little around F. Two triangles, EFB and EFJ, are shared; for example, the angle EFB is a central angle for the polygon centred on F, but a right-hand angle for that centred on E. As there are still four triangles in each polygon which are not shared, the simplest way to distribute the central closing errors is to distribute them among those four. Thus the triangles EFB, EFJ, are now treated as fixed, and in the polygon centred on E, for

20.4 Two Polygons Linked

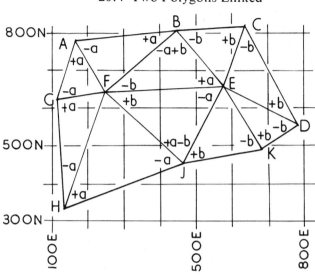

example, the 0·0083° is distributed among the other four central angles, reducing three of them by 0·0021° and one by 0·0020°; the ten-thousandth part of a degree is insignificant, and can be disposed of in any angle without affecting the results. The triangles no longer total 180°, so the right-hand and left-hand angles are all increased by 0·0010° or 0·0011° to eliminate the error. You could if you wished go two steps further, as explained in the next section, to get a rather more even distribution of the errors; but there seems no need to do so in this case.

These adjusted angles are used to calculate the shifts. As will be seen, various approaches which differ in detail are possible, but all depend on the same principle of 'equal shifts'.

The increase, for an increase of 0·01°, in the last three figures of a six-figure 'log sin', is given by 075·8 divided by the tangent of the angle; proof, if you want it, is given in Para. 20.9. So these increases can easily be tabulated; but if you have tables to hand it is quicker to use them as in Para. 20.8 Then assuming that in each polygon there is a shift from right-hand to left-hand angles as shown in Figure 20.4, the relative increase in the 'left-hand' sum of the log sins can be written down.

Each polygon is then solved, using the angles as balanced; the

Table 20.4 Two Polygons Linked

Angles: preliminary balancing.

Triangle	Left-hand Angles Measured	Adjusted 1	2	Central Angles Measured	Adjusted 1	2	Right-hand Angles Measured	Adjusted 1	2	Initial Total
FEJ	43·1967	·2033	·2033	58·2281	·2350	·2350	78·5550	·5617	·5617	179·9800
JEK	51·2667	·2800	·2810	60·5483	·5616	·5595	68·1450	·1584	·1595	179·9600
KED	88·9983	·9917	·9927	30·7717	·7650	·7630	60·2500	·2433	·2443	180·0200
DEC	34·0700	·0783	·0794	97·9083	·9167	·9146	47·9967	·0050	·0060	179·9750
CEB	65·2133	·2067	·2077	63·6400	·6333	·6312	51·1667	·1600	·1611	180·0200
BEF	94·7567	·7567	·7567	48·8967	·8967	·8967	36·3467	·3466	·3466	180·0001
				360·0083						
EFB	48·8967	·8967	·8967	36·3467	·3466	·3466	94·7567	·7567	·7567	180·0001
BFA	35·2317	·2356	·2353	79·5750	·5788	·5795	65·1817	·1856	·1852	179·9884
AFG	48·5600	·5633	·5629	67·8883	·8917	·8925	63·5417	·5450	·5446	179·9900
GFH	92·9550	·9417	·9413	62·8967	·8833	·8840	24·1883	·1750	·1747	180·0400
HFJ	49·9683	·9650	·9646	70·0967	·0933	·0941	59·9450	·9417	·9413	180·0100
JFE	78·5550	·5617	·5617	43·1967	·2033	·2033	58·2283	·2350	·2350	179·9800
				359·9970						

Increase in 4th. to 6th. figure of log sin for increase of $0·01° = 075·8 \div$ tangent.

L. H. Angles	inc	Shift	R. H. Angles	inc	Shift	L. H. Angles	inc	Shift	R. H. Angles	inc	Shift
FEJ 43·2033	81	+b	78·5617	15	+a −b	EFB 48·8967	66	+a	94·7567	−6	−a +b
JEK 51·2810	61	+b	68·1595	30	−b	BFA 35·2353	107	+a	65·1852	35	−a
KED 88·9927	1	+b	60·2443	43	−b	AFG 48·5629	67	+a	63·5446	38	−a
DEC 34·0794	112	+b	48·0060	68	−b	GFH 92·9413	−4	+a	24·1747	169	−a
CEB 65·2077	35	+b	51·1611	61	−b	HFJ 49·9646	64	+a	59·9413	44	−a
BEF 94·7567	−6	−a +b	36·3466	103	−b	JFE 78·5617	15	+a −b	58·2350	47	−a
Totals:	+ 6a + 284b		+ 15a − 320b				+ 315a − 15b		− 327a − 6b		

Relative increase of 'left-hand' sums:
− 9a + 604b   + 642a − 9b

Calculation of Shifts:

Programme	Polygon centre E. Data	Results	Notes	Polygon centre F. Data	Results	Notes
Figs. ÷.	100·00		EF	100·00		FE
Figs. sin. x.	78·5617		JR	94·7567		BR
Figs. sin. ÷.	43·2033		FL	48·8967		EL
Figs. sin. x.	68·1595		KR	65·1852		AR
Figs. sin. ÷.	51·2810		JL	35·2353		BL
Figs. sin. x.	60·2443		DR	63·5446		GR
Figs. sin. ÷.	88·9927		KL	48·5629		AL
Figs. sin. x.	48·0060		CR	24·1747		HR
Figs. sin. ÷.	34·0794		DL	92·9413		GL
Figs. sin. x.	51·1611		BR	59·9413		JR
Figs. sin. ÷.	65·2077		CL	49·9646		HL
Figs. sin. x.	36·3466		FR	58·2350		ER
Figs. sin.	94·7567		BL	78·5617		JL
=.		99·9063	EF		100·0877	FE
Logarithms	1·999 593			2·000 381		

= 2 − ·000 407

So the required Shifts are given by the equations: 9a − 604b = −407
642a − 9b = −381

whence a = −·58 = − ·0058°; b = ·66 = ·0066°

programme is the same as in table 20.2, but for brevity the circumferential lines have not been included. Considering the polygon centred on F, if FE is taken as 100 to start with, its final value is 100·0877. The logarithm of this is 2·000 381, so the sum of the log sins for the left-hand angles exceeds that for the right-hand angles by 0·000 381; the slight difference from the 374 in table 20.1 arises because extra angles have been taken into account in the preliminary balancing. This 381 has to be disposed of by the combined effects of the shifts a and b. Similar reasoning applies to the polygon centred on E, though in that case the 'left-hand' sum is relatively 0·000 407 too small. The simultaneous equations given in table 20.4 can thus be written down and solved for a and b. The method has been described in detail, to clarify the next section, but in practice, with only two polygons, you will almost always get a very close approximation to the correct values by working out the shift for each polygon separately, without considering the effect of the other.

Once the shifts have been found, the procedure is essentially the same as for a single polygon. A little work is saved by starting the calculations for both polygons with the shared line EF.

Although a calculator has been used here, the required equations can also be found by summing log sins as in table 20.1; or a and b can each be made equal to 0·01° and the effects for each polygon found by the method used in table 20.2.

20.8 *Four Linked Polygons.* Any number of polygons can be linked together, and the method of solution remains essentially the same. An example, for four polygons, is shown in Figure 20.5, and the calculations, as far as finding the shifts, are set out in table 20.5. It is assumed for illustration that log tables and a calculator are available.

The advantage of this is that although most calculations can be done much more quickly with a calculator, the changes in the log sin of an angle can be read off directly from tables without any intervening calculation. Since the change varies slowly no interpolation is needed and the measured angles, taken to the nearest minute, can be used in entering the tables.

Having arranged the blank table for your calculations, and ringed the shared triangles, you convert the measured angles into decimals of a degree and enter them in the section for preliminary balancing, and at the same time list them to the nearest minute in

Table 20.5 Four Polygons Linked
(a) Balancing Angles

Preliminary balancing:

Triangle	Left-hand Angles Measured	Adjusted 1	3 & 5	Central Angles Measured	1	Adjusted 2	3 & 4	Right-hand Angles Measured	Adjusted 1	3 & 5	Initial Total
BFA	35·2317	·2356	·2355	79·5750	·5788	·5793	·5790	65·1817	·1856	·1855	179·9884
AFG	48·5600	·5633	·5632	67·8888	·8917	·8922	·8920	63·5417	·5450	·5448	179·9900
GFH	92·9550	·9417	·9416	62·8967	·8833	·8838	·8835	24·1883	·1750	·1749	180·0400
(HFJ)	49·9683	·9650	·9693	70·0967	·0933	·0938	·0935	59·9450	·9417	·9372	180·0100
(JFE)	78·5550	·5617	·5597	43·1967	·2033	·2038	·2052	58·2283	·2350	·2351	179·9800
(EFB)	48·8967	·8967	·8942	36·3467	·3466	·3471	·3468	94·7567	·7567	·7590	180·0001

Central angles total: after 1st. adjustment 359·9970; after 3rd. adjustment 360·002

(BEF)	94·7567	·7567	·7590	48·8967	·8967	·8953	·8942	36·3467	·3466	·3468	180·0001
(FEJ)	43·1967	·2033	·2052	58·2283	·2350	·2336	·2351	78·5550	·5617	·5597	179·9800
(JEK)	51·2667	·2800	·2796	60·5483	·5616	·5602	·5634	68·1450	·1584	·1570	179·9600
(KED)	88·9983	·9917	·9863	30·7717	·7650	·7636	·7624	60·2500	·2433	·2513	180·0200
DEC	34·0700	·0783	·0796	97·9083	·9167	·9153	·9141	47·9967	·0050	·0063	179·9750
CEB	65·2133	·2067	·2079	63·6400	·6333	·6320	·6308	51·1667	·1600	·1613	180·0200

Central angles total: after 1st. adjustment 360·0083; after 3rd. adjustment 360·004

(EJF)	58·2283	·2350	·2351	78·5550	·5617	·5583	·5597	43·1967	·2033	·2052	179·9800
(FJH)	70·0967	·0933	·0935	59·9450	·9417	·9383	·9372	49·9683	·9650	·9693	180·0100
HJN	35·9550	·9517	·9540	72·4133	·4100	·4065	·4054	71·6417	·6383	·6406	180·0100
NJM	70·3083	·3128	·3150	60·1583	·1628	·1594	·1583	49·5200	·5244	·5267	179·9866
(MJK)	53·4150	·4228	·4328	37·6567	·6644	·6610	·6598	88·9050	·9128	·9074	179·9767
(KJE)	68·1450	·1584	·1570	51·2667	·2800	·2765	·2796	60·5483	·5616	·5634	179·9600

Central angles total: after 1st. adjustment 360·0206; after 3rd. adjustment 360·004

(EKJ)	60·5488	·5616	·5634	68·1450	·1584	·1538	·1570	51·2667	·2800	·2796	179·9600
(JKM)	37·6567	·6644	·6598	88·9050	·9128	·9082	·9074	53·4150	·4228	·4328	179·9767
MKL	55·3933	·3833	·3860	50·2800	·2700	·2655	·2647	74·3567	·3467	·3493	180·0300
LKD	48·6650	·6717	·6744	63·6833	·6900	·6854	·6846	67·6317	·6383	·6410	179·9800
(DKE)	60·2500	·2433	·2513	88·9983	·9917	·9871	·9863	30·7717	·7650	·7624	180·0200

Central angles total: after 1st. adjustment 360·0229; after 3rd. adjustment 360·00

Increase in 4th. to 6th. figure of log sin for increase of one minute, from tables.
Angles are entered to nearest minute.

	L. H. Angles	inc	Shifts	R. H. Angles	inc	Shifts
BFA	35° 14'	179	+a	65° 11'	058	-a
AFG	48° 34'	112	+a	63° 32'	063	-a
GFH	92° 57'	(-06)	+a -c	24° 11'	281	-a
HFJ	49° 58'	106	+a	59° 57'	073	-a
JFE	78° 33'	026	+a-b	58° 14'	078	-a +c
EFB	48° 54'	110	+a	94° 45'	(-11)	-a+b

527a - 26b - 106c   -542a - 11b + 78c

Relative increase of 'left-hand' sums:

1069a - 15b - 184c

	L. H. Angles	inc	Shifts	R. H. Angles	inc	Shifts
BEF	94° 45'	(-11)	-a+b	36° 21'	172	-b
FEJ	43° 12'	135	+b-c	78° 33'	026	+a-b
JEK	51° 16'	101	+b -d	68° 09'	051	-b+c
KED	89° 00'	002	+b	60° 15'	072	-b +c
DEC	34° 04'	187	+b	48° 00'	114	-b
CEB	65° 13'	058	+b	51° 10'	102	-b

11a + 472b - 135c - 101d   26a - 537b + 51c + 7

- 15a + 1009b - 186c - 173d

	L. H. Angles	inc	Shifts	R. H. Angles	inc	Shifts
EJF	58° 14'	078	-a +c	43° 12'	135	+b-c
FJH	70° 06'	046	+c	49° 58'	106	+a -c
HJN	35° 57'	174	+c	71° 38'	042	-c
NJM	70° 19'	045	+c	49° 31'	108	-c
MJK	53° 25'	004	+c-d	88° 54'	002	-c
KJE	68° 09'	051	b+c	60° 33'	071	-c+d

- 78a - 51b + 488c - 94d   106a + 135b - 464c
                                         +71d
Relative increase of 'left-hand' sums:

- 184a - 186b + 952c - 165d

	L. H. Angles	inc	Shifts	R. H. Angles	inc	Shifts
EKJ	60° 33'	071	-c+d	51° 16'	101	+b -
JKM	37° 39'	164	+d	53° 25'	094	+c-
MKL	55° 24'	087	+d	74° 21'	035	-
LKD	48° 40'	111	+d	67° 38'	052	-
DKE	60° 15'	072	-b +d	30° 46'	212	-

- 72b - 71c + 505d   101b + 94c - 494d

- 173b - 165c + 999d

Table 20.5 Four Polygons Linked
(b) Calculation of Shifts

Programme	Data		Data		Data		Data	
Figs. ÷.	100·00	FE	100·00	EF	100·00	JK	100·00	KJ
Figs. sin. x.	94·7590	BR	78·5597	JR	60·5634	ER	53·4328	MR
Figs. sin. ÷.	48·8942	EL	43·2052	FL	68·1570	KL	37·6598	JL
Figs. sin. x.	65·1855	AR	68·1570	KR	43·2052	FR	74·3493	LR
Figs. sin. ÷.	35·2355	BL	51·2796	JL	58·2351	EL	55·3860	ML
Figs. sin. x.	63·5448	GR	60·2513	DR	49·9693	HR	67·6410	DR
Figs. sin. ÷.	48·5632	AL	88·9863	KL	70·0935	FL	48·6744	LL
Figs. sin. x.	24·1749	HR	48·0063	CR	71·6406	NR	30·7624	ER
Figs. sin. ÷.	92·9416	GL	34·0796	DL	35·9540	HL	60·2513	DL
Figs. sin. x.	59·9372	JR	51·1613	BR	49·5267	MR	51·2796	JR
Figs. sin. ÷.	49·9693	HL	65·2079	CL	70·3150	NL	60·5634	EL
Figs. sin. x.	58·2351	ER	36·3468	FR	88·9074	KR	100·0338	KJ
Figs. sin.	78·5597	JL	94·7590	BL	53·4328	ML	—	
=.	100·0941	FE	99·9047	EF	99·9703	JK		
Logarithms	2·000 409		1·999 575		1·999 881		2·000 147	

$$= 2\text{-}\cdot000\ 425 \qquad = 2\text{-}\cdot000\ 119$$

So the Shifts are given by the equations

$$1069a - 15b - 184c \qquad\quad = -409$$
$$-15a + 1009b - 186c - 173d = +425$$
$$-184a - 186b + 952c - 165d = +119$$
$$-173b - 165c + 999d = -147$$

which can be re-written as

$$a = \qquad\quad 0\cdot014b + 0\cdot172c \qquad\qquad - 0\cdot383$$
$$b = 0\cdot015a \qquad\quad + 0\cdot184c + 0\cdot171d + 0\cdot419$$
$$c = 0\cdot193a + 0\cdot195b \qquad\quad + 0\cdot173d + 0\cdot127$$
$$d = \qquad\quad 0\cdot173b + 0\cdot165c \qquad\qquad - 0\cdot147$$

Step-by-step solution:

		a	b	c	d	Total Change	Approx. Value	
	a	—	+ 0·014	+ 0·172	—	—	- 0·383	a
Coefficients and	b	+ 0·015	—	+ 0·184	+ 0·171	—	+ 0·421	b
first approx.	c	+ 0·193	+ 0·195	—	+ 0·173	—	+ 0·125	c
	d	—	+ 0·173	+ 0·165	—	—	- 0·147	d
First change,	a	—	+ 0·006	+ 0·022	—	+ 0·028	- 0·355	a
caused by	b	- 0·006	—	+ 0·023	- 0·025	- 0·008	+ 0·413	b
first approx.	c	- 0·074	+ 0·082	—	- 0·025	- 0·017	+ 0·108	c
	d	—	+ 0·073	+ 0·021	—	+ 0·094	- 0·053	d
Second change,	a	—	neg.	- 0·003	—	- 0·003	- 0·358	a
caused by	b	neg.	—	- 0·003	+ 0·016	+ 0·013	+ 0·426	b
first change.	c	+ 0·005	- 0·002	—	+ 0·016	+ 0·019	+ 0·127	c
	d	—	- 0·001	- 0·003	—	- 0·004	- 0·057	d
Third change,	a	—	neg.	+ 0·003	—	+ 0·003	- 0·355	a
caused by	b	neg.	—	+ 0·003	- 0·001	+ 0·002	+ 0·428	b
second change	c	- 0·001	+ 0·002	—	- 0·001	neg.	+ 0·127	c
	d	—	+ 0·002	+ 0·003	—	+ 0·005	- 0·052	d

The final values should be checked by substitution in the original equations.
To the second decimal place the Shifts can be taken as:

$$a = -0\cdot35'; \quad b = +0\cdot43'; \quad c = +0\cdot13'; \quad d = -0\cdot05'.$$

20.5 Four Polygons Linked

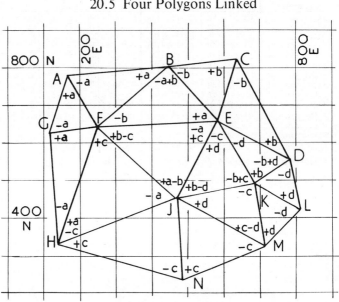

the section for calculating the effect of shift (table 20.5a). The change in log sin per minute change in angle is then filled in, after which the tables can be put aside.

The next step is to give the angles their preliminary balancing. To exemplify method, this has been taken through five stages, but to stop at the third would often be legitimate; it may perhaps give undue weight to the measured angles in the shared triangles.

The method is essentially the same as that given previously; illustrated figures are mostly taken from the polygon centred on K. Although the description of the procedure sounds complicated it will be found simple and automatic if followed step by step.

(i) Adjustment 1 brings each triangle to a total of 180°. Thus in triangle EKJ, which is 0·0400° too small, each angle is increased by 0·0133° or 0·0134°. The odd one ten-thousandth of a degree is insignificant, and can be disposed of in any angle without affecting the results.

(ii) When this has been done, the central angles no longer add up to 360°. Since three of the angles round K, for example, are shared, to treat those as fixed would involve a disproportionately large adjustment to the remaining two. So the central angles are *all* given a second adjustment, − 0·0045° or 46 round K, and similarly for the other polygons.

(iii) The arbitrary decision is now taken to give one more adjustment, 3, to the two triangles EFJ and EJK which are shared between three polygons, and then to keep their angles fixed. Taking the *central* angles in these triangles as having the values found after the second adjustment, those for EJK add up to 179·9905°, so each is increased by 0·0031° or 32. These, the third adjusted angles, are entered in the appropriate columns, ringed and henceforth left unaltered. Triangle EFJ is treated similarly.

(iv) The central angles for each polygon are then added up again, replacing the second adjustment for the shared triangles by the ringed figures. Angle EKJ, for example, has increased from 0·1538° to 0·1570°, so the total around K is 0·0032° too great; each of the remaining four central angles is therefore reduced by 0·0008°. This is the fourth adjustment, and applies only to the central angles, but the resulting figures must be entered in the appropriate columns for the other shared triangles. Thus JKM is a Central Angle at K, and has the value 88·9074° after the fourth adjustment; but it is also a right-hand angle in the polygon centred on J, so ·9074 is entered in that column. Similarly, the fourth adjusted value 35·6598 for the central angle MJK is entered as a left-hand angle for the triangle centred on K. All these angles are underlined; they are given no further adjustments.

(v) Finally, keeping these angles fixed, the triangles are once again balanced. For triangles such as JKM, shared by two polygons, only one angle remains available for adjustment, but unless some mistake has been incorporated in the calculations this fifth adjustment will be small.

Each polygon is then solved, using the same programme as in the last section; to save space, no separate column has been provided for 'Results'. The simultaneous equations for the shifts can then be written down.

The solution of four simultaneous equations by normal methods is laborious, but fortunately these are of a type which can be solved step by step. Each unknown is much the most important quantity in one equation, so as a first approximation the rest can be neglected. Each first approximation can then be substituted in the equations, and will produce a change in the approximate values. Then inserting these first changes in the equations a second change is found, and so on. As will be seen from the table, further changes soon become negligible. The final approximate values are substituted in the original equations, to make sure that they are in fact sufficiently accurate solutions.

20.9 *Derivation of Formula.* For the sake of completeness, and for the benefit of those not willing to take it on trust, the derivation of the formula used in Para. 20.7 is given here.

$$\text{The first differential of } \log_e \sin x = \frac{1}{\sin x} \frac{d}{dx} (\sin x)$$
$$= \frac{\cos x}{\sin x}$$
$$= \frac{1}{\tan x}$$

But this is the change of the logarithm to base e for a change in angle of 1 Radian.

$$\log_{10} \sin x = 0.4343 \log_e \sin x$$

$$\text{and } 0.01° = \frac{\pi}{100 \times 180} \text{Radians}$$

So change in $\log_{10} \sin x$ for one-hundredth of a degree change in

$$\text{angle} = \frac{0.4343 \times \pi}{18,000 \tan x}$$
$$= \frac{0.000\ 075\ 8}{\tan x}$$

Part VI
MISCELLANEOUS TECHNIQUES

21 Plotting from Oblique Aerial Photographs

21.1 *Introduction.* All archaeologists are familiar with the overwhelming mass of information, much of it new, yielded by aerial photography, but most of these photographs have of necessity been taken obliquely and without the exact records of height and other details needed for stereogrammetric plotting (Para. 22.1). Nevertheless, subject to two conditions which are very often satisfied, a reliable plan can be drawn using such a photograph, without the need for any complicated apparatus.

Two methods have been described by I. Scollar (*Aerial Reconnaissance for Archaeology*, ed. D. R. Wilson, CBA 1975, pp. 52-9) and a supplementary alternative has been given by R. Palmer (*Journal of Archaeological Science*, vol. 3 (1976), pp. 391-4). These authors have also given computer programmes (Scollar, *Aerial Reconnaissance* and *World Archaeology*, vol. 10 (1978), pp. 71-87; Palmer, *JAS* vol. 4 (1977), pp. 283-90) but these fall outside the scope of this book. Other methods which do not require a computer are described below.

One condition which must be satisfied is that four points, identifiable on the photograph, must also be identifiable on an accurate plan; usually a 1/2,500 map will provide these, but they can of course be surveyed. The points should lie at the corners of an (imaginary) quadrilateral which encloses most of the features to be plotted.

The second condition is more restrictive. The ground photographed *must* be a plane surface, not necessarily horizontal but flat. Fortunately, most crop-mark sites, for which these methods are particularly useful, occur on such terrain. The principles are equally applicable to a flat wall, and can therefore often be used to draw the elevations of a building, but generally there are simpler ways of doing this. Theoretically, given enough landmarks, a curved ground surface could be replaced by several intersecting planes, each of which would be treated separately; where these overlap the lines plotted would diverge and would be 'smoothed in' by eye. In practice, save in exceptionally simple cases, this seems unlikely to be a useful approach.

In any plot of this kind, one rule must be absolutely invariable: a copy of the original print must be kept entirely free from any marking. If you do not keep to this rule, you will discover that you have been carefully transferring to the plan a pencil mark you made a few days ago; or worse still you will not discover it, and the mark will be recorded as a genuine feature. The ideal is to have a good glossy enlargement to be kept virginal, and a matte enlargement on which to work; but if only one print is available the relevant detail should be very carefully replotted as a working drawing.

In the figures relating to the examples which follow, the upper part of the diagram relates to the photograph, the lower to the map. All are based on a genuine site, though details have been simplified.

21.2 *The Network Method (The 'Möbius' Network).* This, first published by Scollar, is easy and versatile. It is the method of choice for simple sites, unless great accuracy is needed. Straight lines photograph as straight lines (accurately enough, with the type of camera used for this work). So if you imagine a network of straight lines joining up features on the ground (or on the map), a corresponding network can be drawn on the aerial photograph; the angles and lengths will be different, but every line will be identifiable. So will every intersection, and these can be joined up to give secondary lines, and so on almost indefinitely. Using this method, the more identifiable points you have the better, so you may find it worth while to measure in features such as trees or gate posts which are recognisable on the photograph but which do not appear on the map.

In the example (Figure 21.1), six points are used, all being the junctions of field boundaries except D which is a ruined wind-pump. Consider the large subrectangular enclosure. Suppose ae and bd intersect at 1, be and cf at 2, ab and ef at 3, ac and df at 4, and ac and be at 5. Then secondary lines can be drawn: b to 4 cuts ad at 6, 2 to 1 cuts ad at 7 and df at 8. The tertiary lines, 5–6, 6–8, 8–c, and d–2, frame the enclosure; more lines can be drawn if

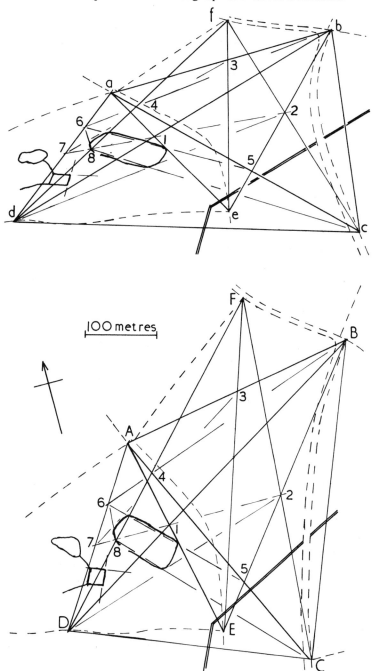

100 metres

desired. All the corresponding lines can be drawn on the map, and the true outline of the enclosure can be sketched in quite accurately.

In addition to its simplicity, this method has a particular merit when several different photographs are available, for the same network can be established on all of them. All other approaches involve separate treatment of each photograph. In fact, even where other methods are used, it is very well worth while to mark the main network on the plan and photographs, as a guide to the reliability of the results.

Two points may be noted at this stage, though they are applicable throughout what follows. The first is obvious: any or all methods described here can be used in conjunction.

The second is equally so, when stated: if the photographs are being used as a guide for excavation, any of these constructions can be carried out on the ground; there is no need to transfer the information to a plan, as an intermediate stage. One precaution is advisable: the poles used should be distinguished by different coloured flags (or rags) to avoid confusion between different alignments.

21.3 *The Paper Strip Method.* This also is described by Scollar, who gives references to earlier publications.

Suppose that we wish to fix the position of the bend in the parch-mark caused by the Roman Road (X in Figure 21.2). This can be done provided that we can draw lines BX and DX on the map corresponding to bx and dx on the photograph. For simplicity only two lines have been drawn on the diagram, but in practice three should always be used; a small triangle of error will result.

To draw the line BX, a strip of paper is placed on the photograph, and the points a, d, c, x, marked where the rays ba, bd, bc, and bx cross its edge. The strip is then transferred to the map and moved so that a lies on BA, d on BD, and c on BC; then the line BX, through x on the strip, corresponds to bx on the photograph.

The method is very simple, though rather laborious if many points have to be located. A proof of its validity is outlined in Para. 21.5.

21.4 *Palmer's Method.* Imagine that the ground carries two or more pairs of widely spaced parallel lines. In an oblique

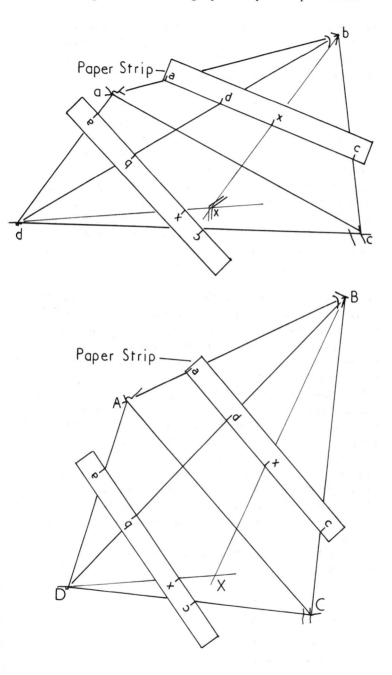

photograph, each pair will converge to meet at a point. The two points define the Vanishing Line. For any line parallel to the vanishing line, the scale on that particular line is uniform; that is, equal divisions on the ground appear as equal divisions on the photograph.

In Palmer's Method, having established the vanishing line (see below) one or more parallel lines are drawn, and the corresponding scales found by measurements on the map and photograph. Rays can then be drawn from known points, and required points fixed by intersection (see Paras. 21.10 and 11).

This method is limited in its application, for except in areas with much modern detail it is seldom possible to establish two pairs of parallel lines, even though the restriction imposed by Palmer, that they must form the sides of a rectangle, is not necessary. A more widely applicable numerical method of establishing lines of constant scale is given in Paras. 21.8 and 9.

21.5 *Theory.* In addition to their other merits, the network and paper strip methods involve no arithmetic. The two which follow are essentially numerical, and this section explains their theoretical basis. It can be skipped, for all the formulae are repeated where relevant; but some readers will prefer to understand them, rather than to use them blindly.

If you imagine that your eye is at the focal point of the camera, then a transparent positive print held in front of you could be arranged so that every point on it was exactly in line with the corresponding point on the ground (Figure 21.3), or alternatively on a map; the theory is unaffected. We are therefore concerned with the properties of lines cutting across 'pencils' of rays diverging from a point. All that follows depends on the 'a/sin A' formula (Para. 16.6). With a few obvious exceptions, lower case letters refer to points on the photograph, capitals to corresponding points on the ground (or plan).

First consider a single pencil of rays OA, OB, and OX, all in one plane and cut by the line axb.

$$\text{Then} \frac{AX}{\sin AOX} = \frac{OA}{\sin AXO}$$

$$\text{and} \quad \frac{XB}{\sin BOX} = \frac{OB}{\sin BXO}$$

21.3 Oblique Aerial Photographs: Theory

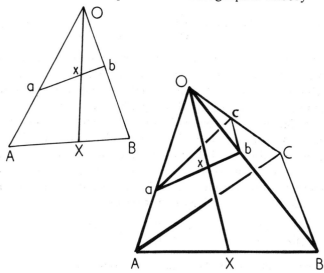

Since $AXO = 180° - BXO$, $\sin AXO = \sin BXO$

So $\dfrac{AX}{XB} = \dfrac{OA}{OB}\dfrac{\sin AOX}{\sin BOX}$

Similarly $\dfrac{ax}{xb} = \dfrac{Oa}{Ob}\dfrac{\sin aOx}{\sin bOx}$

For any given lines AB, ab, $\dfrac{OA.Ob}{Oa\ OB}$ is constant; so these equations can be written

$$\frac{AX}{XB} = R_{AB}\frac{ax}{xb}$$

where R_{AB} is constant. This holds for any position of X, whether between the points AB or outside them.

The same reasoning shows that provided the lines Aa, Bb, and Xx all converge, not necessarily at the focal point of the camera, then the same relationship must hold. This is the theoretical basis of the paper strip method.

Now suppose that O forms the vertex and ABC the base of an unsymmetrical pyramid. The vertices of a smaller triangle a, b, and c lie on OA, OB, and OC respectively. Then

$$R_{AB}.R_{BC}.R_{CA} = \frac{OA.Ob}{Oa.OB} \cdot \frac{OB.Oc}{Ob.OC} \cdot \frac{OC.Oa}{Oc.OA} = 1$$

Although the relationship $\frac{AX}{XB} = R_{AB}.\frac{ax}{xb}$ is probably the most convenient way of defining the ratio of measurements on the map to those on the photograph, we usually need AX in terms of ax, ab, and AB (or conversely). A simple graphical construction is shown in Figure 21.4; it has the disadvantage that except when R = 1 a separate diagram has to be made for each point. Lines of lengths DB and db are drawn at an angle, with B and b coincident. We wish to make the ratio DP : PB equal to R_{DB} times the ratio dp : pb, which is known. Mark p on db, and make d_1p equal to $R_{DB} \times dp$. Then if pP is drawn parallel to d_1D, P is the required point on DB.

Alternatively, the equation can be rewritten as

$$R_{DB} \times \frac{PB}{DP} = \frac{pb}{dp} \quad \text{or} \quad R_{DB}\left(\frac{DB}{DP} - 1\right) = \frac{db}{dp} - 1$$

which can easily be worked out either longhand or with a calculator. A suitable programme would be: enter figures for db; ÷; enter dp; —; 1; ÷; enter R_{DB}; (or: x: enter R_{BD};) +; 1; ÷; enter DB; =; take reciprocal. If several such calculations are to be made for the same pair of lines, then assuming that only two memories are available whichever of the three quantities DB, db, and R_{DB} has fewest digits is entered each time it is needed; the other two can be stored.

21.4 Graphical Construction for Ratios

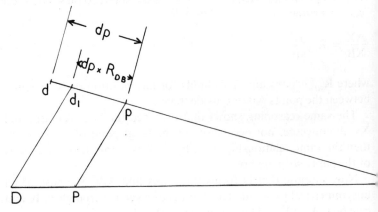

21.6 *Applications of Equations.* There are several different ways of using these equations, but basically they reduce to two: direct comparison of distances, and establishing lines of constant scale: these are described in the following sections. The necessary measurements can be made with any closely graduated scale. Although not essential, it is advisable to use the same scale for measuring the photograph and the map; this obviates the risk of finding that you have used, say, the 'map' scale on the photograph. In all the calculations which follow, the original measurements were taken with a 1/2,500 metric scale. Usually there is no need to give more than the number, but when necessary dimensions on the photograph (top in the diagrams) are stated in 'units' and on the map in 'metres'.

21.7 *Direct Comparison of Distances.* Suppose that we wish to fix the north-east corner of the small square crop-mark (Figure 21.1). This can be done by finding the intersection of its sides, produced, with lines DB and DF; so we require the relation between measurements on those lines and on db and df, on the photograph. There are several corresponding points on these pairs of lines. The measurements to them, and quantities derived from those measurements, are set out in table 21.1 and are plotted in Figure 21.5.

Provided no great accuracy is needed, the simplest method is to draw a smooth curve relating the known measurements on the map to those on the photograph. A better result is obtained by plotting $\frac{XD}{XB}$ against $\frac{xd}{xb}$; or by plotting their logarithms. The first plot should give a straight line passing through the origin and having slope R_{DB}. The second should give a straight line at 45° to the axes, and the value of $\frac{XD}{XB}$ when log. $\frac{xd}{xb} = 0$ gives R_{DB}. The results obtained are also set out in table 21.1.

One warning must be given. The value of R is very susceptible to small errors in measurement, and while this will not have much effect on the positions of points fixed by this method provided they lie between the ends of the line, the inaccuracy increases rapidly outside those limits.

21.8 *Lines of Constant Scale: Theory.* The advantages of lines of constant scale (that is, lines parallel to the vanishing line) were pointed out by Palmer (Para. 21.4). This method differs from his

21.5 Oblique Aerial Photographs: Direct Comparison of Distances

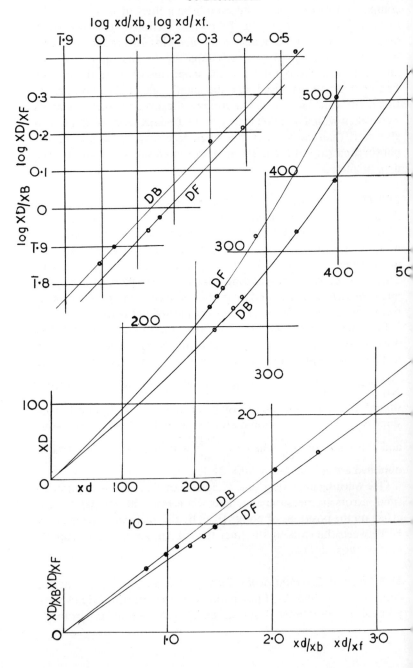

Table 21.1 Oblique Aerial Photographs: Direct Comparison of Distances

Line DB	cut by	D	AE	AC	Fence	FE	FC	B
Measurements:	Photo (xd)	0	226	253	265	342	396	510
	Map (XD)	0	198	227	240	327	395	547
	Photo (xb)	510	284	257	245	168	114	0
	Map (XB)	547	349	320	307	220	152	0
Ratios:	Photo xd/xb	0	0·7958	0·9844	1·0816	2·0357	3·4737	∞
	Map XD/XB	0	0·5673	0·7094	0·7818	1·4864	2·5987	∞
Logarithms:	xd/xb	− ∞	$\bar{1}$·9008	$\bar{1}$·9932	0·0341	0·3087	0·5408	+ ∞
	XD/XB	− ∞	$\bar{1}$·7538	$\bar{1}$·8509	$\bar{1}$·8931	0·1721	0·4148	+ ∞

Line DF	cut by	D	AE	AC	Fence	AB	F
Measurements:	Photo (xd)	0	221	231	239	287	403
	Map (XD)	0	227	241	251	321	516
	Photo (xf)	403	182	172	164	116	0
	Map (XF)	516	289	275	265	195	0
Ratios:	Photo xd/xf	0	1·2143	1·3430	1·4573	2·4741	∞
	Map XD/XF	0	0·7855	0·8764	0·9472	1·6462	∞
Logarithms:	xd/xf	− ∞	0·0843	0·1281	0·1635	0·3934	+ ∞
	XD/XF	− ∞	$\bar{1}$·8951	$\bar{1}$·9427	$\bar{1}$·9764	0·2164	+ ∞

Plotting Ratios gives: $R_{DB} = 0·735$ $R_{DF} = 0·662$

Plotting Logarithms gives: $R_{DB} = 0·733$ $R_{DF} = 0·652$

From calculation, Table 24: $R_{DB} = 0·7209$

Intersects to locate N.E. corner of small square enclosure (to nearest metre).

	E. side	N. side		E. side	N. side
From d, on db	85	126	From d, on df	114	96
Hence from D on DB:			Hence from D on DF:		
reading off curve	70	105	reading off curve	105	90
$R_{DB} = 0·735$ or $0·733$	70	106	$R_{DF} = 0·662$	108	89
$R_{DB} = 0·721$	69	105	$R_{DF} = 0·652$	106	88

approach in that the lines are established by calculation. The only requirement, apart from flat ground, is that four points, at the corners of a fairly large quadrilateral, shall be identifiable on the map and on the photograph. There is no need to identify two pairs of parallel lines, and the method is applicable to nearly vertical views in which the vanishing line is inconveniently far from the print. In principle, the accuracy of this method is only limited by the precision of measurement possible on the photograph.

In Figure 21.6, suppose AM and am are a corresponding pair of lines of constant scale; stated another way, R_{AM} is unity. Since $R_{AB} \times R_{BM} \times R_{MA} = 1$ (Para. 21.5),

$$R_{MB} = R_{AB}$$

Also $R_{AB} = R_{AX} \times R_{XB}$ or $R_{AX} \div R_{BX}$

Keep in mind throughout what follows that $R_{AX} = 1/R_{XA}$

Hence if AX, BX, CX, and DX, and the corresponding lengths on the photograph are found, the values of R can be calculated for

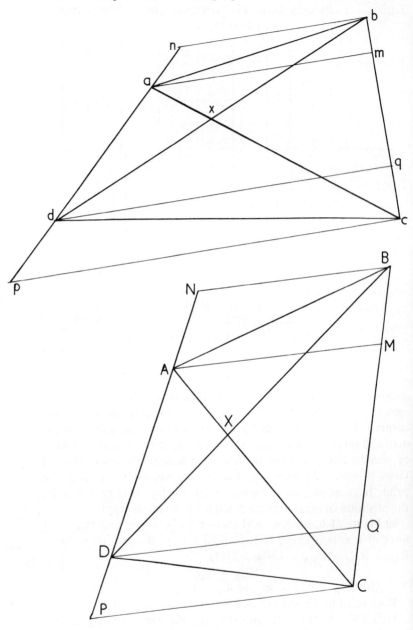

all the lines in the diagram. The necessary lengths can be determined by measurement, or more accurately by calculation.

Expressions for BM and bm can be found as follows:

$$\frac{BC}{CM} = R_{BM} \times \frac{bc}{cm} \qquad \text{or rearranging} \quad R_{BM} \times \frac{CM}{BC} = \frac{cm}{bc}$$

$$\text{and similarly} \quad R_{CM} \times \frac{BM}{BC} = \frac{bm}{bc}$$

Adding: $\quad R_{BM} \times \dfrac{CM}{BC} + R_{CM} \times \dfrac{BM}{BC} = \dfrac{cm + bm}{bc} = 1$

Now writing CM = BC − BM this gives

$$\frac{BM}{BC} = \frac{R_{BM} - 1}{R_{BM} - R_{CM}} = \frac{R_{BX} - R_{AX}}{R_{BX} - R_{CX}}$$

for $R_{BM} = R_{BA} = R_{BX} \times R_{XA}$

and $R_{CM} = R_{CA} = R_{CX} \times R_{XA}$

This expression may be described verbally as giving the distance from B at which a line of constant scale (through A) cuts the line BC. The order in which the angles of the quadrilateral are named in this sentence is the same as that in which they occur in the right-hand side of the equation; this simplifies writing down the expressions for AN, CQ, and DP.

A similar argument, starting with $R_{MB} \times \dfrac{cm}{bc} = \dfrac{CM}{BC}$ leads to the corresponding expression

$$\frac{bm}{bc} = \frac{R_{XB} - R_{XA}}{R_{XB} - R_{XC}}$$

These equations can be rearranged in many different ways, and even more ingenious programmes can be devised for use with a calculator; but the following scheme seems to introduce the least risk of mistakes:

$$BM = -\frac{R_{AX} - R_{BX}}{R_{BX} - R_{CX}} BC \qquad\qquad bm = -\frac{R_{CX}}{R_{AX}} \cdot \frac{R_{AX} - R_{BX}}{R_{BX} - R_{CX}} bc$$

$$CQ = -\frac{R_{CX} - R_{DX}}{R_{BX} - R_{CX}} BC \qquad\qquad cq = -\frac{R_{BX}}{R_{DX}} \cdot \frac{R_{CX} - R_{DX}}{R_{BX} - R_{CX}} bc$$

$$AN = -\frac{R_{AX} - R_{BX}}{R_{DX} - R_{AX}}AD \qquad an = -\frac{R_{DX}}{R_{BX}}\cdot\frac{R_{AX} - R_{BX}}{R_{DX} - R_{AX}}ad$$

$$DP = -\frac{R_{CX} - R_{DX}}{R_{DX} - R_{AX}}AD \qquad dp = -\frac{R_{AX}}{R_{CX}}\cdot\frac{R_{CX} - R_{DX}}{R_{DX} - R_{AX}}ad$$

The factors $(R_{AX} - R_{BX})$, $\dfrac{R_{AX}}{R_{CX}}$ etc. are worked out and listed as intermediate steps in the calculation.

21.9 *Determining Lines of Constant Scale.* Logically, to use several pairs of corresponding points rather than only four ought to give more reliable results, but in practice R is so sensitive to small errors in measurement that to get consistent values is difficult; three values along the sides of a triangle, which ought to give a product of unity, very seldom do so when calculated by the method described in Para. 21.7. By contrast, exact agreement is possible for the angles and sides of a quadrilateral.

If moderate accuracy is acceptable, the lengths ax, AX, etc. from which the other quantities are found can be measured. Table 21.2 gives the relevant calculations. If however, the greatest possible precision is desired, the lengths must be calculated, as in table 21.3; inevitably much more work is involved. Both tables refer to Figure 21.6. The calculations start from the co-ordinates, relative to arbitrary axes, of the angles of the quadrilateral; this obviates the need to 'balance' the sides and diagonals.

Owing to the sensitivity of R, mentioned above, the lines of constant scale as found in table 21.2 diverge quite considerably from their true positions given by table 21.3. Fortunately though, the errors are almost self-compensating. The first example in the next section is at worst only just over a 'unit' away from its true position when drawn out using the table 21.2 figures.

21.10 *Transferring Site Grid to Photograph.* Once the lines of constant scale have been determined, any point can be fixed from two or more intersecting lines. This example and the next will serve to illustrate the method. In both, the calculated results from table 21.3 are used (and see Figure 21.7).

The most usual requirement is to transfer detail from the photograph to the map, but sometimes it is desired to represent a true rectangle, such as a site grid, on the photograph. The principles involved are the same. The rectangle is supposed to

Table 21.2 Oblique Aerial Photographs: Lines of Constant Scale, by Measurement

All measurements are in "metres" on a 1/2500 scale.

Map		Photograph		
AX	115	ax	93	$R_{AX} = \dfrac{AC}{CX}\dfrac{cx}{ac} = 1\cdot0869$
BX	318	bx	254	$R_{BX} = \dfrac{BD}{DX}\dfrac{dx}{bd} = 1\cdot1967$
CX	267	cx	294	$R_{CX} = \dfrac{CA}{AX}\dfrac{ax}{ca} = 0\cdot7982$
DX	229	dx	255	$R_{DX} = \dfrac{DB}{BX}\dfrac{bx}{db} = 0\cdot8584$
BC	428	bc	272	
AD	263	ad	222	

Factors needed in calculations:

$$R_{AX} - R_{BX} = -0\cdot1098 \qquad R_{BX} - R_{CX} = +0\cdot3985 \qquad \frac{R_{CX}}{R_{AX}} = 0\cdot7344$$

$$R_{CX} - R_{DX} = -0\cdot0602 \qquad R_{DX} - R_{AX} = -0\cdot2285 \qquad \frac{R_{DX}}{R_{BX}} = 0\cdot7173$$

Intercepts on BC and AD.

$$BM = -\frac{R_{AX} - R_{BX}}{R_{BX} - R_{CX}} BC = +117\cdot9 \qquad bm = -\frac{R_{CX}}{R_{AX}}\frac{R_{AX} - R_{BX}}{R_{BX} - R_{CX}} bc = +55\cdot0$$

$$CQ = -\frac{R_{CX} - R_{DX}}{R_{BX} - R_{CX}} BC = +64\cdot6 \qquad cq = -\frac{R_{BX}}{R_{DX}}\frac{R_{CX} - R_{DX}}{R_{BX} - R_{CX}} bc = +57\cdot3$$

$$AN = -\frac{R_{AX} - R_{BX}}{R_{DX} - R_{AX}} AD = -126\cdot4 \qquad an = -\frac{R_{DX}}{R_{BX}}\frac{R_{AX} - R_{BX}}{R_{DX} - R_{AX}} ad = -76\cdot5$$

$$DP = -\frac{R_{CX} - R_{DX}}{R_{DX} - R_{AX}} AD = -69\cdot3 \qquad dp = -\frac{R_{AX}}{R_{CX}}\frac{R_{CX} - R_{DX}}{R_{DX} - R_{AX}} ad = -79\cdot6$$

Hence by measurement	AM 289	BN 262	CP 361	DQ 345
	am 312	bn 254	cp 532	dq 474
Scales in units on photo. to 100m.on map	107·96	96·95	147·37	137·39

measure 200 by 150 m, located as shown. The line of the west side cuts AM at U, DQ at V. AU measures 31 m, and 100 m on AM corresponds to 106·5 units on am; so au is 34 units. Similarly DV measures 92 m, the scale is 135·6 units to 100 m, and dv therefore equals 127 units. The line of the east side is fixed in the same way.

The north and south sides cut the lines of constant scale inconveniently far off the map, and this is true even for the diagonals. One method of fixing the angles, and probably the simplest, is to bisect the sides (Figure 21.7) and preferably to extend them for half a length in each direction. The corresponding diagonals can easily be drawn. Thus the lines which cut at Y intersect AM 30 m to the left of A and 114 to the right, and DQ at 178 m to the right of D and 20 to the left; so using the scales as above the corresponding lines fixing y on the photograph cut am at 32 and 122 units from a and dq at 241 and 27 units from d. Plotting

Table 21.3 Oblique Aerial Photographs: Lines of Constant Scale, by Calculation

All lengths in 'metres' on 1/2500 scale; angles in degrees and decimals.
Coordinates from arbitrary axes:

	Map x	Map y		Photograph x	Photograph y
A	278	299	a	240	401
B	579	438	b	540	493
C	532	12	c	586	225
D	195	48	d	106	225

	Coord. difference x	Coord. difference y	Length	Bearing		Coord. difference x	Coord. difference y	Length	Bearing
AB	301	139	331·545	65·2128	ab	300	92	313·790	72·9510
AC	254	− 287	383·256	138·4906	ac	346	− 176	388·191	116·9611
AD	− 83	− 251	264·367	− 161·7021	ad	− 134	− 176	221·206	− 142·7157
BC	− 47	− 426	428·585	− 173·7041	bc	46	− 268	271·919	170·2606
BD	− 384	− 390	547·317	− 135·4441	bd	− 434	− 268	510·078	− 121·6958
CD	− 337	36	338·917	− 83·9025	cd	− 480	0	480·000	270·0000

In triangle ABX	In triangle abx	In triangle CDX	In triangle cdx
$\hat{A}$ = 73·2778	$\hat{a}$ = 44·0101	$\hat{C}$ = 42·3931	$\hat{c}$ = 26·9611
$\hat{B}$ = 20·6569	$\hat{b}$ = 14·6468	$\hat{D}$ = 51·5416	$\hat{d}$ = 31·6958
$\hat{X}$ = 86·0653	$\hat{x}$ = 121·3431	$\hat{X}$ = 86·0653	$\hat{x}$ = 121·3431
AB = 331·545	ab = 313·790	CD = 338·917	cd = 480·000

So using the a/sine A formula:

AX = 117·236	ax = 92·902	CX = 266·019	cx = 295·289
BX = 318·275	bx = 255·269	DX = 229·042	dx = 254·810

Hence, substituting in the expressions given in Table 23:

R_{AX} = 1·09592	R_{BX} = 1·19372	R_{CX} = 0·78236	R_{DX} = 0·86059
BM = 101·895	CQ = 81·506	AN = 109·867	DP = 87·883
bm = 46·151	cq = 71·729	an = 66·276	dp = 103·007

Calculations for scales. From now on, measurement would usually be adequate.

Programme	Triangle ABM Data, etc.		Triangle CDQ Data, etc.		Triangle ABN Data, etc.		Triangle CDP Data, etc.	
Figs.	331·545	AB	338·917	CD	331·545	AB	338·917	CD
F. x/y. Figs.	58·9169	$\hat{B}$	90·1984	$\hat{C}$	46·9149	$\hat{A}$	102·2004	$\hat{D}$
R. (. −. Figs.	101·895	BM	81·506	CQ	109·867	AN	87·883	DP
). F. x/y. P.	292·270	AM	348·854	DQ	268·755	BN	367·665	CP
F. x/y.	76·2890	$\hat{M}$	103·7097	$\hat{Q}$	64·2862	$\hat{N}$	115·7114	$\hat{P}$ External angles

	Triangle abm		Triangle cdq		Triangle abn		Triangle cdp	
Figs..	313·790	ab	480·000	cd	313·790	ab	480·000	cd
F. x/y. Figs.	82·6904	$\hat{b}$	80·2606	$\hat{c}$	35·6667	$\hat{a}$	127·2843	$\hat{d}$
R. (. −. Figs.	46·151	bm	71·729	cq	66·276	an	103·007	dp
). F. x/y. P.	311·302	am	473·177	dq	262·803	bn	548·555	cp
F. x/y.	91·1462	$\hat{m}$	88·8531	$\hat{q}$	44·1223	$\hat{n}$	135·8767	$\hat{p}$ External angles

Units on photo. to 100 metres on map

  AM: 106·51 DQ· 135·64 BN: 97·79 CP: 149·20

If desired, the bearings can be worked out from the results given above.
Relative to the y-axes they are

  AM: 82·5849° DQ: 82·5862° NB: 82·5841° PC: 82·5865°
  am: 81·4068° dq: 81·4075° nb: 81·4066° pc: 81·4076°

showing that the four in each set are almost exactly parallel, as they should be

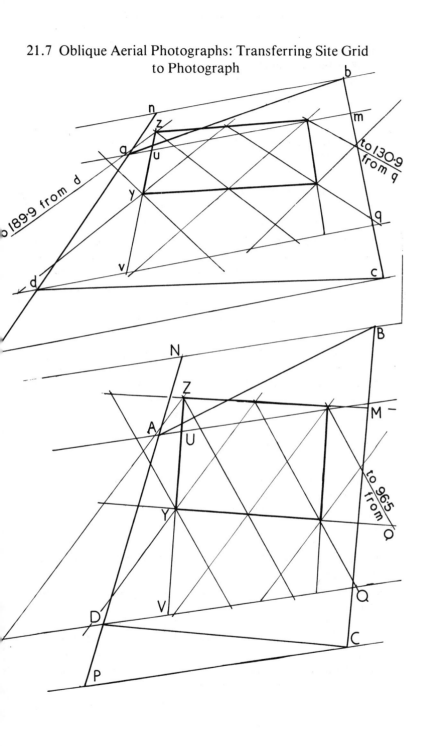

all eight diagonal lines and the east and west sides provides some check against mistakes.

For that reason a graphical solution is always desirable, but if greater accuracy is needed lengths measured along the sides, such as vy, can be calculated. Just as $R_{MB} = R_{AB}$ (Para. 21.8) so $R_{VU} = R_{VA} = R_{DA} = R_{DX} \cdot R_{XA}$, so if the lengths VY, YU, UZ, and vu are known, yu and uz can be found; these calculations are also set out in table 21.3.

21.11 *Transferring Detail from Photograph.* When detail is to be transferred from the photograph to the map, any grid can be chosen. The most convenient arrangement is to impose a square grid on the photograph, with its lines at 45° to the lines of constant scale. In Figure 21.8 this has been done, with diagonals of 50 units. The corresponding spacing along AM is then $50 \div 106 \cdot 5$, that is 46·9 m, and along DQ $50 \div 135 \cdot 6 = 36 \cdot 9$ m. The intersections with dq start at 3 and 14 units from d, corresponding to 2 and 10 m from D. The resulting grids can be repeatedly subdivided, as explained in Para. 26.7.

The advantage of imposing the square grid on the photograph rather than on the map is that the same grid, drawn on transparent material, can be used for all photographs, which can then be kept unmarked. The lines of constant scale are established on a separate drawing on which the grid is superimposed. The co-ordinates of the corners of the original quadrilateral are then noted, and the transparent grid can then be located relative to the photograph.

21.12 *Comparison of Methods.* Recapitulation may be useful. First, remember that no simple method is applicable unless the ground is flat. Subject to that condition, the network method is the simplest and most versatile when nothing more is needed than a good representative sketch-plan. The direct comparison of distances, using merely a smooth curve to relate measurements on photograph and map, will often be a helpful supplement to the network. Palmer's Method requires data which are often not available.

If rather greater accuracy is required, then direct comparison of distances, using one of the methods of finding R, is suitable if only a few points are to be fixed. If there is a lot of detail, a grid can be superimposed on photograph and map as in Para. 21.11, using measurements in the initial calculations.

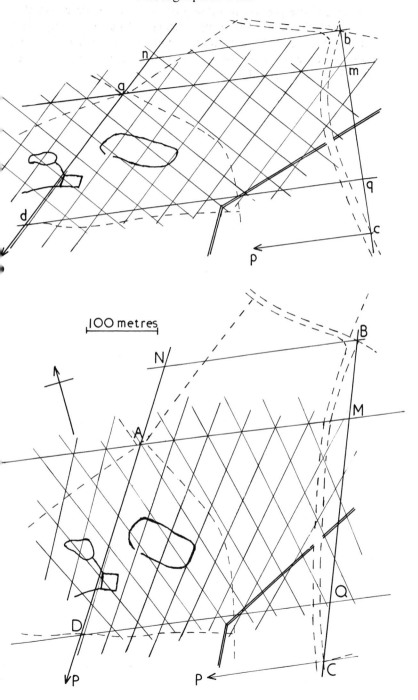

Finally, if the greatest possible precision is to be obtained, the grids should be established using calculated distances throughout, and points of special importance should be fixed either by intersection or by calculation; but if the features are visible a ground survey is always preferable.

22 Other Applications of Photography

22.1 Photogrammetry; 22.2 Conditions Justifying its Use;
22.3 Organising a Photogrammetric Survey; 22.4 Triangulation from
Photographic Pairs.

22.1 *Photogrammetry.* A site with well-defined features, and not obscured by vegetation, can be accurately planned, with contours, from aerial photographs. These are observed stereoscopically, and at the same time twin pointers, one visible in each eyepiece, are adjusted to coincide with features visible on the photographs. The principle is thus simple enough, but the stereoplotter which applies it is a complicated and expensive device, and the necessary photographs have to be taken under carefully controlled and recorded conditions of height and tilt. The actual production of a plan by this method is therefore outside the scope of this book; but it is often worth while to examine the possibility of applying it to a major site.

22.2 *Conditions Justifying its Use.* As will be seen, quite a lot of work has to be done in the field even when the main plan is done by this method. Whether judged in terms of time or of cost, photogrammetry is not always the method of choice.

So many factors will influence your decision that only general guidelines can be suggested. These are summarised below, followed by considerations which justify them or may suggest some modification.

As a rough guide, photogrammetry is only likely to be worth while if contours are needed, whatever the nature of the site. If that condition is satisfied, sites of less than 3 hectares can usually be done more economically with chain and tacheometer, whereas for larger areas photogrammetry is to be preferred; but the critical area is not sharply defined.

The following factors have to be taken into account. First of all, arrangements have to be made with the company who will do the photography and plotting, preferably by personal discussion, which may well take a day unless their offices are close at hand. Next, the necessary ground control work will take about one other day, for two surveyors. Finally, when the photogrammetric plan has been received, at least another day's work in the field by archaeologists will be necessary, more if it is a site with much complex detail (see below). Photogrammetry, therefore, is unlikely to be advantageous from any standpoint if the survey can be done by chain and theodolite in three days or less. If the monetary cost is considered, this three days needs to be considerably increased, for the price of a photogrammetric survey is normally made up of a fairly large basic charge and a relatively small addition depending on the area covered. No exact figures can be given, but the basic charge could well be the equivalent of a fortnight's field expenses. The decision needed here is whether the time saved is worth the extra expense. In this context also, the financial arrangements of the organisation (if any) for which you work may be relevant; for example, photogrammetry may be preferable though more expensive because it is charged under a different subhead in the accounts, or because it sounds so scientific that it impresses those responsible for the allocation of funds.

Reverting to the nature of the site to be surveyed, accessibility is obviously important, but so also is the character of the remains. Massive grass-covered banks and ditches can be plotted direct from the photographs, and require very little checking. On the other hand hut-platforms may well not show up at all, and will then have to be surveyed on the ground; so nearly as much work will be needed as for a complete chain survey. Similarly, the lines of facing which can often be detected in a ruined stone wall will have to be recorded by ground survey. In fact, on dry-stone built structures of the kind common in the Highland Zone almost as much chaining will be needed as if the whole survey were done by that method; the advantage of photogrammetry is that contours are provided automatically.

22.3 *Organising a Photogrammetric Survey.* The first step is to find an organisation which will take the photographs and do the plotting; advice may be sought from the Geography or Civil Engineering Departments of a University or Technical College. If circumstances permit it is worth while to shop around. Cheaper rates can sometimes be arranged by accepting some delays so that your photography can be done during the same flight as other work, or by having several sites in the same region done at the same time.

The firm will need to know *precisely* what you wish to have surveyed, so you should provide at least 'six-inch' or 1/10,000 maps with the outline of the area marked; 1/2,500 maps are much better. You must also specify the scale required. Personal discussion with the firm's representatives is very desirable.

If the site to be surveyed is under your control, you should arrange at this stage where the ground control points are to be located. Each should be marked on the ground with a peg at the centre of a white-painted cross, so that they are clearly visible in the photographs. To be able to do this is very unusual, and normally these points have to be located at features visible on the photographs (see below).

The next stage is for the firm to take the necessary photographs and send duplicates to you; one print should preferably be matte to receive annotation. On one set of prints, unless ground control has already been marked, the firm will have indicated the points between which they require measurement and those where they wish for levels. Usually they will need two measured base lines and a ring of spot levels enclosing the site; rather surprisingly, they do not generally ask for a summit level when the plan represents a hill.

The control points for base line measurements will be sharply defined, such as gate or fence posts, corners of electricity pylons, or even one corner of an angular boulder. For levelling, less precision is needed; the centre of a gateway, for example, would be adequate. If for some reason the exact point specified is not accessible, another near by will be suitable, provided of course it is identifiable on the photographs; there is no need to consult the firm before using such an alternative. You will now measure the base lines and take the ring of spot levels, making sure of all the necessary checks.

I hope that it will never be useful for you to know that a gross mistake in chaining a base line may be indicated, when the site is being plotted, by what appears to be a mistake in levelling; but if a levelling mistake should be suspected, check the base line measurements before setting out to relevel the complete circuit.

At this stage you must also decide what points you will need in order to survey the detail. Posts or well defined angular boulders are to be preferred, but if nothing better is available the inter-section of two sheep-tracks or anything which defines a recognisable and sufficiently permanent feature can be used. These points should be ringed on the matte print and listed, and will be plotted by the firm on the plan.

The annotated matte prints, as well as the data concerning base lines and spot levels, are all returned to the firm, who will prepare the plan, and send it to you. They should be asked to show top and toe of scarps and ramparts, for these do not appear clearly from contours. Obtain also at least two photoprints, one to take into the field and one for plotting detail. The main original plan should be kept unmarked.

Detail is then surveyed in the ordinary way, using the points chosen earlier. The results are plotted on one of the photoprints.

To make the final plan for publication, the chosen points are traced in pencil from the main plan, and using these the detail is copied from the photoprint. The contours and other features are then traced from the main plan.

22.4 *Triangulation from Photographic Pairs.* If the optical properties of a camera are known, a photograph provides, among other information, a permanent record of numerous angular measurements, but for the field archaeologist the advantages of such a camera, or its adaptation to a 'photo-theodolite', would not justify its high cost.

Nevertheless, on occasion a series of paired photographs taken with an ordinary hand camera may offer a convenient time-saving alternative to more conventional methods of surveying. An obvious application is to record a feature such as a ditch exposed in a working quarry face.

The photographs are taken from two fixed points (for example, fence-posts) which will form the ends of the base line. Their distance apart must be known. They need not be at the same height above Ordnance Datum, but the camera must not be tilted.

In addition to the feature to be recorded, each photograph must include at least one, and preferably two or three, permanent sharply defined landmarks, not necessarily the same for both views. The bearings of these landmarks relative to the base line must be determined, preferably with a theodolite though the average of three or four careful prismatic compass observations could be acceptable in an emergency.

The camera can be calibrated by photographing a range of five evenly spaced poles, set upright at (say) 100 m from the camera and on a line perpendicular to that joining the middle pole to the camera; but this is not essential.

22.1 Triangulation from Pairs of Photographs

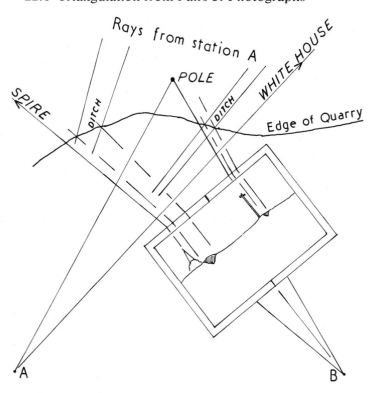

Few modern hand cameras take large negatives, so enlargements will be needed. It is very desirable that all should be to exactly the same magnification and they must not be trimmed or masked, so that the actual edges of the negative appear on the enlargement.

As an example, (Figure 22.1) assume observations are being made on ditches exposed in a quarry face. Two fence-posts, A and B, are taken as ends of the base line. The 'landmarks' visible in photographs are the gable of a (distinctive) white house from A only, a church spire from B only and pole (for electricity cables) from both. Suppose that the rays from A have been drawn, and we are dealing with the photograph taken from B, which is represented greatly simplified in the figure. The vertical axis of the photograph is drawn; it corresponds accurately enough to the line half way between the edges of the photographic image. Also , all the relevant points — the spire, edges of ditches, and pole — must be projected upwards perpendicularly to the edge of the photograph. Work is simplified if these points and the axial line are transferred to a sheet of tracing paper, either directly or by measurement; if measured, the scale can be increased.

The print or tracing is then slid over the plan until the points corresponding to the spire and pole lie on the relevant rays, and the axial line produced passes through B. The rays corresponding to the ditch edges can then be drawn, and their intersections with the rays from A fix the required points on the plan.

Up to a total of about half a dozen, the more 'landmarks' the better; but even if only one is available the method can still be used, with rather less accuracy, provided the camera has been calibrated as described above. The difference in bearing between the axial line and the spire (say) is known from the calibration, so the direction of the axial line can be drawn on the plan.

23 The Plane Table

23.1 General Remarks: 23.2 Description; 23.3 Use.

23.1 *General Remarks.* The plane table has a respectable ancestry, and many good-looking plans have been prepared by means of it, but it has serious disadvantages, especially for fieldwork in this country; I would most strongly advise against its use. Nevertheless, as there is a risk that you may find yourself persuaded or compelled to work with one, some account of it must be given.

The advantages claimed are that the method of use is simple and easily understood, and that since the plan is drawn directly in the field time is saved and possible mistakes in booking are avoided. Although I have never had an opportunity to compare a chain and a plane-table survey made on the same site, I think it is probably true that the *total* time required to produce a pencil draft ready for tracing is rather shorter by the latter method.

The counterbalancing disadvantages make a longer list: the instrument is cumbrous to transport, though perhaps not much more so than a theodolite; slight rain, and anything more than a moderate wind, make it unusable; the size of the plan is limited to the size of the board; although the *total* time required to produce the pencil draft may possibly be less, the time spent *in the field* will be longer than would be required for a chain or theodolite survey; to produce a clean and legible plan working in the open air is far more difficult than to do so indoors; and to balance errors is difficult and adds considerably to the work involved. Even the supposed advantage, that the plan develops before the surveyor's eyes while he is on the site, is open to the objection that this offers an almost irresistible temptation to sketch in detail by eye instead of measuring it, thus perhaps establishing on the plan a subjective and possibly mistaken interpretation of the remains. Finally, although the method is certainly simple, it is no simpler than chain surveying, and it is very much more difficult to adapt to single-handed work.

To sum up, a beginner should avoid the plane table; its use will establish faulty techniques, and he will have difficulty in extending his work to large sites. An experienced user of the instrument can produce satisfactory plans, and will no doubt be reluctant to change his methods, though for fieldwork in Britain he would be well advised to do so.

23.2 *Description* (Figure 23.1). The table itself is essentially a drawing-board, from about 40 cm square up to 80 by 60 cm, fitted with a spindle so that it can be rotated about a vertical axis and clamped as desired. In the simplest instruments the spindle rotates in a socket in the tripod head, but usually there is a set of levelling screws, or similar device, as for a theodolite or level.

Observations are made with an alidade or sight-rule. In its simplest form this is a ruler, 40 to 60 cm long depending on the size of the board, fitted with a sight at each end; one, corresponding to

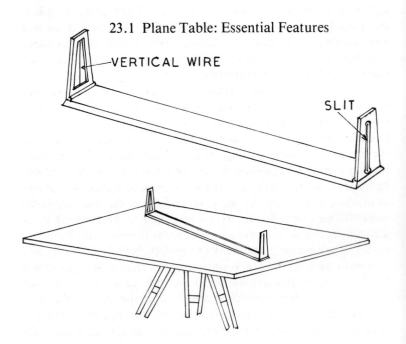

23.1 Plane Table: Essential Features

VERTICAL WIRE

SLIT

the eyepiece, is a narrow vertical slot, the other a wider slot with a wire stretched vertically along it. These give the line of sight, which must be parallel to the edge of the ruler. The ruler may be graduated with any convenient scale, or a separate scale can be used.

The sight-rule can be modified by fitting a telescope and vertical circle of the kind used on any theodolite, from the simplest up to the complications of a self-reducing instrument, with a corresponding increase in the versatility of the equipment. Levels and distances can then be found as with a tacheometer. The cost is comparable to that of a similar theodolite, as also is the inconvenience of transport, to which must be added the need to carry the table itself. Moreover, the sight-rule is not attached to the table, and the risk of several hundred pounds worth of instrumentation falling to the ground is appreciable.

The sight-rule usually carries a spirit-level, axis parallel to that of the ruler, which is used in setting up the plane table; a second spirit-level, with its axis at right angles to the above, is an advantage. The spirit-level can, however, be separate. The method of levelling is the same as for a level or theodolite.

The final essential is a compass, to orient the board approximately. The prismatic compass can be used, but greater accuracy is obtained with a trough compass, in which the needle, about 15 cm long, is contained in a narrow box with sides parallel to the meridian when the needle is pointing to zero; but the compass should invariably be used only to fix a rough orientation.

For large-scale work, a plumbing fork may be useful. This consists of two long arms, nearly parallel, joined rigidly together by a short rod. The free end of the upper arm rests on the table, and vertically beneath it the lower arm carries a plumb-line. Usually, with the scales employed, the relative position of points on the table and on the ground can be estimated accurately enough without the need for this device.

As a drawing surface, paper is not satisfactory for outdoor work unless the weather is reliably fine and dry; a non-absorbent synthetic material is to be preferred. It will usually need to be fixed to the board with drafting-tape sealing the edges completely; some boards have a clamping device. If paper is used it should preferably be damped before being fixed in position, and left to dry for a day. Then, provided it has not torn the fixing loose, it will have a taut smooth surface.

23.2 Use of Plane Table

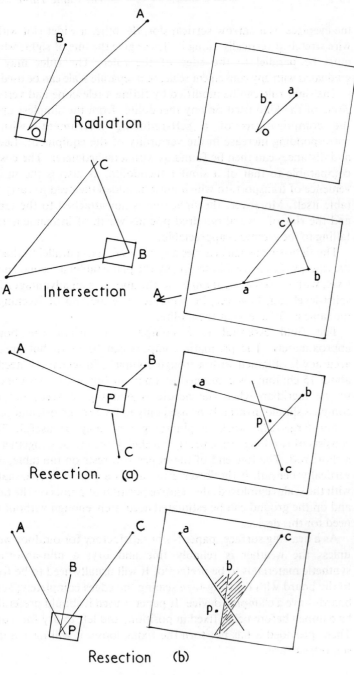

Radiation

Intersection

Resection. (a)

Resection (b)

23.3 *Use.* As with all other methods except photogrammetry, the preparation of a plan consists essentially of locating isolated points, which are then joined up to give the outline of the feature to be represented. With a plane table the required points can be fixed in three different ways (Figure 23.2); these methods can of course be combined. In what follows, capital letters refer to points on the ground, lower case to corresponding points on the plan.

(a) *Radiation.* The board is set up at some chosen point, O say, and oriented, either by sighting to a known point or magnetically. Then the direction OA can be sighted and the corresponding distance measured, so that the direction oa and the position of a can be marked on the plan. The distance can be taped, or if the scale is so small that the inaccuracy is unimportant it can be found tacheometrically.

(b) *Intersection.* Two points A and B are taken as the ends of a base line; they can be deliberately laid out as such or can be points fixed earlier in the survey.

The board is set up with a over A, and oriented so that ab is sighted along AB. By sighting the alidade towards C, ac can be drawn. Repetition of the same procedure at B gives bc, which fixes C. As always, the triangles should be 'well-conditioned'.

(c) *Resection: The Three-Point Problem.* The plane table is set up at P so that three (or more) known points (a, b, c) are visible. The problem is to fix p on the plan corresponding to the position of the plane-table. The solution for accurate surveying has already been described (Para. 17.10), and the same essential condition holds: the plane-table must not lie on (or too near to) the circle passing through the three known points.

The simplest solution is by systematic trial and error. Initially, the board is oriented as accurately as possible with the compass. Rays are then drawn through a, b, and c, towards A, B, and C; they will form a triangle of error near the correct position of p. A better position for p is then selected, according to the following rules:

If p lies within the triangle a b c it also lies within the triangle of error; its distances from the rays through a, b, c are proportional to the lengths pa, pb, pc.

If p lies outside the triangle a b c (which is not such a good arrangement for fixing the required point), a further rule is needed. Imagine yourself standing at a, b, c in turn looking towards p; then the correct position for p is either to the left of all three rays or to the right of all three, so it cannot lie in any part hatched in the diagram. The other rule shows that it lies in roughly the position shown (Figure 23.2, bottom), for it must be nearer to the ray through b than to either of the others.

Having estimated a better position for p, the alidade is laid along the line joining p to the most distant of the three points, and the board reoriented. Rays are then drawn through the other two points. If there is still a triangle of error, the procedure is repeated.

This method is useful for adding detail to an existing map, especially when the scale is small enough to justify sketching most of the detail. In suitable weather conditions the results should be more accurate than can be obtained with a prismatic compass.

24 Underground Surveying

24.1 *General Remarks.* Unlike the rest of this book, this chapter is second-hand; for it has been my good fortune never to have had to survey an underground structure. Nevertheless, some notes will be useful, in case you are unlucky enough to have to undertake such a job.

Apart from the difficulties caused by darkness and often extremely unpleasant physical conditions, the arrangement of the survey itself offers problems. In general triangulation is impossible, and detail has to be based entirely on traverses (Chapter 19), often linked only at one end to the network used for an associated surface survey. Moreover, the link may well be *via* a vertical shaft, probably less than two metres in diameter, which gives a very short base by which to connect the surface and underground surveys.

24.2 *Degree of Accuracy needed.* Even moderate accuracy is much more difficult to attain in underground work than on the surface, so the first thing to consider is how much precision may reasonably be sacrificed, especially as regards angular measurement. A degree corresponds to 1·75 m in 100, so for a system of short tunnels which do not need to be related to surface features an accuracy of half a degree might be acceptable, assuming that no 'ritual' function is suspected. By contrast, much greater accuracy would be needed in dealing with an extensive system formerly served by vertical shafts which are now blocked and invisible from above but which need to be located precisely relative to surface features. Two widely separated links with the surface, on the other hand, allow the errors in the underground work to be balanced (Paras. 19.3–5), and thus again justify rather less accuracy. No general rule can be given, but fortunately most artificial features in Britain, other than mine-works, are fairly short.

24.3 *Methods of Measurement.* For linear measurement, the chain remains the method of choice, provided the floor of the tunnel is dry. If, as all too often, it is deeply concealed by water and liquid mud, the tape is preferable, for it can be pulled tight and kept above water level. Unless an extra helper is available to hold it, some device will be needed for anchorage. Probably the simplest is a deep wooden box, with a hook on one edge to anchor the tape and rope handles for carrying. This can be filled with stones on the site. Indeed, it would probably be worth while to make a 'nesting' pair of such boxes, so as to free both surveyors for detail measurements. A strong bulldog clip will be useful to hold the case end of the tape.

Tacheometric measurements are hardly accurate enough for this sort of work.

Offsets can be measured either with another tape, a pole or half-pole, or a folding rule, whichever is the most convenient.

For angular measurement, a theodolite gives the best accuracy, though it may prove rather unmanageable in difficult conditions. Apart from provision for illumination (Para. 24.4) it should preferably carry a magnetic compass, which will give appreciably more accurate readings than a prismatic compass. This is desirable, for in order to reduce the risk of mistakes and of cumulative errors *all* sights in underground surveying should have the magnetic bearing recorded.

Since many sites are small, though, prismatic compass observations are often adequate. The sights should be taken in both directions, preferably about half a dozen times each way, and averaged.

24.4 *Illumination.* In addition to lights to see where you are going, and to book your records, others are needed to illuminate the instruments and stations.

As station marks, a candle or a small electric hand torch can be used, but a white-painted board with a black X is better; the light is shone on to the board; cross-hairs can be more easily seen against an illuminated white background. The board can be provided with props, or can be suspended.

If you are doing a lot of underground work, it will be worth while to get a theodolite fitted with a device to illuminate the cross-hairs, but for occasional use these can be made visible by shining a torch obliquely into the object-glass.

If you are working with a prismatic compass, remember that the section of the graduated circle which you read is that beneath the prism.

24.5 *Marking Stations.* If the floor of the cave or tunnel is earth, or even bare rock, stations can be marked with a peg or spike, but often this will be impossible. If the roof is sound, a spike can be driven into it, if possible with a hooked head so that a marker can be hung from it. Alternatively, a reference point can be marked, with paint, crayon, or a spike, on the wall of the passage, the actual station being recorded as a specified distance perpendicular from the wall at that point. If the passage is not too wide, spikes can be driven into each side of the passage, slightly projecting, and the station established on a piece of wood cut to fit between them. If, as may be convenient, the wood is movable, care must be taken always to replace it the same way round, unless the mark is exactly central.

24.6 *Plumbing Down a Shaft* (Figure 24.1). Occasionally, you may need to relate the underground and surface surveys more accurately than magnetic observations permit, and the only possible link is by plumbing down a single narrow shaft. Two plumb-lines, 1 and 2, corresponding to points P and Q in the survey, are suspended from fixed supports just above the top of the shaft, the line PQ pointing roughly along the line of the underground tunnel. The upper ends of the lines are stationary, and can be tied into the surface survey without difficulty. Observation of the lower end gives an extremely thin and ill-conditioned triangle, but if PQ and QX are known (the theodolite being set up at X) then PQ sin QPX = QX sin PXQ. The angle QPX, giving the direction of PX relative to PQ and hence to the surface features, is thus found accurately.

Unfortunately, the plumb-lines are unlikely to be exactly stationary. The movement of the plumb-bobs can be damped by putting them in pails full of water. Alternatively, and rather more accurately, a horizontal scale readable through the theodolite can be fixed behind each plumb-line. Several successive readings of the plumb-line against the scale are taken for the limits of the swing and averaged (note that the last reading *must* be on the same side as the first, so there will be one more reading on that side). The mid point between the two averages gives the exact plumb. For example, if successive readings on the scale in centimetres, are 3·5, 22·1, 3·7, 21·8, 3·8, 21·7, 4·1, 21·5, 4·3 (alternately to left and

24.1 Plumbing down a Shaft

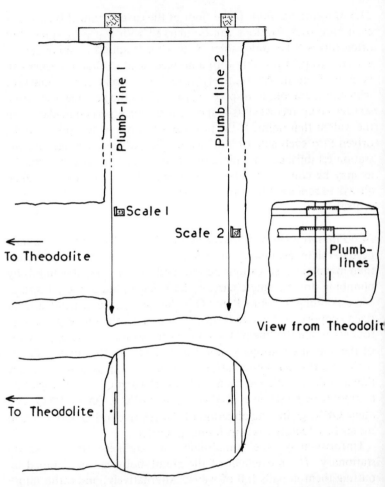

right), the mean value of the five left-hand values is 3·88, and of the four right-hand values 21·78. So the true vertical reading would be 12·83.

24.7 *Levelling*. Apart from illuminating the staff and cross-hairs, no special precautions are needed in underground levelling. If the staff is held inverted, to fix the level of the roof, the reading should not only be marked −, but should be ringed to reduce the risk of a mistake when working out levels. For rough work, especially on small sites, a clinometer is often adequate.

Bench marks or change-points at the top and bottom of a shaft can usually be located so that they can be related directly by taping vertically.

Part VII
RECONNAISSANCE AND ROUGH SURVEYS

25 The Ordnance Survey and Reconnaissance

25.1 Introduction; 25.2 The Ordnance Survey; 25.3 The Current
Standard Maps; 25.4 Obsolescent Large-scale Maps; 25.5 The
Prismatic Compass; 25.6 Reconnaissance; 25.7 Example.

25.1 *Introduction*. Among the most important objectives of field
archaeology are the discovery, identification, and location of
previously unrecorded structures. The first two are not specifically
problems for a surveyor. Discovery results from a combination of
luck and experience, and will be assisted by a study of the two
books mentioned in Para. 28.4; these also form the best brief
introduction to identification of remains. Experience supplemented
by critical comment from fellow archaeologists is also necessary,
and after many years of work mistakes are still possible. Nevertheless, however accurate the identification may be, it is not of
much use if the position of the site is wrongly given, whereas if the
location is correct the identification can always be checked,
provided the structure still exists.

This chapter is concerned with simple methods for fixing the
positions of sites on the ground (the complementary problem, of
making rough plans, is discussed in the next). Much useful
reconnaissance can be done with nothing more than a 1/25,000
map, but the addition of a prismatic compass to your equipment
will be found very helpful indeed, especially in wild or mountainous
country; it is also a valuable safeguard against getting lost in mist.

25.2 *The Ordnance Survey*. British archaeologists are exceptionally
fortunate; wherever they may choose to work in this country, an
accurate large-scale map is available, with most known field-
monuments marked upon it. They owe this good fortune to the
Ordnance Survey.

The indebtedness of British archaeologists to that body cannot
be exaggerated. Not only did the Survey provide, in their old six-
inch to the mile maps, what was probably the finest *complete* large
scale coverage of any country in Western Europe if not in the

265

world, they marked, as a regular practice, all known antiquities. The general accuracy of all this information was maintained by the Archaeology Division (now, 1979, being disbanded) who also prepared the incomparable series of Period Maps. Only the current standard scales will be discussed in detail here, but reference should be made to an extremely valuable booklet *The Historians Guide to Ordnance Survey Maps* (published for the Standing Conference for Local History by the National Council of Social Service, 1964) which describes all maps at a scale of one-inch to the mile or larger, *with dates of the various editions* and other information (by J. B. Harley), and includes a section on the Period Maps (by C. W. Phillips).

25.3 *The Current Standard Maps.* These are as follows:

The 1/50,000 superseding the former 'one-inch'. This is useful for finding one's way about the countryside and for visiting known sites, but is on too small a scale for original fieldwork.

The 1/25,000 or 'Two-and-a-half-inch' (*sc.* to the mile). This is now the basic map for fieldwork. All field boundaries are shown, though somewhat generalised, and 10 m corresponds to 0·4 mm on the map, so eight-figure grid references are possible.

The 1/50,000 and 1/25,000 both give details of magnetic variation.

The 1/10,000 map is nominally the successor to the 'six-inch', but is excessively generalised. It shows no more detail than the 1/25,000. Except that it is rather easier to read, it offers the fieldworker nothing to counterbalance the extra cost and bulk (see also below, in 25.4).

All the above maps are intended to cover the whole country.

The 1/2,500 (or 25-inch). This is an accurate and detailed map, covering all cultivated or built-up areas, but not moor or waste land. Spot levels are shown, but no contours. Most features are shown exactly, but earthworks may be somewhat generalised. For some areas the new edition (on national grid lines) has not yet replaced the older County sheets.

For some major towns and cities, maps are available at 1/1,250; they are essentially an enlargement of the 1/2,500 maps.

25.4 *Obsolescent Large-scale Maps.* The older large-scale maps, on county sheet lines, remain of value to fieldworkers and are often available for reference in libraries or in the offices of County Authorities. They are now irreplaceable reference documents, and should be treasured as such, especially in the case of the 'six-inch'.

Details of the history of these maps are given in the *Historians Guide* mentioned above (Para. 25.2), as well as lists of those towns for which very large scale plans are available, at 1/500, five feet, and ten feet to the mile; these may be useful for the study of town defences or industrial remains. As regards the 'six-inch' and '25-inch', some matters of particular interest to fieldworkers deserve mention.

The Ordnance Survey does not enforce copyright on maps published more than 50 years ago (see *Current Archaeology*, vol. V no. 53 (November 1975), p. 190) so copies of these can be used as a basis for maps or plans without charge; it is courteous to acknowledge the use of such material. The 'gridded' six-inch county sheets state the exact co-ordinates of their corners, so the National Grid can easily be superimposed on the older sheets, and on the '25-inch' sheets, each of which coincides with a quarter of a 'six-inch' sheet.

All except the very latest of the county-sheet series indicate bench marks, and these are now again being shown on the 1/10,000 maps. At one stage they were omitted, and a fee was charged for the information. For most practical purposes, the bench marks on the County sheets are adequate. Note, though, that the older editions work from a different datum.

If you are working in open moorland or similar country the absence of landmarks will often cause inconvenience. You may then find it worth while to transfer to your field maps details which are shown on the County sheet series of 'six-inch' maps but which are now omitted, such as sheep-folds or ruined buildings. Among the less obvious of such reference points are bench marks. These are not always easy to find, but as a general guide, in the sort of country considered they will be cut on a fairly conspicuous outcrop or immovable boulder and will be visible to someone looking in the direction of the 'arrow' symbol. Some appear on the oldest editions but are not repeated on the later maps.

From the point of view of the fieldworker, the 1/10,000 map which has replaced the 'six-inch' is very unsatisfactory indeed. It is highly generalised, so that for example a small church of typical irregular outline may be shown as a simple rectangle, touching the side of a road even though there is in fact a space between them. Roads and lanes tend to be shown as of constant width, the variations which are often informative being suppressed. The conventional signs are very coarse; that for rocky ground, for example, can be misinterpreted as a group of oval sheep-folds.

Criticisms of this kind could be multiplied. Nevertheless, having regard to the extremely high quality of most of their work, the Ordnance Survey staff are unlikely to be directly to blame for this distressing (and one hopes temporary) collapse in standards; one may reasonably suspect that they, as well as the users of their maps, are victims of an external directive which they were not allowed to disregard.

25.5 *The Prismatic Compass.* Although this is not a precise measuring instrument, it gives results which are accurate enough for reconnaissance. With its use, points can almost always be located on the map within about 10 m, that is, closely enough to establish an eight-figure grid reference. The standard prismatic compass (Figure 25.1) comprises a graduated compass-card in a

25.1 Prismatic Compass: Diagram of Main Feautres

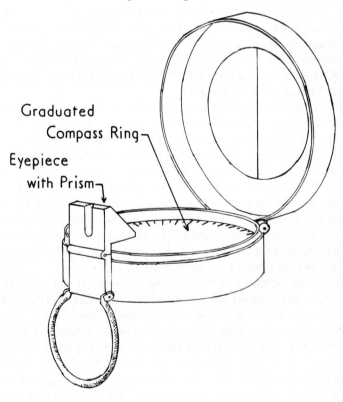

Graduated
    Compass Ring
Eyepiece
    with Prism

glass-topped box about 6 cm in diameter, fitted with a prism so arranged that the graduated circle can be observed through a lens at the same time as a view forwards through a sighting-line. The prism usually moves on a slide so that it can be focused on the graduations, and there is a ring to fit over your thumb. The cheapest type, with 'dry' suspension, has a small button with which the oscillation of the needle can be damped, but the small extra cost of a 'liquid' suspension is well worth while, as in it the oscillations are eliminated almost at once. Larger types are available, including models which can be used on a tripod, but these sacrifice the great advantage of portability.

Get accustomed to using the compass with your non-writing hand, thus leaving your writing hand free to take notes without having repeatedly to disengage your thumb. Also, to avoid the risk of dropping the compass when in use, attach it to your clothes or to the carrying-case by a loop of string through the ring.

25.6 *Reconnaissance.* Pacing and the prismatic compass together are adequate for almost all reconnaissance work. You should try to establish the length of your normal walking pace under various conditions; it is unlikely to be the same, for example, when you are climbing a steep heather-covered slope as when you are crossing a level pasture. Nevertheless, even when you have a fairly good idea of the length of your pace, you should always try to start and finish at a known point, as this reduces the effect of any uncertainty.

It is impossible to cover every contingency, but the examples discussed below will suggest methods of approach. In general, obviously, the nearer the known landmarks, the greater the precision with which a point can be located; and since all observations are rather rough, at least one redundant measurement should be made, preferably two. Usually your objective will be merely to fix the national grid reference of some features, but in some circumstances you may need to publish, or to put on permanent record in some archive, the actual measurements you made. In the first case discussed, for example, x might be the find-spot of some relic; excavation might be desirable, and the point could be located more precisely on the ground from a record of the actual pacing than from a statement of the grid reference. Another possible example is that of an obscure site in open country which may be located on the ground, by reference to some obvious feature not shown on the map, more easily than from the grid alone.

Probably the simplest case is when the feature (x here and subsequently) stands in a field with defined angles ABCD (Figure 25.2a). If P is lined in with x and C, x can be located quite accurately by pacing AP, PD, PX and XC. If the distances involved are small, fewer measurements may be adequate; even if your assumed pace differs by as much as 0·2 m from its real value, 50 paces will be only 10 m wrong.

An alternative way of fixing x would be by taking prismatic compass sights from x to A, B, C, and D (Figure 25.2b), and correcting them for the magnetic variation by means of the information given on the 1/50,000 or 1/25,000 map. Theoretically, of course, two sights are adequate, but as errors are almost certain

25.2 Reconnaissance: Methods of Fixing Points

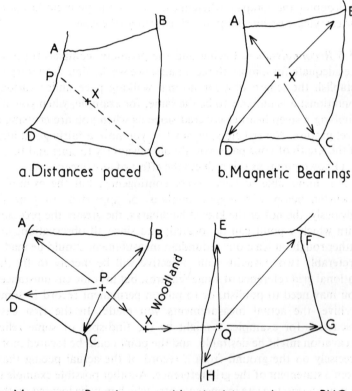

a.Distances paced   b.Magnetic Bearings

c.Magnetic Bearings combined with pacing on PXQ

to occur a third is taken, and if x on the map is placed in the resulting triangle of error, the accuracy should be improved. Provided the triangle of error *is* small, the fourth sight is not needed; but some time you will almost certainly make a mistake such as misreading 5°. With three sights, one wrong, the triangle will be large, and you will have no way of deciding which of the three vertices is the right one; but the fourth sight will almost always make it clear.

Obviously other ways, combining the use of pacing and compass bearings, can be devised; bearings and paced distances of AX and of XC would be one such way.

Owing to the lie of the ground or to the presence of vegetation direct sights between X and three known points may not be possible. In such a case intermediate 'stations' P, Q etc. can be used (Figure 25.2c), not themselves of any significance but capable of being fixed by observations to known points and themselves linked to X either by compass bearings alone or by bearings and paced distances. Since these more elaborate arrangements increase the risk of mistakes, and since the fact that they are necessary usually implies a shortage of landmarks, particular care is needed to make sure that all measurements are correct.

Finally, the use of the compass and pacing during search needs to be mentioned. Open moorland, and to a lesser extent woodland, often conceals undiscovered remains. In searching for these it is useful to record your course as a paced traverse. Marks, such as heaps of stones, crayon crosses on conspicuous rocks, or blazes on trees, can be left and recorded at suitable points; it is helpful if they can be numbered. These can be picked up by intersecting lines, but loops should be avoided, and each traverse should keep fairly near to a fixed bearing if possible, and should start and finish at points defined on the map. Rather than trying to reduce the traverse to some standard scale it is simpler to plot it to some arbitrary scale, for example 10 paces to a centimetre, and then, using the known grid references of start and finish to superimpose the national grid. The grid references of features discovered can then be read off (see next section).

That is often all that is needed, but if the area is likely to be revisited by you or by a colleague the course followed should be plotted on a record map and on a field map, so that duplication of of work can be avoided and the actual intensity of search is known.

25.3 Reconnaissance Survey

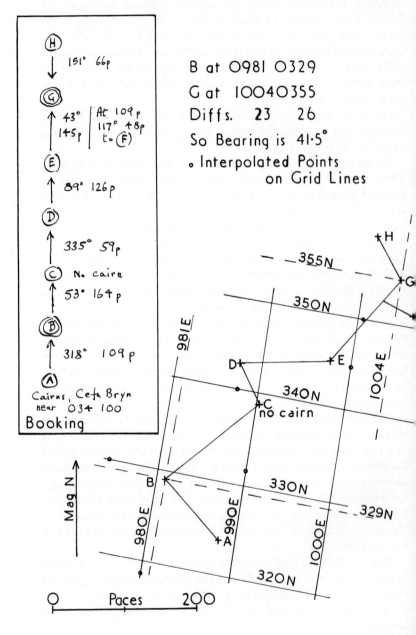

H
↓ 151° 66p
G
↑ 43° | At 109 p
145p | 117° 48p
       | to F
E
↑ 89° 126p
D
↑ 335° 59p
C No cairn
↑ 53° 164p
B
↑ 318° 109p
A
Cairns, Cefn Bryn
near 034 100
Booking

B at 0981 0329
G at 1004 0355
Diffs.   23   26
So Bearing is 41·5°
∘ Interpolated Points
        on Grid Lines

+H
— — 355N
+G
350N
981E
D+   +E
1004E
340N
+C
no cairn
330N
Mag N
980E
990E
329N
1000E
+A
320N

O   Paces   200

25.7 *Example.* Assume that a reconnaissance survey is made of a group of cairns, two of which (B and G) appear on the OS map. The booking appears as a simple linear diagram (Figure 25.3); the description of each cairn is noted separately, and apart from the co-ordinates of B and G need not be repeated here.

The first cairn found (A) is unrecorded. The magnetic bearing to B is 318°, and the distance 109 paces. From B no other cairn except G is visible, so you set off in about that direction, but after 164 paces (that is, at point C) you notice another cairn D on your left; the bearing is 335°, and the distance 59 paces. Thence it is 89° bearing and 126 paces to E. From E you set out towards G, bearing 43°, but at 109 paces you notice that you are passing a cairn (F) on your right. Rather than make a dog-leg in the traverse, you decide to take this by measurement from the line EG. *Before doing anything else* you note 'At 109 p.' in the margin (it is surprisingly easy to forget a number, or to forget to write it down, if you attempt to carry it in your head while you do something else). Next mark your position temporarily (for example by dumping your coat) at 109 p. on EG, and then take the bearing and distance to F. Return to the temporary mark and continue pacing to G. As you are leaving the site you find another cairn H, and locate it by bearing and distance back to G.

Plotting can conveniently be done on ordinary ruled paper, the lines being taken as corresponding to a fixed magnetic bearing. This is usually 0° or 90°, but need not be; in the example given 45° might have been preferable, as BG runs roughly NE. Measurements are plotted as booked, with no attempt to convert paces to metres or to correct for magnetic variation. The traverse is drawn with a protractor (not by calculation) and using any convenient scale. For eight-figure grid references 5 paces to 1 mm is about the smallest which is likely to be satisfactory; the original plot reproduced in Figure 25.3 was at 1 pace to 1 m on a 1/2,500 metric scale.

The grid co-ordinates of B and G are known (in this case 0981 0329 and 1004 0355 respectively), so G lies 1004 − 0981 = 23(0) m to east of B and 0355 − 0329 = 26(0) m to north, whence the grid bearing of BG can be found either graphically or by calculation. It is 41·5°. Hence the grid lines corresponding to 0981 and 1004E, 0329 and 0355N can be drawn through B and G. It is then easy to draw the lines for 0980, 0990, 1000E and for 0320, 0330, 0340, 0350N. This can be done either by calculation or more simply by holding a suitable scale inclined to the grid lines; in Figure 25.3, the ringed dots which fix the positions of the E grid lines correspond to 0, 20, 40, and 60 on a 1/1,250 metric scale held with graduations 1 and 24 at grid lines 981 and 1004. Having drawn the grid to the arbitrary scale used, the eight-figure grid references can be read off and if desired the line of the traverse can easily be transferred to the record map.

The main precaution in using a pace-and-prismatic traverse in this way is that the reference points (B and G here) should lie at or near the ends of the run, since corrections for magnetic bearing and length of pace depend on them. Points A, F and H are not so reliably fixed as the remainder, but your pace may reasonably be supposed not to have differed much when you were fixing them from its value on the run BCDEG. As a check, when the plotting is finished, you should work out the magnetic variation and pace length (9° and 1·22 paces to a metre in the example); if they are wildly improbable a mistake should be suspected. Accuracy can be improved, and the risk of mistakes reduced, by sighting both ways along each line and by repeating the pacing. In booking, you should always write down a measurement immediately you have taken it or if your pacing is interrupted; any distraction, such as sudden recognition of a 'new' cairn, can very easily make you fail to record some essential figure.

Traverses of this kind can intersect to form a network. Suppose that cairn D were included in a similar run between known points P and Q. The grid reference for D would first be found independently for both runs, and the average value would be treated as a new 'fixed point'.

Although results are rather more reliable if the 'fixed points' are actual features shown on the map, spots fixed merely by bearings to known sites can be used if necessary.

26 Rough Surveys

26.1 General Remarks; 26.2 'Improving' the Ordnance Survey;
26.3 Methods of Measurement; 26.4 The Main Outline; 26.5 Detail;
26.6 Controls; 26.7 Plotting; 26.8 Enlarging a Plan; 26.9 Profiles
with a Clinometer.

26.1 *General Remarks.* Lack of time may often prevent you from making an accurate survey of a site, but even a rough plan is more informative and valuable than a long verbal description, subject to one absolutely essential requirement: the standard of accuracy must be explicitly stated.

The following examples will make this clear; the techniques involved are discussed in greater detail later. The plan of a hill-fort taken without alteration from one of the older 1/2,500 maps will usually be accurate in scale and general outline, but may well omit details which are archaeologically important. To fix our ideas, suppose that you find on inspection that there is a faint unrecorded bank curving away from the main rampart to form a large annexe. For publication, therefore, you could either use the copy of the 1/2,500 outline unaltered and supplemented with a description, or 'improve' it by sketching on the annexe by eye without measurement, or improve it still more by using the original outline as a control with detail added from a 'pace-and-prismatic' traverse. If the hill-fort were newly discovered, a pace-and-prismatic survey by itself could give a good indication of shape and entrance arrangements, but the actual dimensions might be wrong by as much as 10 per cent, and the area by twice that proportion. If such a survey is checked by a more accurate control measurement of overall length, this uncertainty will be greatly reduced.

All these different types of rough plan are useful, but only if their limitations are known. For example, a detailed statistical study of hill-fort areas would find the unimproved 1/2,500 plan reliable, but could be falsified if the uncontrolled paced traverse were taken as exact; by contrast, the latter might be more helpful in showing whether the outline is polygonal or curvilinear.

26.2 *'Improving' the Ordnance Survey.* Waste ground is not covered by the 1/2,500 maps, but despite this limitation most of the major field monuments in Britain are represented on this valuable series. On the latest edition the plans prepared under the direction of the staff of the Archaeology Division are likely to be as accurate as anything that can be hoped for, short of a complete new *ad hoc* survey; they are of course copyright (see Para. 25.4). Much of the country, though, is still covered only by older editions, and the representations of earthworks will often need to be 'improved'.

A simple systematic method of doing this was described by one of the pioneers of field archaeology, J. P. Williams-Freeman, in his excellent work *Field Archaeology as Illustrated by Hampshire* (Macmillan, 1915). Details are given in his Appendix I (pp. 329–33), all of which deserves study but which can only be summarised here.

Williams-Freeman's method was to work on a tracing of the 1/2,500 map; a photoprint, not available in his day, would save work, but an enlargement (Para. 26.8) would give more room for annotation. The tracing was fixed on one side of a small drawing-board, and a sheet of paper for note taking on the other. He walked round the earthwork, sketching corrections on the plan and making notes where more detailed explanations were needed. He rightly recommends that *before leaving the site* the fieldworker should 'complete and verify the notes, repair omissions, and write a short description of the camp . . .'

Williams-Freeman also described a step by step method of sketching profiles: a short measuring-rod was held vertically, at the toe of a slope, and the point on the slope and level with the rod's upper end was fixed by eye; the rod was then moved to that point, and the procedure repeated as necessary. By noting the corresponding horizontal distances, the profile could be sketched. Such sketches, especially for multivallate defences, display a lot of information very concisely, but my own view is that having regard to the large inherent inaccuracies they tend to give an unrealistic impression of precision; it seems preferable simply to state that the overall height is 'about' so many metres (but see Para. 26.8).

26.3 *Methods of Measurement.* Williams-Freeman's method requires very little actual measurement, but it is not applicable to a newly discovered site or to one outside the area covered by the 1/2,500 maps. In such circumstances a rough paced survey is always worth while; it may occasionally form the only record of an important earthwork. Rough surveying depends primarily on your pace for long distances and your foot for short ones. In booking, these should be specified as p. and f. (not ft for your foot is not necessarily standard). You should have noted, from previous work, what p. and f. correspond to in metres; if two people are working together, the relevant units should be distinguished by booking them as ps. and pj. say (for Smith and Jones) but it is assumed throughout this chapter that you are working single-handed. Distances measured with your foot, by stepping out heel to toe, are fairly accurate, but unless you have military training your pace will vary considerably according to the nature of the ground and your physical condition; some form of check on a paced survey is always very desirable.

Although a plan can be made with pacing only, a prismatic compass is a great help, and since the need for emergency rough surveying usually arises during a planned campaign of fieldwork you will probably have it available. Similarly a tape or chain is useful. The latter is to be preferred if you have to make a long check measurement, but is otherwise less convenient than a tape. Sometimes you may find it useful to cut a sapling to form a rod '5f.' long, for example if you wish to make fairly accurate measurements on steep slopes or over marshy ground.

Rough surveying falls essentially into three parts: the main outline, detail, and checking. This is illustrated by a genuine example, though it has been simplified for brevity.

26.4 *The Main Outline.* After making a rough sketch for reference (not reproduced), the shape is established by a pace-and-prismatic traverse. The starting-point and most (preferably all) of the other stations should be indicated by some temporary expendable marker, such as a wand or a pile of stones. The more important should be 'named' either with crayon on a stone or with a piece of paper threaded on to the wand; other distinctive marks will suggest themselves. These can be put in while making the traverse, but sometimes it is useful to mark particularly important points during the preliminary examination of the site. This examination can be dispensed with, but if so, very detailed notes will need to be made during the traverse.

In the example (Figure 26.1) the traverse is started at A (the middle of the entrance, which happened to be at the north-east vertex of the enclosure) and proceeds clockwise round the crest of

26.1 Rough Survey: Booking

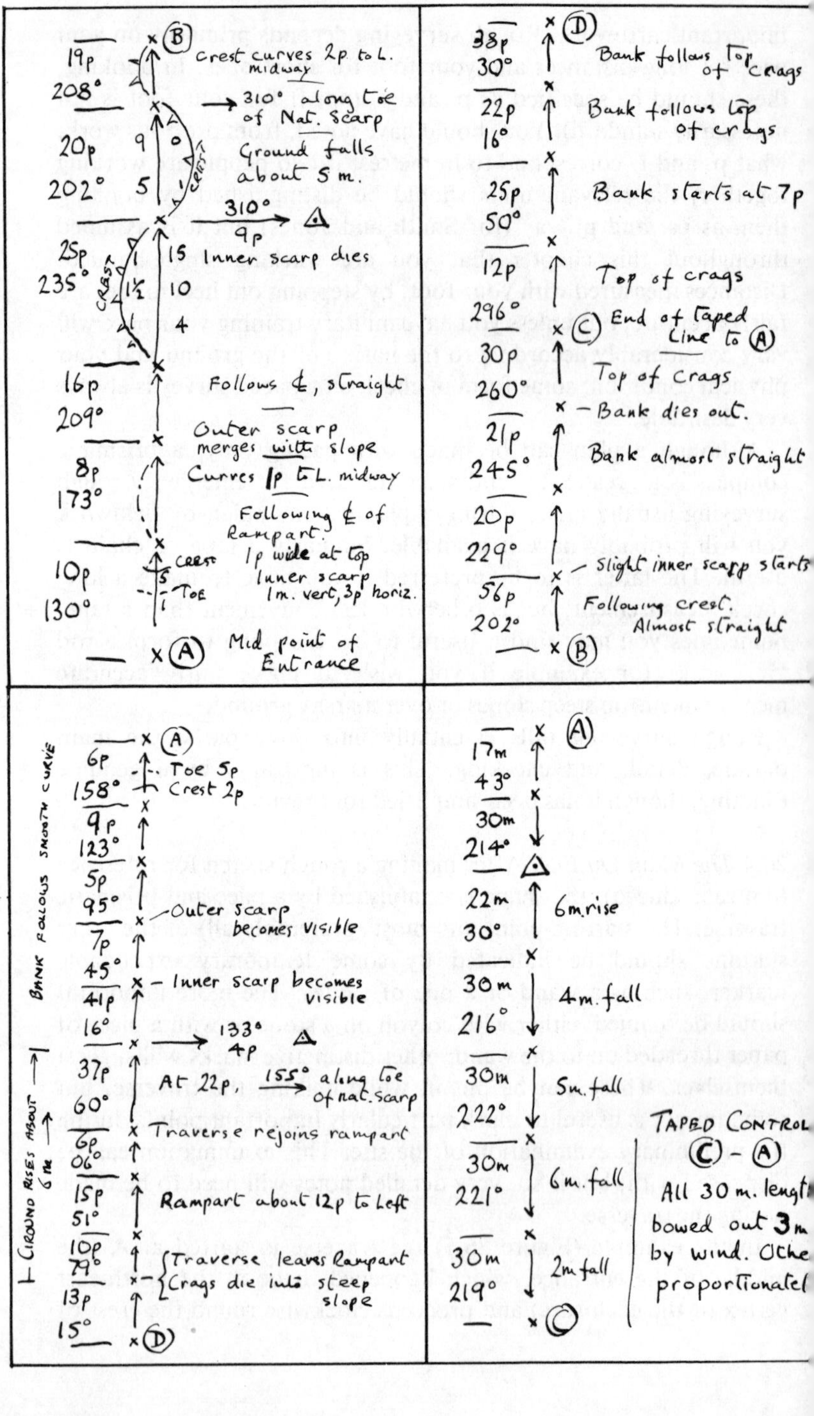

Top-left panel:

B (crest curves 2p to L. midway)

19p
208°

→ 310° along toe of Nat. Scarp

Ground falls about 5 m.

20p
202°   9   0   5   1

310° → Δ
9p

25p
235°   CREST   1   1½   1   15 10 4   Inner scarp dies

16p
209°   Follows ₵, straight

Outer scarp merges with slope

8p
173°   Curves 1p to L. midway

Following ₵ of Rampart.

10p
130°   crest / Toe   5   1   1p wide at top
Inner scarp 1m. vert, 3p horiz.

x A   Mid point of Entrance

Top-right panel:

D

38p
30°   Bank follows Top of crags

22p
16°   Bank follows top of crags

25p
50°   Bank starts at 7p

12p
296°   Top of crags

C   End of taped Line to A

30p
260°   Top of Crags

— Bank dies out.

21p
245°   Bank almost straight

20p
229°   — Slight inner scarp starts

56p
202°   Following crest.
Almost straight

x B

Bottom-left panel:

BANK FOLLOWS SMOOTH CURVE

x A

6p
158°   Toe 5p
Crest 2p

9p
123°

5p
95°   Outer scarp becomes visible

7p
45°   Inner scarp becomes visible

41p
16°   → 133° Δ
4p

37p
60°   At 22p, 155° along toe of nat. scarp

6p
06°   Traverse rejoins rampart

15p
51°   Rampart about 12p to Left

10p
79°   Traverse leaves Rampart
13p   Crags die into steep slope

15°   x D

GROUND RISES ABOUT 6 m.

Bottom-right panel:

x A

17m
43°

30m
214°   Δ

22m
30°   6m rise

30m
216°   4m. fall

30m
222°   5m. fall

30m
221°   6m. fall

30m
219°   2m fall

— x C

TAPED CONTROL
C – A

All 30 m. lengths bowed out 3 m by wind. Other proportionate[l] the rampart. Each leg of the traverse is aimed ahead, and the bearing measured *and recorded at once*. Features such as a small bush, or even a conspicuous tuft of grass, will serve to mark the direction. A suitable distance is then paced out, any relevant information being noted on the way, until a change in direction seems desirable, in this case after 10 paces. That distance is noted, and the next leg is then started. No attempt is made to vary the space allotted in the notes according to the length of the leg. The general arrangement will be obvious from the figure. The last station on each page is 'named', to ensure that the record is followed correctly, as also are any stations which may require to be used again. In this case, C is important as it is at the south-western apex of the enclosure and is to be used as one end of a taped measurement (see Para. 26.5); but it is often useful to run a linking traverse to join two opposite points on the main circuit. In this case, such a link is provided by measurements to the OS Trigonometrical station (indicated by the conventional triangle). The traverse is continued to close on its starting point.

26.5 *Detail*. Features of special importance, as for example entrances, often deserve a more accurate survey than the main outline. Provided a tape is available, that can be weighted down to act as a chain line, and offsets measured 'heel-and-toe'; remember to record in the field book that the offsets are in 'f.' (your feet), while the chainages are in metres. Lacking a tape, wands or even stones can be set at measured intervals in a straight line as a substitute 'chain line', and all measurements made in 'f.'. Any such detailed survey should be tied in to the main outline, and its orientation should be noted.

Where there is a lot of internal detail, such as numerous hut-platforms, the work involved in trying to record it is seldom justified. Usually, all that is needed is to note 'numerous hut-platforms' on the final plan, for a rough survey will not in fact be recording anything more than that; nothing could be deduced from it as to the significance, if any, of their arrangement.

26.6 *Controls*. If a plan is based entirely on pacing, the drawn scale should always be marked as 'Approximate', or more truthfully 'Rough'. With this qualification, such a plan can give a very useful indication of the character of a site. Unfortunately, however careful you yourself may be to specify the inaccuracy of your work, anyone who uses it in a secondary publication is very likely indeed to omit that information. You cannot reasonably be blamed for that, but nevertheless, if you can get the general scale right, one potentially misleading item will be eliminated.

In Britain, most earthworks appear on the 1/2,500 maps (see Para. 25.4 concerning copyright); the Victoria County Histories reproduce nearly all the relevant plans to 1/5,000 in their 'Ancient Earthworks' sections, where these have been published. What is shown on the 1/2,500 maps is almost always accurate; mistakes do occur, but if your plan differs significantly from the Ordnance Survey you are more likely to be wrong, and should check your work. You therefore have a reliable outline plan, and can fit your pace-and-prismatic survey to it, as described in the next section.

Sometimes in Britain, and almost always abroad, no such outline plan is available, so if you wish for a check on the scale you will need to measure one of the major dimensions of the enclosure. Ideally, of course, the distance should be chained, but the assumption here is that you are in a hurry.

In the example given, the OS showed no detail south of the trigonometrical station, so marks were left during the paced traverse at the north-east (A) and south-west (C) ends of the enclosure, and the distance between these was taped; the trigonometrical station lay near the line.

A fairly conspicuous pile of stones was built at C (in other circumstances a wand might be used) and the end of the tape was marked with a piece of white rag, and tied to a moderately heavy rock. Thirty metres length was then measured in roughly the right direction, another pile of stones (the '30 m mark') was built, and the magnetic bearing back to C recorded. Owing to windage, the tape was bowed out an estimated 3 m from the straight line; this was noted, as well as the rough difference in level between C and the 30 m mark (see next section). The tape was then pulled on until the white rag was at the 30 m cairn, the 60 m mark was placed, and a bearing taken on the 30 m mark. The measurement was continued in this way, though at the 120 m mark it was more convenient to take a forward bearing to the trigonometrical station. It was also convenient to take that station as the start of another 30 m length, and again to take a forward bearing from that point to A. When plotting, the measurements must be corrected. Thus the length from the 30 to the 60 m mark is reduced by $6^2/2 \times 30 = 0.6$ m for slope and by 0·8 m to allow for the displacement caused by the wind (see Appendix IV).

The result is of course rough. In the conditions which obtained in this case, the accuracy was probably worse than one part in a hundred, though on level ground and in sheltered conditions one in two hundred or even better might be attained. Nevertheless, it is appreciably better than relying on pacing alone. In a survey of this kind, if time permits, a second taped line running roughly at right angles to the first would ensure a better representation of the shape of the enclosure. In the example, such a line could have been run from B through the '90 m mark' to D.

26.7 *Plotting*. If you have no background control for scale, you must convert all paced distances to metres; the easiest way of doing this is to make a scale of your paces on a piece of thin card, to whatever reduction factor you intend to use for your plan. Such a home-made measuring scale can always be used, but if you have a control, some simple conversion factor which can be applied mentally is almost always adequate. In this example, 10 paces were taken as 9 m, so to correct the distance the whole number of paces is measured on the metre scale and one-tenth of the number counted back.

For most purposes 1/1,250 is a useful scale for plotting, allowing reduction to 1/2,500 for publication; this is probably the most widely used scale for earthworks, where any standard scale is attempted.

The traverse is first plotted to the chosen scale, marking the lines and 'stations' clearly. Again, ordinary ruled paper forms a convenient background, as the rulings can be taken as east-west or north-south and the magnetic bearings drawn with a protractor, without correction. The traverse, and the draft plan, are not intended for publication. In preparing the final tracing (not reproduced) these would be supplemented by notes made during the examination of the site, as for example those relating to the size of the rampart.

For convenience in tracing, the traverse should be plotted in separate parts (Figure 26.2), each part overlapping its neighbour by one leg. Thus in the example, where A and C are control points, one part would run from 6p. before A to 12p. after C, the other from 30p. before C to 10p. after A. If the cross-measurement BD

26.2 Rough Survey: Plotting

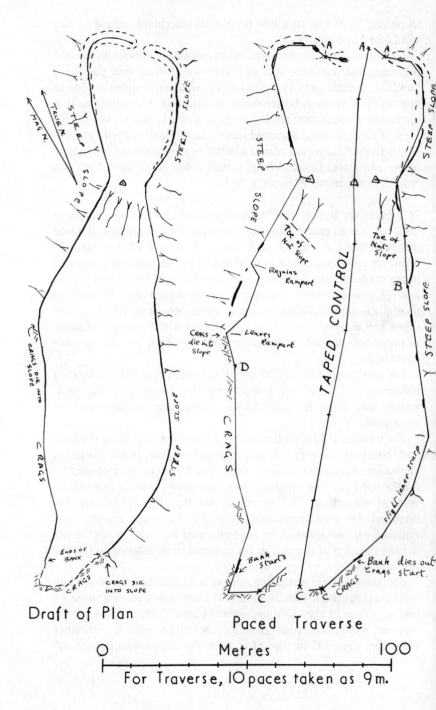

Draft of Plan

Paced Traverse

Metres

0   100

For Traverse, 10 paces taken as 9m.

(Labels within figure:) MAG. N., TRUE N., STEEP SLOPE, Toe of Nat. Slope, Rejoins Rampart, Leaves Rampart, CRAGS die into Slope, TAPED CONTROL, CRAGS, STEEP SLOPE, CRAGS DIE INTO SLOPE, slight inner scarp, ENDS OF BANK, CRAGS DIE INTO SLOPE, Bank starts, Bank dies out & crags start., A, B, C, D

had also been taken, the parts would have run from 6p. before A to 56p. after B, 19p. before B to 12p. after C, and so on. If there is no control, the plots run from vertex to vertex, again with a slight overlap; in this example they would be as before, from near A to near C. If a map is available as control, any two halves are suitable. The reason for drawing the traverse in two parts is to avoid confusion caused by the closing error, and the overlap is to simplify 'smoothing' the detail in the final tracing. Any subsidiary linking traverses are also plotted independently. After this has been done, the detail is added, care being taken not to obscure the actual lines of the traverse.

If a taped control is being used, the control points are plotted and then traced, and the detail from the traverse is copied on to the same tracing, the errors being distributed by eye. In the example, A, C and the trigonometrical station (TS) would be accepted as controls. Starting with A, the detail near A would be traced. Then A and TS on the tracing would be placed roughly equidistant from A and TS on the traverse plot, and detail covering about the middle third of the interval between them copied. Then the tracing would be moved again and detail near TS traced, and so on until the circuit was completed.

With no control, if one point (TS say) is made to coincide, the two halves of the traverse will give different positions for A and for C; the averages of these are then taken as the 'fixed points', and errors distributed as before. If in addition, B and D had been linked by a paced traverse two more 'fixed points' would have been obtained by taking the average positions of the ends of the direct traverse BD (placed as symmetrically as possible relative to the main traverse) and the corresponding points on the main traverse.

If a 1/2,500 map is available, it will need to be enlarged (see next section) and a tracing made of the outline. Detail is then added in essentially the same way as that already described. Recognisable features, such as entrances or angles, are traced first, and then detail from sections midway between them.

On 1/2,500 plans, modern features such as walls or buildings are most accurately shown. Next come the centre-lines of banks or ditches, after those the crests of scarps; in these, minor irregularities, which may none the less be archaeologically important, are sometimes smoothed out. Toes of scarps, however, are often extended further than an archaeologist would accept as justified, so banks may appear wider on the OS map than on your plan.

26.8 *Enlarging a Plan.* This is often necessary. For example, if your 'improved' 1/2,500 plan is to be published at that scale, it will need to be drawn at 1/1,250, and you will need a pencil outline of that scale as basis. The enlargement can be done optically or with a pantograph or similar device, but it can also be done very easily without any such elaboration; an objection to the pantograph is that it also enlarges every slight error in positioning the tracing-point.

The simplest method, and the one which I prefer, is to super-impose a grid of squares on the original, and to transfer the detail to a corresponding grid of larger squares, points which have to be located precisely being fixed by measurement of co-ordinates (Figure 26.3). If the enlargement is to a simple multiple, such as two to one, there is no need to relate the size of square to the scale, but usually it is more convenient to do so. If you are enlarging to a rational scale from a plan published at an awkward one 'to fit the page', the squares superimposed on the original should correspond to some definite dimension in metres (or feet); this can be repro-duced easily on the enlargement. Most of the necessary co-ordinates can be measured and plotted by using scales marked on the corner of a thin card. To avoid defacing the original, a suitable grid can be drawn on transparent material.

The grid can also be subdivided by diagonals (Figure 26.3 bottom). By this means the original large grid can be broken down into smaller sections almost without limit, without the need for further measurement. I find the multitude of small divisions confusing, but the choice of method is a matter of personal preference.

In drawing out the enlargement it is advisable first to complete the circuit of some well-defined outline, such as the crest of a rampart, before adding more detail; this gives a general guide to the shape of the structure, and reduces the risk of plotting a feature in the wrong square.

Although an enlarged drawing is easier to work on, a slight loss in accuracy is unavoidable. Generally, therefore, there is little point in enlarging the original in a ratio exceeding 2:1, and the final plan as published should not be on a larger scale than the original.

26.9 *Profiles with a Clinometer.* For many ramparts, although the profile obtained with a clinometer is not exact, it is perfectly adequate; and the instrument is far more easily portable than a level and staff.

26.3 Methods of Enlarging Plan

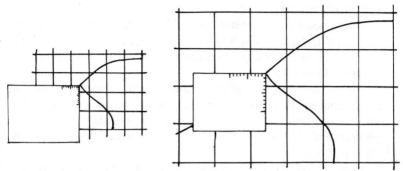

Using cards as movable scales

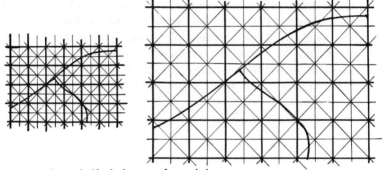

Repeated subdivision of grid

Owing to the inaccuracy of measurement, the instrument should be used sparingly, most levels being fixed by lining in. For a low rampart poles are set up at each end of the profile, and the vertical angle measured from the 1·5 m point on one pole to the same (or if preferred a lower point) on the other; several readings should be taken, and averaged. Levels are then taken by sliding a pencil or chain book up and down a pole held upside-down at an intermediate point until the pencil or edge of the book lines in between the two marks. The height is then noted, as well as the distance (which will usually be horizontal, but can be along the line of sight). The actual heights of the line of sight on the poles at each end must also be recorded; it will be rather less than 1·5 m, as those poles are fixed in the ground. The profile can then be plotted without difficulty. At worst, the only substantial error will be a slight tilt in the assumed 'horizontal'; the relative heights will be very nearly correct.

This method is less suitable for multiple defences with ditches of considerable depth, but if it has to be used for such, spot levels can be fixed on the crests of the ramparts, the ditch bottoms being observed from these.

The method can be applied single-handed, though it is rather more troublesome. The intermediate poles are set upright in the ground, and the depths to which they are inserted are recorded. The observer then has to estimate the heights at which they are cut by the line of sight.

Alternatively, Williams-Freeman's method (Para. 26.2) can be made accurate enough for most purposes if instead of depending on levelling by eye the clinometer is set to zero and is used as a level to fix the point at which the horizontal line through the top of the measuring-rod cuts the slope. Small nontelescopic hand-levels are also available. These are essentially Abney levels with a fixed spirit-level and of course no graduated scale. They are relatively inexpensive, but their possible applications are so limited that they are not really very useful items of equipment.

Part VIII
RECAPITULATION

27 Excavation

27.1 *The Purpose of this Chapter.* Many (too many?) archaeologists
are concerned with surveying only in so far as it applies to
excavation, but to arrange this book with that restricted objective
in mind would have made its use by others too difficult. This
chapter summarises the type of work likely to be needed on a dig,
with references back to the relevant sections. My concern is
exclusively with surveying; I intend no implications of any kind
relative to the merits of different research techniques except to
emphasise that where the need for accurate measurement is not
appreciated the validity of all other information given must be
doubtful. Nevertheless, the recommendations made here are
necessarily generalised, and must be considered in the context of
the site.

Philip Barker's *Techniques of Archaeological Excavation*
(Batsford, 1977) will be in the hands of all excavators, even though
they may differ from him in detail. His Chapter 8 especially is
essential reading (though his Figure 53b should be amended; see
Figure 7.6d above) and amplifies from the archaeological standpoint much that is said here.

27.2 *The Initial Survey.* On anything other than a 'salvage' dig or a
crop-mark site, an accurate survey of the surface features ought
invariably to precede the actual excavation; it should not, as it too
often does, form a rather reluctant afterthought. On a complex site
it will often indicate problems which require investigation. As
always, chain survey (part II) is the method of choice if the ground
is not difficult. Whether contouring (Paras. 11.4–6; 14.3) is needed
will depend on the nature of the site. For a large area it is very time-
consuming, and profiles and sections can often be arranged to give
an adequate representation of the topography. For a major

excavation, especially under emergency conditions, the advantages of a professional photogrammetric survey deserve to be considered, even though in normal circumstances it might seem unjustified (Para. 22.2).

The pegs defining the grid or other co-ordinate system used in the excavation should always be tied in to the survey stations, not to secondary features such as wall-junctions; the latter method introduces cumulative errors. Similarly, features revealed in excavation, or the outlines of new areas to be examined, should always be measured from the pegs defining the co-ordinate system, never from the sides of excavations, however carefully these may have been cut.

27.3 *Continuity of Record*. Save for a small structure such as a burial-mound, or a site destroyed by quarrying, an excavation is hardly ever 'complete'. Some decades later, further work will be desirable. However careful the earlier records may have been, their value will be greatly reduced if they cannot be linked to the later discoveries. At least some of the stations used, therefore, ought to be made recoverable, especially those near the area excavated. What follows relates to stations used in the plan; levels are considered later.

The ideal permanent station for a long-term excavation is a steel tube, large enough to take the end of a ranging-rod, and set in a block of concrete, the top being at ground level. Expense, and the normal use of the ground, will usually make these impossible. An alternative, nearly as satisfactory, is a substantial steel rod driven into the ground; this was, I believe, first used by Dr Willoughby Gardner at Dinorben, some 60 years ago. Unless the ground is certain to remain undisturbed, the rod should be driven into the bottom of a pit dug to well below plough level; to discourage potential treasure-hunters from digging up 'a Roman Javelin' some old tins might be added before refilling to show that the deposit is modern.

More commonly, especially when a survey is made without a forthcoming excavation in mind, less satisfactory controls have to be accepted. Anything on or near the survey area can be used, provided it is a sharply defined point and likely to survive. Examples are the corner of a building, a stone gate-post, an OS bench mark whether current or disused, or a mark cut on a rock outcrop. These must be tied in as accurately as possible to the main survey, but need not be on it, though it is more convenient if they are.

Details of these permanent points need not be included in the published report, but the fact that they exist should be mentioned, so that any future investigator will be aware that information can be found in the record files relating to the work.

If excavation is expected to take place in a decade or so, wooden pegs may be good enough. In good conditions oak pegs may still be identifiable after 20 years, but soft wood, or pegs cut on site from branches, will probably vanish in less than half that time.

The remarks on recording station-pegs (Para. 7.2) apply particularly to those intended to be permanent. The rediscovery of steel rods is simplified by the use of metal detectors.

27.4 *Excavation Co-ordinates.* Although a co-ordinate system as a basis for records is now used on many excavations, it is not essential, and individual parts of the work can be tied in with reference to separate pairs or groups of pegs incorporated as points in the main survey. Even when co-ordinates are used, it is again not always absolutely essential to set out a complete grid. If relatively few features have to be recorded, the total work involved may well be reduced by measuring from pegs whose co-ordinates are known but random, rather than by setting out the grid on the ground. To determine the co-ordinates of pegs set more or less at random is enormously less laborious than to set out a truly rectangular grid, assuming the same degree of accuracy in each case.

Nevertheless, for some excavations a grid is very desirable indeed (Barker, *Techniques*, pp. 146 ff), sometimes absolutely necessary, as when the position of every stone has to be plotted. The procedure for setting out the main framework has been described in Chapter 15; the high degree of accuracy assumed there can often be reduced (Para. 7.5).

The objective is usually to break down the whole area into squares of one or two metre side. Since setting out pegs with real accuracy is very laborious, a first subdivision can be made with pegs at 10 m intervals. Metre divisions are then marked, usually with large nails, first by measuring along an adjacent pair of lines ten metres apart, and then across between corresponding nails. A string-line is used to get the alignment, and a builder's level (Para. 15.2) is preferable to a plumb-bob. As a check, make sure that the spacing along diagonals is 1·414 m.

If only a few features have to be recorded, 10 m squares can be used, and individual points measured in, either by co-ordinates or by triangulation using at least three of the four corners.

The final breakdown into 10 or 20 cm squares is done by a grid of strings suitably spaced on a frame (Barker, *Techniques*, p. 150). Usually the frame is exactly either 1·0 or 2·0 m square internally, and the corners are placed over the appropriate nails. A preferable arrangement is to make it 1·2 or 2·2 m squares, the 1 (or 2) m square being indicated by strings of different colour or thickness. This makes possible a smoother transition in drawing when a feature crosses from one square to the next. Detail is plotted directly on squared paper.

Provided the surface to be planned is fairly flat, so that the strings (which can be elastic) lie in contact with it, one grid is adequate, but if the surface is irregular the frame should be deep, perhaps five centimetres from top to bottom, with a string grid on each face. Parallax can then almost be eliminated by making sure that the upper square over the area being drawn is symmetrically centred over the lower square.

As excavation proceeds, the pegs and nails will have to be removed and replaced at lower levels. This can be done as described in Para. 15.7, but rather than drive temporary pegs the transfer marks can be made on suitable stone slabs or bricks. Another possibility is to use adjacent nails as transfer marks. In theory, the errors introduced at every transfer should tend to cancel out, but in practice they are more likely to accumulate, so the grid should be checked occasionally.

27.5 *The Site Bench Mark*. The nearest OS bench mark will probably be some distance away, so some reliable site bench mark will need to be established. Anything will do so long as it is not likely to be moved and the staff can be rested on it or against it. Examples are the lower hinge-hanger on a gate-post, a spike driven into a mortared (not dry-built) wall, a doorstep, or a conspicuous boulder. Less obvious, perhaps, is a cut on the trunk of a mature tree; provided this is not near a root the *vertical* movement over years is very small.

Although the level of any point can be defined precisely relative to Ordnance Datum, at least in principle, levels relative to site datum (taken as 100·00 say, to avoid negative levels) are often fully adequate for the excavation report. In that case the unpublished record file should contain full details of the position and nature of the site bench mark, as well as levels on the stations established for permanent reference, such as the tops of the buried steel rods.

In theory, this is not necessary if the site bench mark is tied in to Ordnance Datum, but in practice it remains desirable. Even assuming that your double line of levels (Para. 11.1) connecting with the nearest ordnance bench mark contains neither errors nor mistakes, the possibilities remain that the bench mark may have been moved, or that if you have taken its value from an old map relevelling or a change of datum has altered its nominal level. Your record file should therefore contain a statement such as 'Site BM (on boulder at site co-ordinate 442·2E, 216·4N) 212·23, based on OBM at GR 41452276 on NE corner of Church, taken as 201·45 above OD'. There is no need to publish this; it is only of importance to a possible future excavator. Unless you are working on an aqueduct or something of that kind the immediate value of your report would not be much affected even by a mistake of a metre.

It may well be that no bench mark survives near your work, and that the importance of getting close correlation with OD is not great enough to justify the long runs of levelling which would be needed. An adequate link is often provided by a spot level on a road, or even by the intersection of a contour with a field-boundary (preferably on one of the earlier editions). If these rather rough data are used, they should be mentioned in your report.

Keep in mind that all bench mark levels published on the older maps are in feet above OD so the figures need to be divided by 3·281 to convert to metres.

27.6 *Use of the Level.* In excavations the level is used almost exclusively to establish stratification, usually in drawing sections. Occasional other applications, such as determining the direction of flow in a water-channel, are obvious and need no description.

Sections are usually too complex to be 'booked' for subsequent plotting, and are more conveniently drawn on the site. Strata can be levelled in and plotted directly, but this is very laborious except in unusually simple examples; the normal method is to establish a horizontal string-line (or two or more in deep excavations) and to measure from it. Measurements could, if desired, be made at right angles to, or vertically from, a string-line which followed a defined slope, but it is hard to see any advantage in such an arrangement.

The string-line is stretched between arrows or nails pushed into the face of the section. At least three should be used. They should be spaced at roughly equal intervals of 3 m or less, and not less than three should be used however short the section. This provides an automatic check against mistakes.

The arrows can be located by moving the staff up or down as directed by the man at the level, but to hold a staff upright and at the same time to support it in the air is difficult. A much easier way is to take a level on the bottom of the excavation and then to put the arrow in against the appropriate reading. To draw the profiles of the surface and of the bottom of the excavation independently of the string-line, by levelling, is usually helpful; it provides an outline within which a mistake in plotting detail will become obvious.

Methods of recording stratification in area excavation are fully discussed by Barker (*Techniques*, pp. 78 ff). If they are to be reconstructed from levels on the successively exposed surfaces, time can often be saved by booking the actual staff readings on a drawing of the grid. The profile of each surface can then be drawn without any arithmetic, by measuring down from a line corresponding to the relevant height of instrument above datum. Since the instrument has to be reset, this will differ for every set of levels, so great care must be taken to record it on each sheet; and when plotting successive profiles, rub out one datum line before you draw the next.

28 Part-time Fieldwork

28.1 General Remarks; 28.2 The Nature of Fieldwork;
28.3 Limitations on Research; 28.4 Lines of Research;
28.5 Collecting and Treasure-hunting.

28.1 *General Remarks*. The full-time 'professional' archaeologist seldom has any problem in deciding what work needs to be done; his difficulty is more likely to be how best to do it in the limited time available. Besides the 'professionals' though, there are many 'amateurs' deeply interested in the subject, who would like to make some useful contribution to it in their spare time. This chapter offers some suggestions.

Incidentally, the use of 'amateur' as a derogatory term in contrast to 'professional' seems illogical. Literally, the implication of this would seem to be that the 'professional' only works because he is paid, and does not love the subject (which is untrue). A better distinction would be between 'competent' and 'incompetent', and there is certainly not exact correspondence between that classification and 'professional/amateur' or 'paid/unpaid'.

28.2 *The Nature of Fieldwork*. The amateur is often handicapped not only by insufficient time and funds, but by lack of formal instruction; nevertheless, there is an enormous amount of useful work waiting to be done which requires very little training or equipment, and can be fitted in to week-ends or spare afternoons.

Two books are almost indispensable. One is O. G. S. Crawford's *Archaeology in the Field* (Phoenix House, London, 1953); it is a classic, and conveys better than any other the fascination of the subject and what it is all about. He was one of the founders, perhaps *the* founder, of scientific Field Archaeology in its strict sense as distinct from Excavation. The other is *Field Archaeology in Great Britain* published surprisingly inexpensively by the Ordnance Survey (5th edn, 1973). This describes literally every type of field monument (at least I have found none missing) and it is clear from every page that the anonymous (and possibly composite) official author writes from real personal knowledge. Moreover, unlike many archaeologists, he is aware that there is quite a lot of Britain beyond lowland England; Scotland and Wales get equal treatment. The book includes a very useful section on practical fieldwork, and a full and helpful bibliography.

Even these two excellent works do not provide a complete substitute for personal training, and if at all possible you should try to attend an extramural course, or something similar, on some aspect of local or at least British Archaeology, preferably a course which includes fieldwork. Details are relatively unimportant, for the actual basic techniques of field archaeology are much the same whatever the period being studied. Much of the value of a course comes from the opportunities for discussion and for meeting others with similar interests.

Two warnings may be relevant; if surveying is included in the course, have regard to the comments in Paras. 1.1 and 1.2 above; and despite the great advantage of a colleague when you are engaged in fieldwork, avoid believers in such things as Ley-lines, Zodiacal Landscapes, or Subterranean Currents of Psychic Force.

28.3 *Limitations on Research.* Three considerations will control any research which you may plan. Limiting factors will normally be equipment, helpers, and time.

In developed country, with plenty of landmarks such as field-boundaries, useful reconnaissance is possible with nothing more than a notebook and a 1/25,000 map (Para. 25.3). In open country, a prismatic compass (Para. 25.5) is almost essential, and with it rough surveys become possible (Chapter 26). The addition of a chain, tape, arrows and set of ranging-rods, and preferably a clinometer, will extend your range to accurate plans (without contours) of structures up to about 100 m across (Chapter 8).

All this can be done single-handed, though for any chain surveying a colleague is very helpful. With a colleague, and given enough time, any site can be surveyed with the equipment already listed, though contouring would be very laborious.

Optical surveying instruments are expensive, and worth while only for the most addicted team of 'amateurs'. A level and staff will enable you to draw profiles (Para. 11.2) and sections (Para. 11.3) easily, and to contour simple sites (Paras. 11.4-6), but will hardly justify their purchase unless you are going to help regularly on excavations. A theodolite (Part IV), though less easily portable will fulfil every function of a level and is much more useful; but it is also much more expensive. With it added to the other equipment, and preferably supplemented by a hand calculator, a team of two can make an accurate plan of any terrestrial site.

28.4 *Lines of Research.* No general rules as to suitable lines of research are possible. Apart from the limitations discussed in the last paragraph, much depends on what types of field monument occur in your neighbourhood and what work has been done, or is being done, already. To take an area I know well as an example, it would (I hope) be a waste of time to resurvey structures of which plans are published in the *Glamorgan Inventory*, but such work would be extremely useful in Carmarthenshire or Pembrokeshire. Contact with active investigators can almost always be made through regional museums, county archaeological societies, and the various regional groups of the Council for British Archaeology; but keep in mind that other workers, especially if 'professionals', are usually extremely fully occupied and may be unable to spare time to accompany you into the field.

Ideas for research may be gained from the works listed in the bibliography of the Ordnance Survey's *Field Archaeology.* John Coles, *Field Archaeology in Britain* (Methuen, 1972) is helpful, and is sound on surveying so far as limited space permits, but is largely concerned with excavation. Christopher Taylor, *Fieldwork in Medieval Archaeology* (Batsford, 1974) is valuable for its period in south-east Britain (except on surveying); further books are expected in the series.

One type of investigation, particularly suited to 'amateur' reconnaissance and neglected almost everywhere, is to follow early trackways and to record them in detail. Saxon and other early boundary surveys offer another interesting field for research. Many have been translated and worked out on *maps*, but to follow them step by step *on the ground* can often lead to interesting discoveries. Examples are given by M. Gelling in *Signposts to the Past* (Dent, 1978) especially Chapter 8. All Anglo-Saxon charters and most of the major attempts at tracing the boundaries given in them have been listed by P. H. Sawyer, in *Anglo-Saxon Charters* (Royal Historical Society, 1968). This index is essential for anyone interested; but, unfortunately from the point of view of the fieldworker, it has been arranged primarily with the needs of historians in mind.

Even Roman roads can still repay fieldwork, for I. D. Margary's encyclopedic volume on *Roman Roads in Britain* (London, 1967), though indispensable, is not wholly reliable, and moreover suffers from an extraordinary reluctance to use the national grid.

28.5 *Collecting and Treasure-hunting.* Even to discuss the use of metal detectors is dangerous. To many archaeologists, one of these devices automatically places its owner far below any beast of the field (with the possible exception of the rabbit; but its indiscriminate burrowings have some excuse). Nevertheless, I hope that some suggestions may reduce the archaeological damage liable to be caused.

Anyone who is solely a collector, whether of Old Masters or old bottles, is a menace to the subject in which he pretends an interest. In those particular cases, the damage caused is small, for a masterpiece will ultimately reappear to delight those who appreciate its aesthetic rather than its monetary value, while the disappearance of a nineteenth-century ginger beer bottle is not a great loss to Art or Science. As regards small antiquities such as pottery or metal objects, the position is far more serious, for archaeological knowledge depends to a great extent on these apparently insignificant items and especially on the associations in which they occur. If they are taken from their true contexts into the obscurity of a private hoard much of their archaeological value is lost, even if they escape being discarded as rubbish after the hoarder's death.

A collector of this type is culpable even if he does not use a metal detector, but if he does he will almost certainly cause even more serious damage by burrowing into undisturbed deposits.

Deliberate digging in search of relics, save as part of a properly organised excavation, must be unhesitatingly condemned; but many 'finds' are exposed by ploughing or other accidental disturbance of the surface. The collector who picks up an object exposed in that way may well have saved it from destruction. Archaeologically his sin would consist in his failure to put it on record.

Metal objects are liable to destructive corrosion when exposed, so (subject to the owner's permission, and on scheduled sites to the permission of the Department of the Environment) regular search with a metal detector of a ploughed field or other disturbed *surface* could be valuable, always provided the objects found are recorded. The value of such records is greatly enhanced if, instead of merely recording the field, the actual position is defined. The technique used must depend on the frequency with which objects turn up but in most cases Para. 25.6 would be appropriate.

To emphasise the need for collaboration with an experienced archaeologist, the sad case of a bronze spearhead from Hammersmith deserves mention. It was found complete with a 5 ft wooden shaft, but that was discarded. Since only five other shafts have ever been found, and all have now disintegrated, the destruction must be distressing not only to archaeologists but to the owner who thereby deprived himself of a unique possession and enormously reduced the monetary value of his find. By contrast, collaboration between archaeologists and users of metal detectors on salvage sites, so far mainly in Norfolk, has proved profitable to all concerned, both in additions to knowledge and to collections.

Appendix I: Alternative Units and Conversion Factors

The Metric system for lengths and the Babylonian system for angles are now standard in Britain; but the accuracy of your work depends on you, not on the units used. A metric scale should always be shown on the finished plan, of course.

If you are absolutely certain that you will always be working with the same partner, there is no reason why you should not work in feet, or even in links. Trouble will arise, though, if you have to work with units unfamiliar to you; mistakes are almost certain. So although, in my view, the ideal equipment for this type of work comprises a lightweight 100 foot chain, a theodolite with metric graduation, and a staff showing feet, I do not recommend you to get them. Nevertheless, you may find that nothing else is available, and this appendix will enable you to work with them.

In the 100 foot chain, the links are one foot long, with brass tags every ten feet. The 50 foot tag is round, the others have one, two, three or four points according to their distance from the *nearer* end; the 30-foot tag is sometimes triangular.

In booking feet and inches, the convention is to use a diagonal stroke to separate the units; thus 10/5 indicates ten feet five inches.

'Gunter's Chain' can also be used. This is 66 feet long, divided into 100 links of just under eight inches. It is tagged in the same way as the 100 foot chain. The reason for this odd length was that 66 ft × 660 ft, or 10 square chains, corresponded to 1 acre. By removing some of the small links, evenly distributed over its length, a Gunter's Chain can be converted into a 20 metre (65 ft 7½ ins) chain, but if you should do this be sure to file off the statements of length on both brass handles, and cut M in their place.

Levelling staves graduated in feet are always subdivided decimally, usually with alternate black and white divisions each of 0·01 ft. The system of numbering is standardised: the *top* of each

300

numeral corresponds to the relevant reading. The red figures (feet) are 0·15 ft high, the black (the tenths) 0·10 ft. There is seldom any need to read to a third decimal place. The Scotch staff, of lighter construction, is divided into tenths and twentieths; this is not fine enough for tacheometry.

If working in feet, the ability to convert inches to decimals, and conversely, may be useful. The rule is, take 1/8 inch as 1/100 ft, and count from the nearest of the easily remembered divisions 3 ins = 0·25 ft, 6 ins = 0·5 ft, 9 ins = 0·75 ft. Thus 4¼ ins = 0·25 ft + ten eighths of an inch = 0·35 ft; 0·65 ft = 0·75 − 0·10 = 9 ins − ten eighths = 7¾ ins. This is correct to 0·005 ft.

For plotting to a rational scale, squared paper divided in 0·01 ft is available from specialist stationers, but it is expensive, and probably now obsolescent. Boxwood or plastic scales at 1/2,500 or 1/1,000, in feet, are likely to remain available for some time.

For angular measurements, the grad or grade is often used abroad. For surveying especially it is far preferable to the degree. It is the only metric unit not adopted in Britain, but you may meet with it on some theodolites. It is one-hundredth of a right angle, and is subdivided decimally. The usual notation is (say) 64g·1142, which multiplied by 0·9 gives 57·70278 degrees, or 57° 42' 10''. Confusion is sometimes introduced by calling a hundredth of a grad a (decimal) minute, and a hundredth of that a (decimal) second; the figure above would be written 64g 11' 42''.

Just possibly, you may also meet with the mille (or mil), the angle corresponding to one metre at a thousand metres distance, that is one-thousandth of a radian. It is used on some Artillery Directors, which are essentially crude but robust theodolites, and which may be useful if no better equipment for measuring angles is available.

Finally, an almost forgotten linear measurement deserves mention. Pre-revolutionary French surveyors prepared many plans of castles, other fortifications, towns, and even some hill-forts. Some of the castles are British, and the fortifications in general are of interest to students. The unit of length is commonly the Toise, and it may be useful to record that it was equivalent to 1·949 m (6 ft 4¾ ins), since this information is not readily accessible.

The more usual conversion factors are:

1 metre = 3·2808 feet.

1 foot = 0·3048 metres.

So for rapid visual comparison of drawn scales 100 metres is roughly 10 per cent or 30 ft longer than 300 feet, or 100 ft is 'just a little' (half a metre) longer than 30 metres.

For maps, 1 kilometre = 0·6214 miles or 1 mile = 1·609 km.

For rapid visual comparison, 1 km is roughly 5/8ths of a mile.

For areas: 1 hectare (100 × 100 metres) = 2·471 acres.

Appendix II: Equipment

This appendix recapitulates, chapter by chapter, the chief items of equipment needed, and lists some firms from which they can be obtained; the list is not complete, for specialist suppliers exist in most large towns, and some items, such as tapes, are available at many ordinary retailers. The firms are listed alphabetically at the end, and are indicated by numbers in the list of equipment.

The prices stated have been rounded off upwards. They are intended merely to indicate *roughly* the lowest price at which an adequate piece of equipment could be bought new during 1978. The actual prices for closely similar objects may differ by 20 per cent or more, depending on details of their specification, so a full catalogue of what is available cannot be compressed into a brief appendix. It is hoped, nevertheless, that this summary may be useful to anyone considering the purchase of equipment.

The more expensive instruments can often be bought reconditioned, at about half to two-thirds their new price, depending on age and condition. They can also be hired. As an *extremely* rough indication, the cost of hire per month is about 10 per cent of the price new. A week's hire is half that for a month, a day's half that for a week.

Chapter 3

Chain, 20 metre, £25; tape, 30 metre, £10; arrows, set of 10, £3; poles, 2 metre, £5; 1 metre sections, £5 each; carrying case, £10; stand for use on hard surfaces, £8; Abney clinometer, £30. Available from 1, 2, 3, 6; tape and clinometer also from 5.

Chapter 4

Chain book, £2. Available from 1, 3.

Chapter 6

Scales, £2; (it is *essential* that scales are of 'flat', that is, thin trapezoidal, section; those of oval section are completely unsuitable. Preferably also, they should be figured from right to left as well as from left to right); set squares and protractors, up to £6 depending on size; straight-edge, 1 metre, £35; drawing-board, approx. 80 × 60 cm, £27; 110 × 80 cm, £41; T-square, 80 cm, £10; 110 cm, £12; beam compasses, from £25. Available from 1, 2, 3; straight-edge also from 5.

Chapter 9

Level, dumpy or tilting, £200; automatic, £400; these prices do not include tripods, £60 to £90; staff, 4 m, £50; level book, £2. Available from 1, 2, 4, 5, 6; level book and some types of level from 3.

Chapter 12

Theodolite, £600 upwards; vernier reading types are cheaper than direct reading; tripods, extra, £90; self-reducing tacheometer, £2900; extras for theodolite: illuminated cross-hairs, £15; magnetic compass, £120; prismatic eyepiece, £75; angle book, £2. Available from 1, 2, 5, 6; angle book also from 3.

Chapter 14

Tacheometric tables and slide-rules, £3 upwards; Cox's Stadia Computer (a circular slide-rule) is apparently the cheapest, but is fully adequate. Although not catalogued, these should be available through any firm supplying tacheometers.

Chapter 15

Steel band, 50 m, £60; tension handle, £15; clamp handle, £2. Available from 1, 6.

Chapter 16

Chambers' Six-figure Mathematical Tables (with positive characteristics) ed. L. J. Comrie (W. and R. Chambers) £2.50 (in 1978). Available from 3. Electronic calculator, as specified, £25 to £30 in 1978 but now cheaper. New models are frequent, and prices for the same type may differ by 30 per cent depending on the supplier. See advertisement in press.

Chapter 22

Plane table, complete, from £60 upwards. Telescopic or self-reducing alidades cost about the same as a similar theodolite; see Chapter 12. Available from 1, 6.

Chapter 25

Prismatic compass, £35 upwards. Available from 1, 2, 4, 5, 6.

List of firms

1. Chadburn (MDS) Ltd, 24 Trading Estate Road, Park Royal, London NW10 7EG. This firm maintains a stock of reconditioned instruments for sale, as well as for hire.
2. C. Frank, Ltd, 144 Ingram St., Glasgow.
3. W. Heffer and Sons, Ltd, Sidney St., Cambridge. This firm can also supply a very wide range of 'squared paper' with many different spacings, as well as other types of specialist 'graph paper'.
4. W. F. Stanley and Co., Ltd, Avery Hill Road, London SE9.
5. J. H. Steward, Ltd, Enbeeco House, Carlton Park, Saxmundham, Suffolk IP17 2NL.
6. Survey and General Instrument Company, Fircroft Way, Edenbridge, Kent. This firm maintains a stock of reconditioned instruments for sale, as well as for hire.

Appendix III: Data Used in Numerical Examples

It is interesting to have some idea of the results given by various methods of balancing 'errors'. Most of the examples in the text have therefore been based on a network with thirteen nodes or 'stations' with specified co-ordinates. From these the true lengths and angles have been calculated, and the 'measured' figures have been derived from these by adding 'errors', which were chosen randomly to give an approximately normal distribution. The results were then rounded off. For lengths, the imposed errors range from 0·5 % to −0·5 % in steps of 0·1 %, the standard deviation being about 0·16 %; for angles similarly, from 0·05° to −0·05°, in steps of 0·01°, s.d. about 0·016°.

STATIONS

	Coordinates E	N			Coordinates E	N
A	169·10	779·25		H	136·75	332·35
B	441·20	801·10		J	470·00	455·00
C	635·80	820·55		K	684·80	494·50
D	781·10	557·75		L	807·25	422·70
E	580·30	659·90		M	711·75	330·60
F	247·70	639·75		N	480·00	235·55
G	114·75	622·75				

LINES

Line	True Bearing Degrees and decimals	Lengths True	Measured		Line	True Bearing Degrees and decimals	Lengths True	Measured
AB	085·4089	272·976	273·00		EK	147·7152	195·646	195·45
AF	150·6013	160·119	159·65		FG	262·7133	134·032	134·05
AG	199·1513	165·669	165·65		FH	199·8461	326·810	327·15
BC	084·2923	195·570	195·75		FJ	129·7294	289·050	288·75
BE	135·4293	198·208	197·80		GH	175·6667	291·232	290·95
BF	230·1769	251·945	252·20		HJ	069·7943	355·104	355·45
BJ	175·2432	347·296	348·70		HN	105·7490	356·638	357·35
CD	151·0621	300·293	300·90		JK	079·5802	218·402	218·40
CE	199·0586	169·967	170·15		JM	117·2295	271·879	271·90
DE	296·9631	225·289	225·05		JN	177·3909	219·678	219·90
DK	236·7030	115·214	115·20		KL	120·3857	141·948	142·35
DL	169·0413	137·558	137·00		KM	170·6624	166·101	166·65
EF	266·5331	333·210	334·20		LM	226·0383	132·675	132·70
EJ	208·2941	232·702	233·15		MN	247·6995	250·485	250·75

The co-ordinates assigned to the stations, the corresponding true lengths and bearings of the lines, and the 'measured' lengths, are tabulated below. The shape of the network is given in Figure 27.1, and the 'measured' angles are all set out in table 20.4, so they are not repeated here. The true angles can easily be found from the bearings. Further, by using these data, it is easy to devise problems with known solutions, in order to gain experience in applying the numerical methods described in the text.

Appendix IV: Corrections to Linear Measurements

The corrections should always be deducted from the Measured Length to give the correct Horizontal distance. The effects of Slope and Sag can be added to give the total correction.

The following data are adequate for ordinary chain surveys:

For gentle slopes, of less than 4° (about 1 in 15), or more than 20 paces to eye level, the correction may be neglected.

For steep slopes, over 15° (about 1 in 4), or less than 8 paces to eye level, measurements should be made in steps.

For intermediate slopes these tables can be used; the corrections are for a 20 metre chain, and can be increased proportionately for greater lengths.

(a) Angle of Slope measured.

Angle (degrees)	4	5	6	7	8	9	10	11	12	13	14	15	16
Correction	0·05	0·08	0·11	0·15	0·19	0·25	0·30	0·37	0·44	0·51	0·59	0·68	0·77

(b) Rough correction.

Paces to eye level.	6	7	8	9	10	11	12	13	14	15	20	25
Correction		1·03	0·75	0·57	0·45	0·36	0·30	0·25	0·21	0·18	0·16	0·09	0·05

Correction for sag is not often needed during a chain survey, but may be useful when measuring across a depression or when a tape is used on a windy site. In the former case the sag will be small, but in the latter it can be considerable. The table gives the corrections for various measured lengths, for sags up to one-twentieth of the measurement, for a catenary.

Normally the sag will be estimated by eye, and the table will be adequate, but if the sag is measured a more accurate correction can easily be worked out. It varies directly as the square of the sag, and inversely as the measured length. Thus for a sag of 4·2 m in a measured length of 28 m the correction would be:

$$\frac{4·2^2}{4·5^2} \times \frac{25}{28} \times 2·22 = 1·73$$

The correct figure is 1·71.

Sag	Measured Length			
	20	25	30	50
0·5	0ʼ03	0·03	0·02	0·01
1·0	0ʼ13	0·11	0·09	0·05
1·5	0·30	0·24	0·20	0·12
2·0	0·54	0·43	0·36	0·21
2·5	0·84	0·67	0·56	0·33
3·0	1·22	0·97	0·81	0·48
3·5	1·68	1·33	1·10	0·66
4·0	2·21	1·74	1·44	0·86
4·5	--	2·22	1·83	1·09
5·0	--	2·76	2·27	1·34
5·5	--	--	2·77	1·63
6·0	--	--	3·31	1·94
6·5	--	--	--	2·29
7·0	--	--	--	2·66
7·5	--	--	--	3·06
8·0	--	--	--	3·49
8·5	--	--	--	3·95
9·0	--	--	--	4·44
9·5	--	--	--	4·96
10·0	--	--	--	5·52

Formulae. For accurate work, as when setting out a grid, the corrected lengths should be calculated using the following formulae; interpolation from tables is seldom accurate enough. The symbols used are:

L = Horizontal Distance

M = Measured Distance

C = M − L = Correction

S = Sag

h = Difference in Level of ends of measurement

a = Angle of Slope (so tan a = h/L)

w = Weight of tape in kilograms per metre.

P = Average of tensions at ends of tape, in kilograms.

Provided that S and h are small relative to M, as almost always when measurements are being made to set out a grid:

$$C \text{ for Slope} = M (1 − \cos a)$$
$$= M − \sqrt{M^2 − h^2}$$
$$= h^2/2M \text{ very nearly}$$
$$C \text{ for Sag} = w^2M^3/24P^2$$
$$= 8S^2/3M$$
$$\text{and Sag} = wM^2/8P$$

Very rarely indeed, a measurement may have to be taken in catenary with a large sag. The accurate formulae are:

$$L = \frac{\sqrt{M^2 - h^2}}{M} \times \frac{M^2 - 4S^2}{4S} \times \log_e \frac{M + 2S}{M - 2S}$$

In this case S is the average sag to the mid point (*not* to the lowest point). That is, if the levels of the ends of the chain or tape are h_1 and h_2 and the level of the chain halfway between the ends is h_m,

then $S = \dfrac{h_1 + h_2}{2} - h_m$

Alternatively, if the chain is supported by a known tension P applied at the upper end,

$$L = \frac{\sqrt{M^2 - h^2}}{2} \times \sqrt{v^2 - 1} \times \log_e \frac{v^2 + 1}{v^2 - 1}$$

where $v = \dfrac{2P - hw}{Mw}$

Index